UKRAINE RISING

Contemporary Creative Culture from Ukraine

gestalten

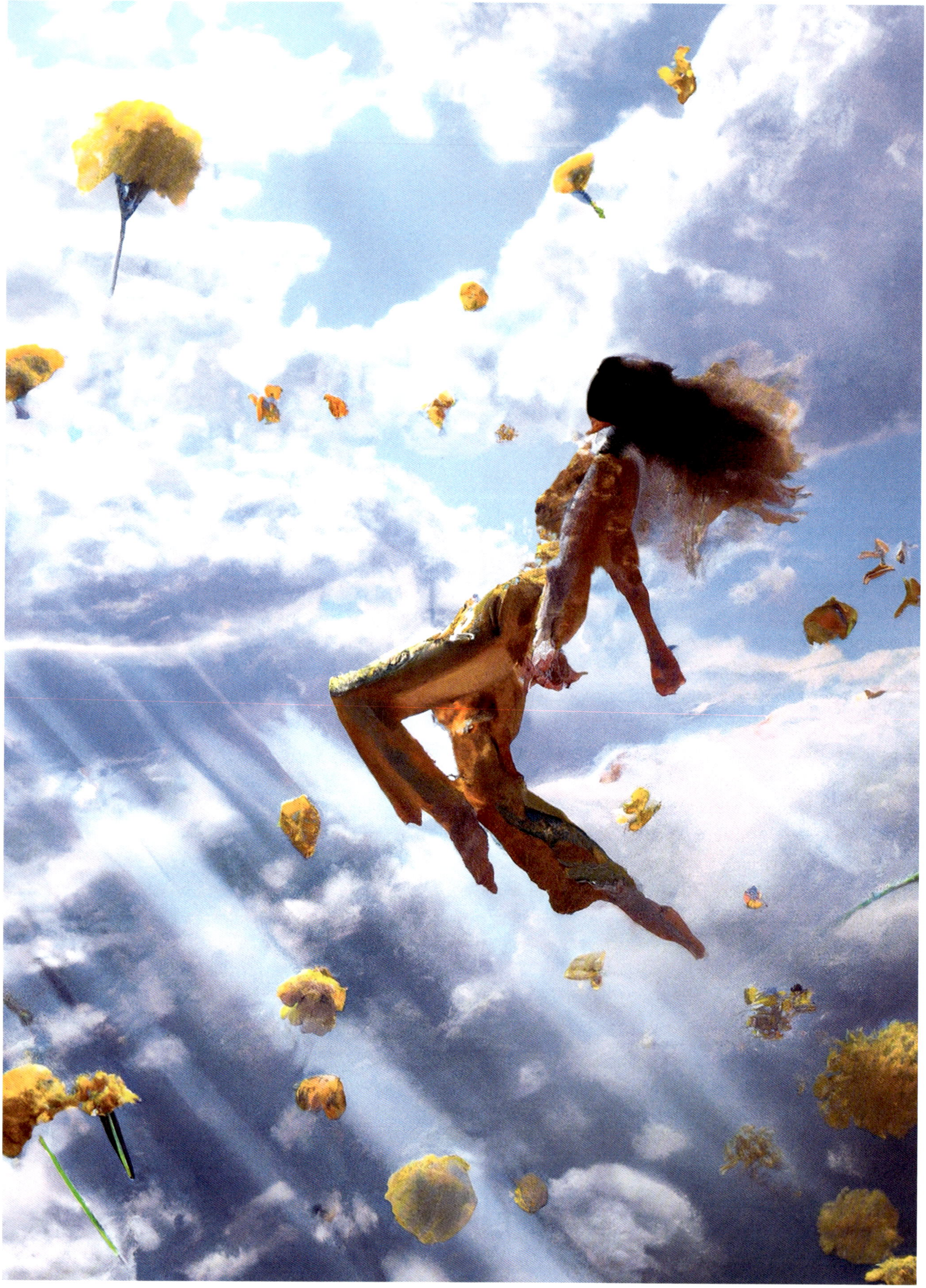

UKRAINE RISING

By Masha Erman and Robert Klanten

What you will discover in the following pages is nothing short of extraordinary. *Ukraine Rising* showcases the pinnacle of creative culture in Ukraine, featuring talents and examples drawn from the fields of architecture, interior design, product and graphic design, crafts, illustration, visual culture, fashion, and fine art.

With the collapse of the Soviet regime in the early '90s, Ukrainians found themselves in a position of reinvention. The somber reality and monotonous certainty of Soviet rule vanished, giving way to the exhilarating unpredictability that freedom, aspiration, self-determination, and prosperity bring about.

At that time, there was no established Ukrainian creative industry—no network of design schools, influential producers, visionary entrepreneurs, existing value chains, marketing strategies, or domestic and international markets for Ukrainian creations. Everything had to be built from the ground up by a young generation eager to live life on their own terms and pursue their dreams.

A country whose most valuable resource is its creative youth must be radical, nimble, and innovative to thrive. And Ukraine has been just that: within a remarkably short span of time, the country has built a reputation among the design, tech, and start-up communities as a hub of exceptional innovation. Over the course of just three decades, Ukraine has transformed into a veritable gold mine of creativity. Individuals who previously had limited access to creative education or the necessary resources are now showcasing their creations at international fashion and design shows and art exhibitions. Paradoxically, this Ukrainian creative evolution seems to have been nurtured by a perpetual state of uncertainty and political turmoil. The Ukrainian spirit has the extraordinary ability to transform oppression and deprivation into powerful sources of creativity and innovation. This serves as a testament to unyielding courage: in any society under an authoritarian regime—whether the Soviet Union or a modern-day dictatorship—creativity becomes the most potent weapon in the fight for self-determination and freedom. Engaging, persuasive, and contagious, culture has the power to change minds, shape politics, and even spark revolution, as was witnessed in 2004 and 2014. Today, Ukraine continues to make its mark on the global stage, with its audacious spirit and resilience acting as a perpetual rebuke to despotic systems around the world.

This distinctive subculture, born out of political upheaval and financial hardship, has learned to harness the power of creativity and to adapt various design elements from around the world. In the process they've forged new directions and national trends from scratch—often with very limited financial means. One could even argue that as soon as budgets come into play, creativity confines itself to the resources available. However, when financial resources disappear, so do the creative limits they impose. Within the following pages, you will witness the result of this intricate set of circumstances: the remnants of the questionable Soviet past juxtaposed with modern design pieces, rough-luxe interiors, and cutting-edge fashion collections created from locally sourced, second-hand clothing. The many handcrafted products and accessories featured in these pages exhibit an extraordinary level of skill and artistry. And while these qualities may sound old-fashioned, rest assured that you will find nothing trivial or outdated in this book.

Having arrived at a crossroads where the future holds infinite possibilities, the independent generation of Ukraine has astutely selected the finest practices and trends from across the globe. By fusing these practices with the richness and diversity of their own culture, the country has charted a fresh, cohesive, and proudly distinctive path. This approach embraces the nation's encumbered past with a touch of irony and strives toward a free and independent future.

Naturally, this generation of artists and designers have not concerned themselves too much with the plans laid out by their parents' generation. Instead, they look to the aesthetic traditions, rituals, and crafts that have defined Ukrainian life and Slavic culture for centuries. Interestingly, the traditional national values of Ukraine align closely with those uniting the international creative community today. Sustainable production, the use of natural materials (such as domestic linen instead of imported cotton), and skilled craftsmanship have always been at the core of Ukrainian creativity—whether driven by a reverence for nature and mastery of craft, or again, a lack of resources.

In a world where trends tend to homogenize creative cultures, Ukrainian creatives stand out with their unique approach. They embrace traditional culture while rejecting any supposed canons or norms, setting themselves apart in the international creative landscape.

Over a short amount of time, Ukraine has become synonymous with freedom, resilience, humor, and a lust for life. This spirit is not only evident on the frontlines but also in the way Ukrainians express themselves creatively. Throughout this book, we invite you to explore Ukrainian creativity and be amazed by the vibrant, thoughtful, and mesmerizing creations that defy the stereotypical public image perpetuated by the news feeds.

Ukraine Rising does not sugarcoat the harsh reality of war that Ukraine and its people face daily. Instead, our goal is to draw even more attention to it, and to expand the understanding of what Ukraine truly is beyond the Russian bombings, atrocities, and occupation. We would like you to see the people behind the news, their creativity, beauty, and humanity. We aim to share with you the pulsating vitality, originality, and proactive spirit that have fascinated us throughout our research.

Working on *Ukraine Rising* has been both a tremendous pleasure and an intense process for our entire team at gestalten. As we delved into the creative world of Ukraine, we found ourselves repeatedly captivated by the images featured here, and engaged in discussions about the exceptional talent and originality displayed. The selection process was both a joy and a challenge since we had an abundance of incredible material, forcing us to make difficult choices. However, we made sure to provide visibility to everyone considered, even if some are showcased more extensively than others. Ukraine's creativity is simply too vast to fit into a single book.

None of this would have been possible without the spirited Ukrainian creatives who contributed to this book. They responded to our requests with unparalleled speed and dedication. We also owe a special acknowledgement to Lucia Bondar, the co-creator of *Ukraine Rising.* With incredible professionalism and enthusiasm, Lucia discovered these talents, facilitated communication, conducted writing, and ensured that this publication would serve as a comprehensive and authoritative guide to modern-day Ukrainian culture.

Now that you have this book in your hands, we leave you to discover and explore Ukraine for yourself. Immerse yourself in the captivating world of creativity, where freedom, resilience, and an unwavering spirit converge to create something truly extraordinary.

We at gestalten would like to dedicate this book to the people of Ukraine, whose bravery, sincerity, and ingenuity set a proud example for us all.

If you'd like to support the creative community in Ukraine with your donation, please see page 320.

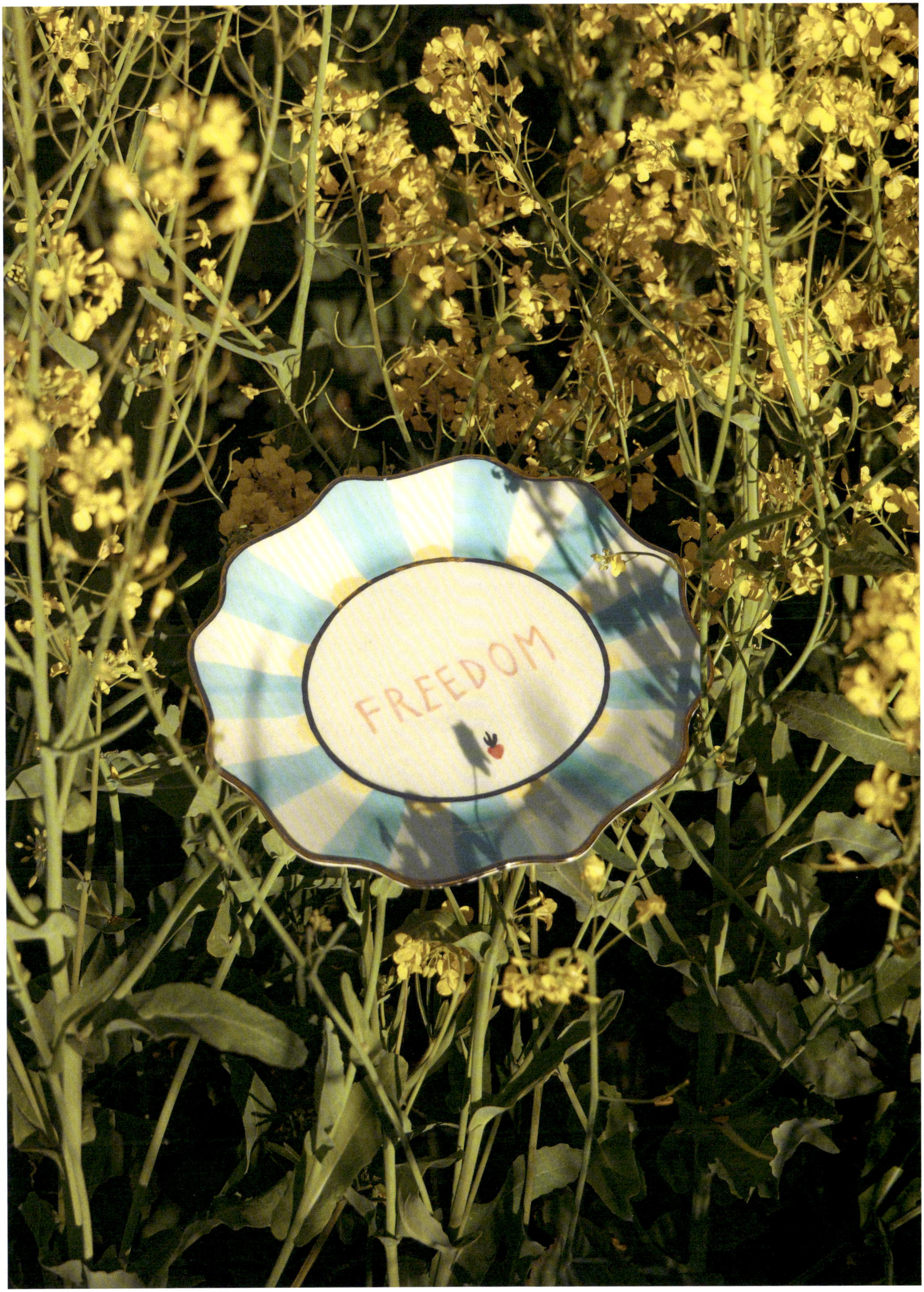
FREEDOM

CRAFTING UKRAINE: WHERE MODERN AND TRADITIONAL COLLIDE

In the aftermath of the Euromaidan Revolution at the end of 2013—the beginning of 2014, Ukraine experienced a creative renaissance that spanned music, design, architecture, fashion, publishing, gastronomy, and even the tech industry. This new landscape of possibilities enabled Ukrainian creatives to reclaim their power and construct a fresh image for their nation.

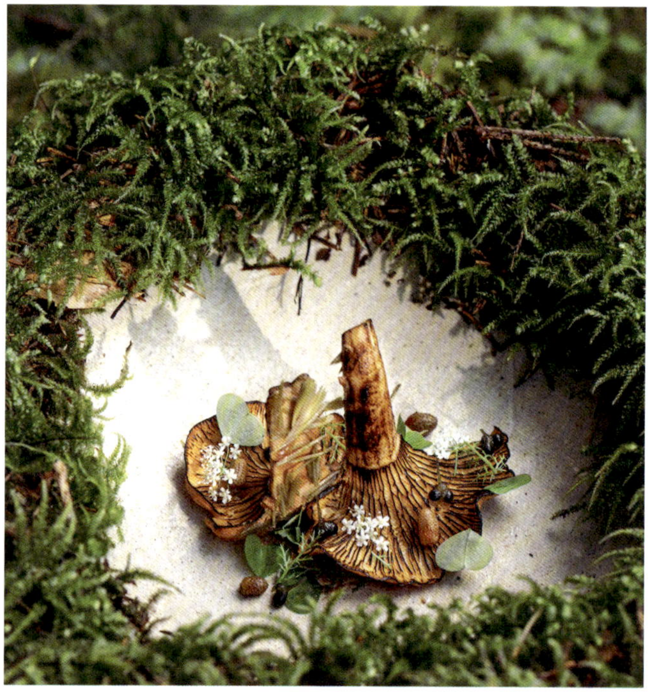

Thanks to photographer Dima Bahta, the culinary traditions of Ukraine are being stylishly documented. Below: Ukrainian folk-rap band Kalush Orchestra, winner of the Eurovision Song Contest 2022.

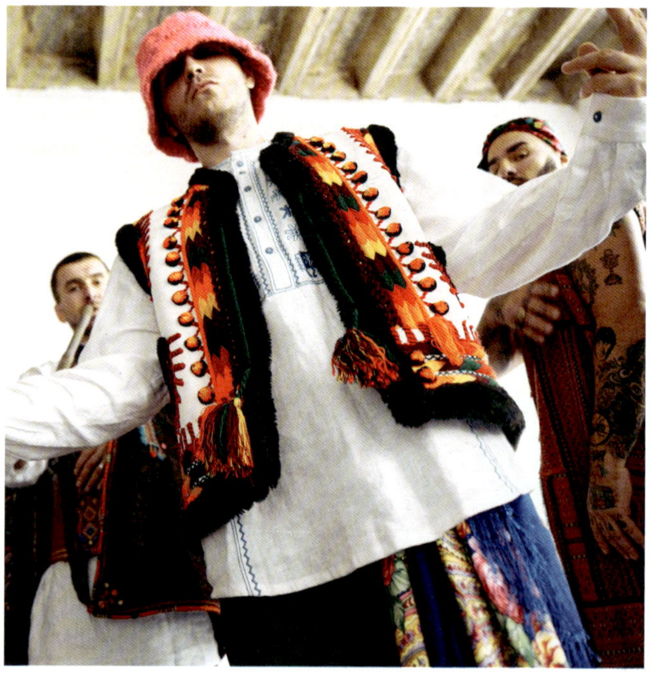

THE EPICENTER OF CREATIVE YOUTH

In the last decade between the revolution and the current war, images and videos of young people dancing at techno parties in industrial spaces circulated widely, portraying Kyiv as Europe's capital of creative youth. Visitors from around the globe, including the United States, Australia, and Europe, were delighted to find a thriving youth culture with its own unique mix of slang, fashion, music, art, and identity.

During this turbulent post-Maidan period, marked by Russia's annexation of Crimea and its military invasion of the Donbas region, Ukraine emerged as a cultural terra incognita, one that suddenly captured the world's attention. Over time, Kyiv became a magnet for tourists interested in contemporary electronic music. Its proximity to European cities (usually a short flight), friendly locals, and open-minded atmosphere contributed to its success on the international electronic music scene.

While the city boasted a wide range of events, it is perhaps best known for the popular Ostrov, Strichka, Brave Factory, Atlas Weekend, and Cxema festivals. First held a few months after the Euromaidan, Cxema has been hosted in various legal and semi-legal venues throughout the years, including skate parks, cinema pavilions, abandoned garages, and warehouses. By repurposing these spaces, the festival has instilled a newfound appreciation for industrial architecture among younger generations, helping them see it as more than just a relic of the Soviet era. With its experimental ethos

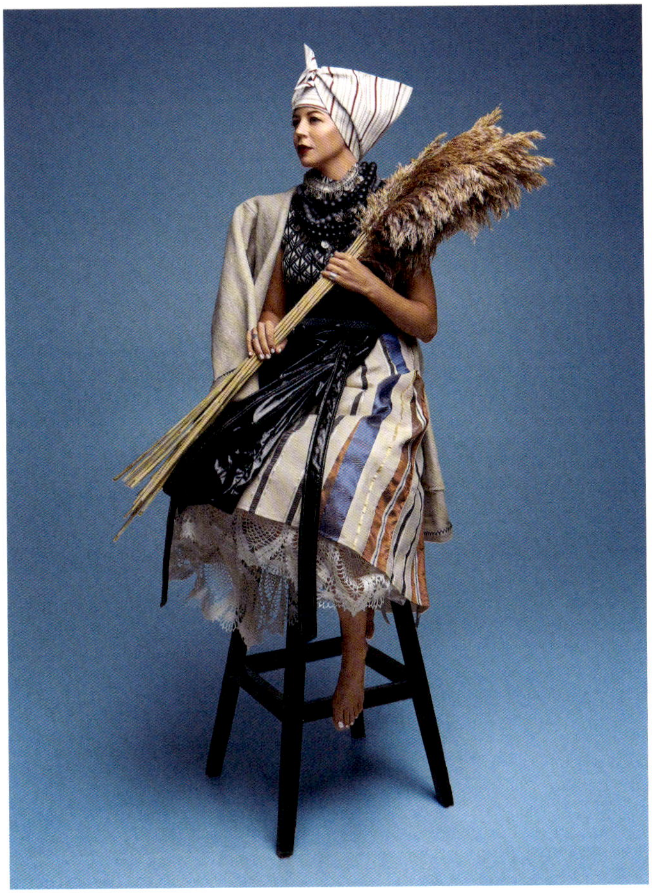

Ukrainian band ONUKA blends national folk motifs with electronic music. Above: Nataliia Zhyzhchenko, frontwoman of ONUKA. Below: ceramic plate by Gunia Project.

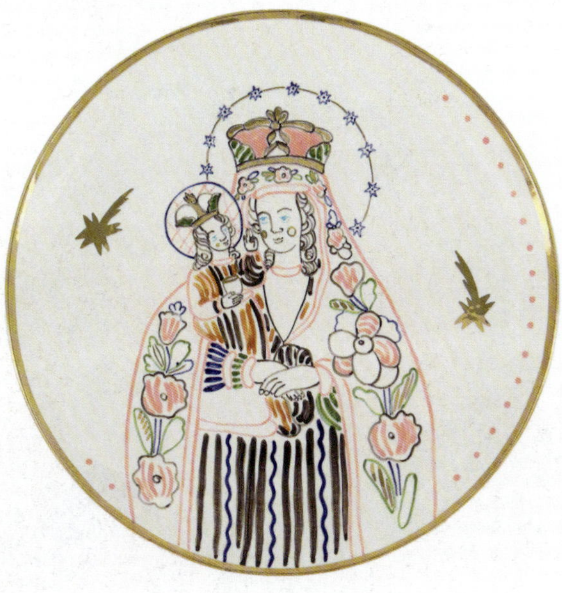

and focus on talented local artists, Cxema has become a springboard for up-and-coming DJs and music producers. While people often come to Cxema to get lost in the music, many leave having felt a deep sense of unity and liberation. Music events like this embody the spirit of change in the country and resonate with other prominent music initiatives in Kyiv, such as the Ukho Music Agency, which focuses on contemporary, classical, and improvised music. The agency has not only put on impressive audiovisual performances, it has also succeeded in uniting an unlikely mix of people: artists, poets, and musicians mingle with techno-club kids, old-school intelligentsia, and trendy bohemians.

The influence of club culture has led to a revival of '90s fashion and an inclusive environment that recognizes all genders, body types, and political expressions. Podil, one of Kyiv's key nightlife destinations, serves as an important meeting place for this movement. By day, the scene moves to the fashionable district of Reitarska, offering cafés, restaurants, and stylish-yet-affordable boutiques. The area is also home to several notable art galleries, such as The Naked Room, whose co-founders, Lizaveta German and Maria Lanko, also curated the National Pavilion of Ukraine at the 59th La Biennale di Venezia in 2022.

CHANGING PERCEPTION

These gatherings were more than parties: they reflected broader societal changes. Ukraine's cultural industries have experienced remarkable growth since 2014, fueled by a community of free-spirited, style-conscious individuals eager to redefine their cultural identity. For this group, it was crucial to shed Russia's imperial portrayal of Ukraine as a mere province. They also sought to break free from the West's post-Soviet gaze, when the countries of the Eastern Bloc were often portrayed as familiar but exotic—a striking blend of brutalist architecture, stagnating suburbs, and a cast of brazen working-class youth dressed in casual sports attire. Ukrainians came to see how lacking this depiction was, profoundly incapable of capturing the full essence of their country.

The urgency to reclaim Ukrainian culture prompted the development of a distinct voice, marked by a blend of patriotism, irony, and an unwavering faith in the nation's uniqueness. This voice is epitomized by books like *Awesome Ukraine* (Osnovy Publishing), a series of unconventional city guides, or *Orthodox Chic* (Osnovy Publishing), which documents new forms of religious architecture, including everything from kiosks to shopping-mall chapels.

Interestingly, the nation's image has also gotten a major boost from its rapidly growing IT sector. The country's strong foundation in math and engineering, inherited from the USSR, has played a significant role in the industry's success. Initially a hub for outsourcing due to relatively low labor costs, IT has evolved into a leading intellectual sector in Ukraine. This progress led to the creation of the Ministry of Digital Transformation, with the goal of making Ukraine a digital state and a frontrunner in cybersecurity—an objective made all the more urgent by the country's ongoing war. An increasing number of Ukrainian companies are now working to develop their own IT solutions and establish Ukraine as a prominent technology hub in Europe. These companies span multiple sectors, from fashion to education and healthcare, and include companies like Grammarly, Reface, Petcube, DressX, 3DLook, People.ai, Delfast, and Esper Bionics, among others.

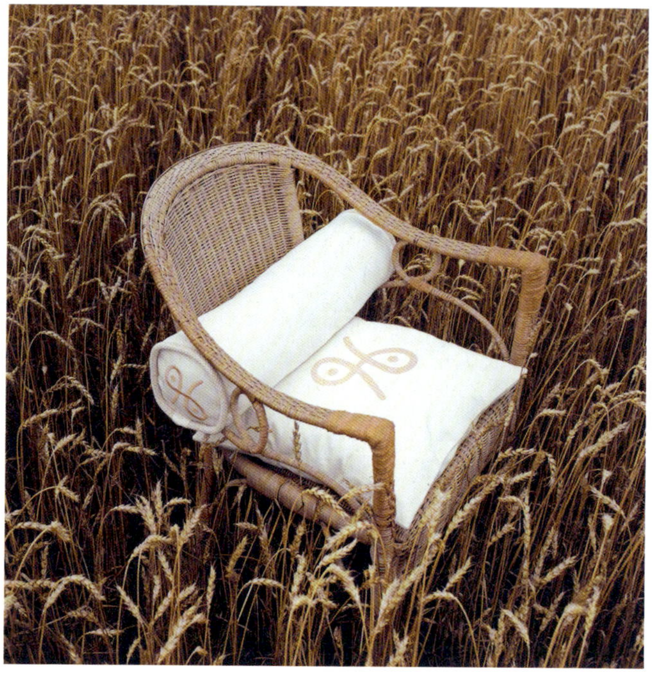

Founded by Iryna Kovalchouk, OSELYA Home and Garden creates modern decor steeped in tradition. Below: each jewelry piece by ZHERNOV Artifactory is a unique work of art.

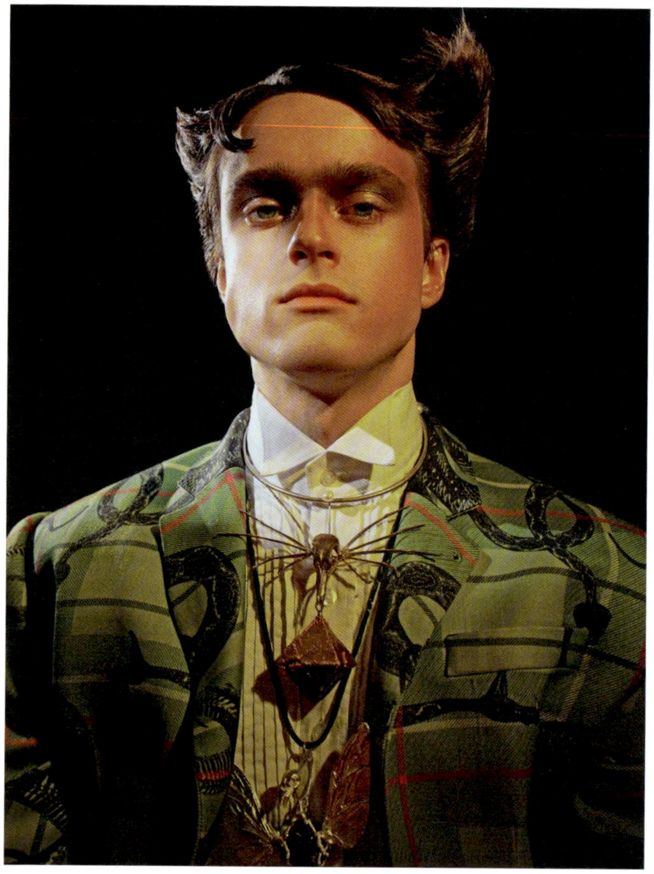

NEWLY ENGAGED WITH THE HERITAGE

In Ukraine it's not uncommon to see people wearing traditional attire simply because they feel like it, without any need for a special occasion. This is a testament to how the ongoing process of creating a new Ukrainian identity is shaped by engaging with its rich heritage. Throughout this process, the country has had to examine and discard stereotypes about Ukrainians perpetuated during the Soviet era. Often these were based on a distorted and oversimplified version of folk culture.

This cultural soul-searching has led to a lasting trend: blending traditional elements into modern culture. This has touched every corner of Ukrainian culture, evident in music, design, cinema, architecture, and gastronomy.

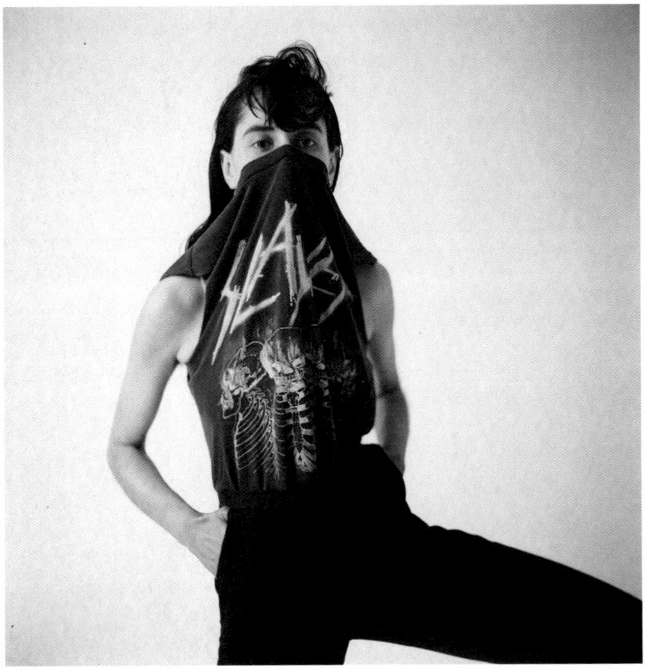

Lena Shkoda, a Ukrainian photographer based in New York, enjoys experimenting with ideas of fashion and sexuality, approaching them with a lighthearted, often ironic touch.

In some instances, this cultural exploration has taken on political significance, as with the case of borshch, the region's renowned local dish. Determined culinary activist, Ievgen Klopotenko, fought to establish its Ukrainian origin and succeeded in having it inscribed on UNESCO's List of Intangible Cultural Heritage in 2022.

This growing interest in Ukrainian history, along with a renewed appreciation for its landscapes and traditions, has given rise to a strong sense of national identity. It has also made Ukrainians more eager to rediscover the natural beauty of their country, from the rolling hills hugging the Dnipro River to the pink lakes near Kherson, and the vast grasslands of the eastern Steppe. Still, the Carpathian Mountains, with their ancient forests and stunning views, continue to be the premier destination for travelers looking to experience Ukraine beyond its urban centers. In addition to offering the tourist trifecta—food, sights, and nature—the region has evolved into a creative hub for artists of all kinds seeking to learn traditional crafts, and to master local techniques in ceramics, glassmaking, weaving, and textiles. For instance, the concept of the Gunia Project, a brand that produces modern household textiles and decor with a traditional flair, was born during such a voyage. The brand was in fact named after a coat traditionally worn by the inhabitants of the region. The garment was also the inspiration behind Gunia Project's first product, a cruelty-free fur coat made from knitted sheep's wool and produced exclusively in the Carpathian Mountains. This eco-conscious approach to authentic crafts aligns with the growing popularity of sustainable production, making the brand all the more relevant today. The passion for handicrafts has led to the creation of various other brands seeking to develop a new Ukrainian style, such as Makhno Studio's furniture and decor, Olk Manufactory's quirky carpets that feature folk ornaments and pop-culture symbols, and the Nadiia project, which connects contemporary creatives with ceramic masters.

Victoria Yakusha, the founder of both the Yakusha Studio and the decor brand Faina, takes things one step further: "Usually, people go somewhere like Mexico or India for inspiration. And I want them to come to us," she says. Committed to turning Ukraine into a global destination for folklore inspiration, she invited international journalists and designers to visit several artisanal spots in the Carpathian region for the 2018–2019 project "Land Inspires." The guests, interior designers and journalists from Sweden, Italy, and the U.K., were astonished that the folk and craft culture in these regions was alive and thriving—a stark contrast to many countries whose folk traditions can only be found behind glass, preserved in museums.

Over the past decade, Ukrainians' euphoric celebration of their country has evolved into a proactive stance, one that has fostered a proud national consciousness and led the nation to pursue ambitious goals, from developing competitive creative and tech industries within Ukraine to defending democratic values worldwide.

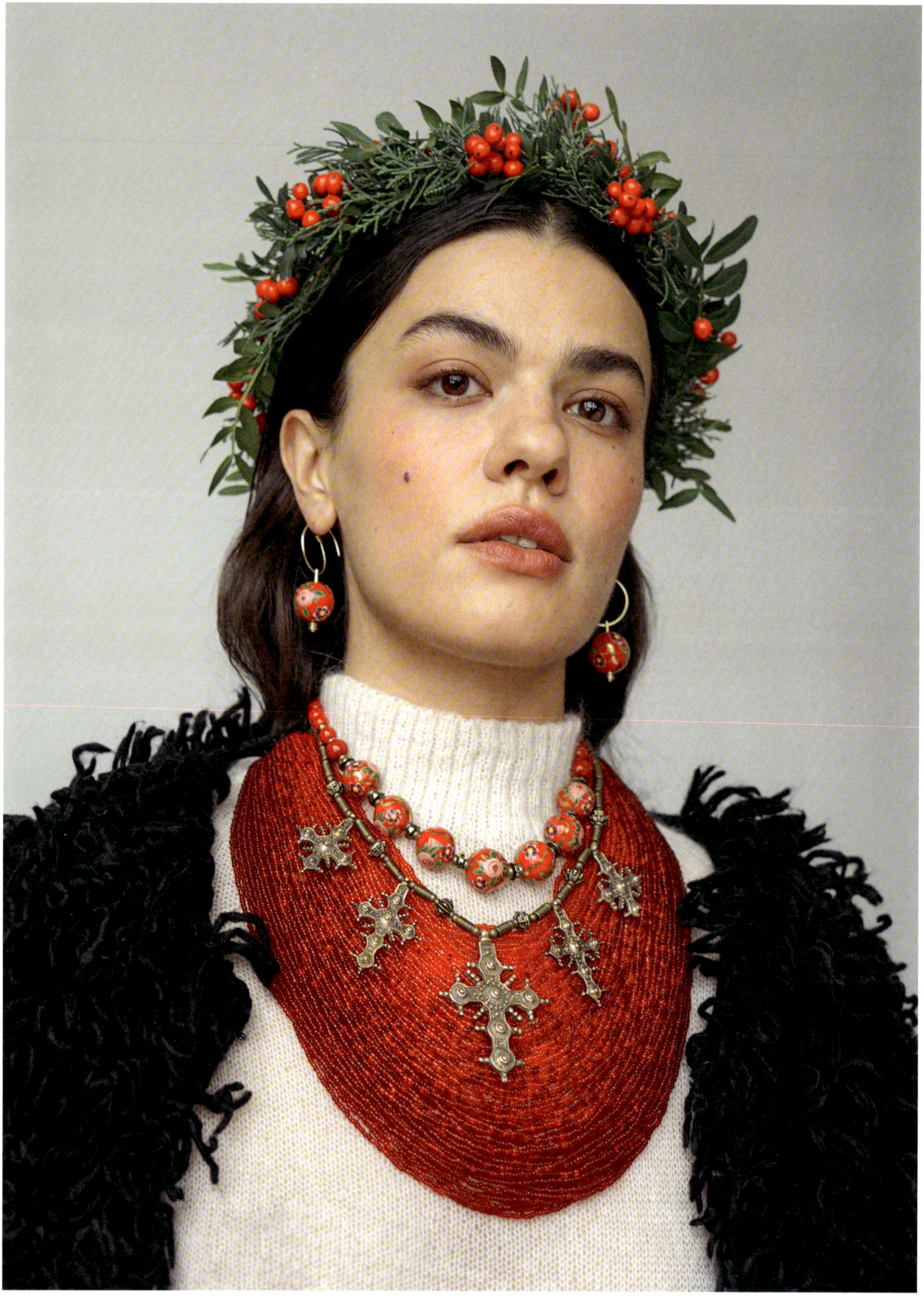

AMULETS OF ANCESTORS

OKSANA BORIYCHUK · *ОКСАНА БОРІЙЧУК*

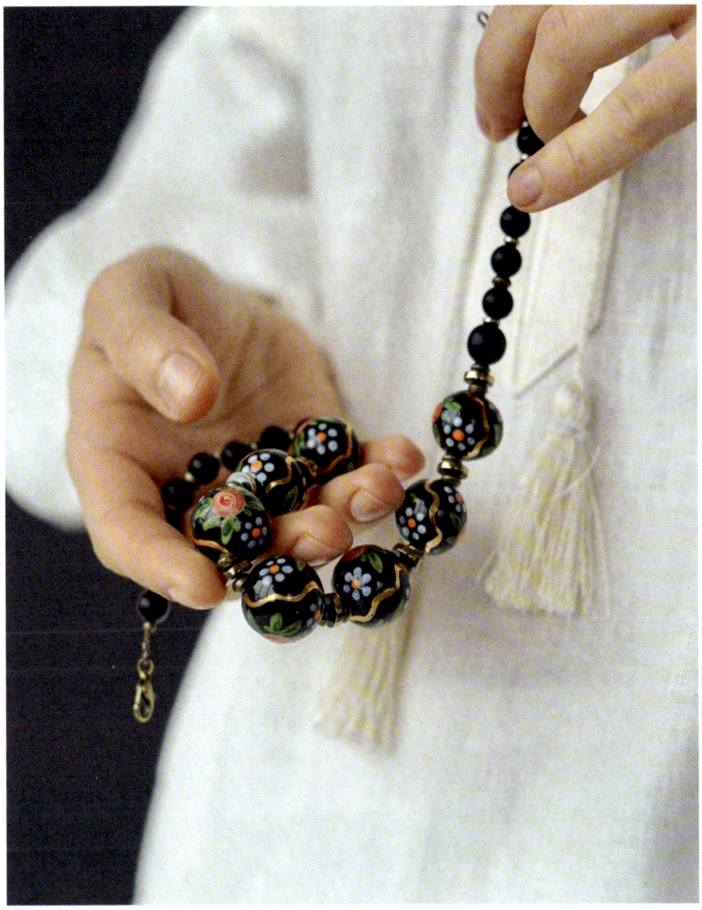

Oksana Boriychuk celebrates her love for Ukrainian heritage and culture through her jewelry, bringing time-honored traditions into everyday life.

Jewelry designer Oksana Boriychuk is almost as passionate about history as she is about her craft, which explains the traditional motifs that permeate her work. Her jewelry seamlessly blends modern aesthetics with a clear homage to the cultural heritage of Ukraine. One of Boriychuk's main goals is to infuse Ukrainians' everyday looks with traditional elements. The designer uses a wide variety of materials to achieve this: cast brass, natural gems, beads, glass, and glazed ceramics. One of Boriychuk's latest collections, titled "Christmas Light," showcases intricate Borshchiv embroidery and uses a striking red and black color palette. Boriychuk chose intricate floral patterns to symbolize hope, and the collection's festive elements are further emphasized by the delightful jingling of brass adornments. In another collection, the designer created ceramic necklaces inspired by traditional painted beads. With their vivid colors, floral ornaments, and gold accents, they are designed to embody the symbolic significance of Ukrainian national identity. Boriychuk envisioned this necklace as both a protective talisman and a manifestation of the unbreakable faith of Ukrainians.

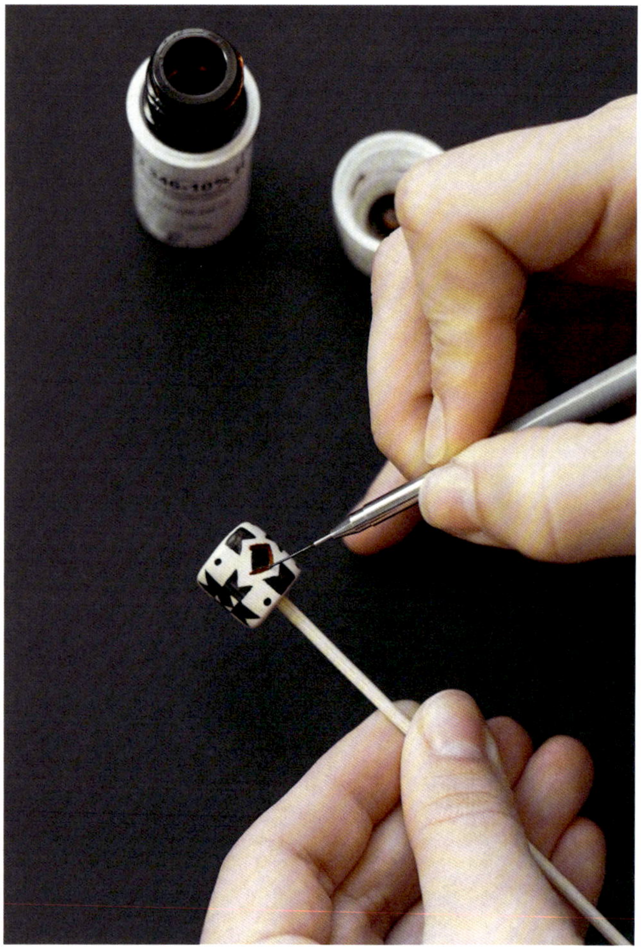

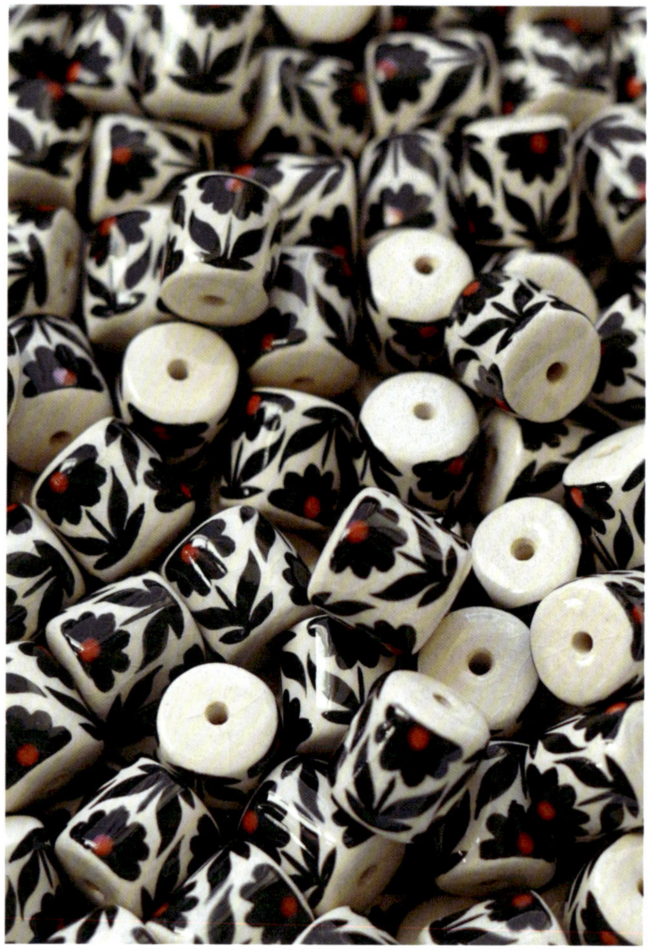

Painted ceramics are a recognizable feature of the Oksana Boriychuk brand. Clay beads are truly magical, because any idea can be expressed through their shape, color, and pattern. This is also meticulous work—each bead is hand-painted with a traditional motif.

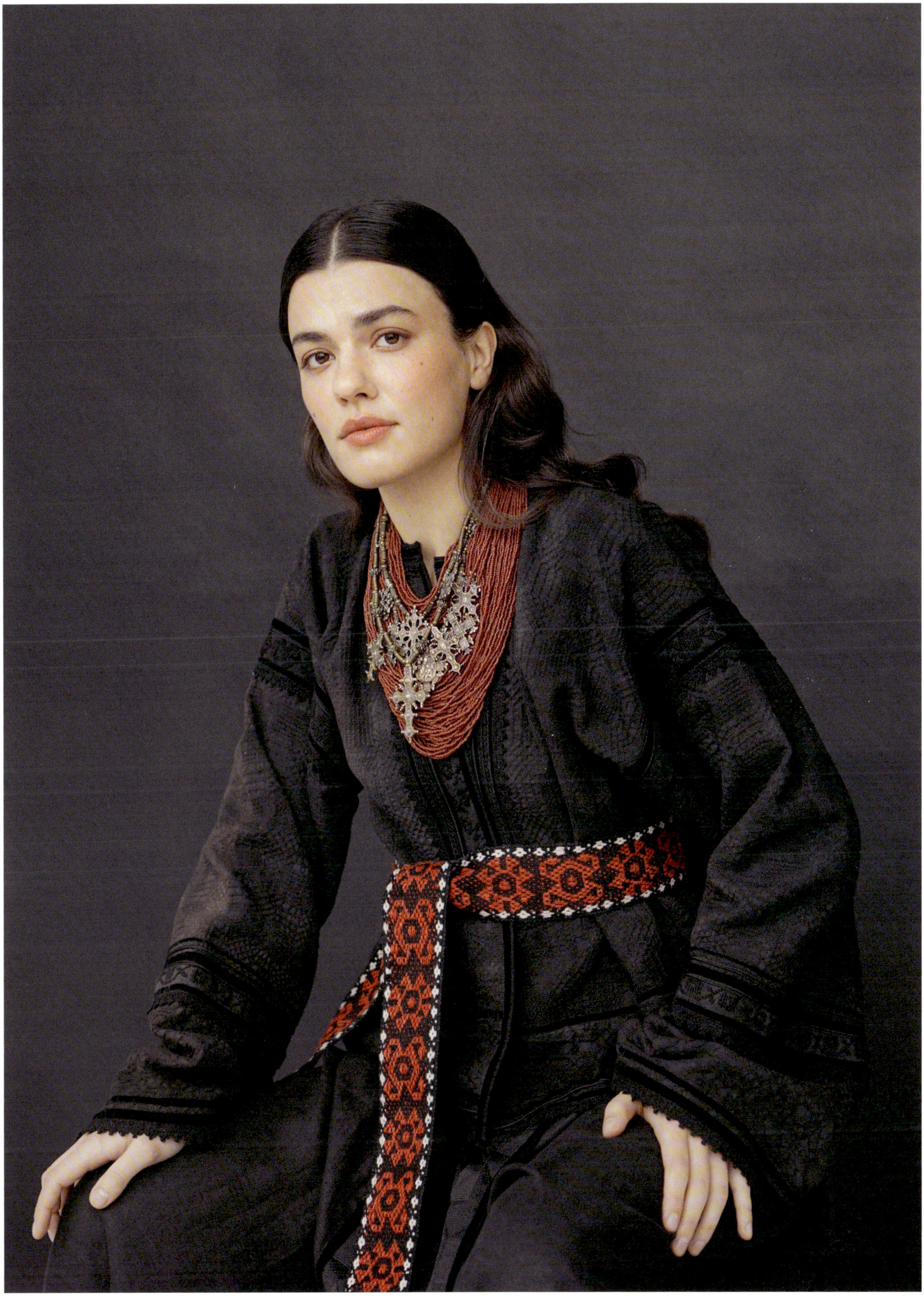

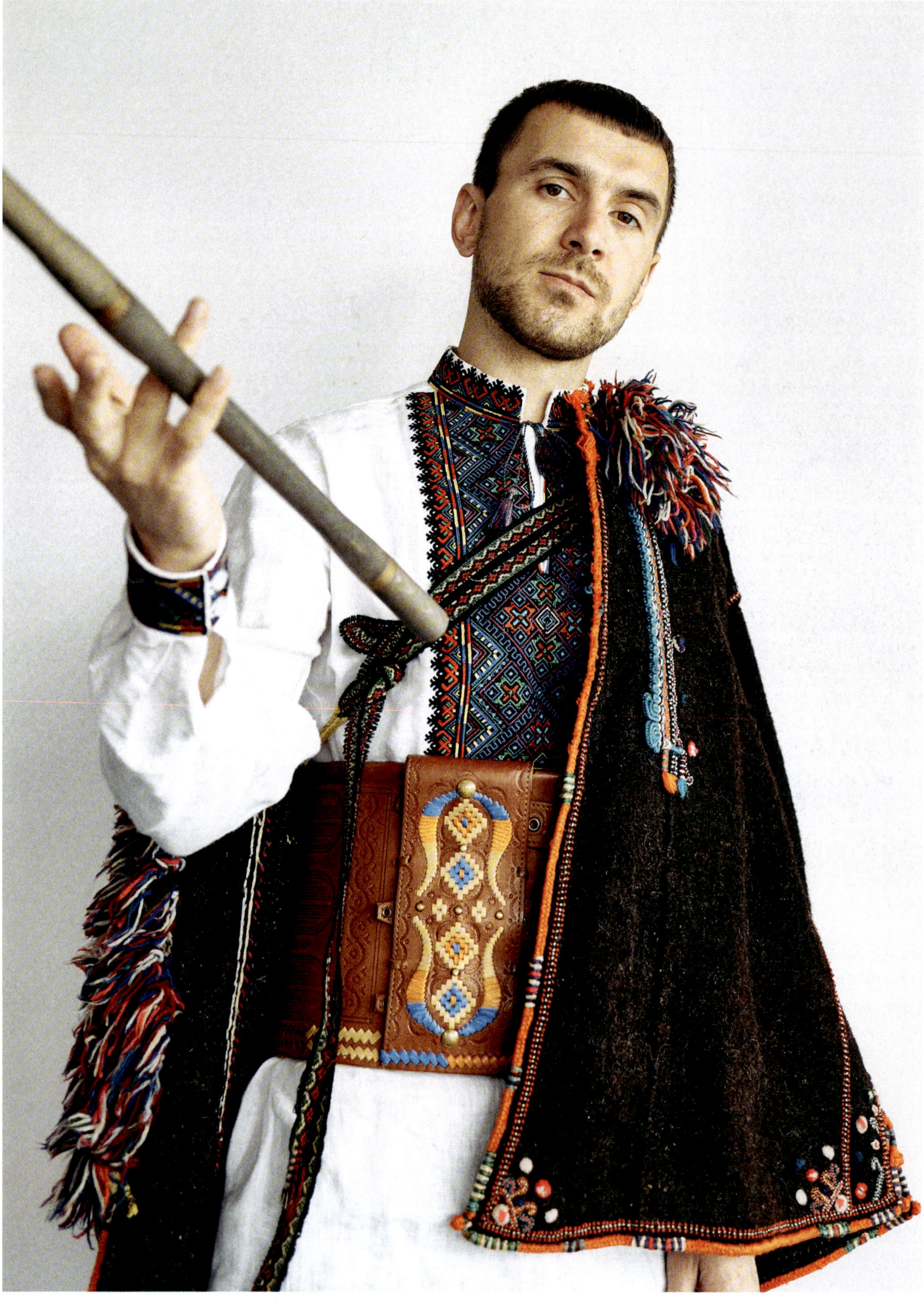

FOLK MUSIC REDEFINED

KALUSH ORCHESTRA

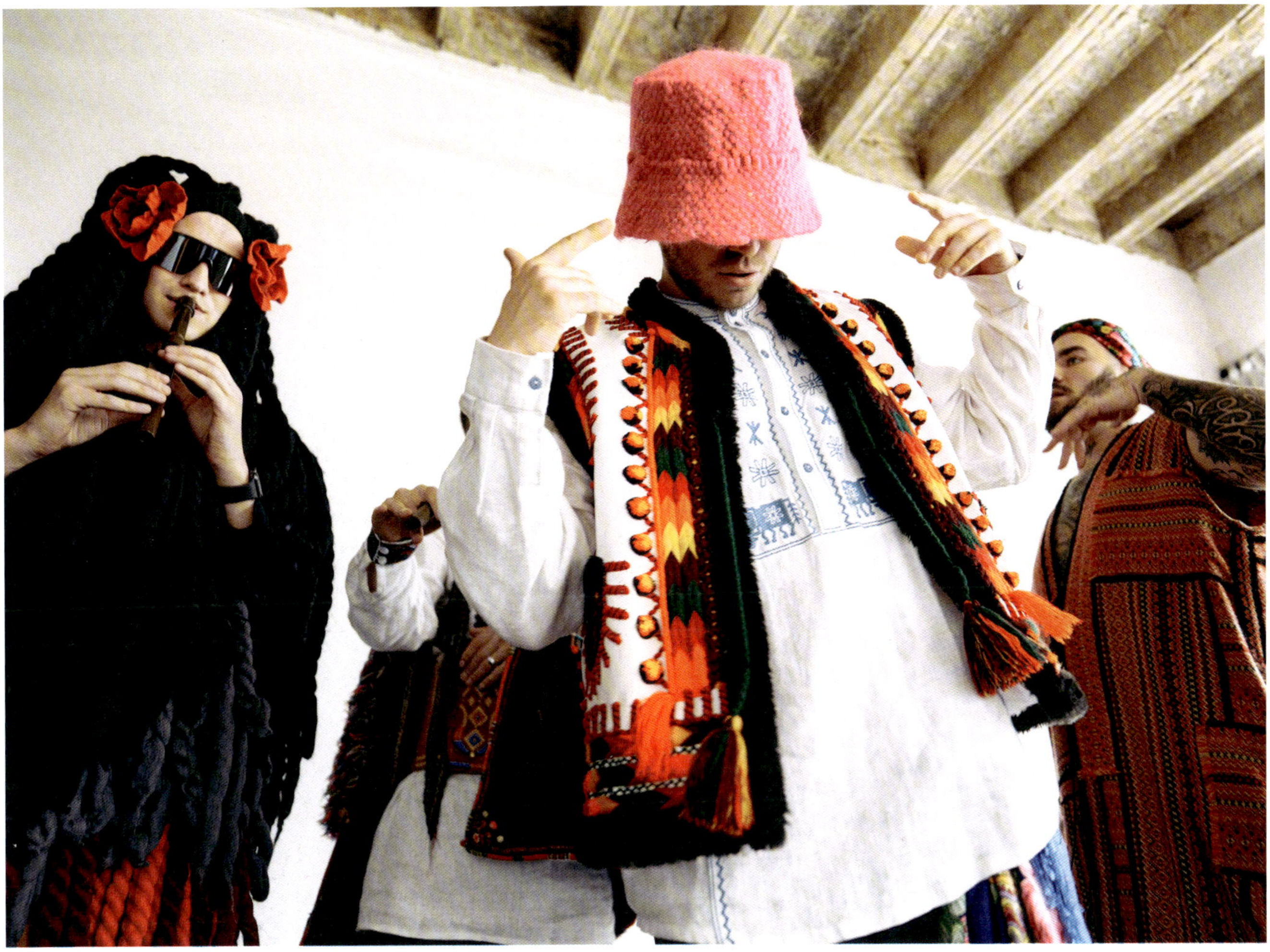

Kalush Orchestra expertly fuses Ukrainian folk music with modern production, blending hip-hop dance, rap, and vibrant traditional attire to create their signature folk-rap style.

Founded in 2021 by rapper Oleh Psiuk, the Kalush Orchestra is comprised of seven musicians (originally six). Named after Psiuk's hometown in western Ukraine, the band takes pride in bridging the gap between old and new: "We are taking old Ukrainian folklore that has been forgotten. We dig it up from many generations and add modern, contemporary elements, rap and instruments. As a result, we have a combination of what our ancestors had and what young people like today," explains Psiuk. Kalush Orchestra won a resounding victory at the Eurovision Song Contest 2022 with the song "Stefania," which masterfully combines rap and folklore in one track. Two traditional Ukrainian woodwind instruments, the telenka and sopilka, feature in the musical composition, and to further showcase their Ukrainian heritage, the band members often don *keptars*, the traditional garb of Hutsul molfars.

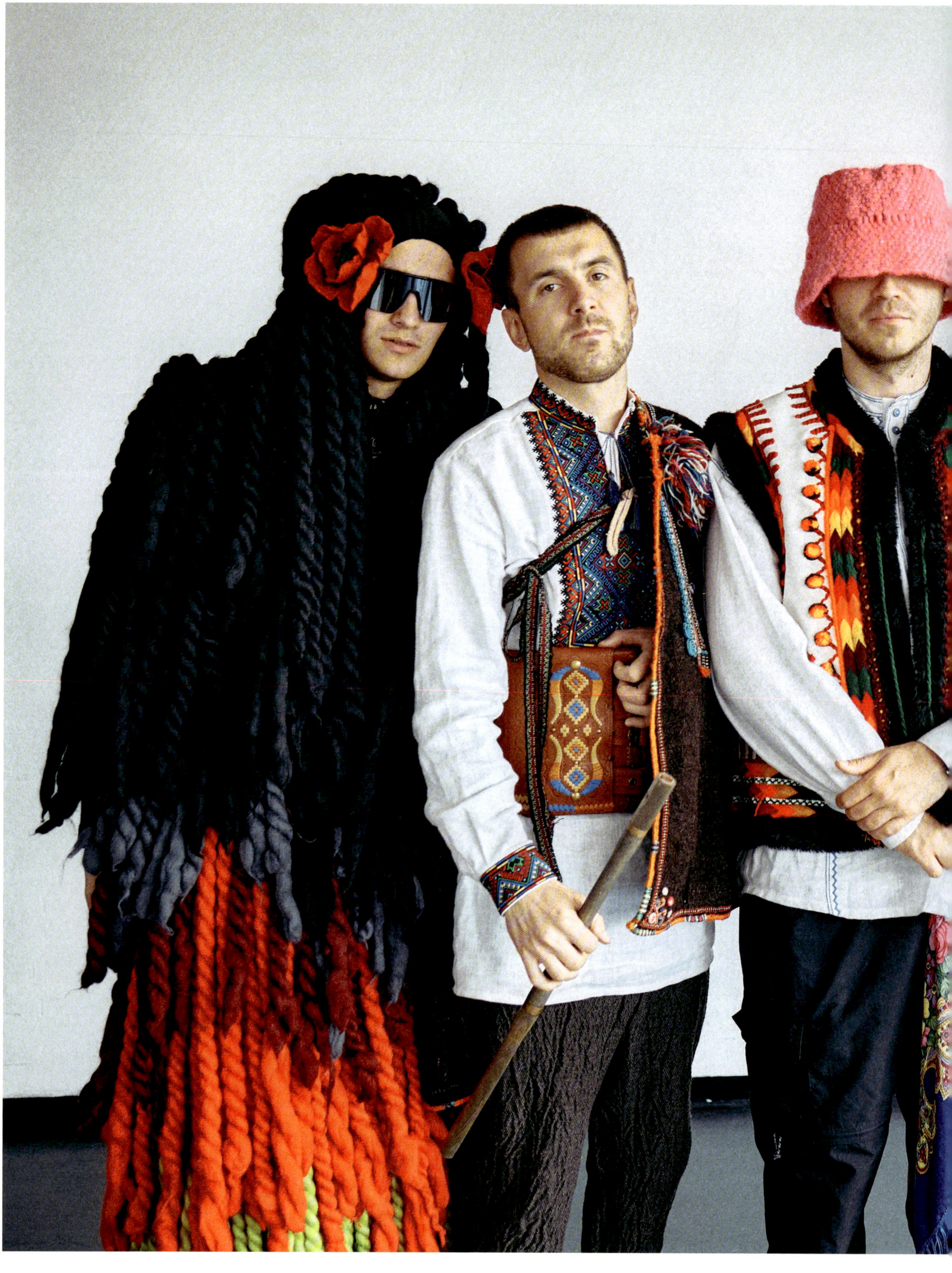

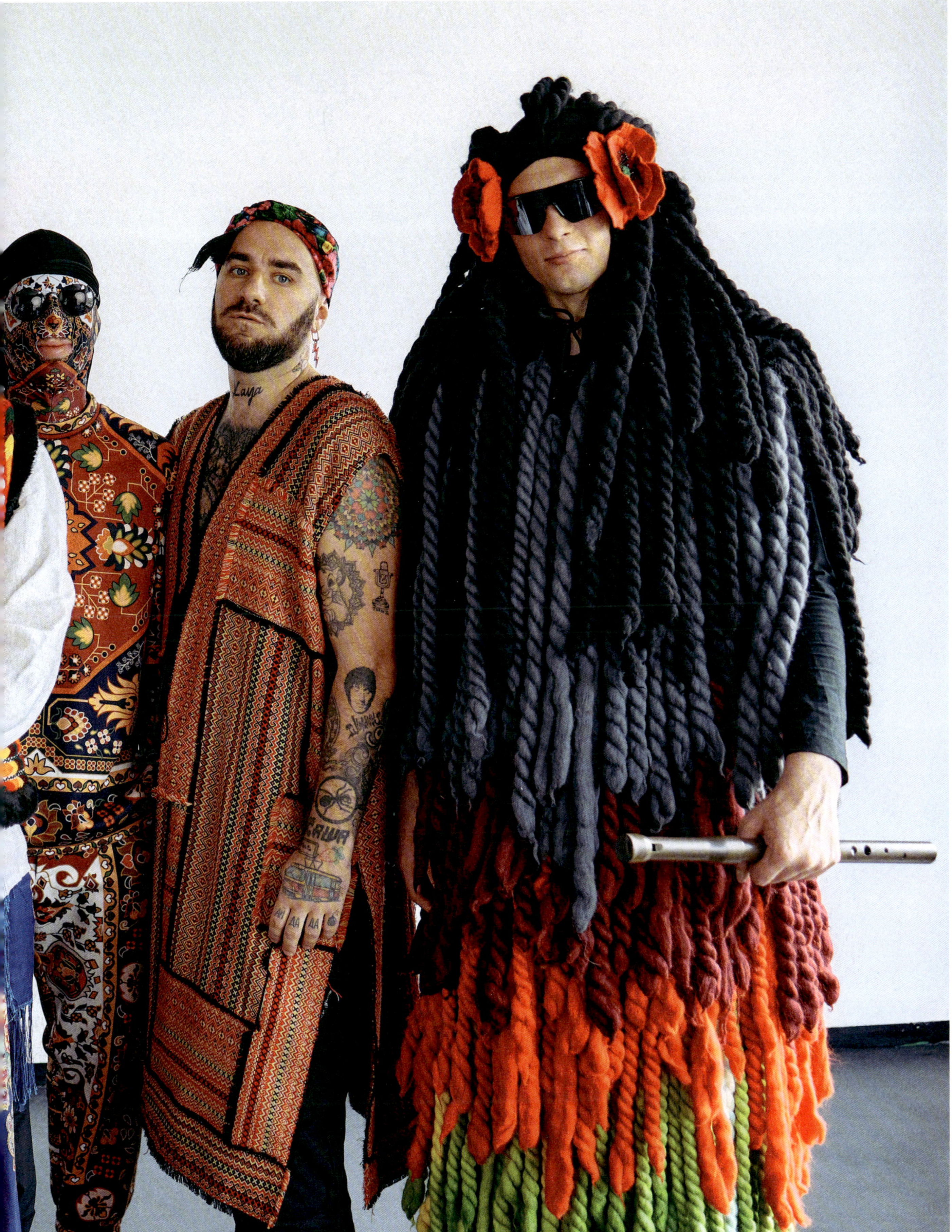

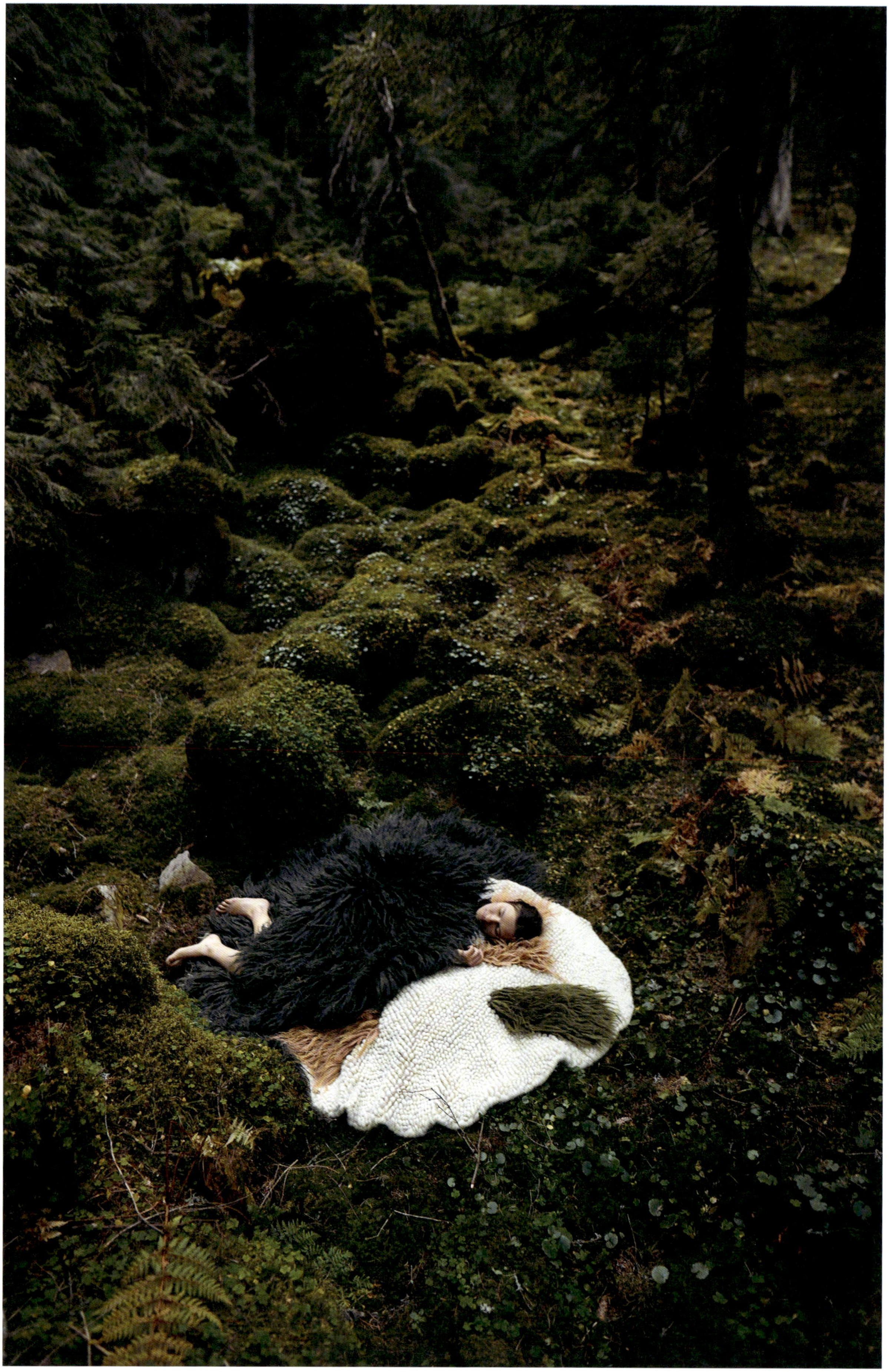

WARM PRODUCTS WITH A HOMEY FEEL

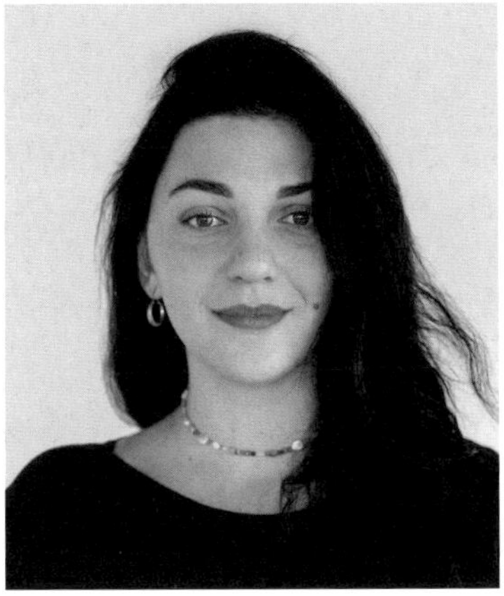 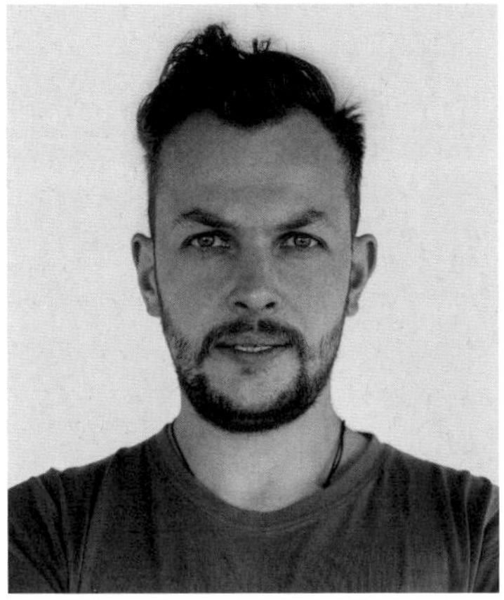

GUSHKA

Handcrafted from natural sheep's wool, Gushka products offer a special sense of peace, comfort, and love.

Founded in 2017 in the village of Yavoriv, Gushka is renowned for its distinctive range of home goods. The workshop is located in Kosiv, nestled among the lush forests and meadows of the Carpathian Mountains. Historically, this area was known for sheep farming and crafts such as blanket making. In the past, nearly every household raised sheep, producing cheese with the sheep's milk and weaving textiles from their wool. Gushka is dedicated to reviving these ancient traditions. Today, a talented team of craftswomen from all over Ukraine is helping Gushka accomplish this goal, often contributing knowledge and skills that they have inherited from older generations. Each Gushka product is a labor of love, with each item carefully handcrafted using age-old weaving techniques and heirloom looms, often passed down from their mothers and grandmothers. The craftswomen also prepare the wool, which involves steaming, dyeing, and raking it to achieve softness and consistency. The company's mission is to preserve the craft, hoping to popularize manual labor and highlight the importance of generational knowledge in the process. Every Gushka collection evokes warmth and belonging, with three distinct series: LIS, HUK, and a range of traditional *lizhnyks*. Drawing from the beauty of nature and the simplicity of everyday life, the brand incorporates these elements into everything they make. The HUK collection, inspired by a roaring river of the same name, highlights the importance of water in the craft. Meanwhile the LIS collection is full of forest imagery, depicting trails, pine trees, moss-covered stones, and dry grass swaying in the wind. Traditionally, *lizhnyk* blankets were not only used for decoration and warmth but also acted as personal talismans, protecting their owners throughout life. The blankets were handed down as treasured heirlooms, given as wedding gifts or to celebrate a birth birth, as dowries, or sometimes accompanied their owners on their final journey.

"Every Gushka product is hard work. Everything is made by hand using traditional weaving technology, on the same looms that our ancestors used. Our mission is to protect this craft and popularize the knowledge shared by past generations."

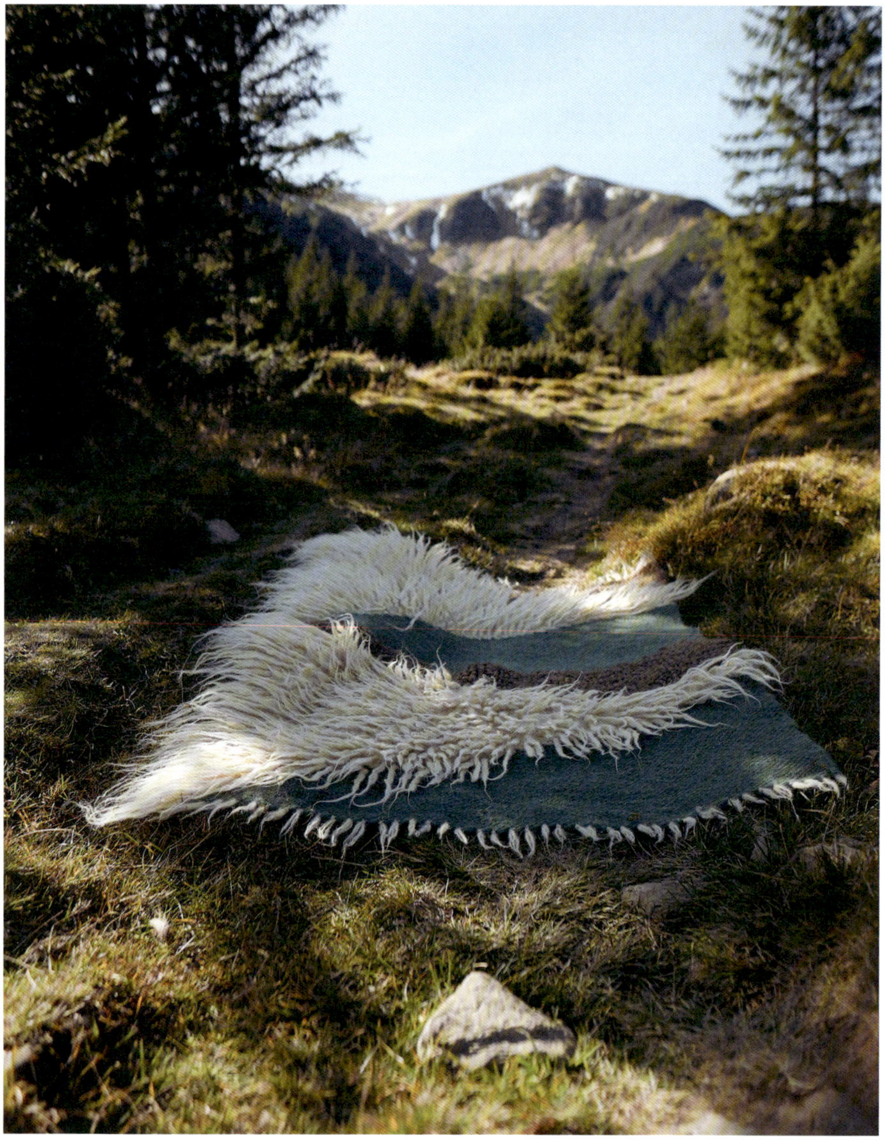

The Gushka project was founded deep in the Carpathian Mountains. The LIS collection (which translates in Ukrainian to "forest") is filled with woodland motifs. Its textures, colors, and patterns conjure everything from forest paths to moss-covered stones.

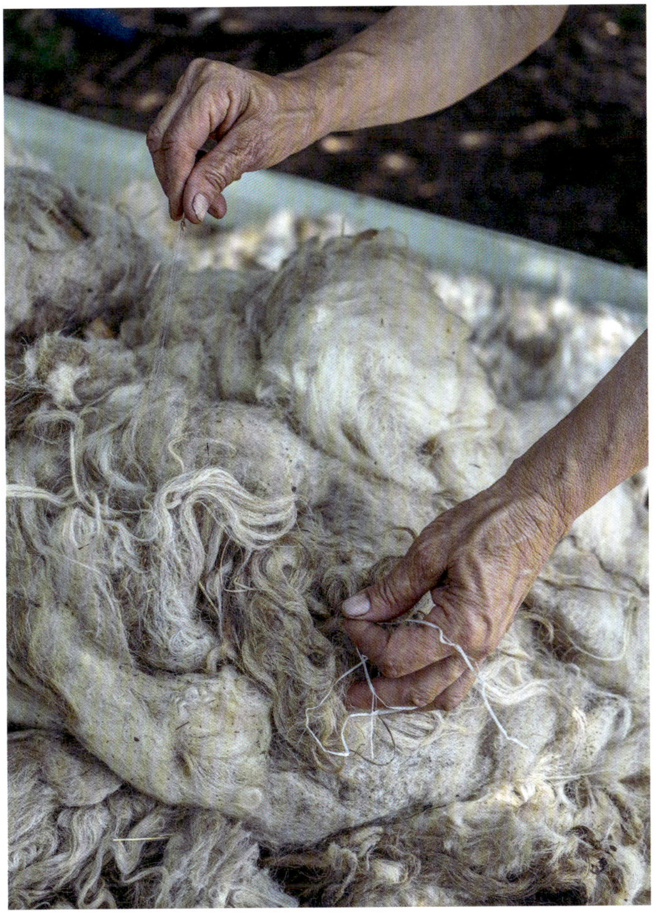
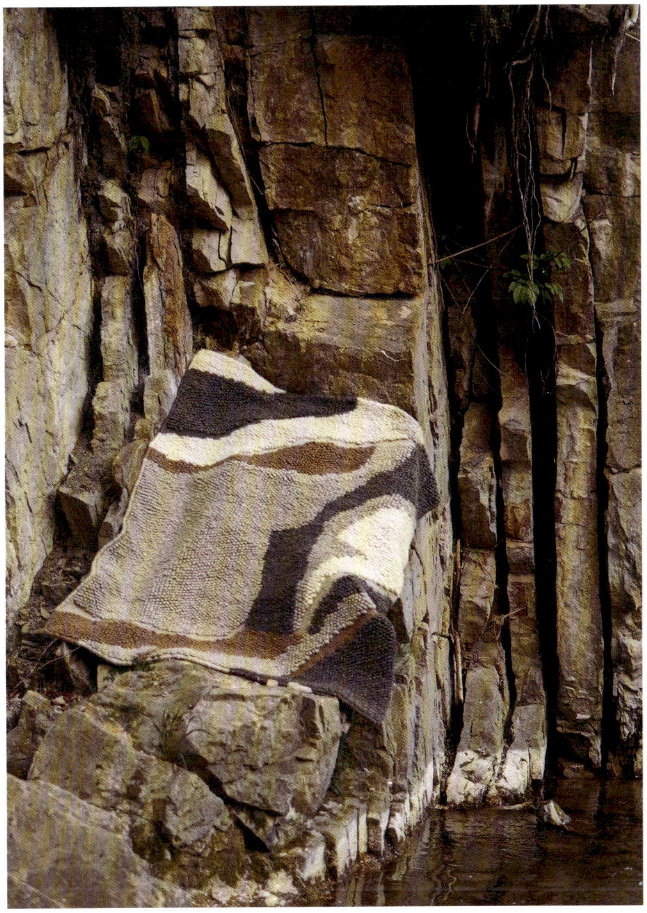
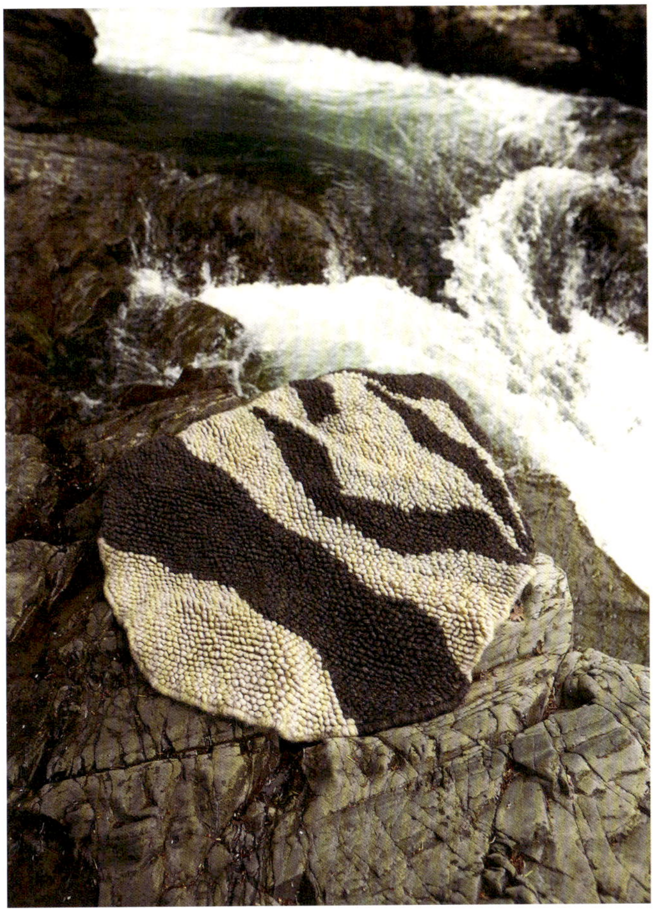
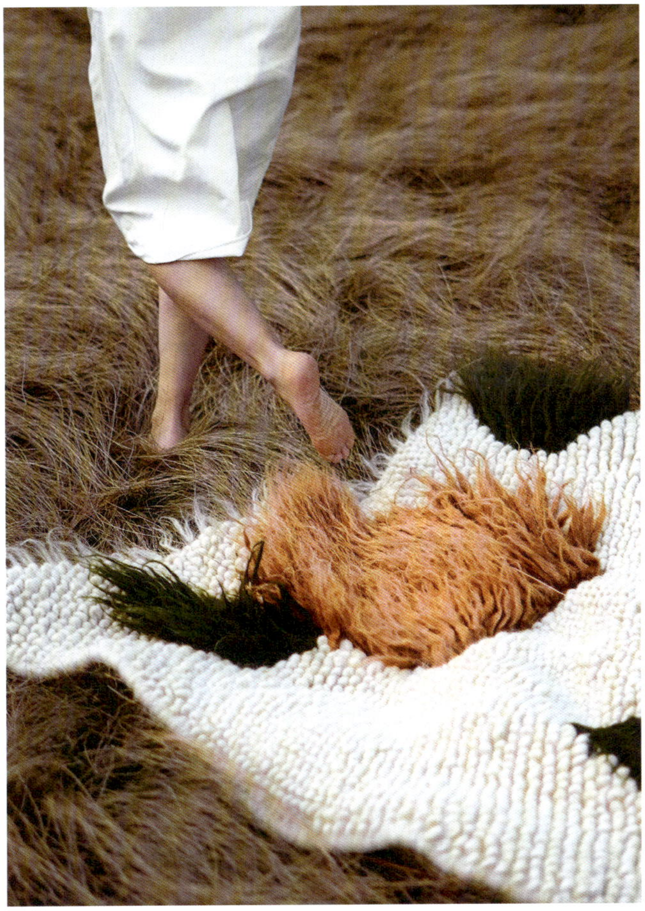

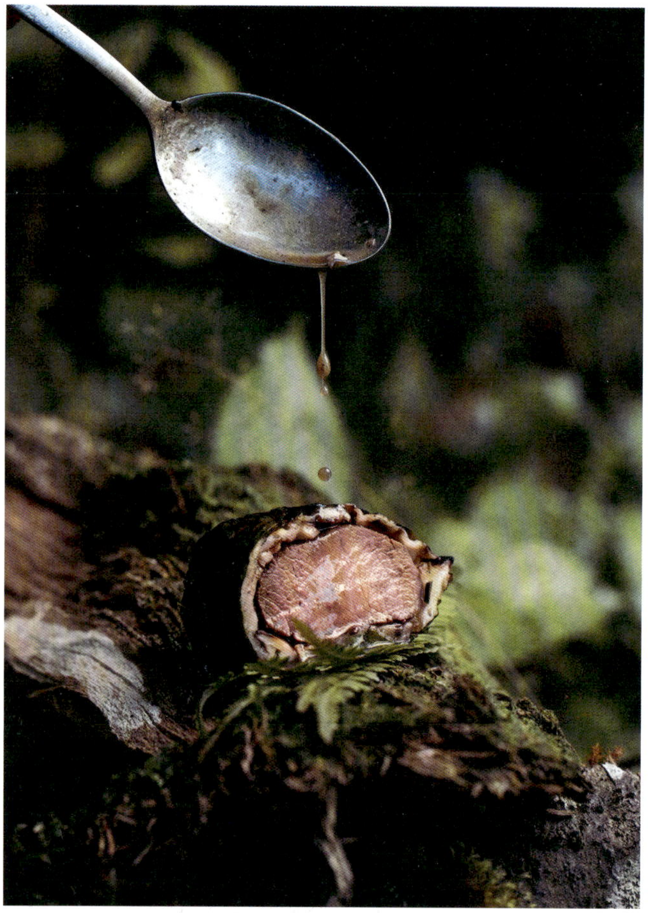

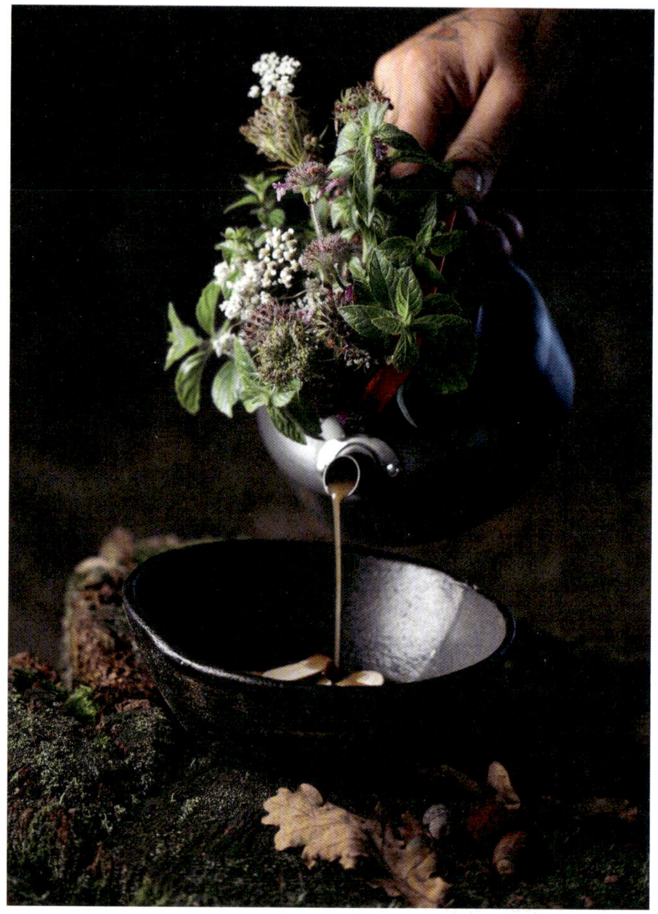

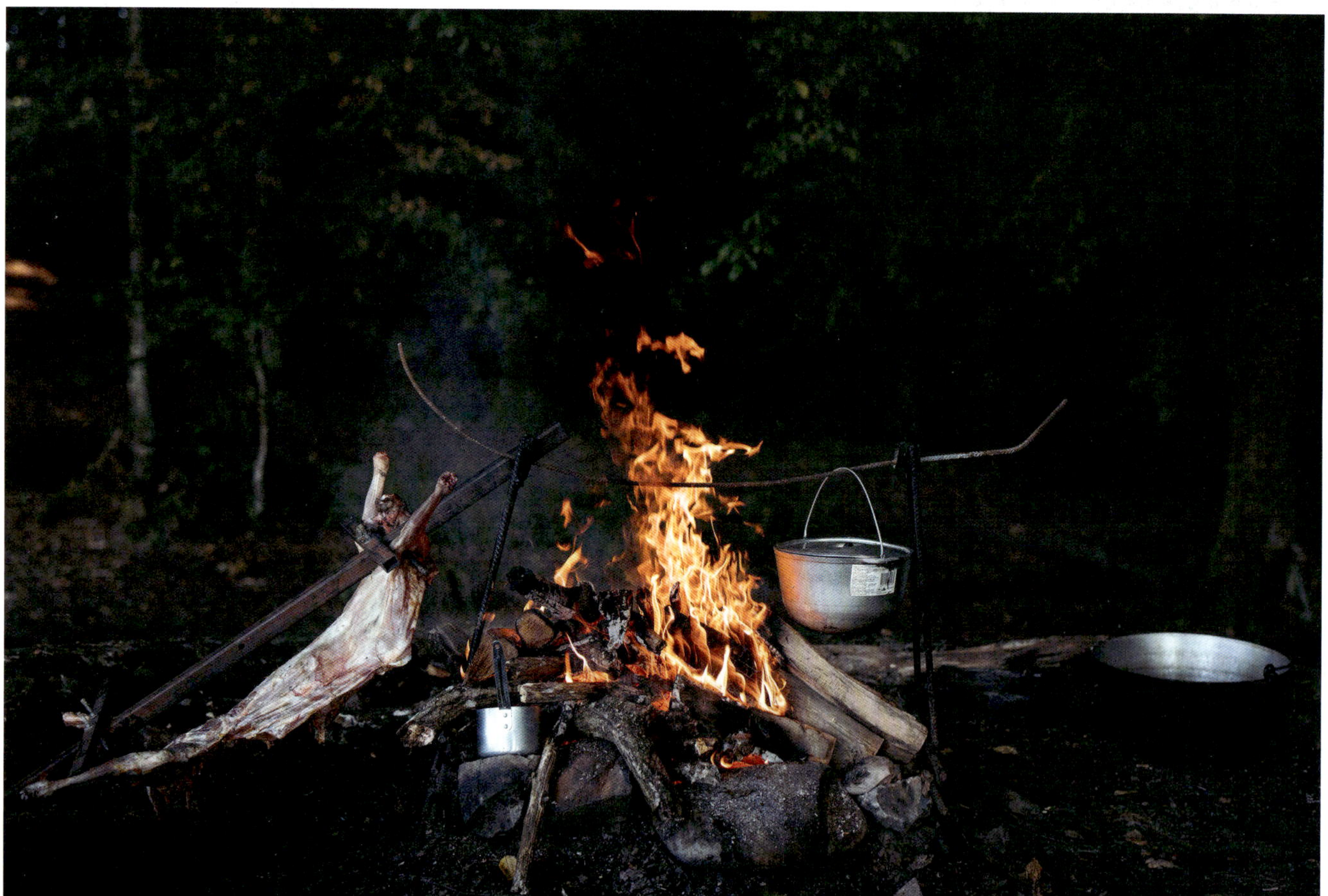

A PHOTOGRAPHER RETURNING TO HIS ROOTS

DIMA BAHTA · *ДМИТРО БАХТА*

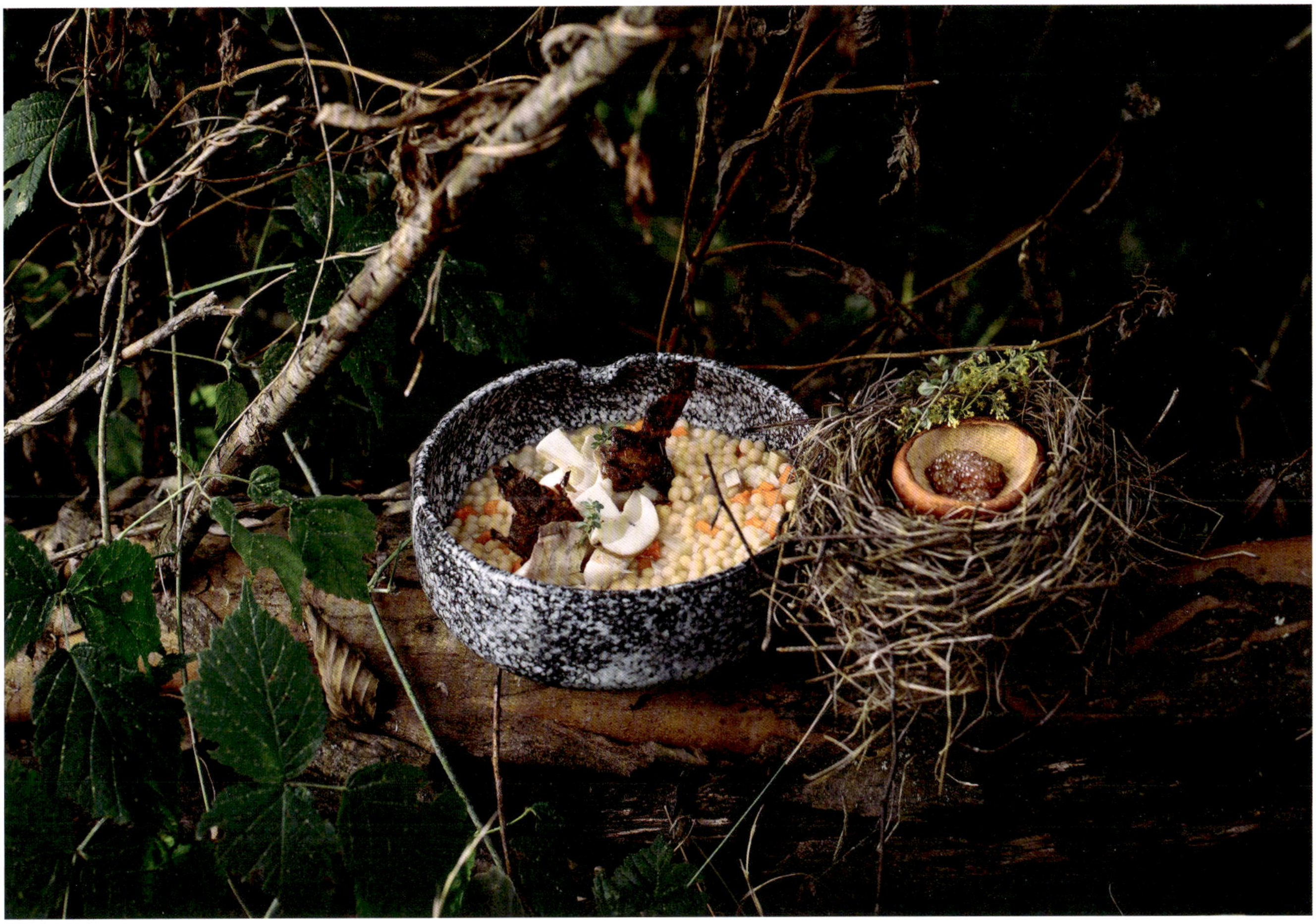

Dima Bahta depicts dishes as works of culinary art, a dance of textures and colors that evoke real emotions.

Throughout his distinguished career, food photographer Dima Bahta has collaborated on over 200 restaurant projects in Ukraine and across the globe. Bahta's professional food photography captivates with its vivid colors, rich textures, and dynamic compositions. Bahta is also actively involved in projects that explore and promote Ukrainian cuisine, local products, and the cultural diversity of the country's different regions. One such project is Topot, which Bahta co-founded with Igor Mezencev (see page 32). Since 2019, they have brought together small teams of chefs from Ukraine and abroad to spend five days immersed in nature, where they cook without modern conveniences and use only foraged and locally available ingredients. When the dishes are done, Bahta uses his expertise to capture their creations on film. The project's main goal is for chefs to rediscover the essence and origins of Ukrainian food culture.

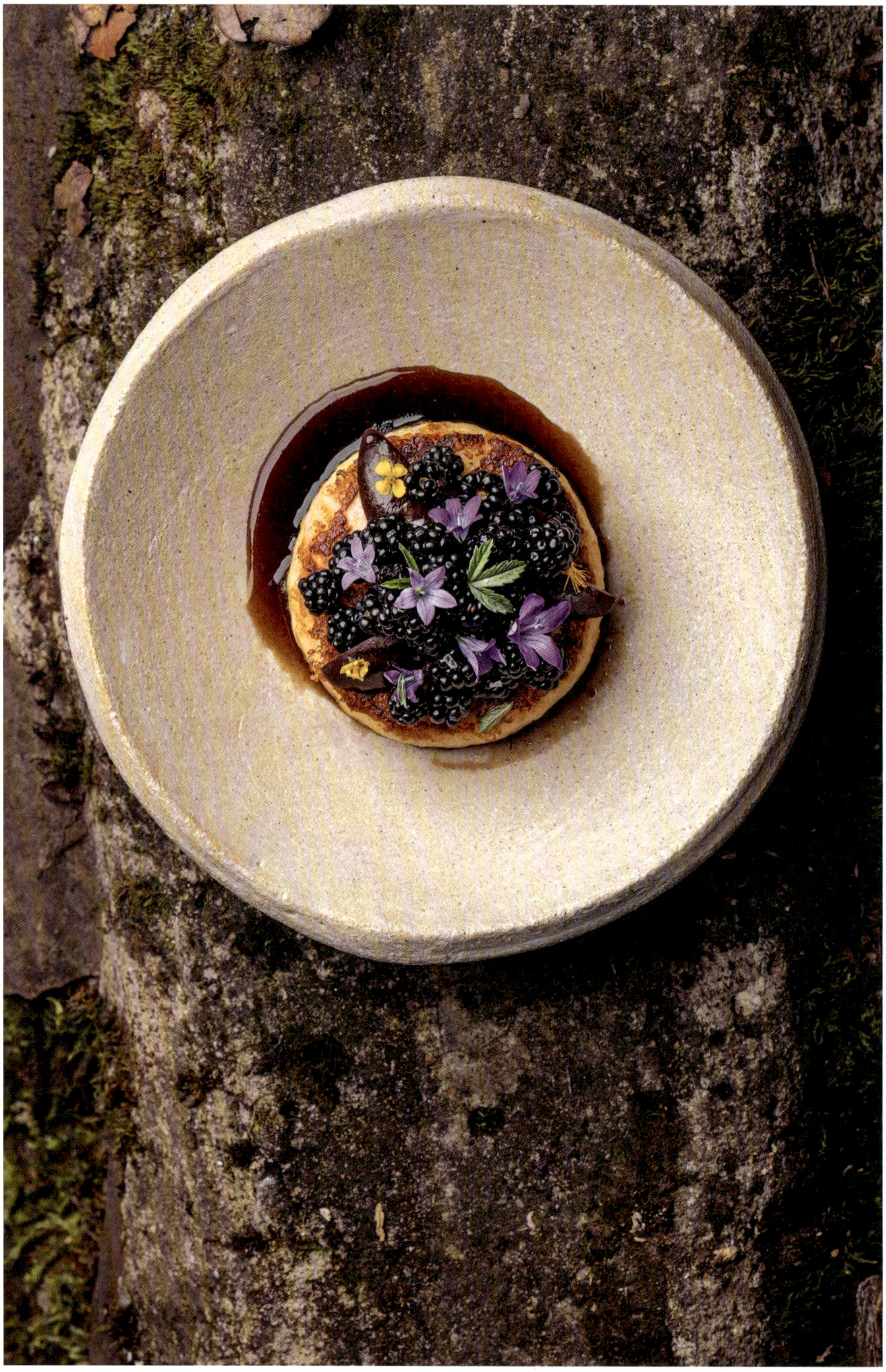

The Topot project focuses on wilderness survival, communal cooking and dining, and environmental stewardship. The project embraces Ukraine's abundant variety of natural landscapes and celebrates the country's rich culinary traditions.

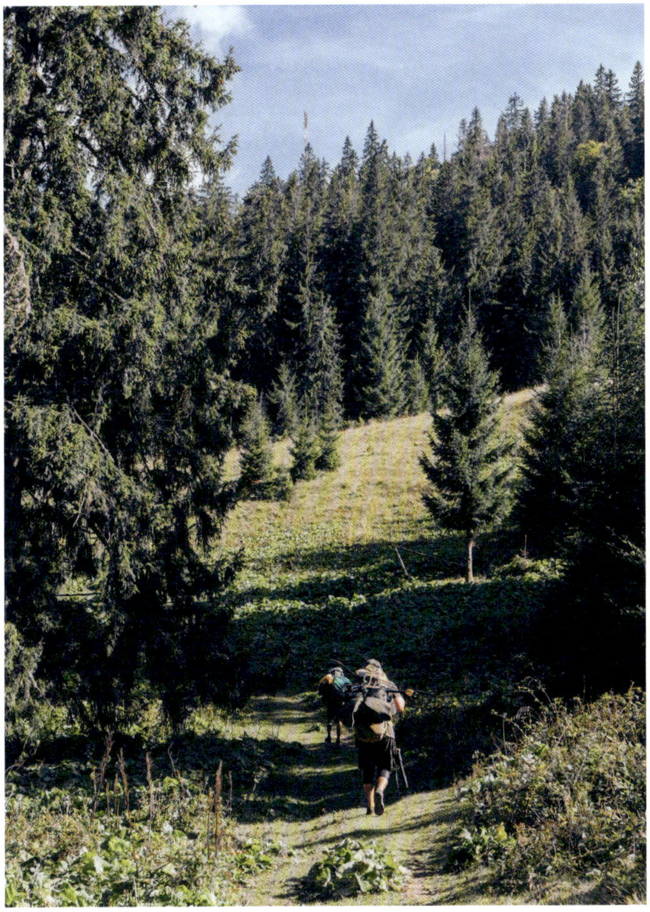
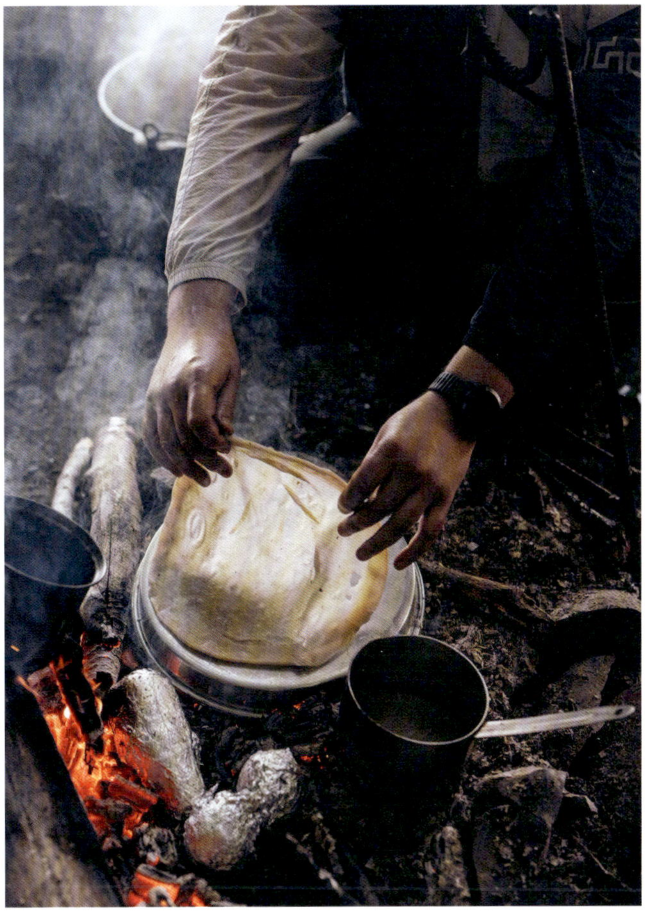
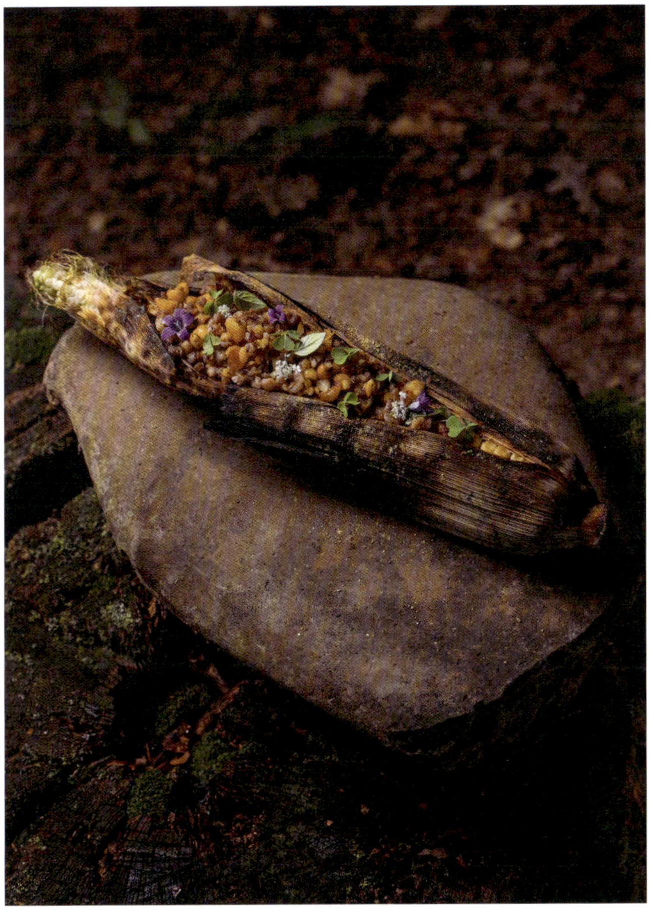
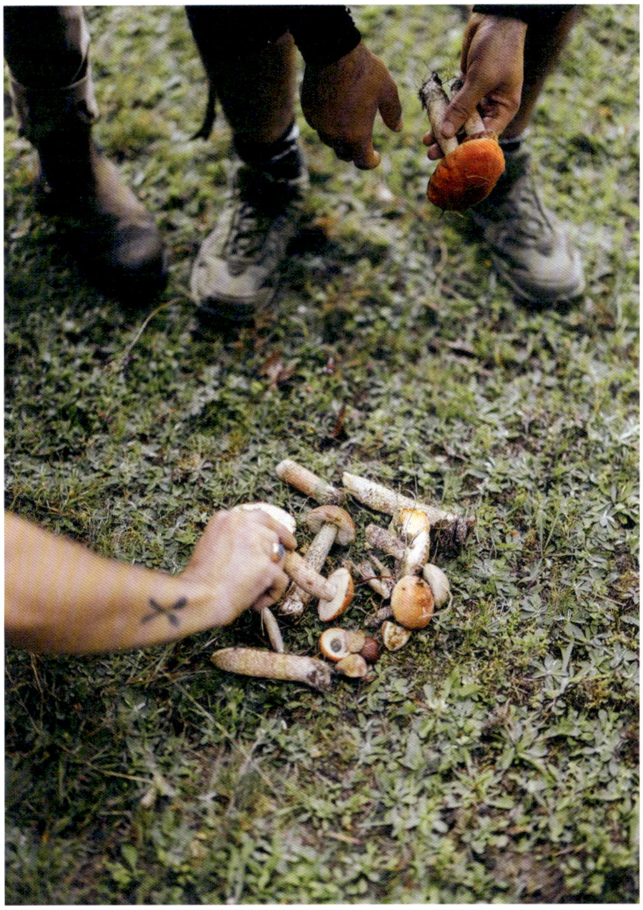

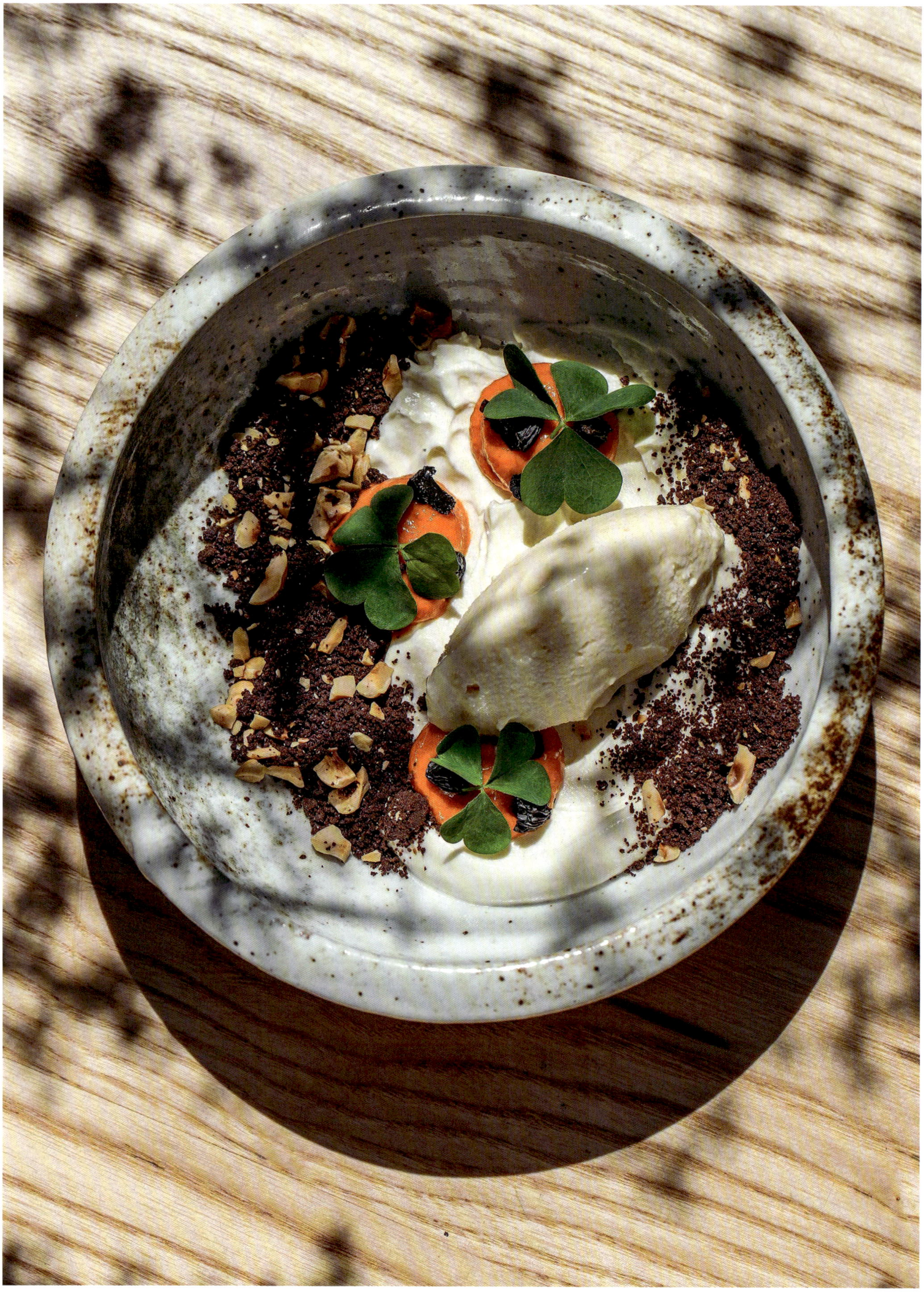

GASTRONOMIC DIPLOMACY AS A CULTURAL TOOL

IEVGEN KLOPOTENKO · *ЄВГЕН КЛОПОТЕНКО*

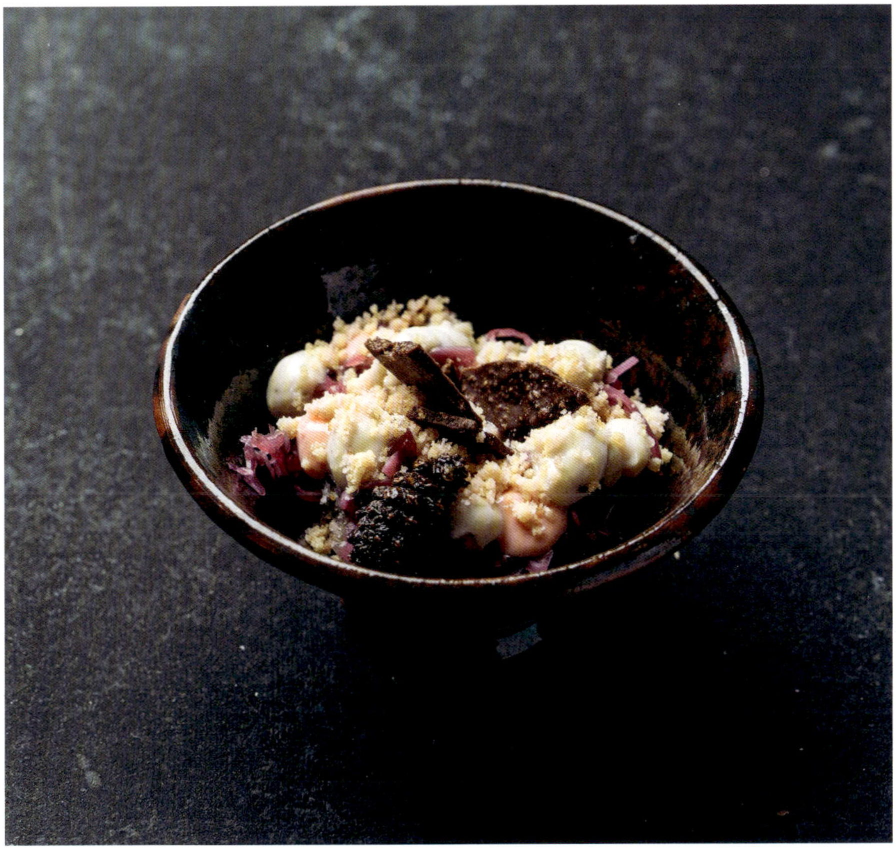

Ievgen Klopotenko studies ancient gastronomic traditions and introduces Ukrainian food culture to the world. His hope is that, one day, every foreigner will burn with the desire to taste *shpundra, vereshchaka,* and *hamula.*

Even as a boy Ievgen Klopotenko had a passion for food. By the age of 20, his love for food had blossomed into a love of cooking. For Klopotenko, the culinary arts perfectly embody creativity, that feeling that there are no limits. It is this state of total freedom that inspired him to revive and popularize Ukrainian cuisine. The young chef is engaged in gastronomic diplomacy, organizing charity dinners, liaising with the media, attending international culinary events, and presenting Ukrainian cuisine to the international gastronomic community. In 2022, thanks to Klopotenko's efforts, the tradition of cooking Ukrainian borshch was added to UNESCO's List of Intangible Cultural Heritage. Borshch, one of Ukraine's oldest and most well-known dishes, is cooked by nearly every Ukrainian. To preserve this culinary legacy, Klopotenko launched a "borshch expedition," where his team collected family recipes from across the country and documented them as part of the nation's collective memory.

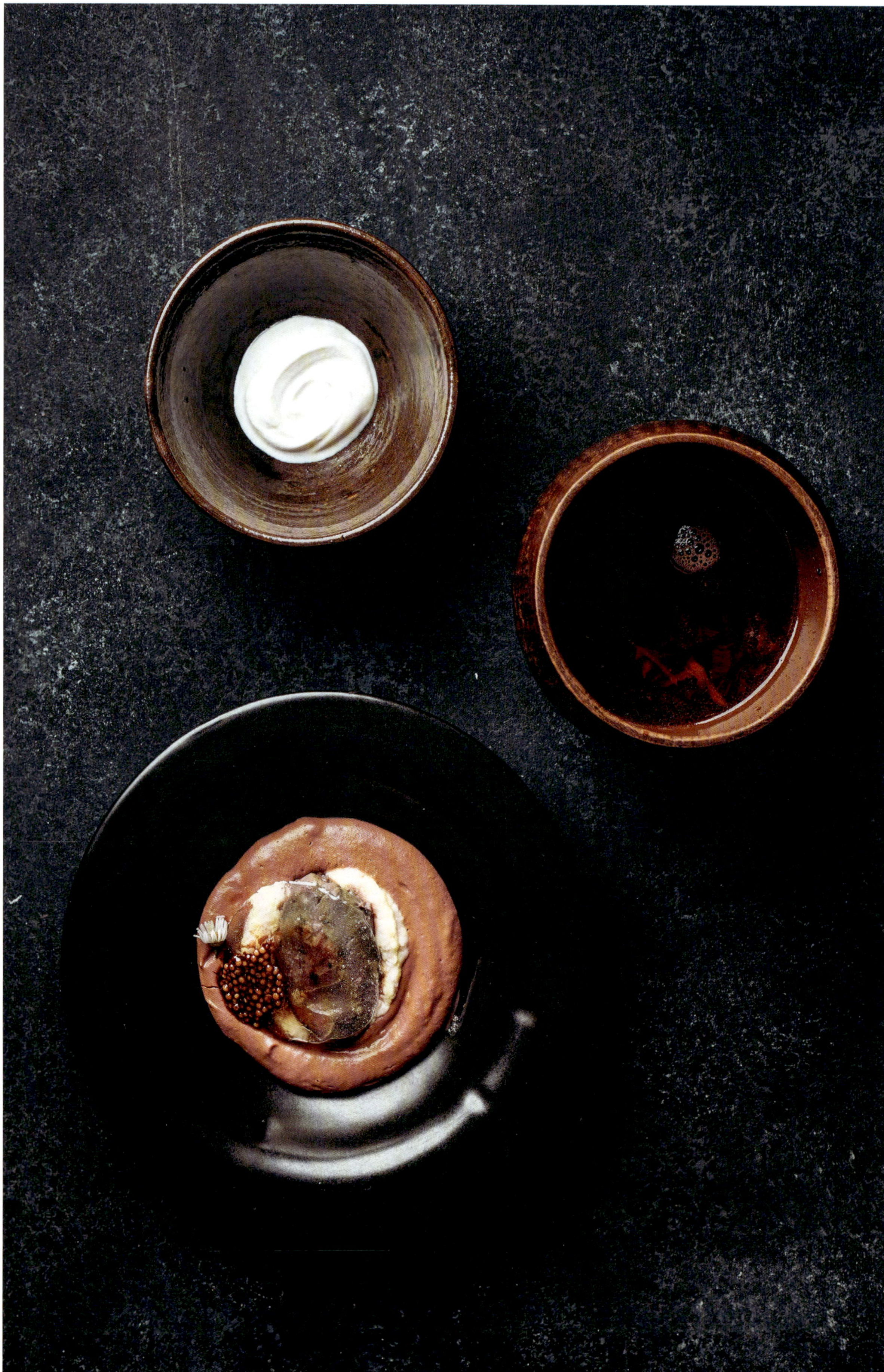

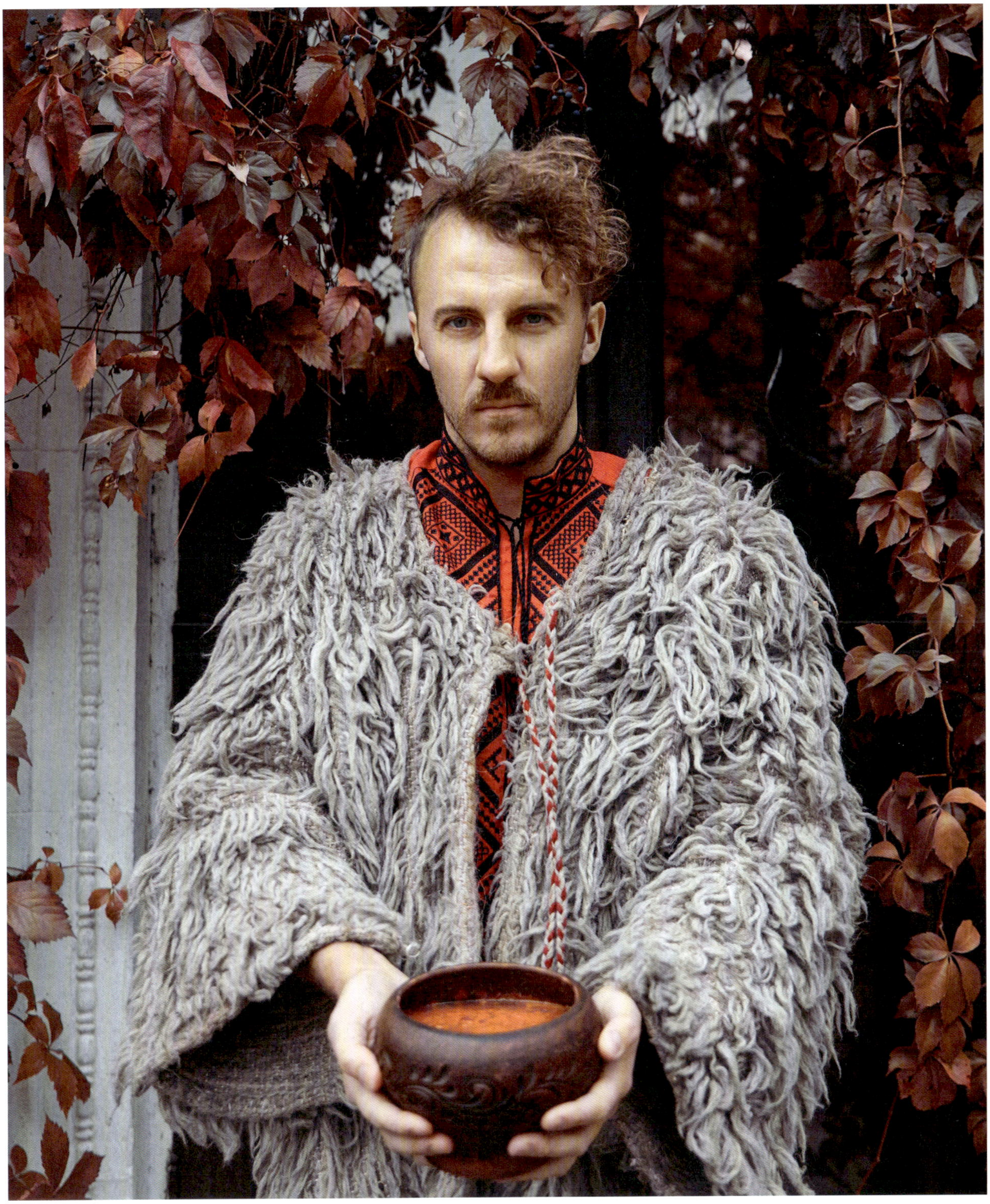

The fundamental value guiding all of Ievgen Klopotenko's pursuits is the Ukrainian spirit. It has inspired him to explore and revive traditional cuisine and give Ukraine's national dishes their due. One day he hopes to popularize them all over the world.

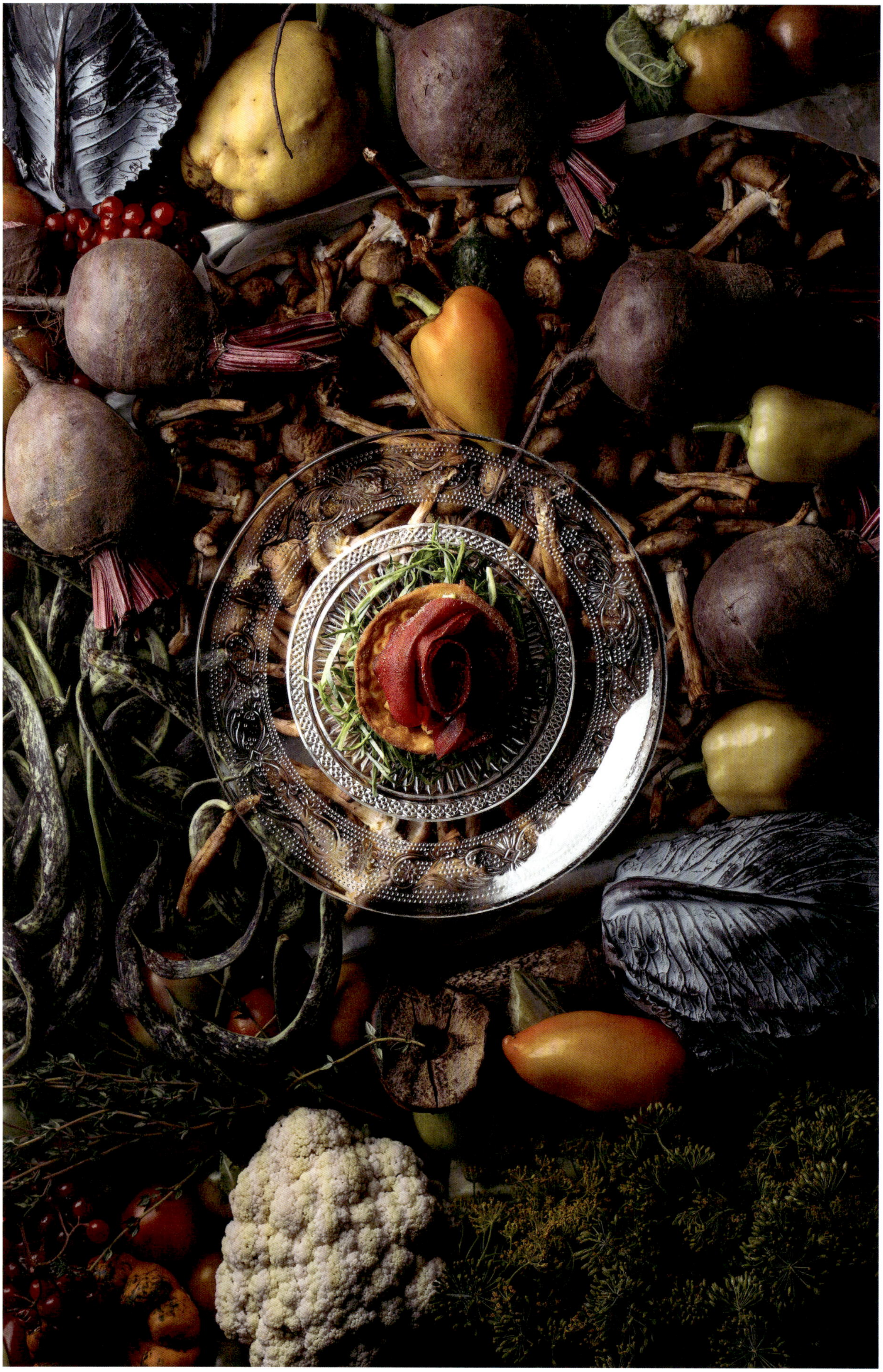

THE ANCESTRAL LEGACY OF UKRAINIAN CUISINE

IGOR MEZENCEV · *ІГОР МЕЗЕНЦЕВ*

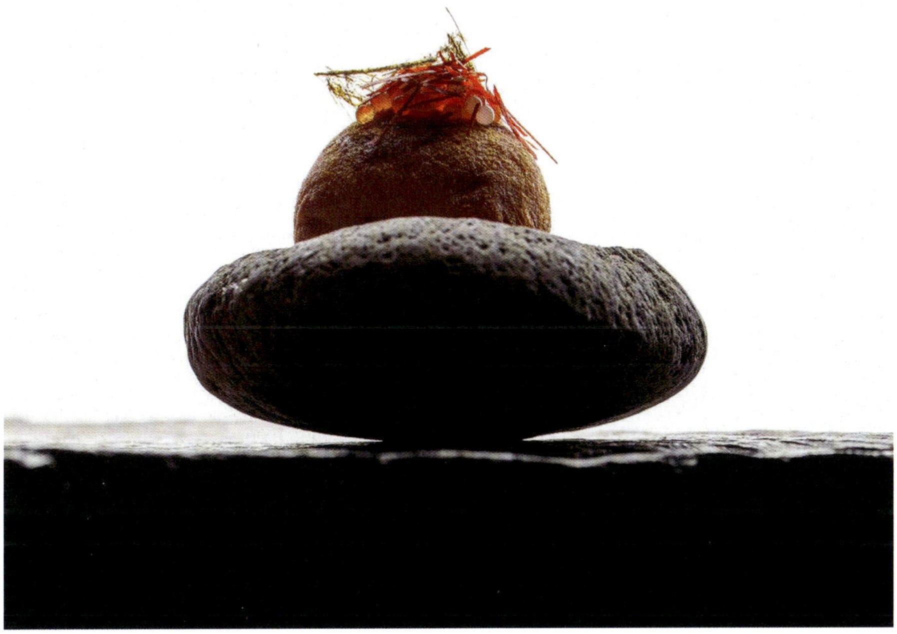

Unearthing culinary treasures, Igor Mezencev revitalizes ancient practices to create a fresh understanding of Ukrainian gastronomy.

In the past few years, Igor Mezencev, a distinguished Ukrainian chef, has dedicated himself to championing Ukraine's national cuisine. Having worked for many years as a chef in various restaurants, he decided to return to his roots. And so, he embarked on a journey to explore distinctive cooking methods and research local ingredients, aiming to gain a deeper understanding of Ukraine's rich culinary history. In 2019, together with project manager Anna Smoliakova and photographer Dima Bahta (see page 24), Mezencev created the groundbreaking Topot project. In 2021, Mezencev and Ievgen Klopotenko (see page 28) organized a gastronomic tour to introduce European journalists to Ukraine's vibrant food culture and elevate its profile on the global culinary scene. Following the outbreak of the war, Mezencev started the Varti project to support Ukrainian chefs affected by the conflict. The initiative consists of a series of dinners hosted by various chefs in cities throughout Ukraine. The dinners, which showcase modern interpretations of traditional Ukrainian dishes, feature local products exclusively sourced from the region where the dinner is hosted.

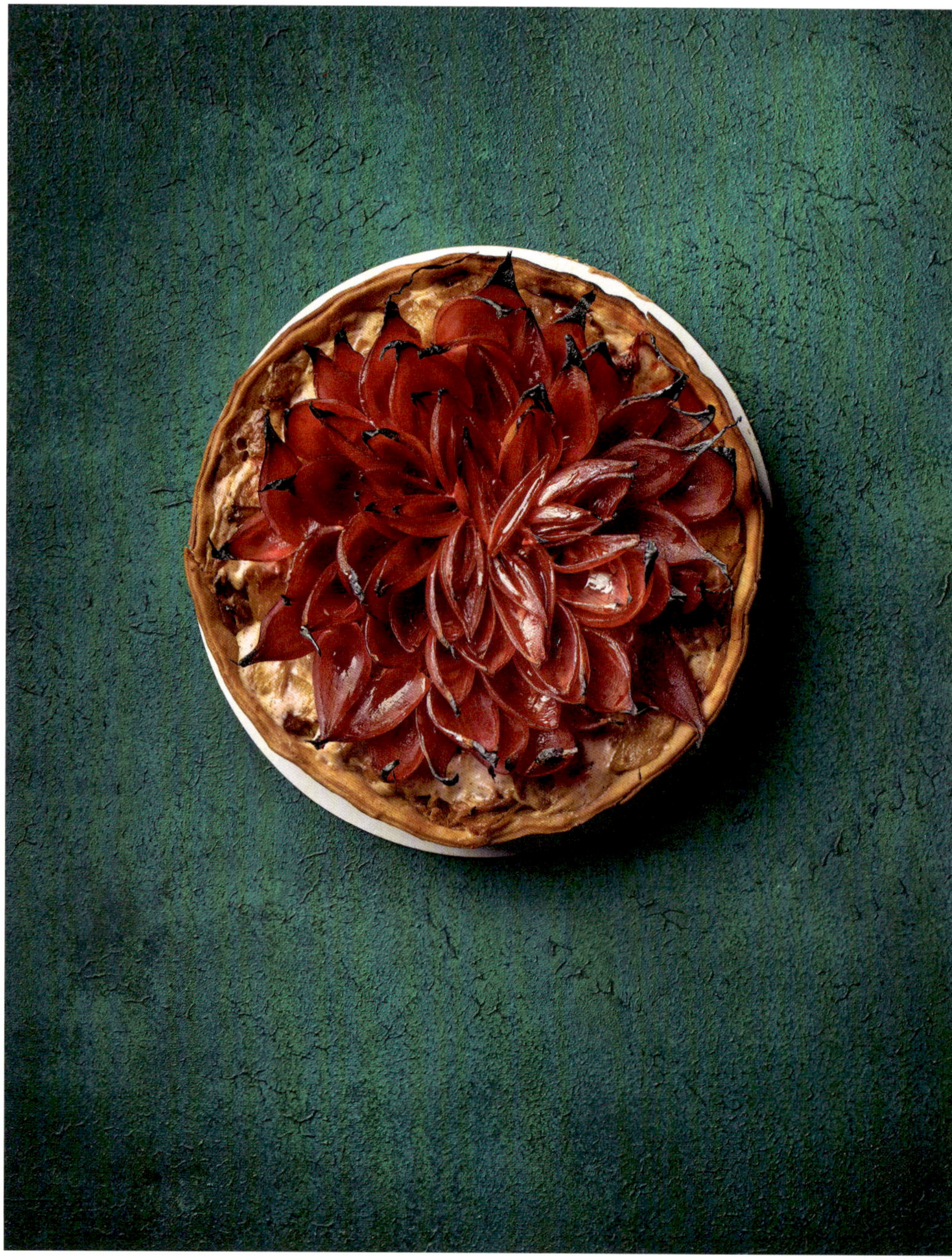

During the war, most Ukrainian chefs began preparing food for refugees and the armed forces in huge quantities. Varti is a project to support chefs, and an opportunity to return to creativity and self-expression in cooking.

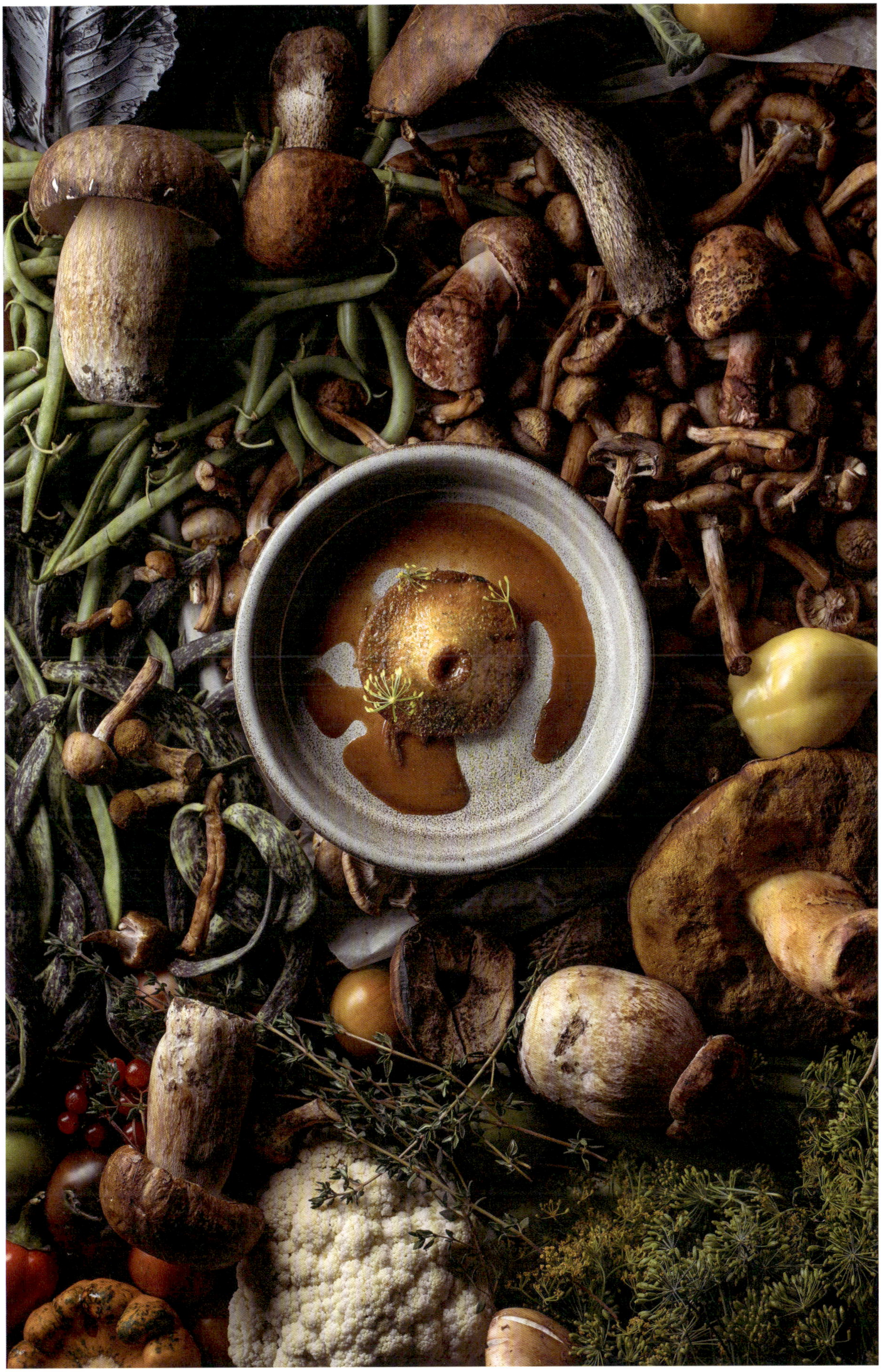

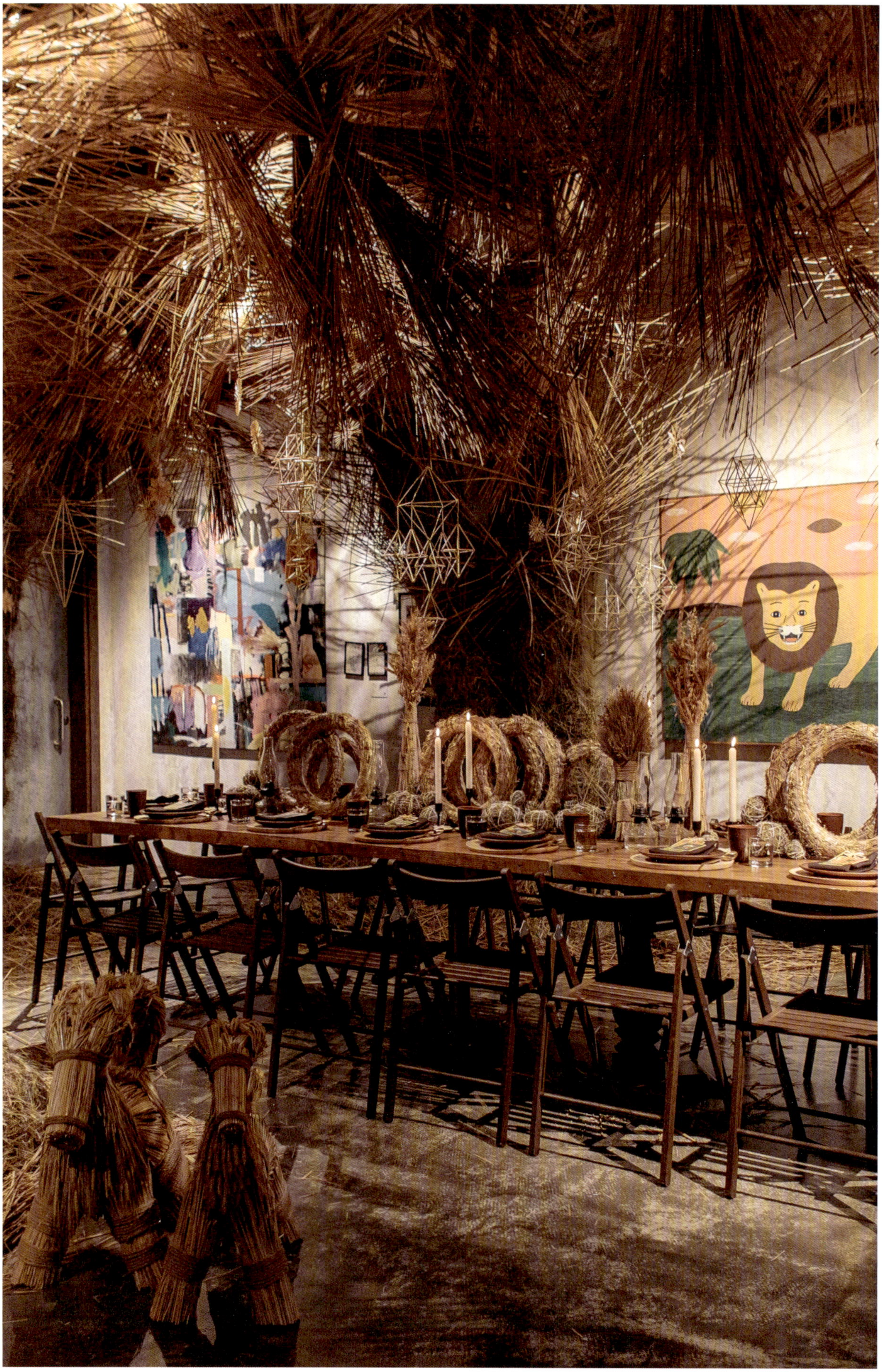

TRADITIONAL ARRANGEMENTS IN A MODERN CONTEXT

KVITKARNYA YU

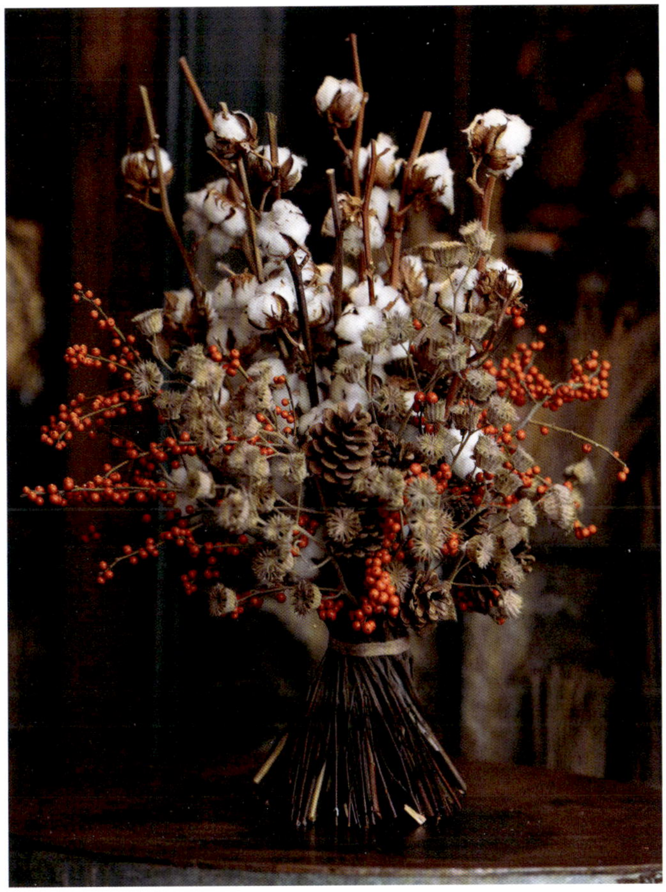

Flower studio Kvitkarnya YU brings the Ukrainian tradition of flower arrangement into the 21st century, all while using local flowers and plants.

Kvitkarnya YU studio creates authentic but modern flower arrangements that breathe new life into time-honored traditions. The founder, Serhii Parfonov, brings 20 years of experience in the flower industry to his new enterprise. The inspiration for Kvitkarnya YU came in 2022 at the onset of the war, as Parfonov began reflecting on Ukrainian self-identity. He started to study unique Ukrainian traditions related to flowers and herbs, immersing himself in the underlying philosophy. The significance of these traditions is evident in the preparations for major celebrations such as Christmas, Easter, and Kupala, where decorations are defined by their use of natural materials—straw, wood, herbs, flowers, and branches. Kvitkarnya YU revives these practices while also supporting local flower farmers and Ukrainian artisans: 80 percent of his assortment consists of local plants, and feature items made by local potters, carpenters, and artists.

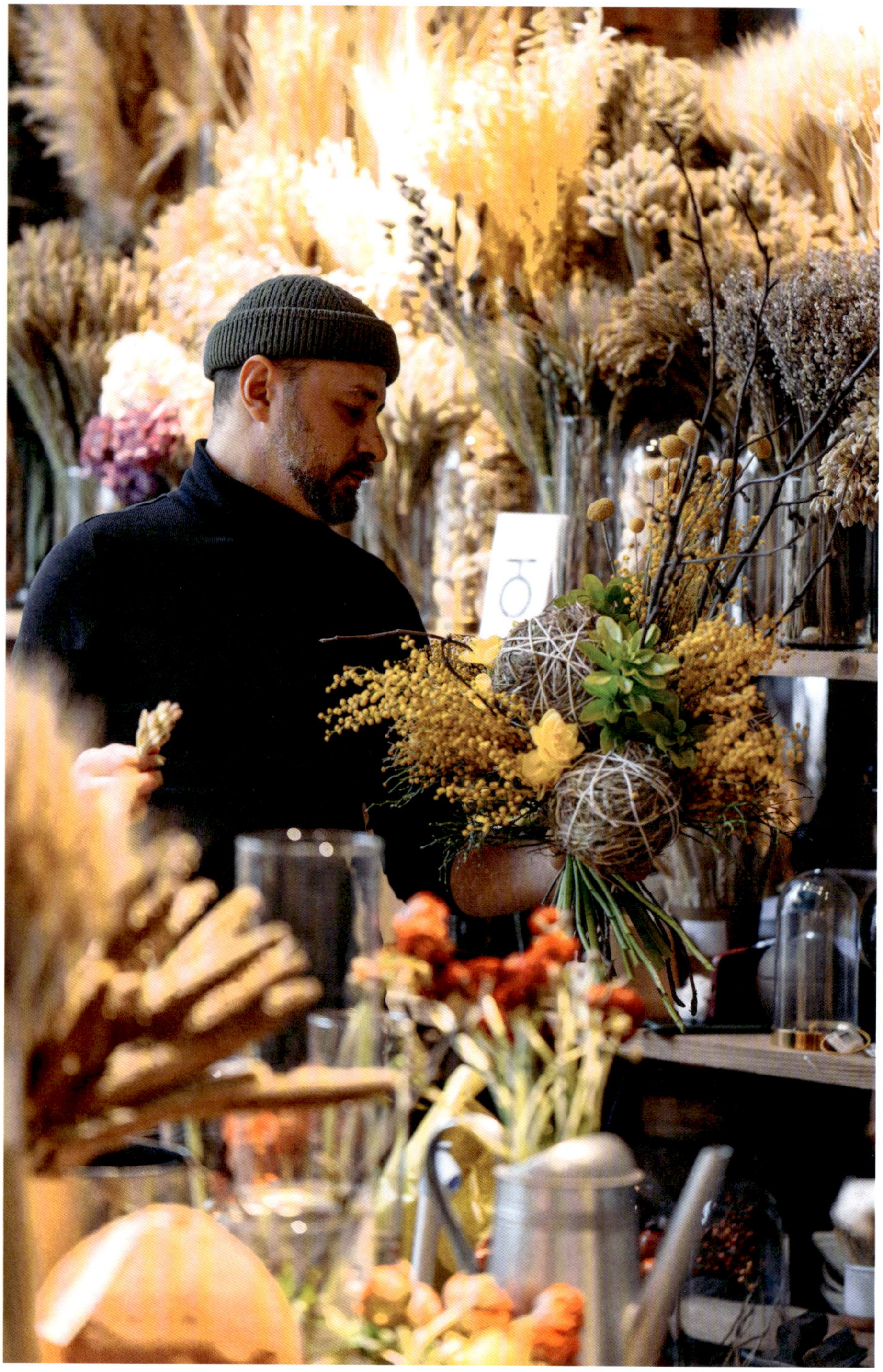

Kvitkarnya YU creates traditional bouquets and stunning organic compositions, using grass, twigs, branches, berries, and other natural materials. The philosophy of YU is to take national traditions and express them in a modern way.

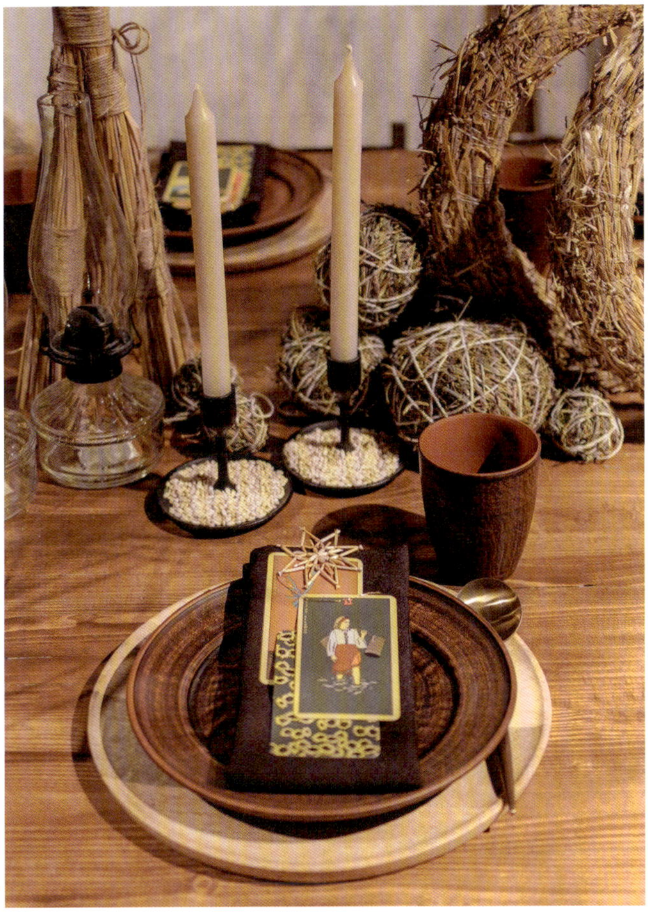
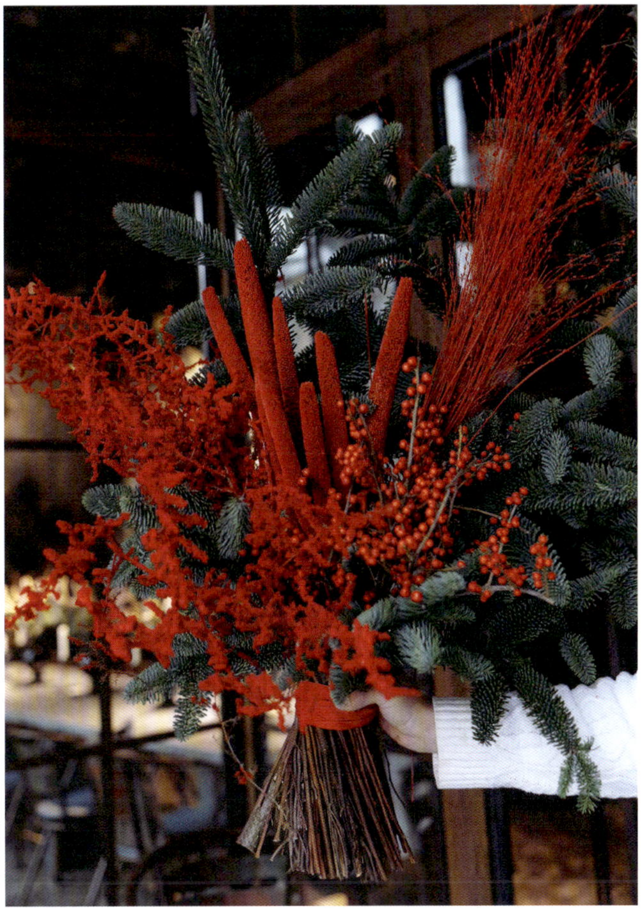
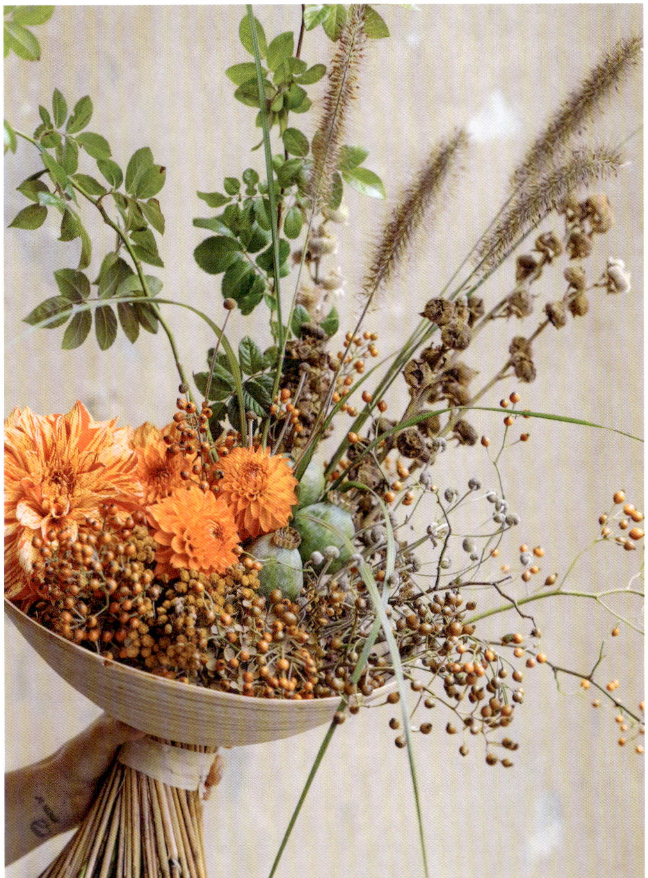
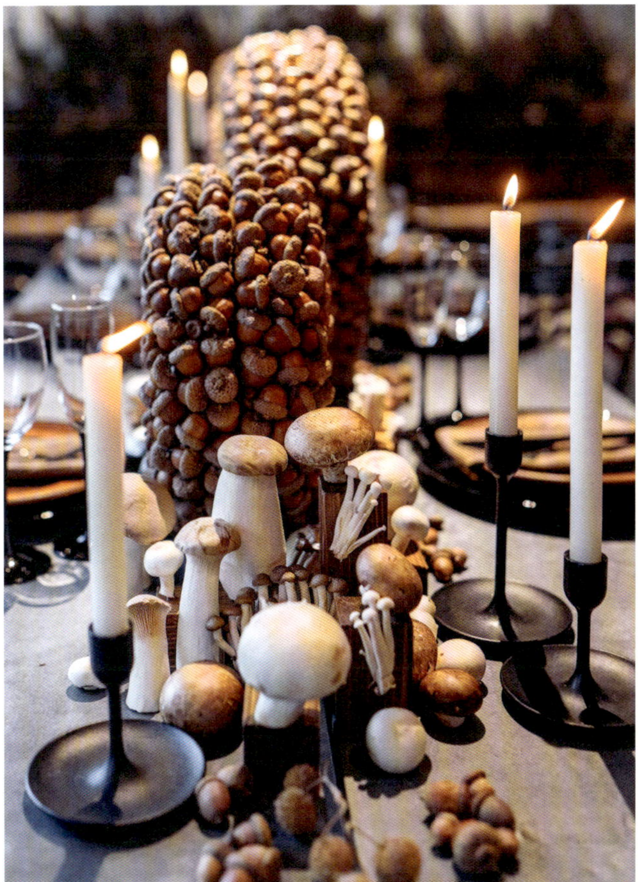

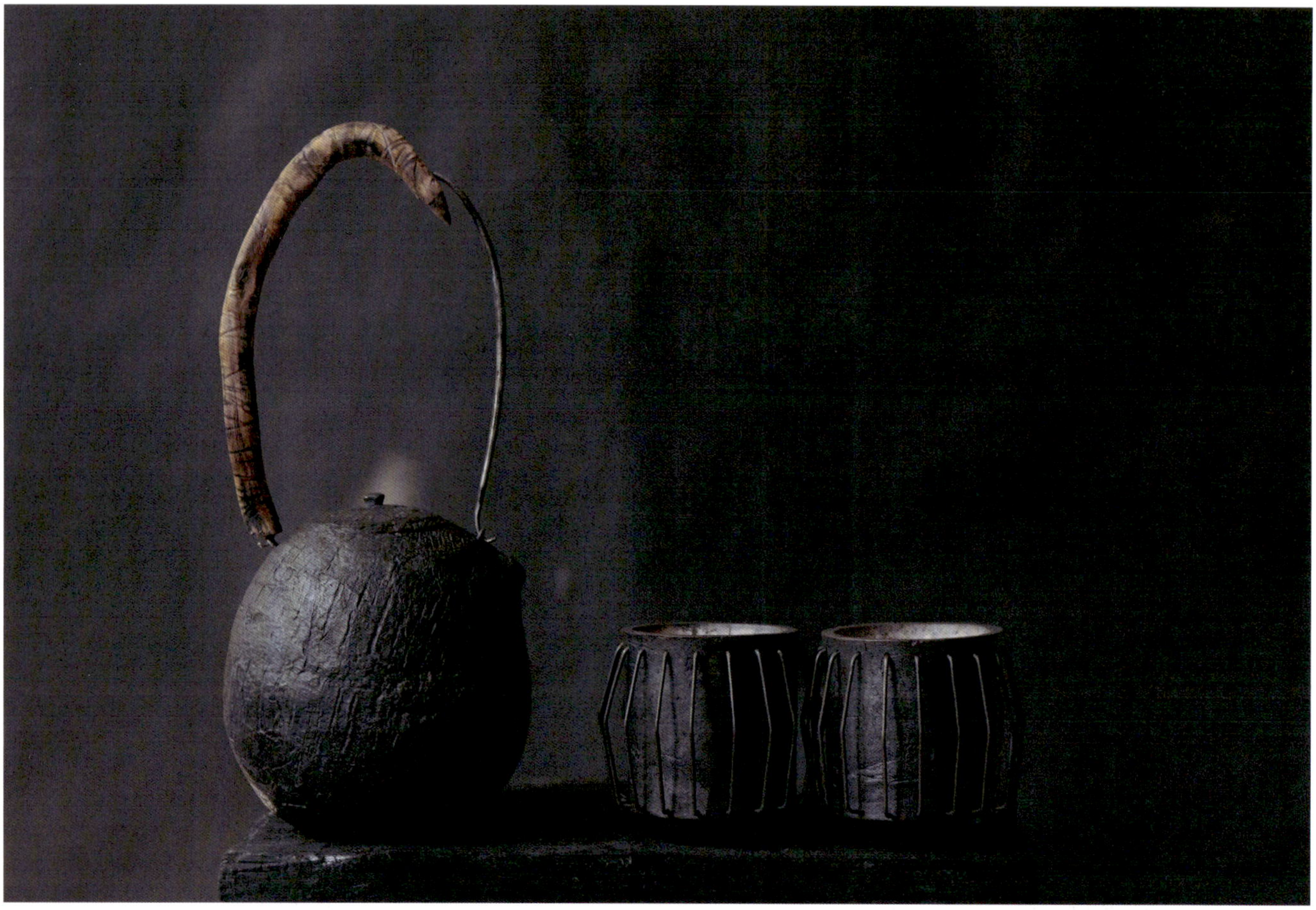

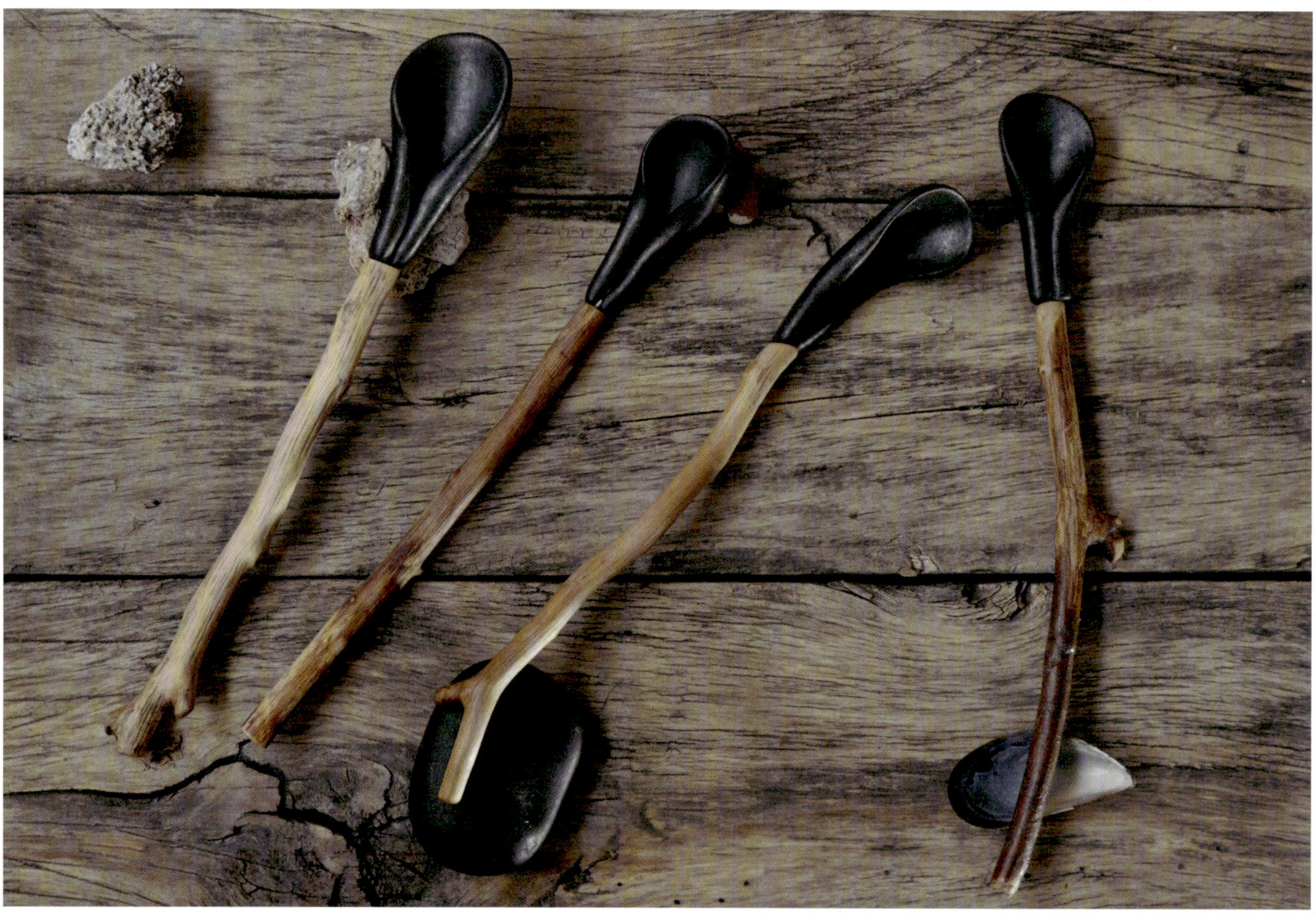

THE CURVES AND TEXTURES OF UKRAINIAN NATURE

VELIKA BOGAIHA

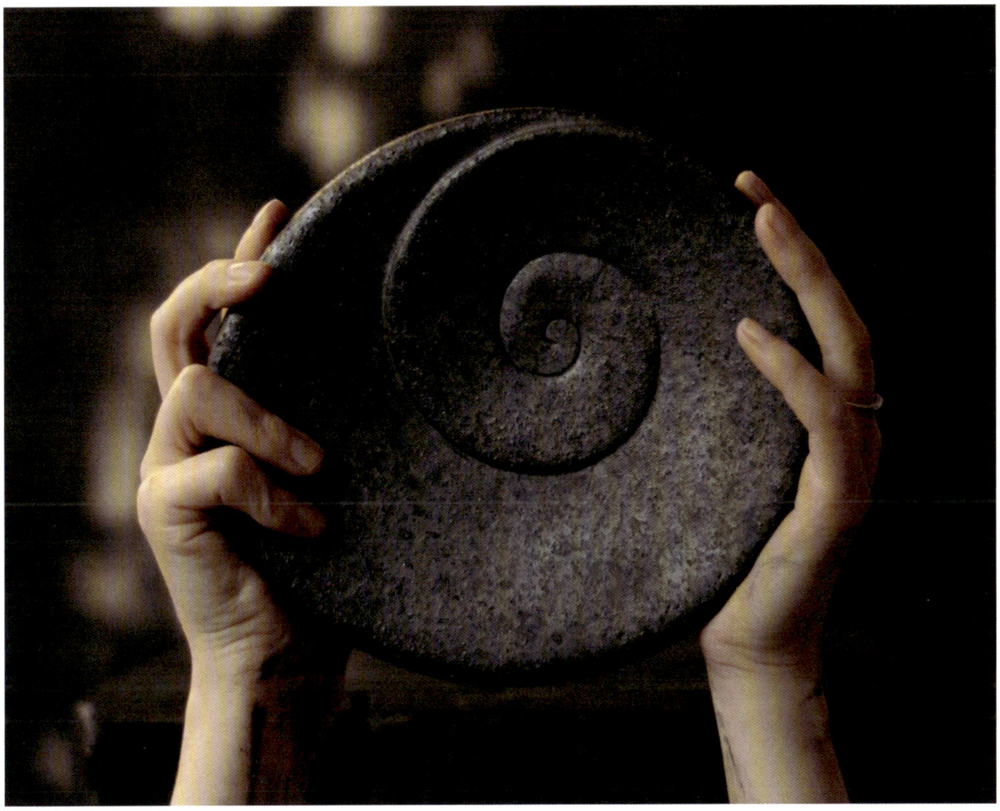

Drawn to the rich heritage of black-smoked ceramics in Ukraine, the Velika Bogaiha studio founders embrace this ancient art form in their contemporary ceramic creations.

The ceramics studio Velika Bogaiha is a family affair, consisting of Marharyta Demianets, Ivan Ivasiuk, and their little daughter Zoriana. This artistic family brings their ideas to life using a variety of materials: branches, bark, plants, shells, stones, and even metal. Nature, particularly its incredible variety of shapes and textures, is apparent in every aspect of their work. Their primary material, though, is of course clay—local, wild clay, which they extract and process themselves. Although the artists have spent years refining their skills, the family believes they are only just now embarking on an exciting, spontaneous journey. The studio's signature product is their black tableware, which embodies the lines, curves, and textures of Ukraine's natural landscape. The black hue allows the forms to take center stage while also conveying an underlying meaning. Velika Bogaiha has participated in several collaborations and international exhibitions, and in 2022, the brand was showcased at the collective Ukrainian stand at Maison & Objet in Paris. Their creations were also featured at the "Terre Libre" exhibition as part of Paris Design Week 2022.

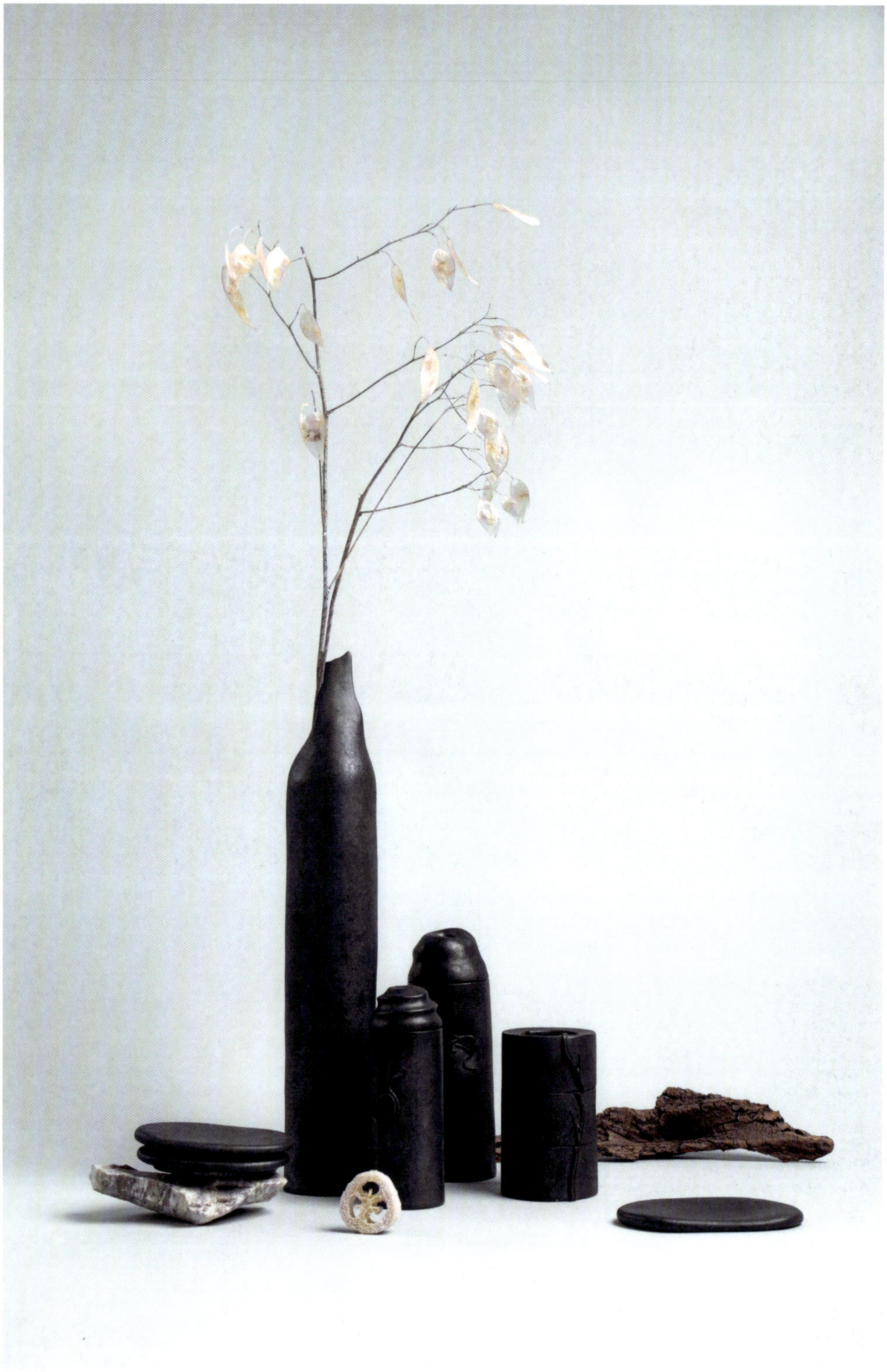

The founders of Velika Bogaiha say they have a profound appreciation for black-smoked ceramics, which have been crafted in Ukraine using traditional methods since ancient times. From fire to water, they believe ceramics embody the power of all the elements.

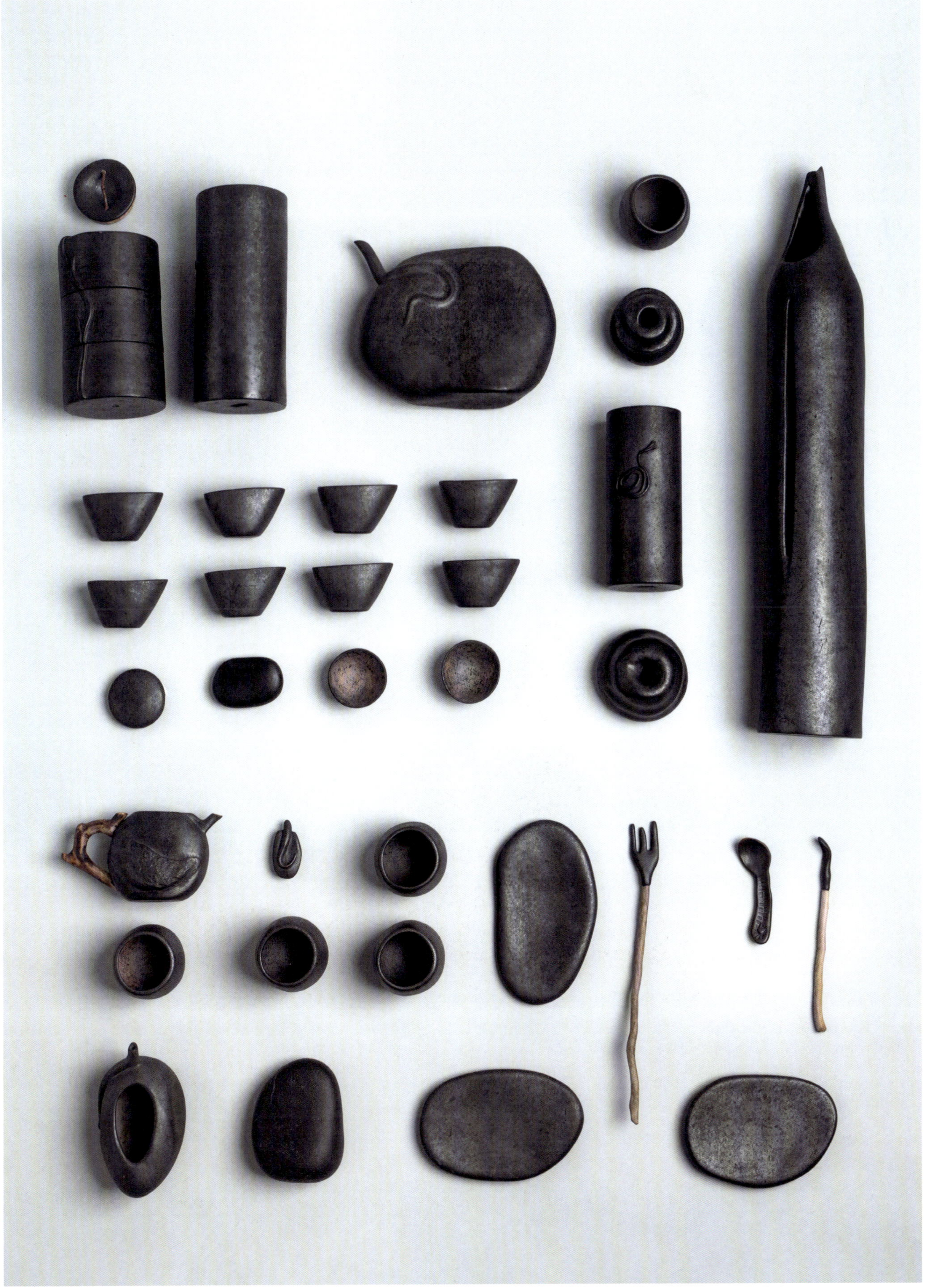

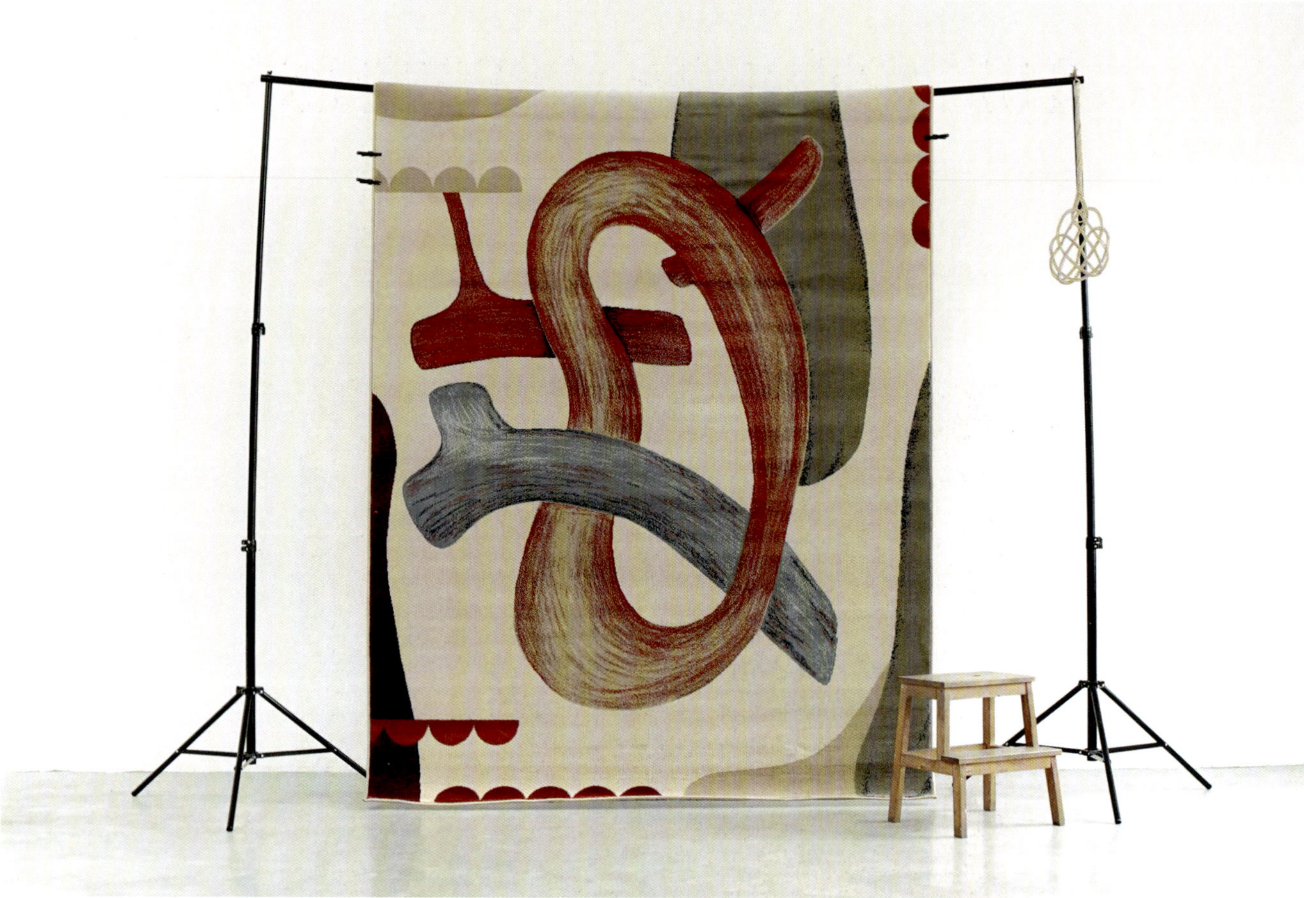

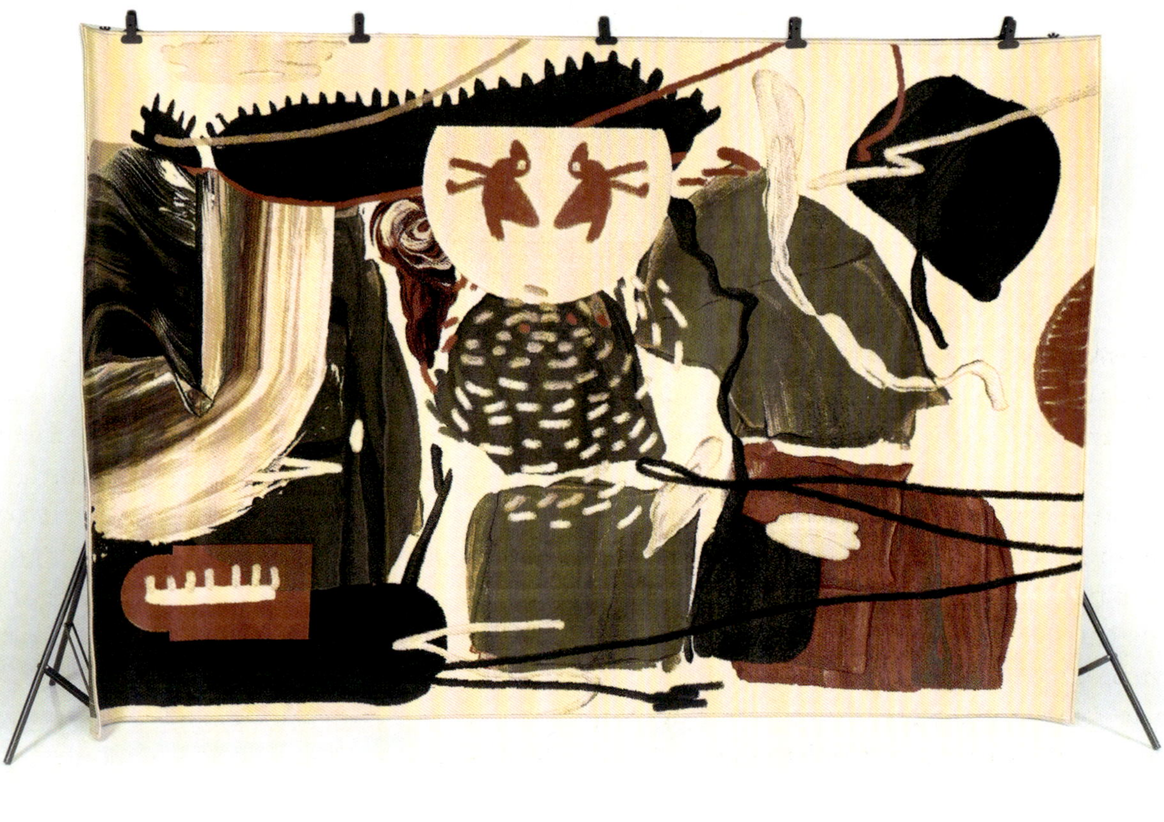

THE ART OF TRANSFORMING AN IDEA INTO FORM

KONONENKO ID

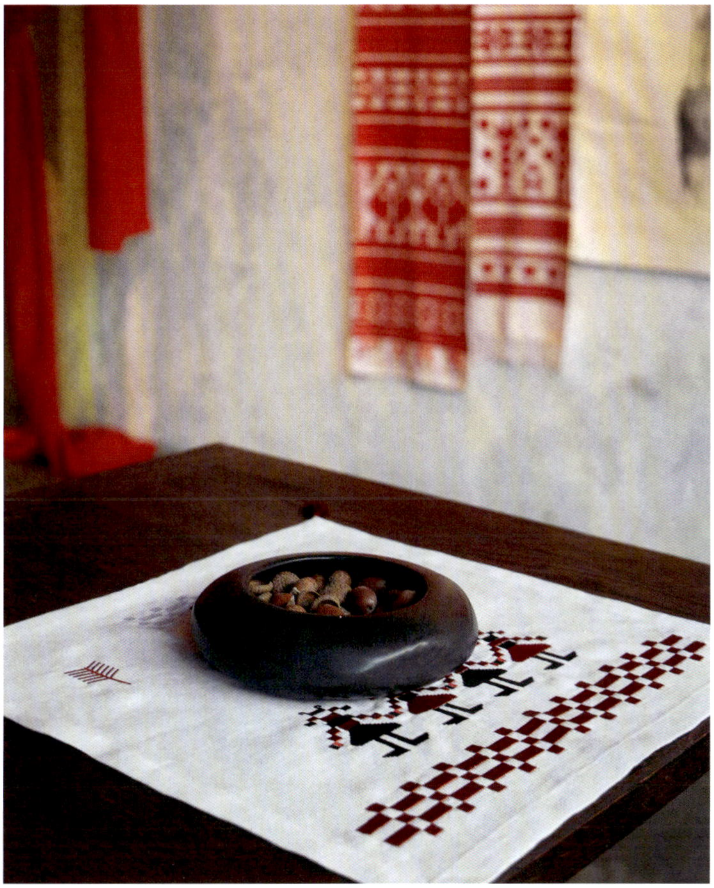

At Kononenko ID, designers take pride in their Ukrainian heritage, drawing inspiration from age-old traditions to craft modern products that celebrate their cultural roots.

Julia Kononenko and Artem Kravchenko, founders of the Kononenko ID studio, follow this guiding expression: "The art of transforming an idea into a form." The duo, whose design style is an amalgam of diverse influences, create stunning contemporary pieces with an emphasis on Ukrainian tradition. In addition to furniture and lighting, the studio designs carpets inspired by ancient cultural heritage and manufactured using advanced weaving technology. The studio's designs have been showcased at prominent international design expos, including imm cologne, Maison&Objet, Paris Design Week, and the Stockholm Furniture Fair. Currently, the studio continues its work in Kyiv, infusing every new creation with artisanal and cultural heritage. For example, in their new Goverla furniture collection, the designers combined Ukrainian minimalism and Scandinavian modernism, creating a functional and sustainable design inspired by the cities, villages, and nature of Ukraine.

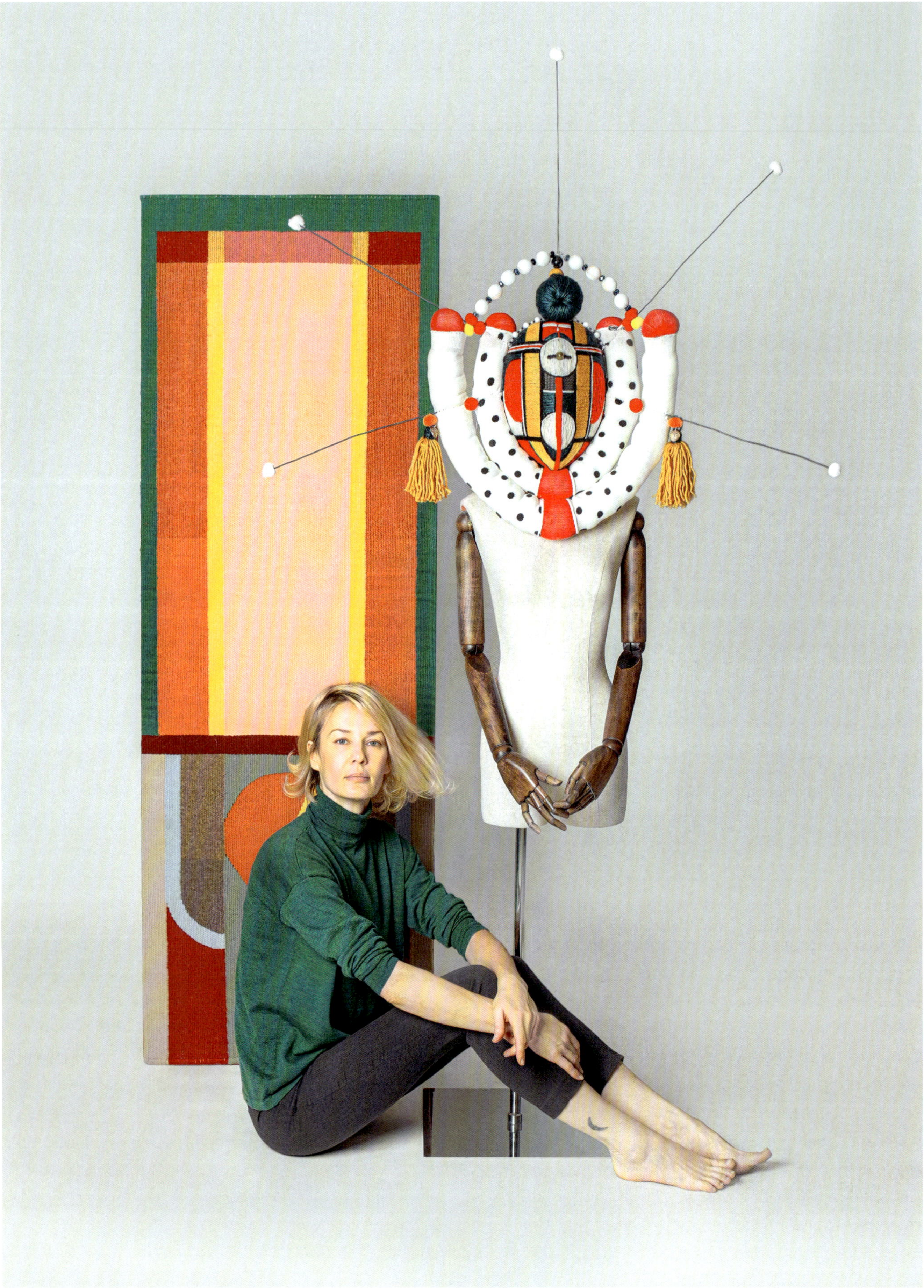

ORIGINAL DECOR WITH POP-FOLK MOTIFS

OLK MANUFACTORY

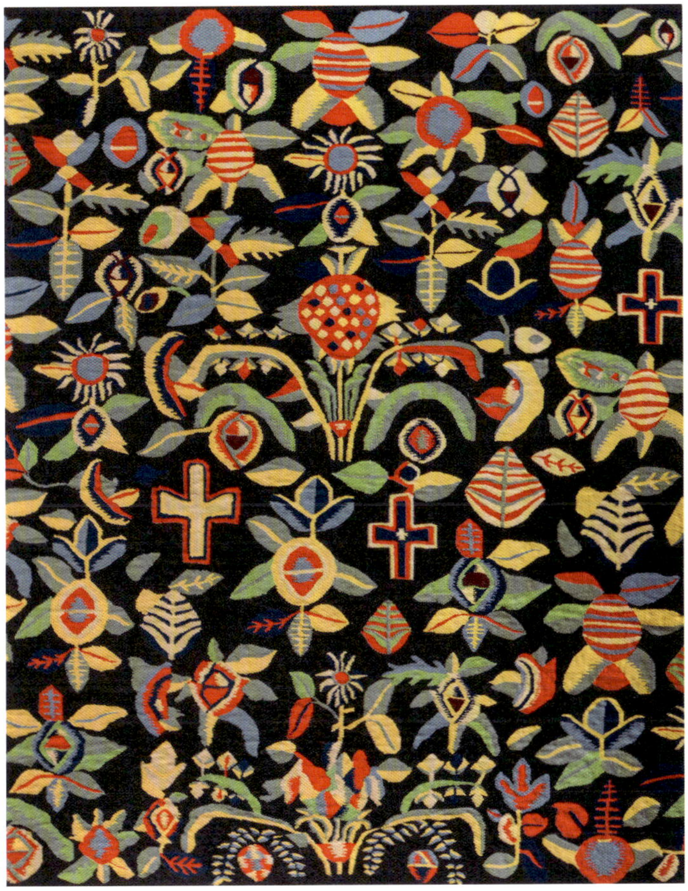

Olk Manufactory blends art and craftsmanship, prioritizing environmental responsibility as they create one-of-a-kind items rooted in tradition.

Olk Manufactory produces *kylyms*, tapestries, and art objects designed by Ukrainian artist Oksana Levchenya. Fascinated by Ukrainian folk art, particularly carpet weaving, Levchenya fuses traditional patterns with modern symbols and techniques, resulting in a unique range of furnishings and decorative objects at the crossroads of art and design. In addition to using traditional weaving patterns, the artist incorporates the aesthetics of Ukrainian Suprematism and Modernism into her creations. Using a mixture of dyed natural wool and plant-based yarns such as hemp thread, Olk Manufactory employs a traditional vertical weaving technique on a modernized vertical loom. Levchenya also makes original art objects, including a series of masks inspired by traditional Ukrainian Motanka dolls. Adorned with bold, geometrically woven textiles and embroidery, these masks symbolize self-defense and the act of going off to war.

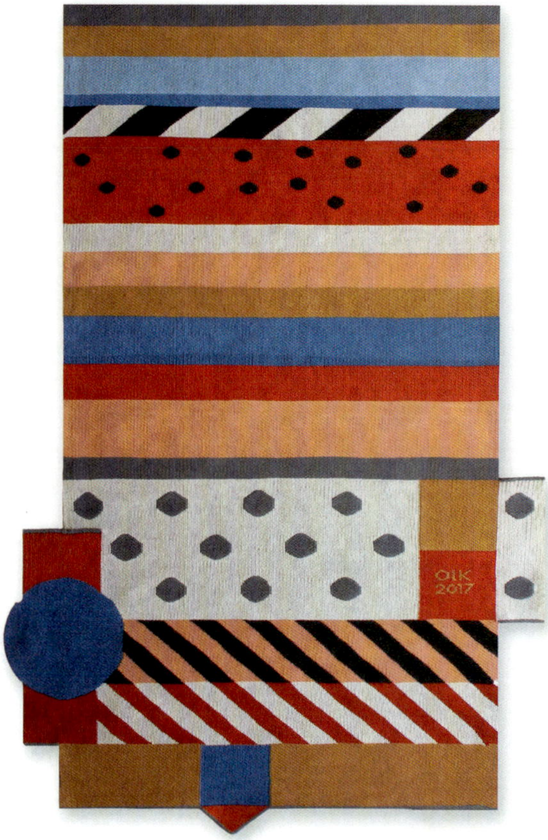
OIK
2017

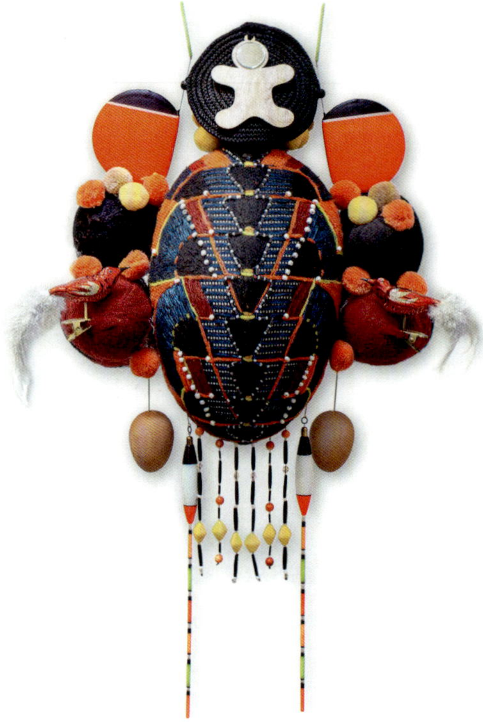

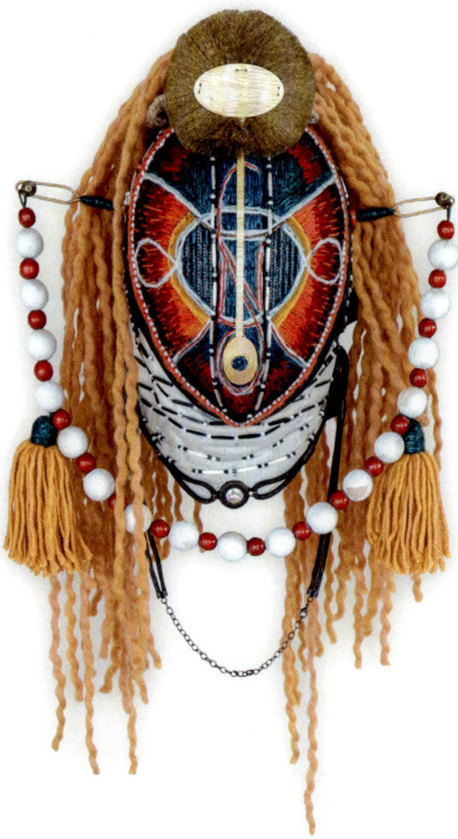

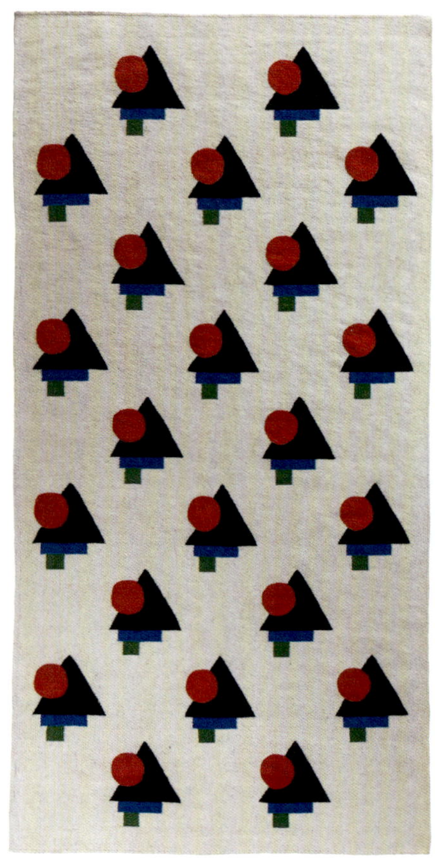

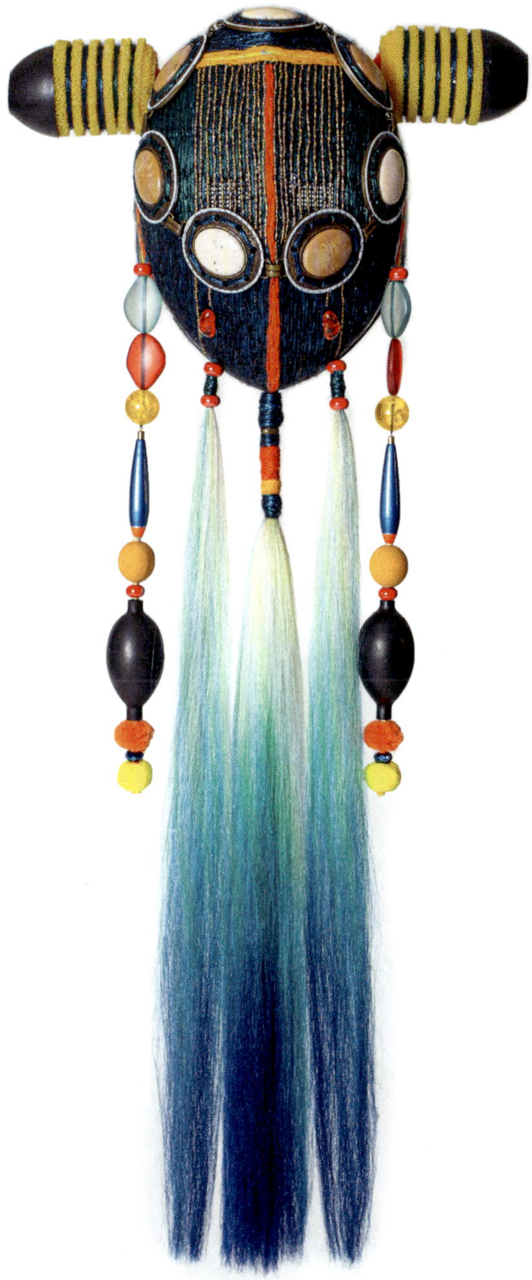

Oksana Levchenya creates masks, contemporary art objects from an imaginary time period. The artist adds traditional geometric embroidery to the base of vintage fencing masks. These objects symbolize the power of self-defense, and the act of going off to war.

THE POWER OF VISUAL CULTURE: PRESERVING AUTHENTICITY

In order to discuss Ukrainian visual culture and art, we must first acknowledge what makes Ukraine such a unique place. One of its defining characteristics, which sets it apart from many other nations, is its desire to balance modernity with tradition. As it seeks to integrate into the European cultural landscape, Ukraine remains fiercely committed to preserving its authentic identity, one deeply rooted in core values such as family, land, and freedom.

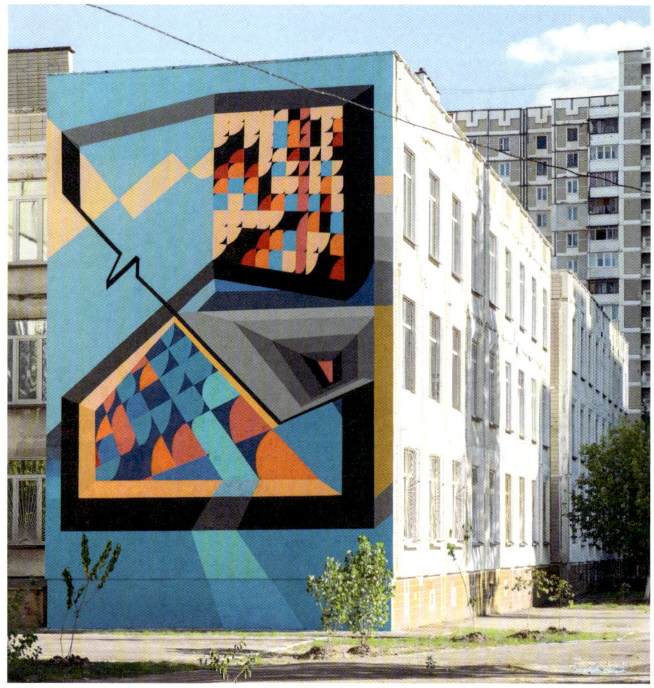

Andriy Kalkov encodes images and symbols in geometric modules, creating optical art. Above: *Circulation*, Kyiv, 2016. Below: Artwork, by Les Panchyshyn, from the "We Will Never Forget" series, 2022.

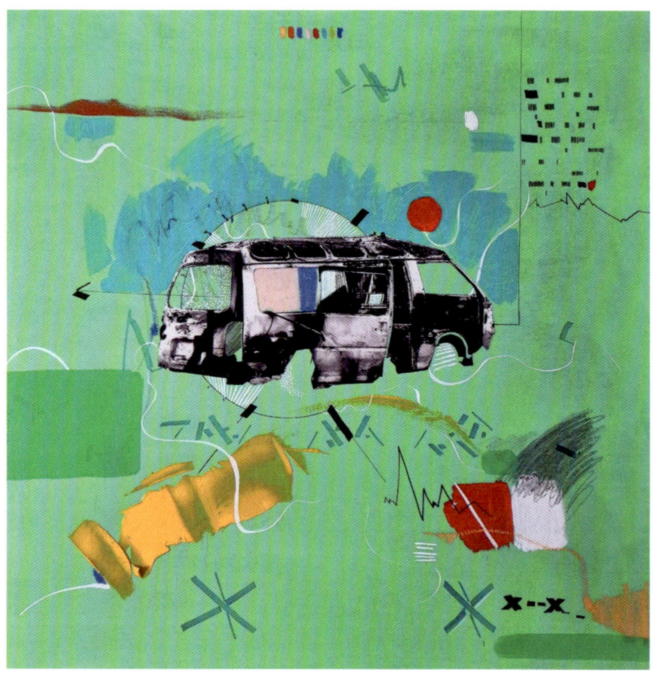

A THOUSAND-YEAR HISTORY OF CULTURE

Ukraine's geographical location and history have significantly contributed to its rich multicultural heritage. Kyivan Rus, a medieval state founded in the 9th century, played a vital role as a major trade and cultural hub in Eastern Europe. The state's influential position enabled the local culture to absorb and adapt elements from various foreign influences, resulting in a rich and diverse cultural identity.

From the 9th to the 20th century, Ukrainian cultural history underwent a series of transformations, closely connected to wider European narratives. In the years following the Reformation, Byzantine architecture and magnificent church mosaics gave way to the stunning baroque era. In Ukraine, as in other countries, the baroque style was defined by highly ornate architecture and sculpture. However, Ukrainian masters did not simply copy Western models: they were able to combine them with their own traditions and in doing so created highly original works. 17th-century Ukrainian engravers have preserved some of the oldest examples of this synthesis, mixing the baroque decoration of the West with the fanciful motifs of the East. This fusion resulted in a distinctly Ukrainian style that culminated in the Cossack baroque style, considered by many to be the epitome of the Ukrainian style. Following the baroque period, the elegant rococo era ushered in fresh ideas and brought

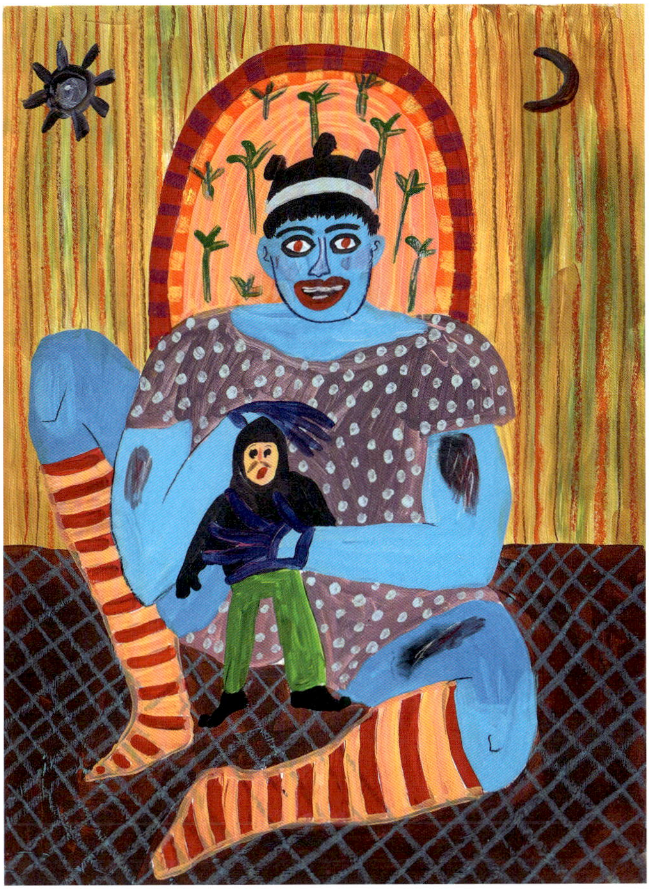

Dzvinya Podlyashetska combines different art influences, creating her own unique, emotive style. Below: In her collages, Olga Zerno often uses old photographs to great effect.

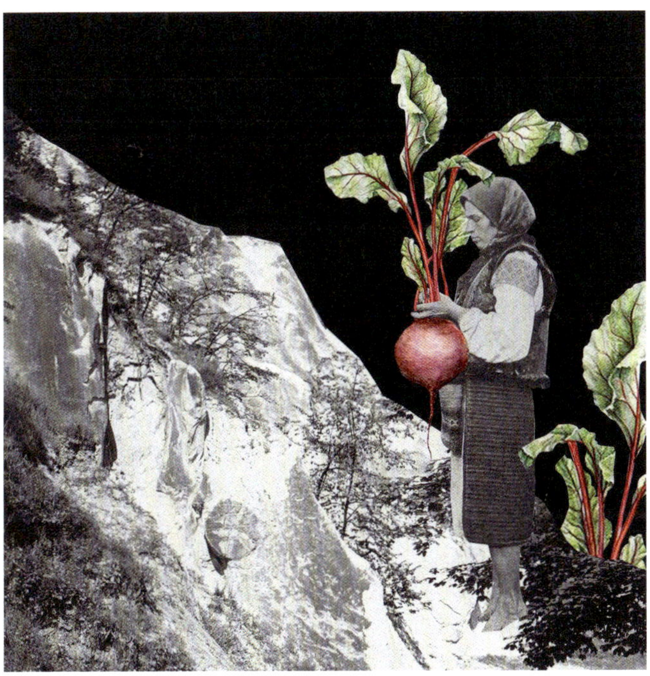

new forms to Ukrainian culture. After this period, artists turned to folklore motifs, historical subjects, and picturesque landscapes, creating art that highlighted the beauty of nature, folk stories, and village life. A notable figure of this period was Mykola Pymonenko, whose works helped to establish a romanticized image of the Ukrainian countryside. A master of his craft, he painted expressive images of Ukraine, celebrating its vibrant people and the charm of his native land.

A CULTURE IN TRANSITION

The turn of the 20th century marked a time of radical change. This period not only brought new, unconventional approaches to the creation and perception of art, but also markedly changed public consciousness. The era of Tsarism had begun to wane, the Russian Revolution was looming on the horizon, and social unrest had reached a fever pitch.

Against this backdrop, the distinctive Ukrainian avant-garde emerged, blending European modernist aesthetics with elements of Ukrainian folk art. The term "Ukrainian avant-garde" was first coined by Franco-Bulgarian art historian Andréi Nakov after visiting the 1973 exhibition "Tatlin's Dream" in London.

Celebrated artists such as Oleksandr Bohomazov, Volodymyr Tatlin, Alexander Archipenko, Alexandra Ekster, and David Burliuk made substantial contributions to the Ukrainian avant-garde movement. Their work still resonates with contemporary artists around the world—evidence of their enduring impact on international art and culture.

FROM CONSTRAINT TO CREATIVITY

Throughout the USSR's seven-decade history, Ukrainian artists grappled with the complex task of defining their identity while also navigating a tumultuous environment marked by genocide, repression, war, revolution, standardized state contracts, double standards, and the restrictive ideologies of socialist realism. This period witnessed rampant human rights violations and the quashing of artistic expression.

Perestroika, which lasted from 1985 until the Soviet Union's dissolution in 1991, marked a critical juncture in the nation's history as it sought comprehensive system reform. The "New Wave" of art evolved amid the collapse of the old system, but it also built upon its remnants. Ukrainian postmodern painting incorporated multi-figured canvases, bright color palettes, bold brushwork, and large formats, all features inherited from socialist realist painting. However, artists subverted these traditional forms, infusing their work with fresh subject material, warmth, and the energy that defined their generation.

In the mid-1990s, Ukrainian cultural life took off—private galleries opened, the first local art fairs took place, and Ukrainian artists were invited to participate in international projects. That said, it was not smooth sailing: the first decade of independence was a turbulent time. A new social order had to be formed, often leaving culture struggling to survive. Nonetheless, the 2000s witnessed the emergence of both private and public cultural institutions, such as PinchukArtCentre, Mystetskyi Arsenal, and M17 Contemporary Art Center, providing a renewed impetus for artistic development. In 2018, the Korsak family opened The Korsaks' Museum of Contemporary Ukrainian Art in Lutsk, Western Ukraine. The first of its kind in Ukraine, it is now the largest world-class museum of contemporary art in the country, and one of the nation's most influential cultural centers.

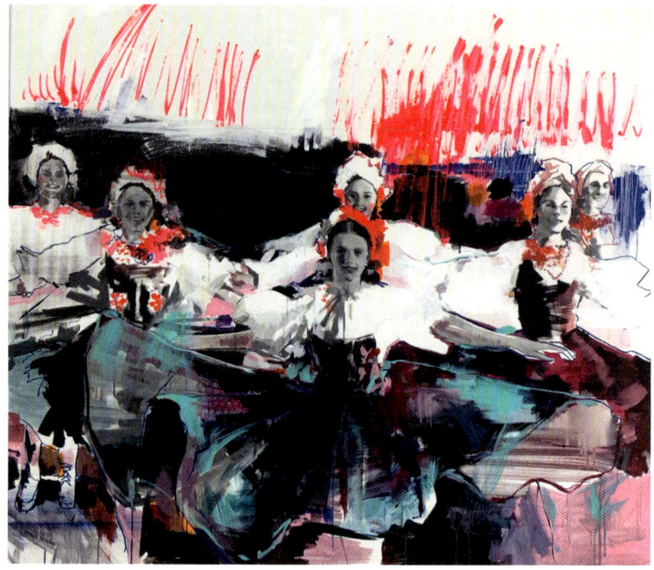

Inna Kharchuk, *Vyr*, acrylic, oil on canvas, 2021. Below: In this photo from the "Young and Free" series, Sergey Melnitchenko captures the freedom and vitality of Ukrainian youth.

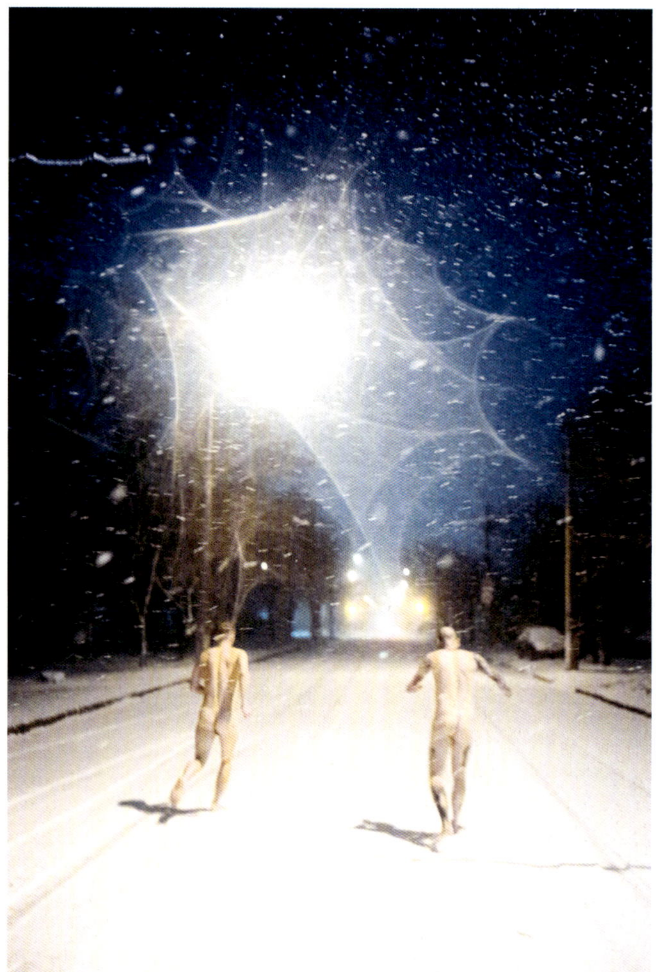

THE ART OF SURVIVAL

The Orange Revolution in 2004 and the Euromaidan Revolution in 2014 were defining moments in Ukrainian history. These critical sociopolitical events set the course for Ukraine's future, giving rise to new principles in governance, culture, civil society, and transforming its international standing.

Both revolutions drew the world's attention to Ukraine and its culture, and served as a powerful reminder of the values underpinning Ukrainians' fight for freedom. Despite the immense social and economic challenges, these periods sparked profound introspection in the art world. Artists candidly portrayed their

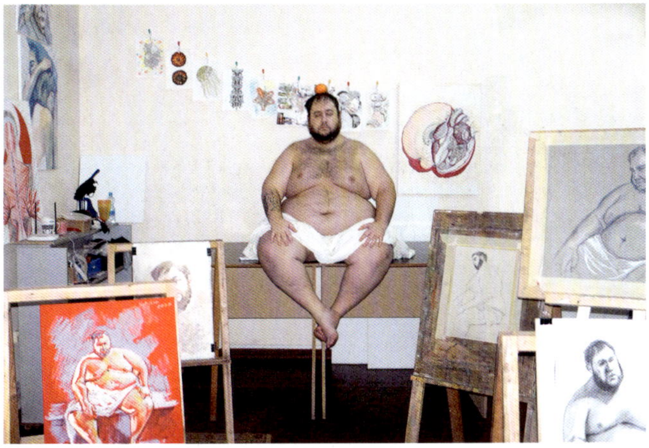

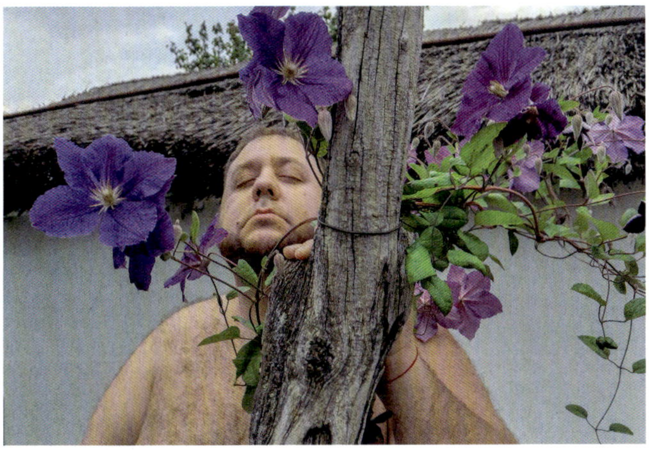

For Artem Humilevskyi, the body communicates sincerity and openness, and aims to be as honest as possible with the viewer. Below: Dilkone, *My Land is My Body, My Soul is My Fire*, ibug 2022, Flöha, Germany.

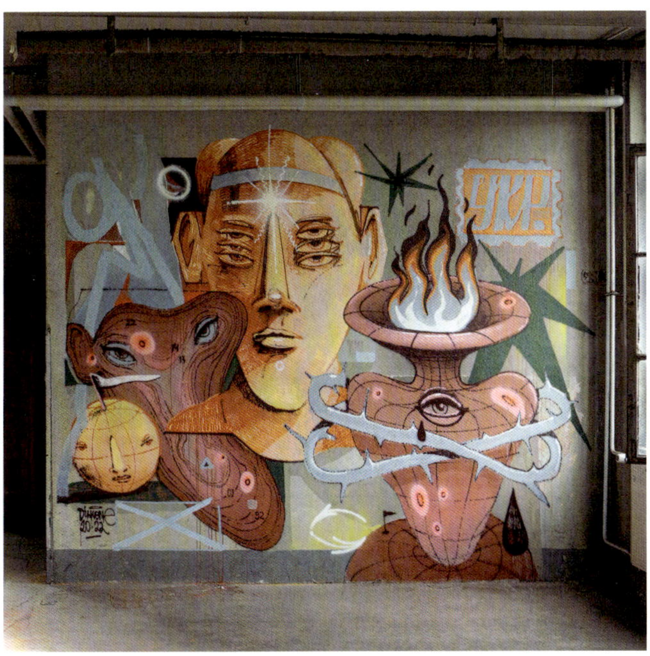

emotions and struggles, demonstrating their resilience and independence. At the same time, this introspection fueled a rich and full cultural life, which in turn attracted the attention of outside observers. Each revolution left its own unique mark: the Orange Revolution gave birth to a surge of activism and led to the founding of the R.E.P. (Revolutionary Experimental Space) group, whose members include the now internationally renowned artists Zhanna Kadyrova and Nikita Kadan. The Euromaidan Revolution was incredibly difficult and painful, giving rise to intense, uncensored portrayals of tragic events, as seen in the photo artworks by the "Shilo" group, and Matvei Vaisberg's famous painting cycle, "Wall." This striking collection of 28 paintings was exhibited throughout the world.

During this period, the art market also experienced a revival, both domestically and abroad. Ukrainian artists participated in auctions held by Christie's, Sotheby's, and Phillips, and Ukrainian galleries were invited to participate in prestigious international art fairs. Meanwhile, exhibitions featuring Ukrainian artists were displayed in prestigious museums and galleries around the world. One such example is the Zenko Foundation's 2018 exhibition, "Permanent Revolution," at the Ludwig Museum in Budapest. This landmark retrospective of Ukrainian art from the last 30 years showcased the country's thriving art scene over multiple generations. The exhibit focused, in particular, on how Ukrainian art was shaped by multiple revolutions and seemingly endless waves of political upheaval and transformation.

Expo 2020 in Dubai featured a full-scale Ukrainian pavilion for the first time, and its Ellipsis Art Project promoted contemporary Ukrainian artists. The project's name, Ellipsis, a reference to the punctuation mark, symbolizes the powerful and unspoken continuity of the past, and the guiding of future events.

NEW GENERATION, NEW RULES

Artists born in an independent Ukraine grew up embracing ideas of freedom, national identity, and independence. Rather than coalescing into a single monolithic entity, artists of this generation are fiercely individualistic, focused on finding their place in the world and discovering new forms of self-expression. As a result, this generation can be hard to pin down. In the absence of state support (and control), these artists have found themselves scattered across multiple movements and orientations, defying easy classification within art history.

The visual language of this new generation often refers to folklore and cultural roots, but also uses the latest technologies and tools, such as digital collage and photography. Taras Haida, a notable artist in this respect, skillfully combines stylish images with Ukrainian ornamentation that disintegrate into pixels. At the same time, Oleksandr Barbolin brings us back to the stories of the Northern Renaissance, combining them with elements of modern design and current trends.

Another crucial figure on the Ukrainian art scene is Waone, a groundbreaking street artist who works effortlessly across several mediums. He adapts his work from urban walls to more traditional canvases all while maintaining his unique style. As one of Ukraine's most influential representatives abroad and on the local scene, Waone has created a world rich with hidden meaning and evocative symbols. In a similar vein, digital art trailblazer, Stepan Ryabchenko, has carved out an incredibly unique artistic universe. Ryabchenko's vibrant and colorful landscapes captivate viewers, transporting them into a new realm of aesthetics. His ability to reinterpret biblical motifs sets his work apart, as seen in his renowned piece "Judgment Day." This approach enables a new generation of artists to freely explore and discover new meanings through innovative mediums, encouraging them to create with unparalleled freedom. By embracing such artistic expressions, we can collectively strive to improve the world, fostering creativity, diversity, and individuality.

Naive art is also experiencing a resurgence, thanks to the vibrant contributions of Iryna Maksymova and Dzvinya Podlyashetska, who have recently garnered global attention for their work. Maksymova, for instance, paints colorful, fantastical animals in a folk-inspired style, often working on an enormous scale. She also occasionally returns to traditional Ukrainian decorative arts, such as hand-made tapestries.

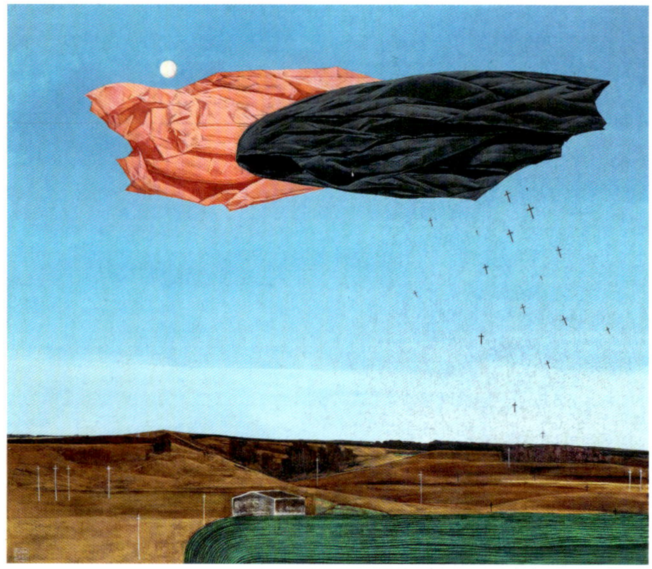

After the war began, an ominous black fabric appeared in Polina Kuznetsova's works. Below: Olga Navrotska uses AI to create her fantasies of traditional Ukrainian fashion.

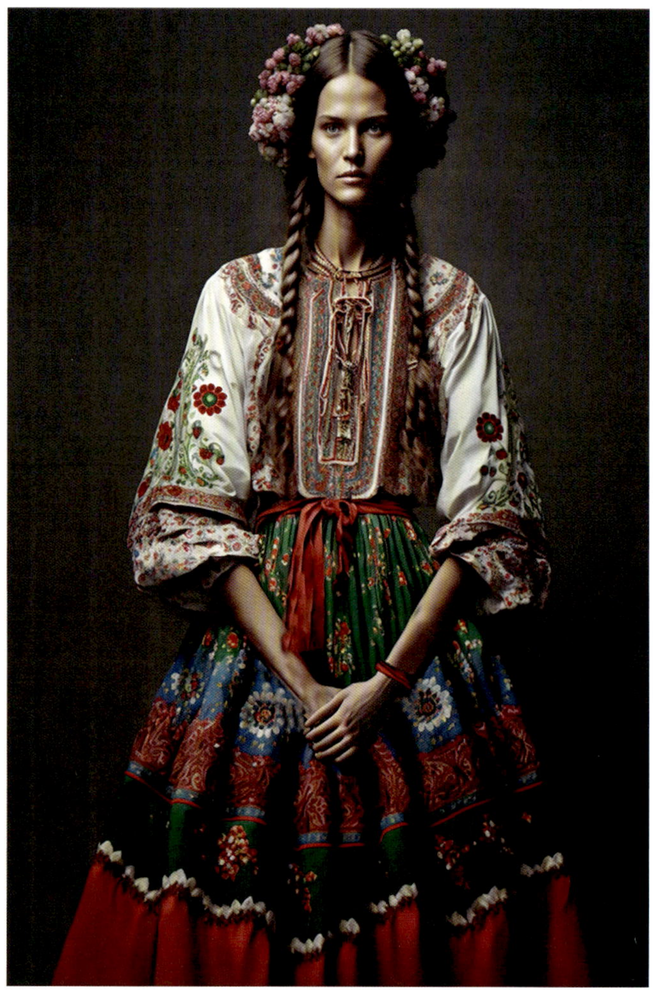

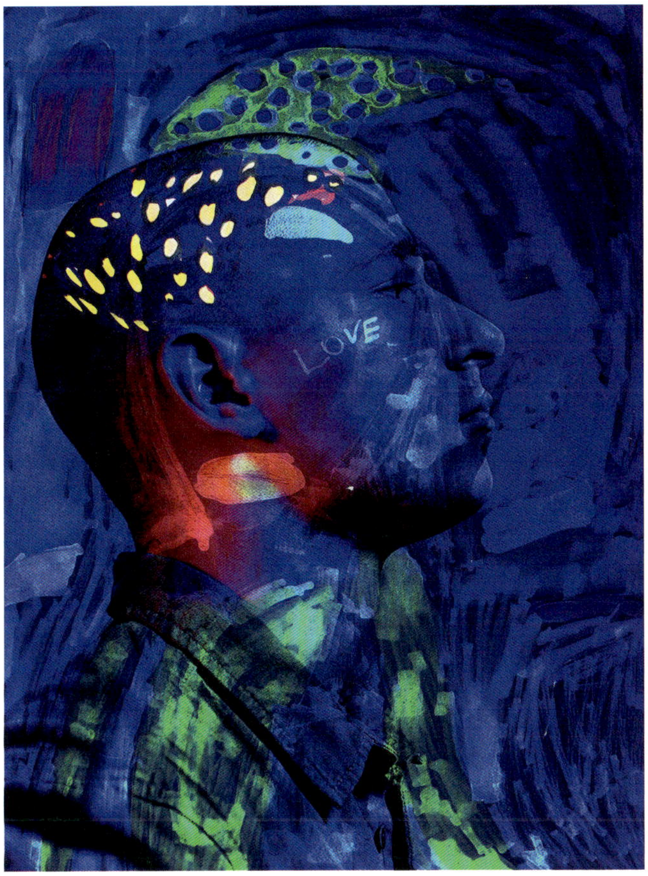

Yevhen Zaiets is a bright representative of an emerging movement that combines photography and digital art. Below: Portions of Waone's mural *From Legend to Discovery*, New York, 2022.

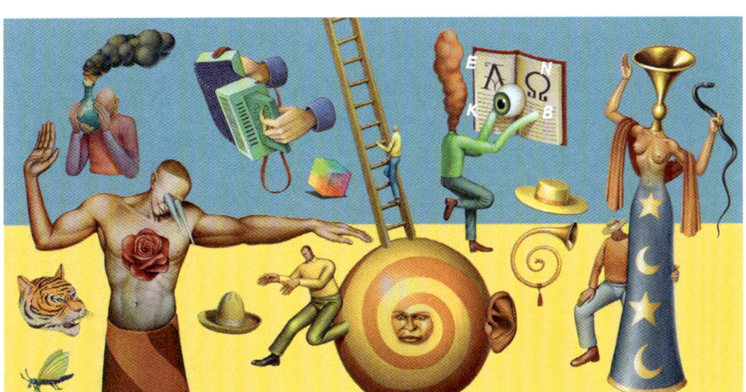

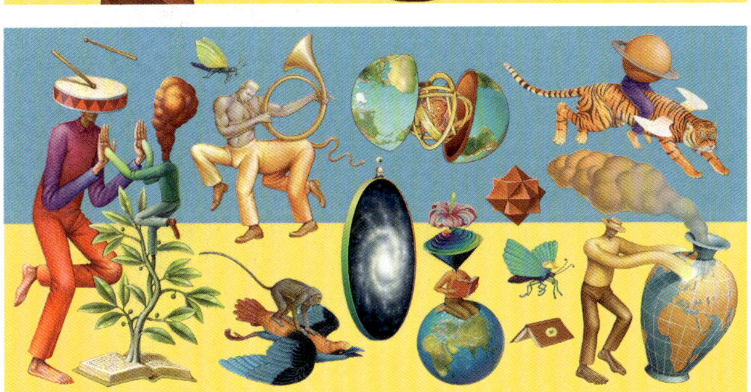

Recent technological progress, with its seemingly endless flow of information and new tools, allows artists to inhabit multiple worlds at once, giving them unprecedented freedom. The boundaries between different types of visual art are increasingly blurring, with graphic design, street art, and illustration gaining prominence alongside traditional painting and sculpture. Often figurative in nature, the art emerging from this movement covers a diverse range of themes and is motivated by the exploration of both national and personal identity.

ENVISIONING A NEW FUTURE

The current generation of young Ukrainians, having lived through various crises, social turmoil, and, most recently, a full-scale war, cannot help but express their inner experiences through art. Many artists reflect on wartime, conveying their feelings and informing the world about the events in Ukraine. One such artist is Polina Kuznetsova, known for her remarkable paintings and evocative performance art. In a recent performance, she locked herself in a cage in one of Tallinn's squares. Caught in the rain and refusing food or an umbrella, Polina demonstrated with visceral urgency what horrors people face during war.

Meanwhile, the Ukrainian illustrators collective Pictoric is engaged in projects that draw the public's attention to current social problems. Graphic designers, who have become active participants in the art scene in recent years, are returning to motifs of folklore and national identity, as well as actively participating in creating new identities for state and private institutions, shedding the last lingering traces of Soviet narratives. A prime example of this is Banda Agency's new identity for the National Art Museum of Ukraine (NAMU).

The history of Ukrainian visual culture is a permanent whirlwind of transformation, exploration, and struggle for its identity, but also a consciously vivid picture of how you can and should fight for those values you hold most dear. The thousand-year development process continues, and the journey, abundant in beauty, truth, and magnificence, appears as enduring as Ukrainian culture itself.

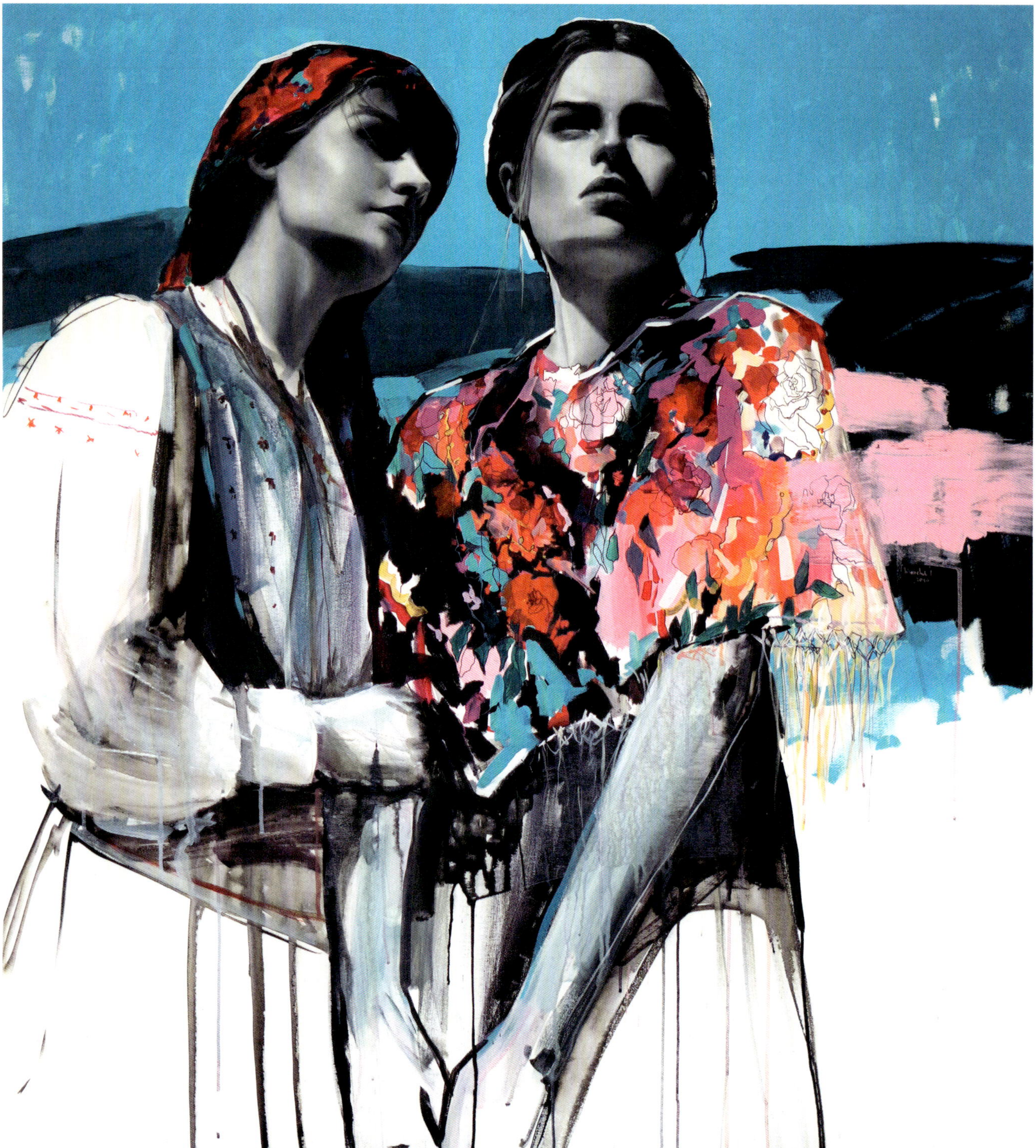

ARTISTIC EXPERIMENTS WITH AUTHENTIC ELEMENTS

INNA KHARCHUK · *ІННА ХАРЧУК*

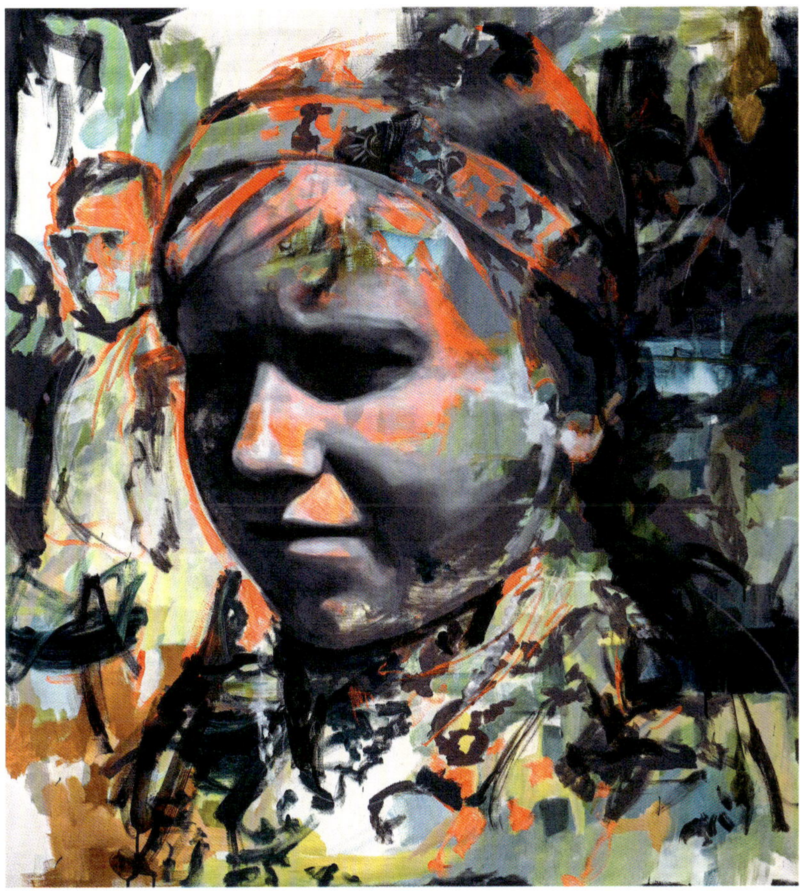

Through artistic experimentation, Inna Kharchuk seamlessly combines elements of realism with bold spectrum colors and figurative abstractions.

The authenticity of Ukrainian culture fills Inna Kharchuk with a special kind of awe; she likes to immerse herself in it, look at it through the prism of modern techniques. National identity is clearly visible in her work, which features scenes related to Ukrainian culture, daily life, and societal values. For a recent series, the painter used archival photographs, exploring not only the unique traditional attire they depicted, but also the circumstances in which each particular picture was taken. Using her own experiences and reflections as a lens, Kharchuk explores issues of self-identity and personal and collective memory. The artist's most recent work created after the war started reveals her ongoing search for new concepts of ancestry, national memory, and loyalty to cultural origins. Kharchuk uses her work to reflect on the unbreakable spirit and humanity of the Ukrainian nation, and she feels it is her duty to express these profound, pressing ideas through her art.

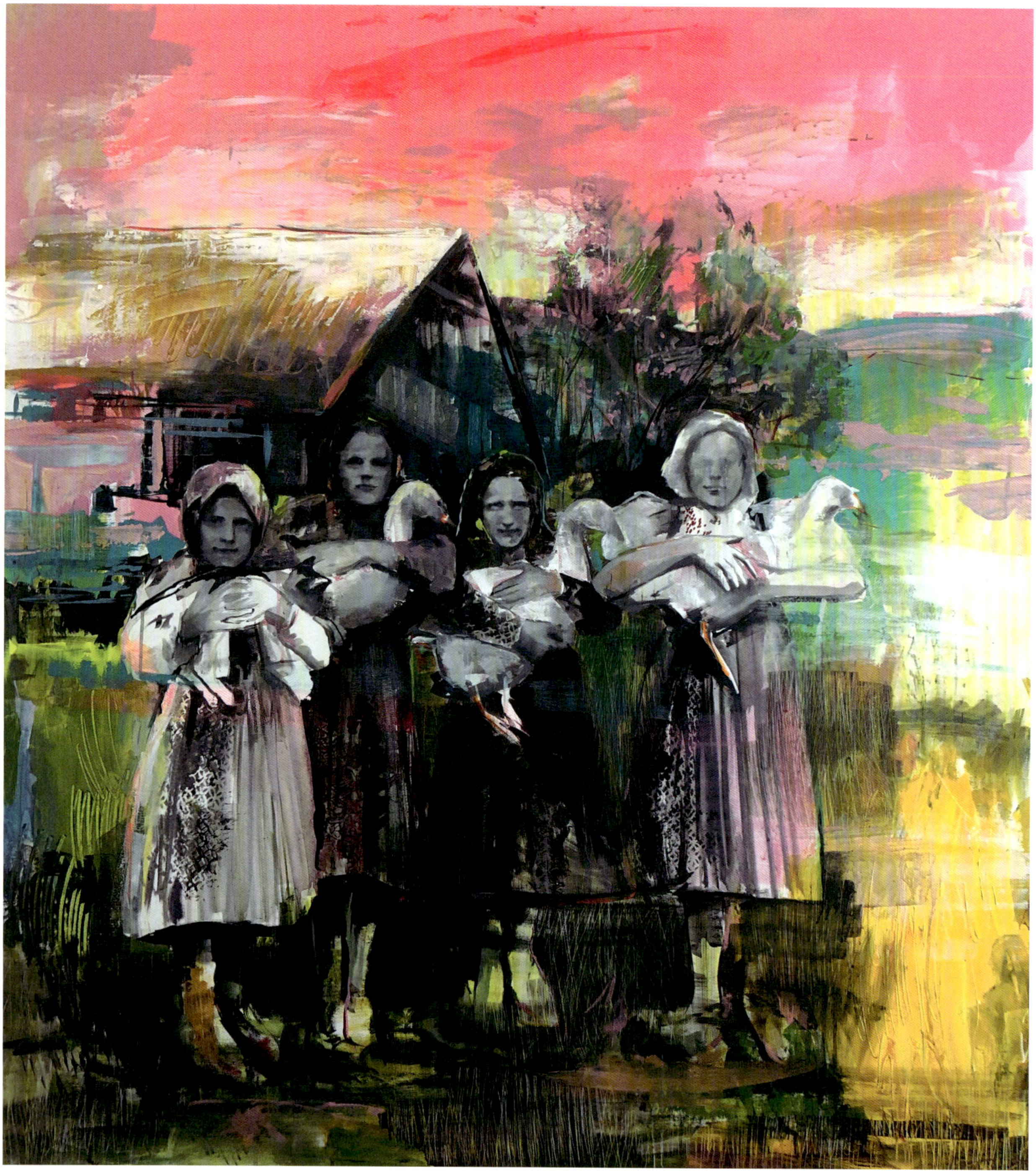

Kharchuk's painting *Berehyni* seems to embody memory itself, with color and detail flashing across the canvas like emotions resurfacing and fading once again. The painting seems to evoke a serene past lost to time's inevitable march. Previous pages: *Ohliadyny*, acrylic, oil, soft materials, and spray paint on canvas, 2020 (p. 56); *Divcha*, acrylic, oil, and pastel on canvas, 2022 (p. 57).

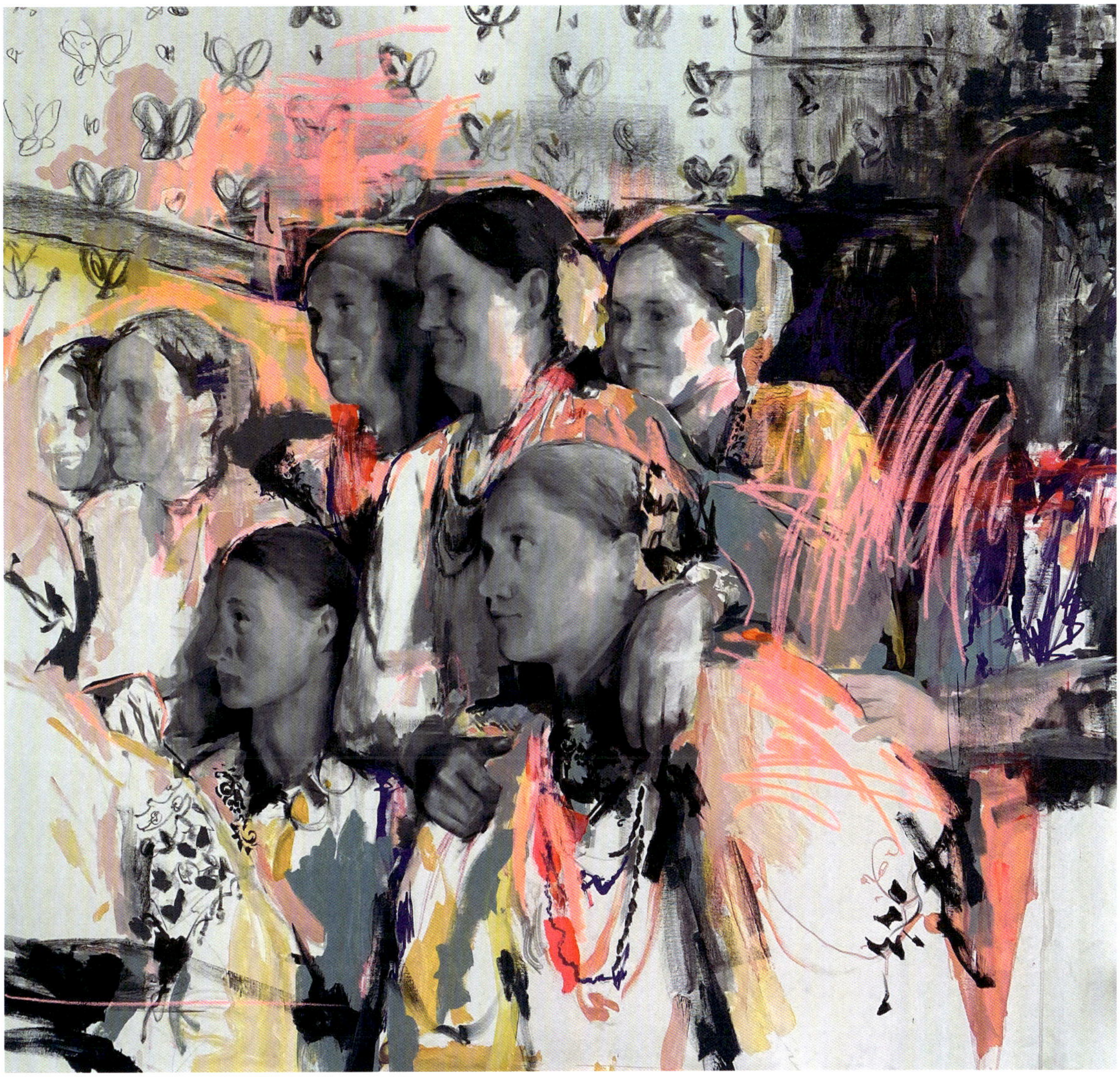

Chary Nochi ("Charms of the Night"), like the artist's other works, reflects a heartfelt love for Ukrainian culture. Long ago she had an irresistible desire to change, and deepen, people's superficial perceptions of Ukraine.

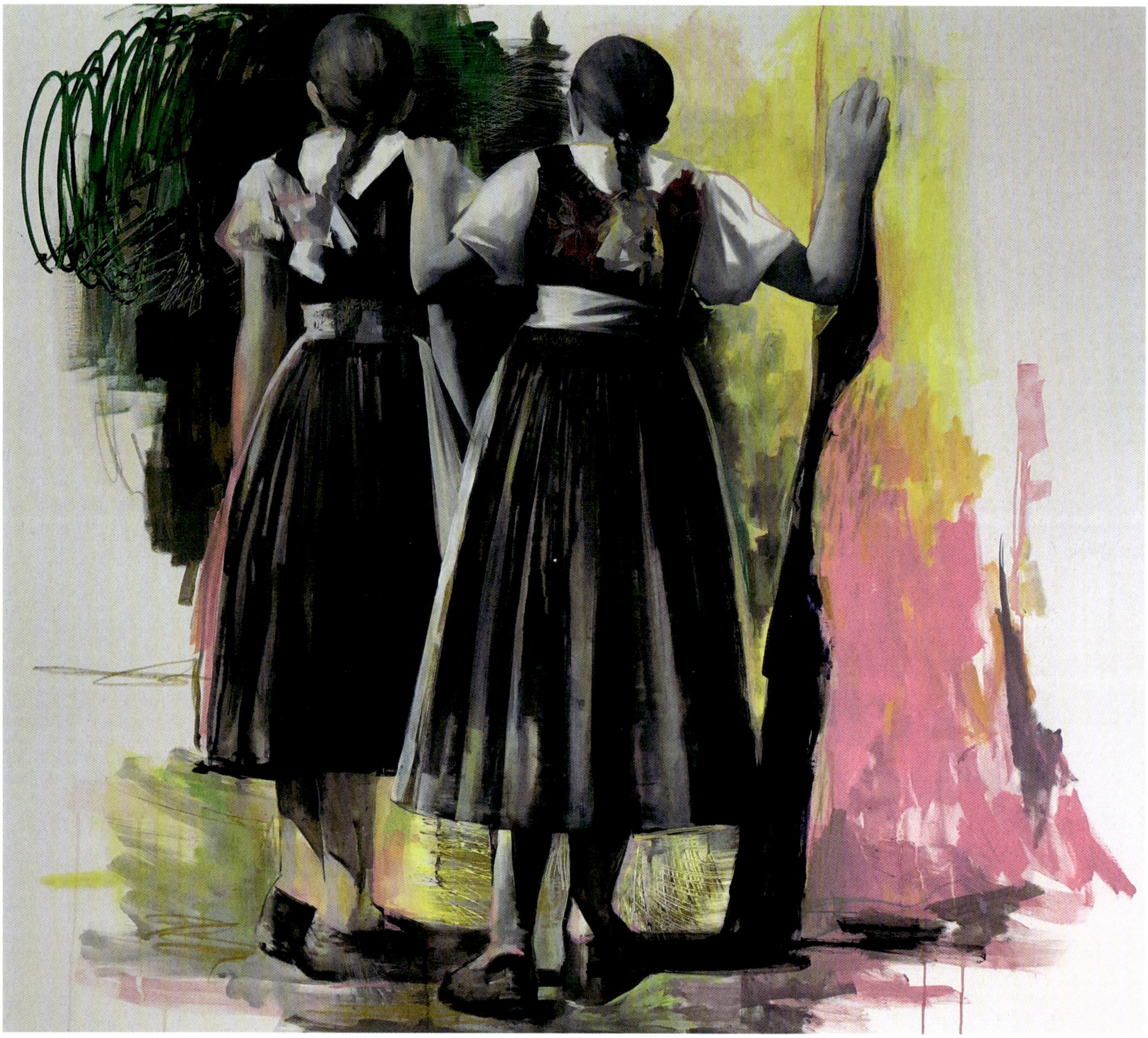

Inna Kharchuk is inspired by archives, color, and a passion for life. She is especially fond of authentic Ukrainian culture and its identity, which she likes to study through the prism of modern techniques. *Sekrety* ("Secrets"), acrylic, pastel on canvas, 2021.

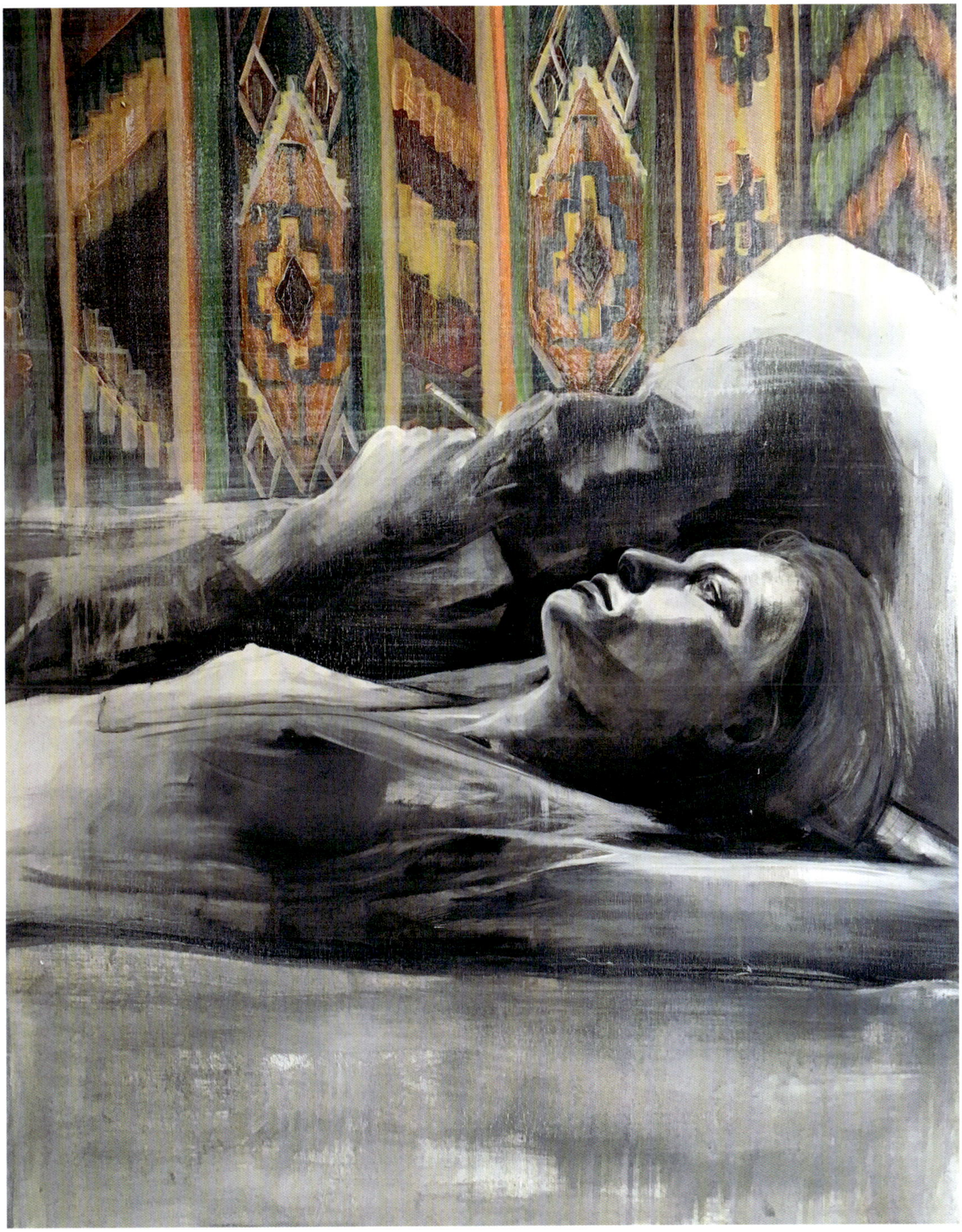

Like any true artist, Kharchuk immerses herself in her feelings and moods, deep reflections, and thoughts, which she depicts in her works. *Dumka* ("Thought"), acrylic, pastel on canvas, 2020.

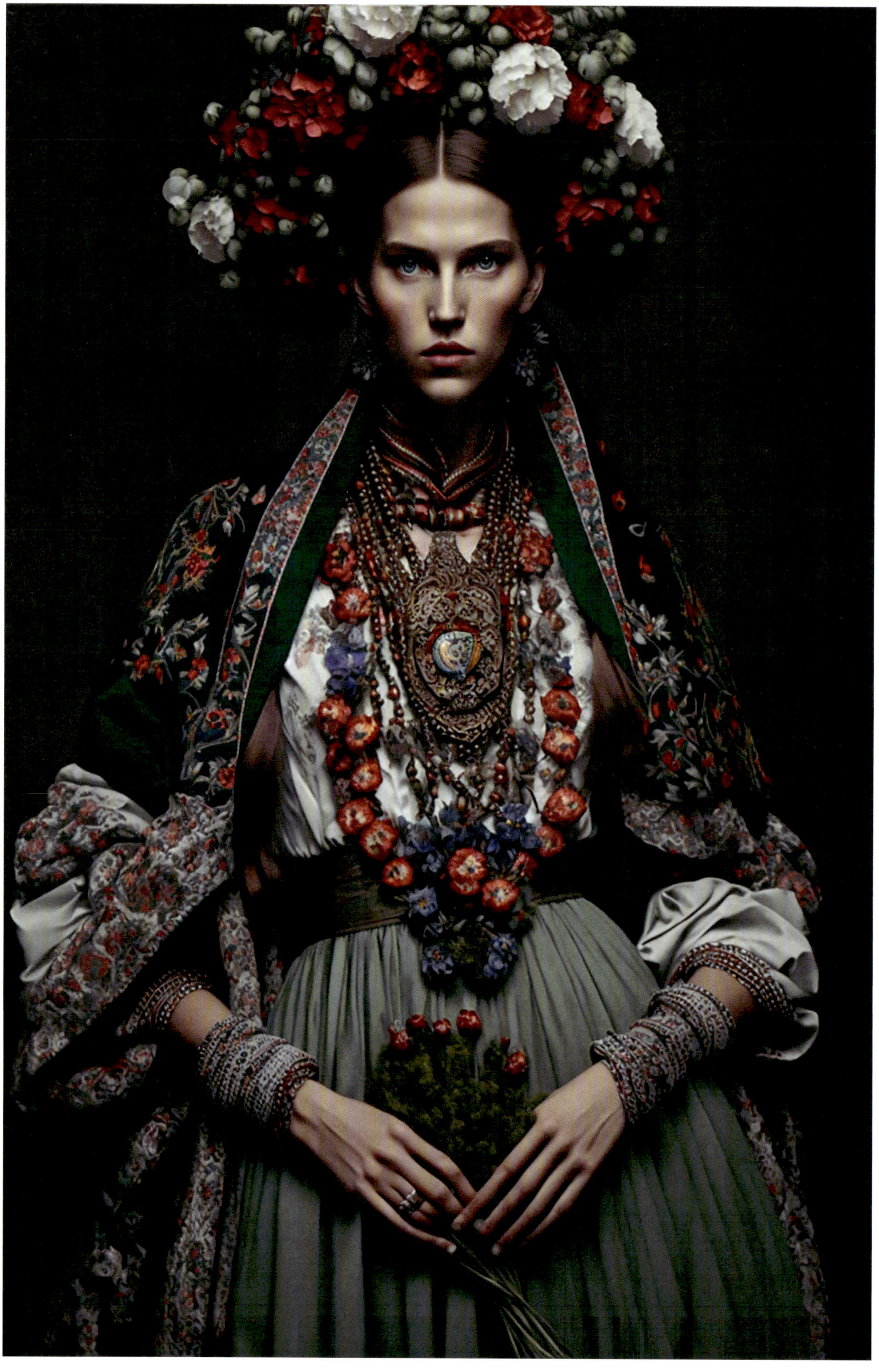

DIGITAL ART MEETS UKRAINIAN FOLK FANTASY

OLGA NAVROTSKA · *ОЛЬГА НАВРОЦЬКА*

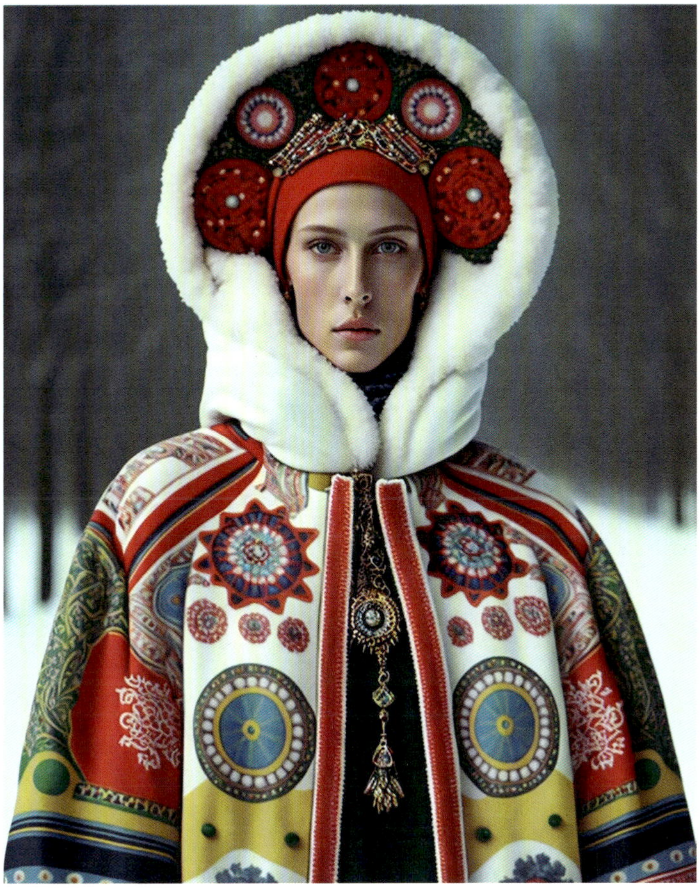

Olga Navrotska uses artificial intelligence to create digital works filled with fantastical interpretations of ancient Ukrainian clothes, jewelry, and embroidery, inventing the art of Ukrainian Folk Fantasy.

In the past, Olga Navrotska worked as a successful fashion designer with her own brand, Navro. Shortly before the Covid-19 pandemic, she decided to explore new creative avenues. Today, she is a writer and show-runner working on the fantasy film project *Chronicles of Power*, based on Ukrainian mythology and history. In the middle of 2022, the artist learned about the possibilities of AI and immediately plunged into the world of technology. Navrotska began to visualize what she saw in her imagination, creating bold and inventive interpretations of Ukrainian folk clothing and cultural symbols. As Ukrainians increasingly return to their roots, interest in Navrotska's ideas has skyrocketed, and her art, which fuses cutting-edge technology with traditional elements, has garnered widespread acclaim. Navrotska views her work as a way to draw people's attention to Ukrainian culture.

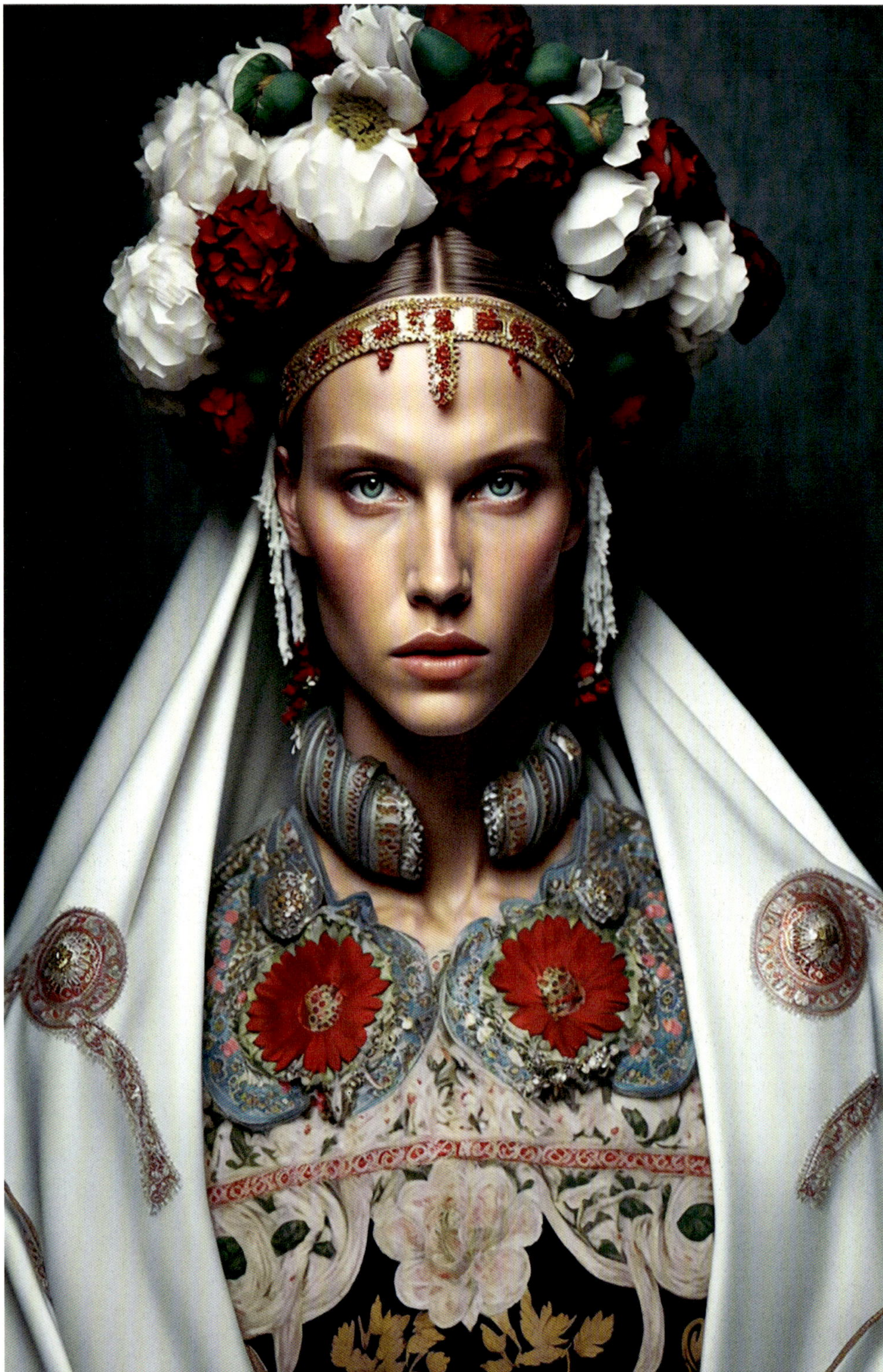

Longing to create something fresh and striking with Ukrainian cultural heritage and traditional attire, Olga Navrotska turned to AI for inspiration. This allowed the artist to develop her distinct style and produce astonishing art that has garnered widespread acclaim.

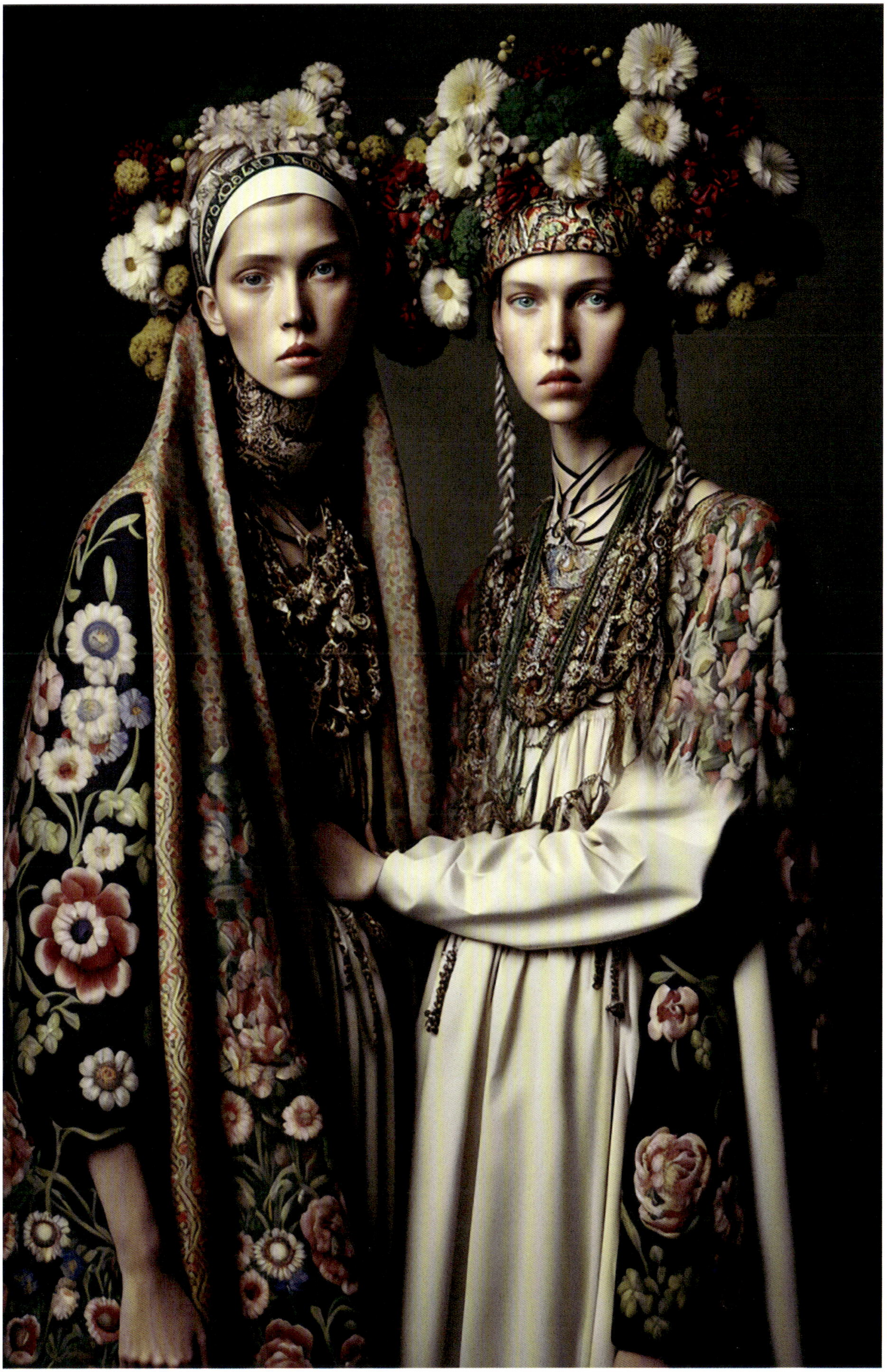

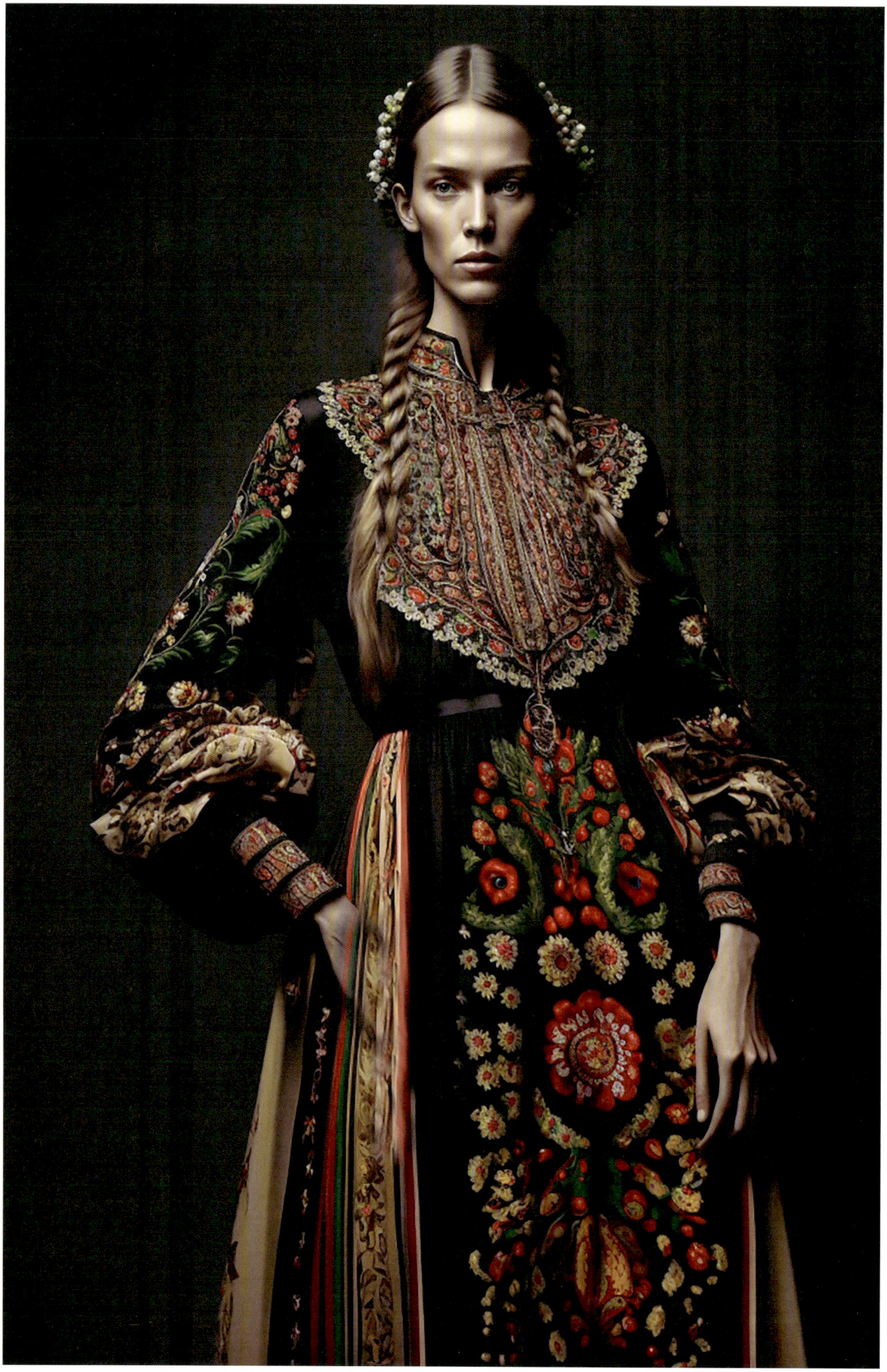

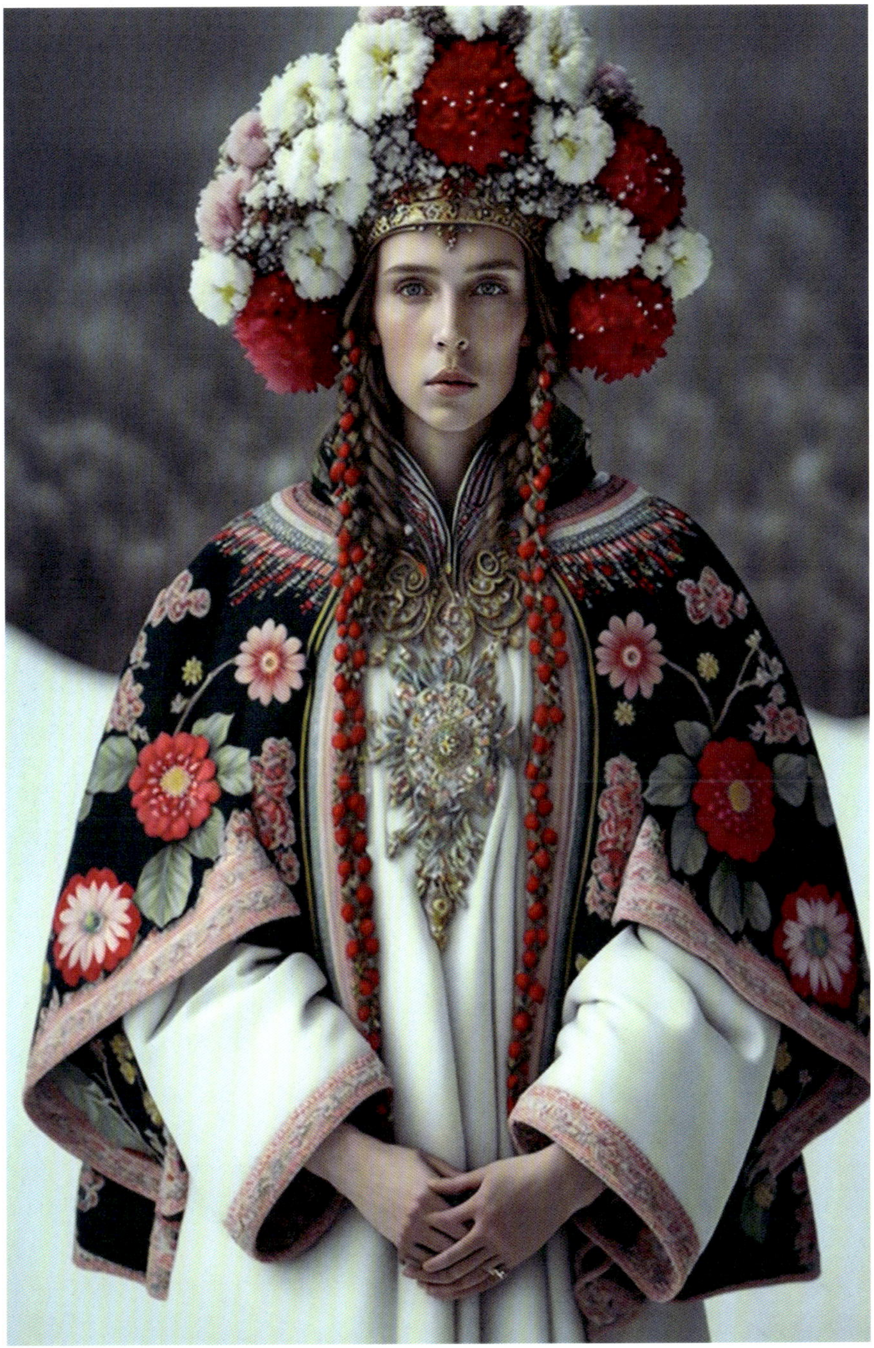

Navrotska's work vividly captures traditional festive folk costumes, showcasing their patterns, materials, ornamentation, and cultural symbols. These works provide inspiration to many artists and designers both in Ukraine and abroad.

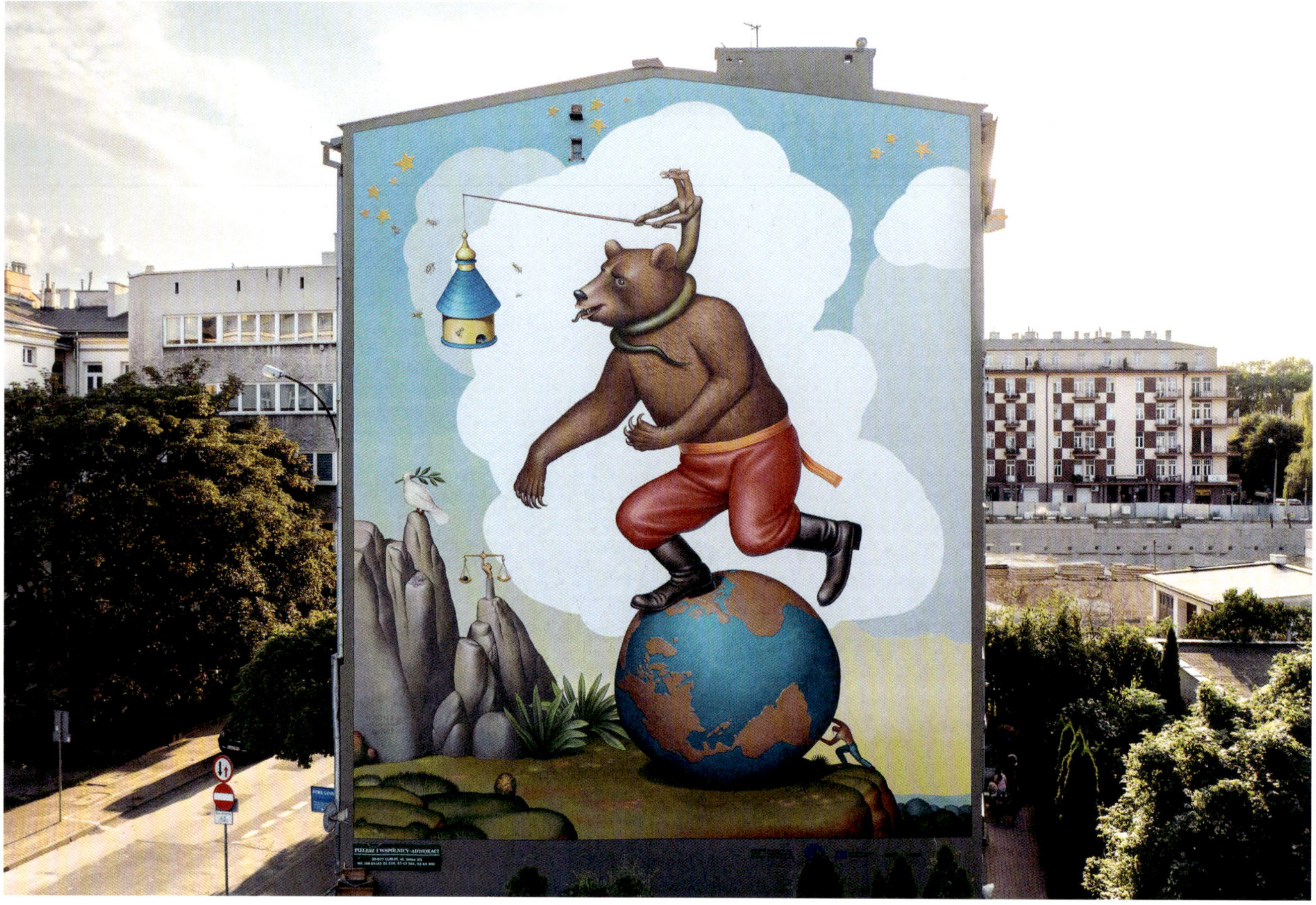

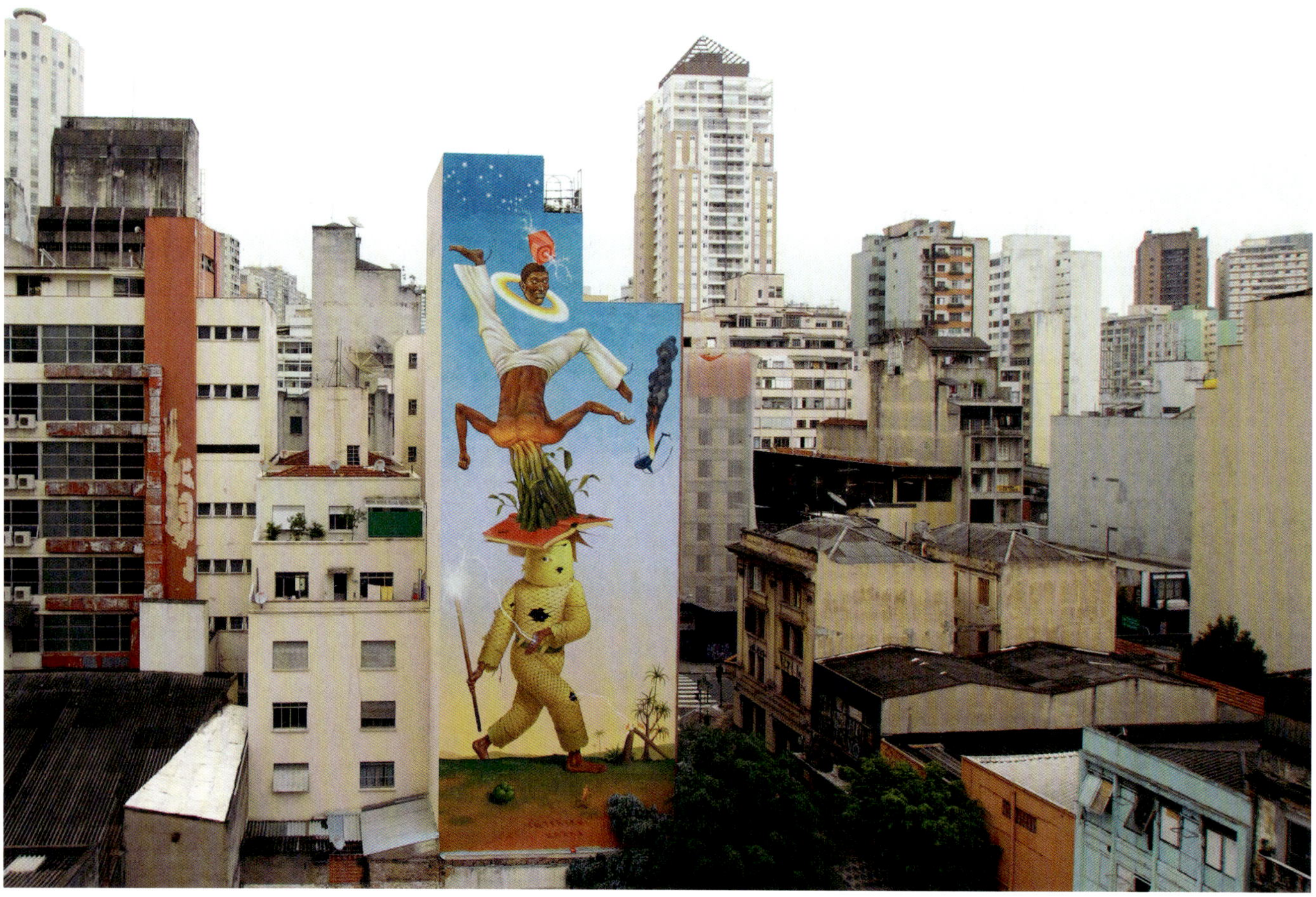

EXPLORING MYSTICAL REALMS THROUGH ART

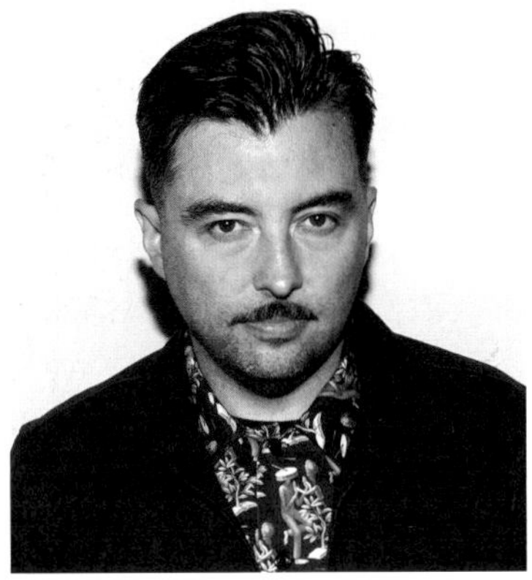

WAONE

Waone's captivating art transports us into a realm of surrealism and symbols, opening doors to the hidden mysteries of the world.

Volodymyr Manzhos, better known as Waone, is a world-renowned muralist and multidisciplinary artist from Kyiv. Working both as a solo artist and as a member of the now-disbanded duo Interesni Kazki ("interesting tales" in Ukrainian), Waone has painted murals across the globe. His visual language is made up of surreal characters, small details, smooth gradients, symbols, and stories. Waone's portfolio spans an impressive range of media, including pencil and ink drawings, lithography and etchings, gouache, acrylic, and oil painting, bronze and ceramic sculpture, and last but not least, digital art. Despite this profusion of different media, the artist divides his art into two simple categories: public and studio work. For public art, he immerses himself in the local context and delves into topics that might be relevant to each location. For his studio work, the process takes center stage. By focusing on process, he partakes in an almost mystical experience, one where the artist dissolves into his work, allowing a project to naturally unfold. Whenever he trusts the process in this way, the result is always impressive. Waone's art is characterized by natural hues, warm, subtle palettes, smooth gradients, and anthropomorphic forms that often merge with the plants, shapes, and architectural forms that surround them. Among his most significant works to date is the "Time for Change" mural series, which highlights various events in Ukraine's history. The first mural in this series, created in India in February 2014, was dedicated to the Maidan events. The second, painted in October 2014 in Kyiv, was influenced by the war in Donbas, and the third, completed in Kyiv in 2022, was dedicated to the Armed Forces and symbolizes the Ukrainian people's faith in victory. Since 2021, Waone has been represented by New York gallery Sapar Contemporary, and in early 2023, he partnered with Idem Paris, an esteemed lithographic studio, for a solo exhibition.

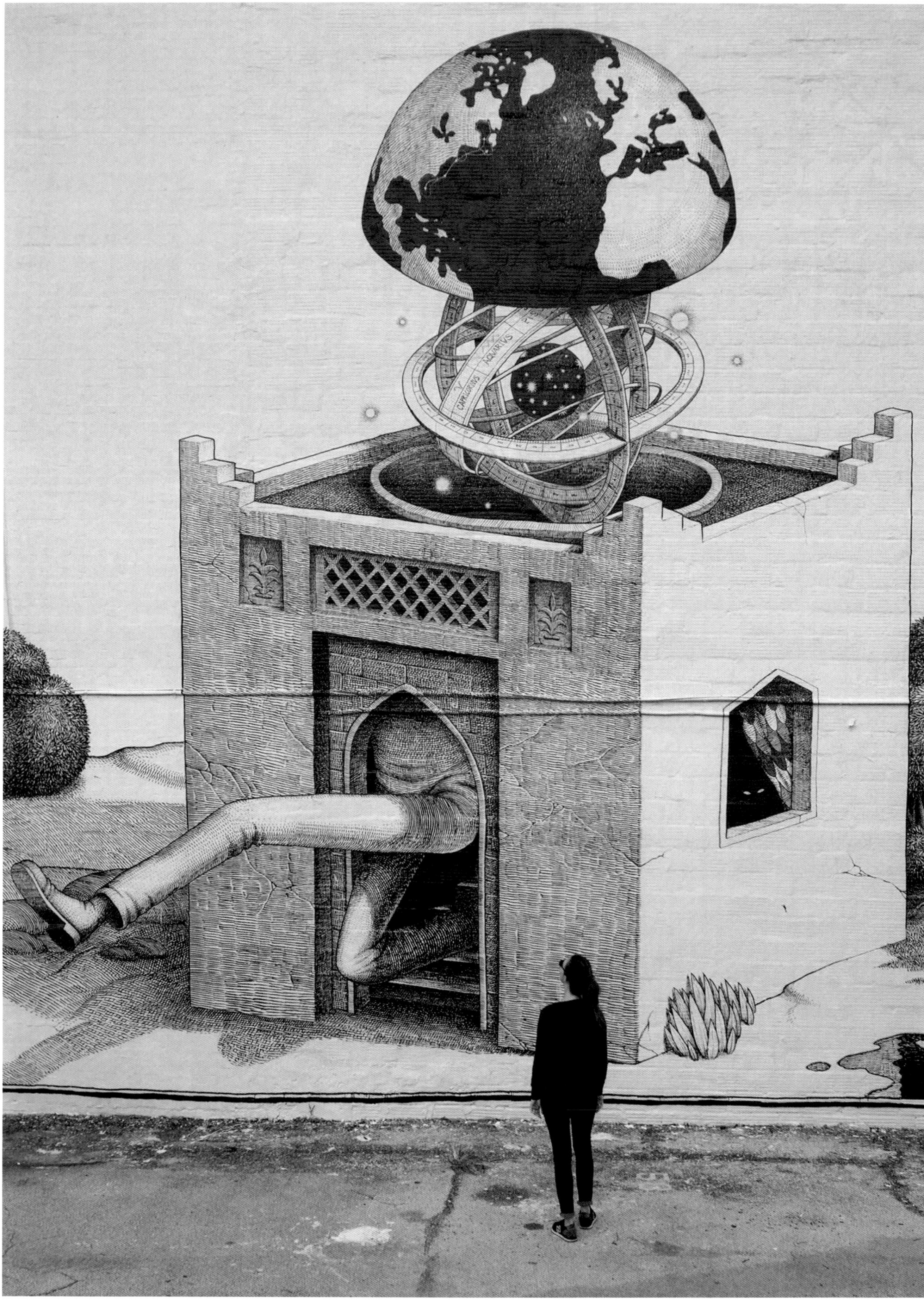
AQUARIUS

"The main goal of my art is to know myself and the outside world. Looking through the prism of the creative process gives me the opportunity to shift the focus from the vanity of life and dive into the depths of the invisible world."

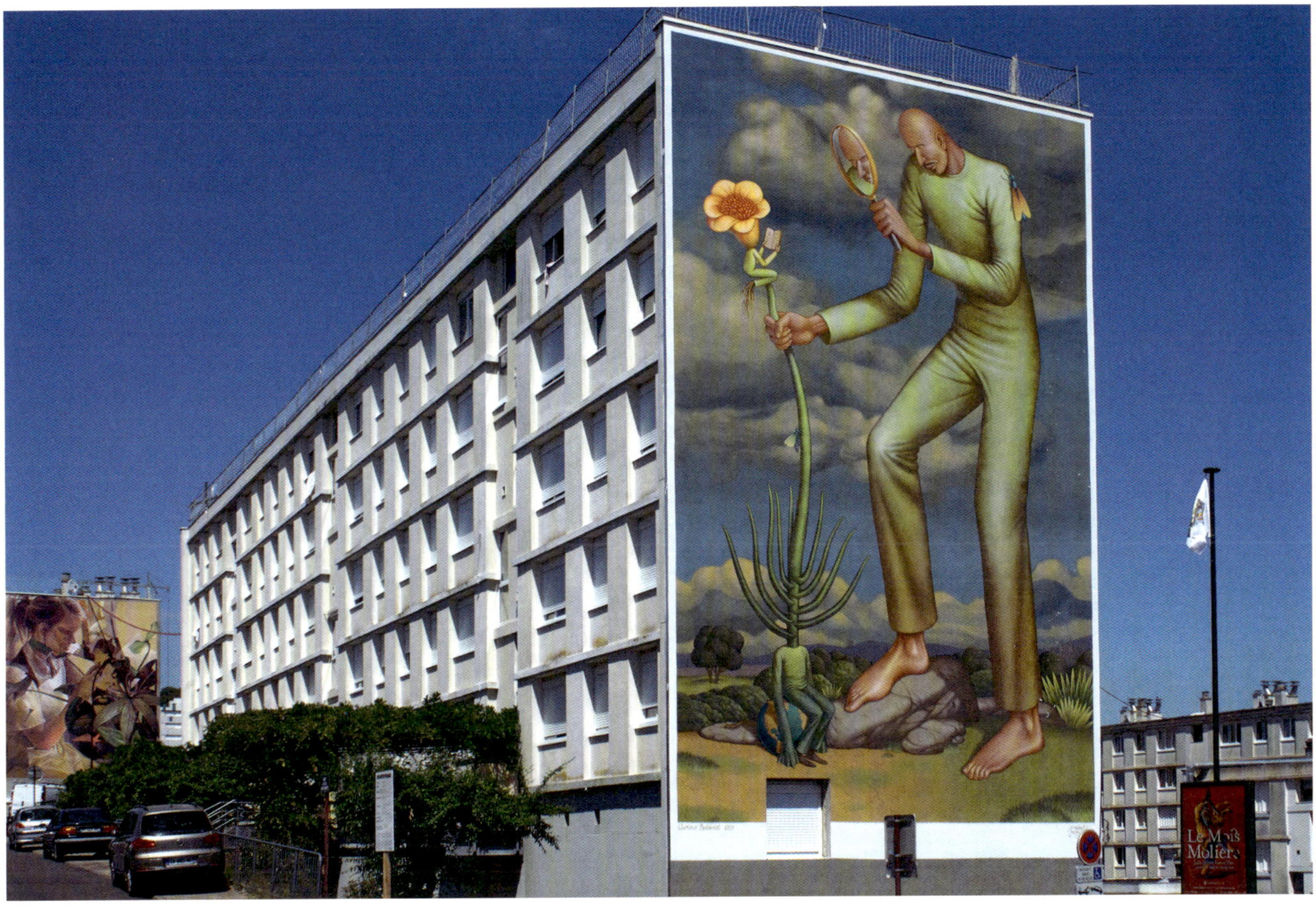

Waone's 2019 *Curious Botanist* mural pays tribute to the celebrated French botanist Bernard de Jussieu. The mural is situated in the Versailles district named in honor of de Jussieu. Opposite page: *Danger of Extinction*, Jacksonville, Florida, USA, 2016. Previous pages: *Deadambitions*, Lublin, Poland, 2022 (p. 68 top), *Capoeira fighter—Bep Cororoti*, São Paulo, Brazil, 2015 (p. 68 bottom).

"I believe that my most important project was the series of murals 'Time for Change,' dedicated to historical events in Ukraine. The second mural from the series was created in October 2014 in Kyiv and was dedicated to the war in Donbas."

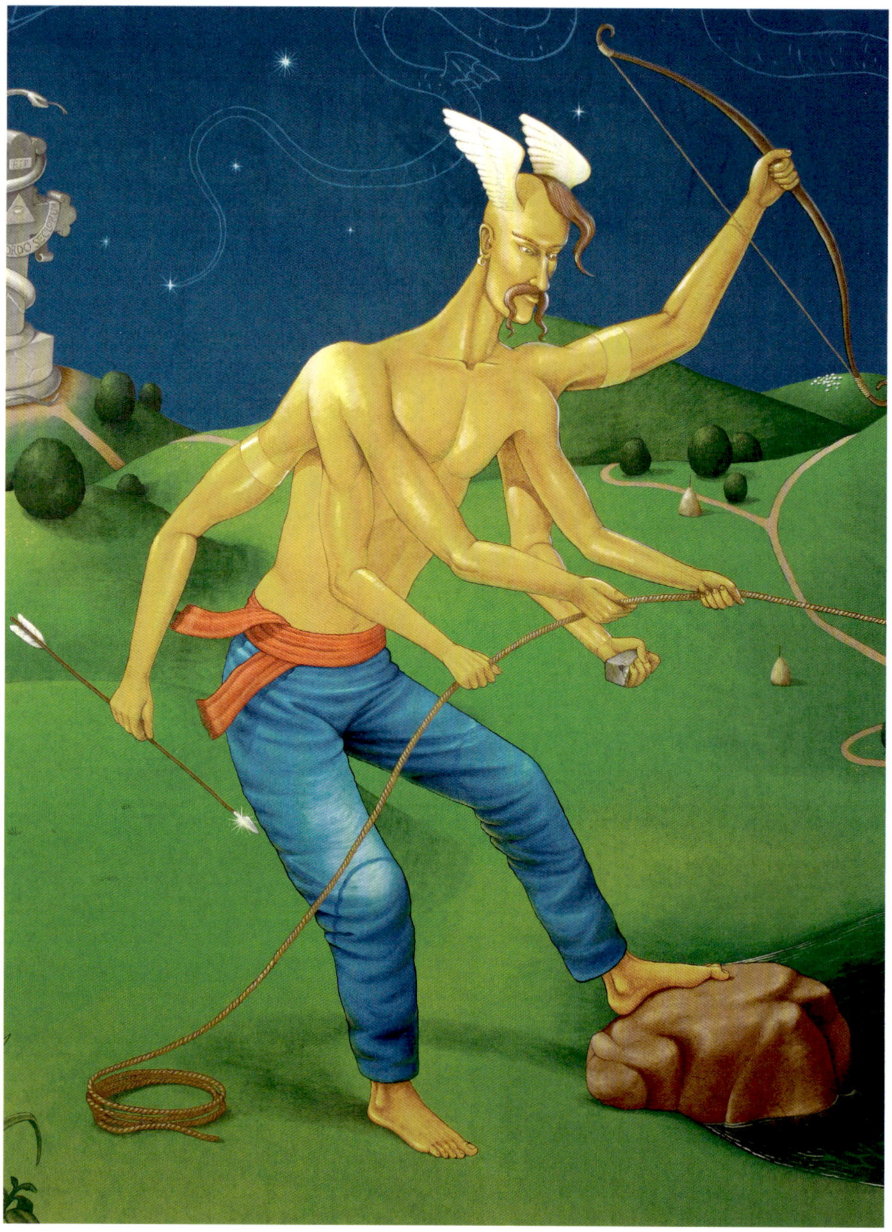

Segment of the mural *Time for Change 2*, Kyiv, Ukraine. Opposite page: *The Magus*, acrylic painting on linen, created in 2012 and exhibited in 2013 in Studio Cromie gallery, Grottaglie, Italy.

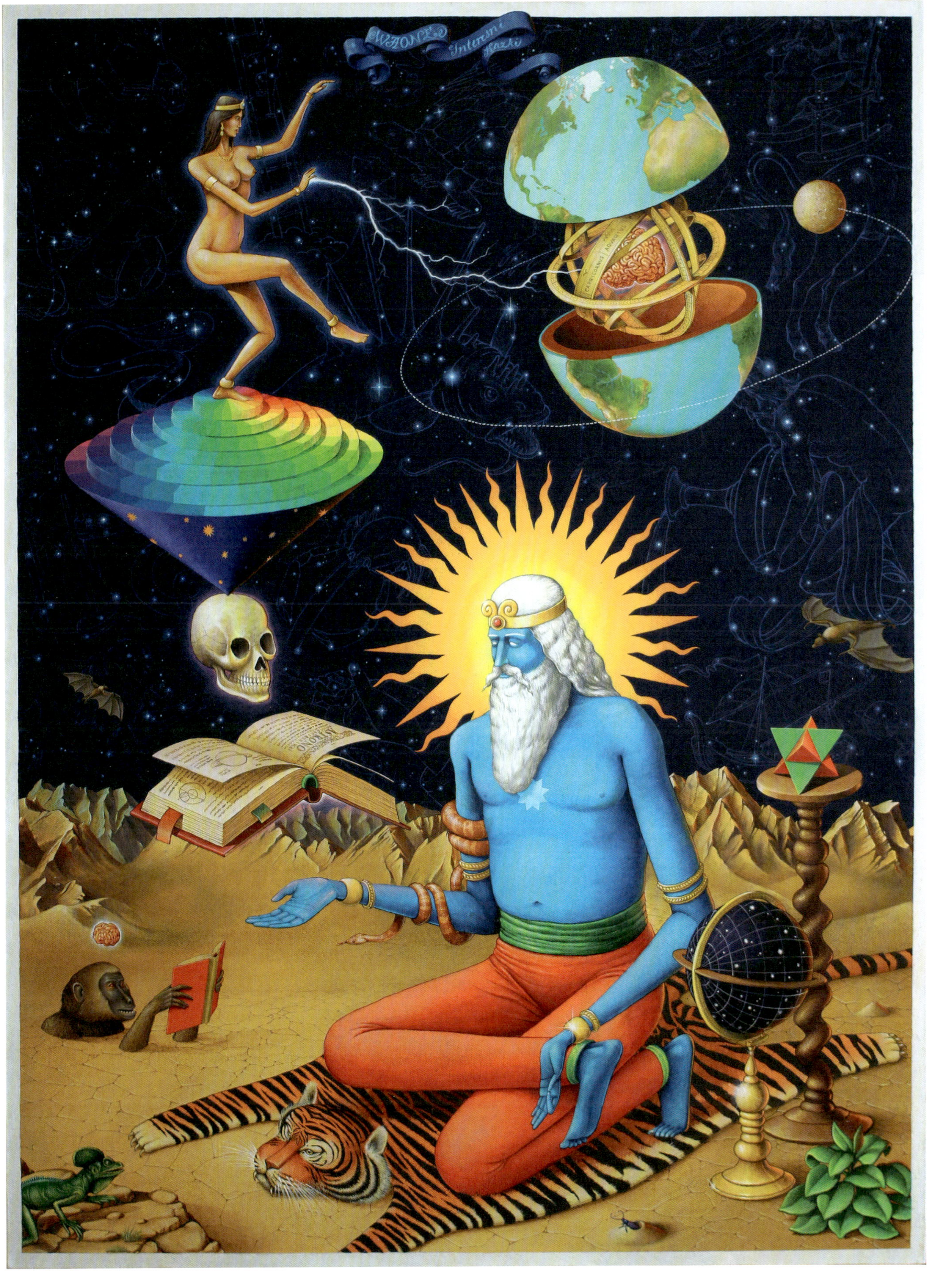

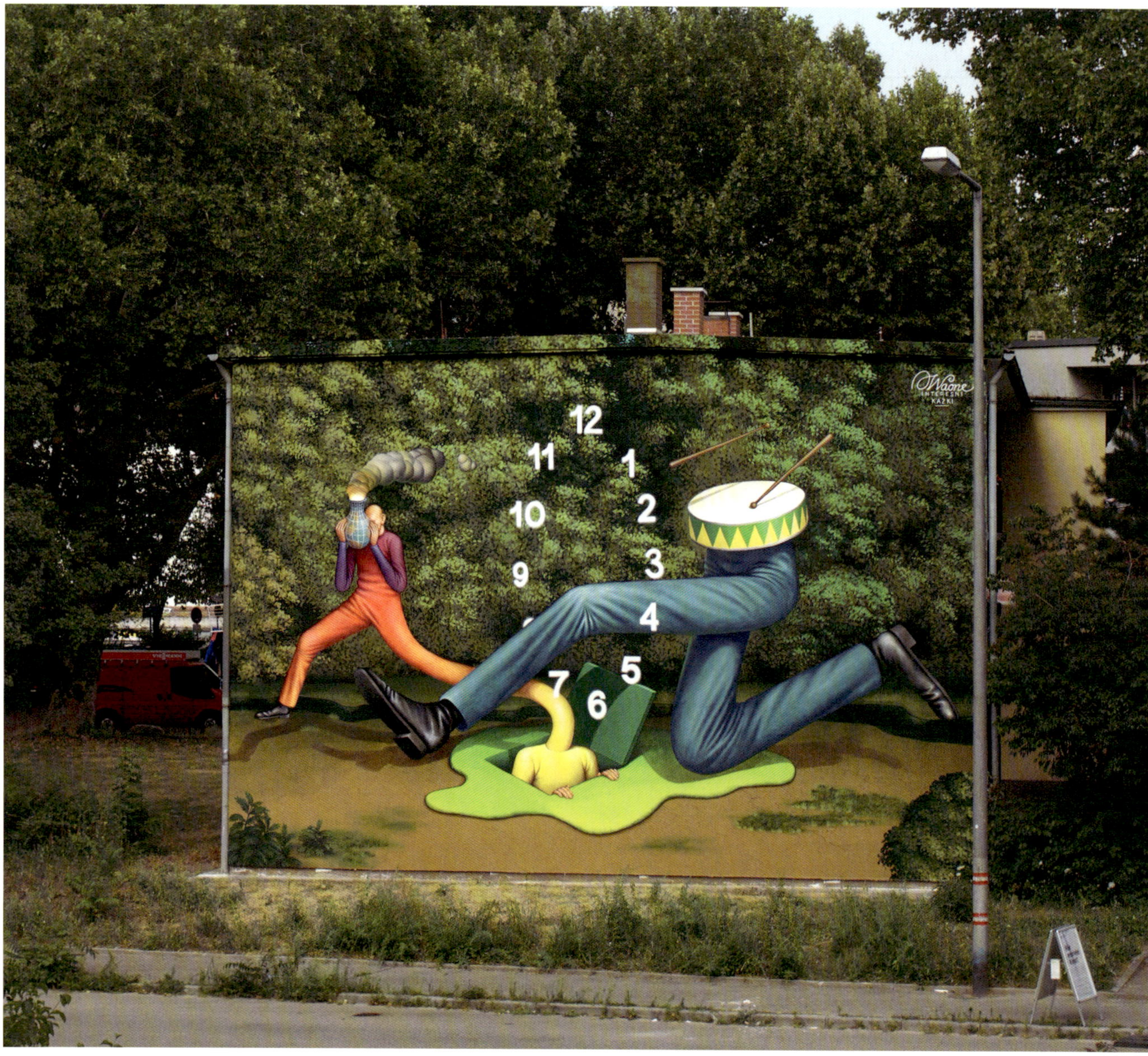

With *Jump Through Time,* Waone transports the viewer to a world of surreal images, providing a brief escape from the hectic nature of daily life. The 26-by-40 foot (8-by-12 meter) mural was created in 2018 in Mannheim, Germany.

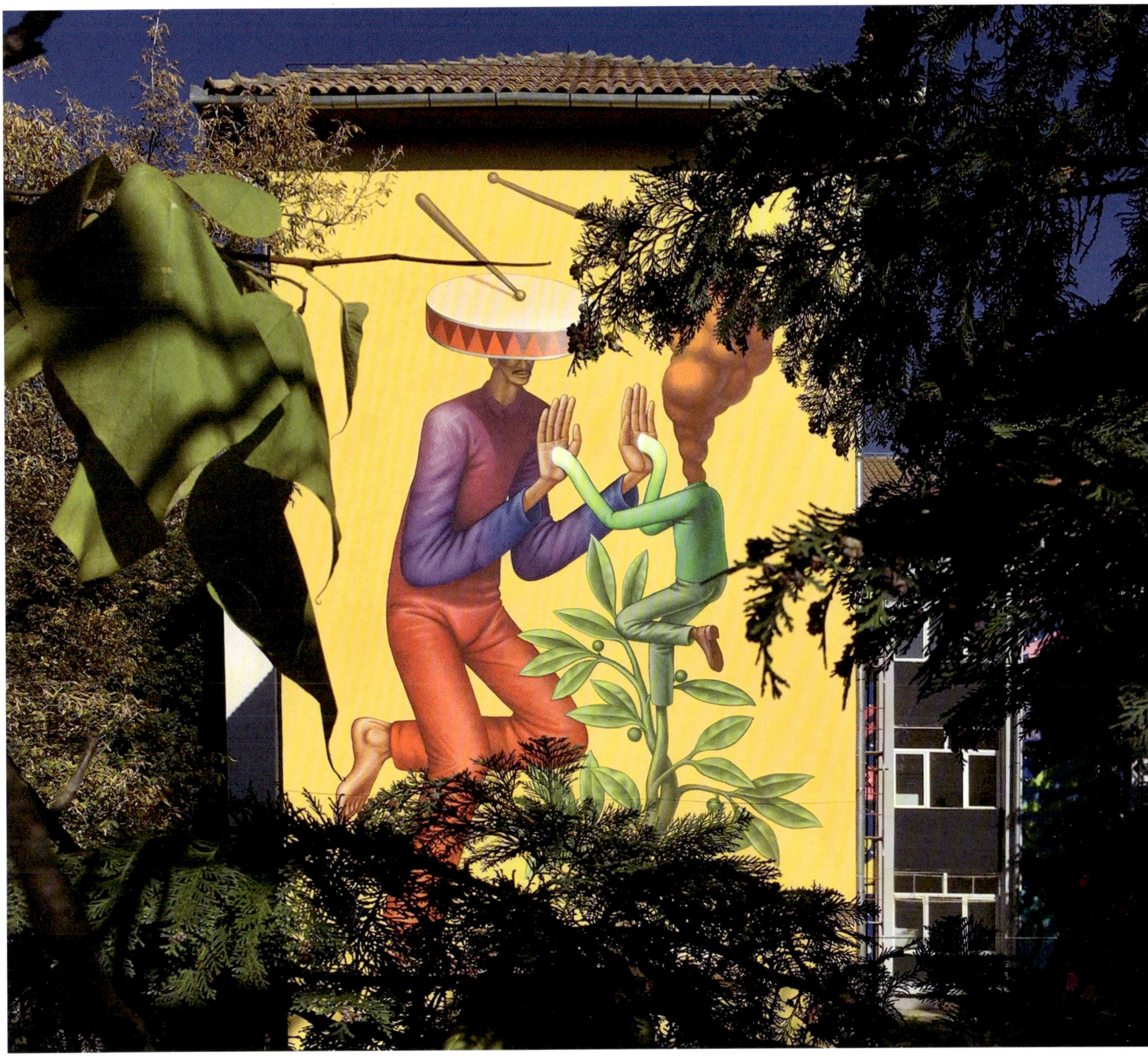

Transcendental Moment adorns the exterior of the Octavian Goga school in Cluj-Napoca, Romania. The work embodies the creative power derived from knowledge, transforming it into a visual delight for all to behold. Next page: *Spark of Life*, acrylic painting on linen canvas, 2015.

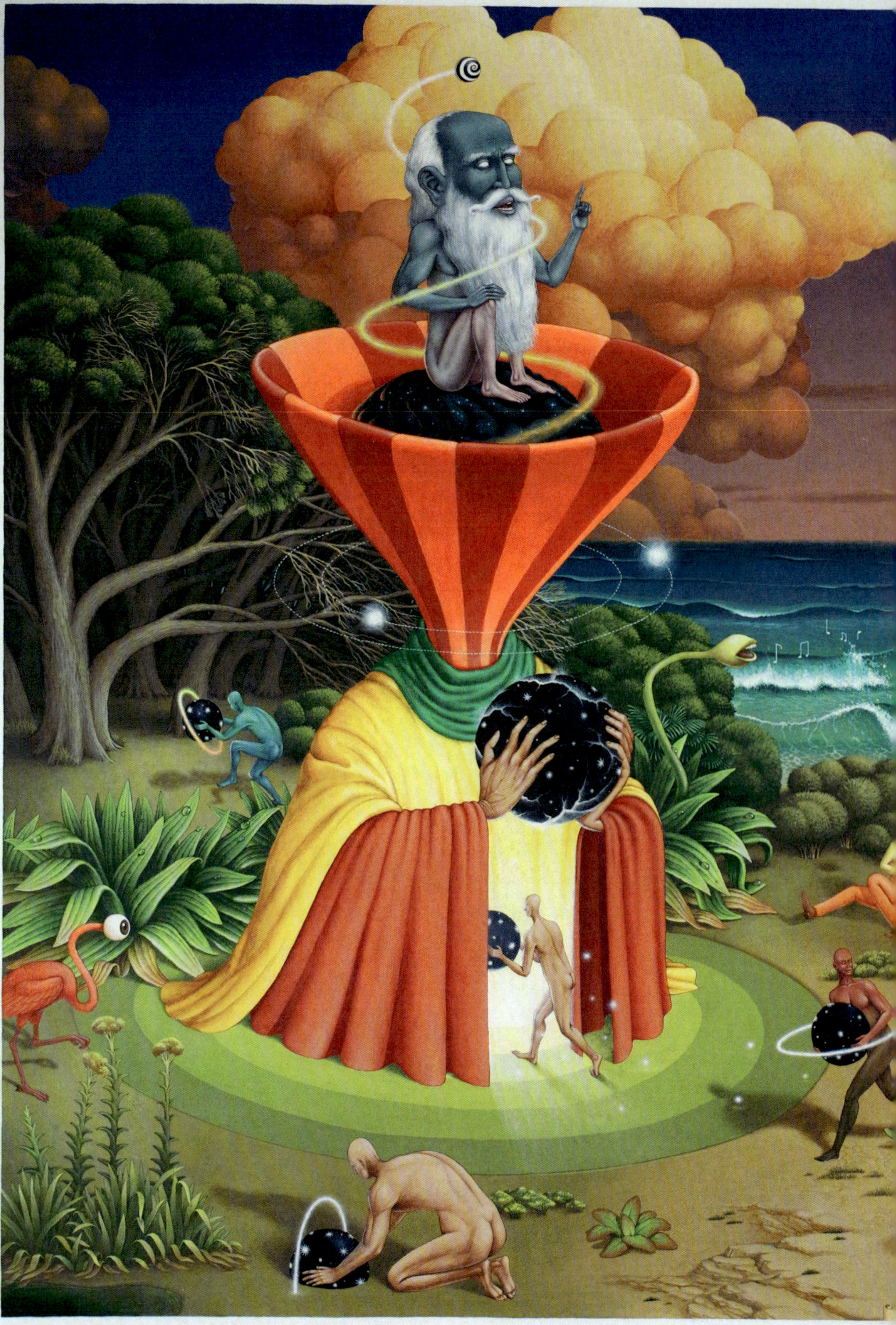

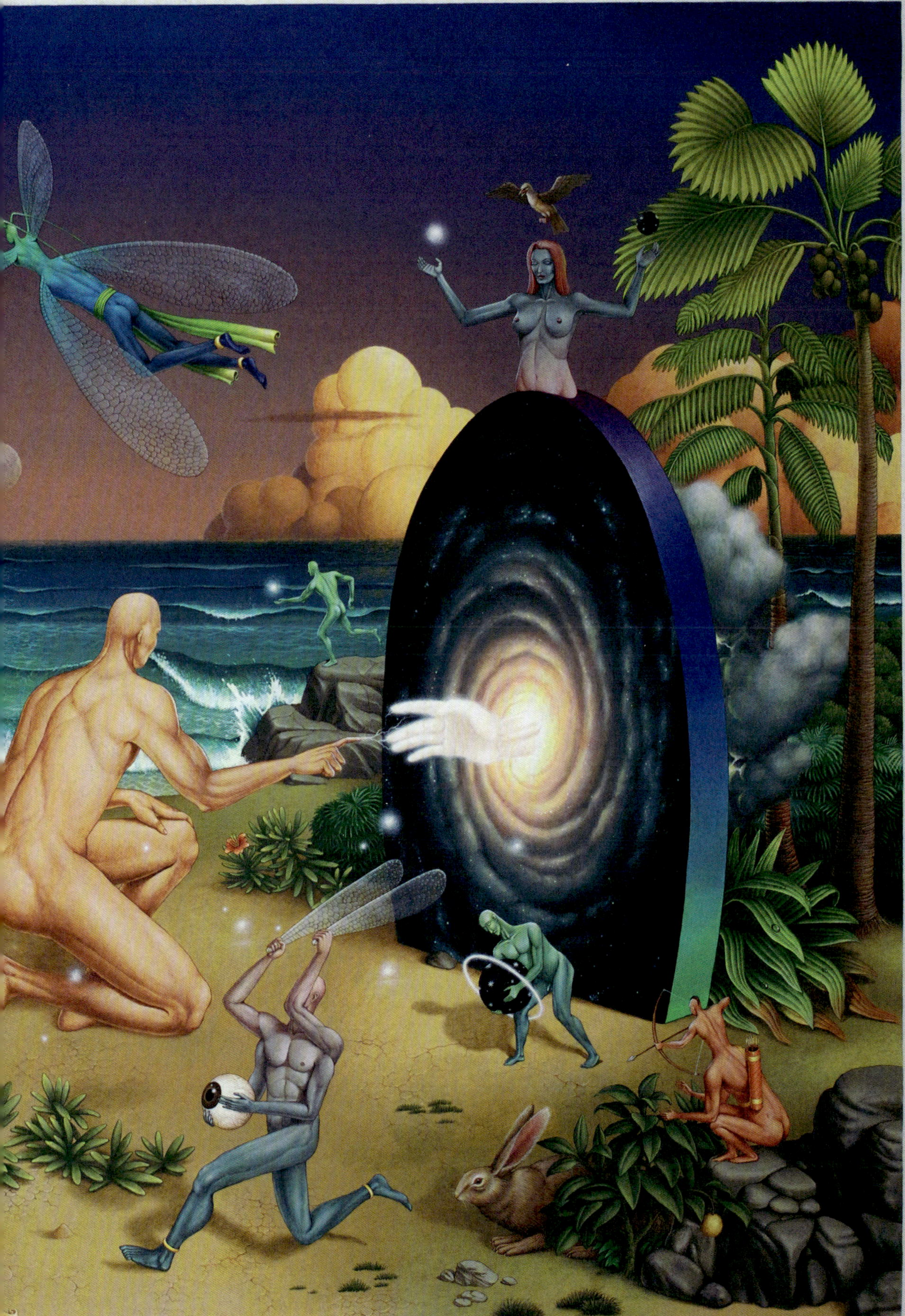

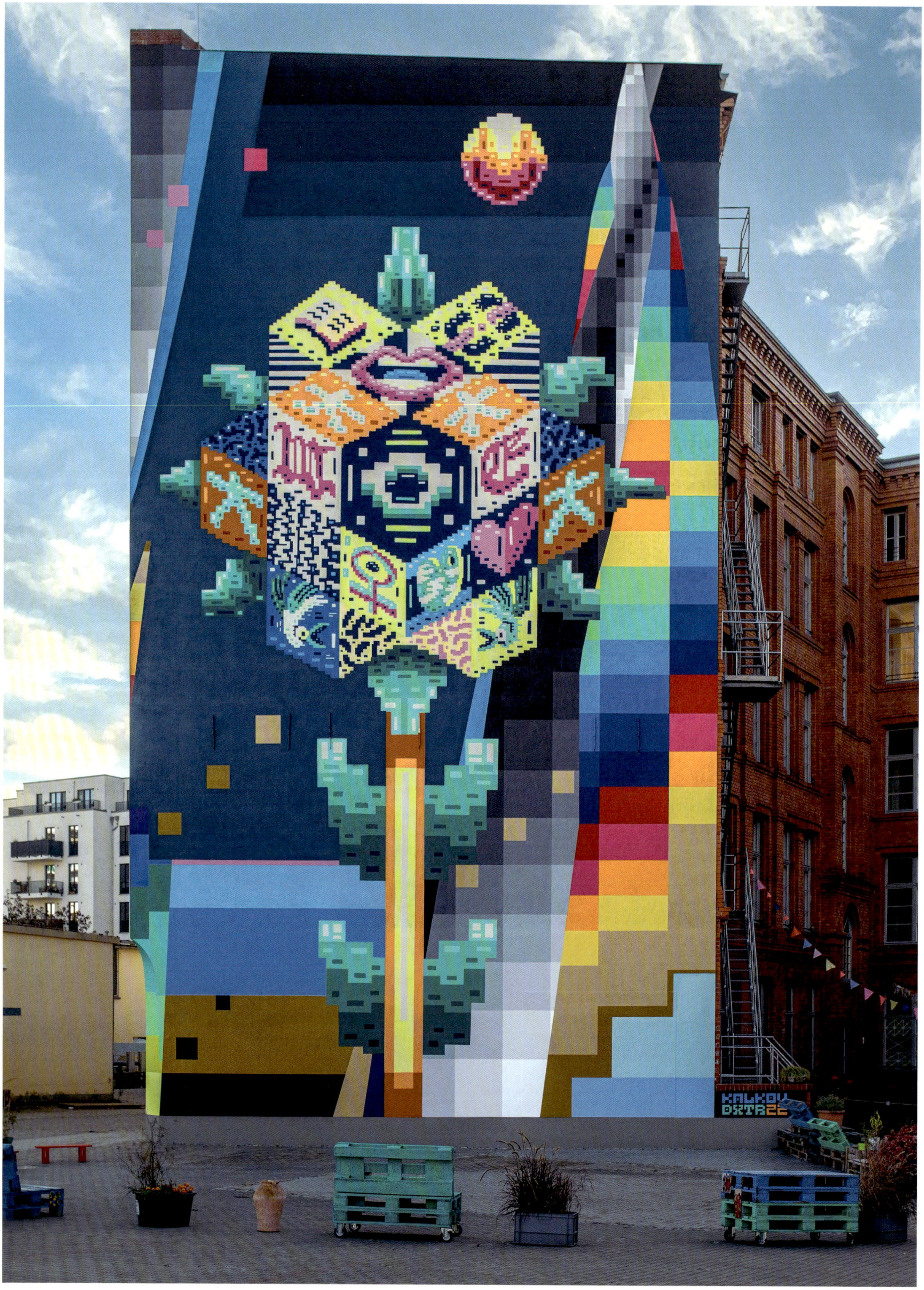
KALKOV
DXTR22

DYNAMIC OPTICAL ILLUSION

ANDRIY KALKOV · *АНДРІЙ КАЛЬКОВ*

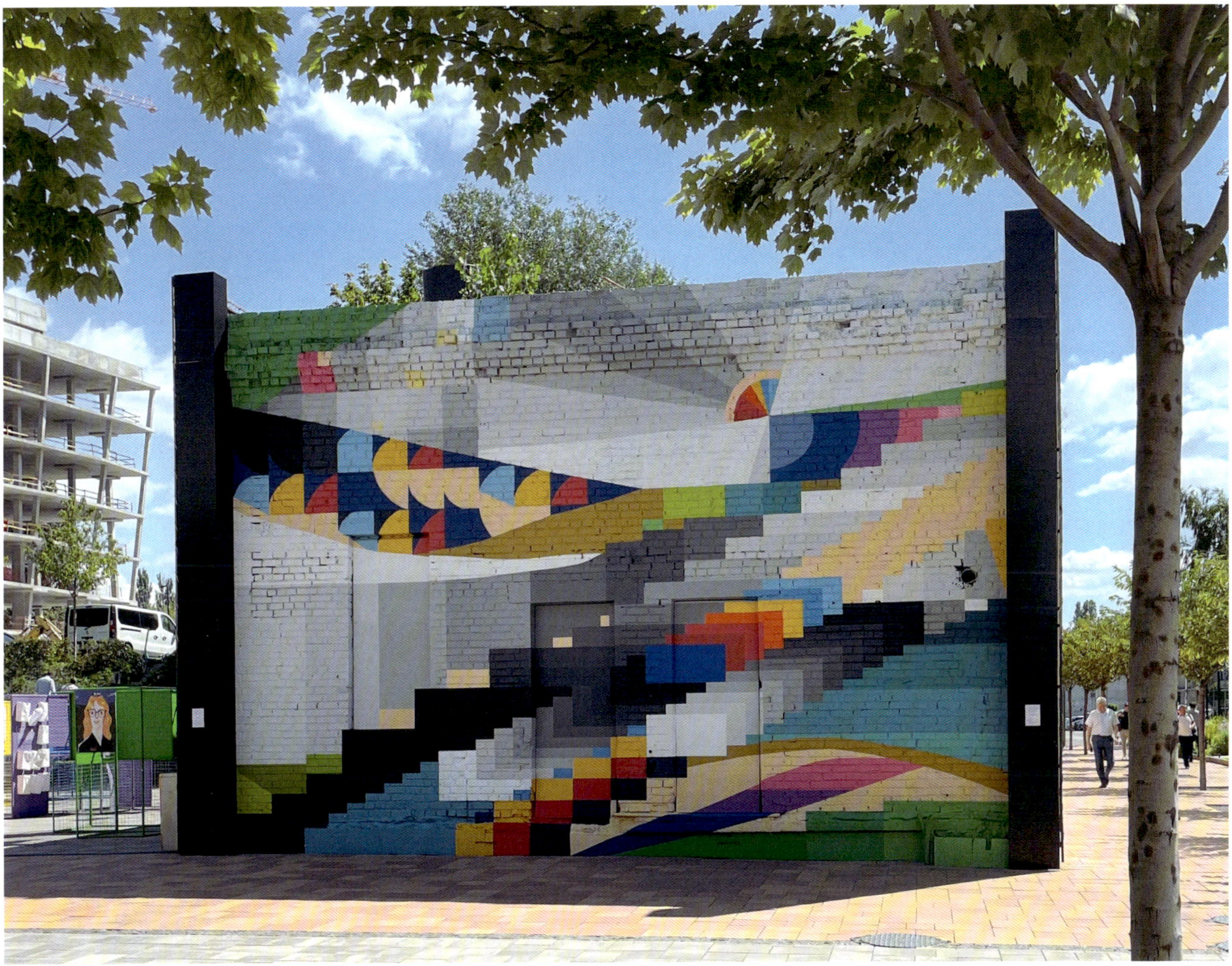

In his lively, colorful works, Andriy Kalkov encodes images and symbols in pixels and geometric modules, creating a novel form of optical art.

Andriy Kalkov, a lifelong resident of Lutsk, works in Ukraine and abroad, creating murals and other art pieces. Kalkov started painting around the year 2000, and a decade later started work on a series called "Circulation." For this series, the artist moved away from traditional graffiti, immersing himself in the world of optical art. At the heart of "Circulation" is the spiral—an eternal symbol of perception and an enduring motif across the centuries. Kalkov's series encourages self-exploration, inspiration, and knowledge sharing, reflecting the spiral's nature of diving in and expanding. Kalkov translates the spiral into pixelated geometric forms, paying particular attention to the arrangement and interplay of color. Above all else, he wants his colors to interact in a way that creates an attractive mood. As for form, it is almost always about dynamics.

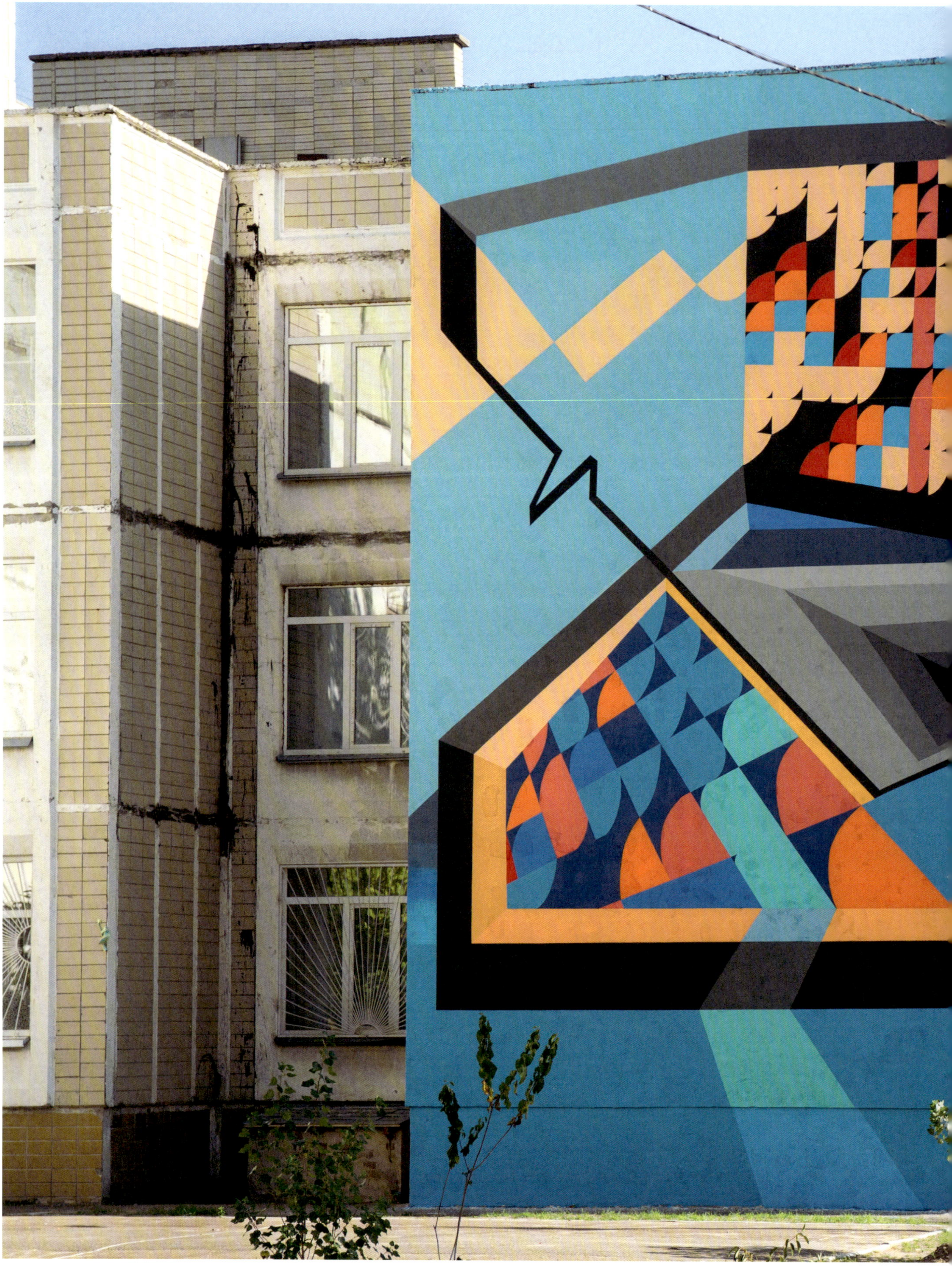

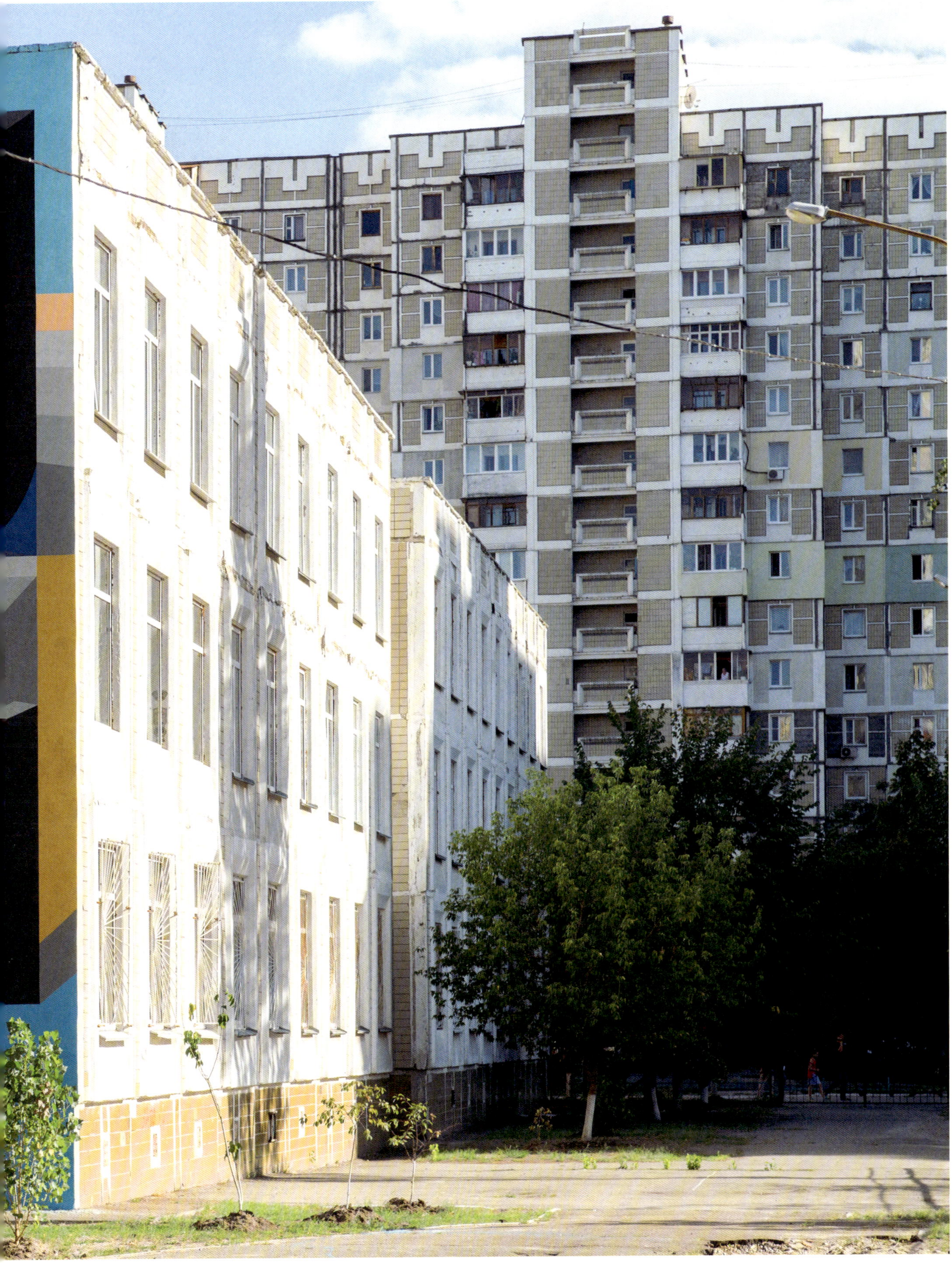

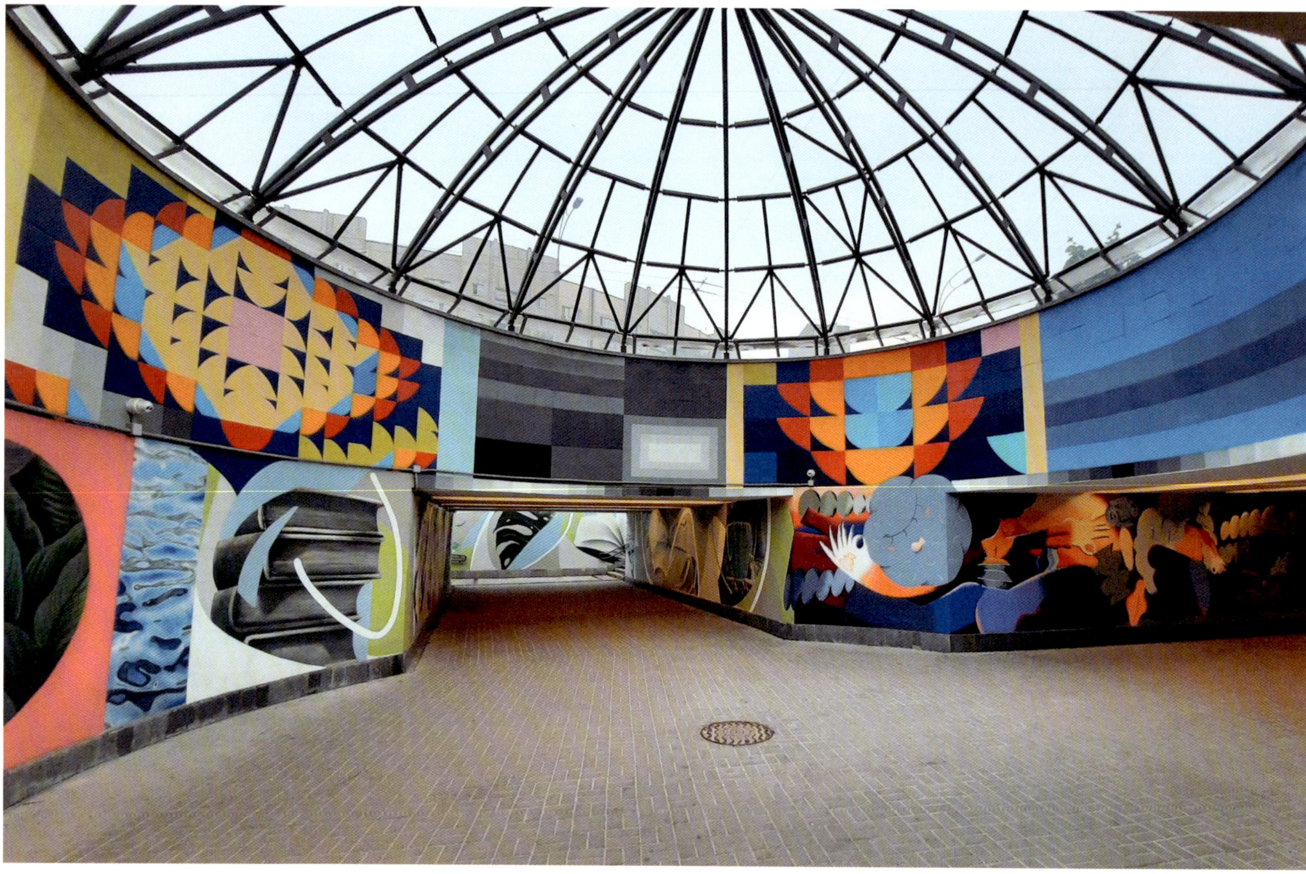

With his striking, energetic artworks, Andriy Kalkov aspires to invigorate the settings that showcase his art. By embellishing mundane urban objects with his street art, he often gives them new identities as local landmarks.

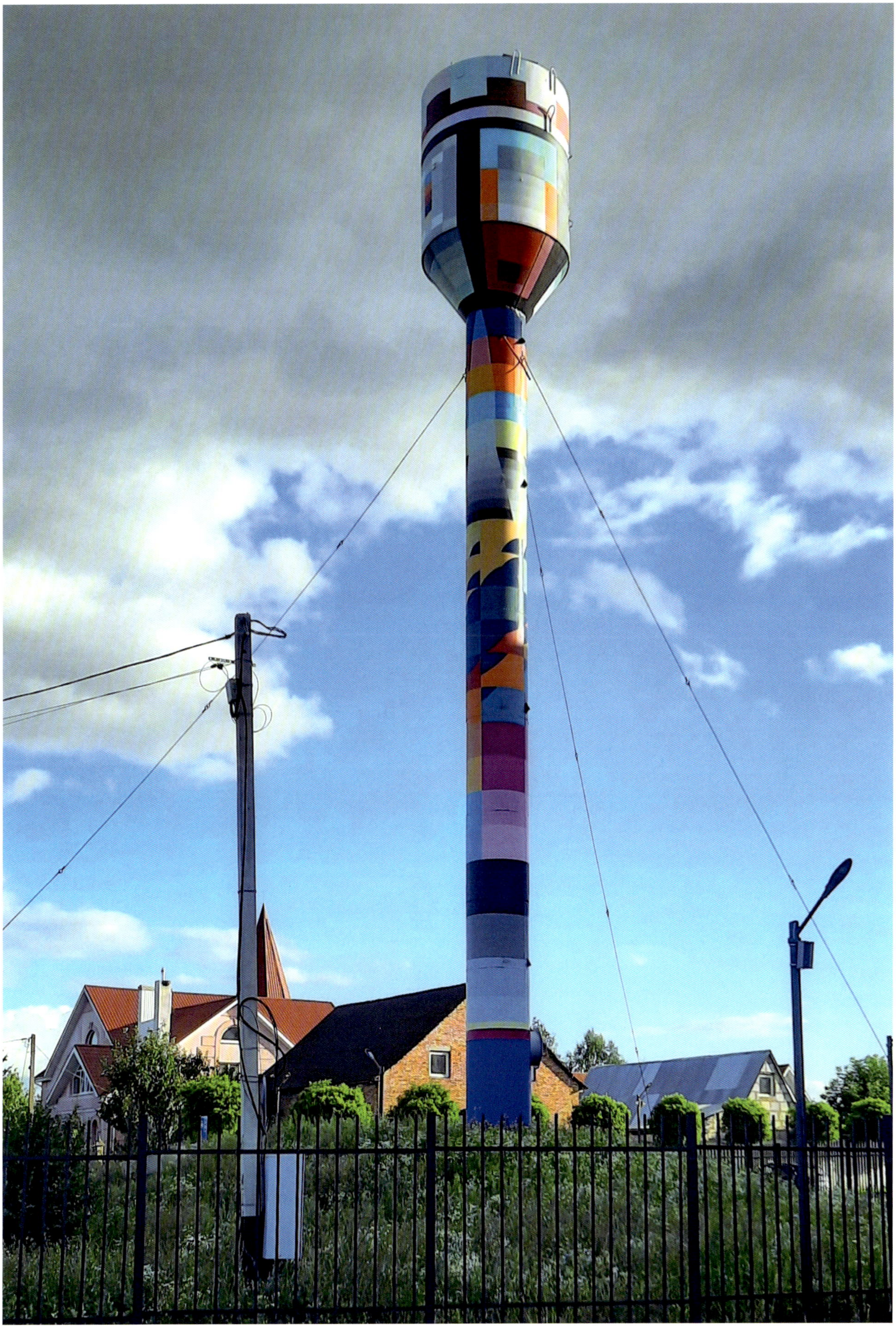

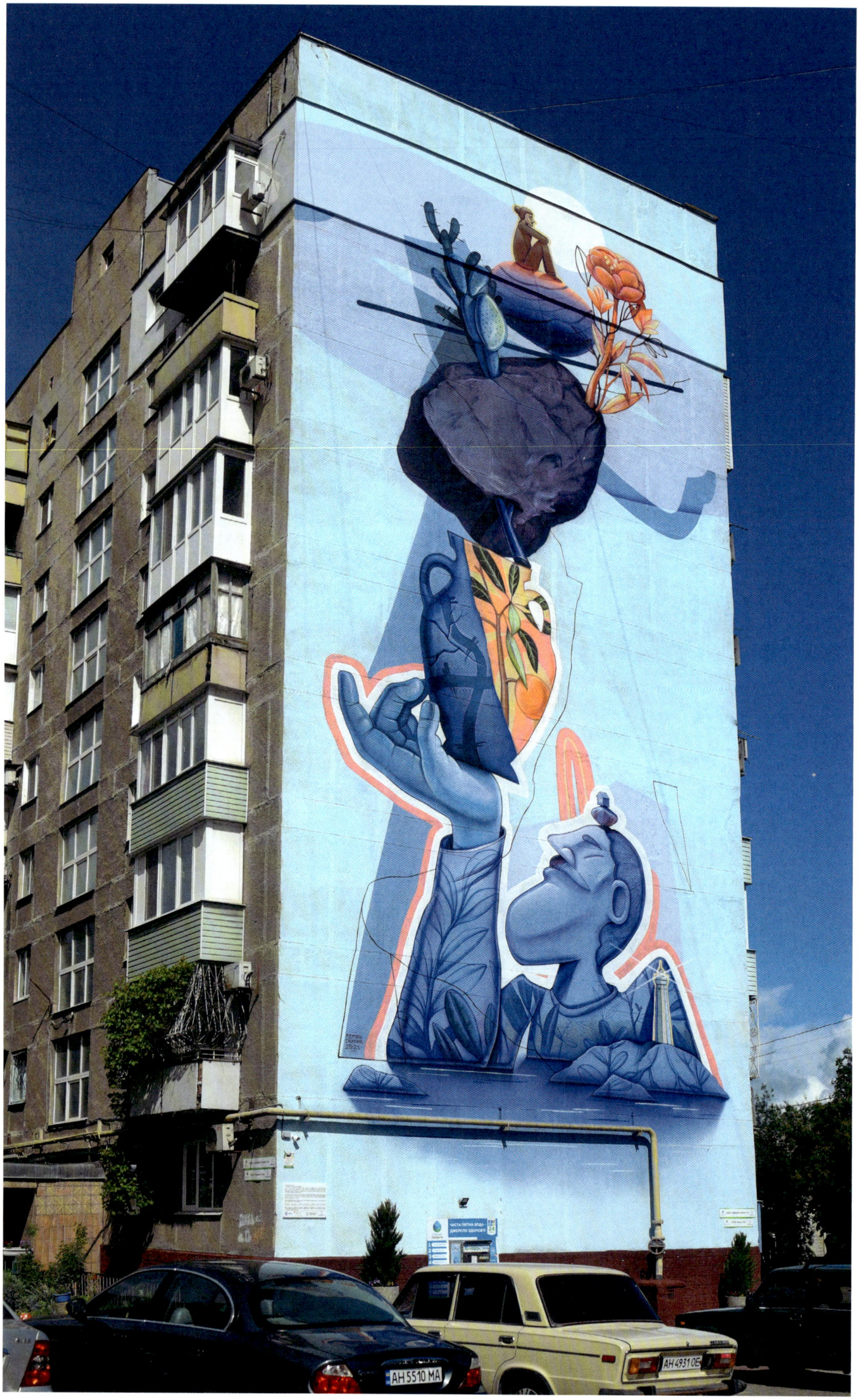
AH 5510 MA
AH 4931 OE

A BRUSH WITH DUALITY: PAINTING LIFE'S CONTRASTS

DILKONE & FEROSONE

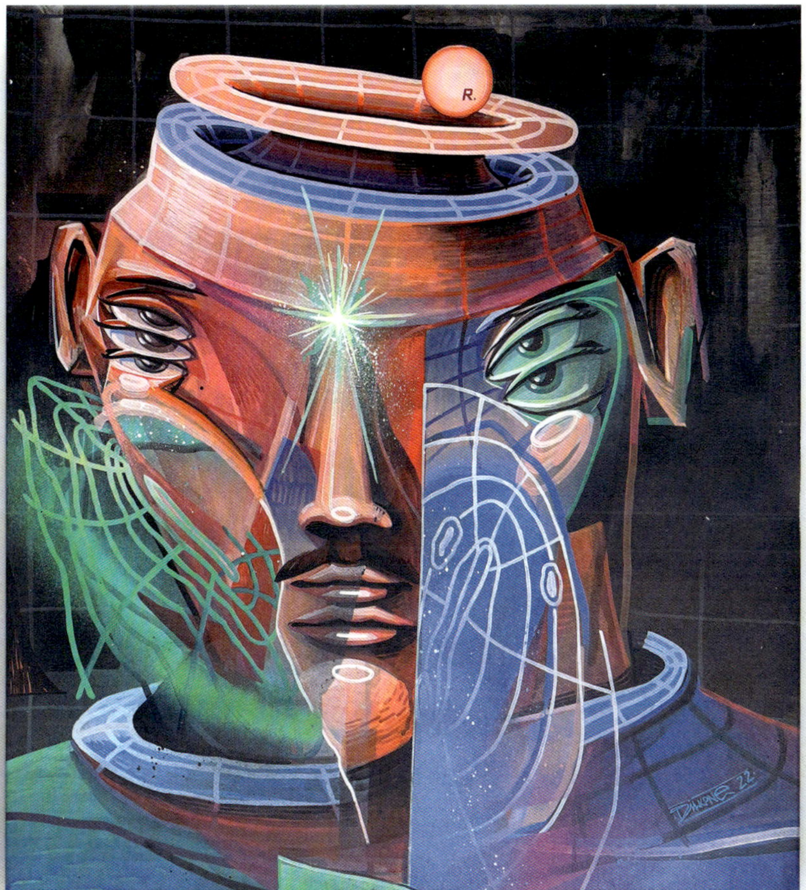

As Dilkone and Ferosone forge a unique visual language to connect with the world around them, the artistic journey is one of both victories and setbacks.

Known by their artist aliases Dilkone and Ferosone, twin brothers Vitalii and Serhii Hrekh have each developed a distinctive, recognizable style. In 2012, they founded the Kickit Art Studio with friends, where they collaborate with each other and other artists, in addition to working independently. The brothers initially discovered creativity through graffiti, but their focus has shifted to murals and large-format canvas paintings. During wartime, their artistic practices have helped them process their heightened emotions, and the ongoing conflict has made them more aware of time's value. They also hope to appeal to the emotions of the viewer: "In figurative works," Ferosone says, "the center for me has become a person and the inner state. I like to create non-banal surreal stories that can be read in different ways." Dilkone adds: "We often paint in public spaces, and this is the case when the artist meets an unprepared viewer. Interesting dialogues often occur."

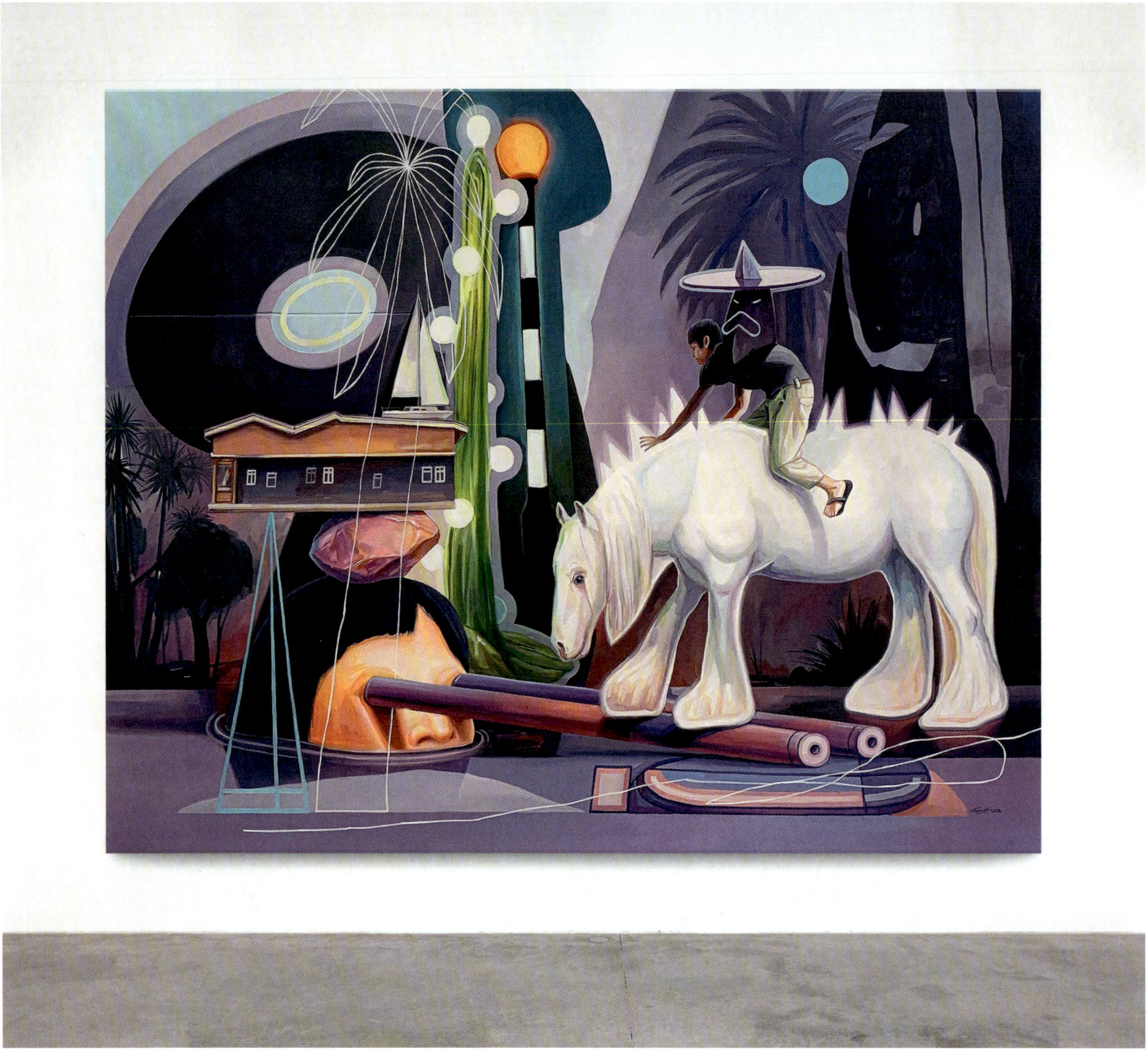

The artwork *Entrance to the Unknown* (opposite page) was created by Dilkone and Ferosone for ibug 2022. The urban art festival, now in its 17th year, took place at a former paper factory in Flöha, Germany. This page: Ferosone, *Walk in an Eclipse*, oil on canvas, 2022.

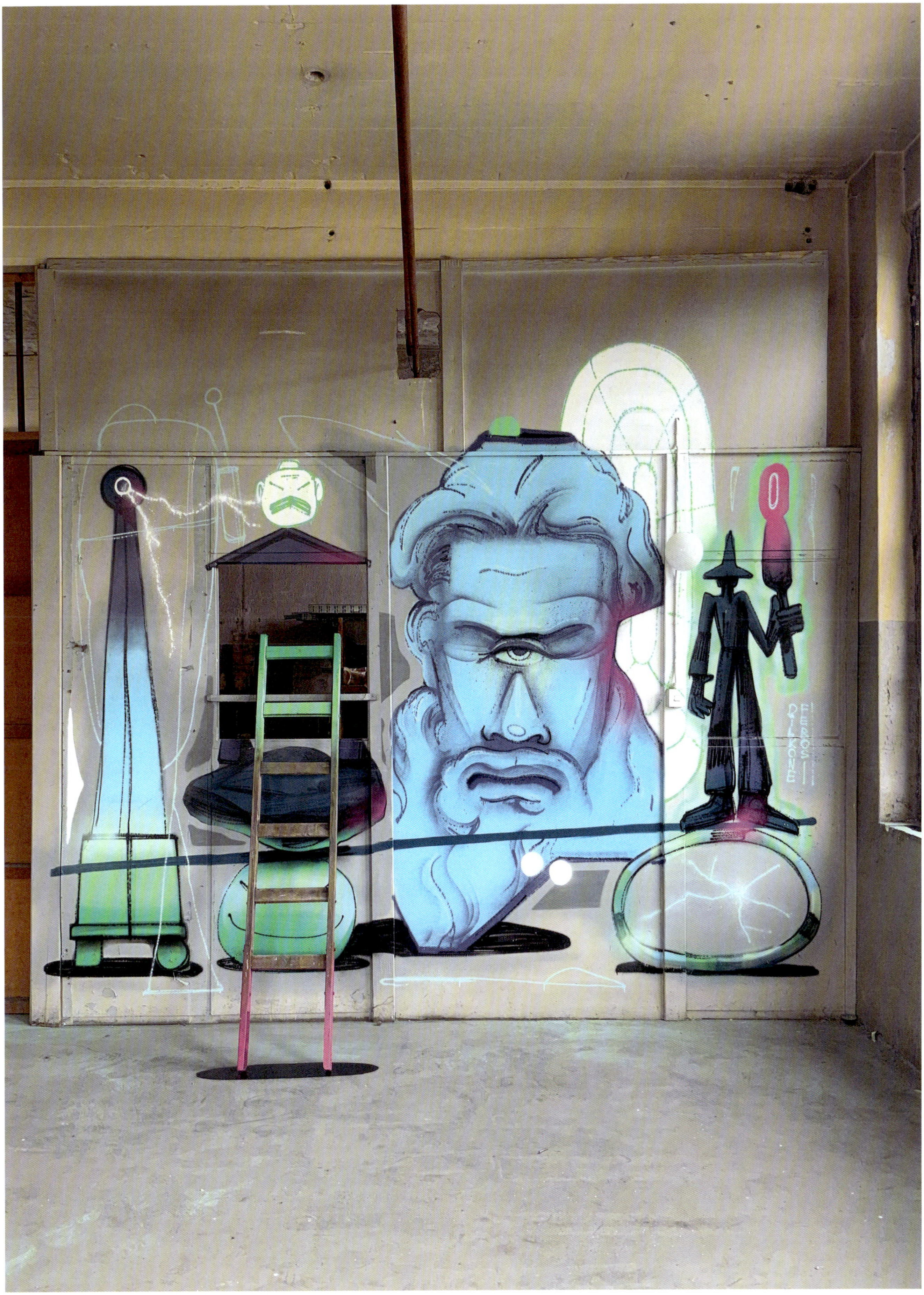

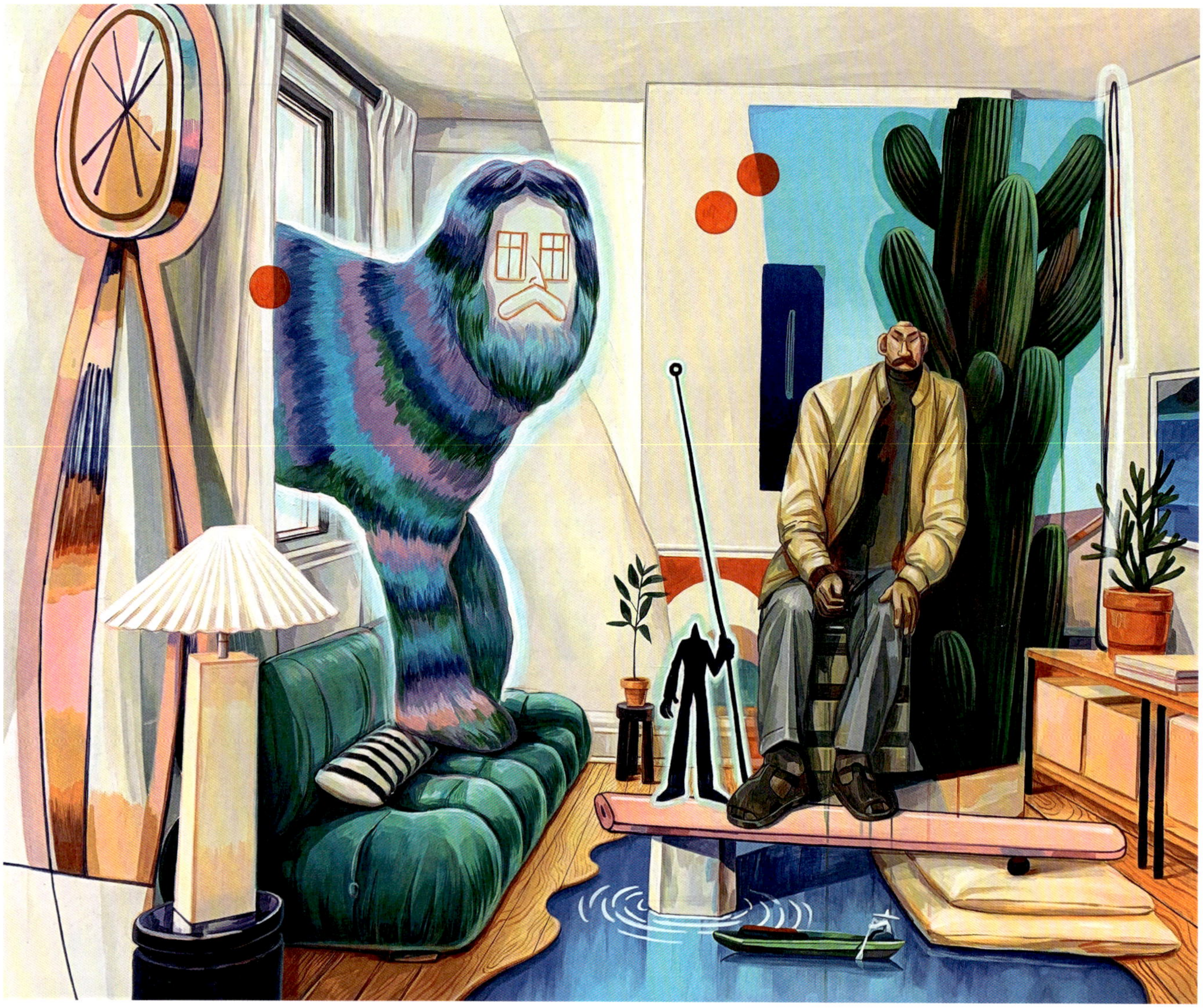

Ferosone claims that his recent creations serve as the ultimate retreat from the harshness of reality, where darkness infiltrates our world without consent, akin to an unwanted visitor. *Guest*, acrylic on canvas, 2022.

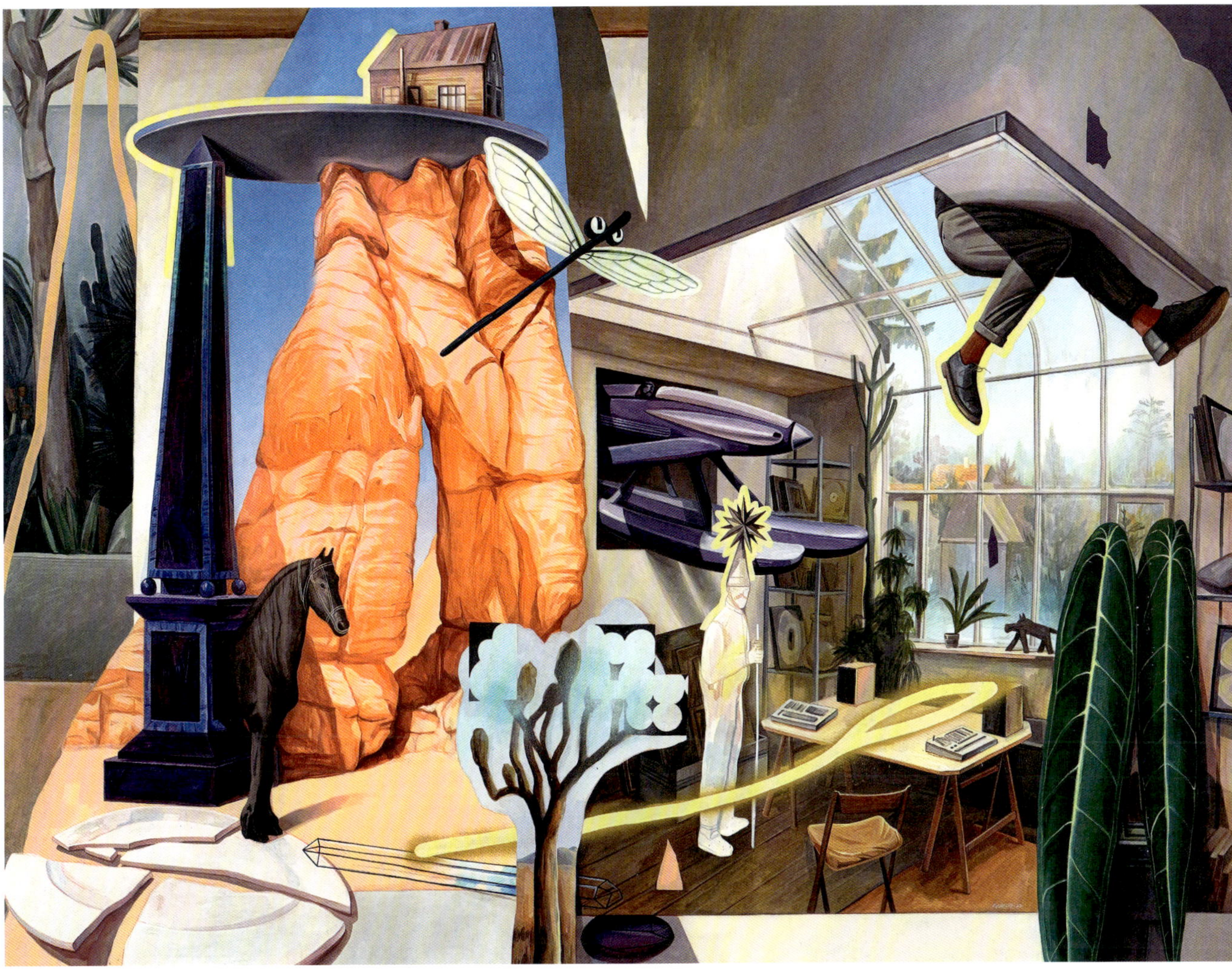

Escape Reality is another painting that embodies Ferosone's reflections on life during wartime. Escape here is a metaphor for utopia—in reality, you cannot run away from this war, because it is existential. *Escape Reality,* acrylic on canvas, 2022.

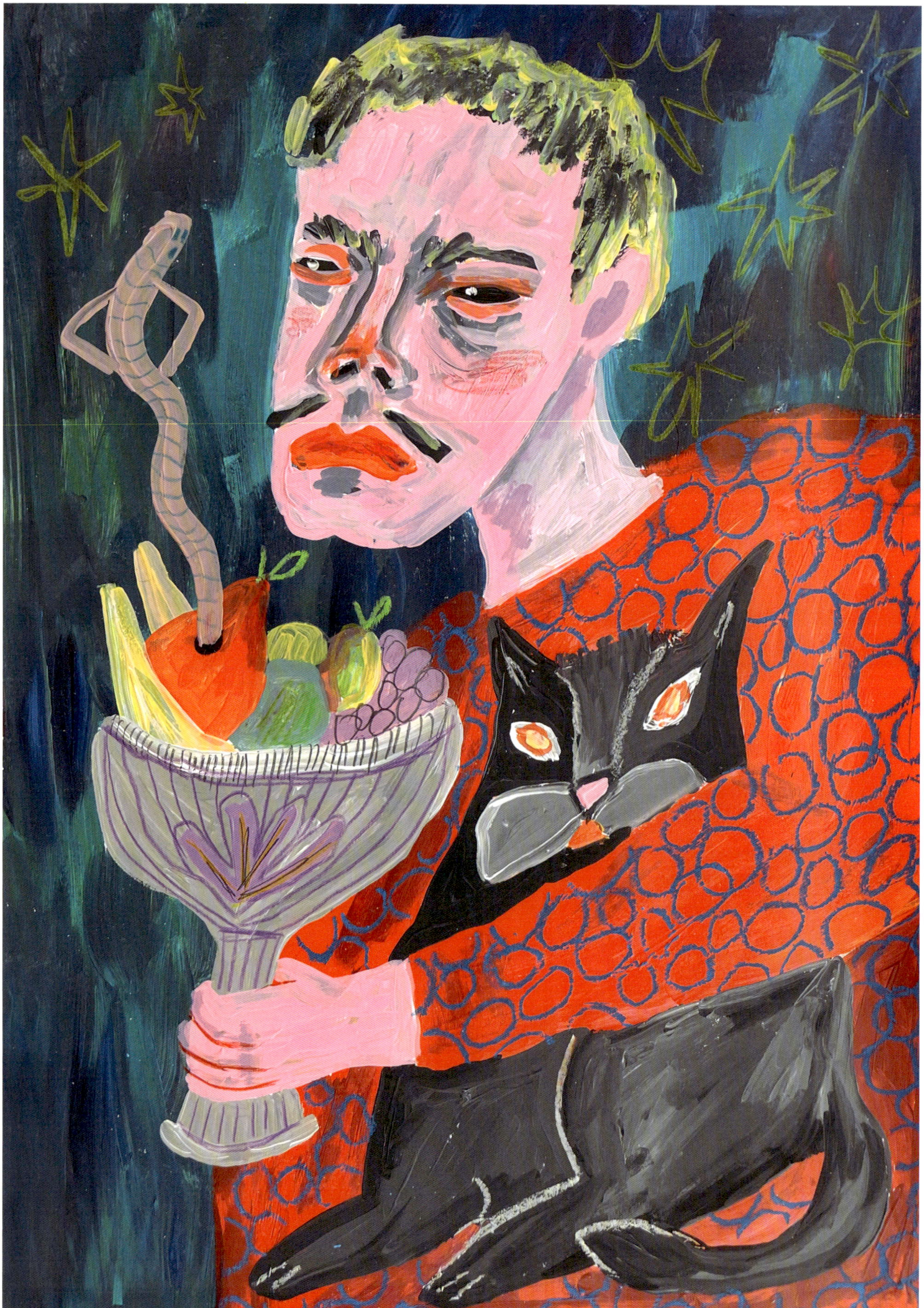

SYMBOLISM WITH FAUVISM INFLUENCES

DZVINYA PODLYASHETSKA · *ДЗВІНЯ ПОДЛЯШЕЦЬКА*

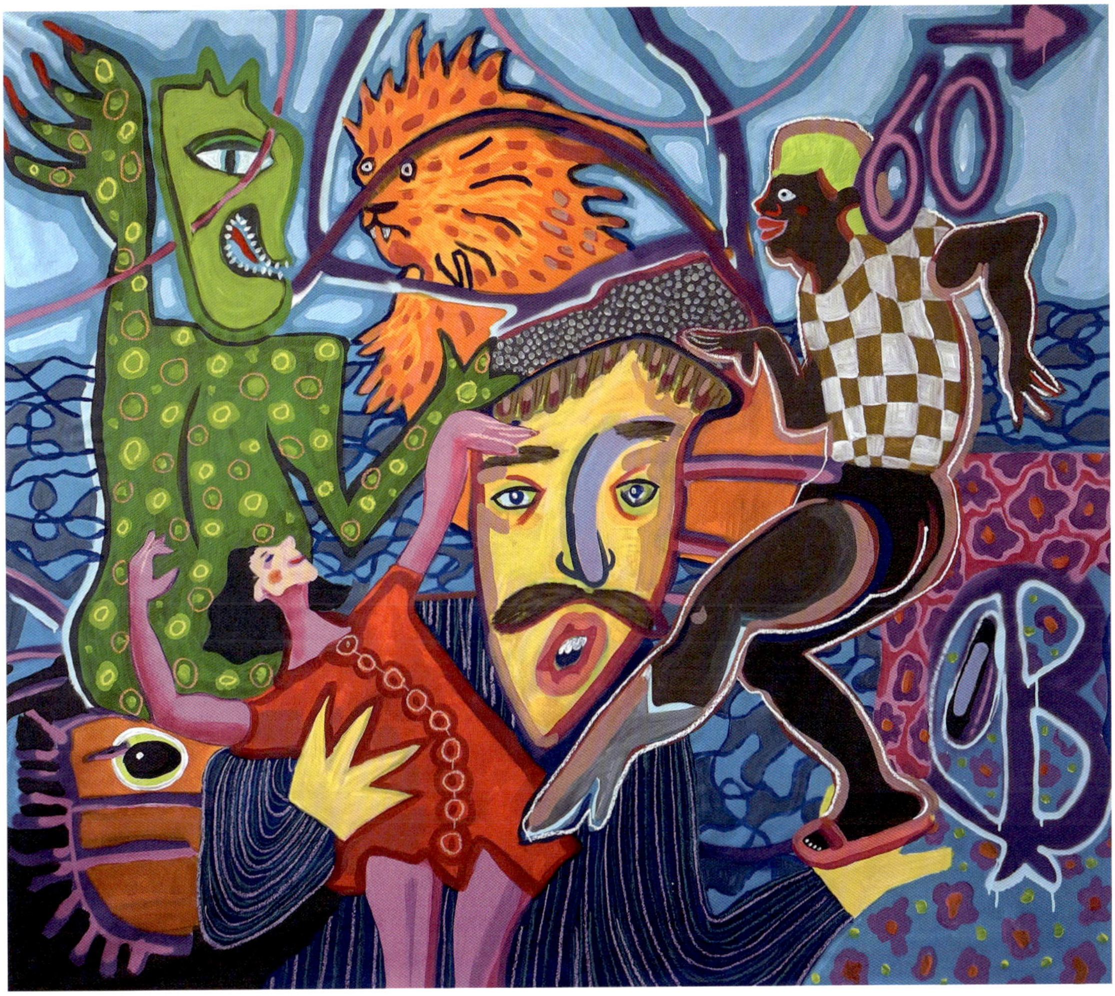

Dzvinya Podlyashetska, a young Ukrainian artist, blends Symbolist, Fauvist, and other art influences to create her unique, emotive style.

Born in Lviv, Dzvinya Podlyashetska graduated from the Ivan Trush Lviv State College of Decorative and Applied Arts and the Ukrainian Academy of Printing. Since 2016, the artist has participated in group and solo exhibitions and projects both in Ukraine and abroad, collaborating with galleries in Europe and in the United States. Prior to the war, she lived and worked in Lviv. Podlyashetska specializes in painting and printmaking, integrating themes of mental health, self-identification, and human interaction into her work. She sees art as a means of gaining self-knowledge and adding meaning, comfort, and pleasure to her life. Her creations stem from her feelings and observations of events, circumstances, and people around her. Because Podlyashetska channels her emotions through her art, the war in Ukraine has had a profound influence on her creative process: her work has taken on a more violent tone, depicting real events unfolding in Ukraine as well as more personal experiences.

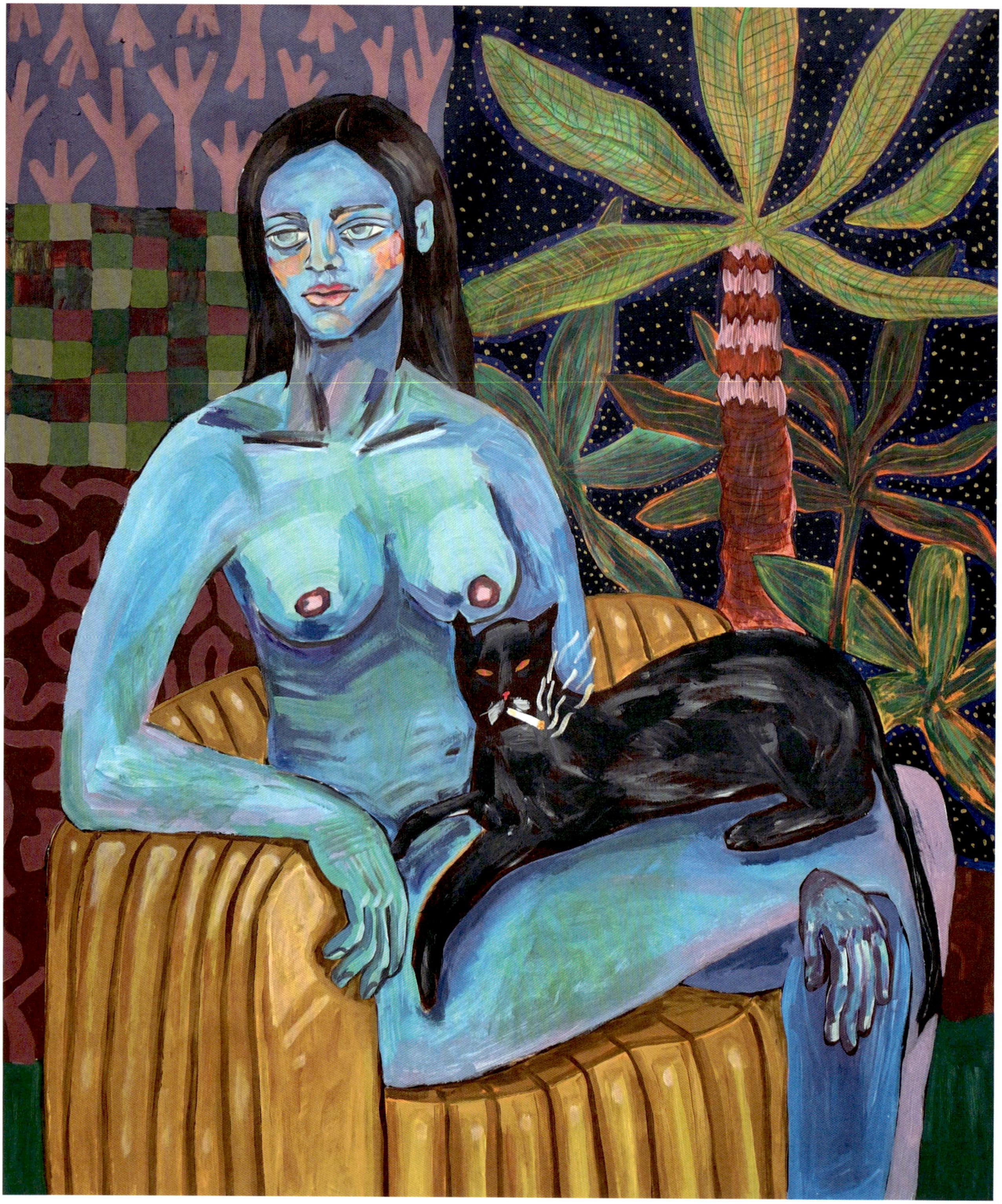

Cat Vasyl, acrylic and oil sticks on canvas, 2022. This painting depicts a vigilant feline guarding a mystical blue being. The cigarette-smoking cat takes its job seriously, looking out with fierce determination. Previous pages: *Quarrelsome Worm*, acrylic, paper, 2021 (p. 90); *Unforgettable Disco*, acrylic, spray paint, and soft pastels on canvas, 2022 (p. 91).

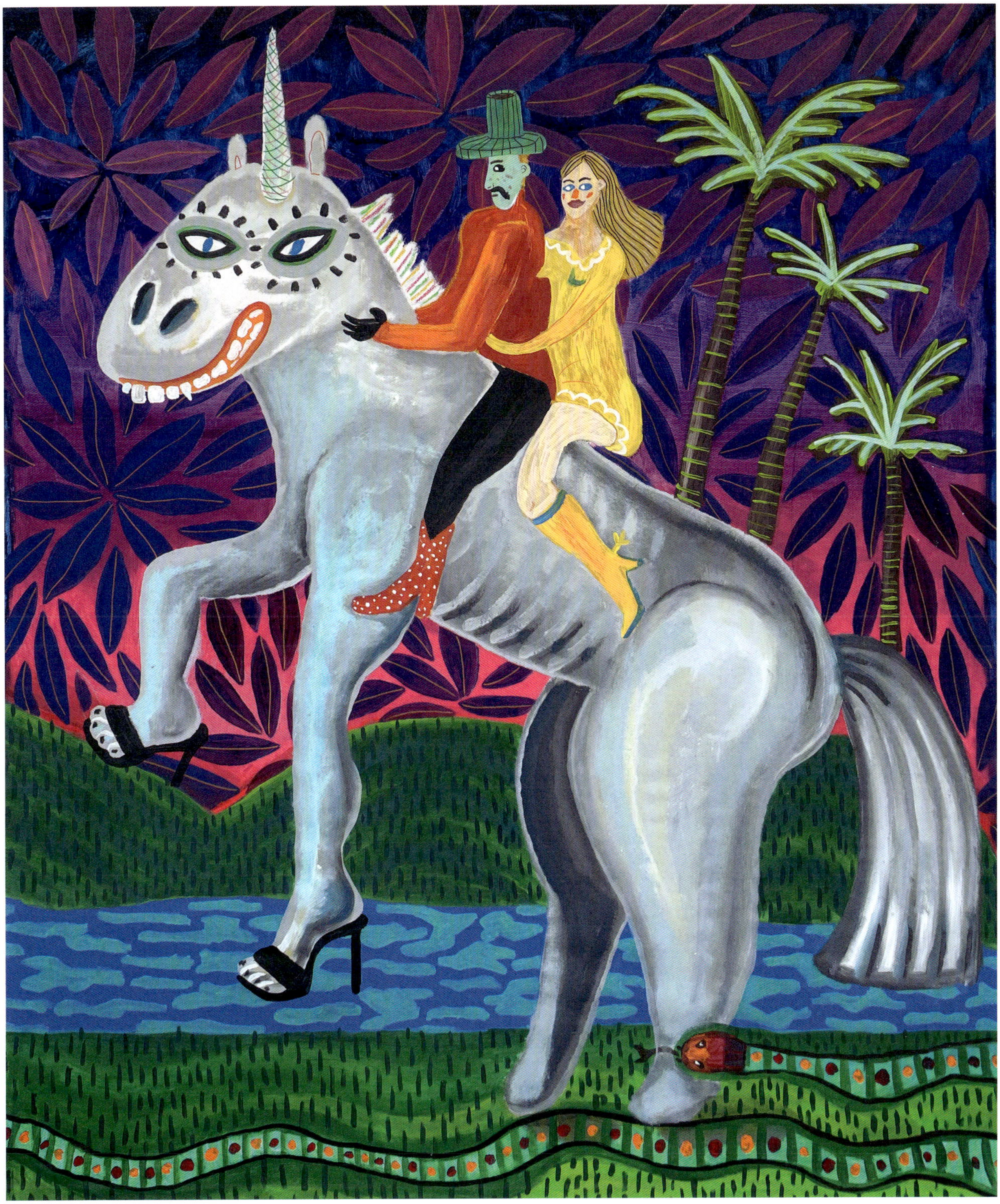

According to the artist, *Snakebite* (acrylic and acrylic markers on canvas, 2022), from a solo exhibition at Breach Miami gallery, is about the fact that there will always be people who will try to pull you down, especially when you start achieving success in life.

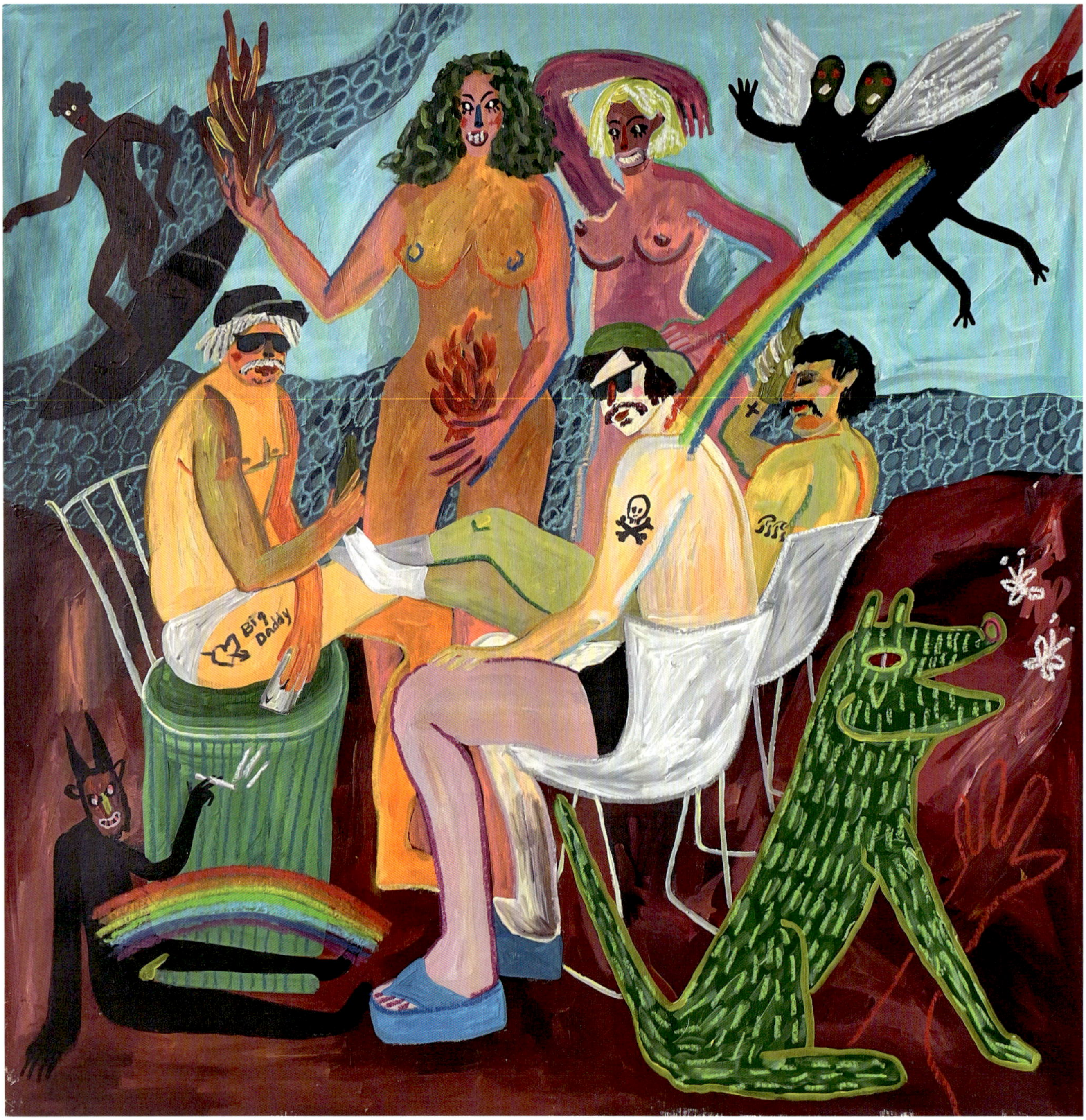

In her tongue-in-cheek artwork *Welcome to the Club* (acrylic and oil sticks on canvas, 2021), Dzvinya Podlyashetska reflects on the themes of leisure and temptation.

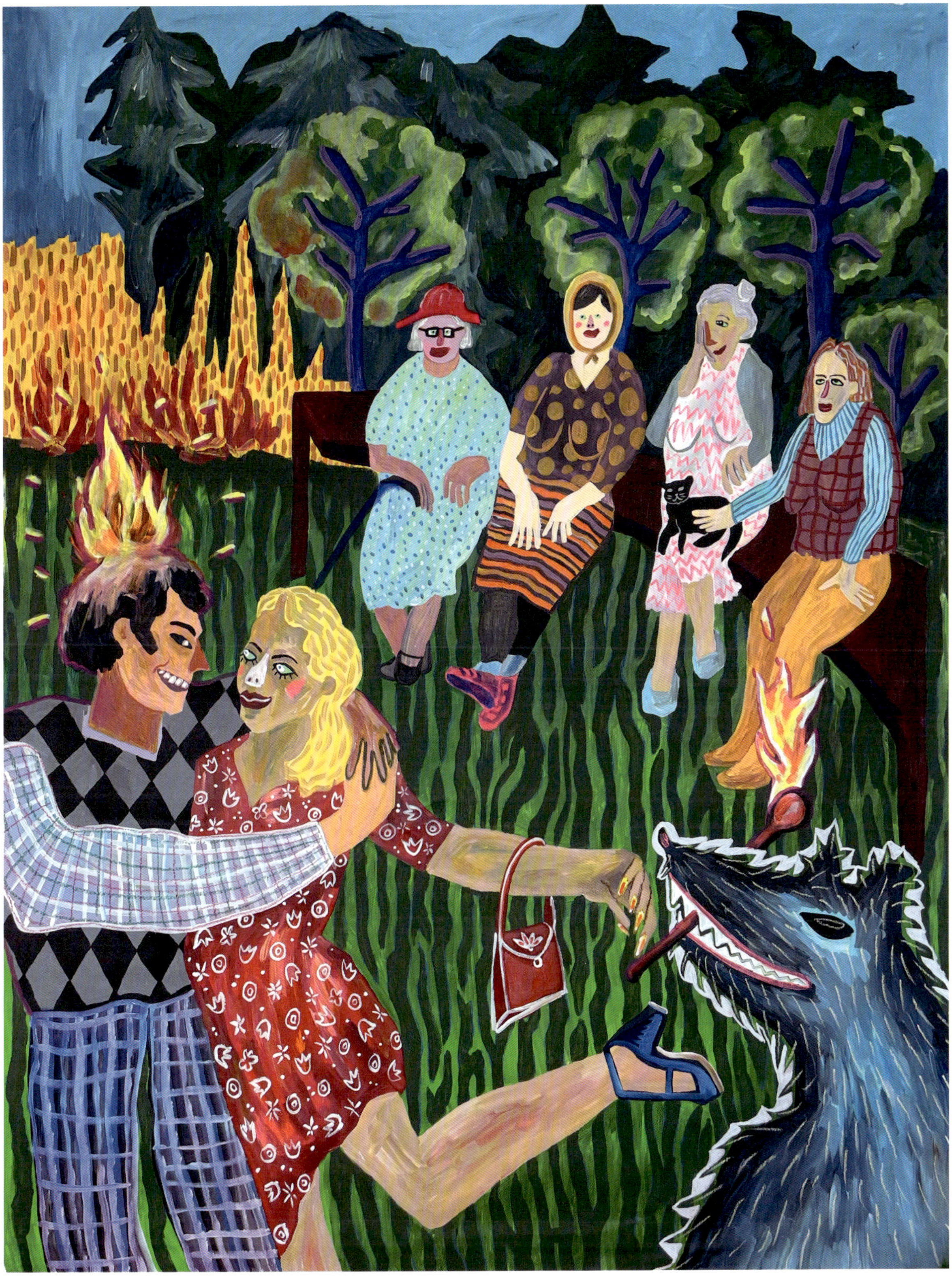

The work *Youth in Full Swing* (acrylic and oil sticks on canvas, 2022) reflects on the vivacity of young people enjoying life, mixing nostalgia with a touch of wicked irony.

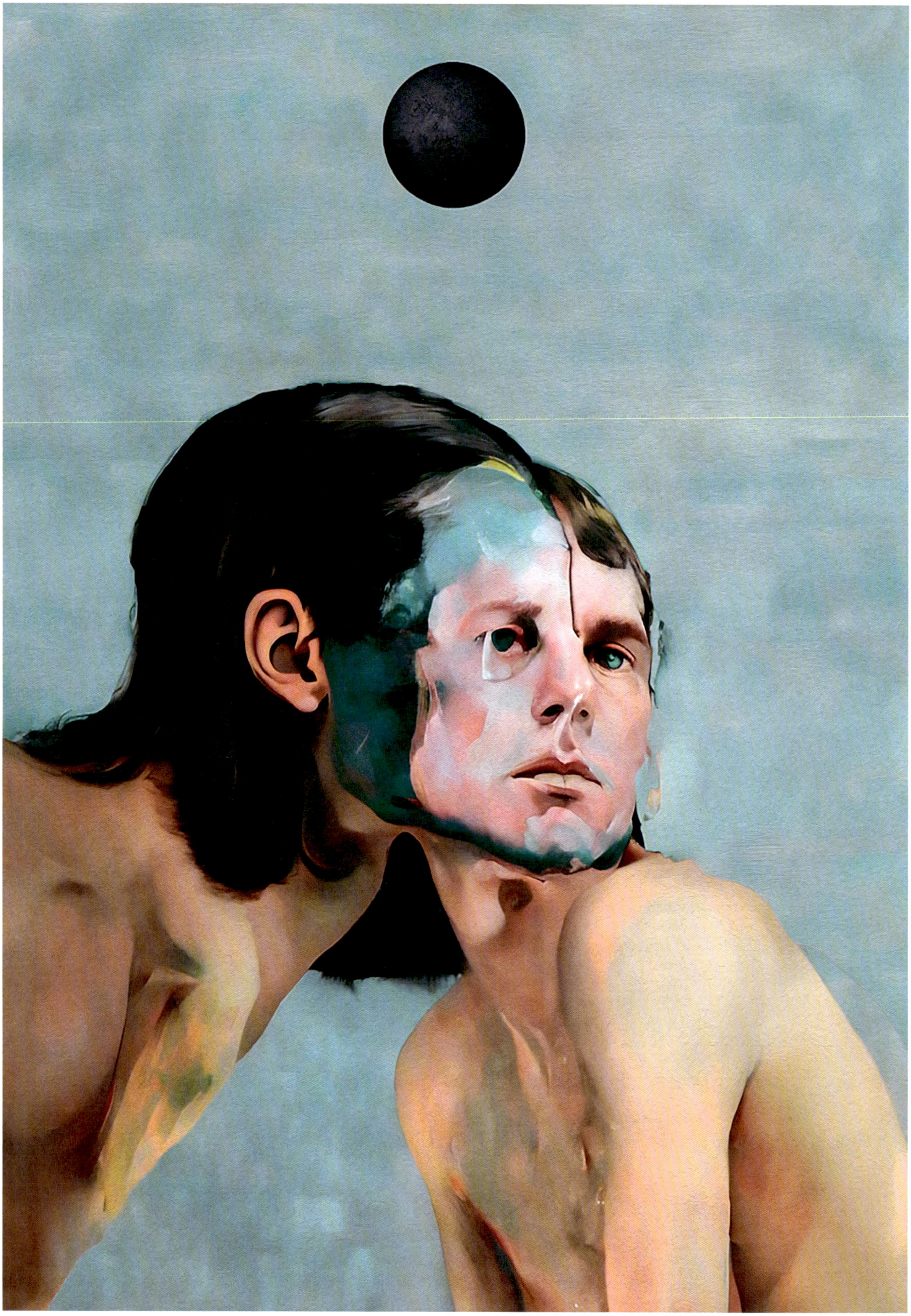

A REFLECTION OF REALITY

OLEKSANDR BARBOLIN · *ОЛЕКСАНДР БАРБОЛІН*

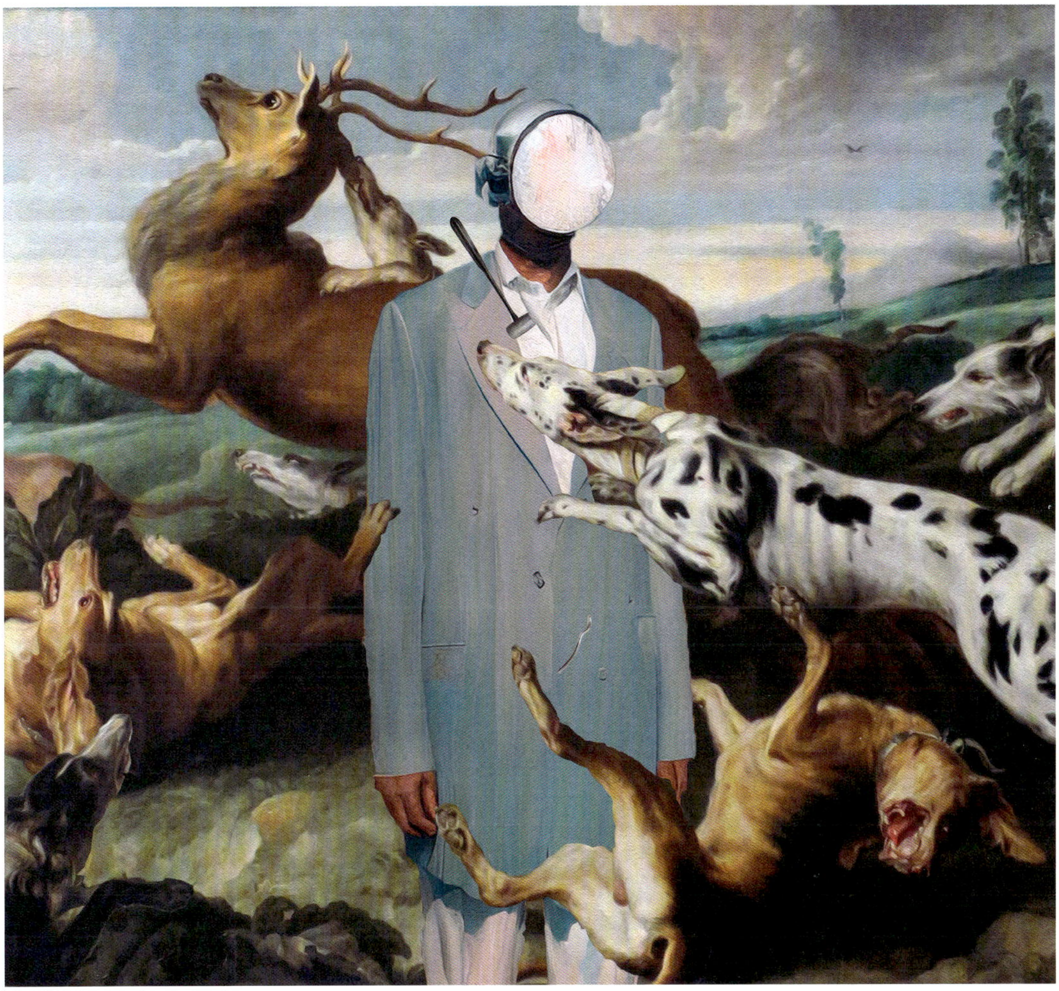

Oleksandr Barbolin believes that art is always a step forward as it seeks out new forms to reflect our reality.

Oleksandr Barbolin was born in Pryluky in the Chernihiv region and now lives and works in Kyiv. A graduate of the Shenkar College of Engineering, Design and Art in Tel-Aviv, where he studied landscape architecture, Barbolin began making collages in 2018. As he sees it, art is an inseparable part of life and an essential form of self-expression. The artist's first works were analogue—he used vintage magazines and retro posters to make collages from clippings. Later, he started using a mixed-media technique, printing a digital collage on canvas then adding acrylic elements and oil paints. Barbolin has a keen sense of national identity, weaving hidden codes—as national colors or images of military gear and weapons—into his work. After the outbreak of the war, he began thinking more about human nature and what drives people to do what they do. Now more than ever, he uses the canvas to analyze his thoughts on complex concepts like collective consciousness, self-identification, and the nature of emotions.

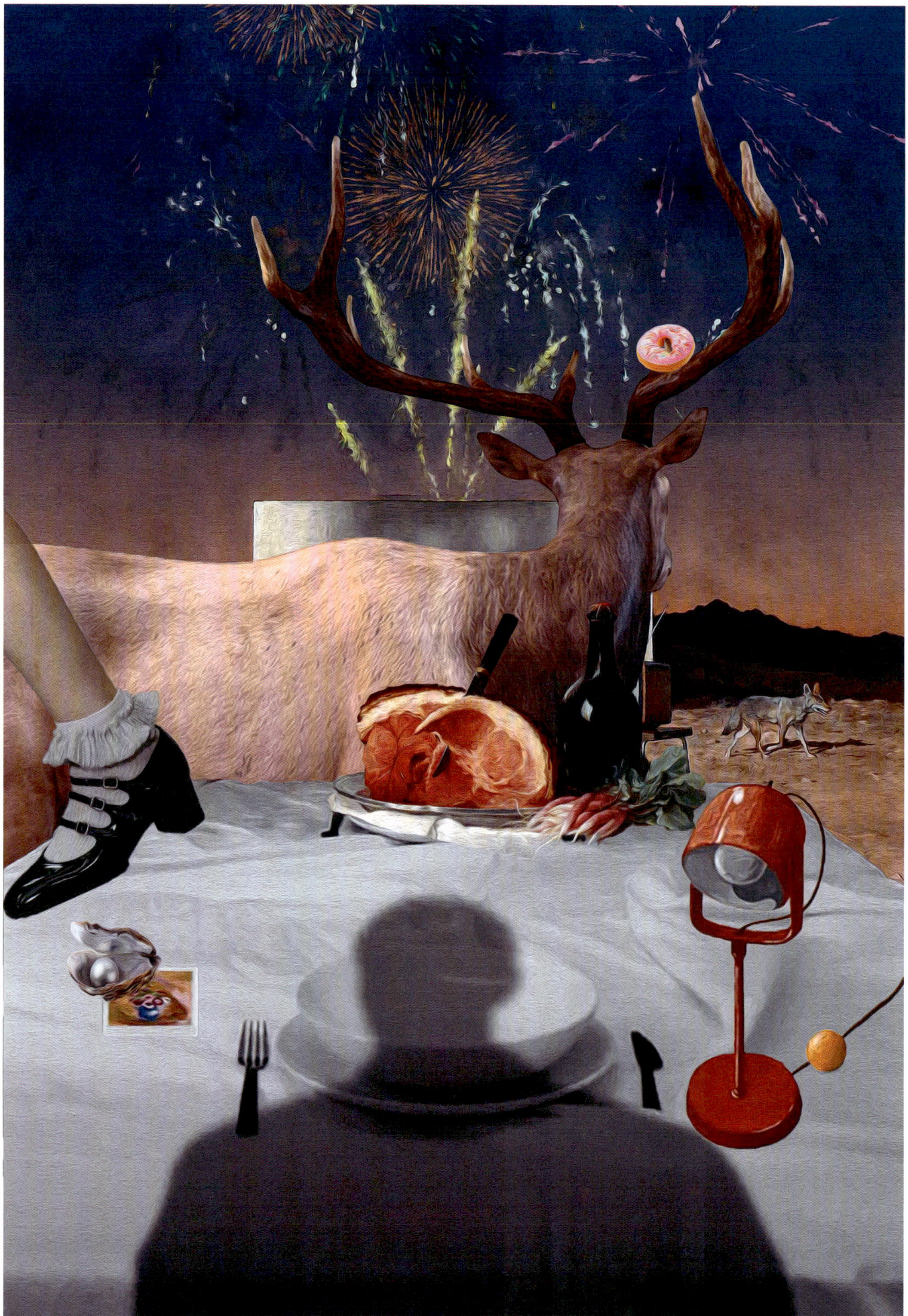

Salute, collage, digital prints and oil on canvas, 2022. Previous pages: *The Siamese Twins*, mixed media, 2023 (p. 96); *Stag Hunt*, mixed media, 2023 (p. 97).

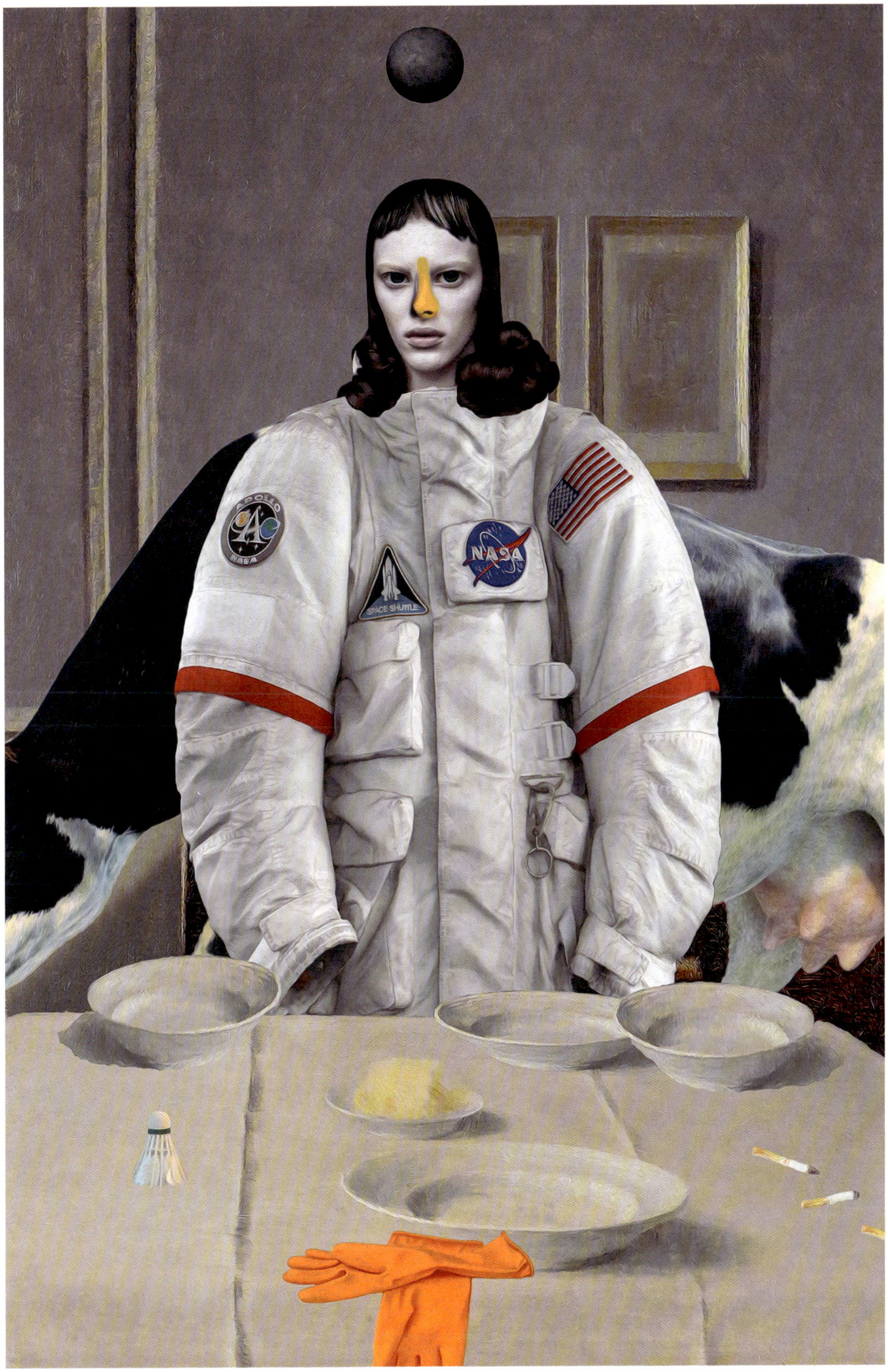

Closed Space, collage, digital print and oil on canvas, 2021.

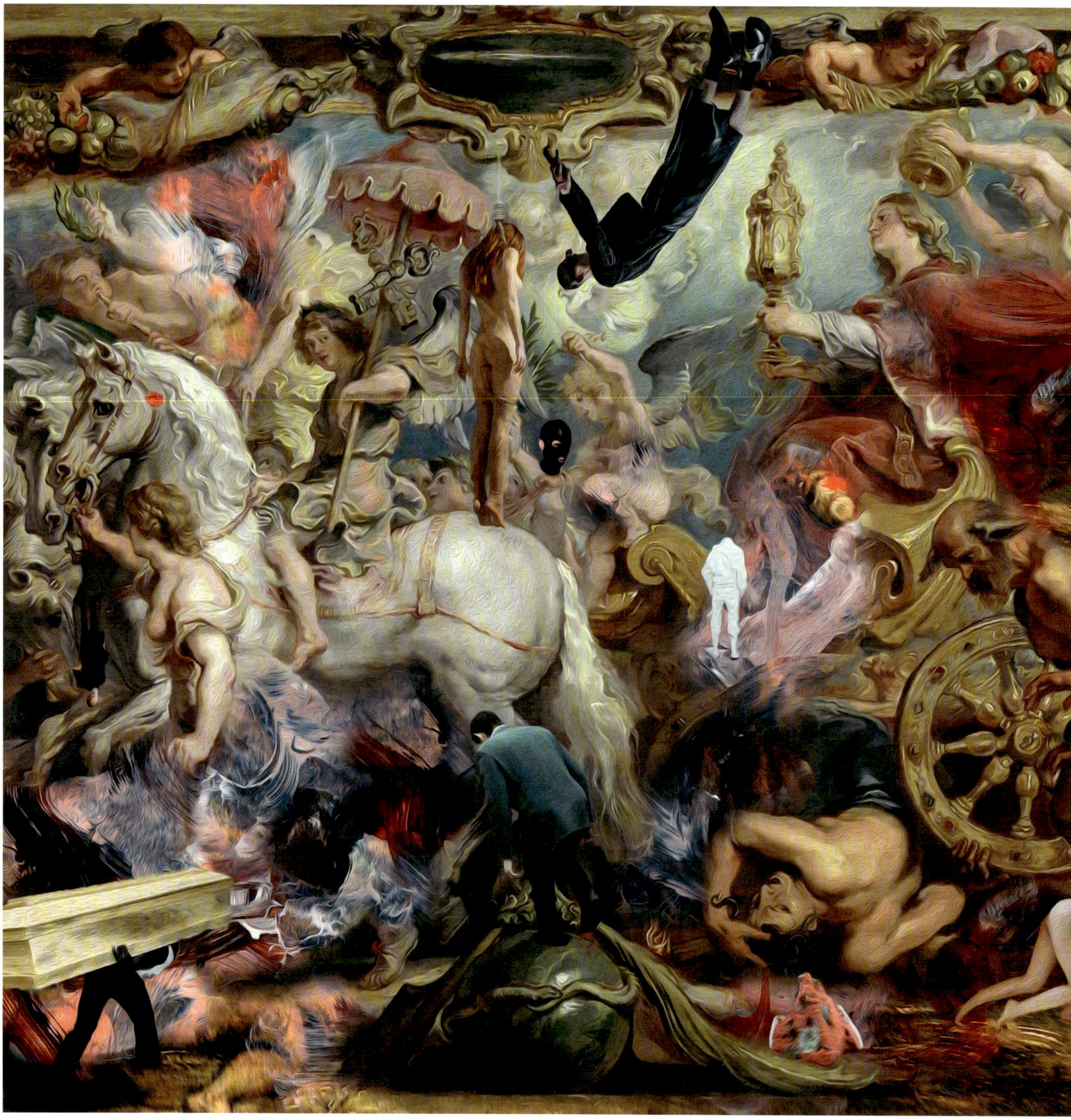

Atonement for Sins, collage, digital print and oil on canvas, 2022.

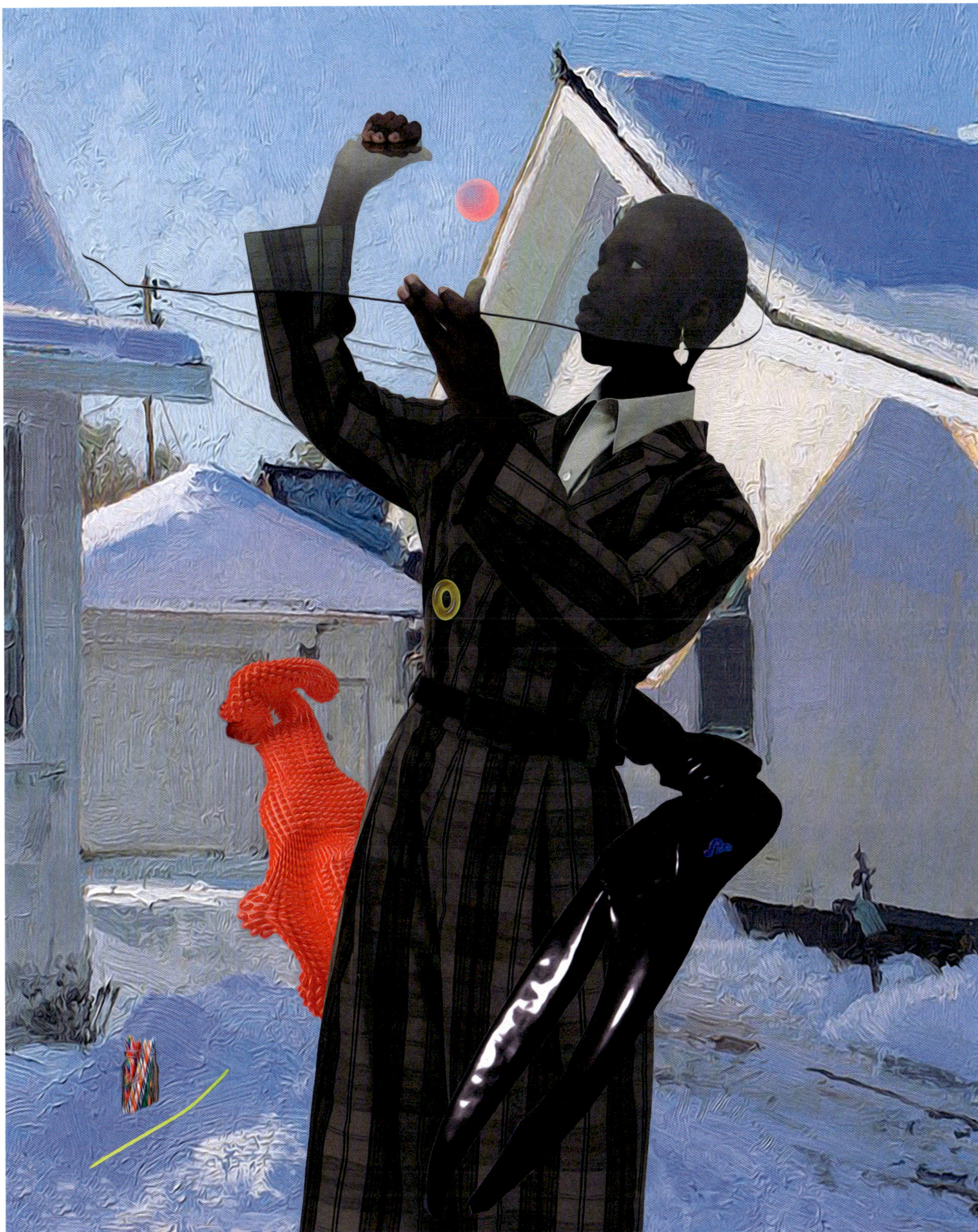

Behind Glass, digital print and oil on canvas, 2022.

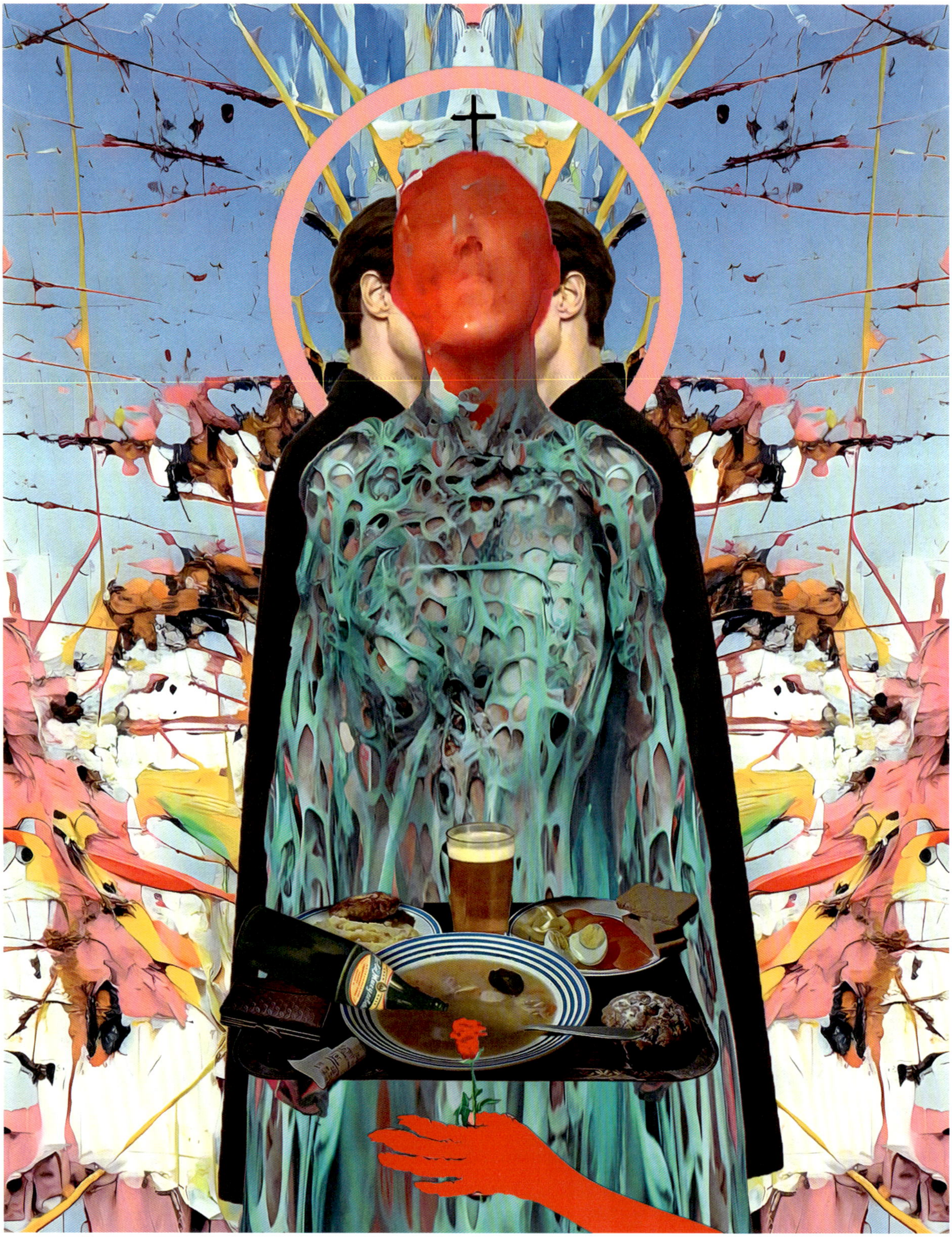

Red Rose, digital print and oil on canvas, 2023.

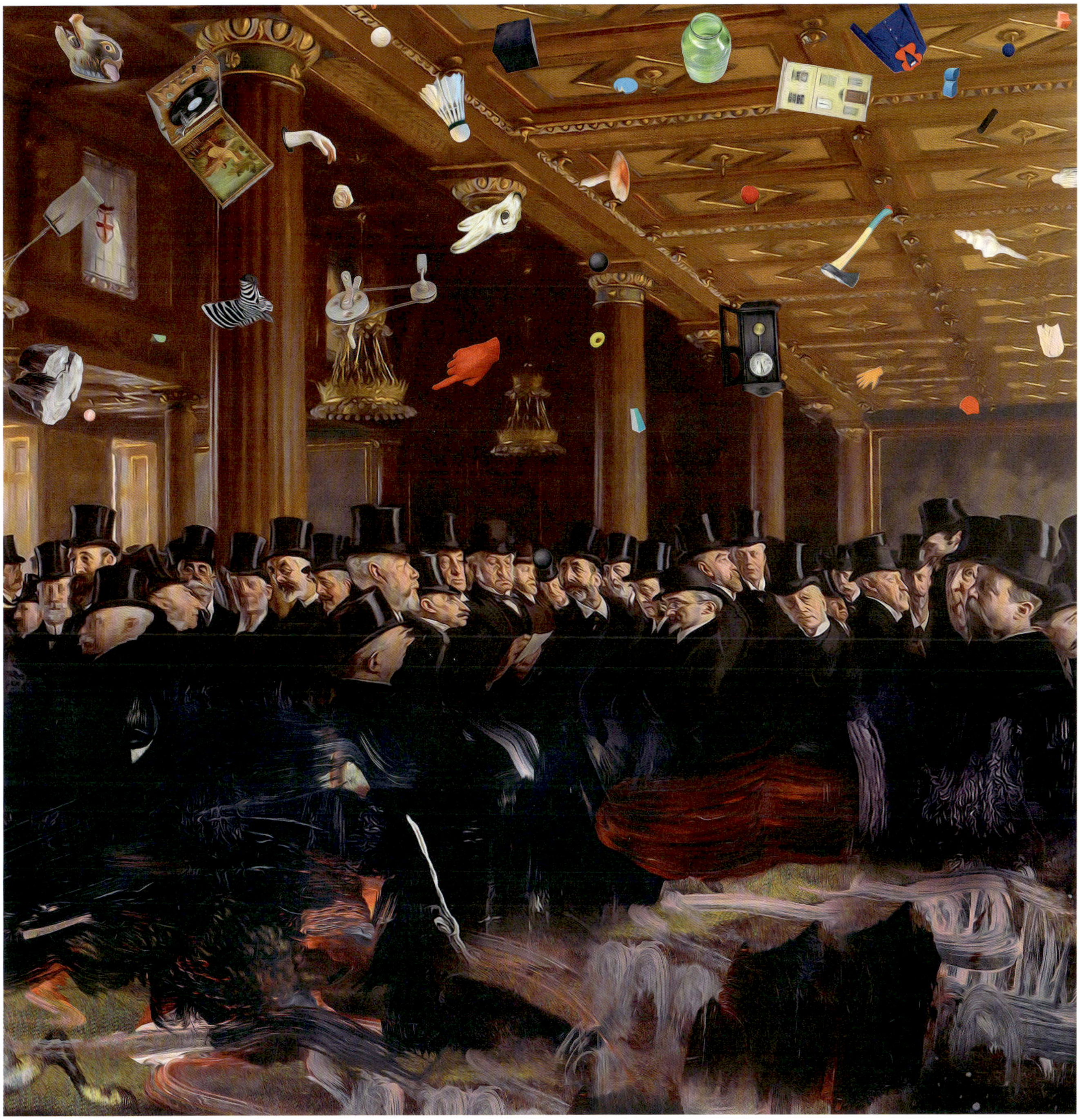

Wingardium Leviosa, digital print and oil on canvas, 2022.

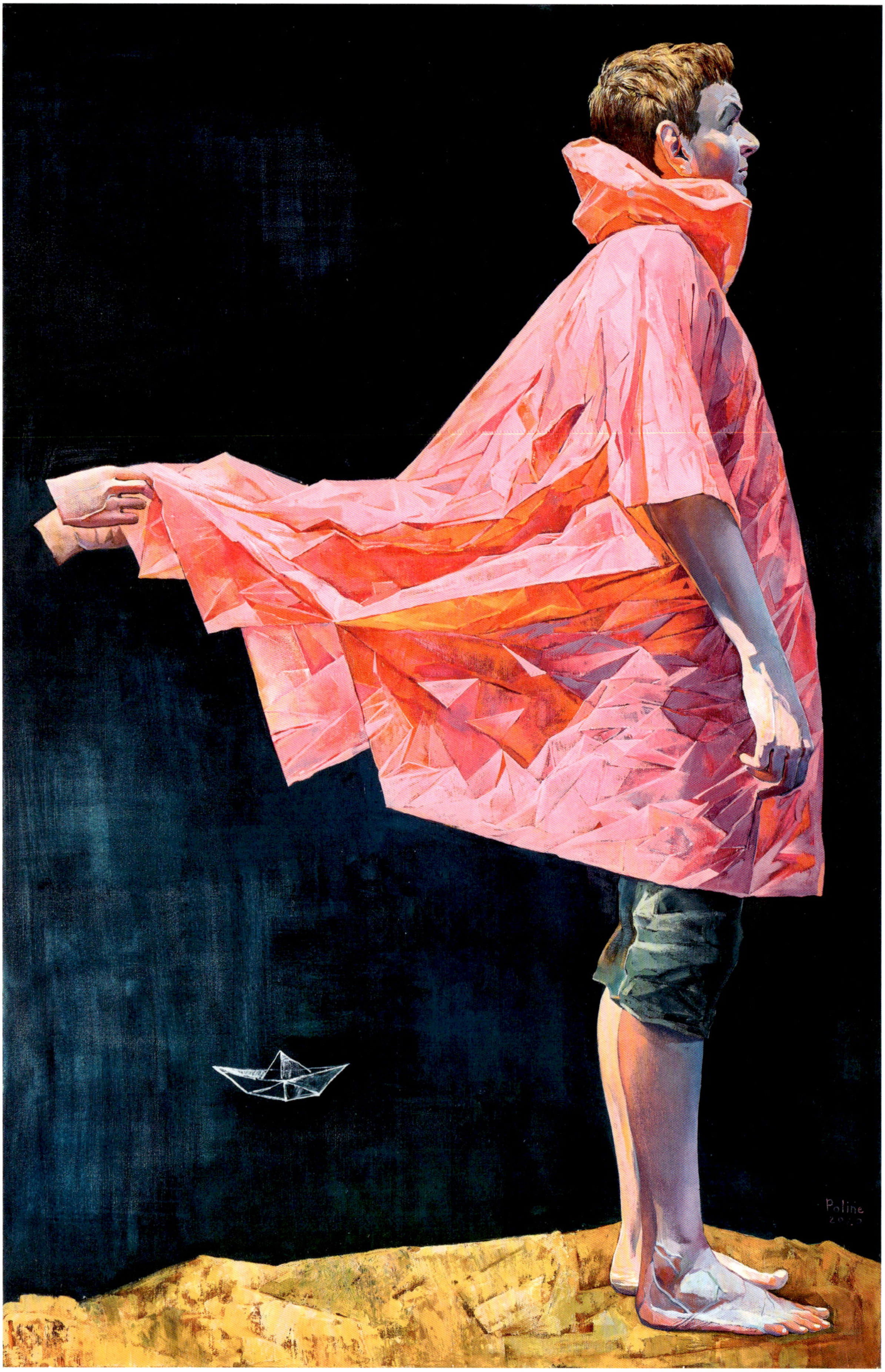
Poline

PINK DREAMS, DARK TIMES

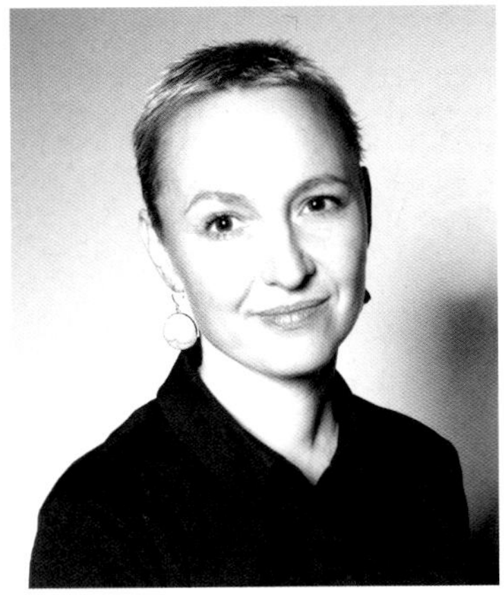

POLINA KUZNETSOVA · *ПОЛІНА КУЗНЕЦОВА*

For Polina Kuznetsova, art is a form of dreaming, allowing her to turn feelings into images. She considers art to be a powerful tool and wants to dedicate her work to preventing war from ever happening again.

Before the Russian invasion, Ukrainian artist Polina Kuznetsova had spent her entire life living and working in Kharkiv. When the conflict erupted, she evacuated to Tallinn, Estonia. However, she returned to Ukraine just seven months later, unwilling to let the war dictate her life choices. The artist has numerous exhibitions to her name, both on the national and international level. Kuznetsova explores various genres, including portrait, landscape, and still life, but has recently been drawn to thematic and conceptual painting, using oil on canvas as her preferred medium. Since the beginning of the war, she has embarked on many projects, addressing both external social issues and the changes occurring within herself. In her opinion, an artist's main responsibility is to evolve internally, to remain curious about the world, and to be sincere in their work. Her pre-war "Dreams" project, which began in 2019, featured a recurrent pink fabric, sometimes floating in a dark, dreamy landscape, sometimes worn as a cloak by a man in existential crisis, enveloped in rose-colored hopes. This project reflected on the nature of dreams and whether they are ultimately helpful or harmful: sure, you can get lost in a dream, unmoored from reality, but you can also use dreams to achieve impossible goals. Kuznetsova continued working on "Dreams," and after the war began, a new black fabric appeared in her work, meeting the pink one and covering it. In 2022, Kuznetsova developed a military-themed project, "Times," a response to historical events and the fact that assessments of current events are only made once they have concluded. The artist is also working on a series of "Magic Landscapes," where she sets out not to reproduce reality or depict specific landscapes, but to convey the emotional essence of the landscapes she paints, and the magic she feels when she is alone with nature.

"The project 'Dreams' was, among other things, a reaction to the presidential elections in 2019. When the majority chose a candidate who was not a politician, who spoke simply and sincerely, there was a feeling that the whole country had chosen a dream."

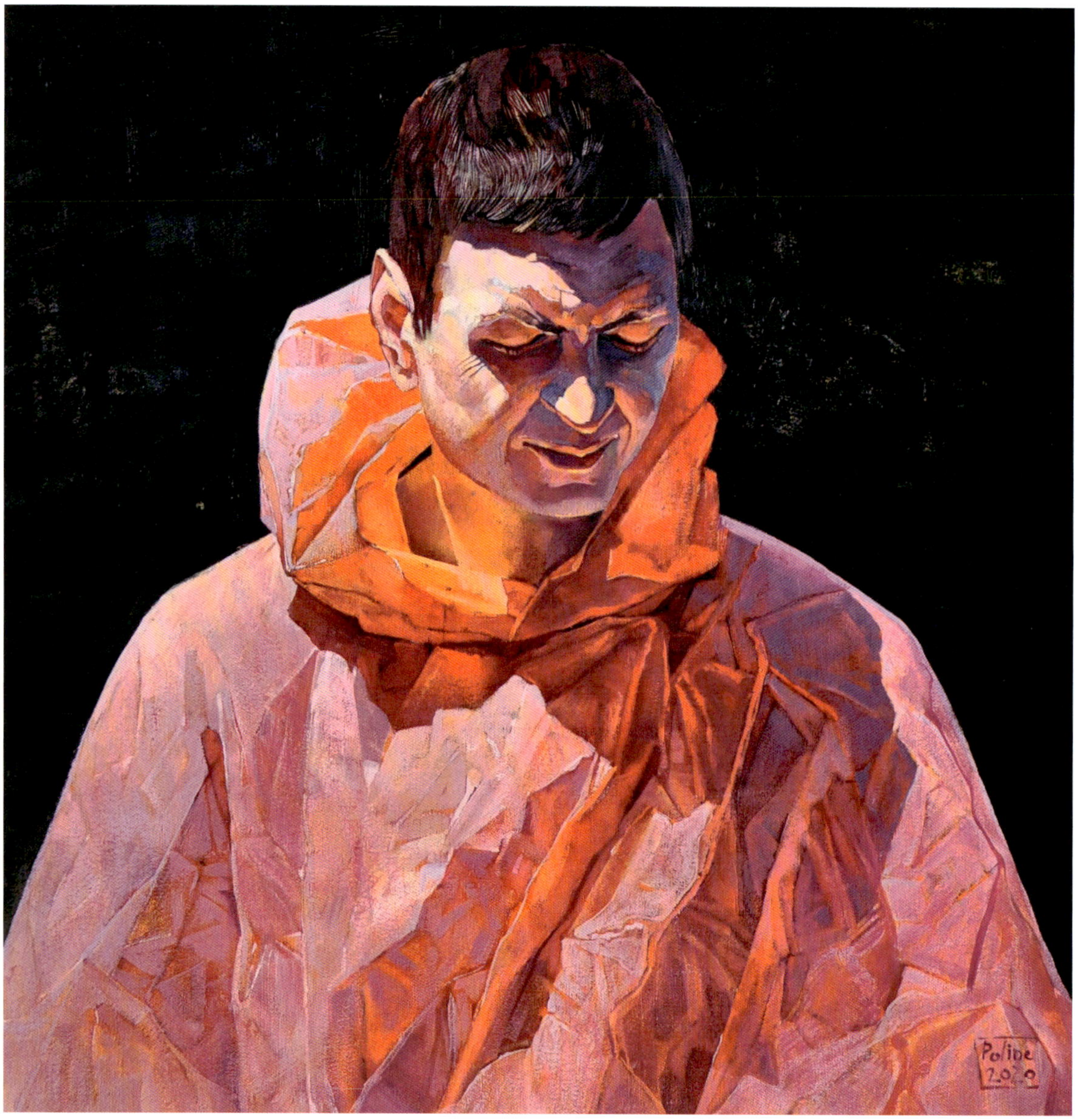

Kuznetsova started the "Dreams" series in 2019. When the war started, the series took on a darker edge, and the newer paintings were filled with brooding symbols, charged with meaning. This page: *Pink*, oil on canvas, 2020. Opposite page: *Dream Ship*, oil on canvas, 2021. Page 104: *Pink*, oil on canvas, 2020.

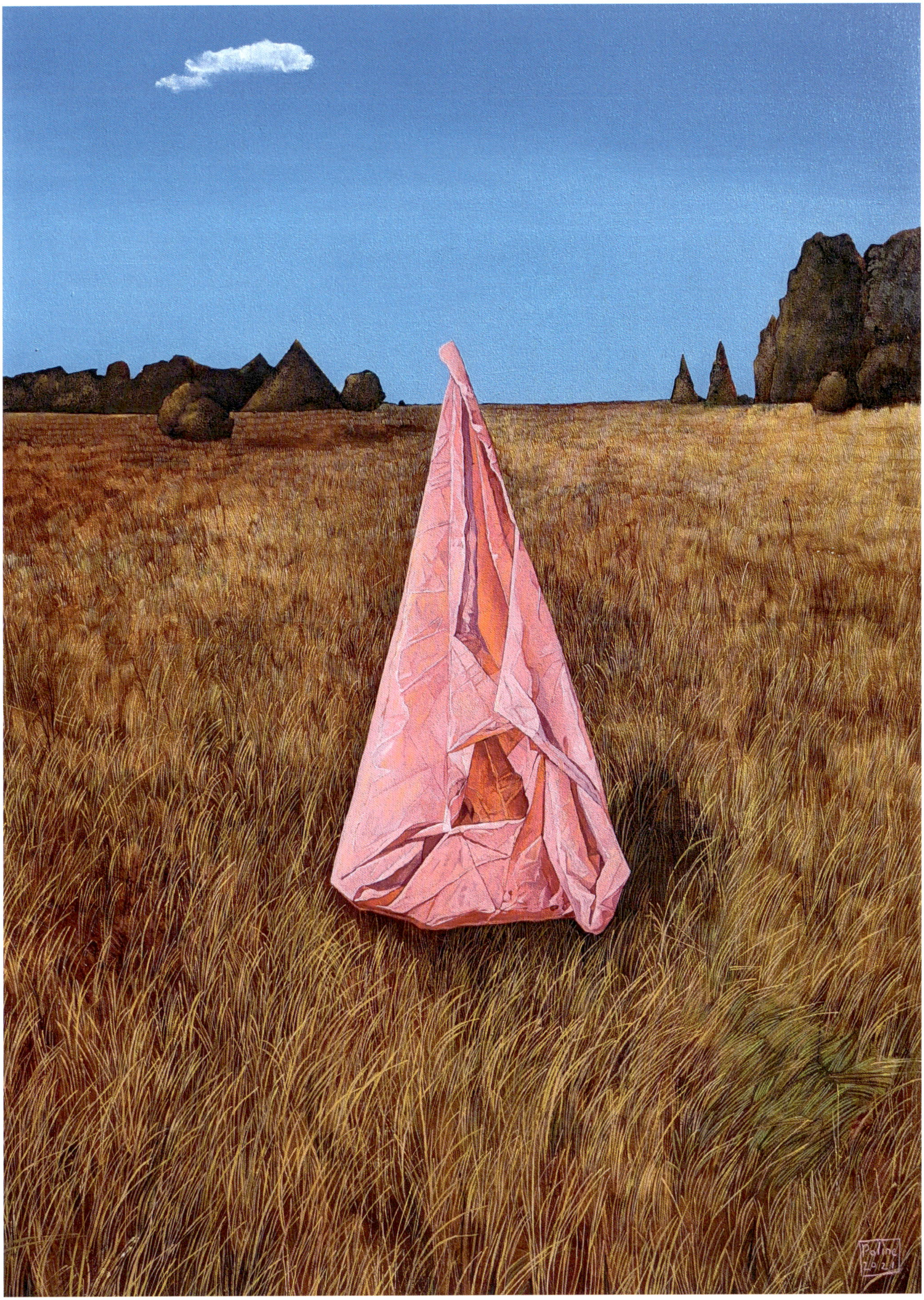
Poline
2021

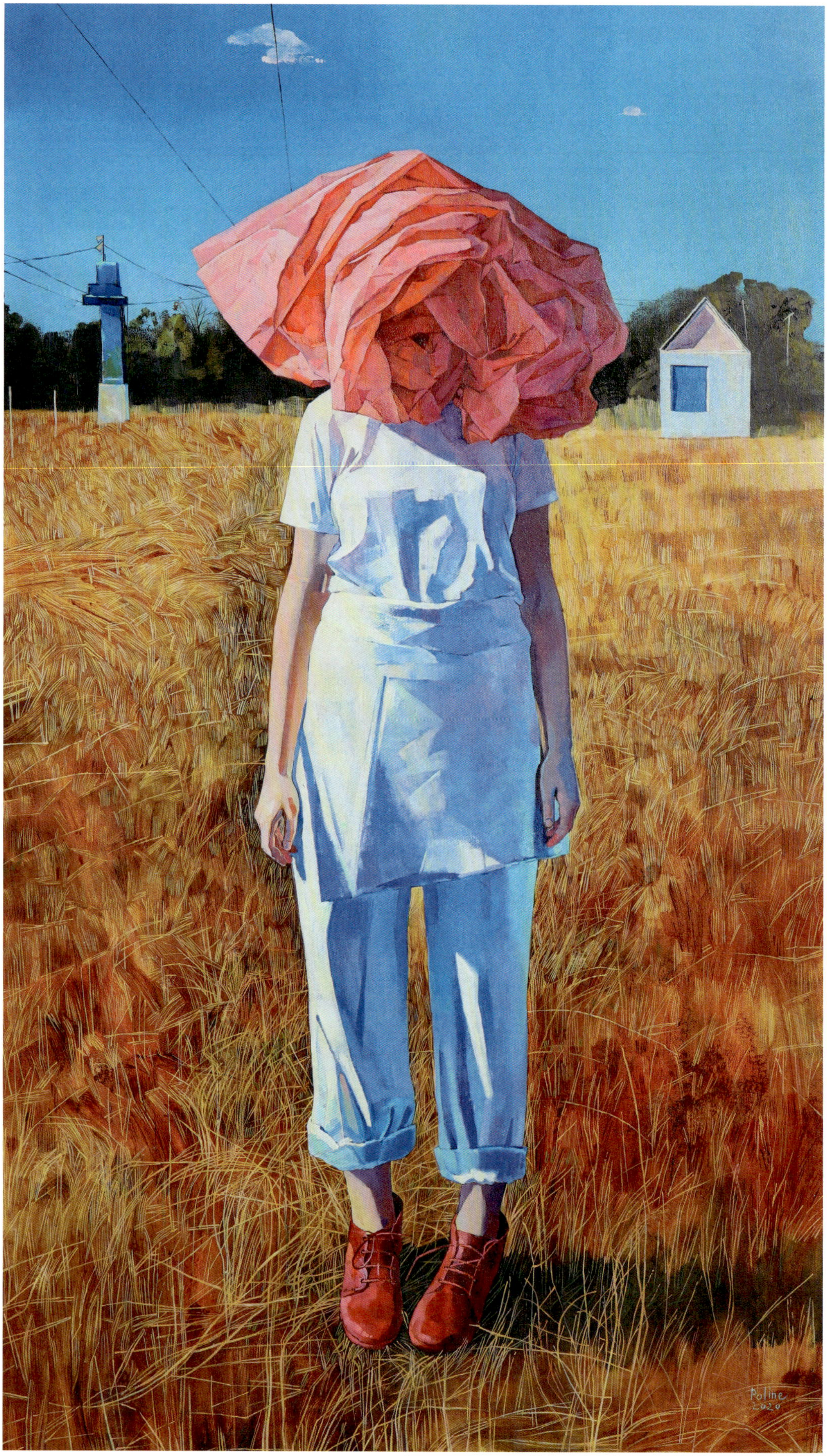
Poline
2020

"Sincerity is probably the main thing that interests me in creativity. When creating art, I constantly check how accurately it corresponds to my inner impulse, how correctly it conveys an emotion or the first image that arose from the depths of the unconscious."

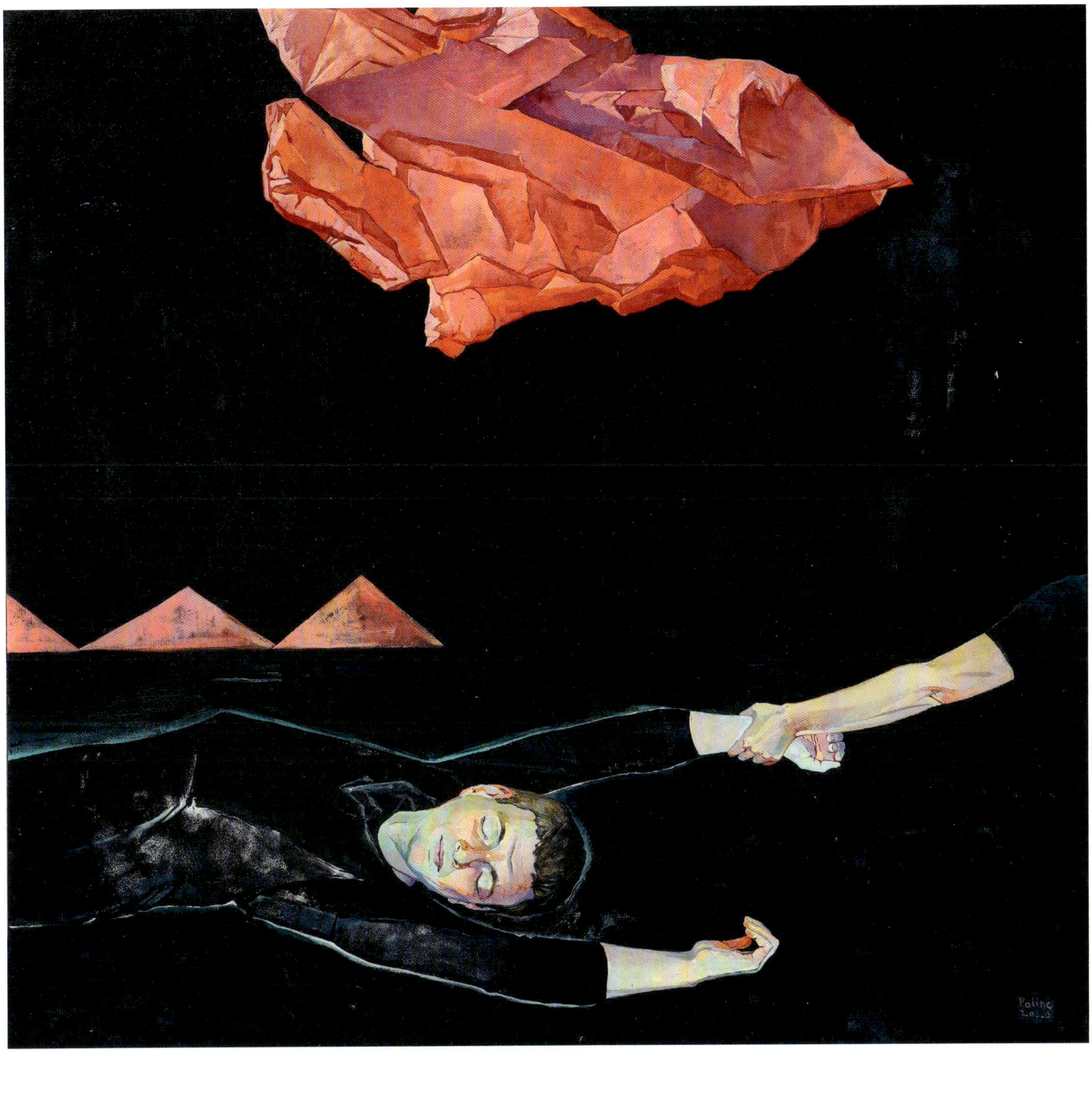

In this 2020 work by Kuznetsova (*Dreams*), a sleeping person floats through a dream world. Meanwhile, an elusive figure, almost entirely off the canvas, gently guides them by the arm. Opposite page: *Flower*, oil on canvas, 2020.

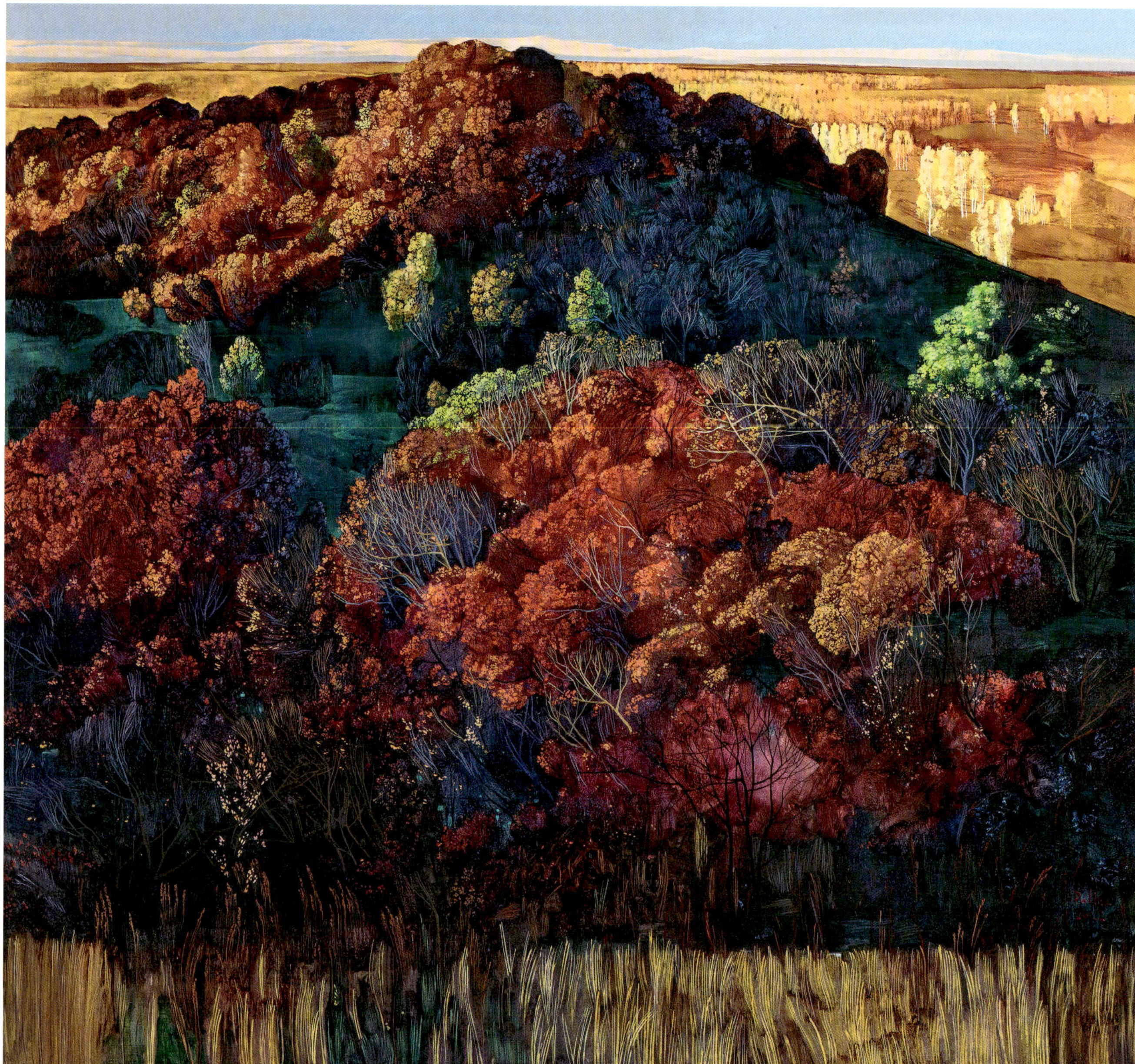

Kuznetsova's "Magic Landscapes" series demonstrates her Ukrainian roots as an artist perhaps more than any other work. Her passion for the landscapes of her native land stems not from patriotic fervor, but from her deep connection to the places where she grew up.

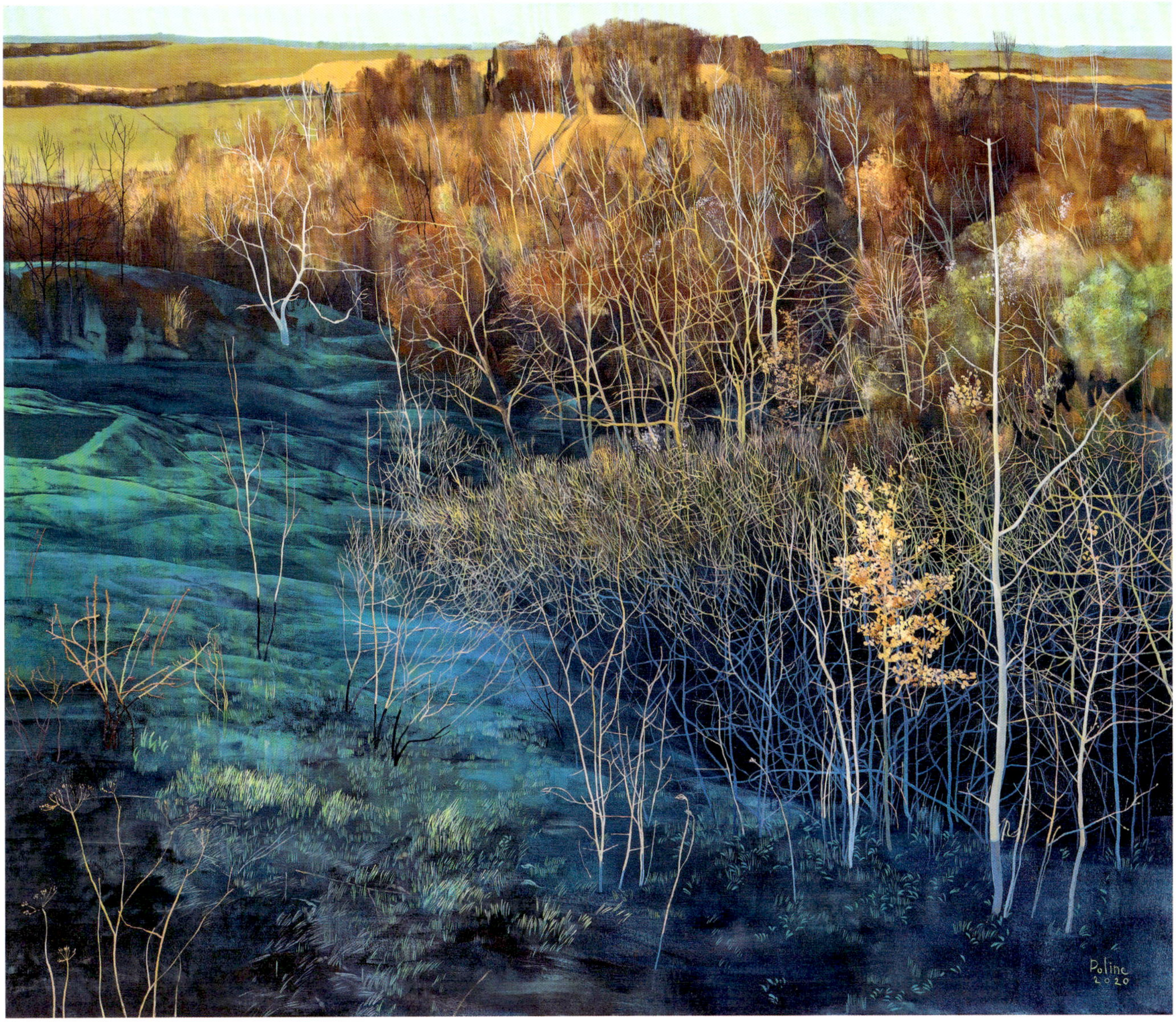

The 2020 painting *Rivers of Shadows* perfectly conveys the spirit of the “Magic Landscapes” series, with the mesmerizing blue of the foreground infusing the painting with a touch of the magical.

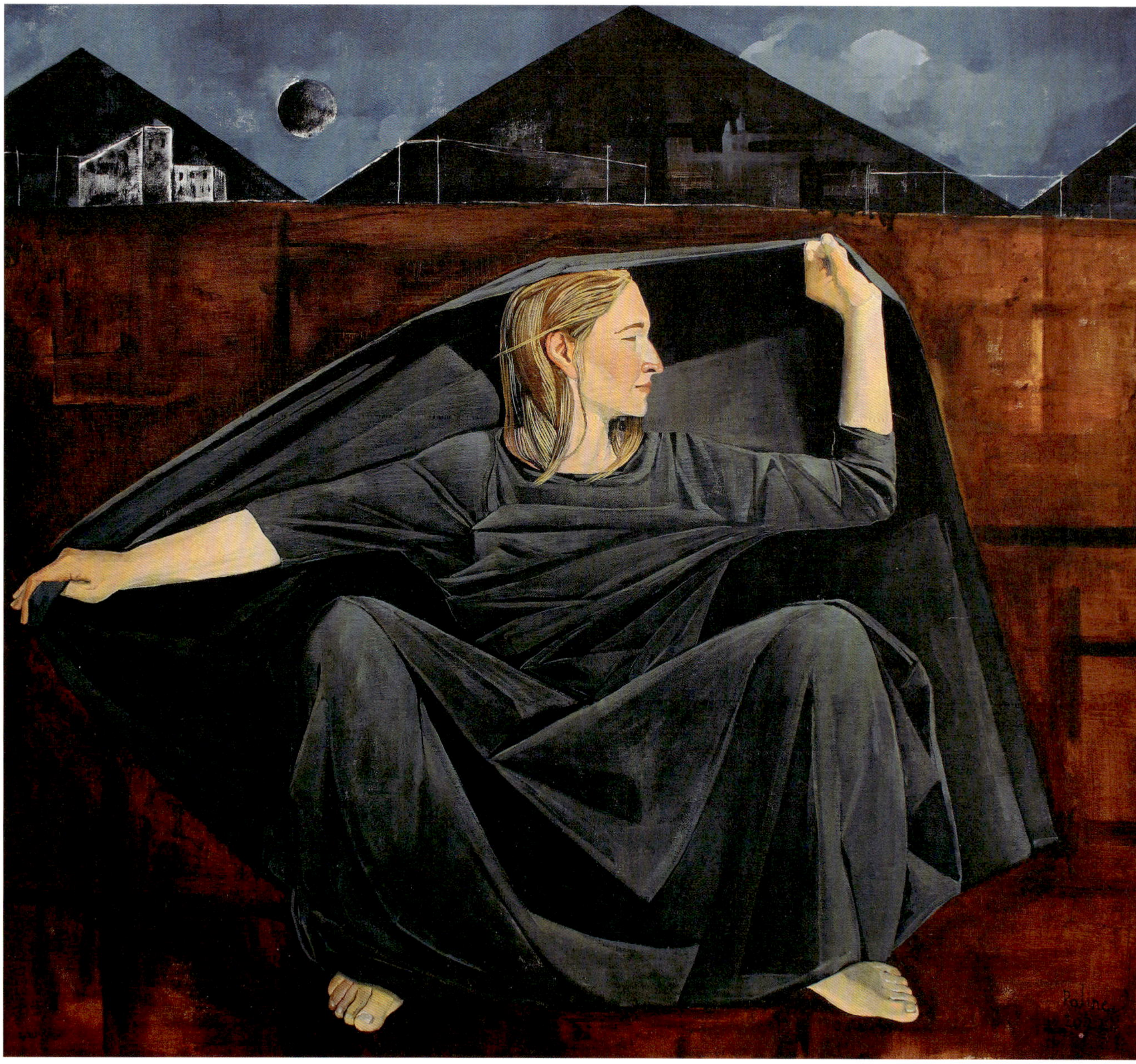

When the war began, a new black fabric appeared in Kuznetsova's art. In this work, entitled *Shelter*, the fabric symbolizes a form of emotional protection for a woman during wartime, highlighting the inescapable impact of war on the lives of everyone it touches.

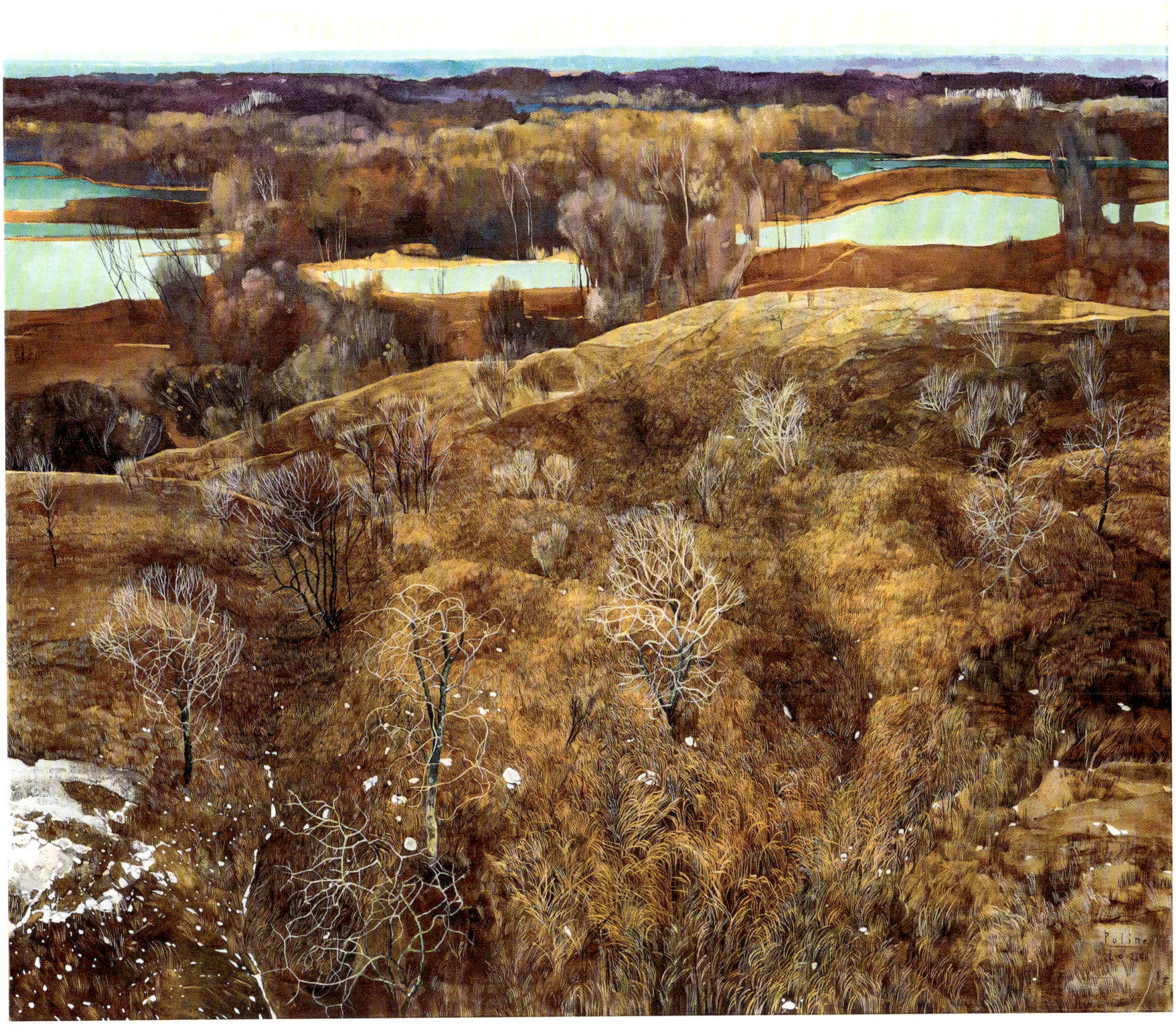

Painting landscapes (above: *Field of Calm*, 2020) has become a way for Kuznetsova to find peace and to focus. She tries to convey the feelings that arise in her whenever she encounters a particular place. To her, the furry body of the earth in winter, when there is neither frost nor snow, looks like a sleeping beast.

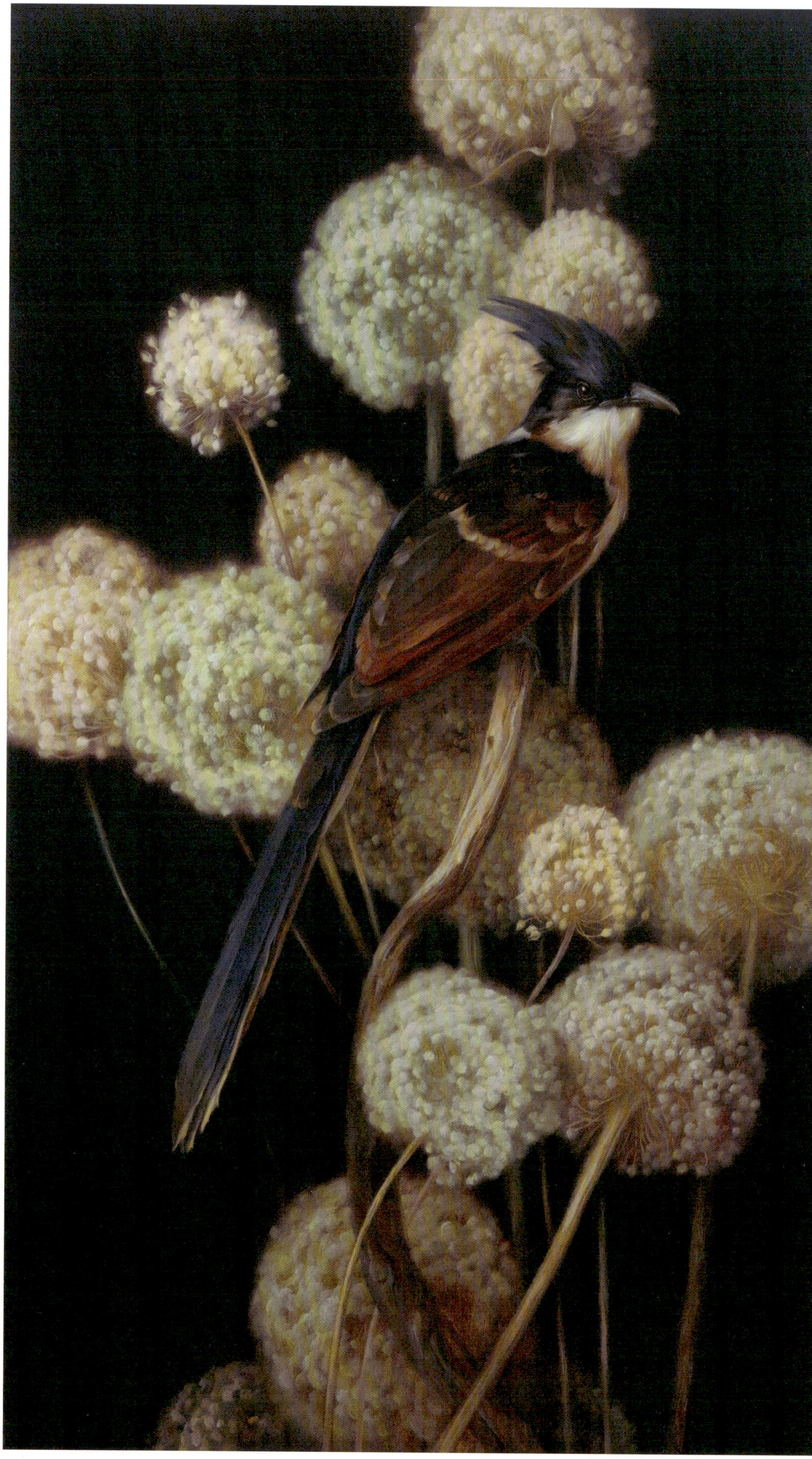

UNVEILING THE HIDDEN BEAUTY

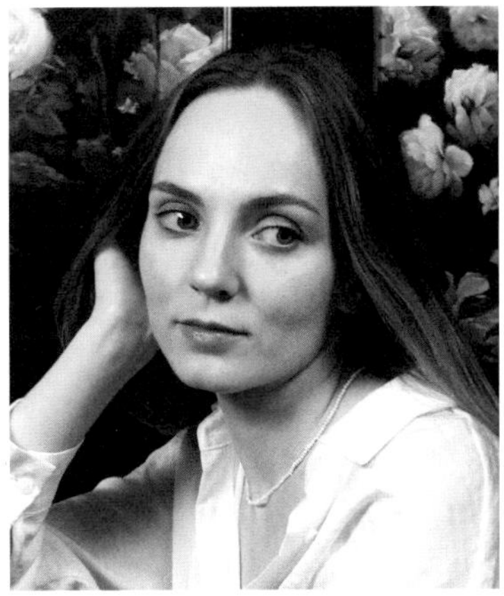

ANHELINA HOLEMBIVSKA · *АНГЕЛІНА ГОЛЕМБІВСЬКА*

In her realistic masterpieces, Anhelina Holembivska infuses images with striking emotions, giving each subject a unique personality.

Painting has always been an integral part of Anhelina Holembivska's life. Raised in a small town near Kyiv, her house was bordered by a field and a river, both of which the artist loved to sketch. Perhaps this early appreciation for nature attracted her to natural forms in her painting later in life. Holembivska believes that the visual images and the architecture we see every day have a huge impact on our perception of the world as a whole. Eager to broaden her horizons, she earned a grant to study at the Accademia di Belle Arti di Firenze and moved to Florence, Italy. For her, it was an incredibly valuable experience to live in the city that gave the world the Renaissance. There, the artist's visual language was directly informed by the masters of the past. Holembivska appreciates a wide range of art styles, but nothing evokes a response in her quite like the Northern Renaissance and the art of the 19th century. She places great importance on the technical aspects of painting and believes that mastery of craft ultimately gives an artist more freedom to express themselves. As a result she has dedicated years to learning various painting techniques, exploring the opportunities offered by each. After years of experimenting, Holembivska has decided that oil painting best suits her passion: still lifes. Working in this genre, the artist strives to capture both the individuality of each object and the general mood. In her flower series, she seeks to imbue each flower with its own distinct character, inviting viewers to reflect on the emotions they convey. Is this a happy flower? Lonely? Sad? Is this flower worried that its petals will soon fall, or is it simply enjoying its own beauty? For Holembivska, it is important that as a Ukrainian artist, she can represent the country on various world platforms. She participated in a group show at New York's Arcadia Contemporary gallery in 2022 and the LA Art Show at Arcadia in 2023.

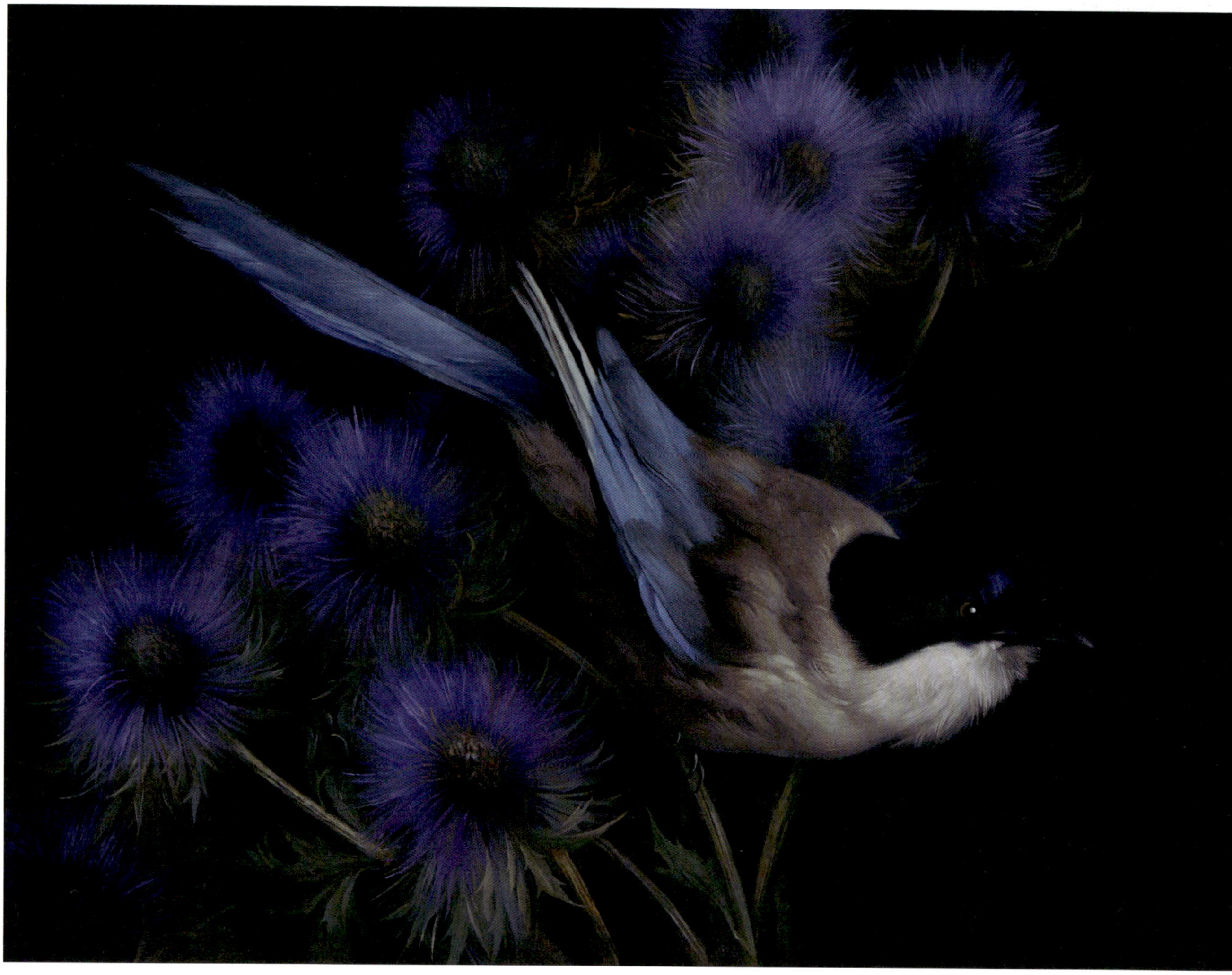

Holembivska's work *Magpie* depicts an azure-winged magpie with mesmerizing realism. It was shown at Arcadia Contemporary gallery in the group exhibition, "The Frame Remains The Same," in 2022. Opposite page: *Poppies*, oil on canvas, 2022. Page 114: *Chestnut Winged Cuckoo*, oil on canvas, 2022.

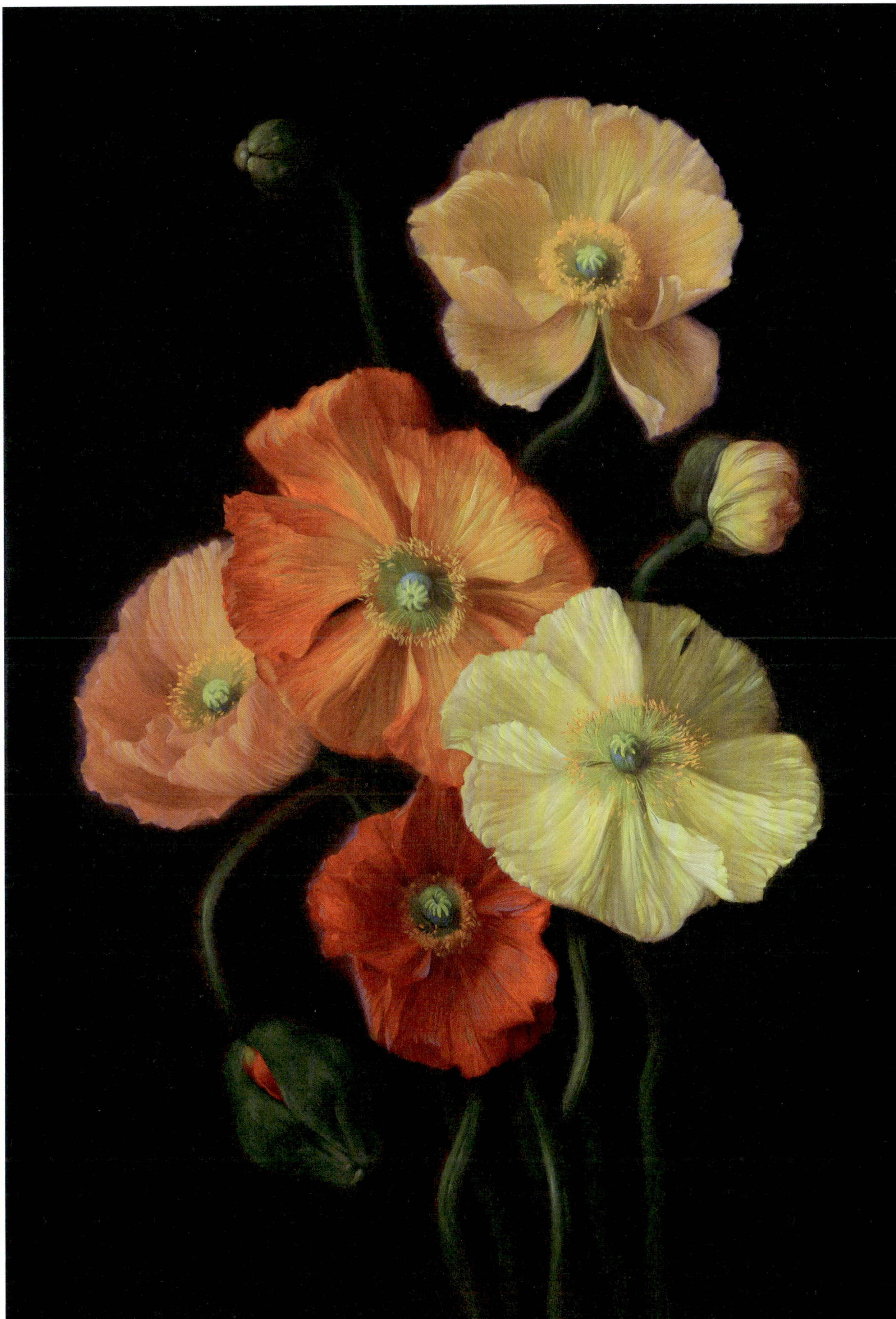

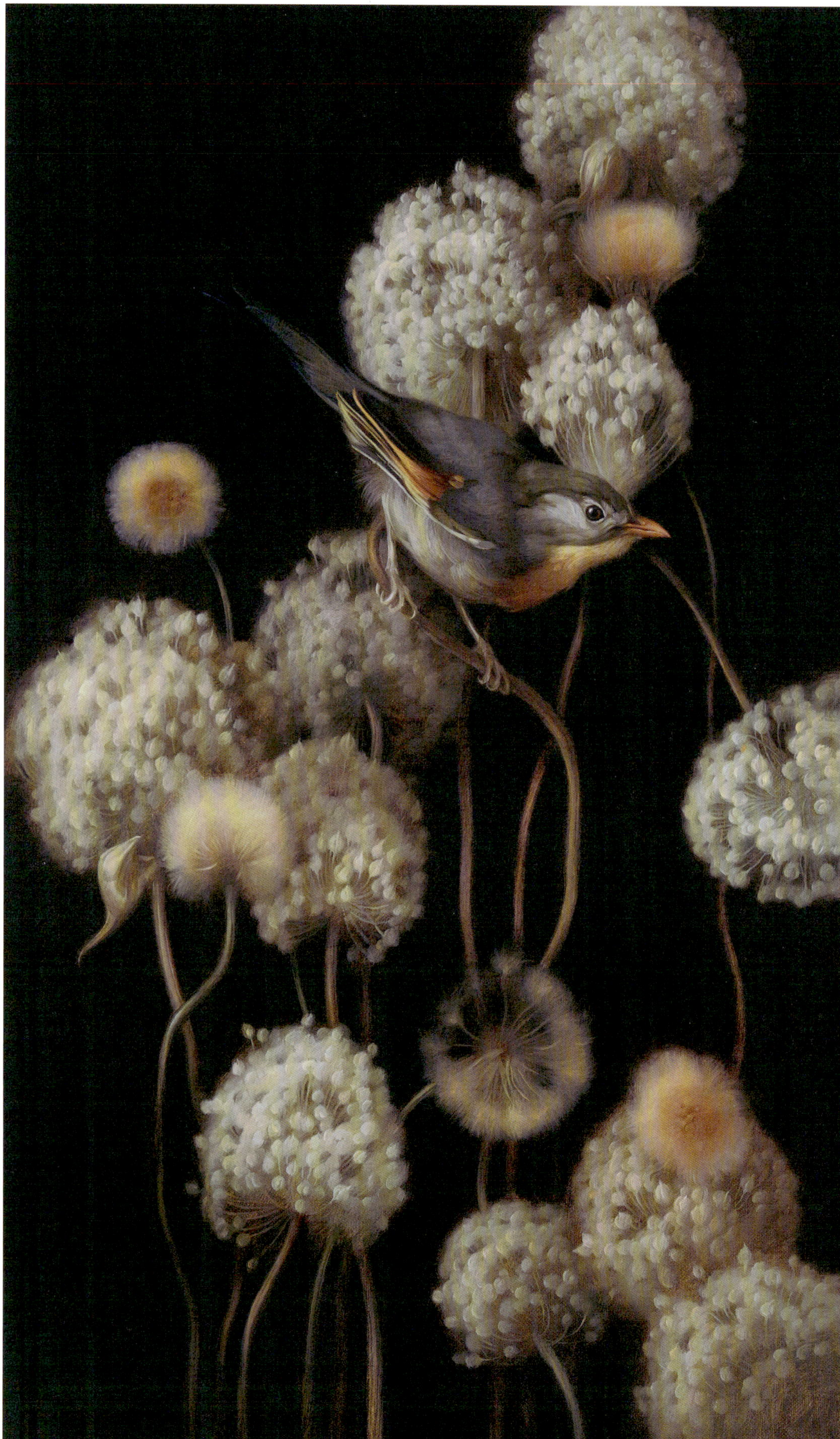

"I look for motifs for my paintings in nature. What fascinates me is often very changeable. And what attracts me to art is the ability to preserve this fleeting beauty. A bright feeling is transferred to the canvas and continues to live."

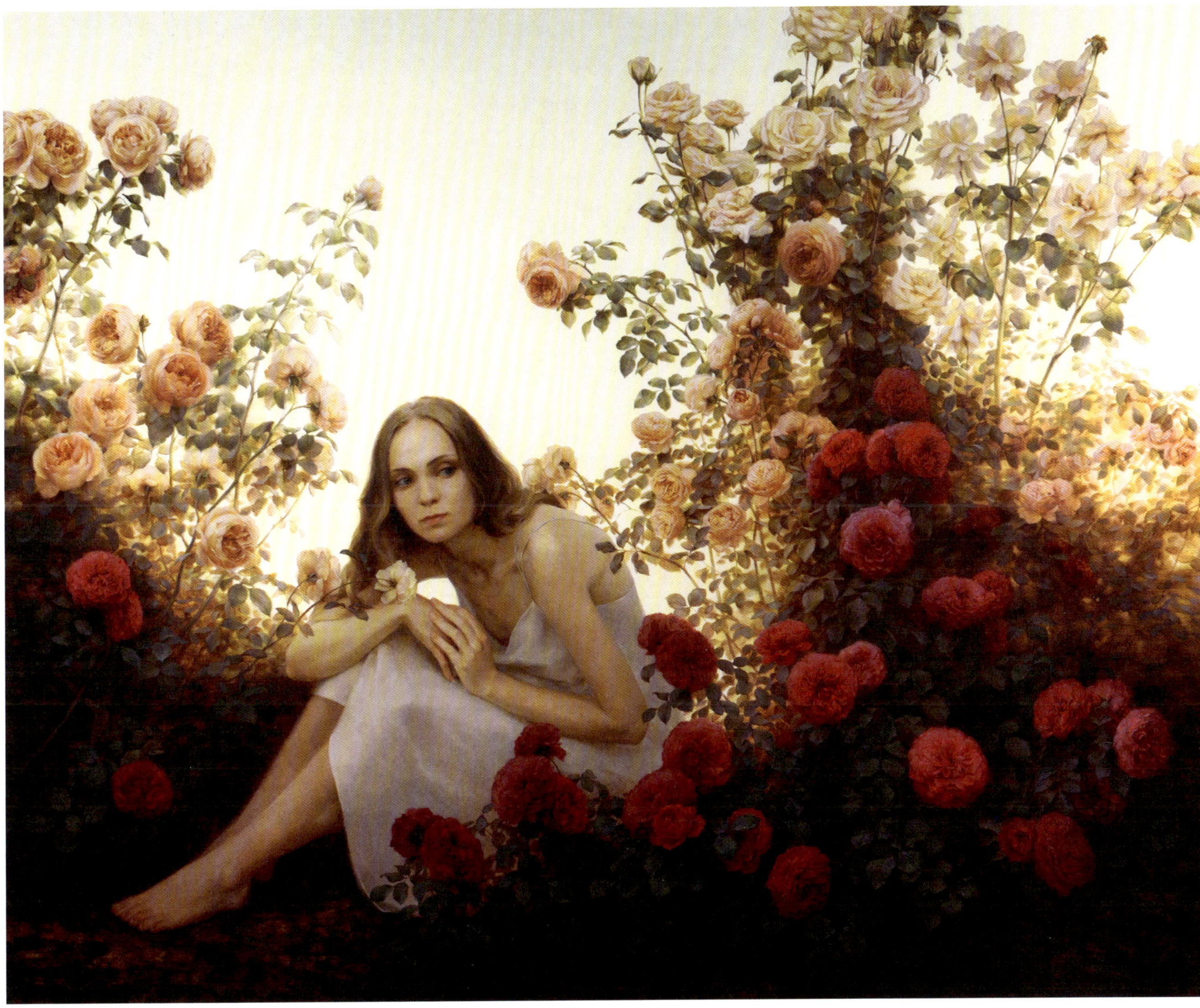

During the war, painting became a refuge for the artist. She tried to cling to "normality," continuing to turn to familiar subjects. She expressed this idea in her work *Hiding Place* (oil on canvas, 2022). Opposite page: *Japanese Nightingale*, oil on canvas, 2022.

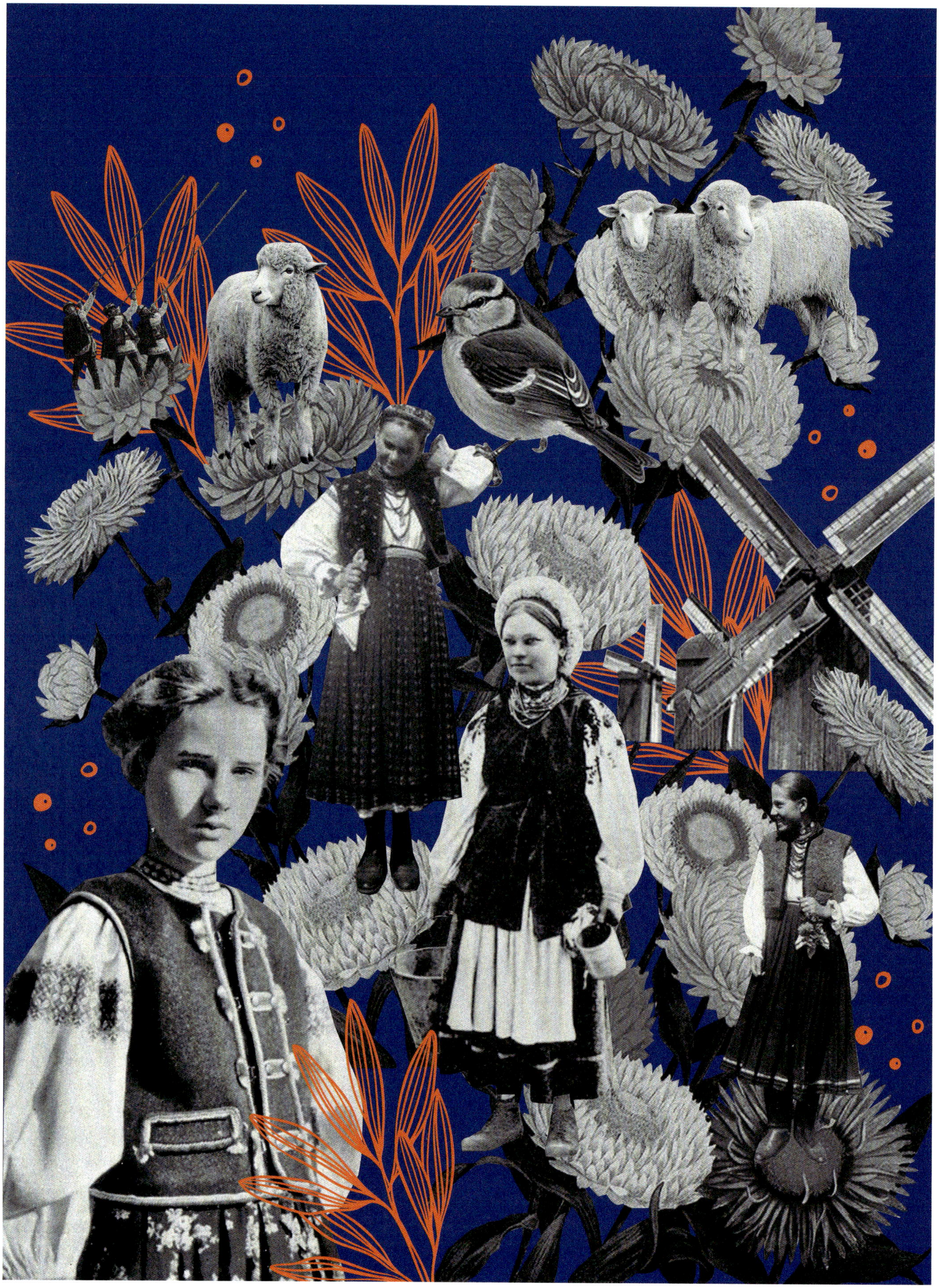

THOUSANDS OF TRAGEDIES, MILLIONS OF STORIES

OLGA ZERNO · *ОЛЬГА ЗЕРНО*

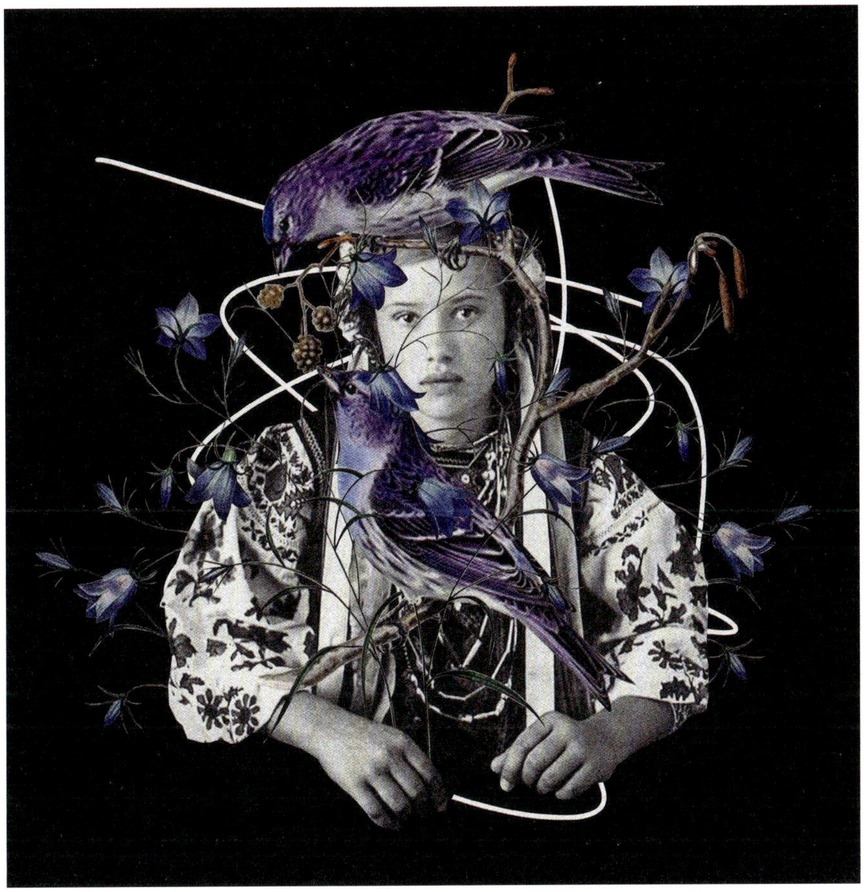

Using old photographs of Ukrainians, Olga Zerno creates refined, smart, and sometimes ironic collages that combine tradition and modernity.

Olga Zerno was born in Berehove in the Zakarpattia region. Until the age of six, she lived in the countryside, surrounded by woodlands. This, she says, inspired in her a great love for nature. She now lives and works in Lviv where she creates collages and digital art; she also works on projects as a designer and illustrator. For Zerno, art is a manifestation of her emotions and a response to what is happening in the world around her. She considers inspiration to be something abstract, so when an idea comes up or something happens, she transforms her thoughts and feelings into art. In her collages, Olga uses photographs of Ukrainians taken over 100 years ago. The collages are an attempt to understand her ancestors—who they were as people and what their lives were like. History is cyclical, so the artist believes that the emotions and feelings experienced by her predecessors can help Ukrainians cope with what is happening today.

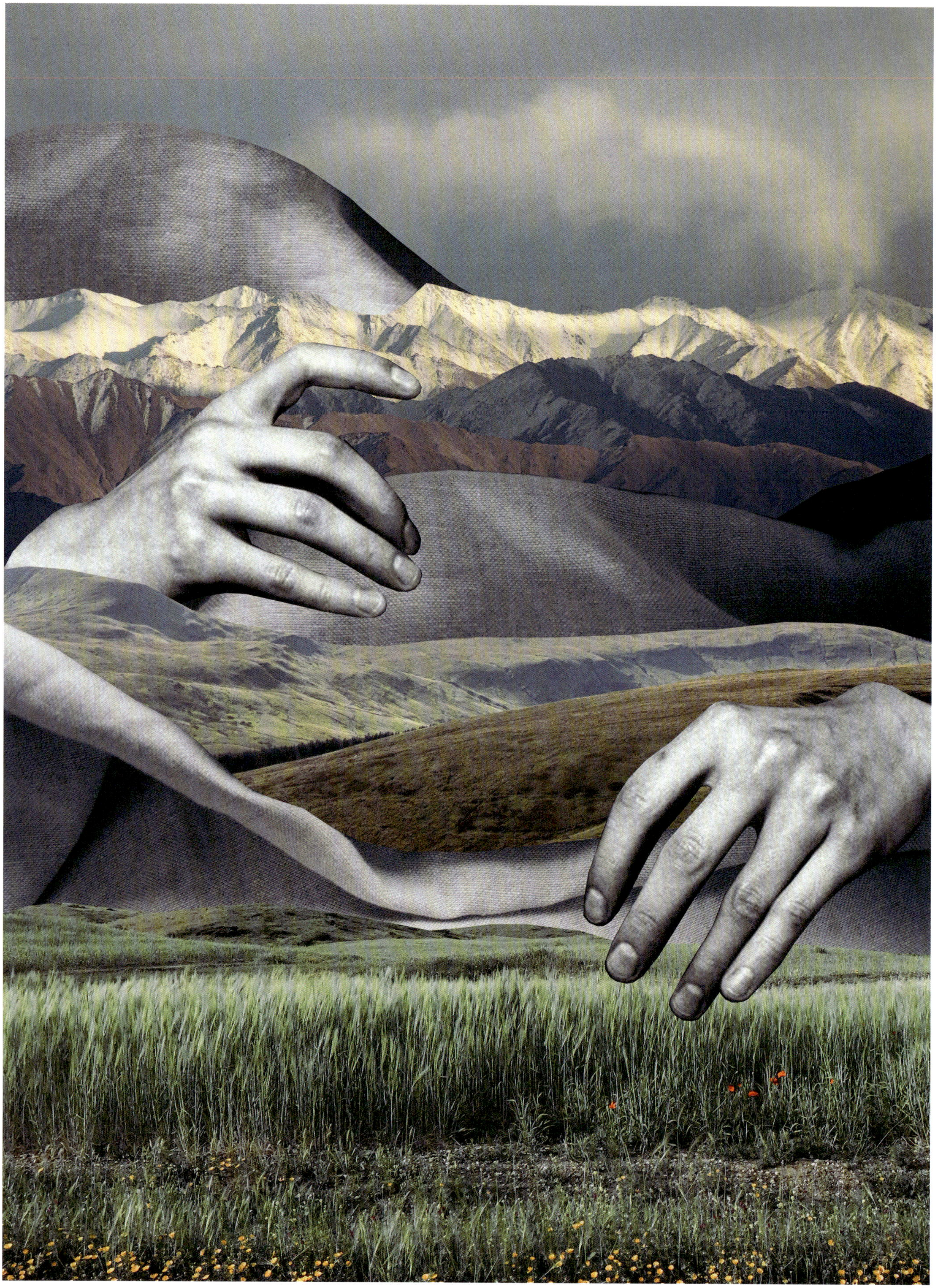

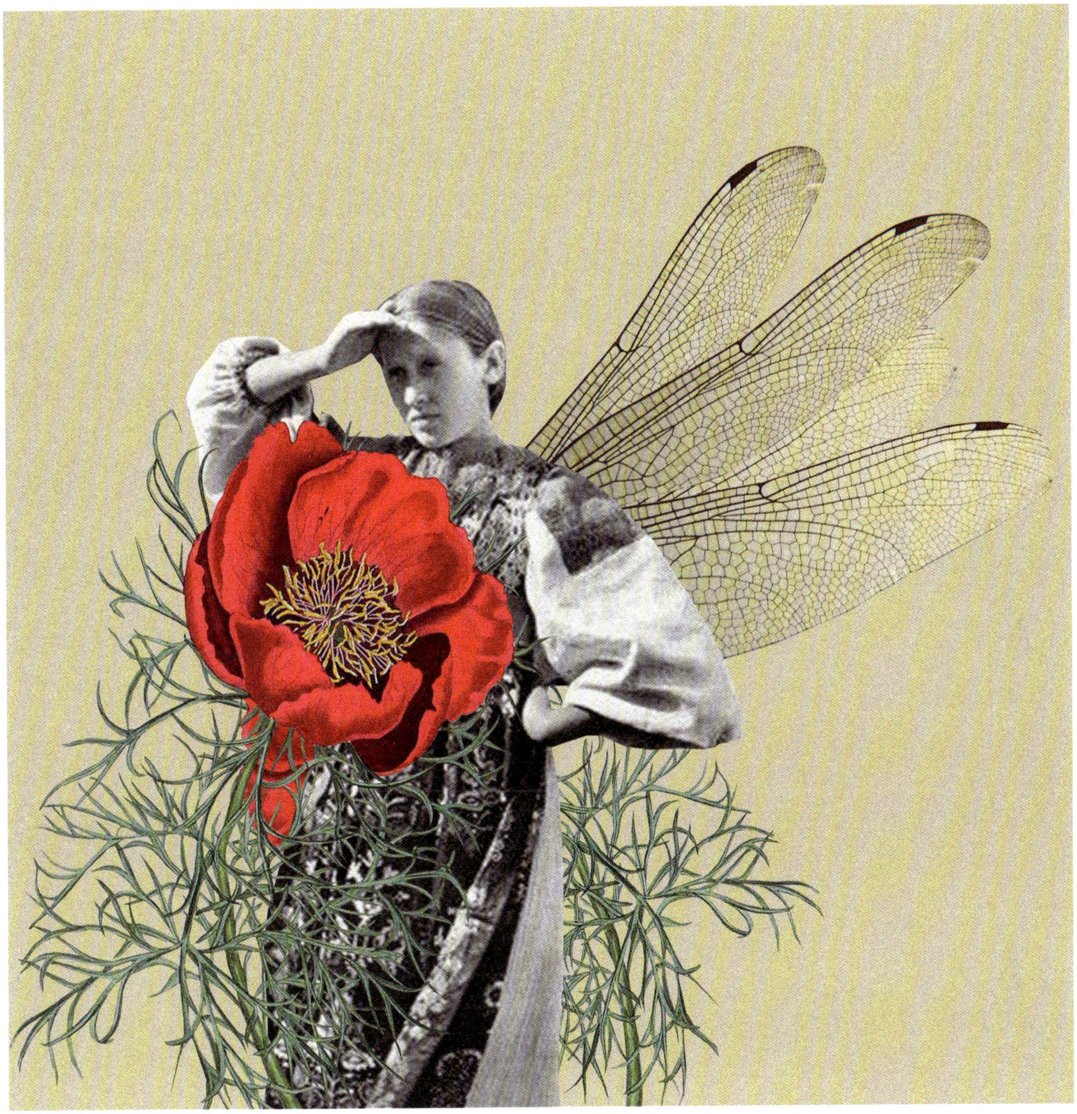

In her art, Olga Zerno uses old photographs of past generations of Ukrainians. This page: *Wings*, opposite page: *Mountains*, both digital, 2022. Previous pages: *Women*, digital, 2023 (p. 120); *Bells*, digital, 2022 (p. 121).

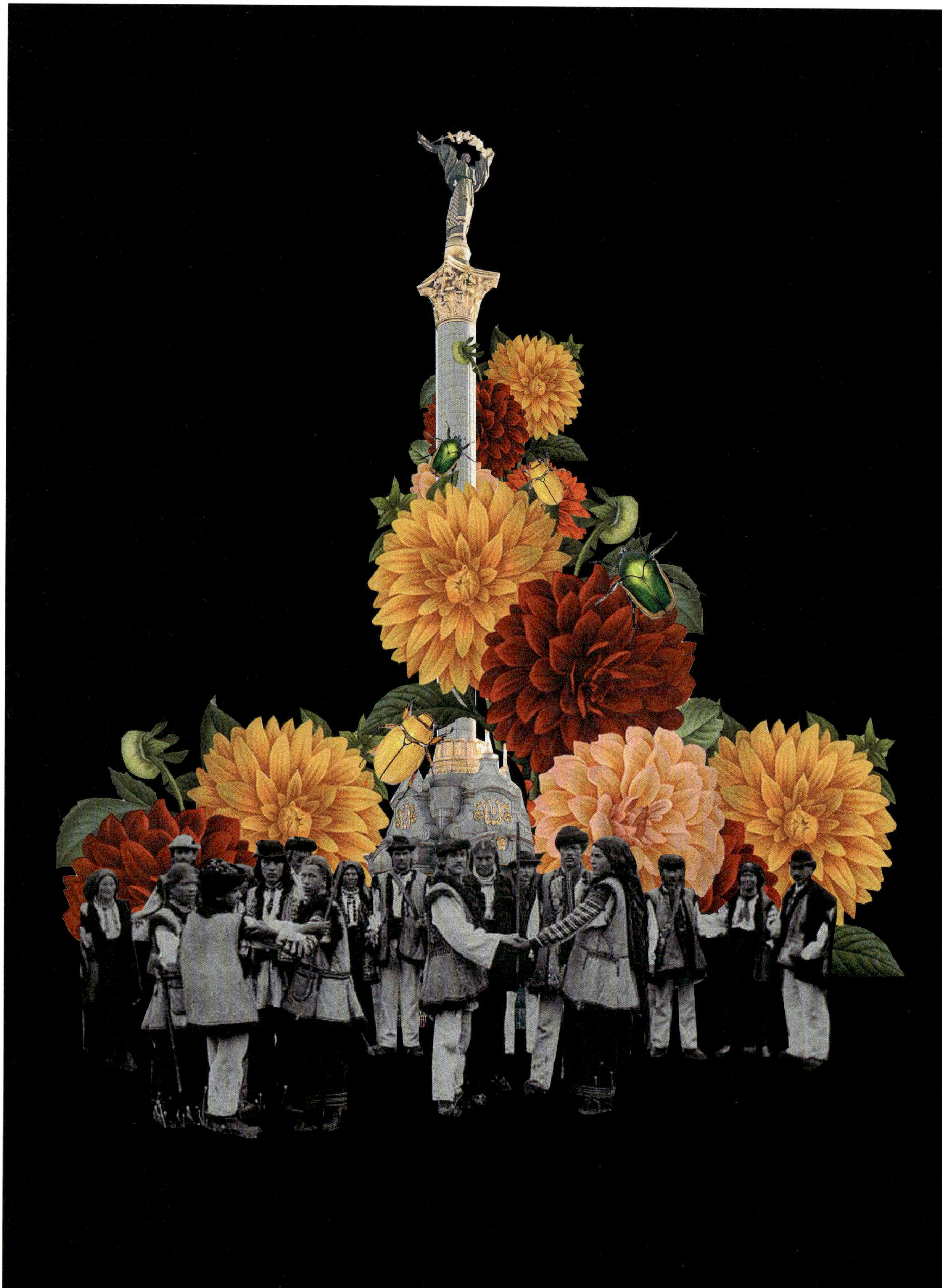

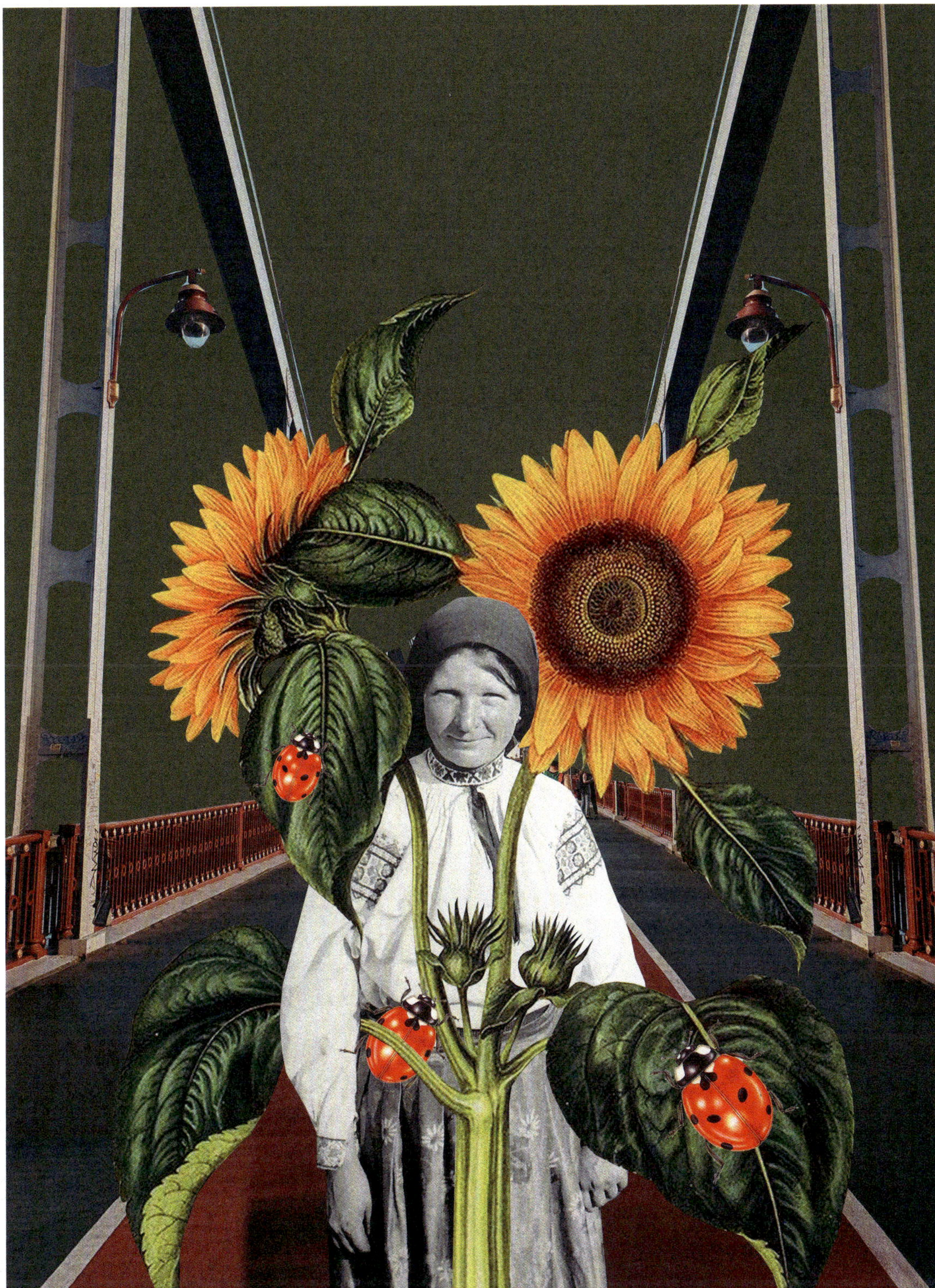

In "Kyiv," a series of digital works, the artist combines black-and-white vintage photos with images of landmarks of the Ukrainian capital, as well as flowers that are considered traditional in Ukraine—chrysanthemums and sunflowers.

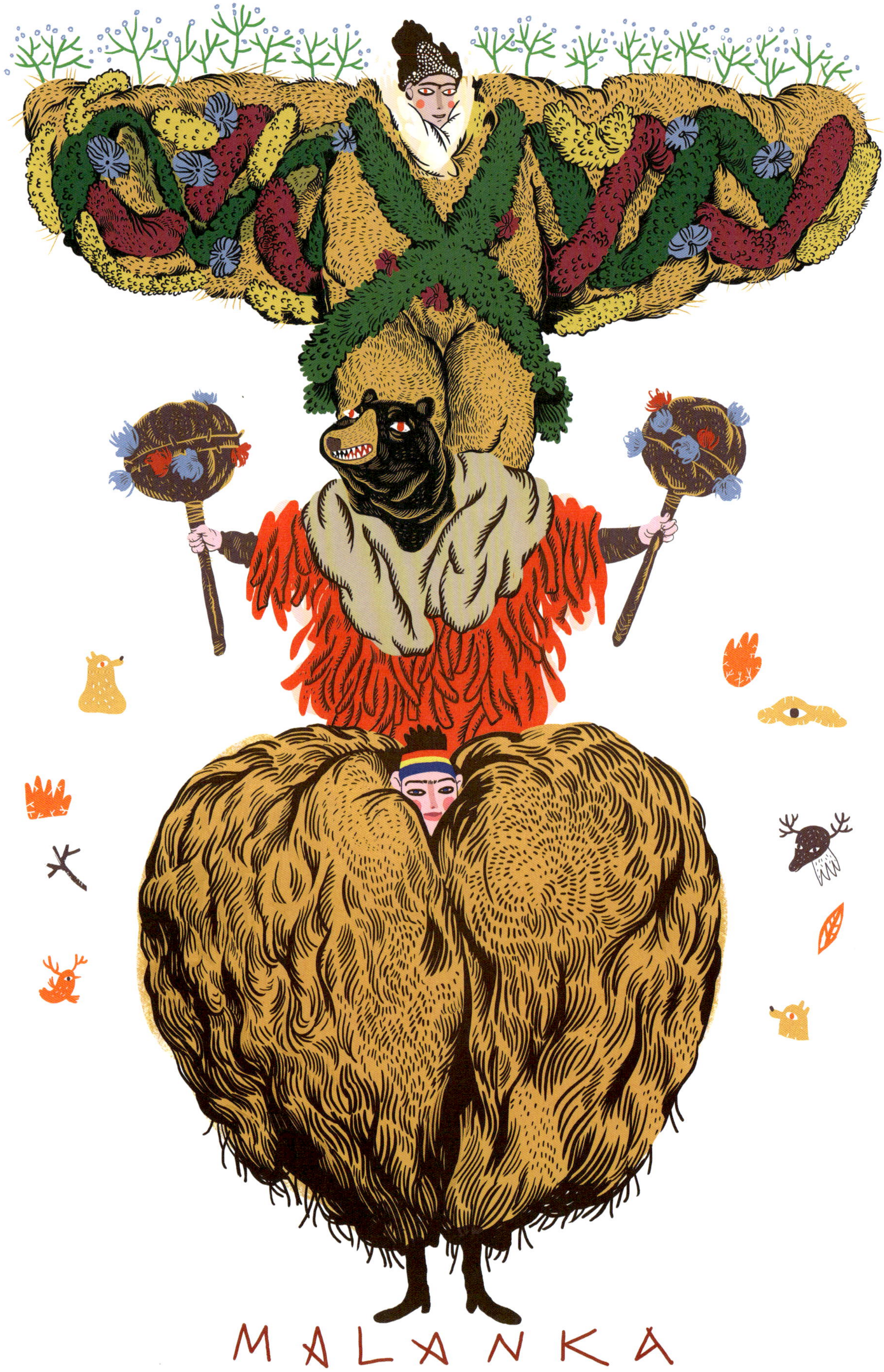

MALANKA

DIVERSITY OF UKRAINE IN YELLOW AND BLUE

PICTORIC

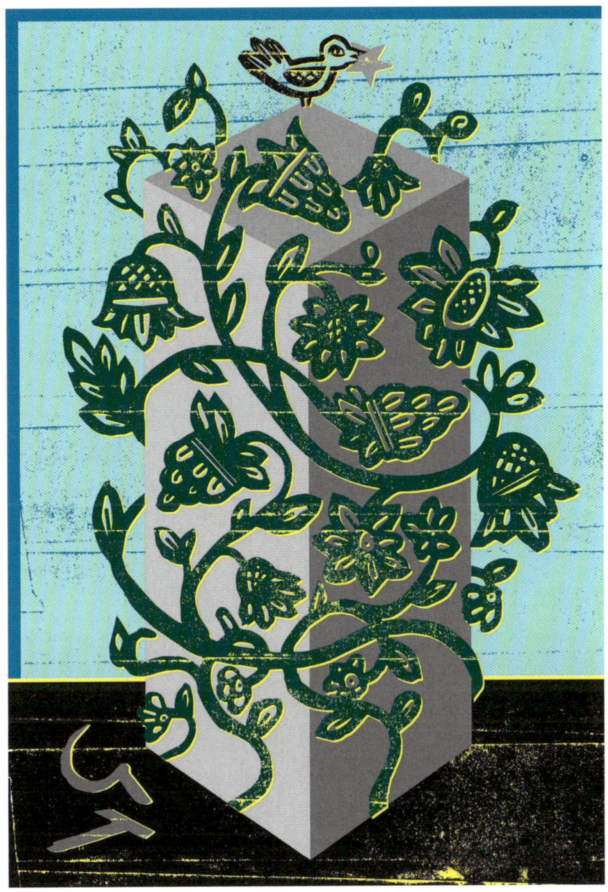

The illustrations in *Yellow&Blue* depict the different regions of Ukraine as well as the cultural practices in place throughout the country's diverse regions. Compiling the work of several illustrators, the volume helps to demonstrate the diversity of modern Ukraine.

In recent years, the field of illustration in Ukraine has risen to new heights, mirroring its growing popularity worldwide. The Pictoric Illustrators Club, founded in 2014 by Oleg Gryshchenko, Olena Staranchuk, and Anna Sarvira, has played a key role in elevating the status of the medium in Ukraine. In 2016 they launched their notable curatorial project "Yellow & Blue," which has been exhibited in numerous countries since. In 2019, Pictoric unveiled the next iteration, "Yellow & Blue Vol. 2," which uses posters and illustrations to depict contemporary Ukraine, highlighting the distinct cultural and social elements of the country's different regions. By examining social groups and their interactions across different cities, the Pictoric Illustrators Club is helping to revive traditions and history, while crafting a fresh urban mythology.

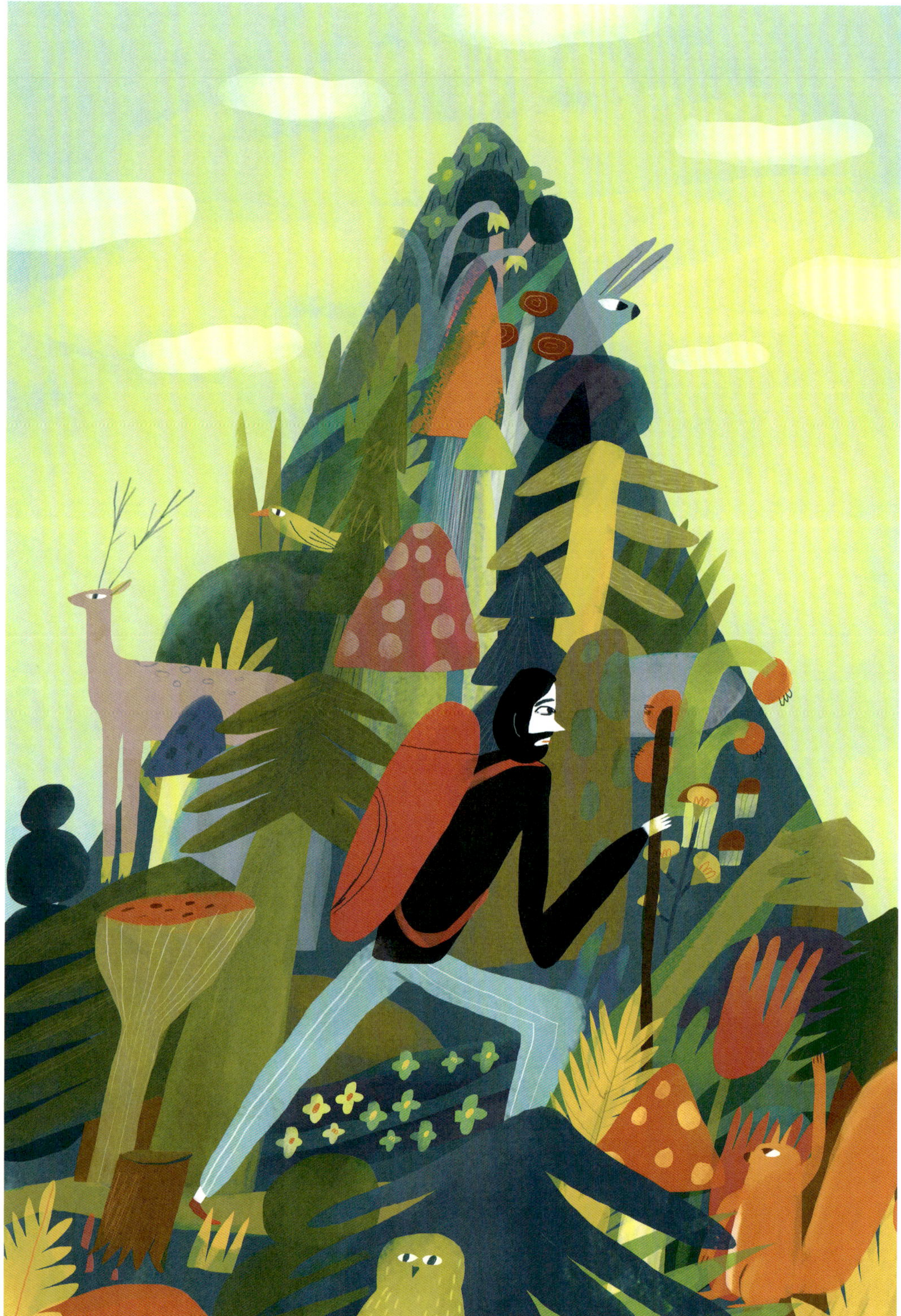

Anna Sarvira, *Carpathians*, “Yellow&Blue” project, digital, 2016. Opposite page: Olga Shtonda, *Wheat*, “Yellow&Blue Vol. 2,” digital, 2021. Previous pages: Yulia Tveritina, *Malanka*, “Yellow&Blue,” digital, 2016 (p. 126), Oleg Gryshchenko, *Decommunization*, “Yellow&Blue,” ink, digital, 2019 (p. 127).

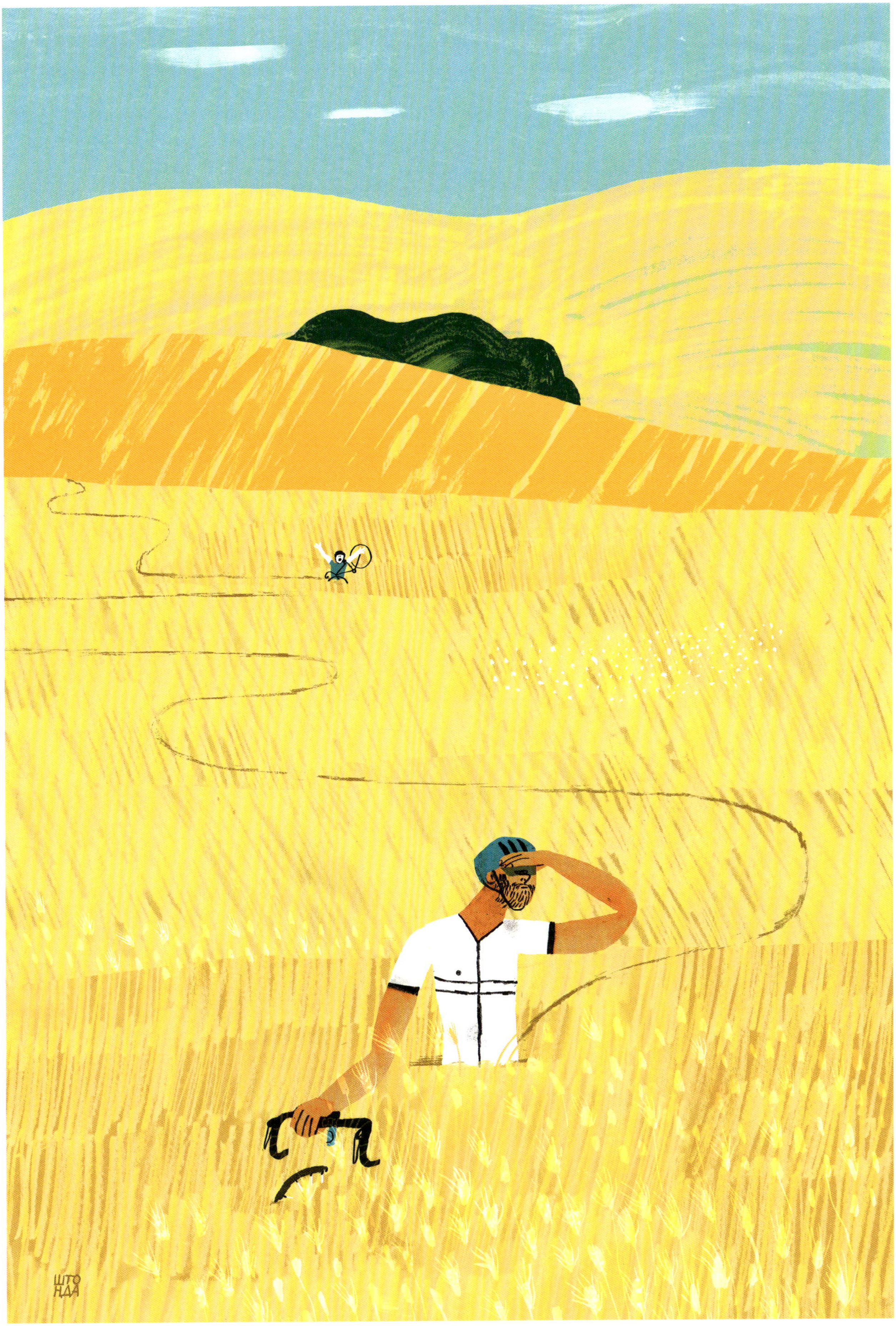
ШТО
НДА

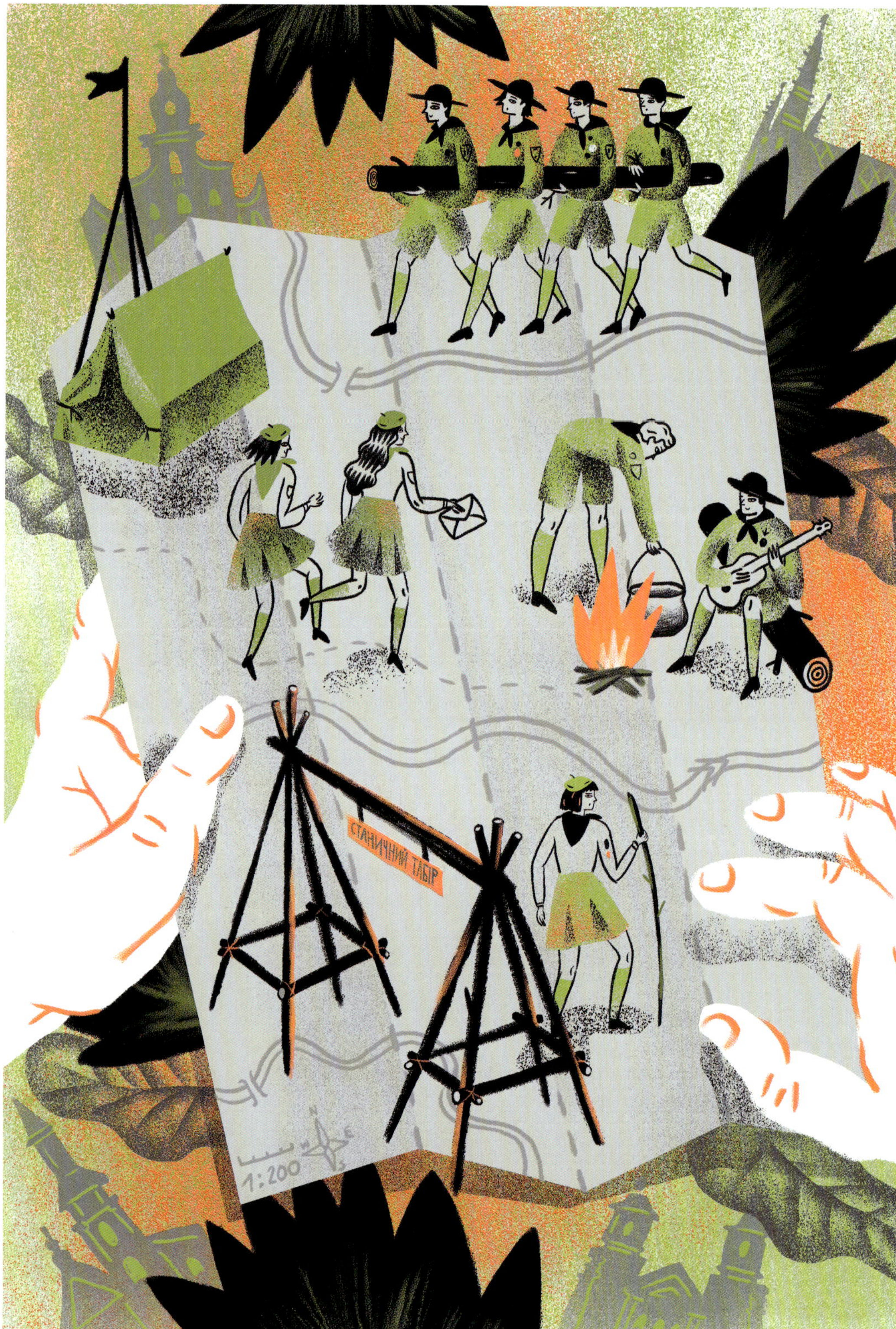

The Ukrainian scouting tradition known as *plast* is depicted here in Olha Hordiienko's illustration: *Plast*, "Yellow&Blue Vol. 2.", digital, 2019. The tradition originated in Halychyna, in western Ukraine, and continues to be practiced today.

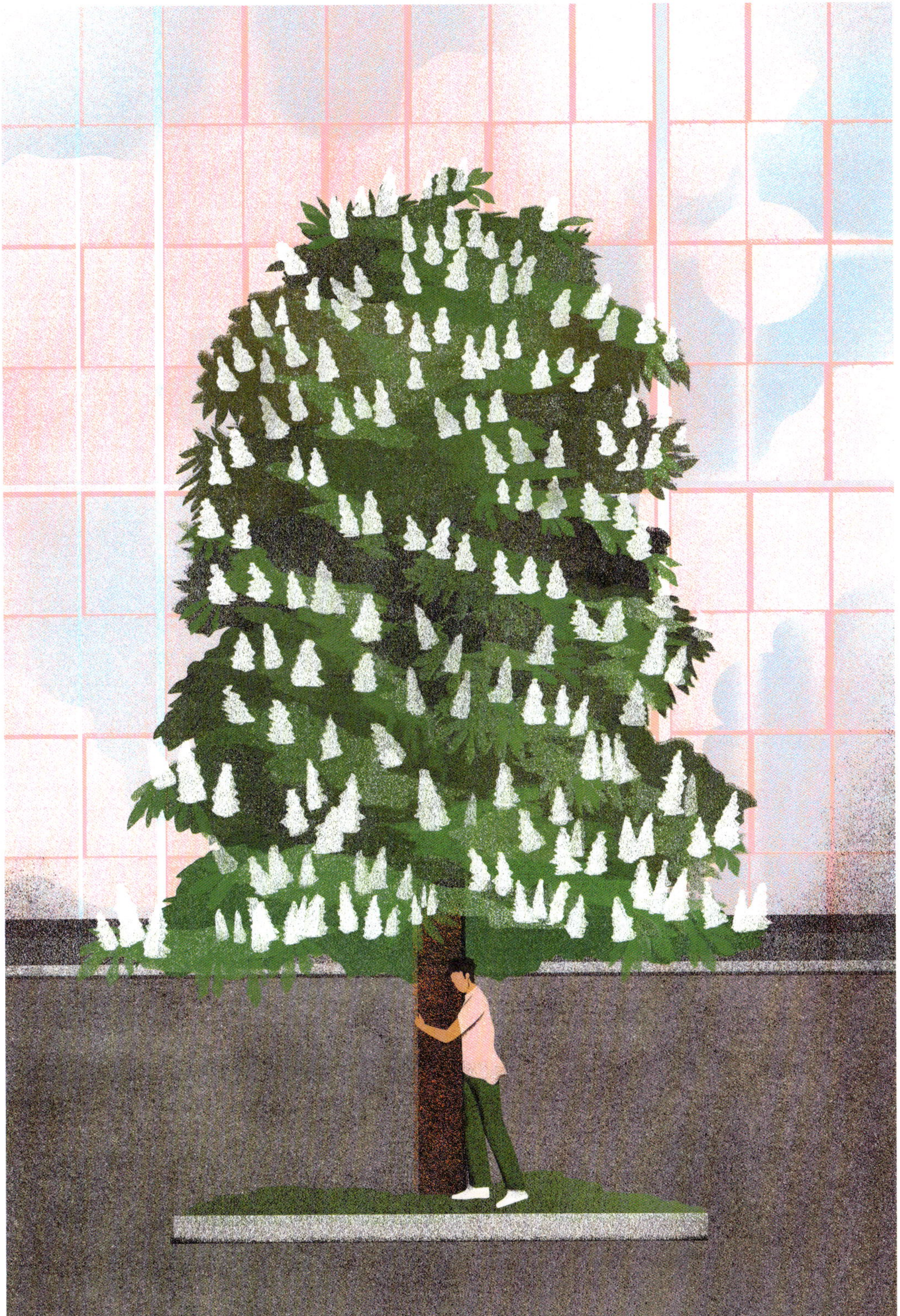

Masha Foya, *Modern Kyiv*, “Yellow&Blue Vol. 2.”, digital, 2021. This poster was created for an exhibition organized by Pictoric in 2021 as part of the Graphic Days festival in Turin, Italy.

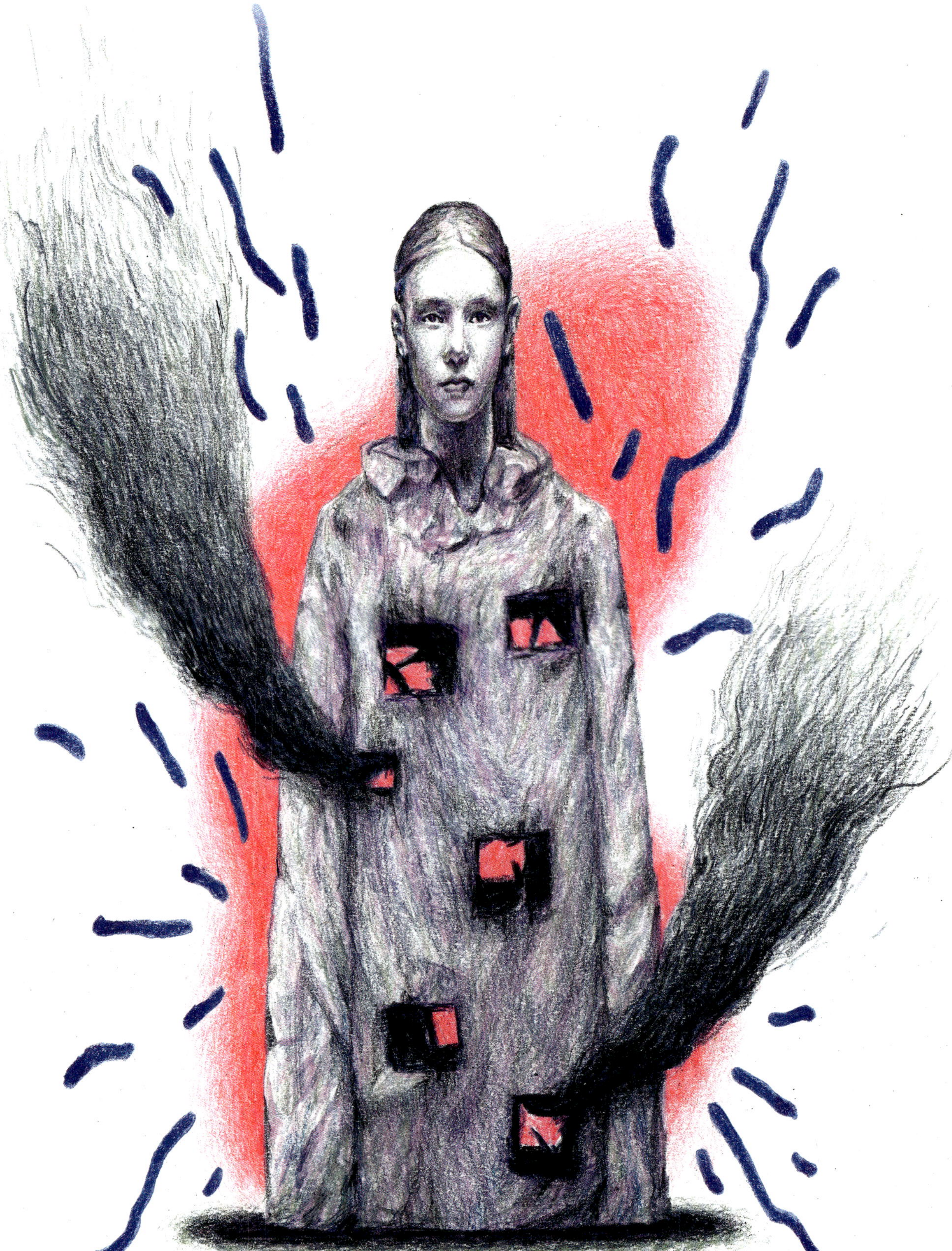

AN ARTIST'S DIARY THROUGH IMAGE AND COLOR

MITYA FENECHKIN · *МІТЯ ФЕНЕЧКИН*

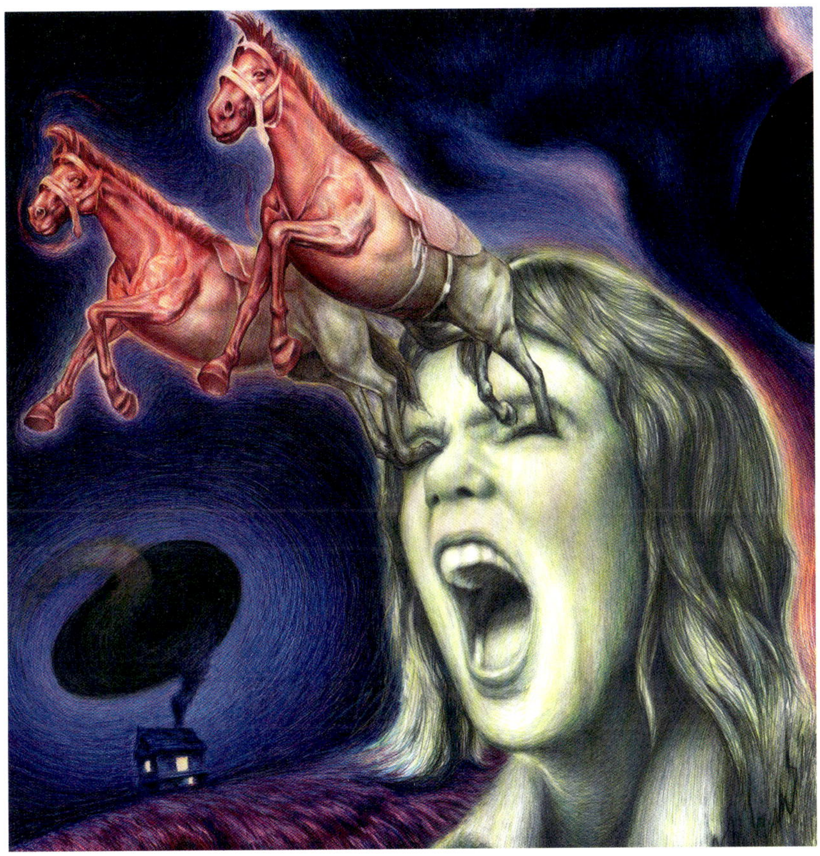

Mitya Fenechkin keeps a visual diary of daily life during wartime, recording his days with intense colors and poignant, often graphic drawings.

Mitya Fenechkin lives and works in Odesa, but considers himself a native of Kharkiv, where he lived for many years. Fenechkin is an artist, designer, and illustrator. He has worked as both an interior and graphic designer, and his work has featured in various art books and album covers. Using image and color, he depicts the complexity of everyday life during the war. After the invasion of Ukraine, the artist found himself unable to make art. However, once the initial shock had passed, Fenechkin began to paint again. At first it was difficult to create images of his own, so he just drew from photographs, recording what was happening, like in a diary. Now he paints mainly with watercolor pencils on paper. In 2022, his work was shown in several international exhibitions. In his work, Fenechkin frequently explores the theme of "home." Perhaps related to his frequent changes of residence, he has a heightened sense of the temporality and transience of home. The artist believes that the concept of the house is one of the boundless anthropological and cultural constants of humanity.

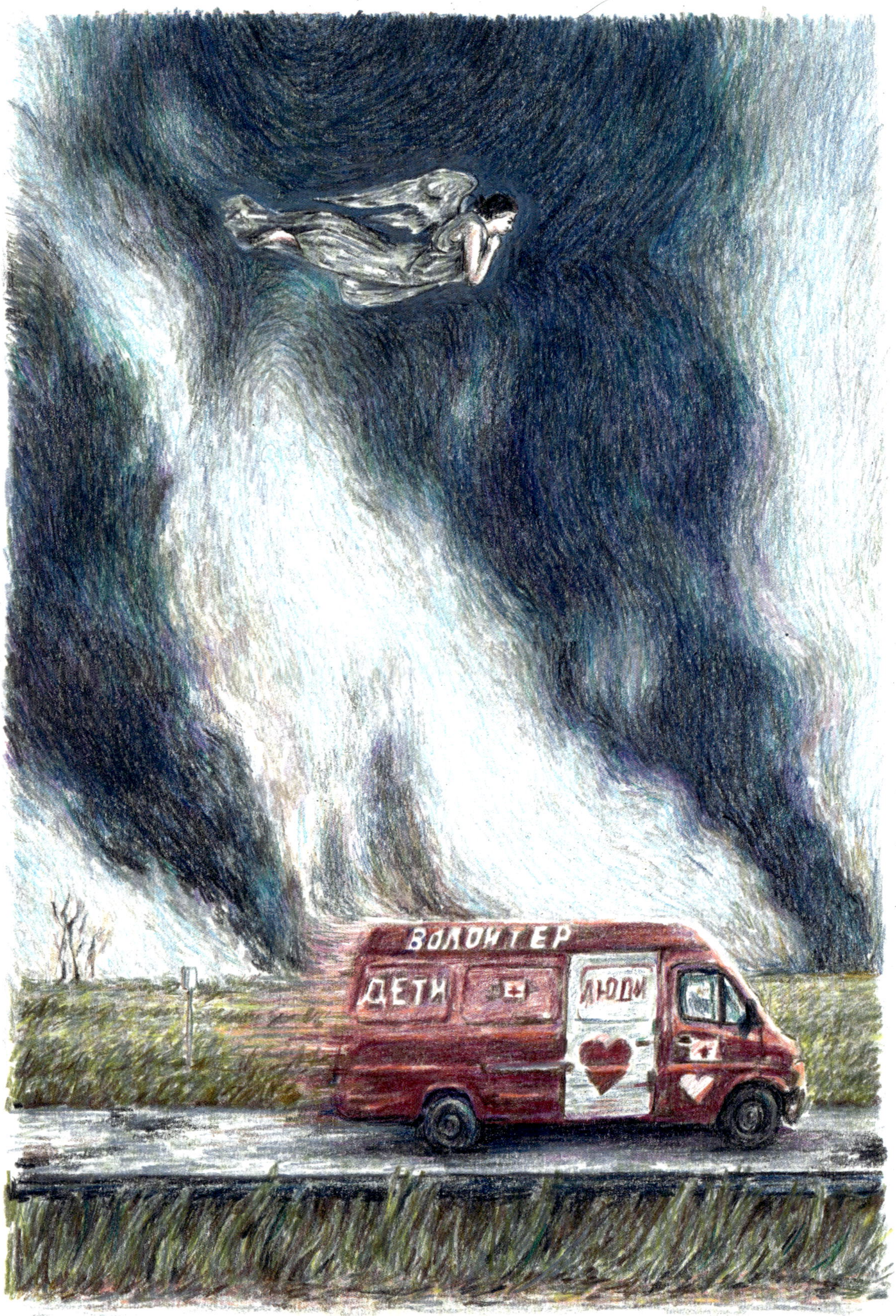
ВОЛОНТЕР
ДЕТИ
ЛЮДИ

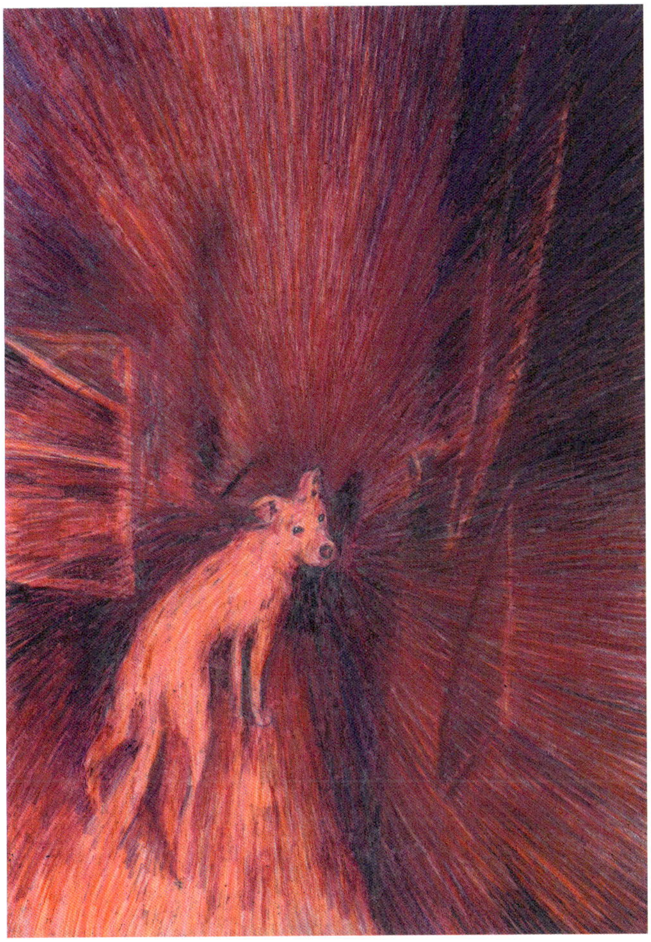

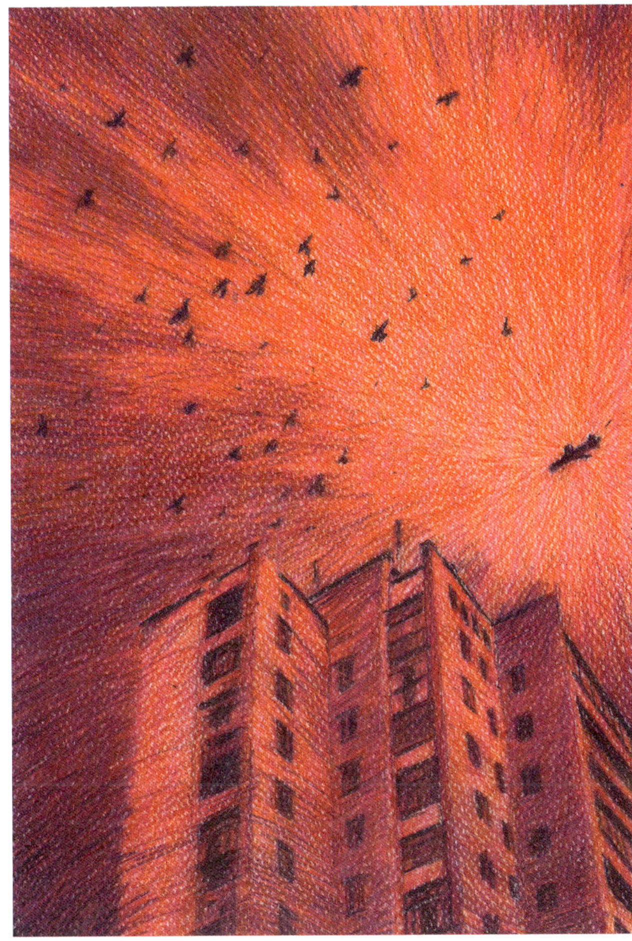

According to the artist, a restrained depiction of the war is impossible. Each of his artworks is bursting with the turbulent emotions Fenechkin has experienced in recent months. Opposite page: *Volunteers*, "Bravery. Made in Ukraine" series. Previous pages: a work from the series "What's Going on at Your Home?," 2022 (p. 132); *Keep Calm*, 2022 (p. 133).

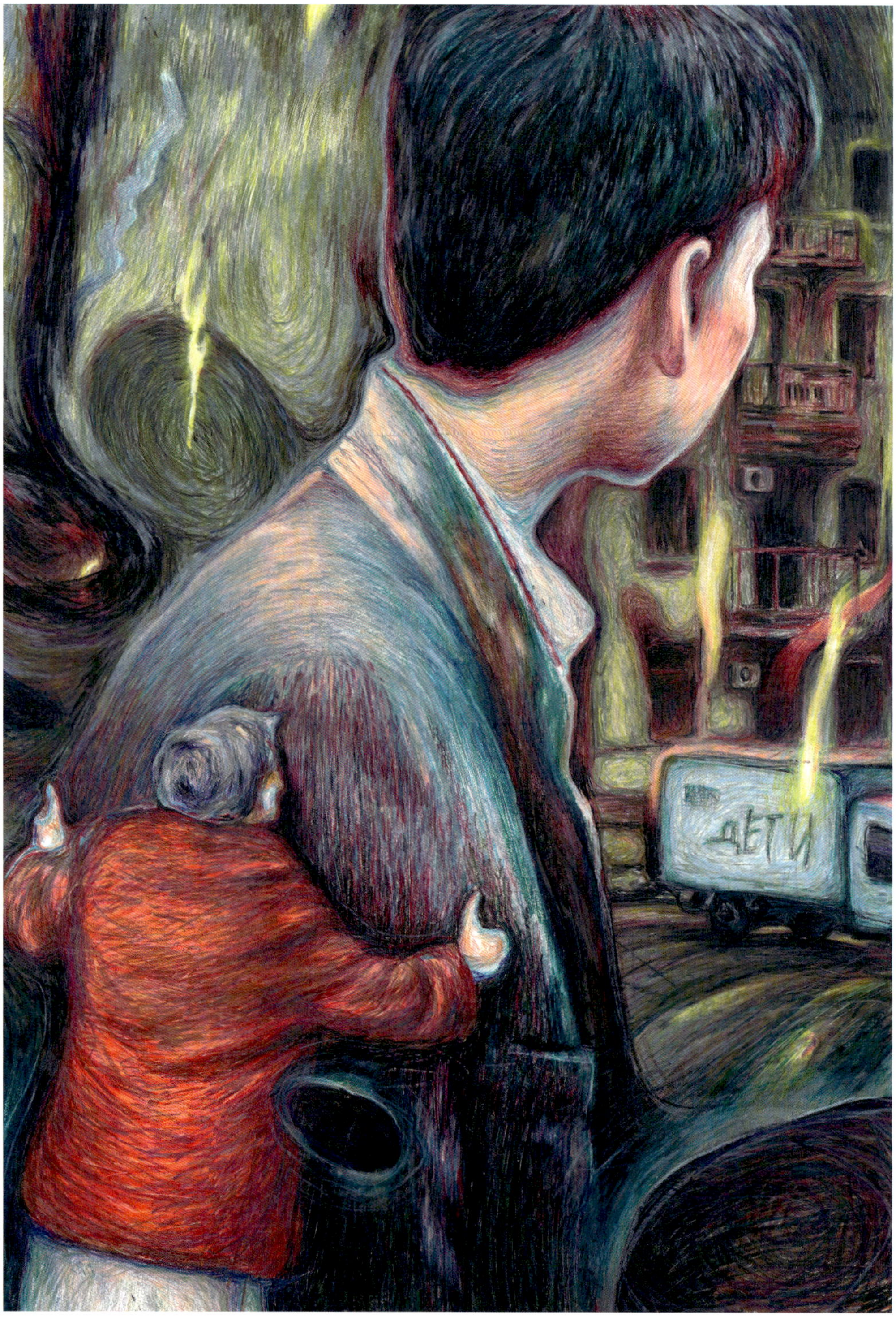

War gives rise to too many images, some of which are forever embedded in the subconscious. The artist was most painfully struck by photos of children who had been injured or killed. Opposite page: From the series “What’s Going on at Your Home?”

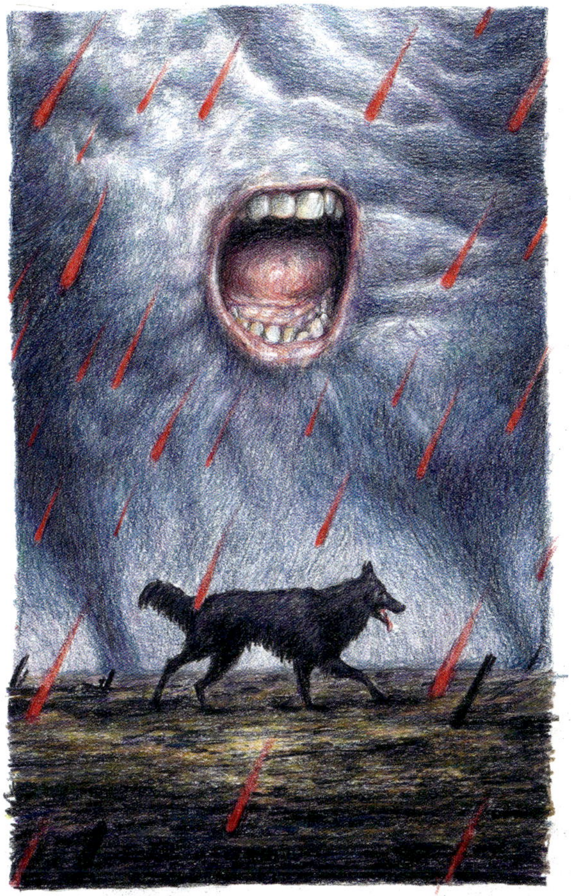
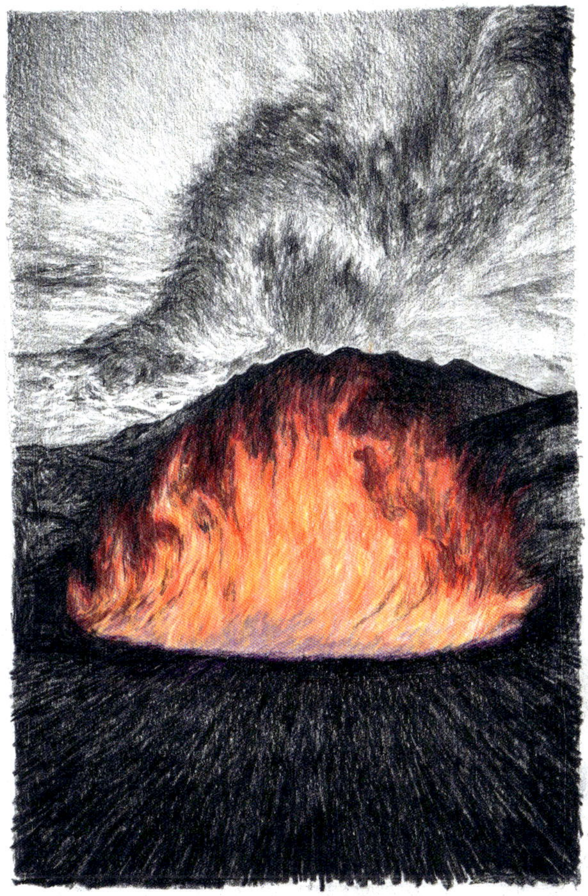
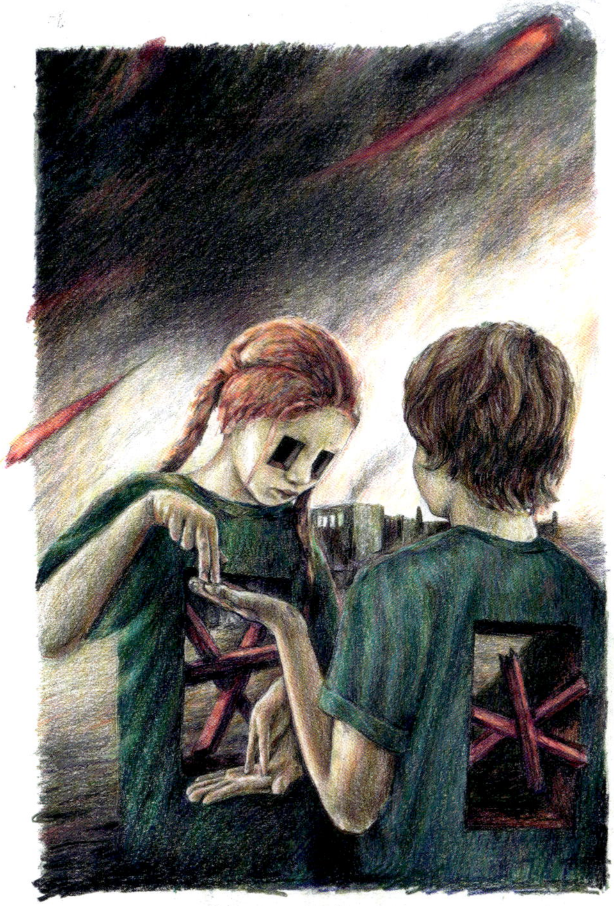
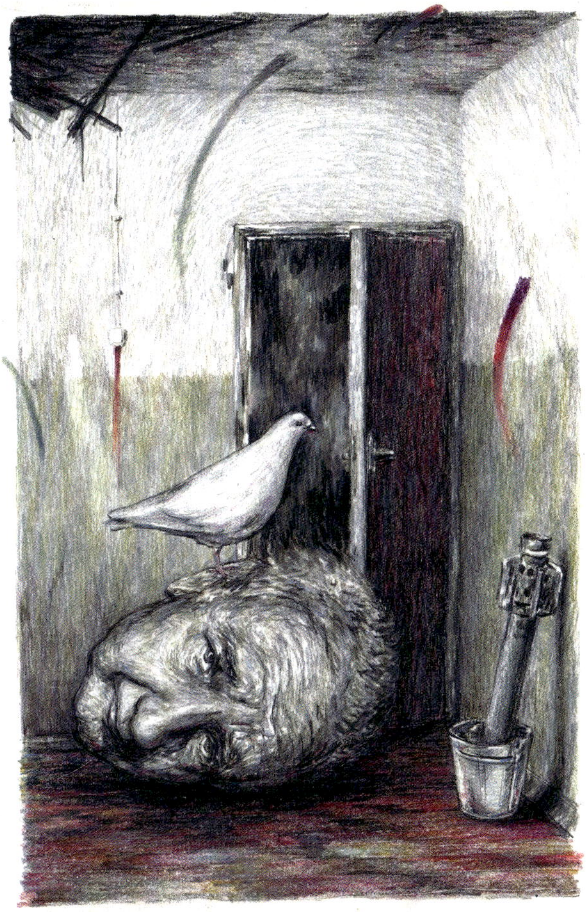

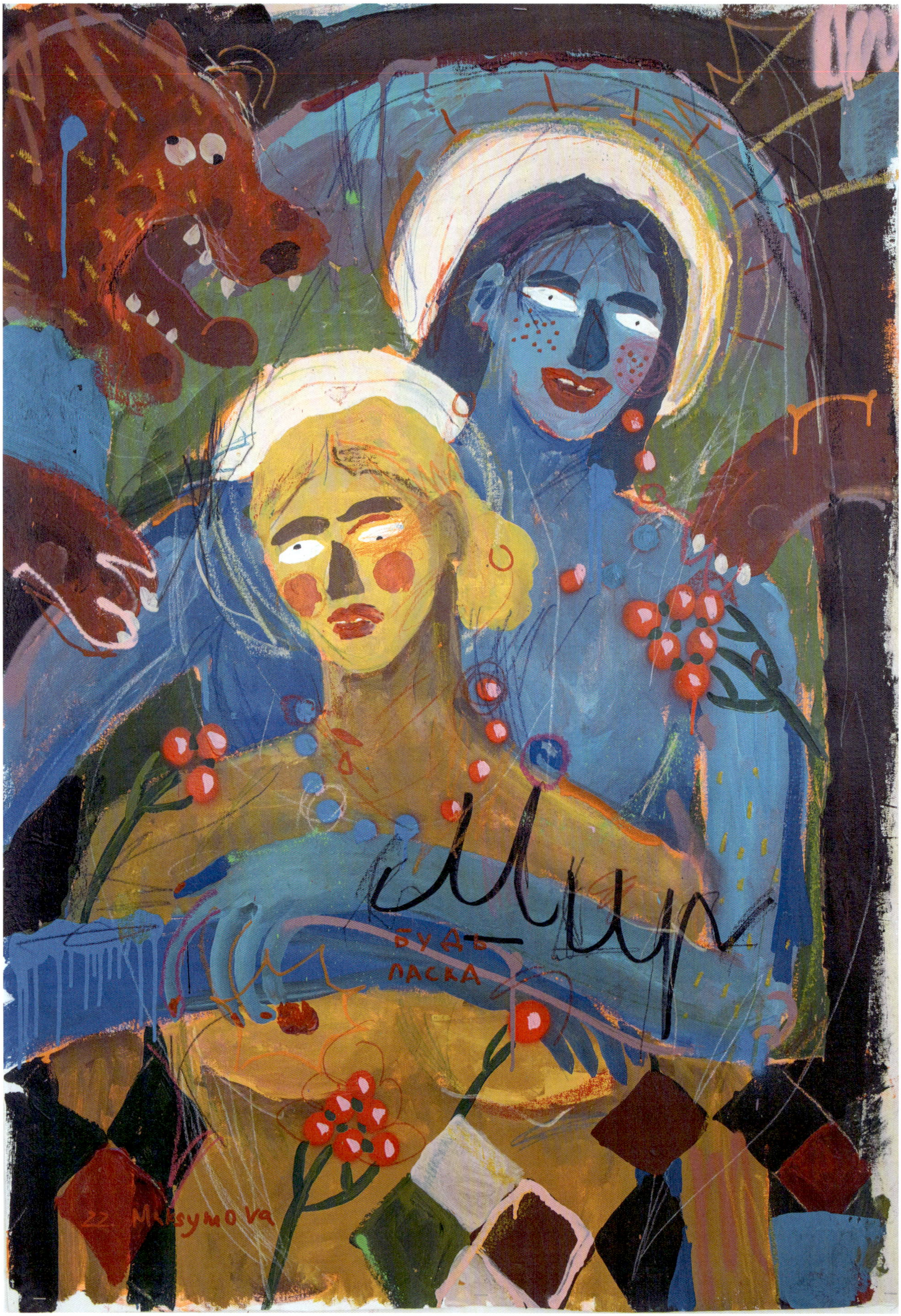
Мир
БУДЬ
ЛАСКА

NEW NAIVE ART

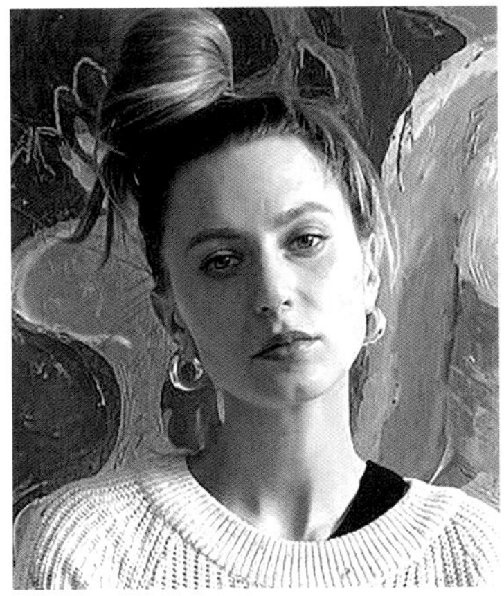

IRYNA MAKSYMOVA · *ІРИНА МАКСИМОВА*

Through her figurative artworks, Iryna Maksymova gives an innocent and candid voice to the global issues that affect her personally.

"Somebody might say that all these themes have been on everyone's lips already for a long time. Although why be silent if you have something to say! Every work is a voice, a manifesto, it's a call for action," Iryna Maksymova says. Maksymova was born and raised in a small town in the western part of Ukraine called Kolomyia. In 2020, the artist had her first solo exhibition in Lviv. Since then, she has had solo exhibitions in Ukraine as well as various group exhibitions in the U.K., Spain, China, the United States, Germany, Australia, and many others. The artist's works are in private collections in almost 25 countries. For Maksymova, art is a way to live her life and express herself, sense the world, and share her thoughts. Her art is lively, almost bursting with vitality. The plots, color contrasts, and characters in the paintings may seem simplistic and playful at first glance, but the works convey profound messages about feminism, sexism, ecology, inhumanity, and cruelty to animals. The artist also explores the female body as both feminine and masculine, valuing equality and interconnection. Maksymova often weaves Ukraine into her work, incorporating Ukrainian words and national symbols into her paintings. She is constantly looking for and developing ways to add traditional motifs to new visual forms, and to cultivate the national vernacular of folk art. When she creates a work, she typically prepares a sketch about a particular theme that's been on her mind, giving careful attention to the composition, the colors, and the main idea. But sometimes this process happens spontaneously: she just comes to her studio and starts putting paint on canvas. Meaning, concepts, and ideas simply arise in the process. Shapes, characters, and objects generate thoughts and new stories. The artist works in a variety of sizes, but prefers to paint on large canvases. Maksymova likes to create depth and dimension and often adds fine details and textures—things that small canvases struggle to accommodate.

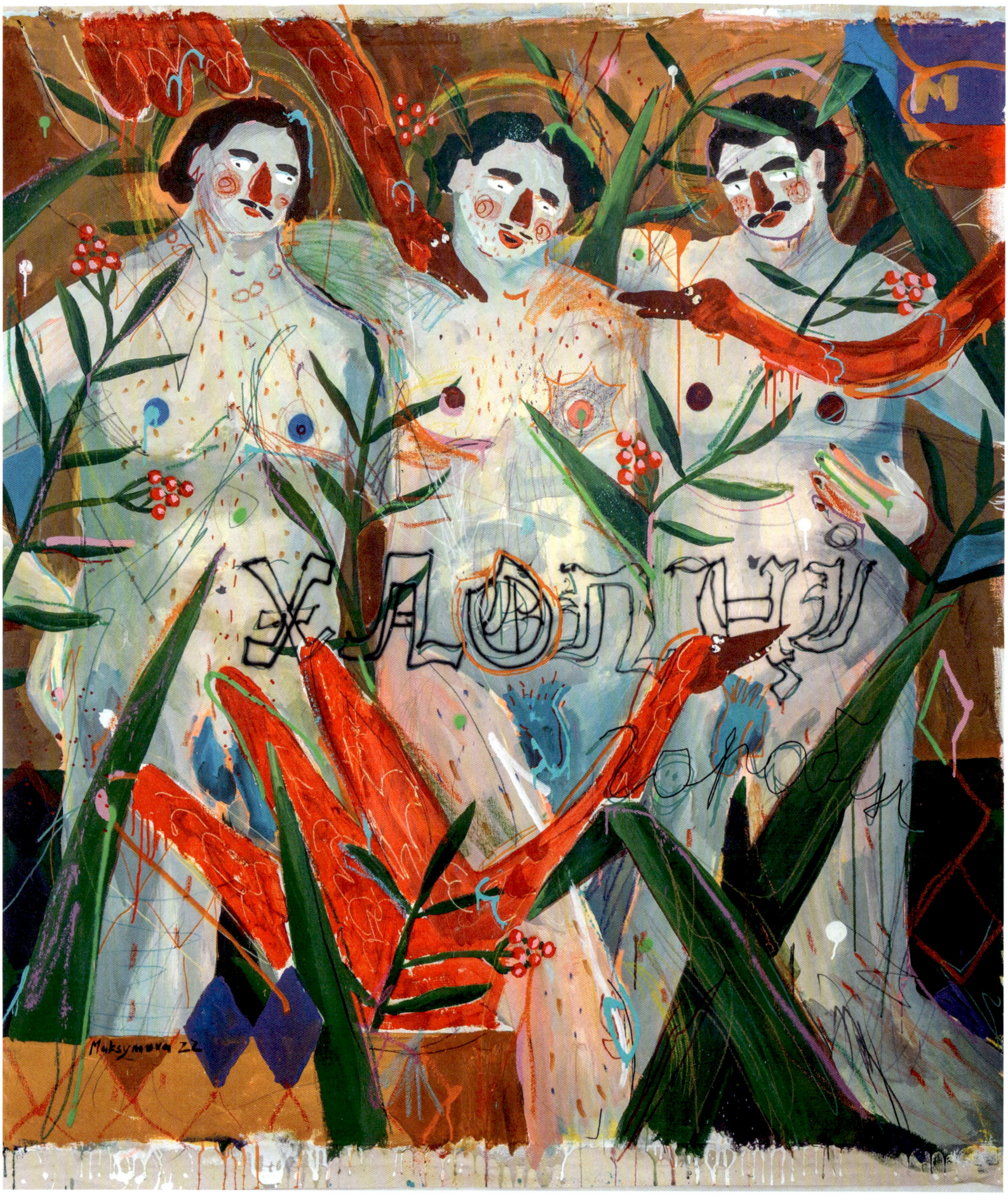
Maksymova 22

"In my works, I want to show a desire for victory and the strength of the nation. In peacetime, I thought about women and their place in everyday life. With the beginning of the war, the woman became for me a symbol of the whole country."

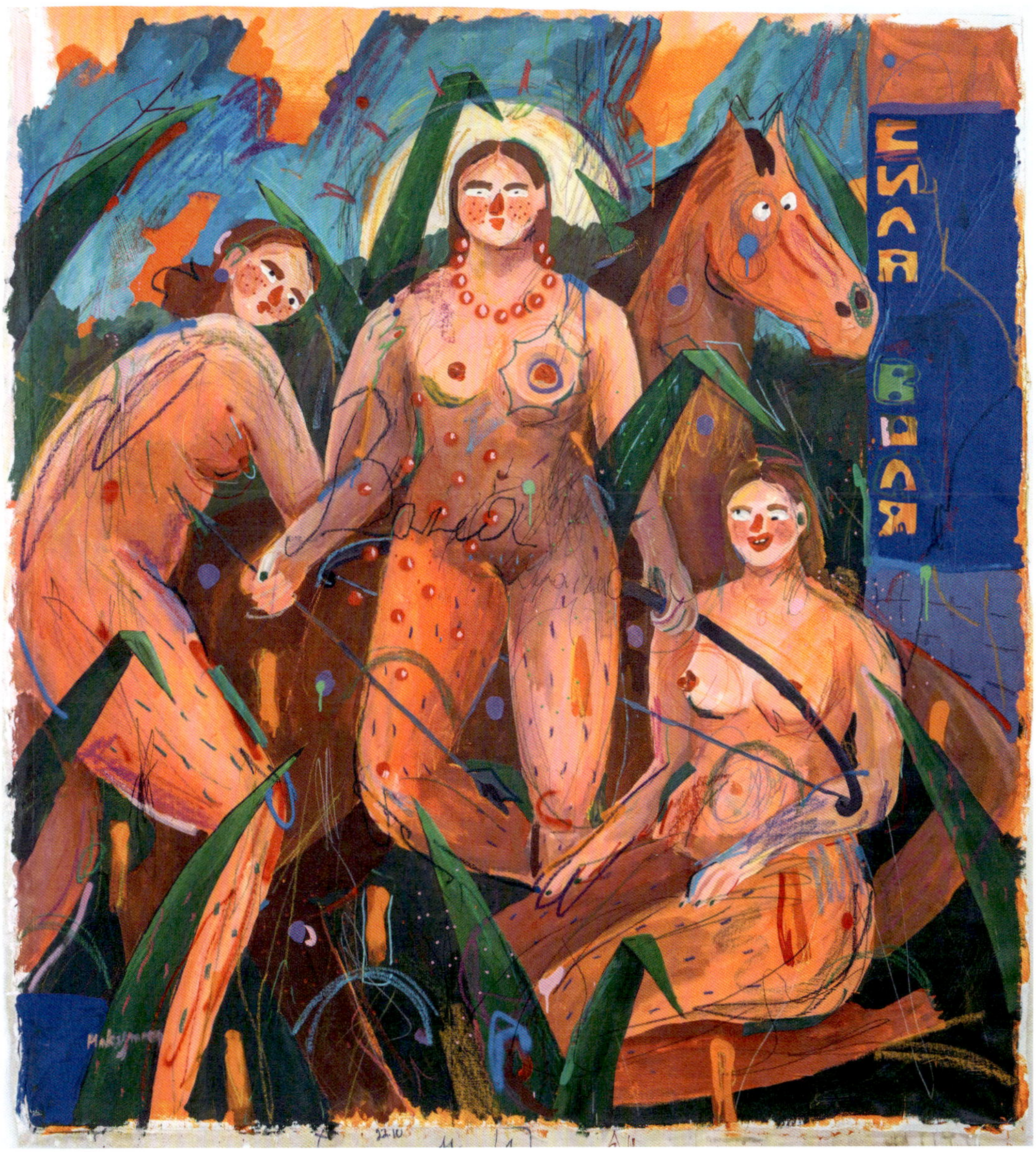

Iryna Maksymova prefers painting on large canvases. Above: *The Archer*, acrylic, pastels, spray, and markers on canvas, 2022. Opposite page: *Boys*, acrylic, pastels, spray paint, and markers on canvas, 2022. Page 138: *Blue and yellow*, acrylic, pastels, spray paint, and markers on canvas, 2022.

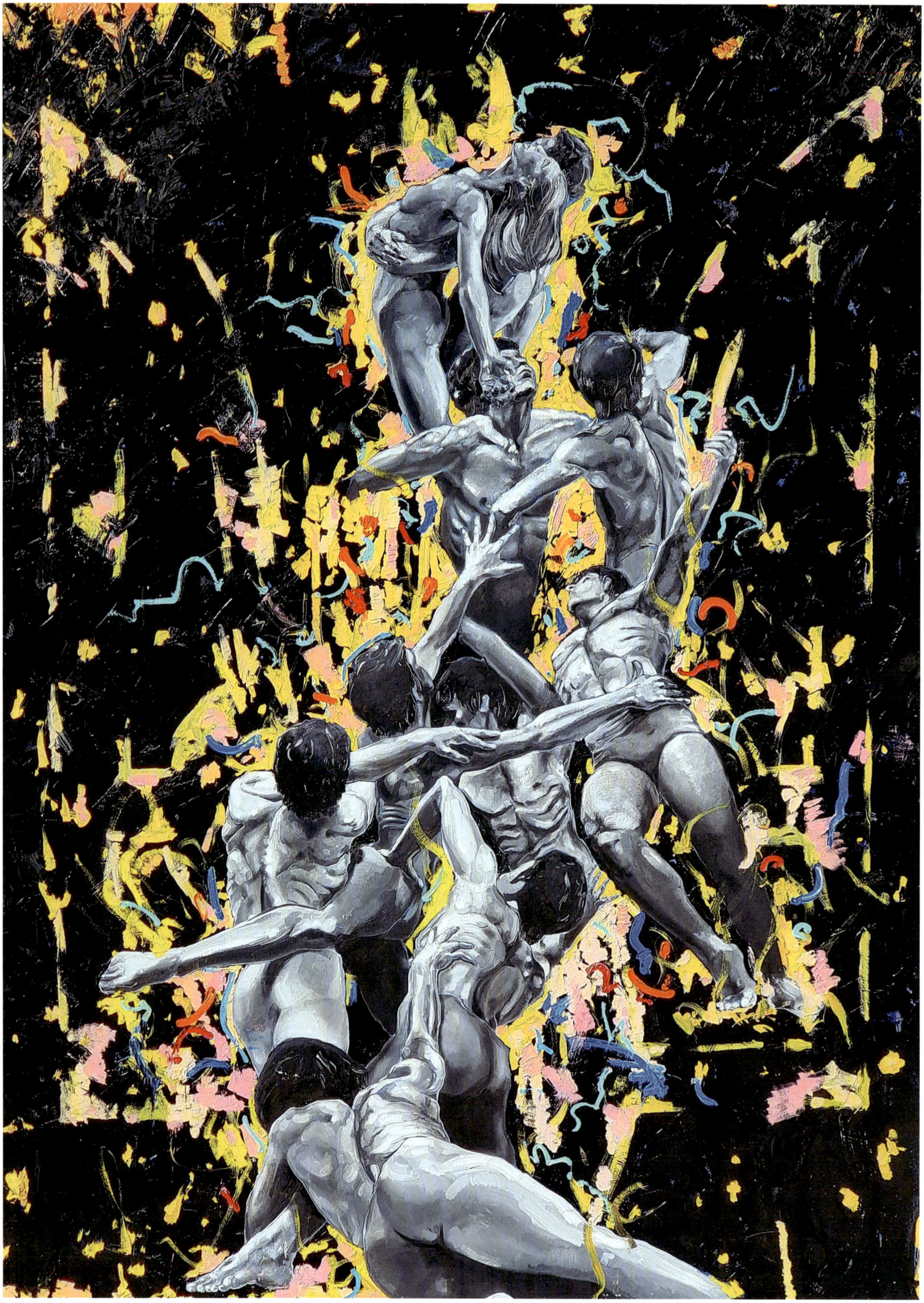

CAPTURING LIFE'S ENERGY THROUGH COLOR AND CONTRAST

LES PANCHYSHYN · *ЛЕСЬ ПАНЧИШИН*

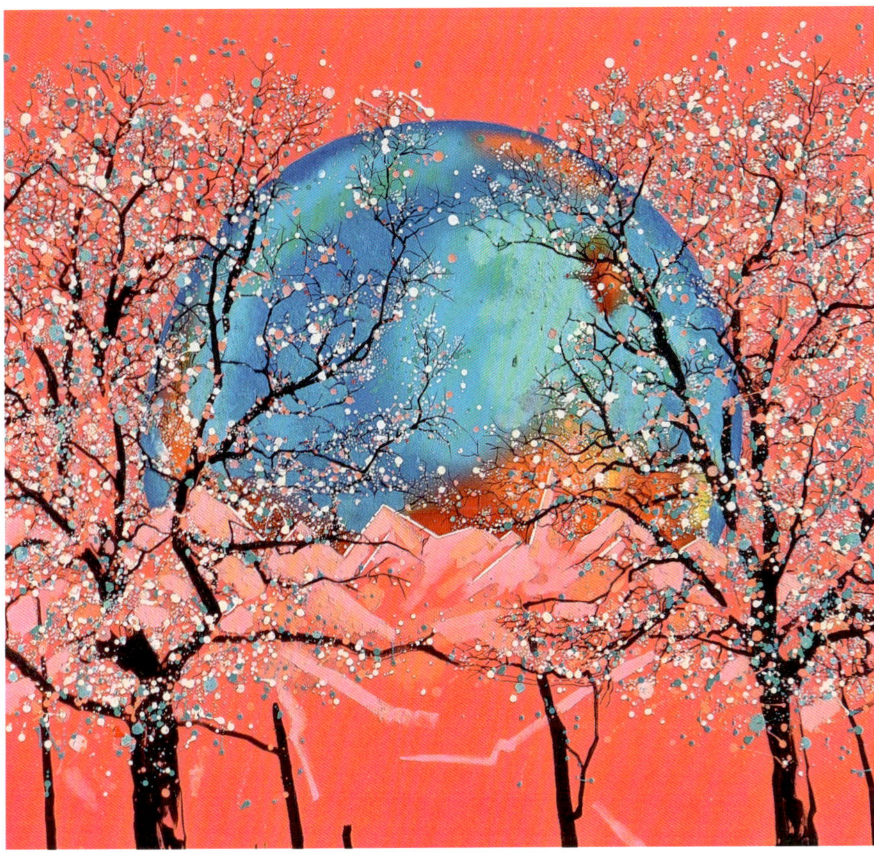

Les Panchyshyn's art is vivid, bold, and animate, full of contrasting colors, energy, and emotions. He explores all manifestations of nature and mankind and reflects the surrounding world in his works.

Born in Novyi Rozdil in the Lviv region, Les Panchyshyn spent his entire youth exploring various forms of creative self-expression. He participated in a folk-dance troupe, studied painting and sculpture, and developed an interest in photography as a student. Later, he became more serious about painting, his preferred medium these days. Panchyshyn uses bold, contrasting colors, with bright shades of red, blue, and yellow dominating his palette. Employing playful shapes and vibrant colors, Panchyshyn paints scenes of flora and fauna, as well as the human form. His paintings of people explore human nature and how it manifests through movement and gesture. Panchyshyn has also used his distinctive style to depict the events of the war in Ukraine. In his series "We Will Never Forget," Panchyshyn depicts scenes of destruction in vivid colors; the jarring contrast between the dark subject matter and the bright colors powerfully highlights the stark disparity between everyday life and the horrors of war.

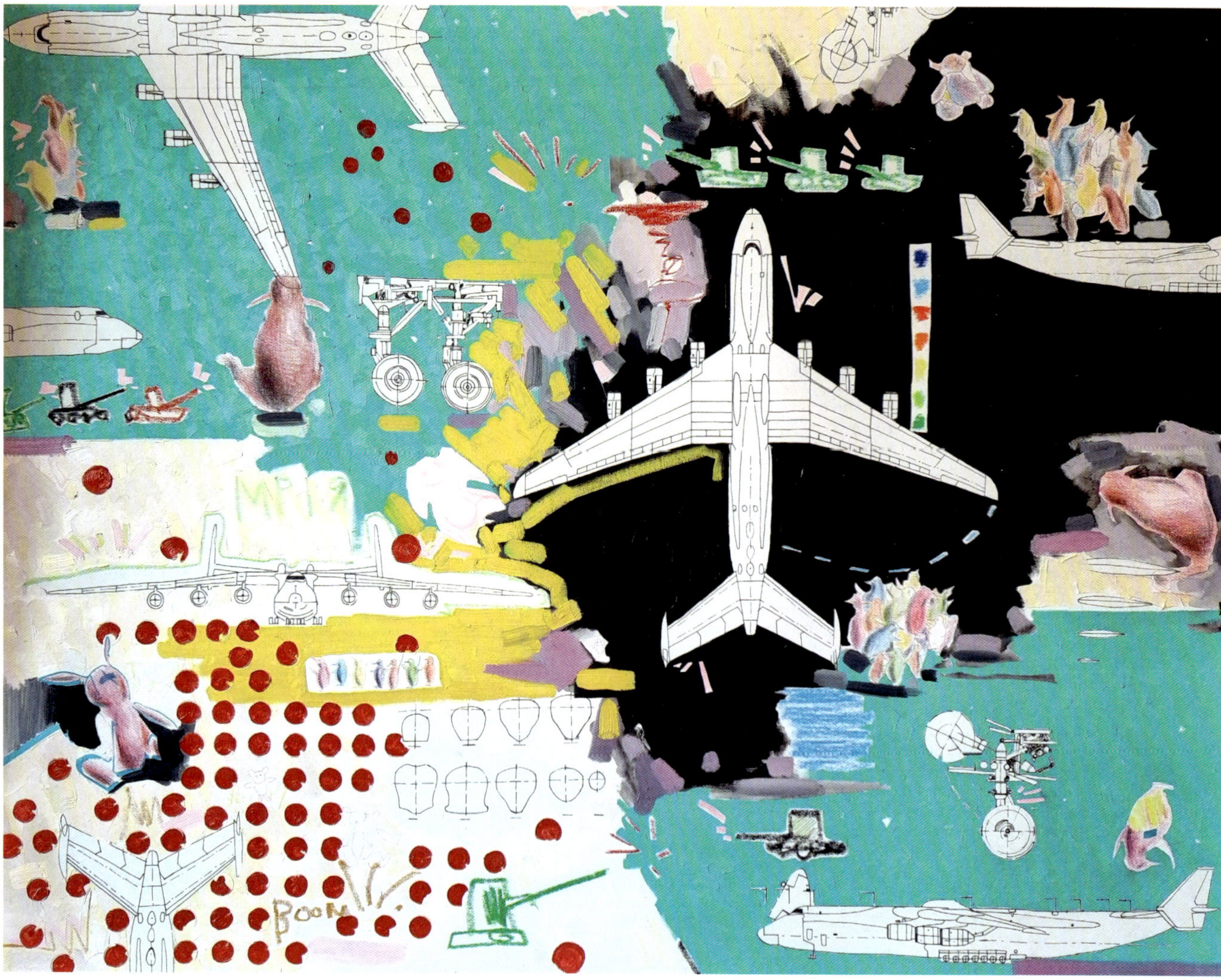

The work *Mriya* shows drawings of the world's largest plane, the Antonov AN-225, destroyed in the first days of the Russian invasion of Ukraine. The enormous aircraft, named Mriya ("dream" in Ukrainian), has acquired cult status in the aviation world. Previous pages: *Volia*, oil on canvas, 2022 (p. 142); *Mountain Cherry Blossoms*, oil, acrylic, and spray paint on canvas, 2022 (p. 143).

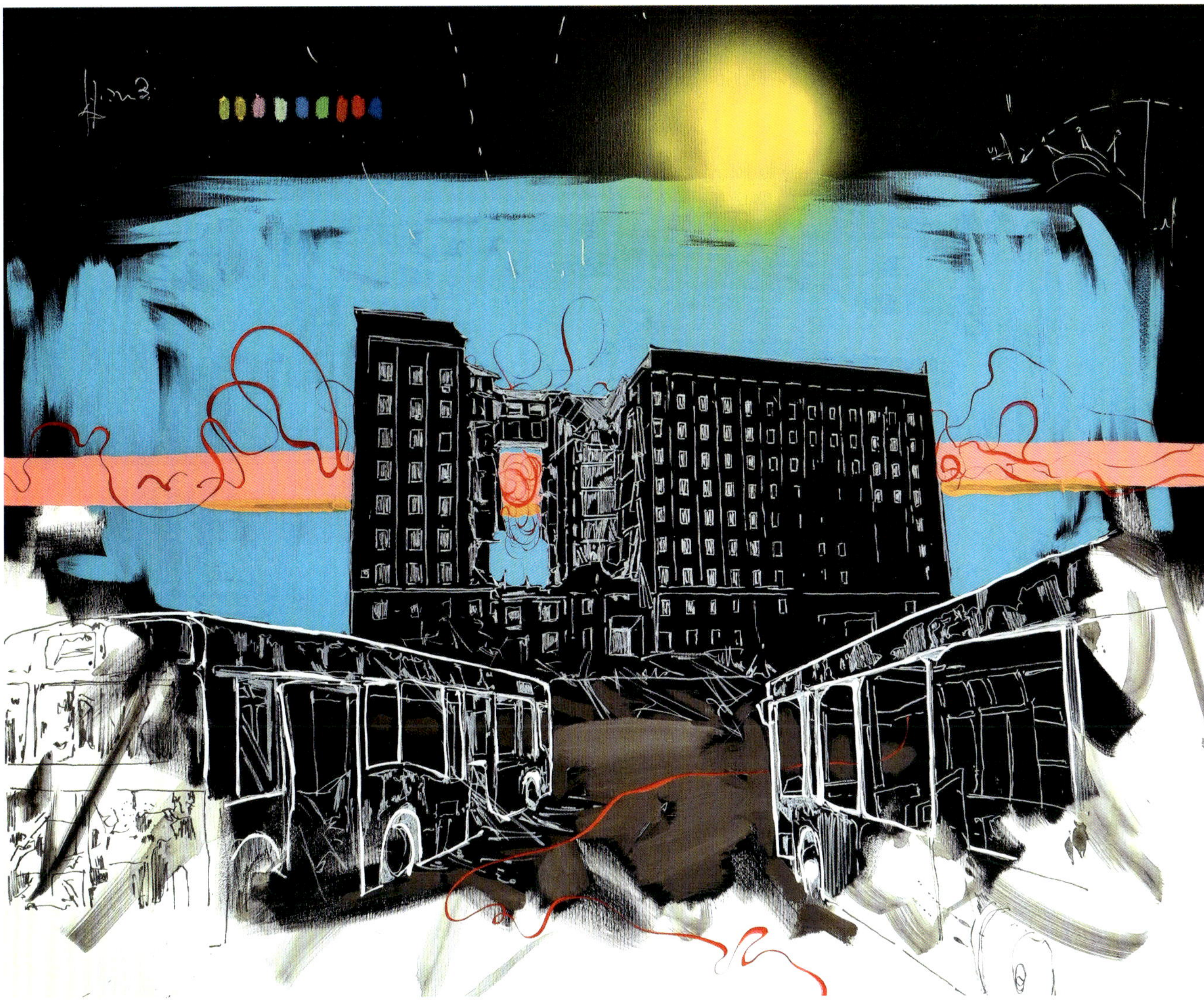

In his paintings about the war, Panchyshyn documents the crimes of the Russian Federation against Ukraine. The painting *Mykolaiv* portrays the Mykolaiv Regional State Administration's headquarters after being hit by a missile.

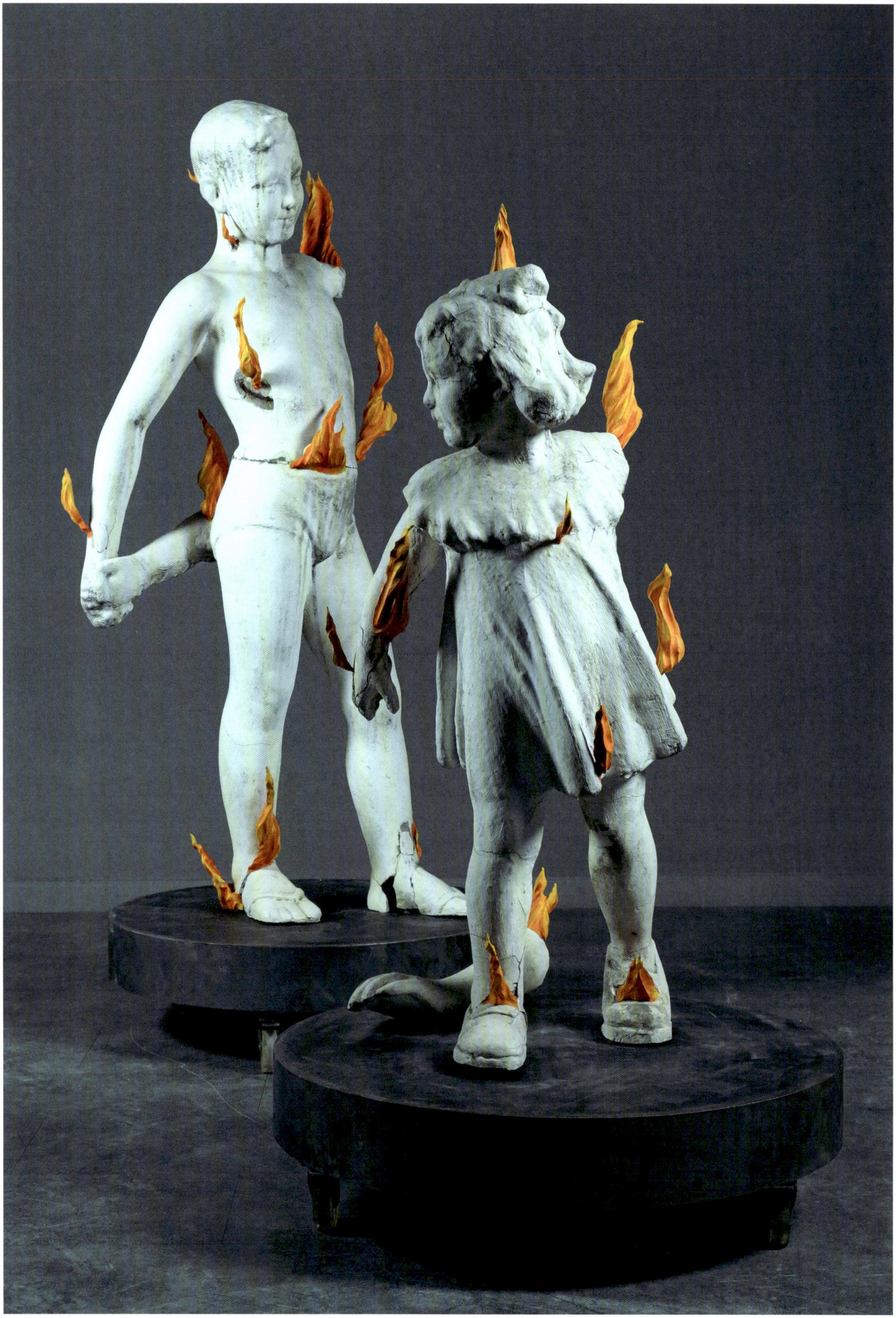

INDUSTRIAL SYSTEMS VS. NATURAL ENVIRONMENT

VASYL DMYTRYK · *ВАСИЛЬ ДМИТРИК*

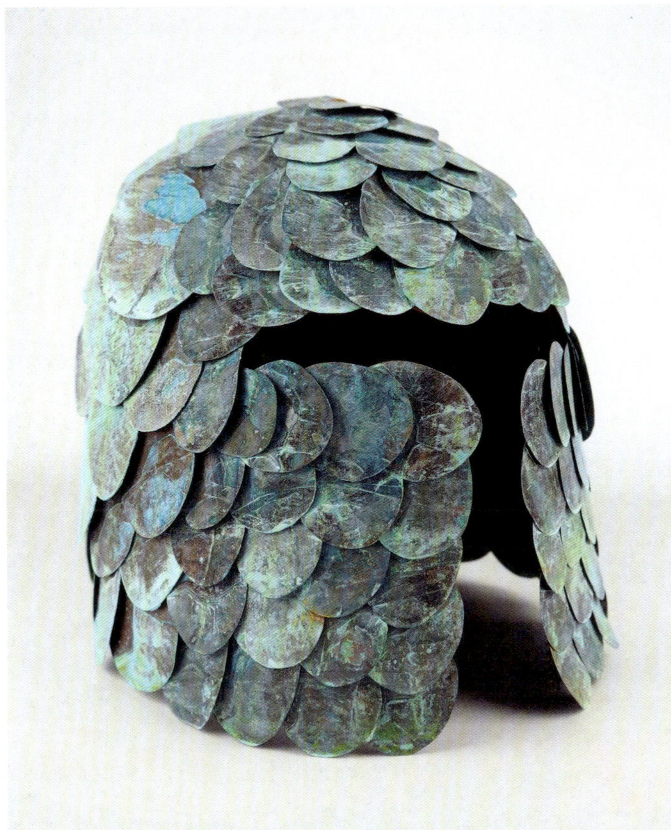

In his artistic practice, Vasyl Dmytryk often explores the interplay between industrial systems and the natural environment, especially where new harmonised connections emerge between them.

Born in Ivano-Frankivsk, Vasyl Dmytryk now lives and works in Odesa, where he is a member of the creative community SRZ-2. He works mainly in sculpture and art installation, using wood, metal, composites, found objects, and various other materials. His work, which can be found in private collections and museums around the world, draws on the artistic traditions and visual imagery of several cultures and historical periods. For Dmytryk, art is the search for the fundamental connections between the elements of a given work, be it an assemblage, installation, or sculpture. As he creates, he also tries to find the links between himself and his work, and between the work and the viewer. He believes that a person or society does not have a fixed identity; identity is always in flux, and because of this, its manifestations are sometimes invisible; while at other times, like in today's Ukraine, they can be perceived by everyone. Since the outbreak of the war, Dmytryk has switched to other media: for example, he has begun to paint more.

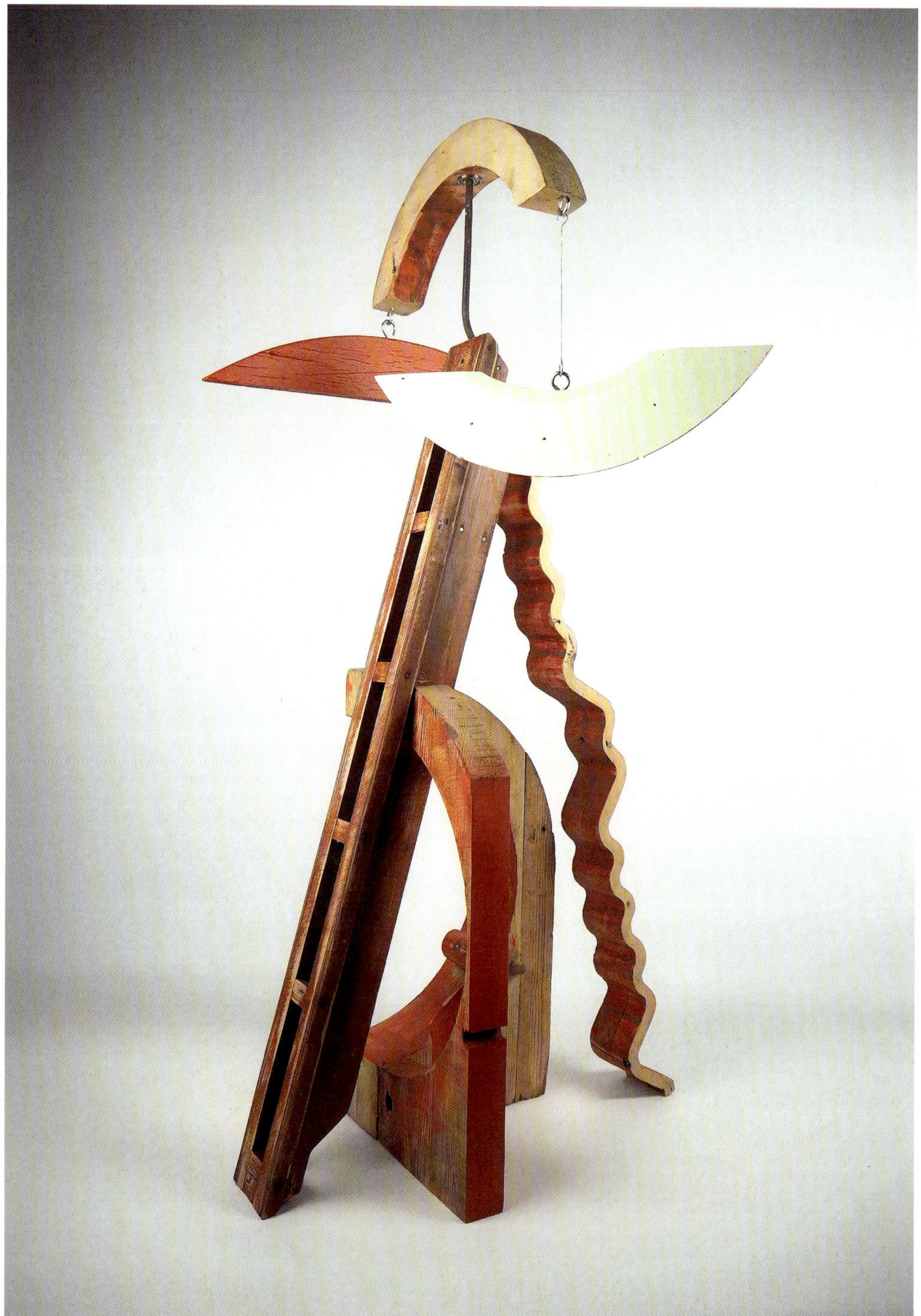

The materials used for objects from the *Industrial Fairytale* installation are wooden models, and molds found on the territory of a former shipyard. The sculptor transforms these objects, referring to his creative imagination and cultural memory of this place.

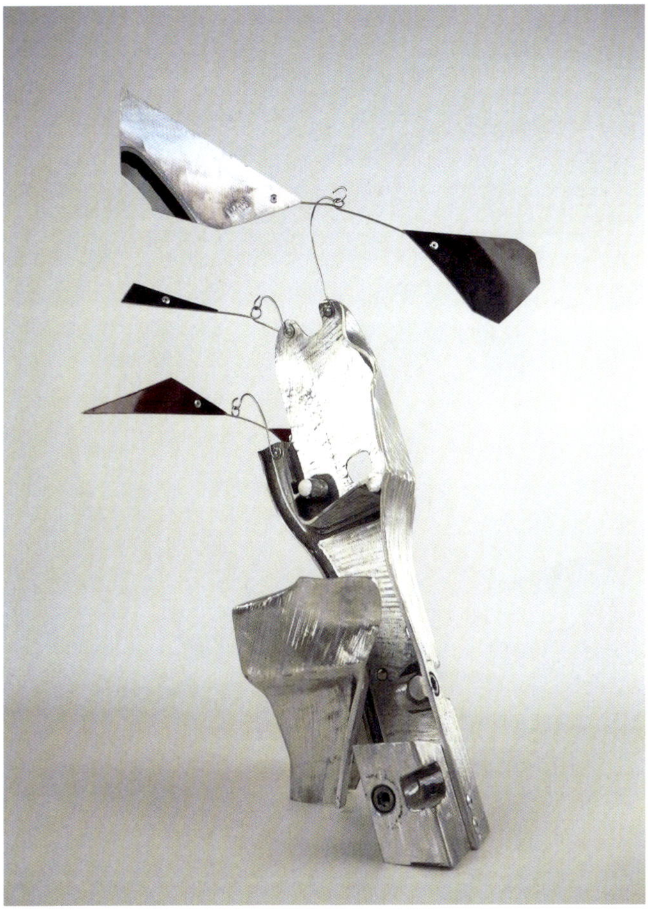
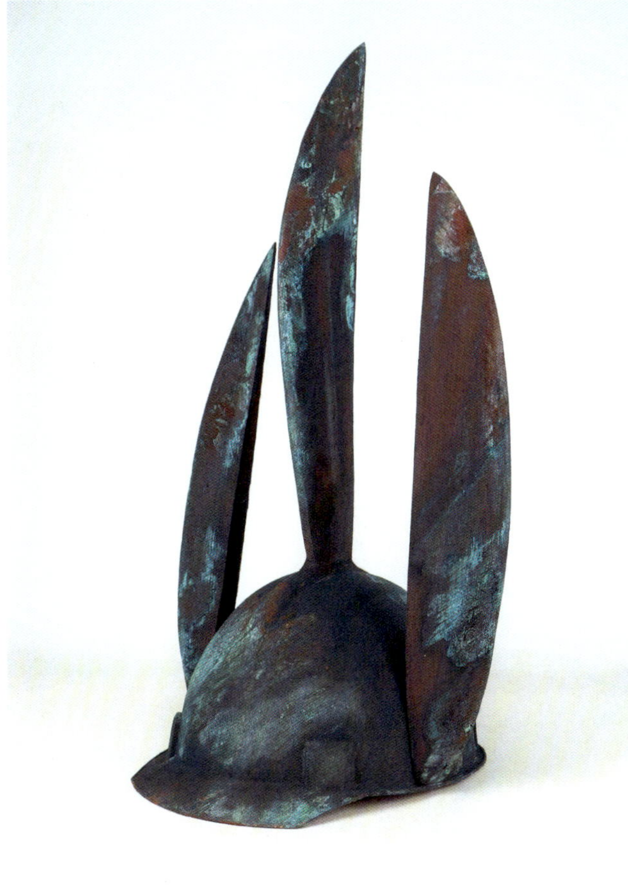
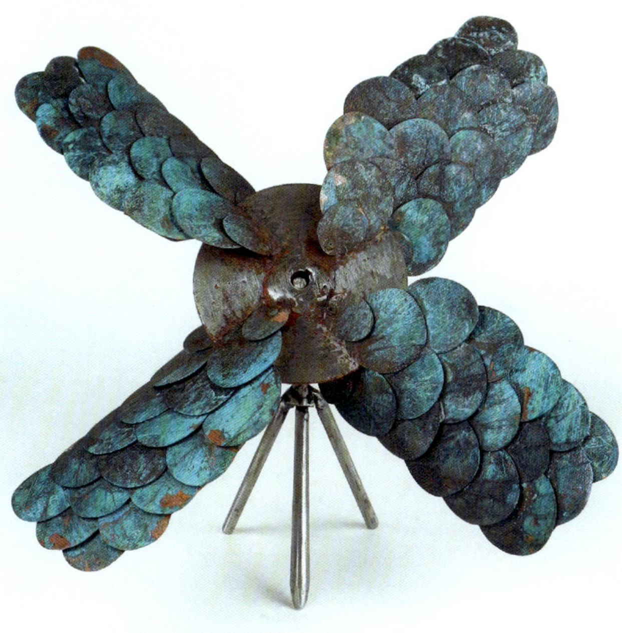
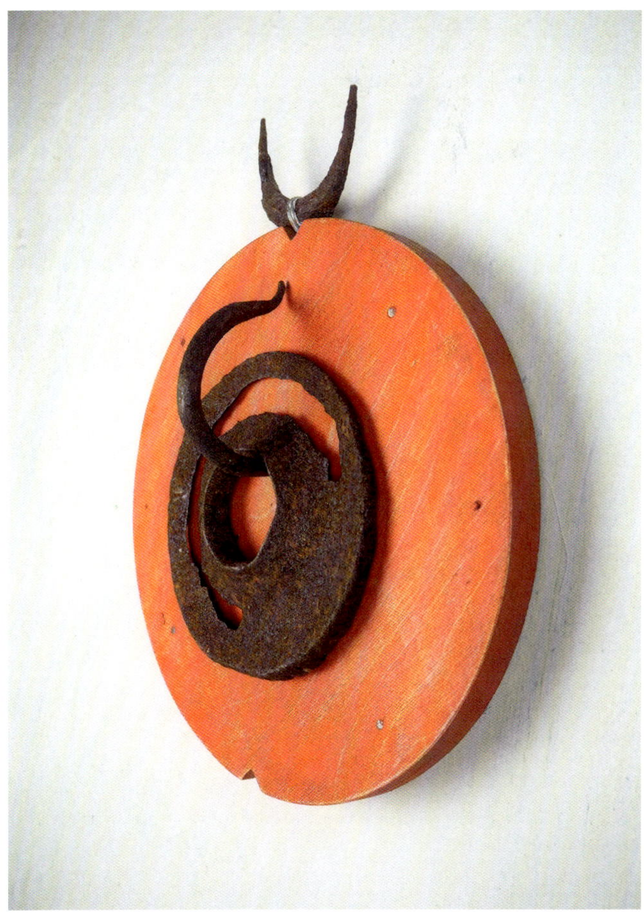

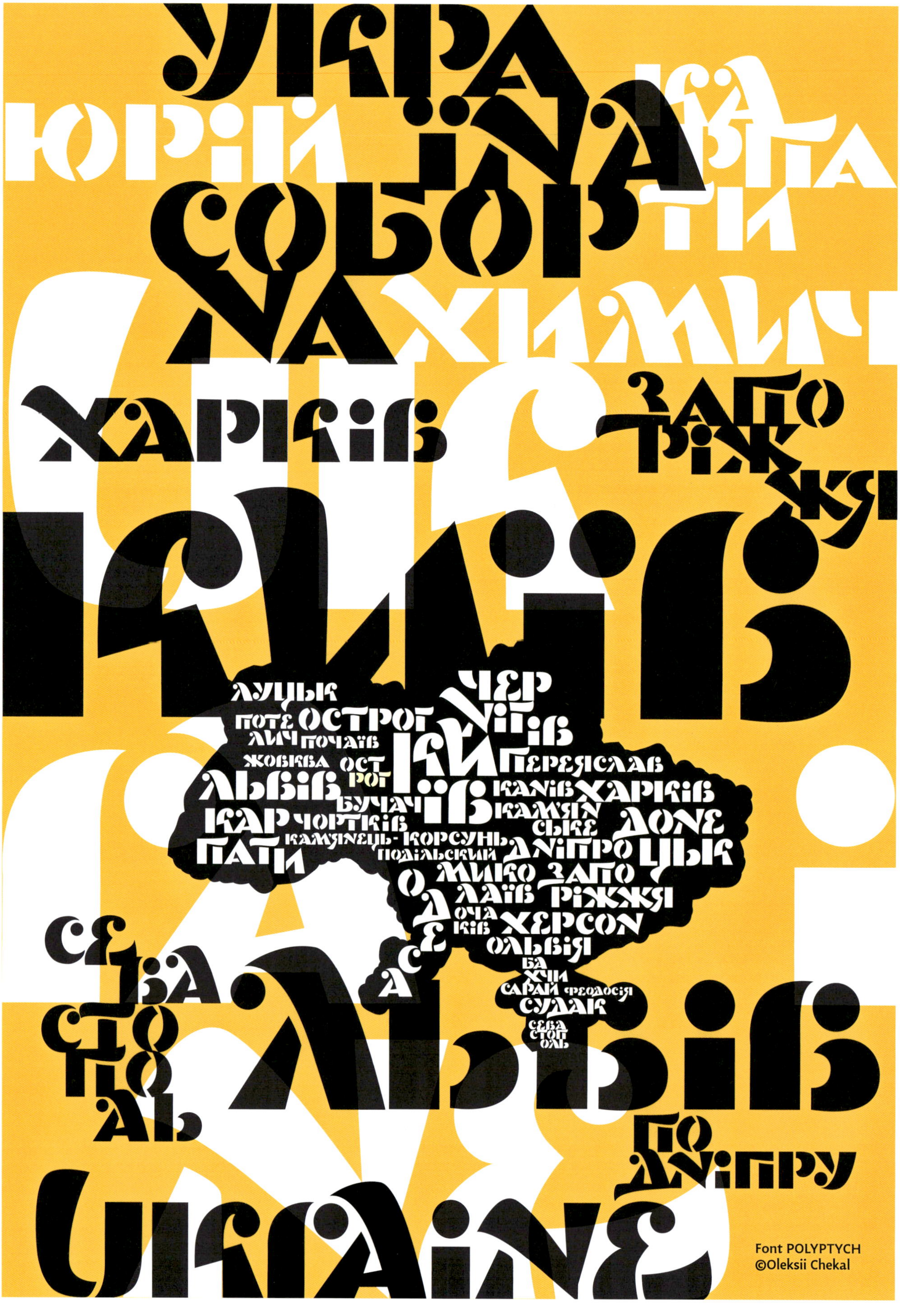
УКРАЇНА
ЮРІЙ
СОБОР
ХАРКІВ
ЗАПОРІЖЖЯ
КИЇВ
ЛУЦЬК
ПОТЕЛИЧ
ОСТРОГ
ПОЧАЇВ
ЧЕРНІГІВ
ЖОВКВА
ЛЬВІВ
ПЕРЕЯСЛАВ
КАНІВ
ХАРКІВ
БУЧАЧ
КАРПАТИ
ЧОРТКІВ
КАМ'ЯНСЬКЕ
ДОНЕЦЬК
КАМ'ЯНЕЦЬ-ПОДІЛЬСКИЙ
КОРСУНЬ
ДНІПРО
МИКОЛАЇВ
ЗАПОРІЖЖЯ
ОДЕСА
ОЧАКІВ
ХЕРСОН
ОЛЬВІЯ
БАХЧИСАРАЙ
ФЕОДОСІЯ
СУДАК
СЕВАСТОПОЛЬ
СЕВАСТОПОЛЬ
ЛЬВІВ
ПО ДНІПРУ
UKRAINE
Font POLYPTYCH
©Oleksii Chekal

UNITING WORLDS THROUGH CALLIGRAPHY

OLEKSII CHEKAL · *ОЛЕКСІЙ ЧЕКАЛЬ*

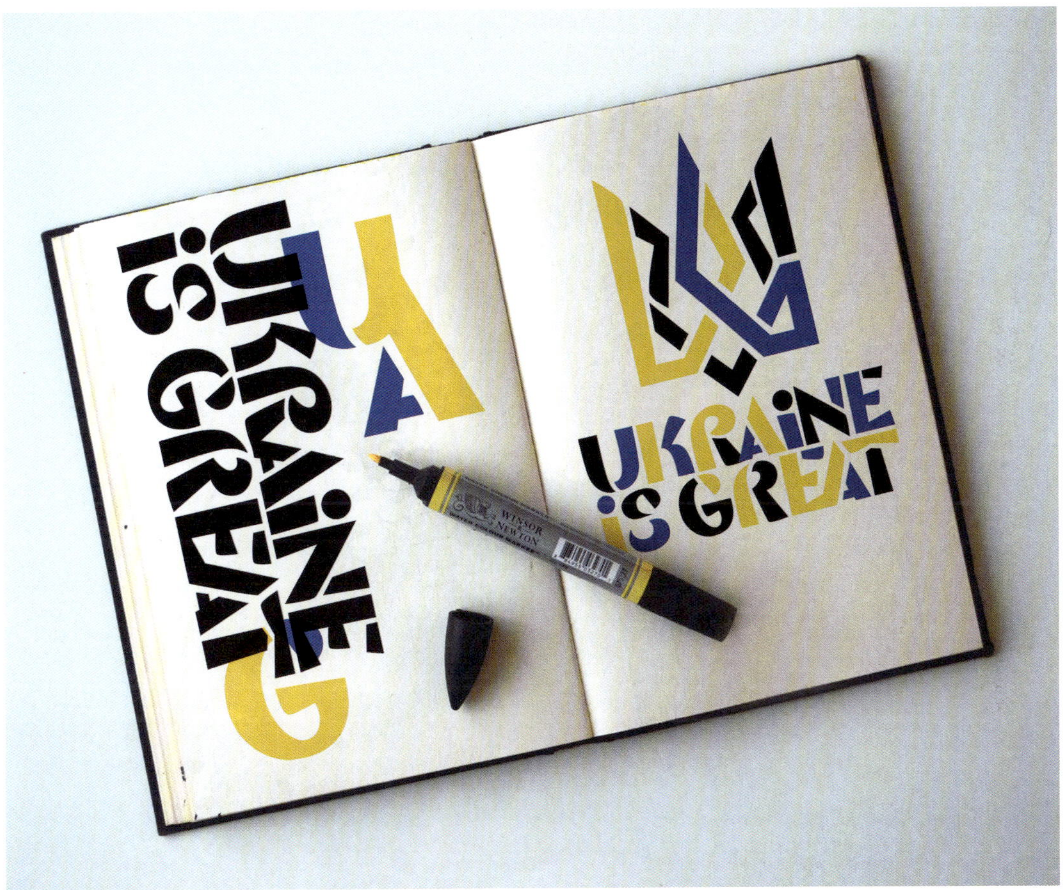

Thanks to his research of different scripts and cultures, Oleksii Chekal has created a highly specialized niche at the intersection of design, science, philology, and religion.

Oleksii Chekal, a self-proclaimed cross-cultural designer, works across various disciplines, including science, religion, and the museum world. He produces typography and calligraphy in several scripts, including Latin, Greek, Cyrillic, Hebrew, Arabic, and Syriac, referring to himself as an "itinerant calligrapher." Chekal first discovered his passion for paleography and calligraphy while studying icon painting and sacred art. Since then he has built a broad portfolio, including exhibition design about Stalin's purges and the history of Passover, church design and calligraphy, tattoo designs in Greek and Syriac, historical decorations for a conference in Oxford, Italian jewelry design, and Arabic calligraphy for books on Muslim culture. Since the war began, he's spent his time designing military chevrons and leaflets that are scattered in occupied territories, and creating logos for charity projects dedicated to helping refugees.

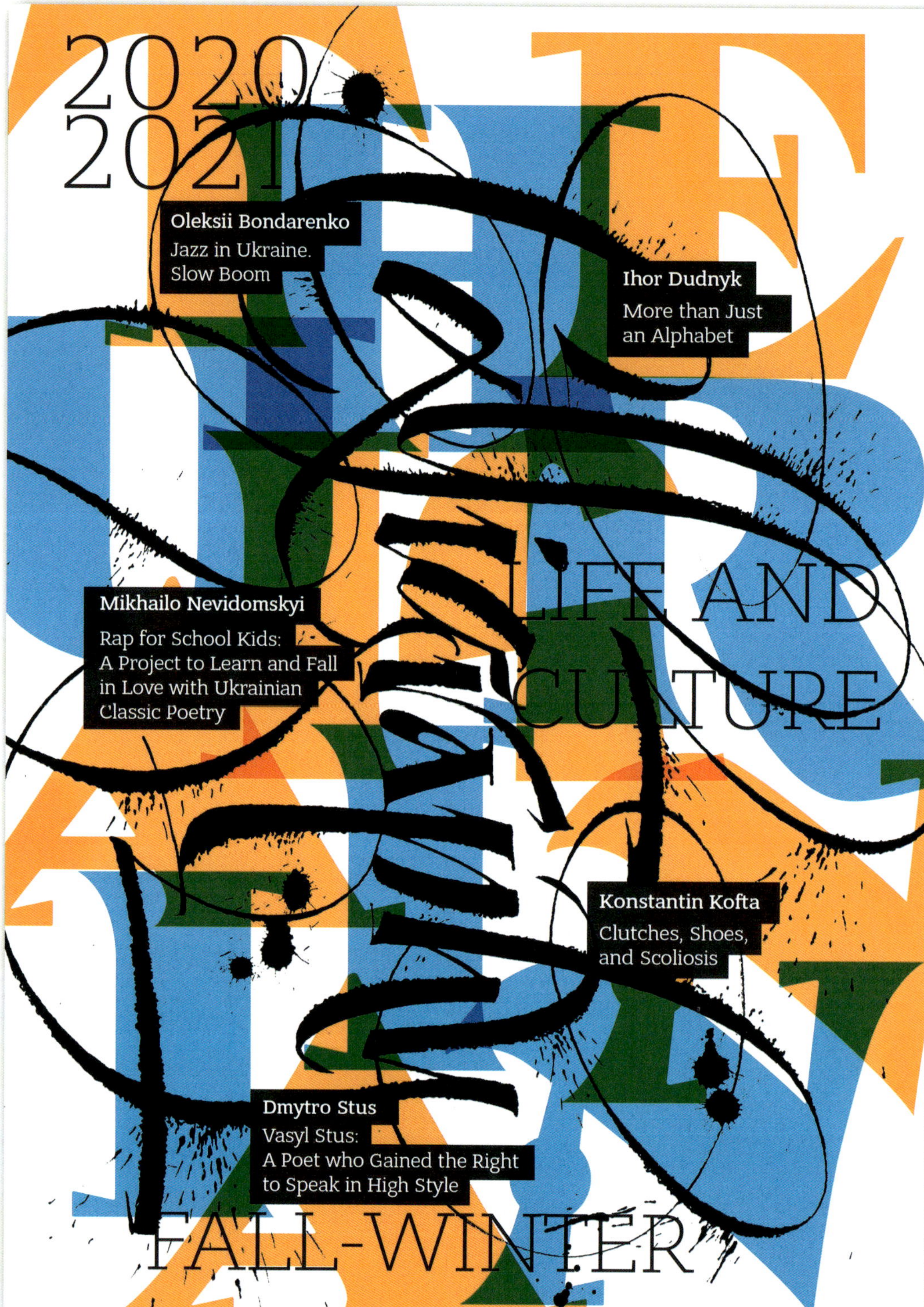

A series of covers designed by Oleksii Chekal for *The Ukrainian: Life and Culture*, an American-Ukrainian cultural magazine. London, Tbilisi, Kyiv, 2019–2020.

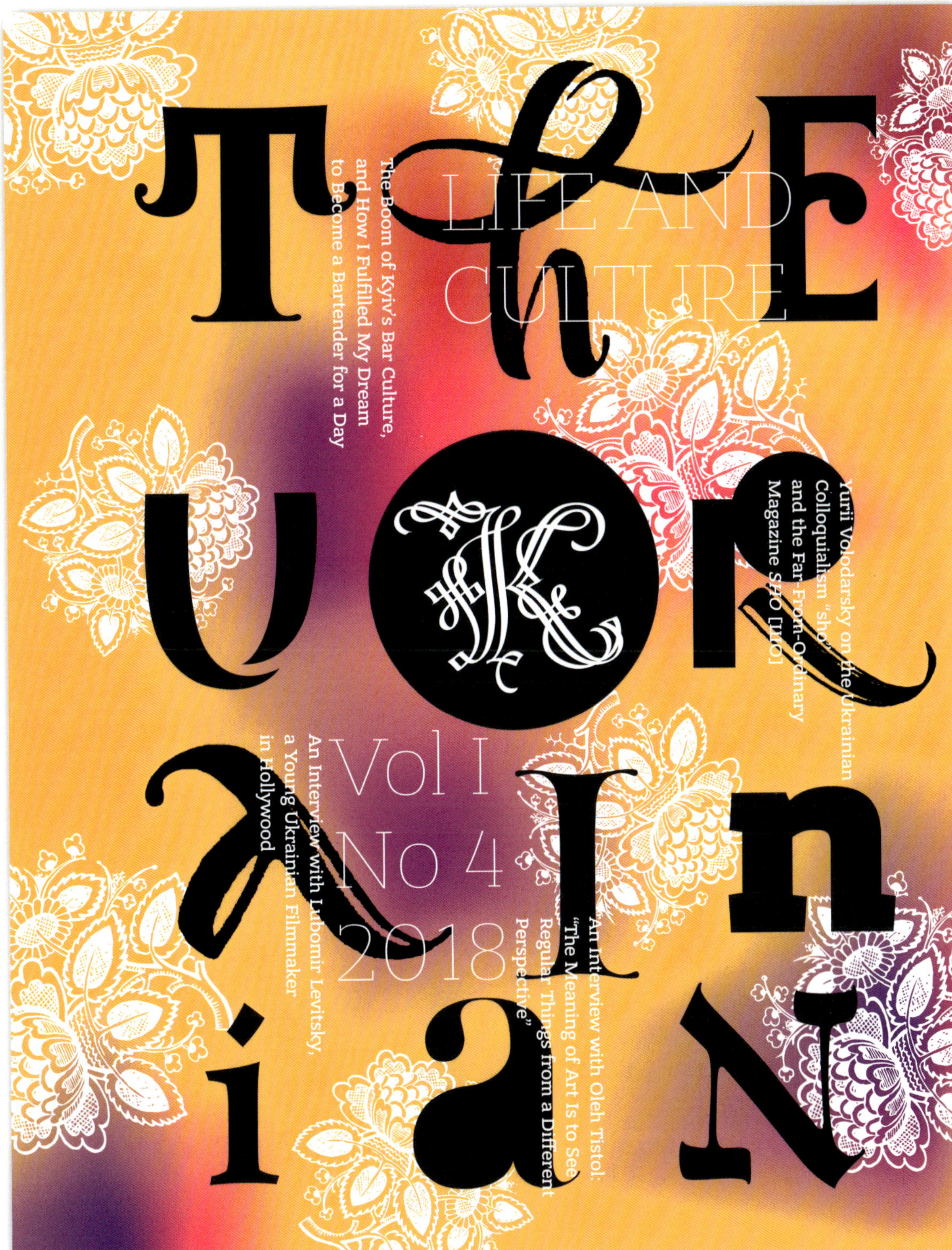

In 2023, Oleksii Chekal received a Certificate of Typographic Excellence in Magazine Design from the esteemed Type Directors Club for his work on the quarterly magazine *The Ukrainian: Life and Culture.*

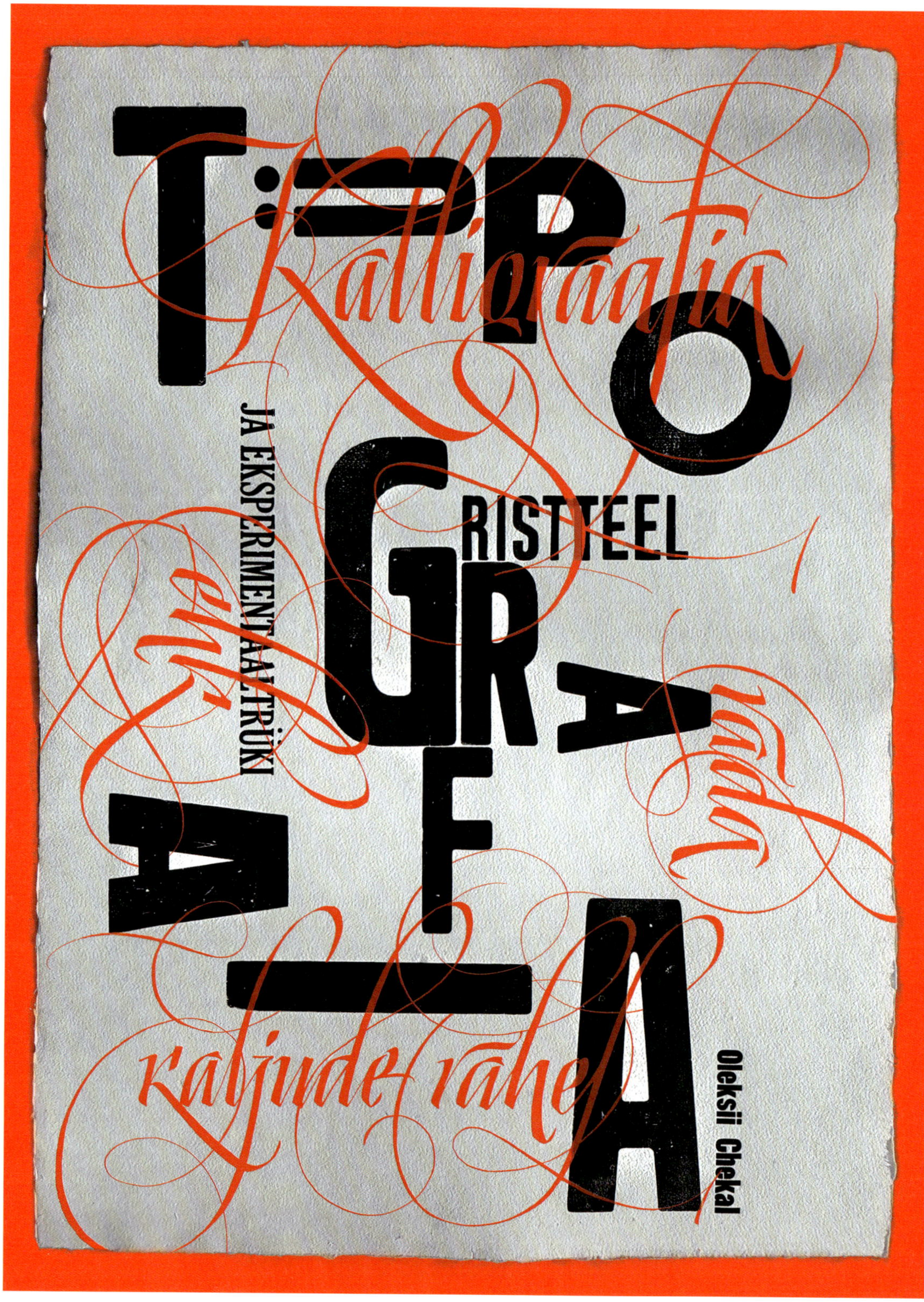

A poster for Chekal's workshop in Tallinn: "The Crossroads of Typography, Calligraphy and Experimental Printing, or The Path between the Rocks." Letterpress printing and calligraphy, 2020.

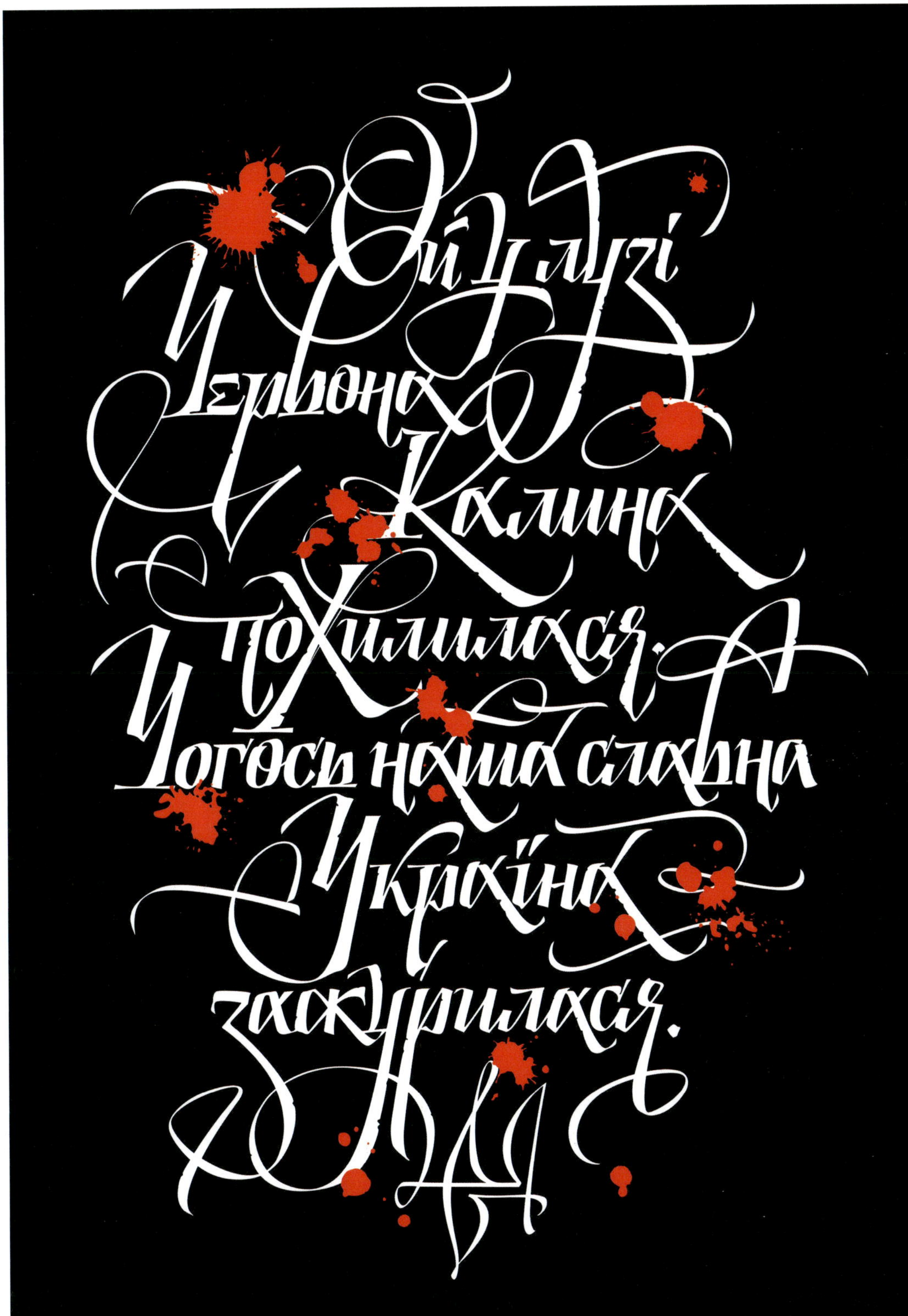

Oh, the Red Viburnum in the Meadow—calligraphy for the "Brush with Silence" project, organized by calligrapher Brody Neuenschwander in Belgium. This work became part of the "Andrii Khlyvniuk 'Boombox' Charitable Fund" project. Kyiv, 2022.

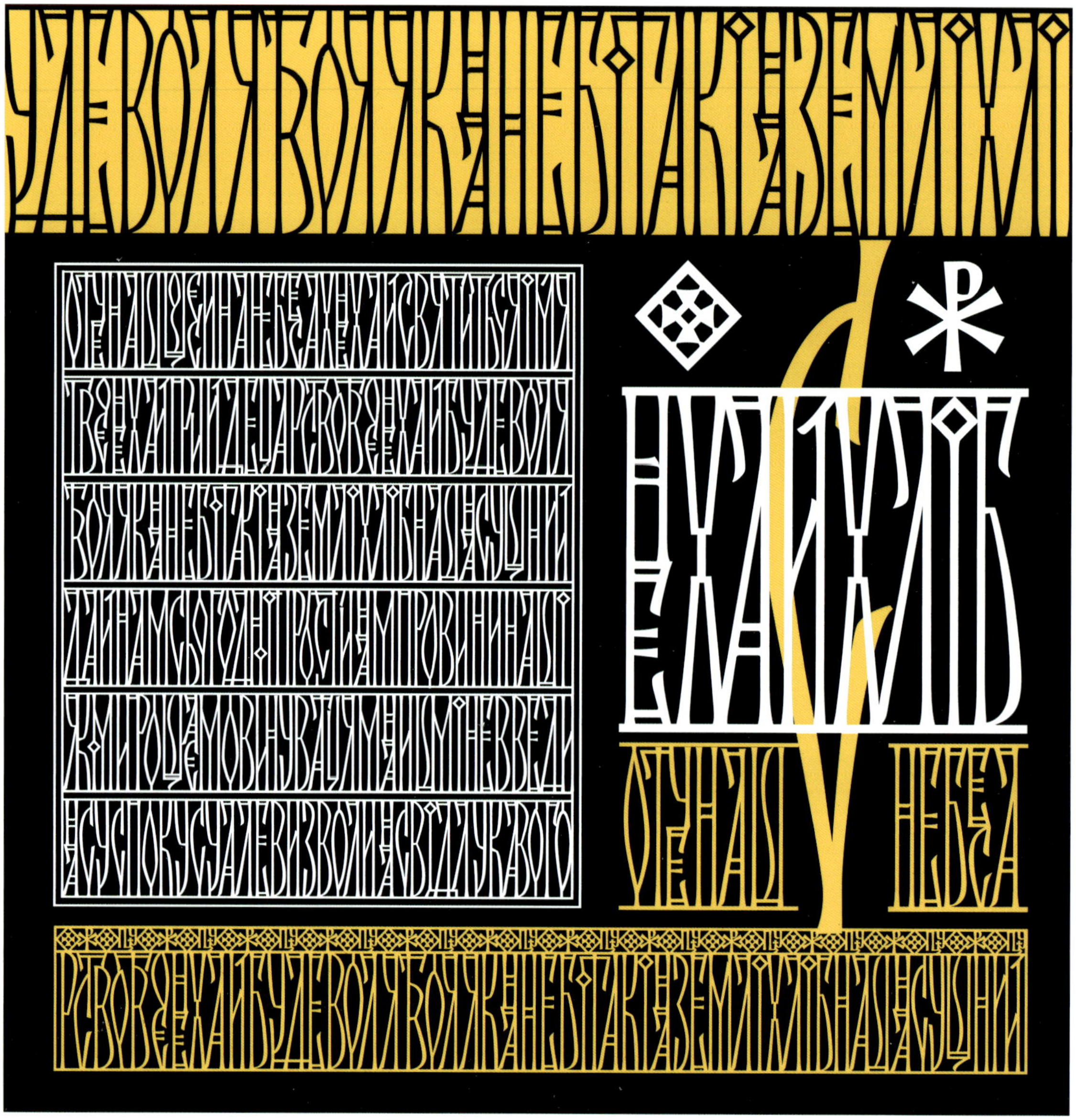

Chekal designed this font for a church fence in Kharkiv. The design follows the calligraphic traditions of ancient Ukrainian script while also evoking the avant-garde geometry of Jacques Hnizdovsky's iconic fonts. The text above is an excerpt of the Our Father prayer.

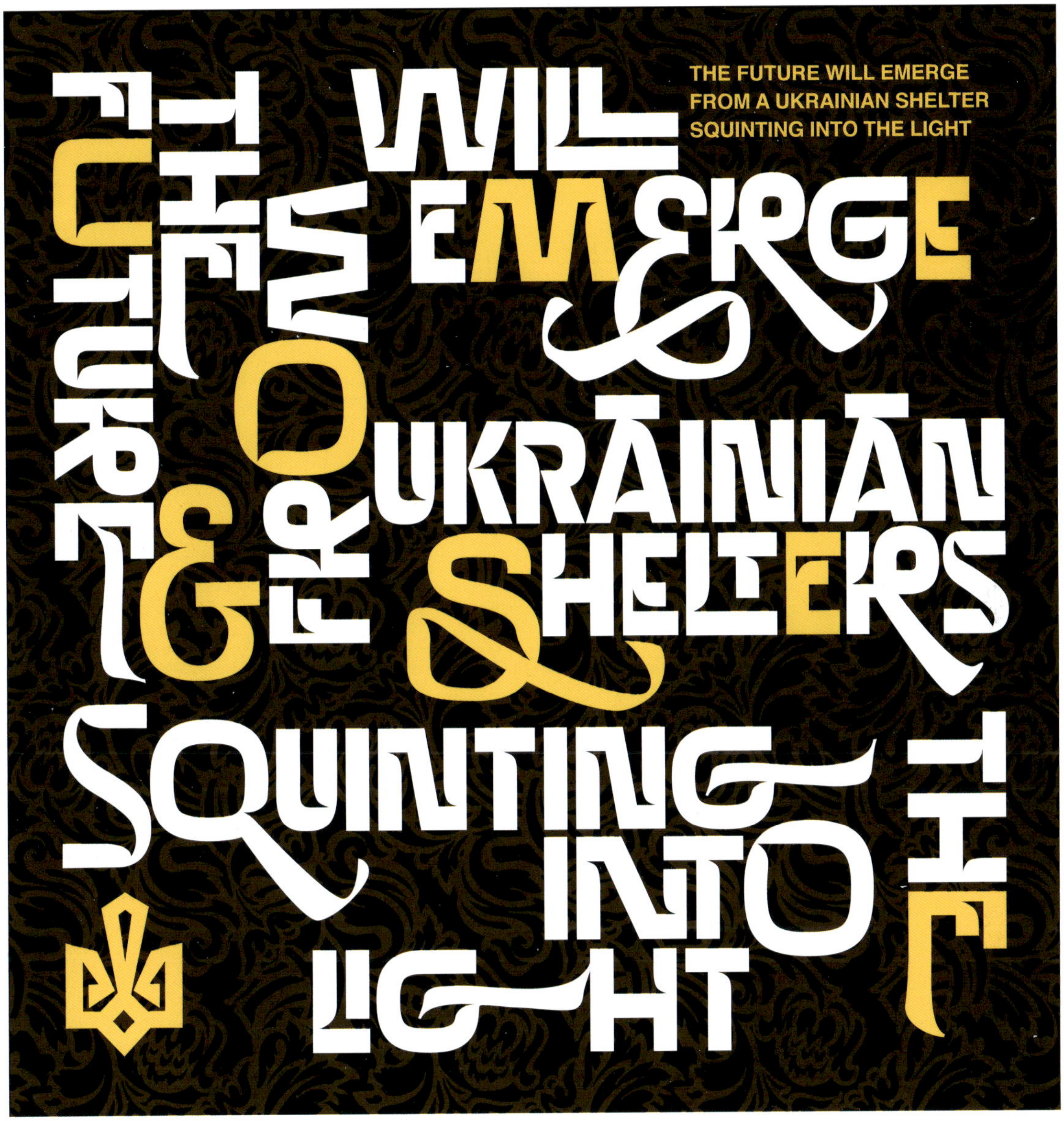

Font design and lettering on glass for an investment project in the field of Ukrainian economy and culture. The text reads: "The future will emerge from Ukrainian shelters squinting into the light."

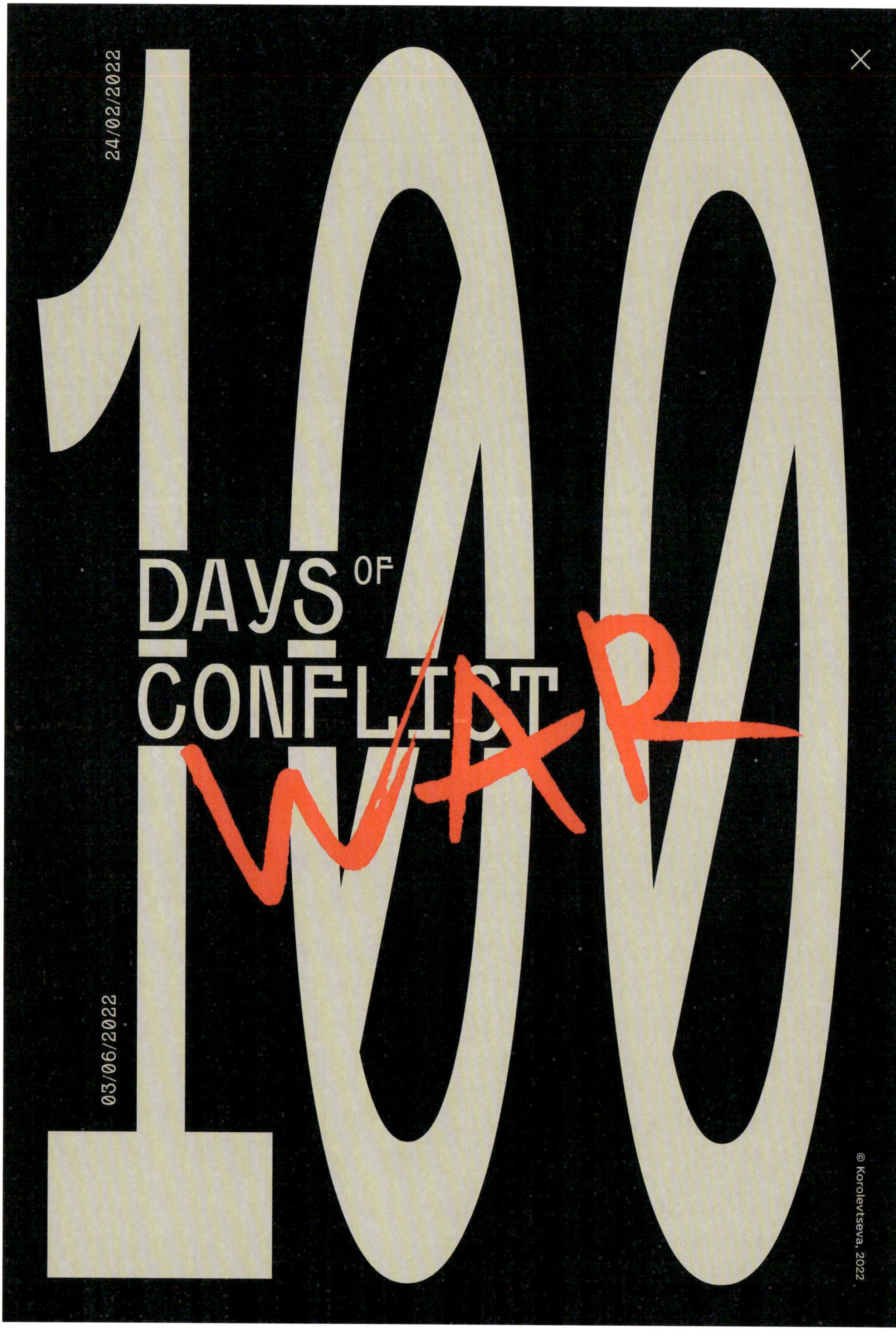
24/02/2022
100
DAYS OF
CONFLICT
WAR
03/06/2022
© Korolevtseva, 2022

WHERE LETTERS SPEAK LOUDER THAN WORDS

KATERYNA KOROLEVTSEVA · *КАТЕРИНА КОРОЛЕВЦЕВА*

In many of her projects, Kateryna Korolevtseva focuses on typography and letters in all forms, embodying and reinterpreting the history of Ukrainian font and visual language for the modern day.

Kateryna Korolevtseva, an independent brand designer and art director, specializes in type design and typographic projects. Korolevtseva, who has received numerous design awards for her work, believes that designers can elevate people's tastes and enhance their minds by creating responsible brands, ethical advertising, and clever communication. One significant aspect of her work involves examining Ukrainian typographical heritage and reinterpreting it for contemporary contexts. In light of the war, it has become increasingly important to Korolevtseva to showcase the rich history and identity of the Ukrainian language as a countermeasure to Russia's long-running campaign to portray it as inferior. One of Korolevtseva's latest art projects was her 2022 "Ukrainian Letters (temporary) Museum." Housed at the art space 11m3 Projektraum in Weimar, Germany, the project featured 33 letters of the Ukrainian alphabet, hand-picked from the works of prominent Ukrainian graphic artists. The letters were sourced from vintage book covers and other printed materials, ranging from 1917 (the time of the Ukrainian National Republic) to present-day Independent Ukraine. The project was funded by Kreativfonds Scholarship of Bauhaus-Universität Weimar.

Latin

ABCDEFGHI
JKLMNOPQ
RSTUVWXYZ

Accents

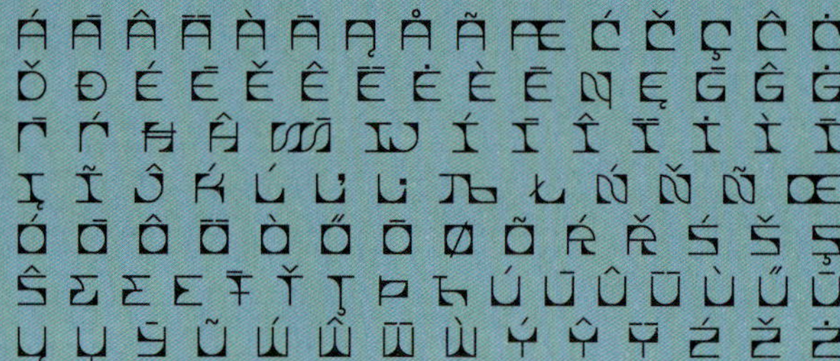

Cyrillic

АБГҐДЕЄЖ
ЗІЇИЙКЛМ
НОПРСТУФ
ХЦЧШЩЬЮЯ

Alternates

Numerals

0 1 2 3 4
5 6 7 8 9

Punctuation and symbols

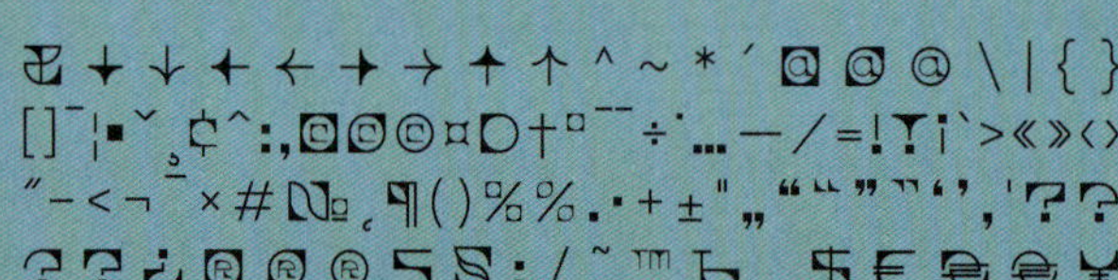

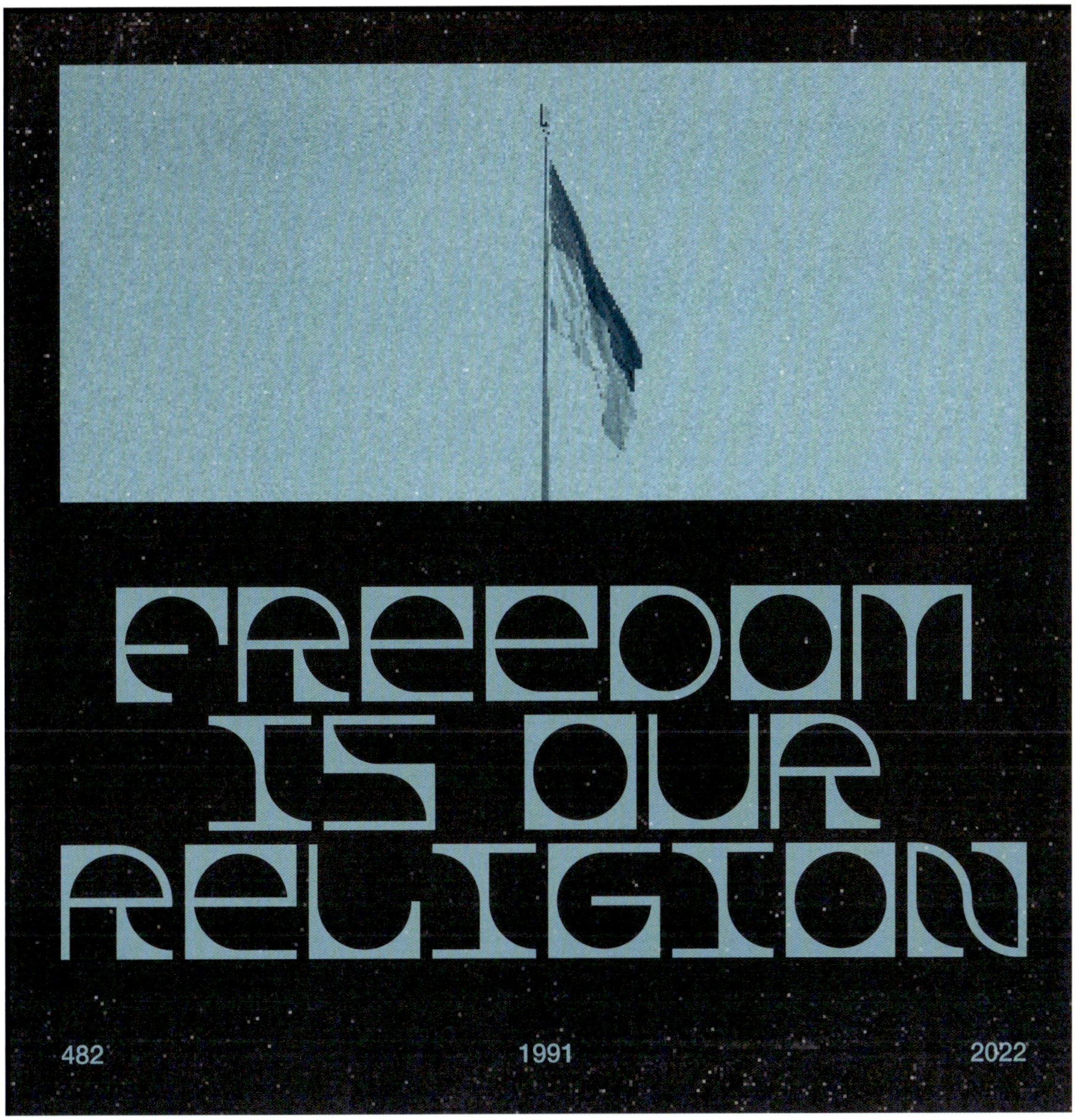

Kateryna Korolevtseva's Kreis is an ultramodernist typeface inspired by the shape of old-school CDs. As a modular display font, its sharp, modern design uses three primary modules, each based on square and circular forms.

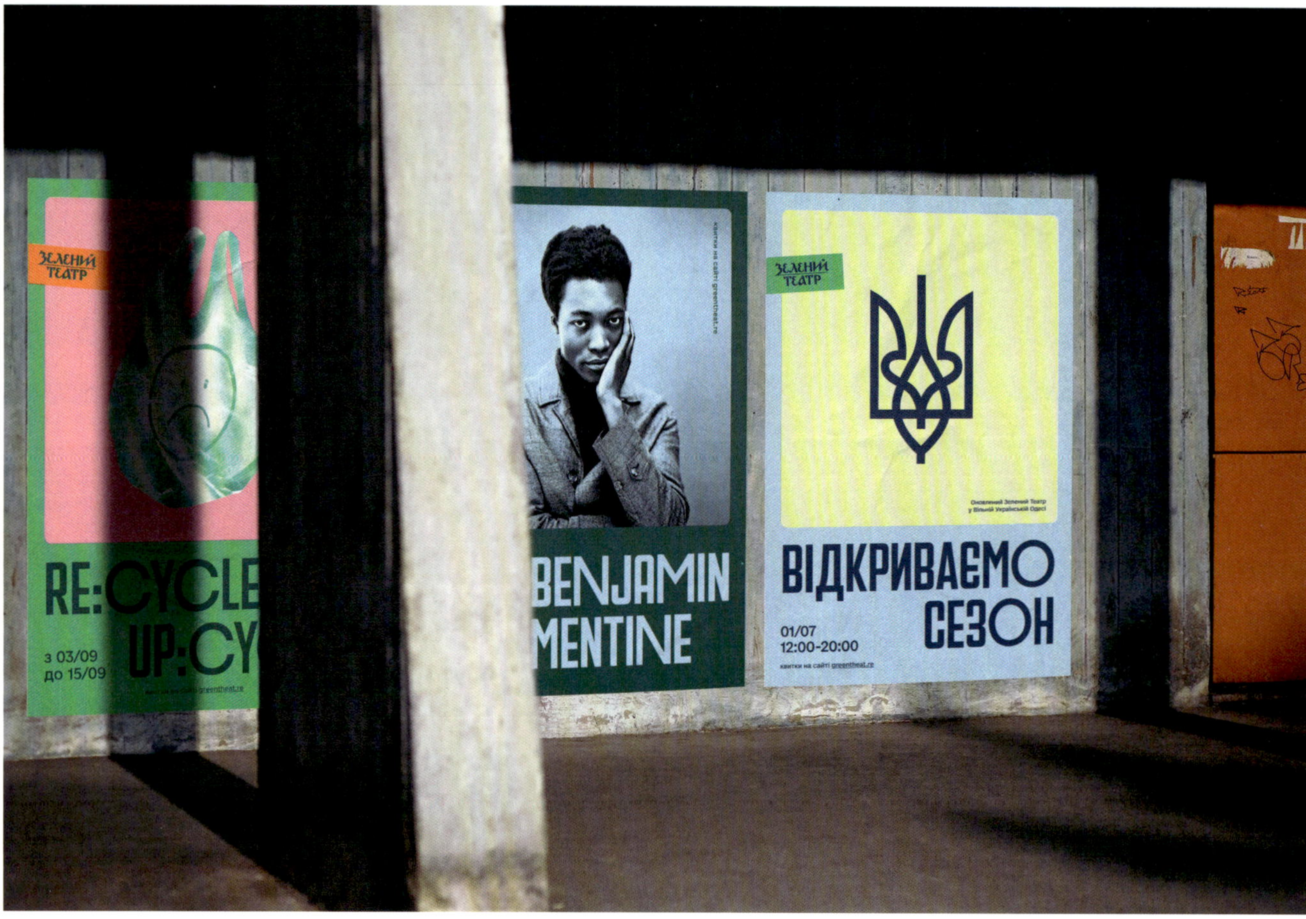

Korolevtseva designed a rebranding project and a custom font logo for the legendary Green Theater in Odesa, which was built in 1936. Opposite page: One of the artist's war posters. It reads, "Armed Forces of Ukraine. Brave, Strong, Invincible. Ukraine Thanks Everyone."

ЗБРОЙНІ

ВІДВАЖНІ СИЛЬНІ НЕПЕРЕМОЖНІ

СИЛИ

ГЕРОЇ

УКРАЇНА ДЯКУЄ КОЖНОМУ

УКРАЇНИ

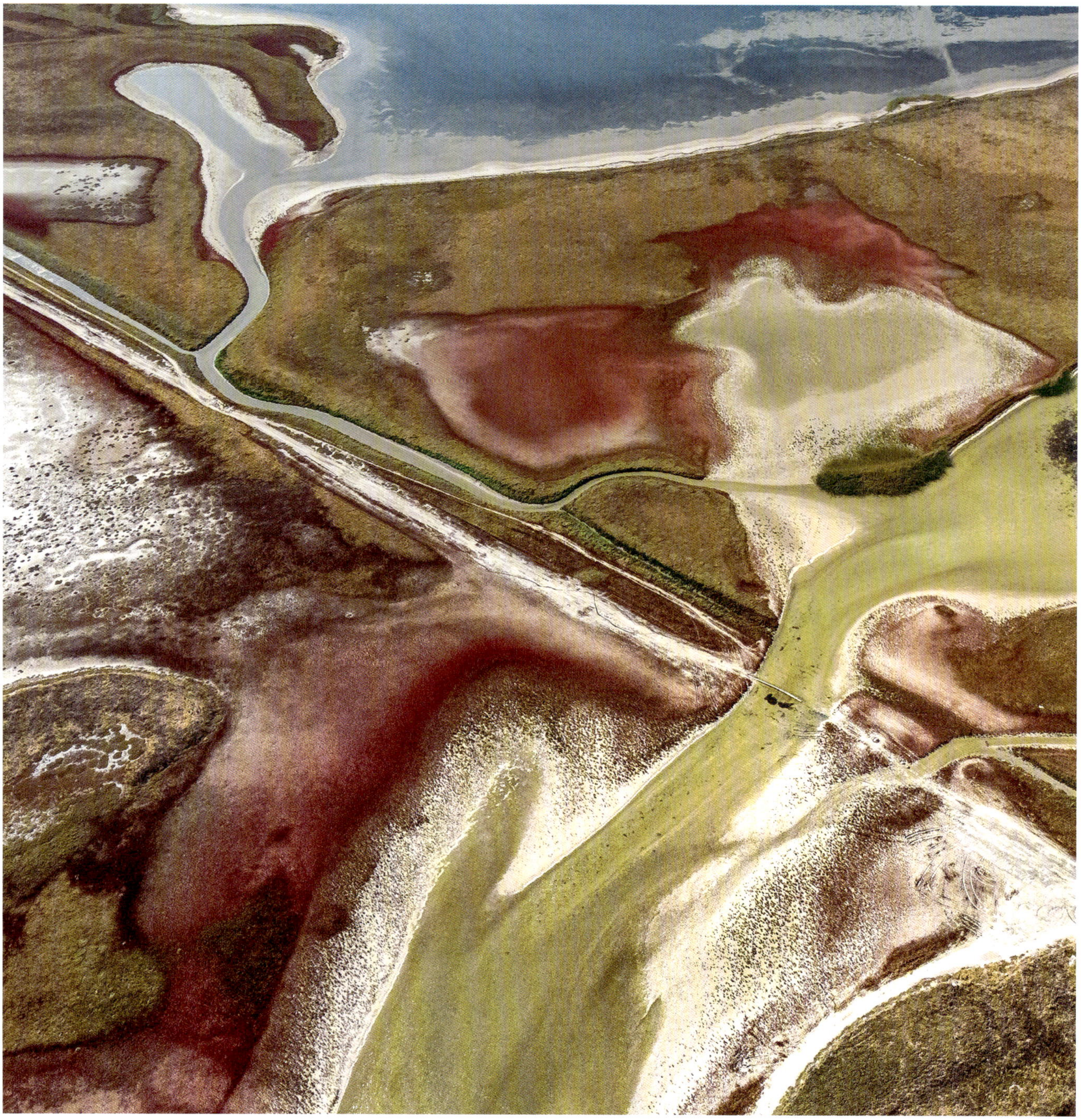

ON THE PINK PLANET

YEVHEN SAMUCHENKO · *ЄВГЕН САМУЧЕНКО*

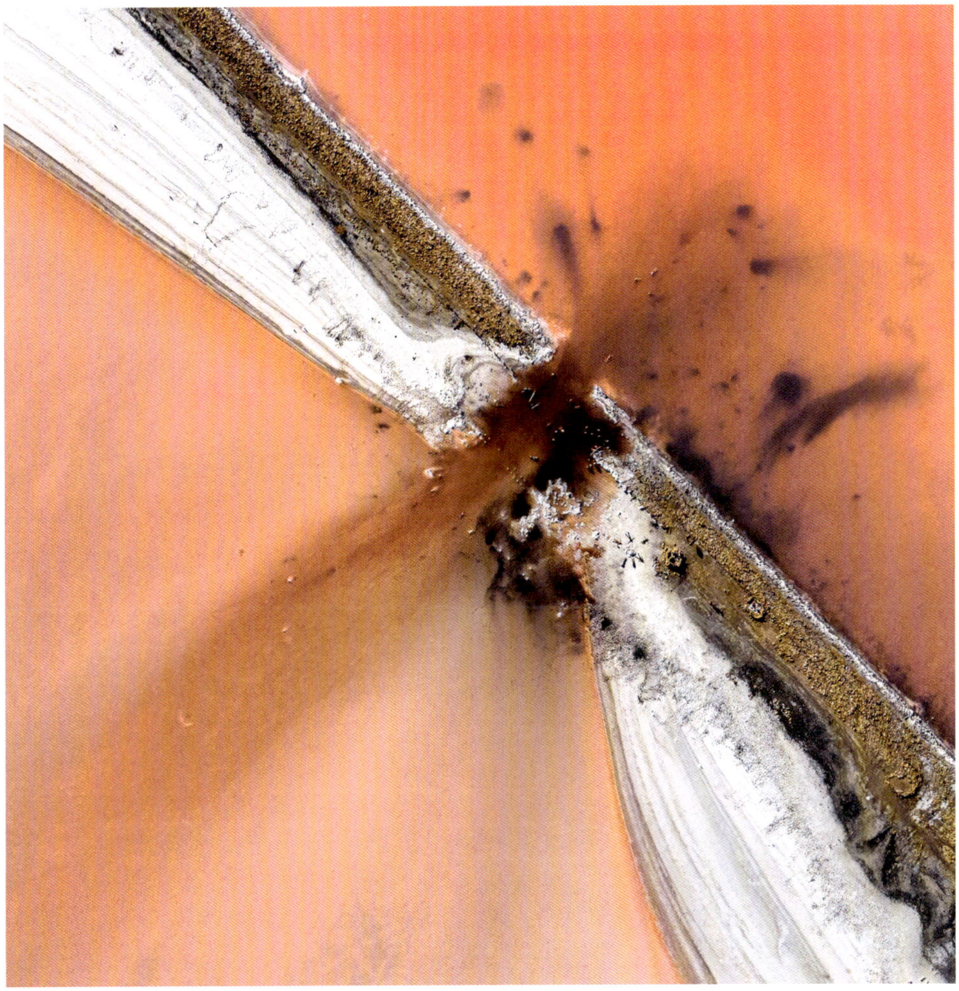

Using aerial photography, Yevhen Samuchenko captured one of the most stunning natural sights in Ukraine—the pink salt lakes in the Kherson and Odesa regions.

A native of Odesa, Yevhen Samuchenko is a photographer specializing in travel, aerial, and night photography. His photographs have won numerous international awards in more than 60 competitions and have been shown in solo and group exhibitions all over the world. Samuchenko's photographs have appeared in a great number of some of the world's leading print and online publications, and he's also served on the jury for several photo competitions in Ukraine and abroad. "Pink Planet," one of Samuchenko's better-known photo series, depicts the fantastic beauty of the pink salt lakes in the Kherson region. In his photos, the lakes take on an abstract, almost alien appearance. The unique pink hue of the lakes is due to the presence of algae, which produce carotenoids under the sun's rays. As temperatures rise, water evaporates from the lakes, intensifying their color and creating a stunning visual display that has been beautifully documented by Samuchenko.

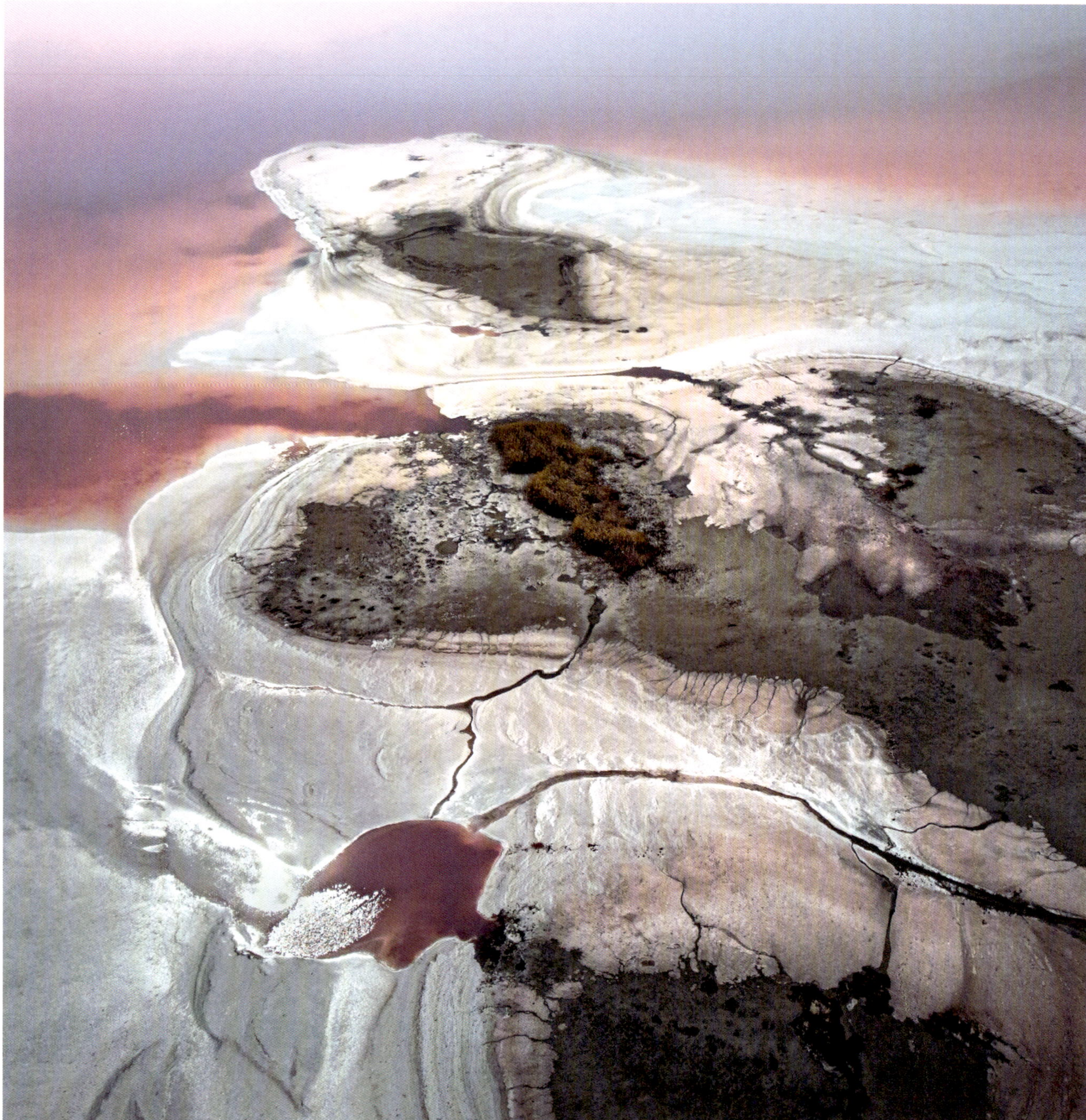

Pink Planet Patterns, Lake Lemuria, Kherson region. In the summer months, microscopic algae cause the water to turn a vivid hue of pink. Aerial photography conveys the extraordinary atmosphere of this place.

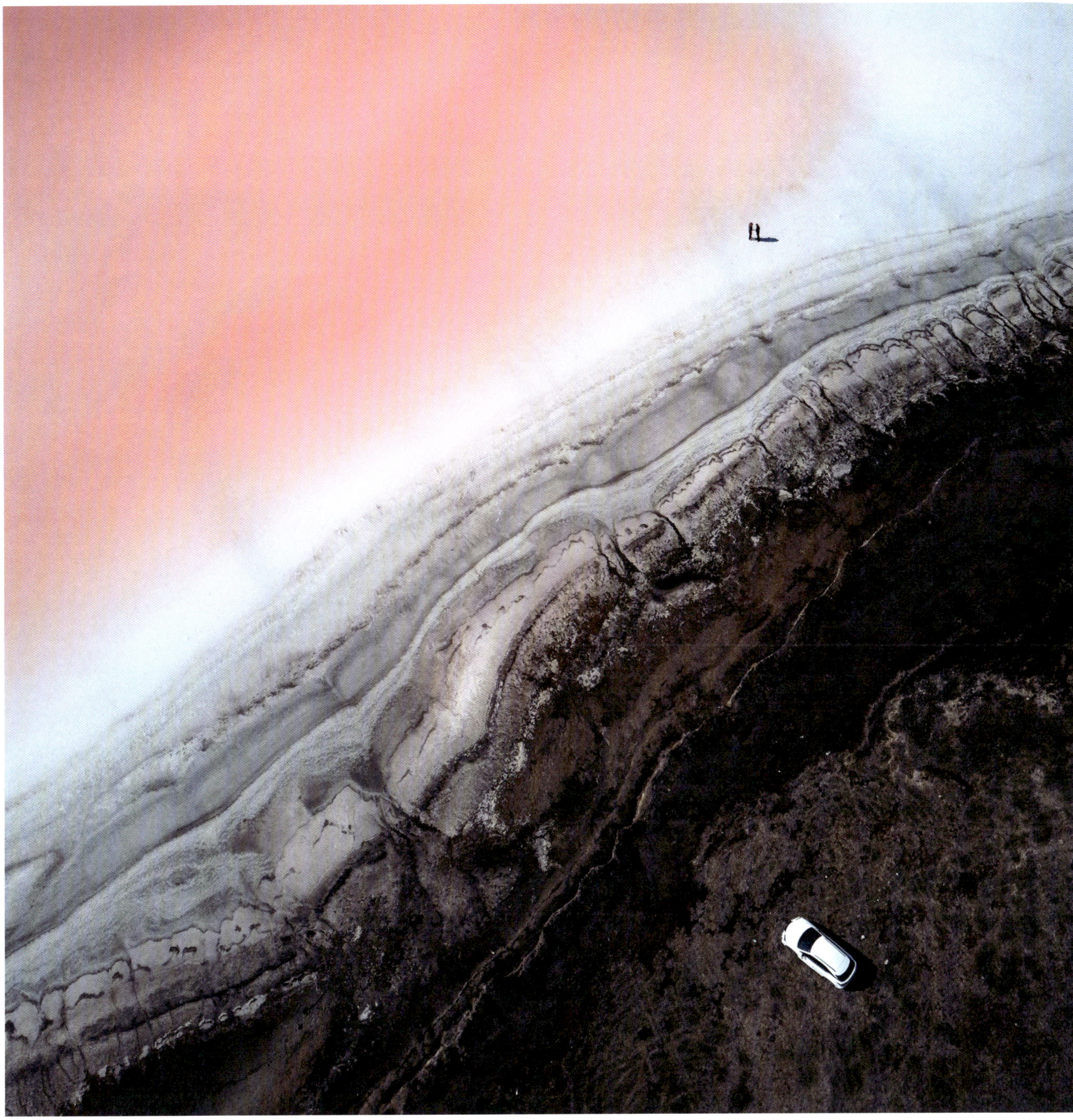

White Car & Two People, Lake Lemuria, Kherson region. This photo received the Highly Commended distinction at the Travel Photographer of the Year awards in 2021.

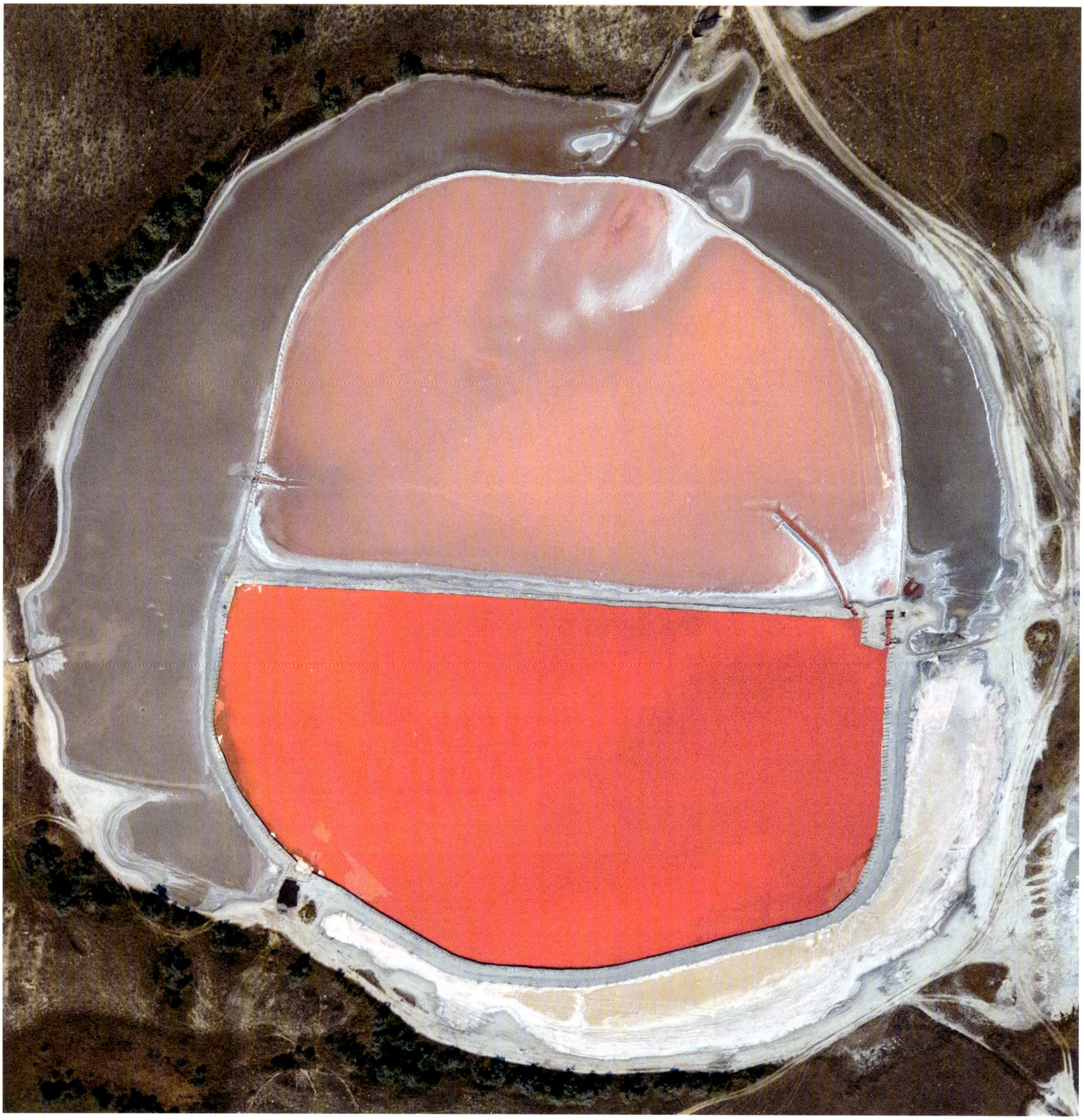

Embryo, Heroiske, Kherson region. This picture was taken above the pink lakes of the Kinburn Spit, near the village of Heroiske. Due to the war, the unique nature of the Kinburn Spit Regional Landscape Park has been greatly affected.

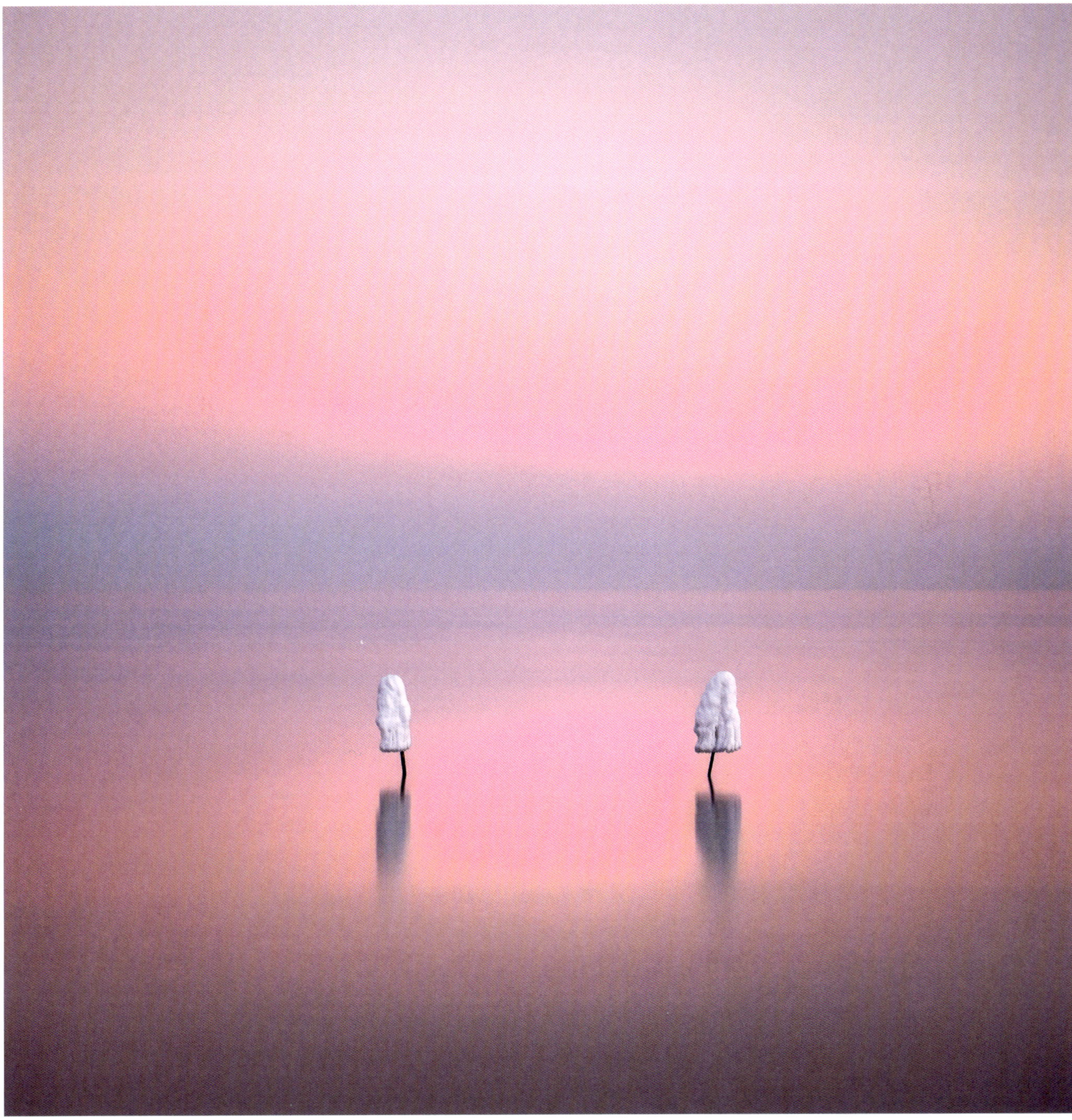

Two Ice Creams, the Black Sea, Odesa. This photograph has won numerous awards and was exhibited at the Museum of East Asian Art in the United Kingdom.

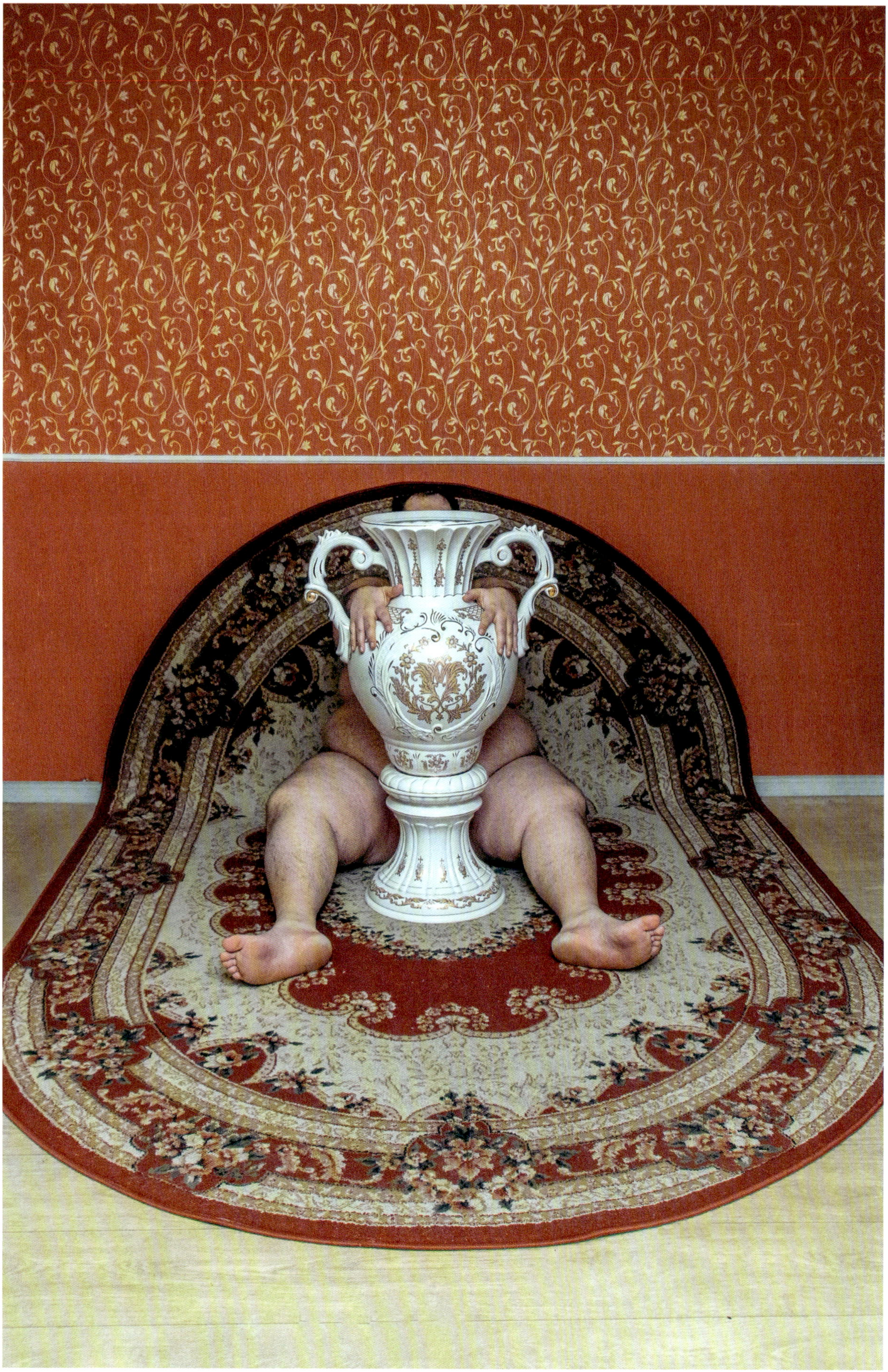

THE NAKED TRUTH

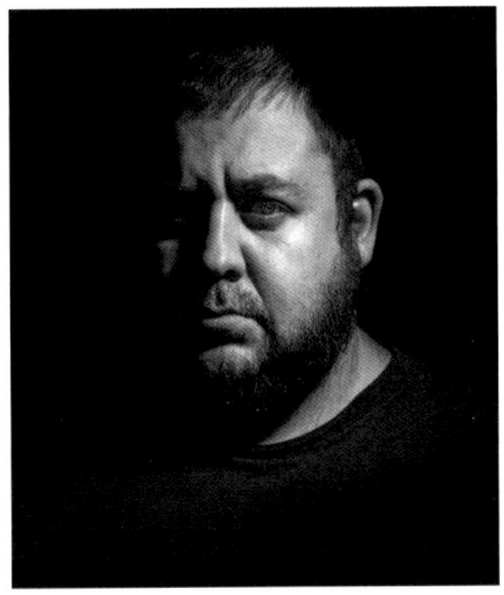

ARTEM HUMILEVSKYI · *АРТЕМ ГУМІЛЕВСЬКИЙ*

The "Giant" project by photographer Artem Humilevskyi is primarily about self-perception and personal freedom.

Artem Humilevskyi, originally from Mykolaiv, discovered photography unexpectedly while working as a senior manager at an agricultural company. Now Humilevskyi resides in his wife's family home in a village in the region of Odesa. In 2019 he began to pursue a career in commercial photography, and decided to hone his craft at the MYPH school of conceptual and art photography under Sergey Melnitchenko's guidance (see page 180). There, he was instantly drawn to conceptual photography and devoted himself to creating conceptual projects of his own. His early project, "Giant," secured him the Global Peace Photo Award 2022. Developed in 2020 during the Covid-19 pandemic, the series started as a humorous collection of self-portraits during lockdown. However, as time went by, the series acquired other implications for the artist. In the pictures, the artist explores his own physicality and vulnerability, appearing nude throughout. Humilevskyi views the naked body as a symbol of sincerity and openness, qualities that he always strives to convey in his photographs. The project lasted until February 2022, when the invasion made its carefree nature impossible to reconcile with his current reality. In the first weeks of the war, Humilevskyi thought a lot about how to help his country, and as a non-documentary photographer, he decided to capture the events through the lens of his own creativity. He examined himself and his reflections on society, noting a surge in cultural pride and unity among Ukrainians. This inspired the project "Roots," in which Humilevskyi studies the symbolism of Ukrainian folk traditions, merging them with his own reflections on the war. The series highlights the artist's deep connection to tradition and nature, and while he still appears nude, Humilevskyi sees his body in this project not as a central theme but a vehicle for broader creative expression.

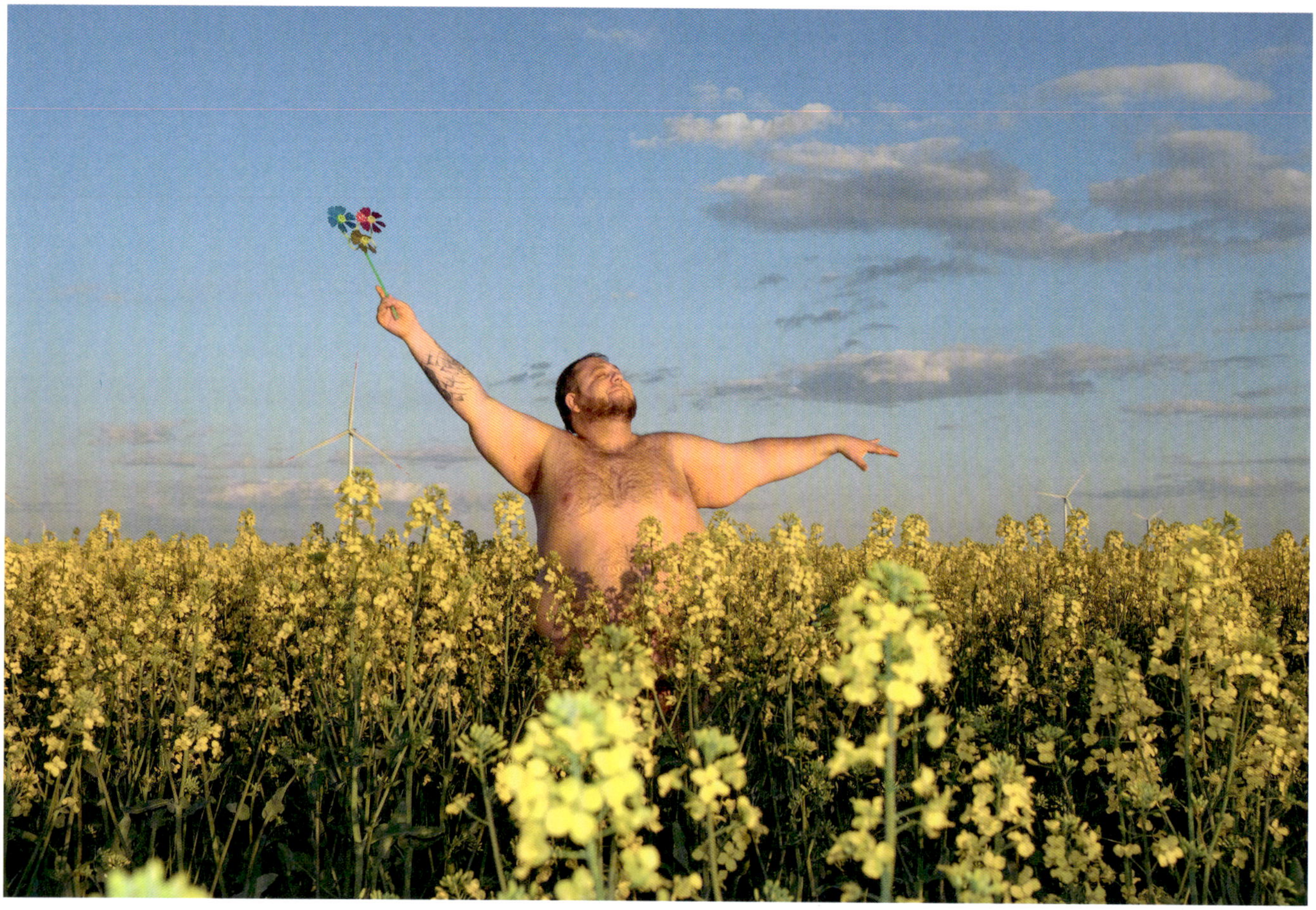

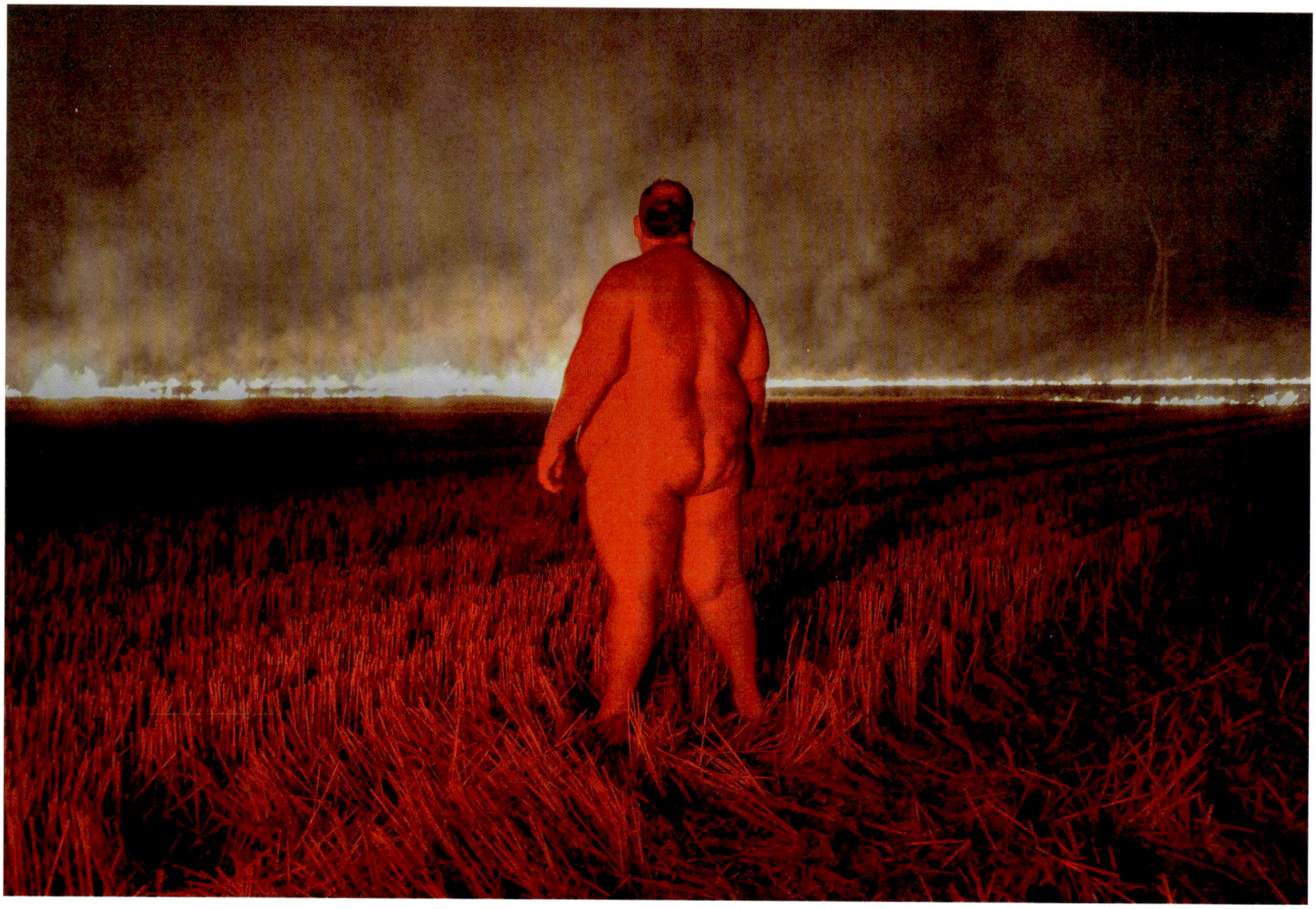

"With the beginning of the war, I completed my 'Giant' project, because it was primarily about self-perception and personal freedom, and began to study myself and my reflections as part of society."

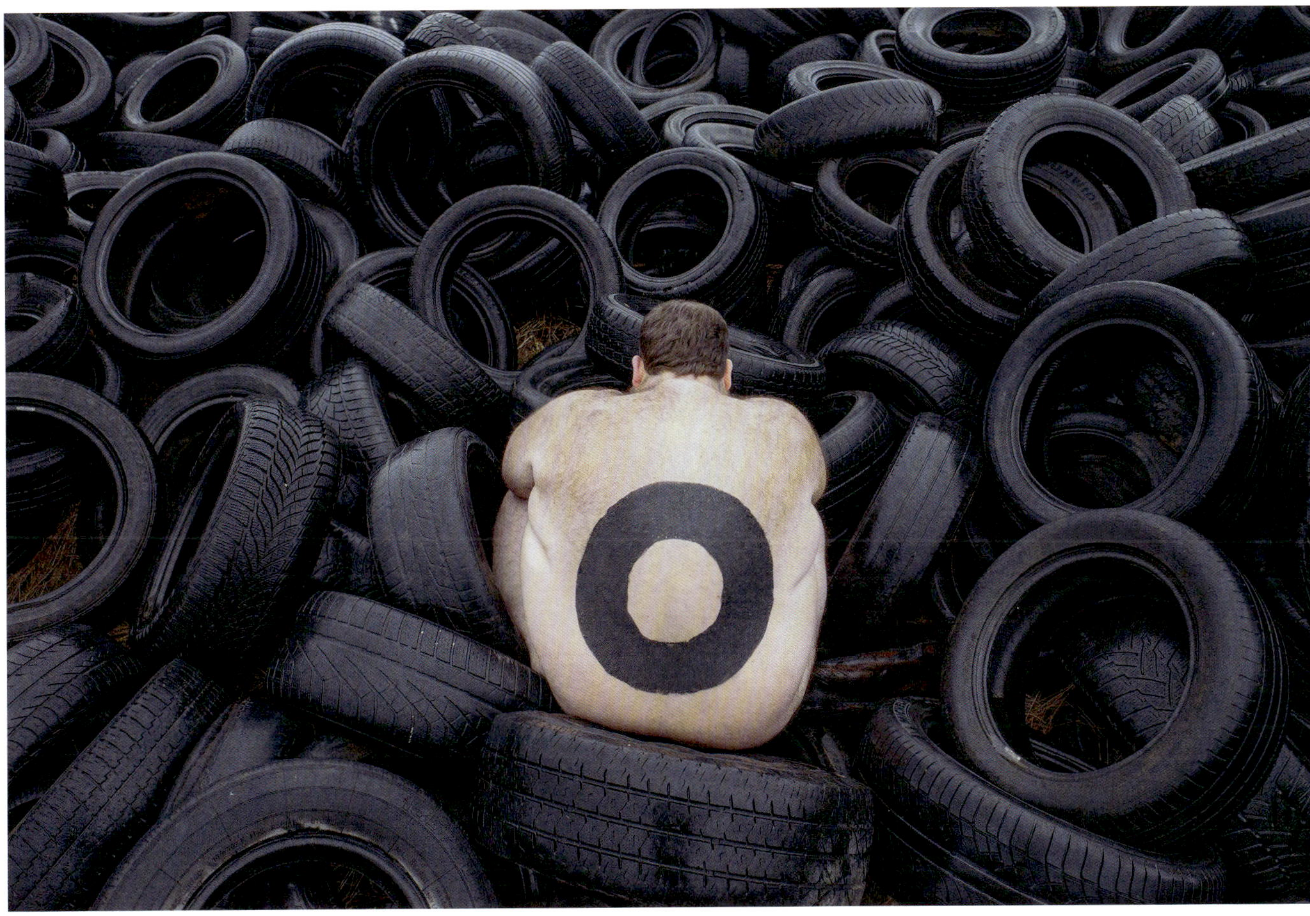

In his projects, Humilevskyi presents an ironic view that challenges unrealistic societal standards of beauty through playful photography. The photos capture inner freedom and the personal journey toward self-love and accepting your body.

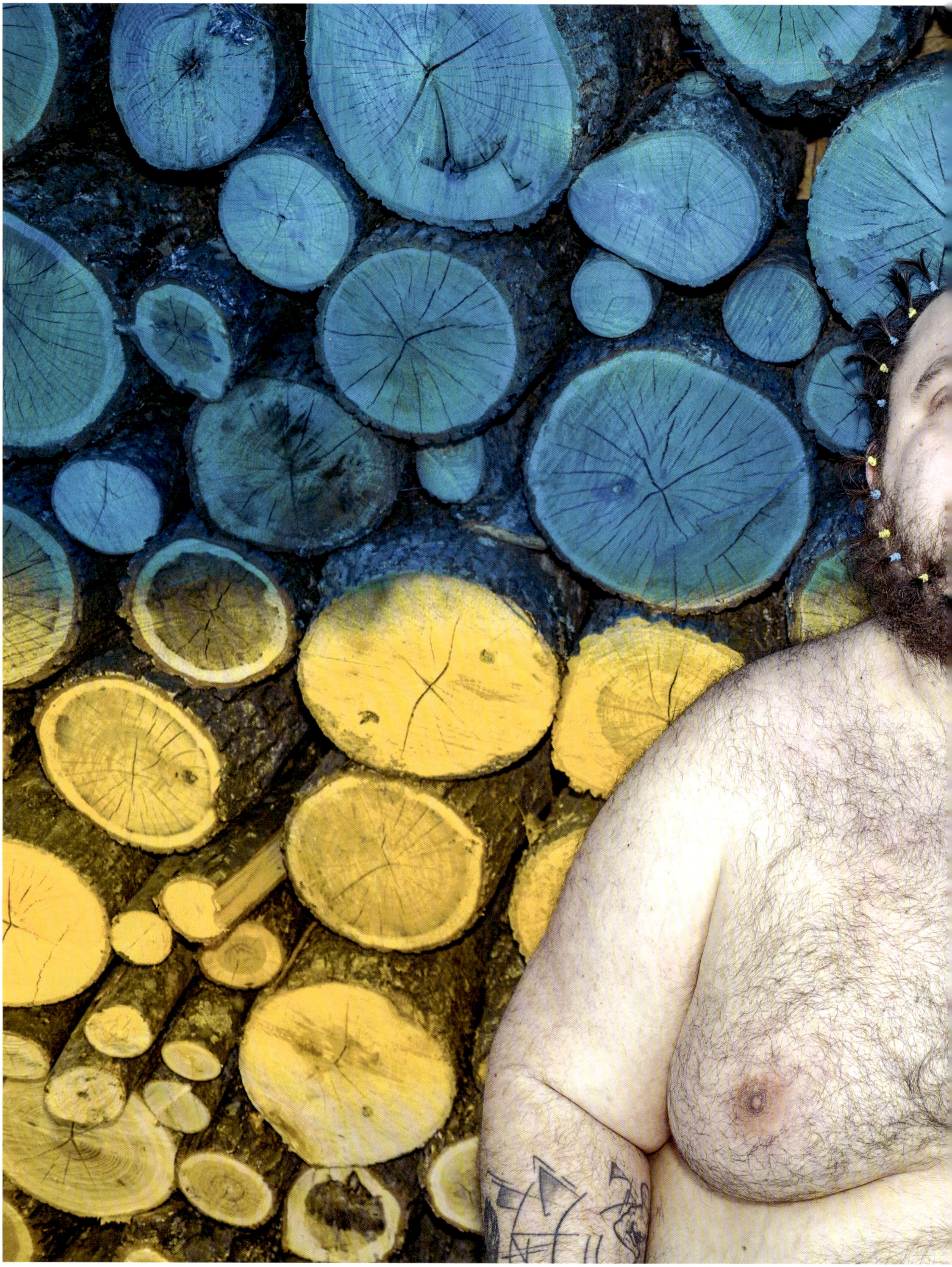

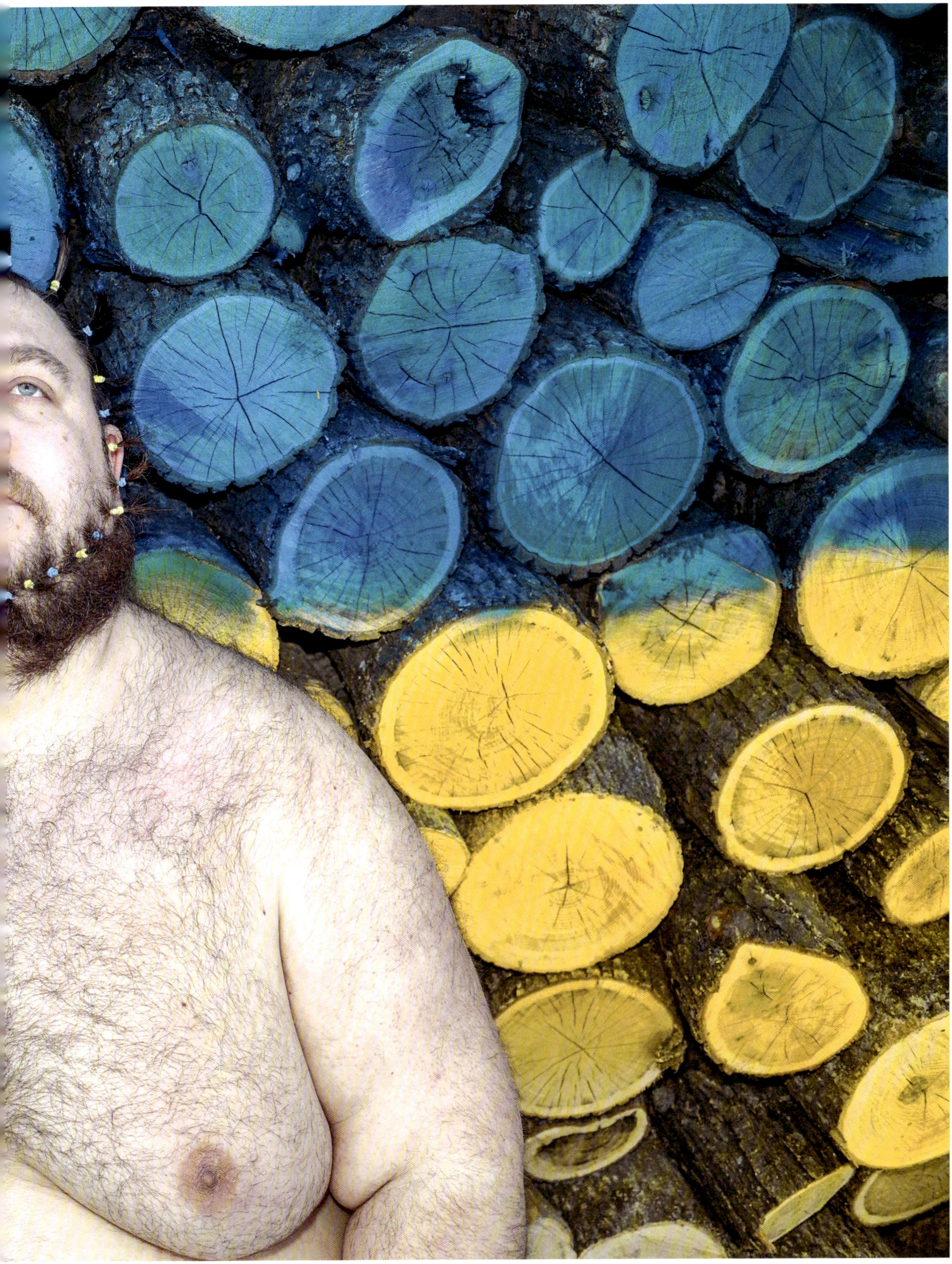

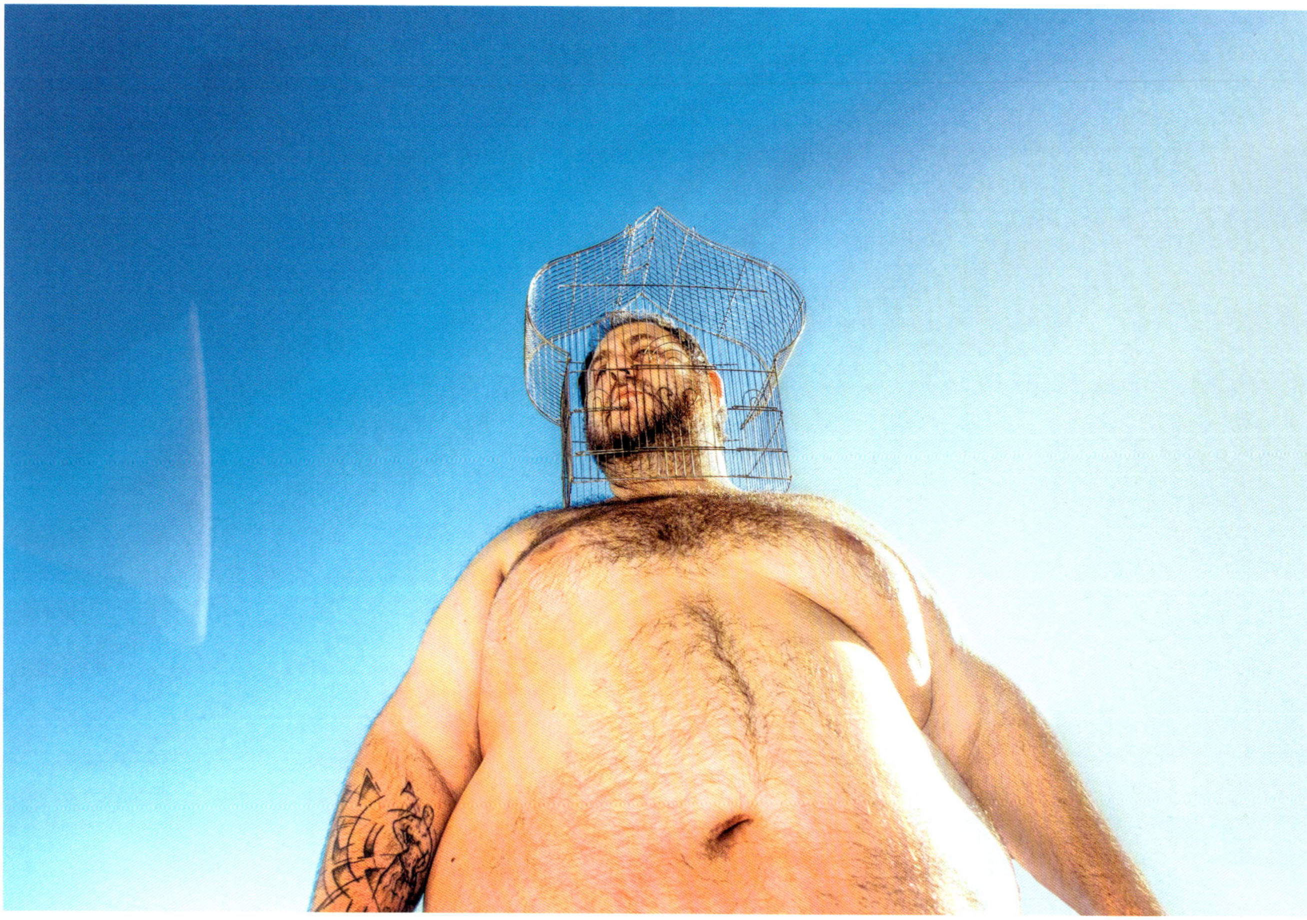

In his "Roots" series, Humilevskyi explores and interprets Ukrainian symbols and traditions, displaying them in a playful manner. For example, the stork (opposite page) has long been a symbol of familial harmony, fertility, and devotion to one's homeland.

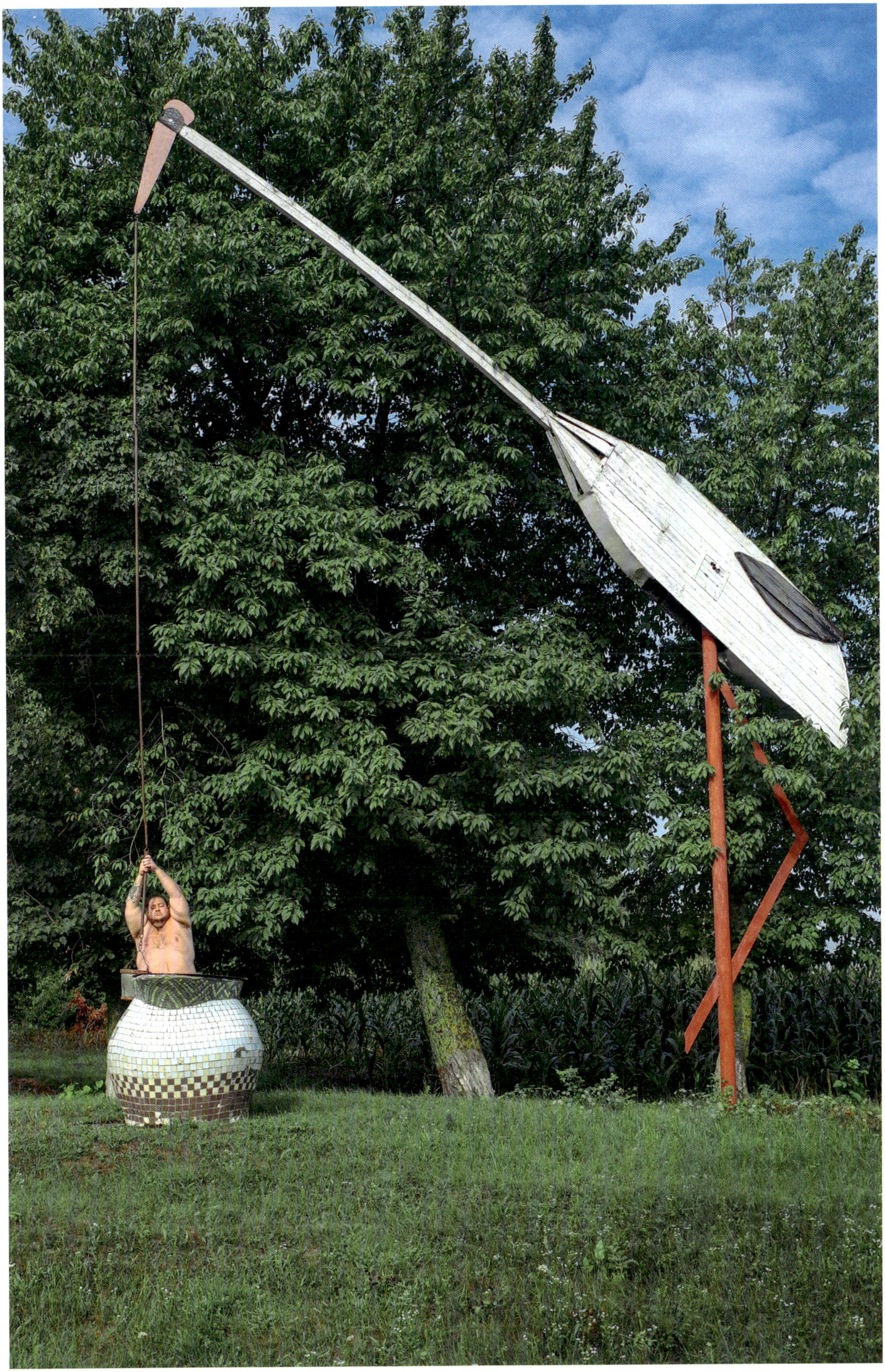

"Like most Ukrainians, I feel a strong sense of belonging and a deep connection to tradition. This is how the project 'Roots' appeared. I also take nude photos, but now it is no longer a central focus of my work, but rather a means of conveying my creative thought."

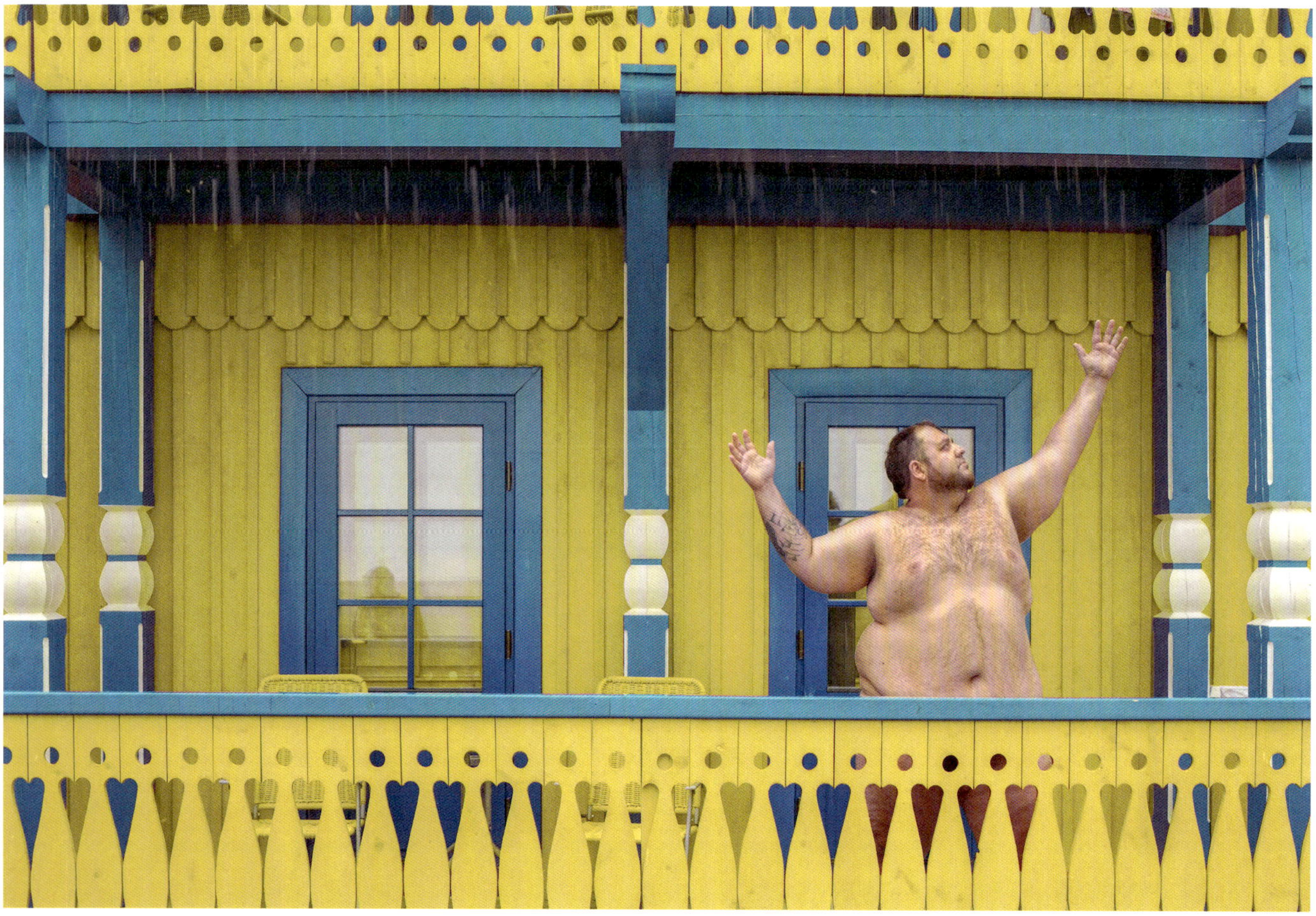

Opposite page (bottom): A reaction to the atrocities uncovered in Bucha, this work shows the artist lying at the edge of a wheat field, his mutilated body sewn together with bright red thread—a poignant symbol of the war's effect on Ukrainian society.

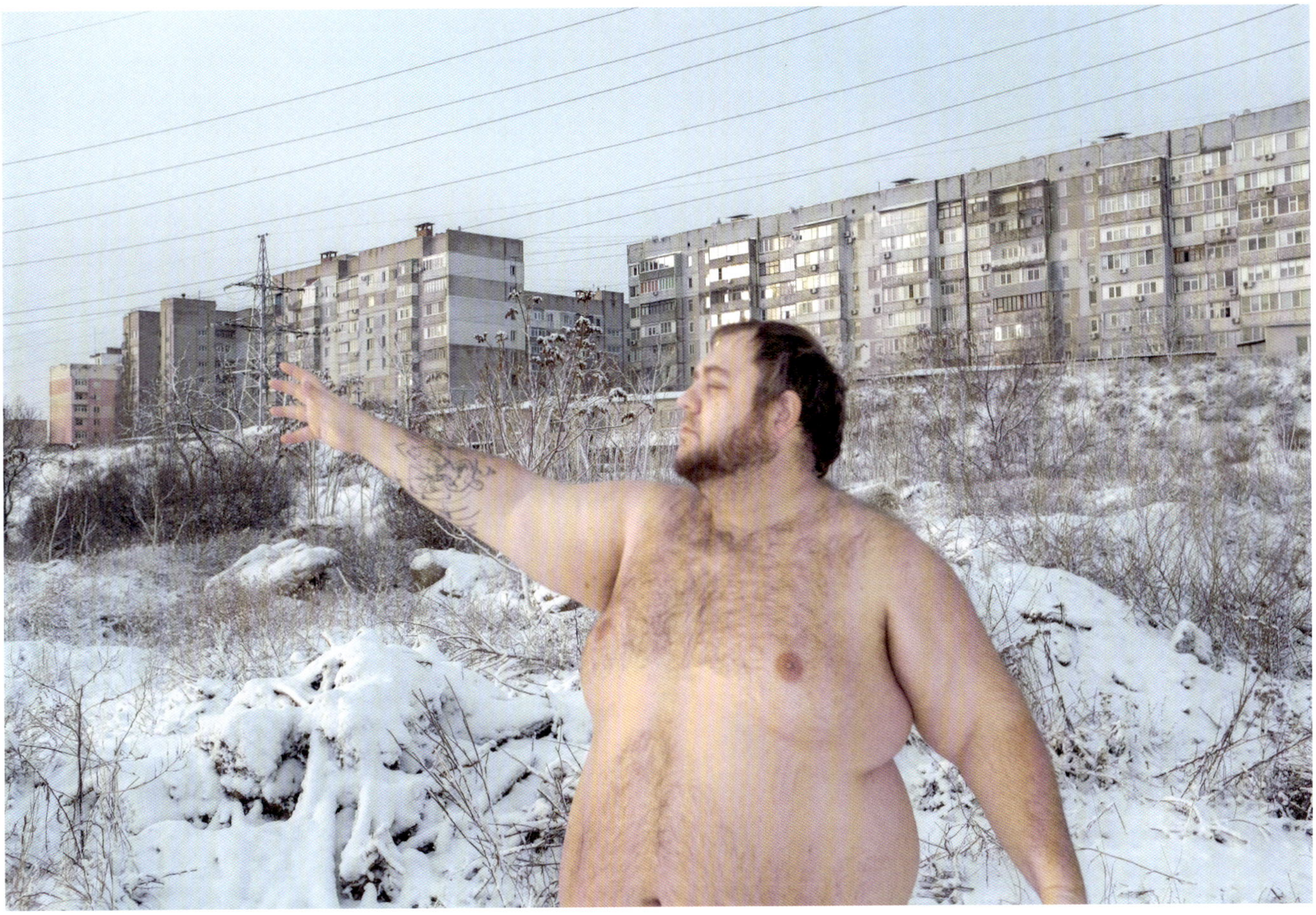

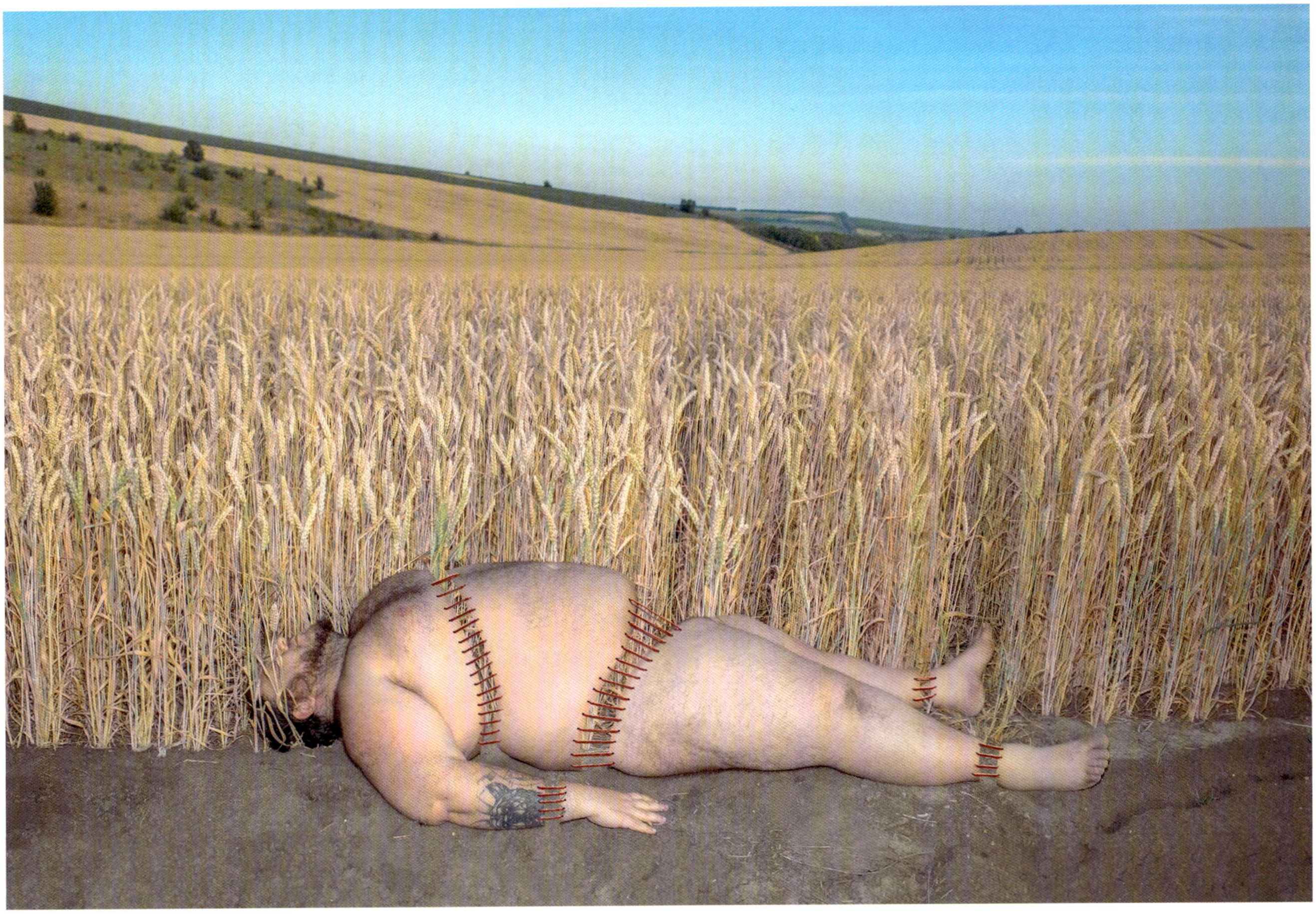

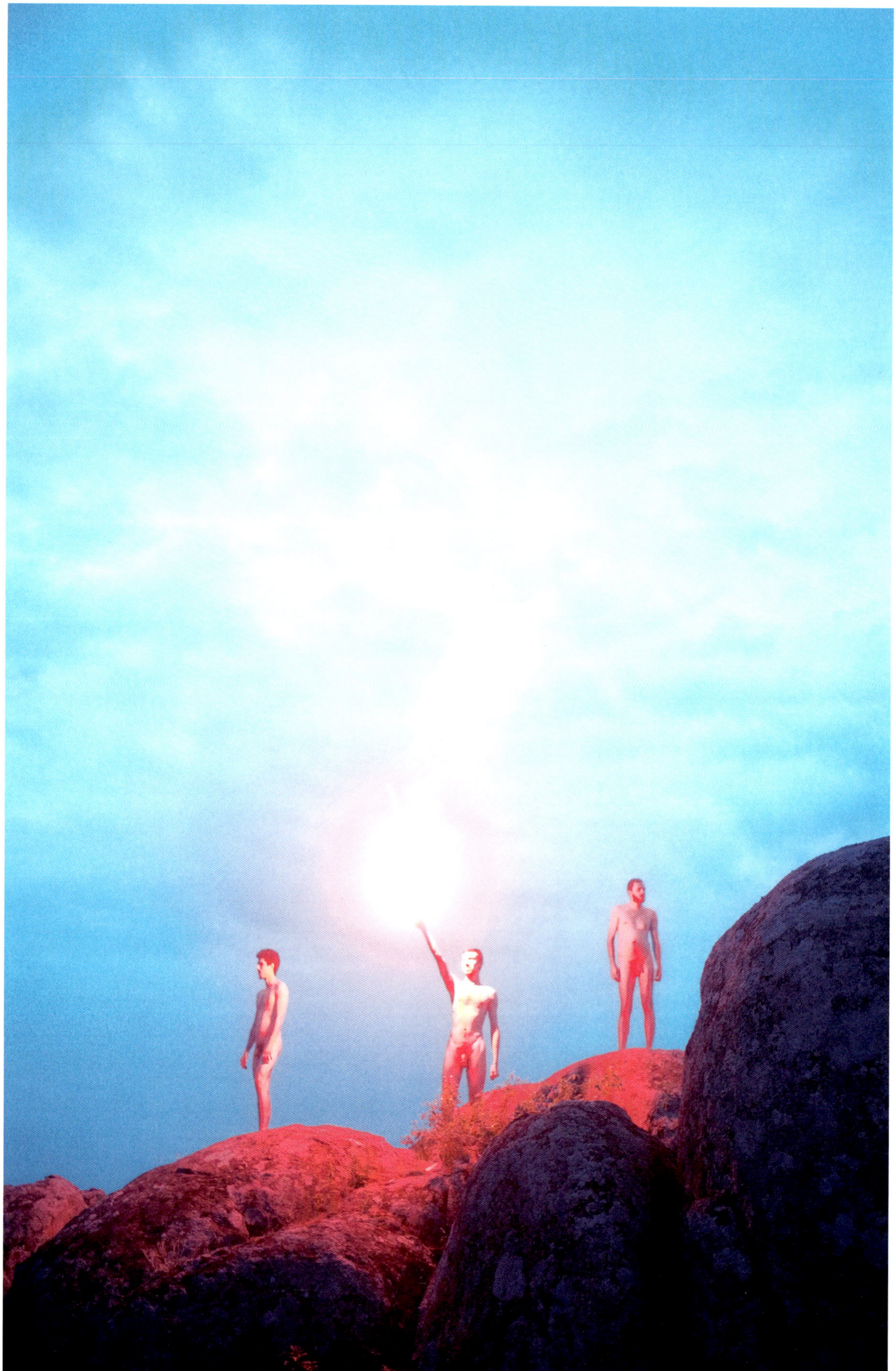

YOUNG AND FREE

SERGEY MELNITCHENKO · *СЕРГІЙ МЕЛЬНИЧЕНКО*

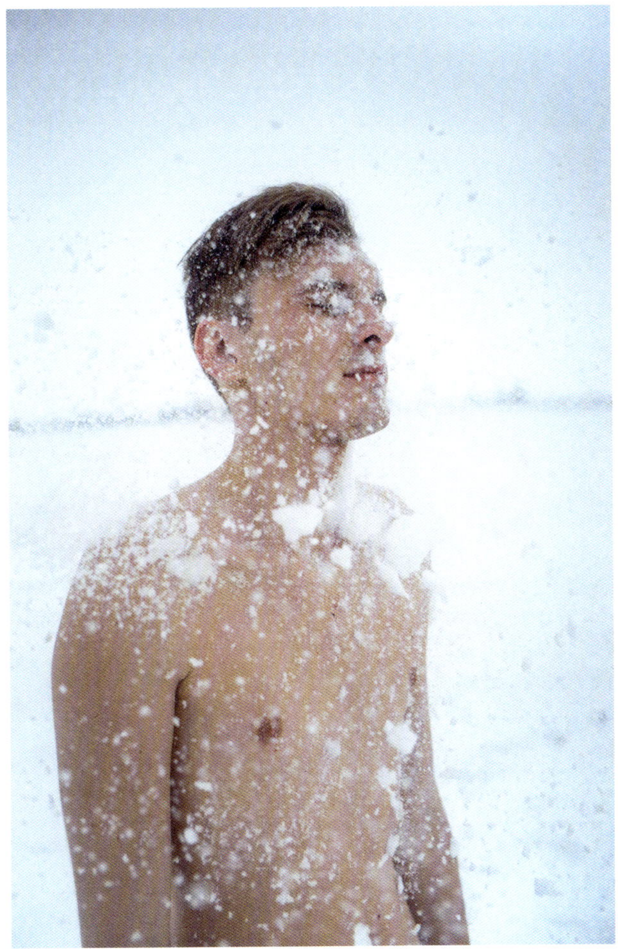

Sergey Melnitchenko, renowned Ukrainian photographer and founder of the MYPH school of conceptual and art photography, captures the freedom and passion of Ukraine's younger generation through his art.

Sergey Melnitchenko, born in Mykolaiv, first discovered his passion for photography in 2009 and began experimenting with analog photography in 2010. His artistic approach transformed in 2012, when he transitioned toward conceptual photography. Since then, Melnitchenko has participated in more than 150 personal and group exhibitions, fairs, and festivals worldwide. In addition to his work as an artist, he also serves as a teacher and curator at MYPH, the school of conceptual photography he founded, where he has discovered and mentored many emerging talents. As an artist, Melnitchenko works in a wide range of styles and mediums—from purely documentary photo series to complex conceptual projects that combine fake documentation, 3D animation, and drawing. Despite their stylistic differences, all of his works share a common thread: a profound interest in the intimate nature of the medium. Fittingly, Melnitchenko delves into various aspects of corporeality, from the sensual nature of the body to its social dimensions.

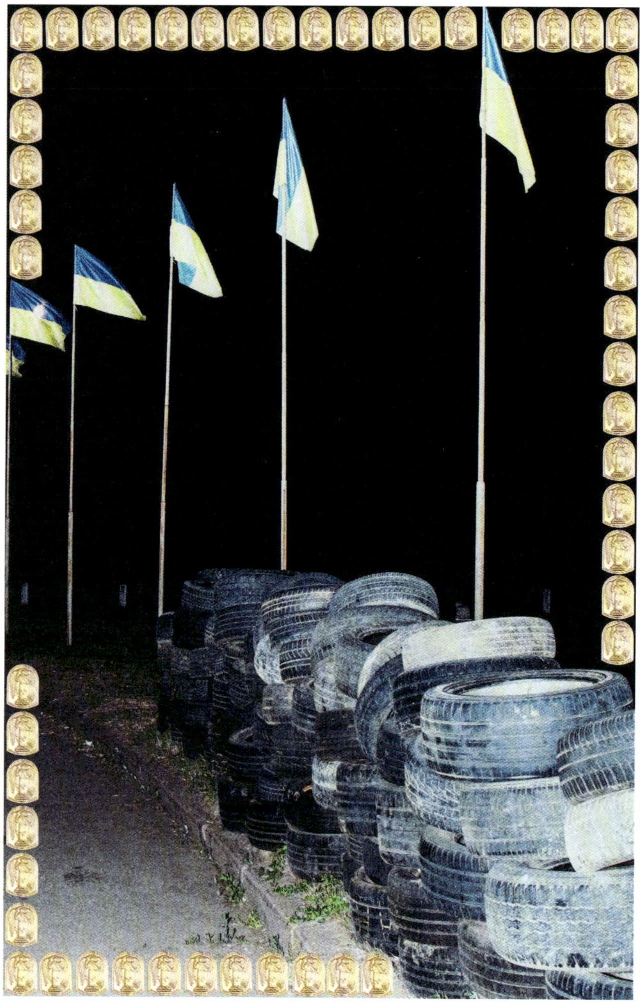

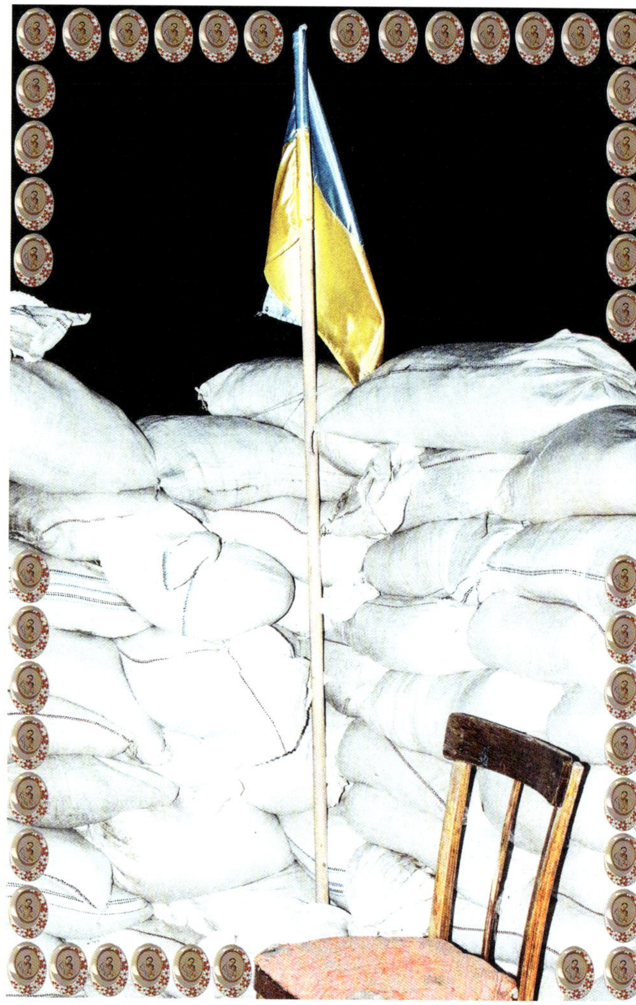

Military Commissariat, 2014. This project tells the story of ordinary young men, of whom there are millions in Ukraine. In early 2014, tanks and weapons might have seemed like mere play things. Soon they would become a brutal fixture of these young men's lives.

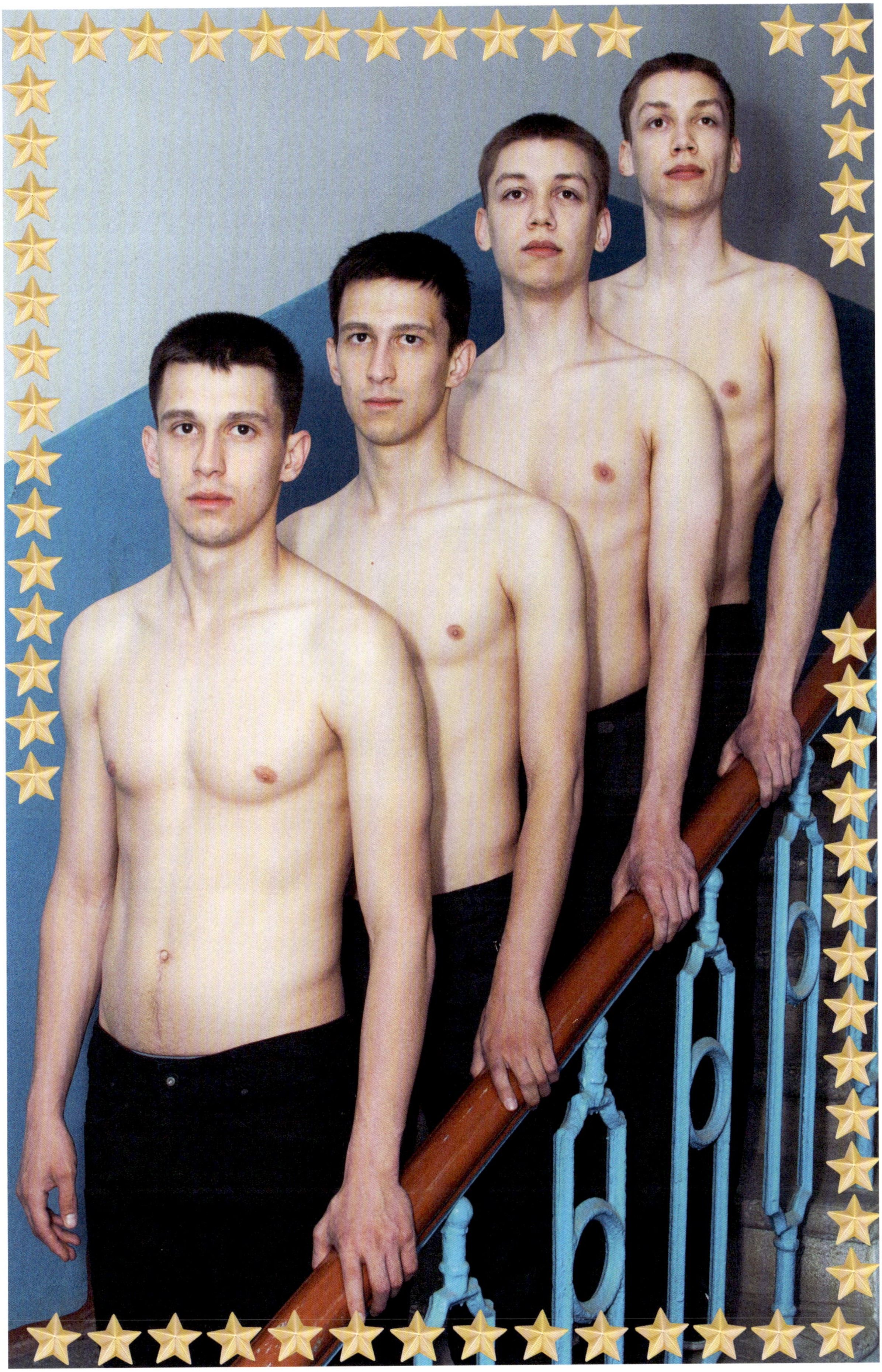

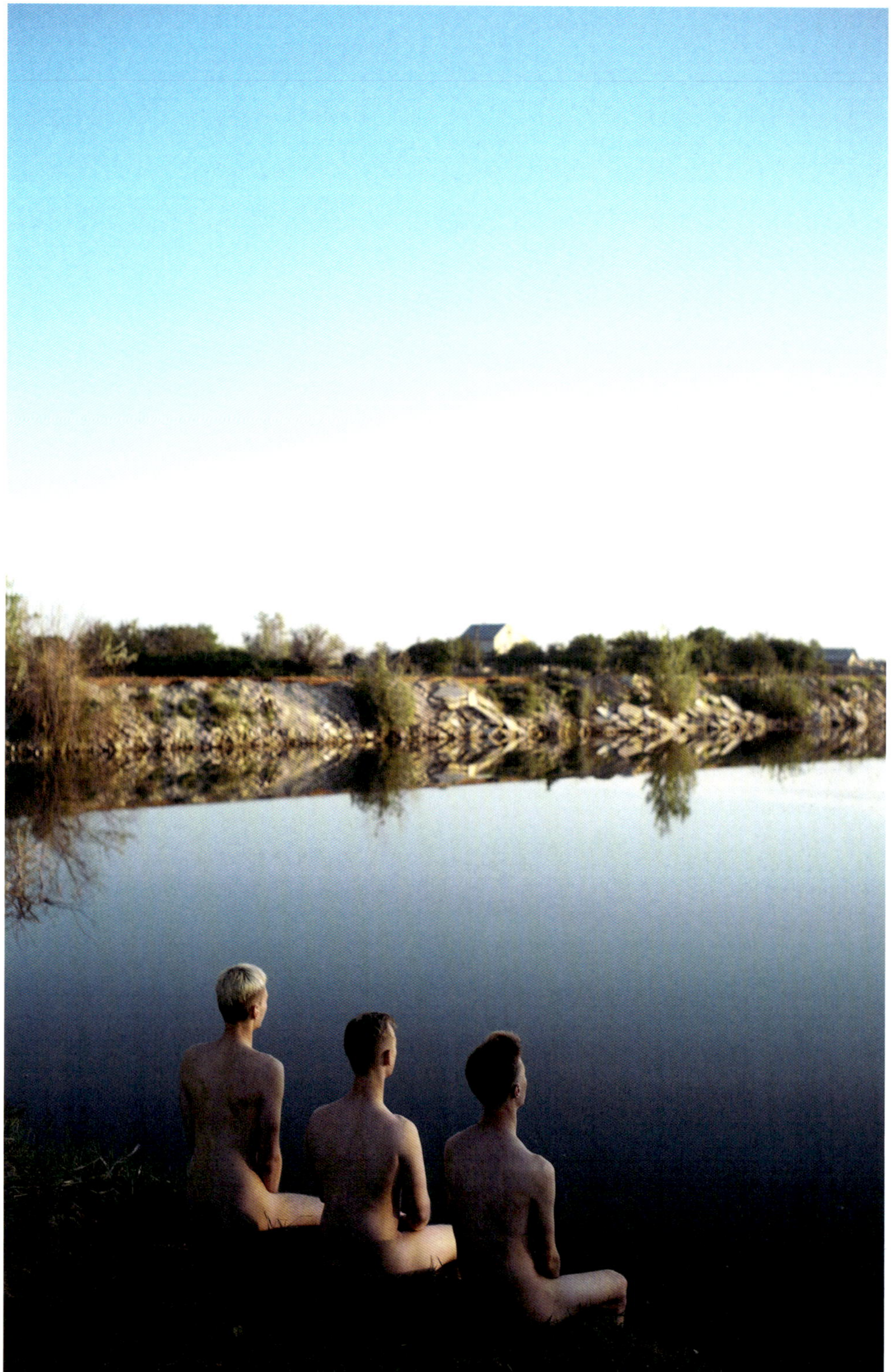

The images from the "Young and Free" series engage a generation of young men caught up in the changing history of their country, but who are determined to live freely. In these photographs, this freedom finds a symbolic form in nakedness. See also pages 180–181.

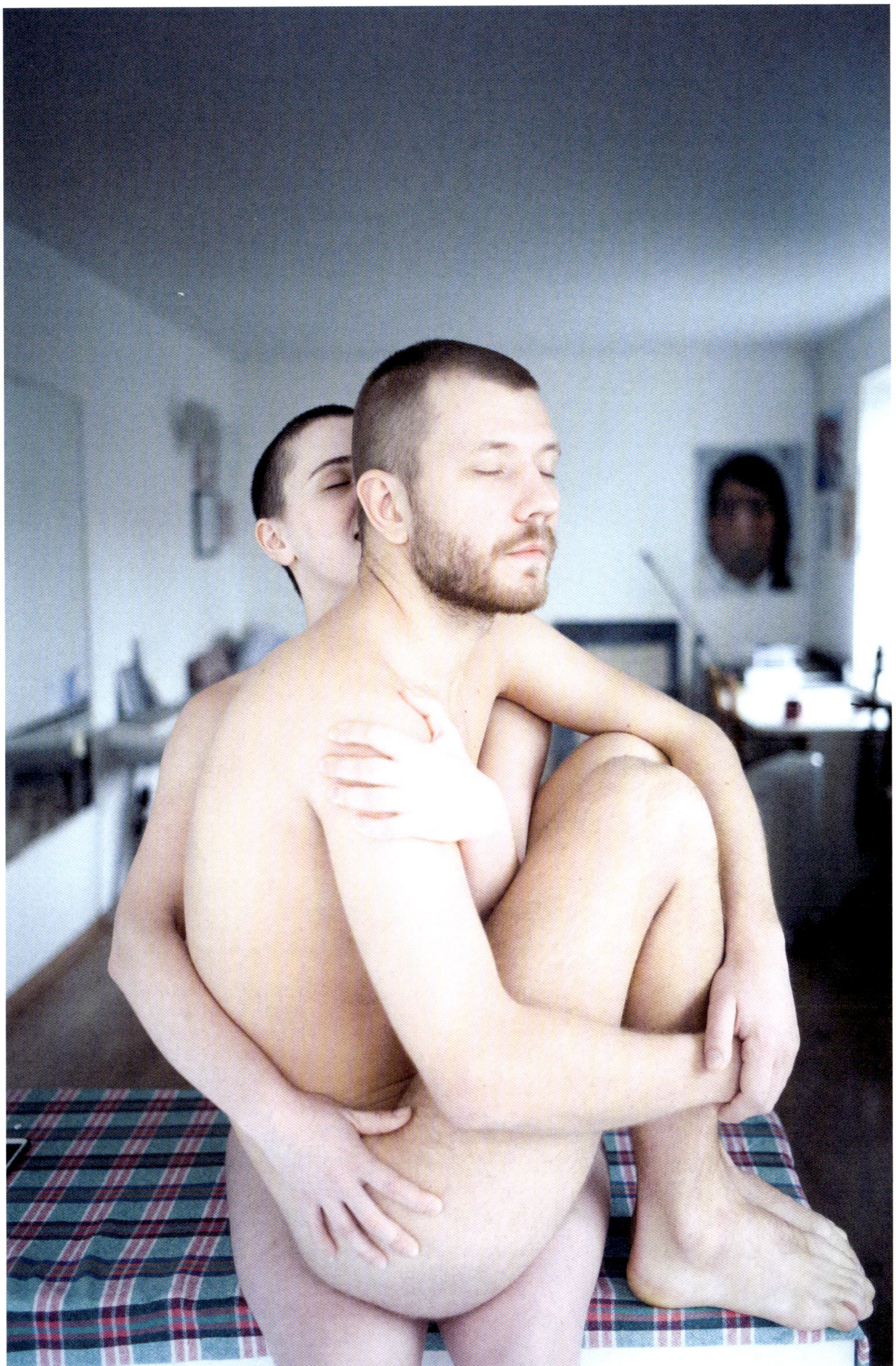

Freed from the symbolic meaning attached to clothes and uniforms, these young people assert themselves as individuals independent of wider social constructs. And in doing so, they manage to appear innocent yet provocative at the same time.

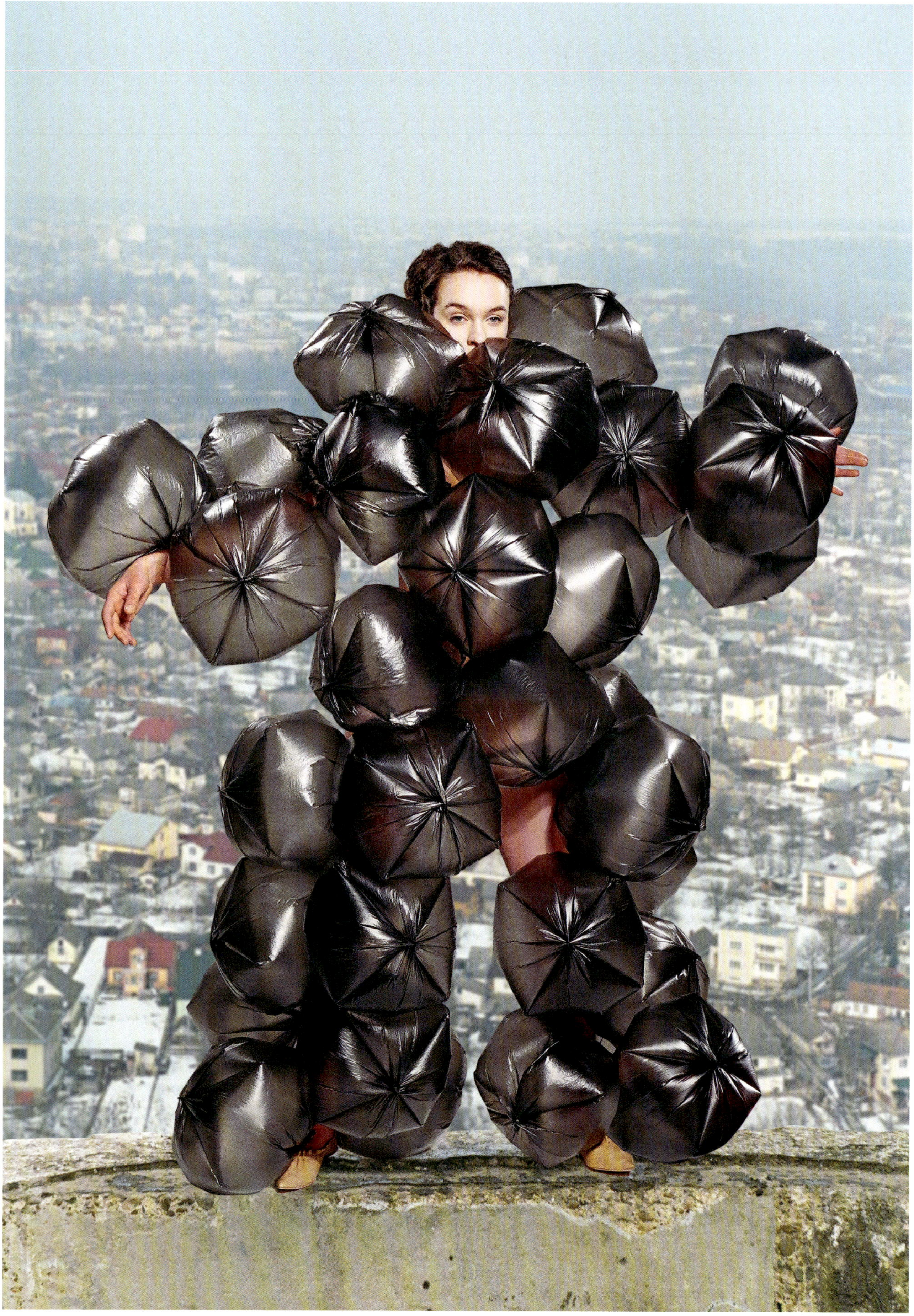

DISCOVERING THE NATURAL WORLD THROUGH ART

SYNCHRODOGS

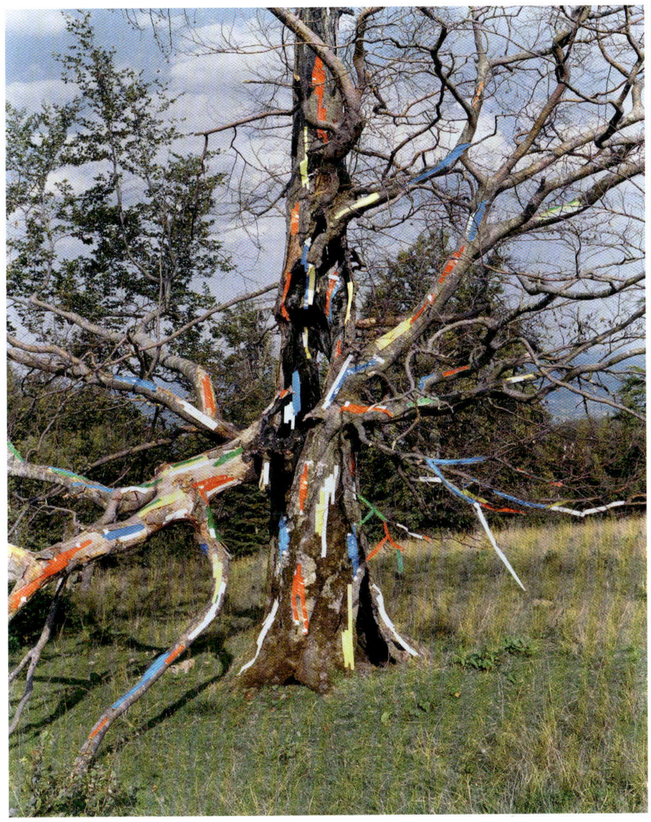

The artist duo Synchrodogs has always been interdisciplinary, working with mixed media, video, CGI, land art, artificial intelligence, installation, and even animation.

Synchrodogs, a duo of visual artists, consists of Roman Noven and Tania Shcheglova. These visionaries and creative directors from Ukraine have been collaborating since 2008. Together, they pursue issues of environmental awareness and education through art, exploring the complex relationship between humans and nature by juxtaposing the natural and the artificial, the real and the surreal through an interdisciplinary artistic approach. In 2020, they created a book about Ukraine for Louis Vuitton's Fashion Eye collection, a series of travel books that highlight various countries and regions through the lens of fashion. By 2022–2023, the duo was invited to the prestigious Media Slopes Conference in the United States, curated by art consultant Beth Fiore. Working as guest artists, they created a brand-new project, "Aura," to be exhibited at the conference. Additionally, the award-winning duo has presented their work at NFT.NYC and at Photo London, and has shot ad campaigns for KaDeWe and other big brands. They also participated in the AFAA art residency, where they studied 100 sports cars to create an art project inspired by automobile design and technology.

FASHIONING A NATIONAL IDENTITY, ONE GARMENT AT A TIME

Built from the ground up during the years of independence, fashion has become one of Ukraine's most significant creative industries, teeming with talent and shattering stereotypes along the way.

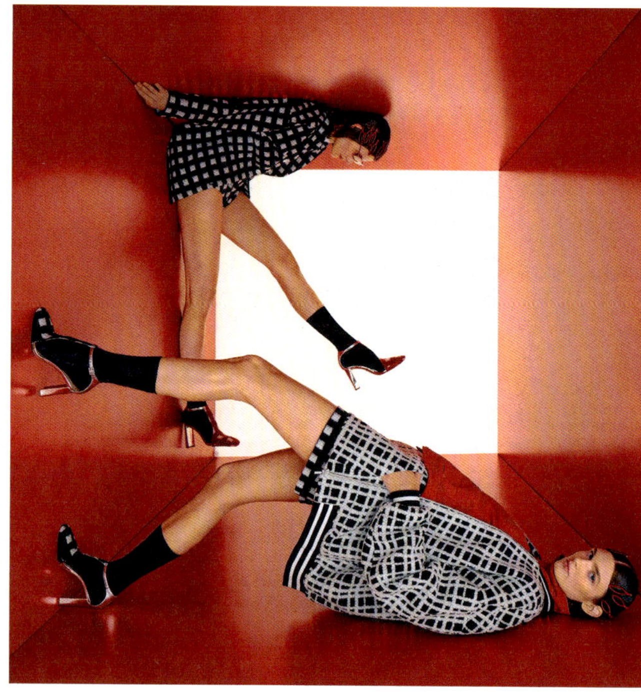

Each collection by the COAT, a brand by Katya Silchenko, is a bold statement aimed at drawing attention to Ukrainian modern culture. Below: fashion photography by Lena Shkoda.

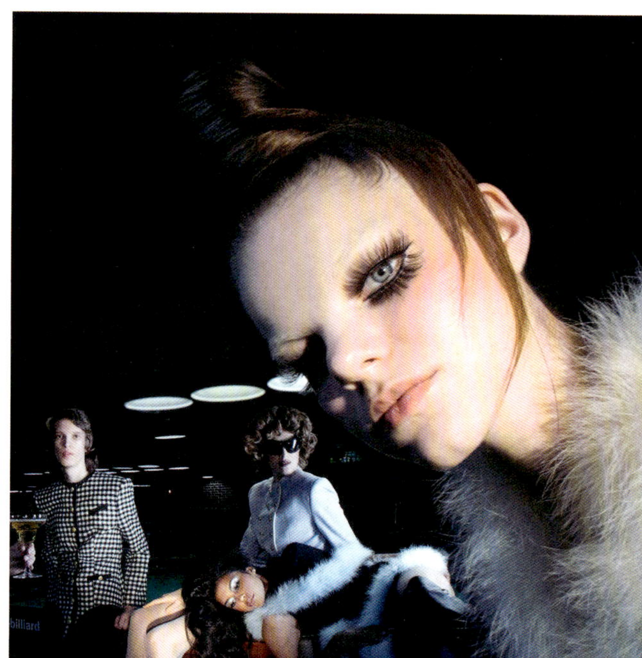

BY THE BOOTSTRAPS

Thirty years ago in Ukraine, the only entry point to the fashion world was to train as a tailor or seamstress. There were no schools offering comprehensive fashion education, guidance, and connections to budding designers, stylists, marketers, buyers, and fashion journalists alike. There was also no developed textile or production industry to speak of. This meant that the two main pillars of any thriving fashion scene—education and industry—simply did not exist. Despite these limitations, Ukraine has built a robust fashion scene from next to nothing, fueled by a mixture of intense enthusiasm, tireless work, and a passion for learning. Thirty years later, Ukraine is now home to a remarkably versatile and renowned fashion scene.

In the years following the country's independence, Ukrainian fashion consisted of small niche brands that catered to a select group of customers willing to take a risk and support local brands over better-known luxury labels. Now, three decades later, fashion has become one of the most vital creative industries in the country. It has also been instrumental in conveying to the rest of the world the essence of Ukrainian culture: youthful, culturally rich, and resilient in the face of economic and political challenge.

"POOR BUT COOL"

In 2015, fashion designer Anton Belinskiy decided to make a collection of dresses, hoodies, and parkas featuring the phrase: "Poor but Cool," a motto he'd borrowed from his friend, the visual artist Vova Vorotniov,

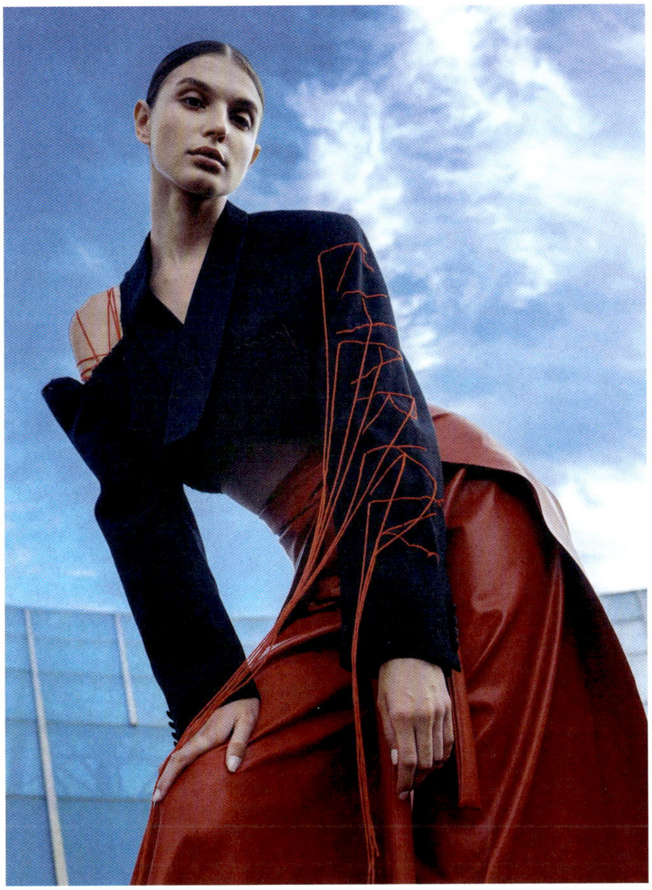

Maria Starchak created her upcycling brand to advocate for mindful consumption. Below: photo by renowned visual artist and fashion photographer Lena Shkoda.

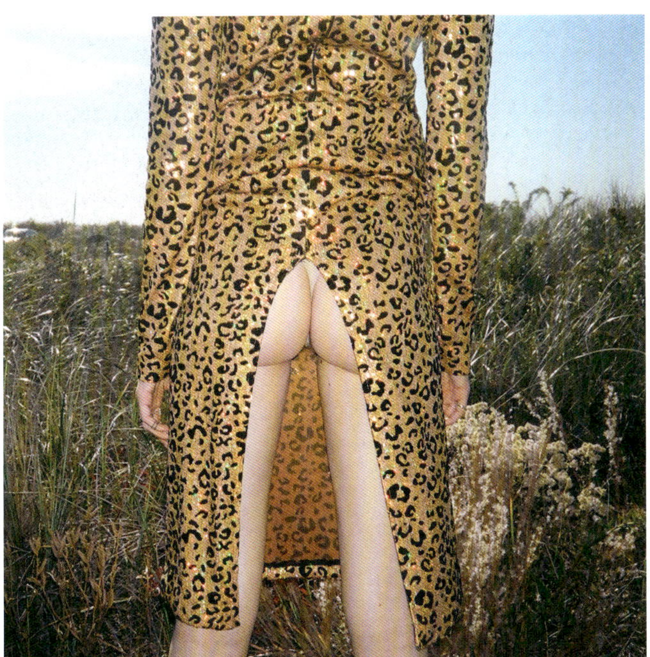

who himself had used the phrase on a popular series of graphic T-shirts. This bold statement, with its political overtones and a message of hope rather than hype, instantly became the unofficial slogan of Ukrainian fashion on the international scene. It perfectly described the vibrant and daring community of homegrown talent determined to succeed despite the lack of finance or established connections.

Vogue Ukraine, launched in 2013, has also boosted the country's fashion movement. The publication gradually made a name for itself among the larger Vogue family as one of the most artistic magazines in the franchise. Particularly committed to showcasing up-and-coming photographers, stylists, journalists, and designers, the magazine featured talent from all over the world as well as local artists and designers, providing rising stars in Ukraine with a chance to get noticed by the international fashion community. The pages of *Vogue Ukraine* were filled with a new generation of creators keen on developing new narratives in Ukrainian fashion and visual culture. Among these trailblazers was the Cat-b agency, whose founders Marija Pogrebniak and Anja Borovska hired models for their charisma rather than conventional good looks. Julie Poly, a photographer, also made a significant impact with her "mockumentary" photo series "Ukrzaliznytsia," which features staged photographs taken aboard trains—a nod to her former experience as a train conductor. The highly stylized yet emotionally raw images depict marginalized local characters and stereotypes using the visual language of fashion photography. Similarly, photographers Kristina Podobed and Genia Volkov, along with stylists Stas Soulkeeper and Sonya Soltes, strove to capture the essence of their generation while being an integral part of it themselves.

ON A MISSION TO REPRESENT THE NATION

It's impossible to describe Ukrainian fashion as having a single unified aesthetic. Nevertheless, one notable trend has emerged in the wake of the Euromaidan in 2014: a renewed passion for traditional culture and motifs. In the years following this revolution, many designers felt inspired to integrate folk elements, rare traditional techniques, and traditional silhouettes into their work. During the revolution, this reinterpretation of Ukraine's cultural legacy played a pivotal role in how Ukraine was depicted on the global stage; it became a symbol of unity at home and an instrument of cultural diplomacy abroad. In 2014, as images of the Kyiv riots filled the front pages of international newspapers, the culture and fashion sections displayed street-style photographs of fashionable women in Paris and Milan dressed in solidarity with Ukraine, wearing the latest collection of Vita Kin linen embroidered dresses—virtuose stylistic interpretation of folk culture, dripping with Ukrainian flair. The stark contrast underscored the nation's rich cultural legacy and inspired empathy for its quest for independence, revealing the influential role of fashion in advocating for Ukraine and in raising its profile internationally. Fashion has acquired a wholly new significance.

Interestingly, the process of fashioning Ukraine's national identity coincided with a broader dismantling of gender stereotypes within the industry. Several generations of womenswear designers were eager to present their own take on femininity. Some tackled clichés about Ukrainian beauty, others were keen to overcome patriarchal ideas of conventional beauty, while others still embraced effortless or even openly provocative sexuality. Whether in Bevza and Six's sleek designs, or Anna October's alluring, fluid dresses, or Frolov's curvaceous silhouettes, these designers exemplified the various forms of expression that have emerged as fashion mirrors the process of societal liberation. That said, the process is not over, and the tension between myth and reality persists, leaving space for future interpretations.

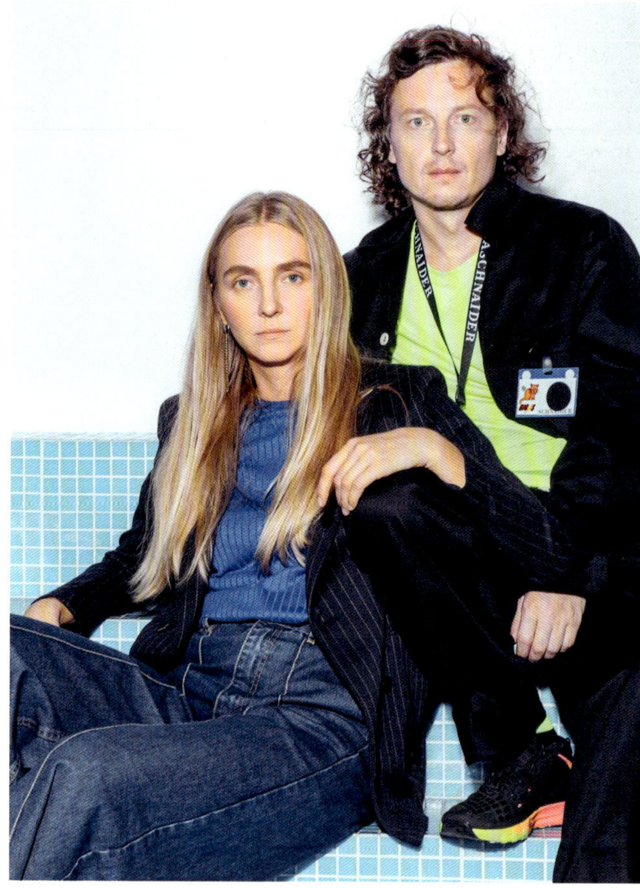

Kseniaschnaider fashion brand is built on sustainability. Below: a campaign image created by the artist Elizaveta Litovka, aka Floweirdy, which reflects the creativity of two Ukrainian creators.

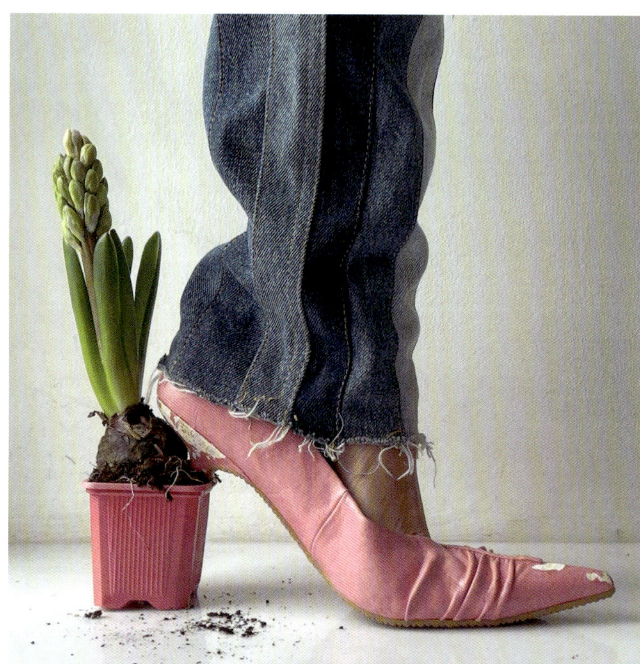

A LAND OF TREASURE

In Ukraine, fashion extends beyond the catwalk to the suburbs, where second-hand shops and vintage markets abound. Ukraine has consistently ranked as one of the top five importers of second-hand clothes. While this risks turning the country into a dumping ground for worn clothes, local designers, stylists, subculture

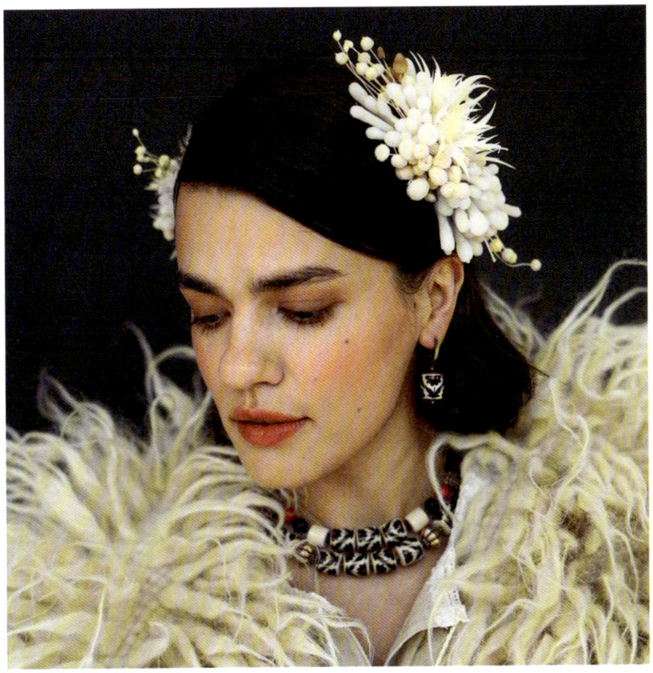

Oksana Boriychuck's contemporary jewelry takes inspiration from traditional Ukrainian accessories and motifs. Below: An iconic white dress by Bevza.

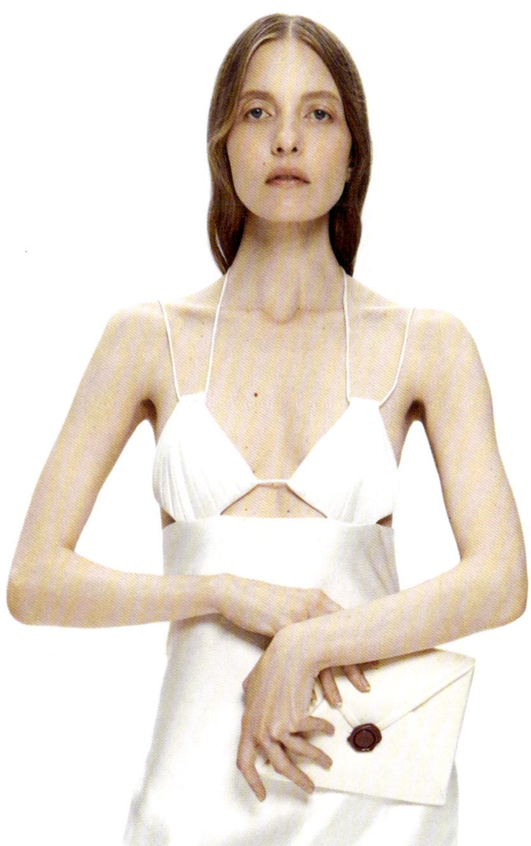

enthusiasts, and fashion lovers all view it as a veritable goldmine. Long before upcycling became trendy, they were perfecting all manner of techniques to refurbish, restyle, and repurpose used clothing.

The legendary Lisovyi Market in Kyiv, thanks to its unique mix of affordable prices and unexpected finds, has become an essential stop for tourists seeking undiscovered local gems. Despite the fact that thrift shopping has been historically associated with poverty ever since the Soviet era, Lisovyi Market has long been a hub for designers looking to upcycle clothing for their collections. These innovators used the market not only for inspiration but as an ingenious response to financial limitations. Sasha Kanevskyi, now a head designer at Stone Island (and previously at Yeezy), used to travel to Lisovyi as a budding designer to find outerwear garments to repurpose. Meanwhile the Kseniaschnaider brand gained international attention with its iconic demi-denim pants made from second-hand jeans. The brand's founders, Ksenia and Anton Schnaider, even created a special position called "the hunter" for someone skilled in finding high-quality used denim at markets. And Yasia Khomenko of RCR Khomenko, celebrated for her innovative techniques in breathing funky new life into shirts, once contemplated building a "church of upcycling" to advocate for widespread upcycling in Ukraine. And last but not least is the fashion brand bettter, founded by the former fashion director of *Vogue Ukraine*, Julie Pelipas. Bettter has made a name for itself by turning unsold men's suits into chic, sustainable masterpieces. Pelipas, so the legend goes, could be spotted early in her career picking out old suits from the racks of Lisovyi.

Until recently, the label "Made in Ukraine" was more likely to be found on clothes of international brands chosing to outsource their production. But now, several young Ukrainian companies have shaped their image on recognizable products. By carving out an image for themselves, they have put a spotlight on the country and established a creative connection with the international scene, shipping their items—proudly designed and produced in the Ukraine—worldwide. The dignity of "Made in Ukraine" has been reclaimed and transformed.

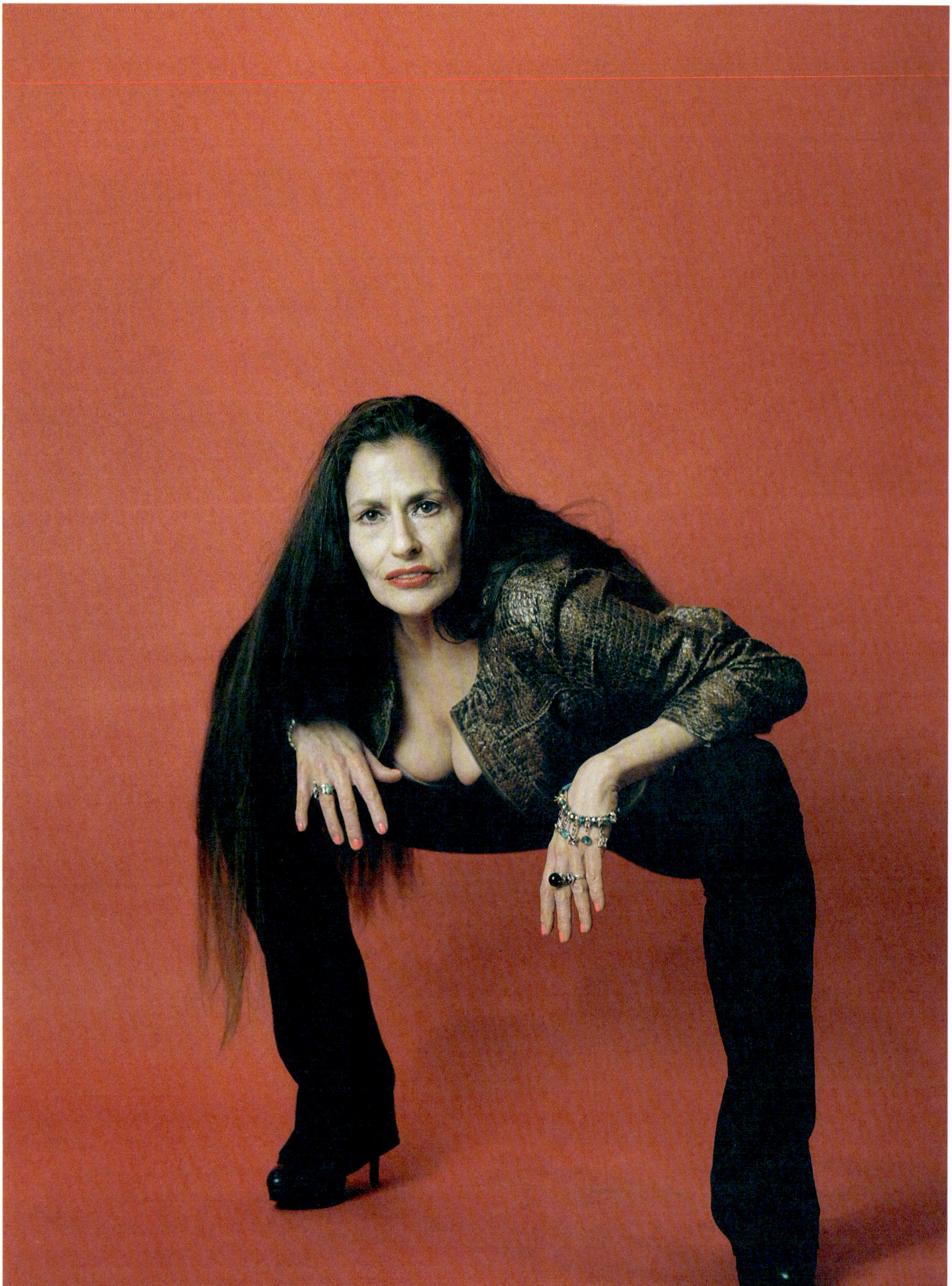

FASHION PHOTOGRAPHY, WITH A TWIST

LENA SHKODA · *ОЛЕНА ШКОДА*

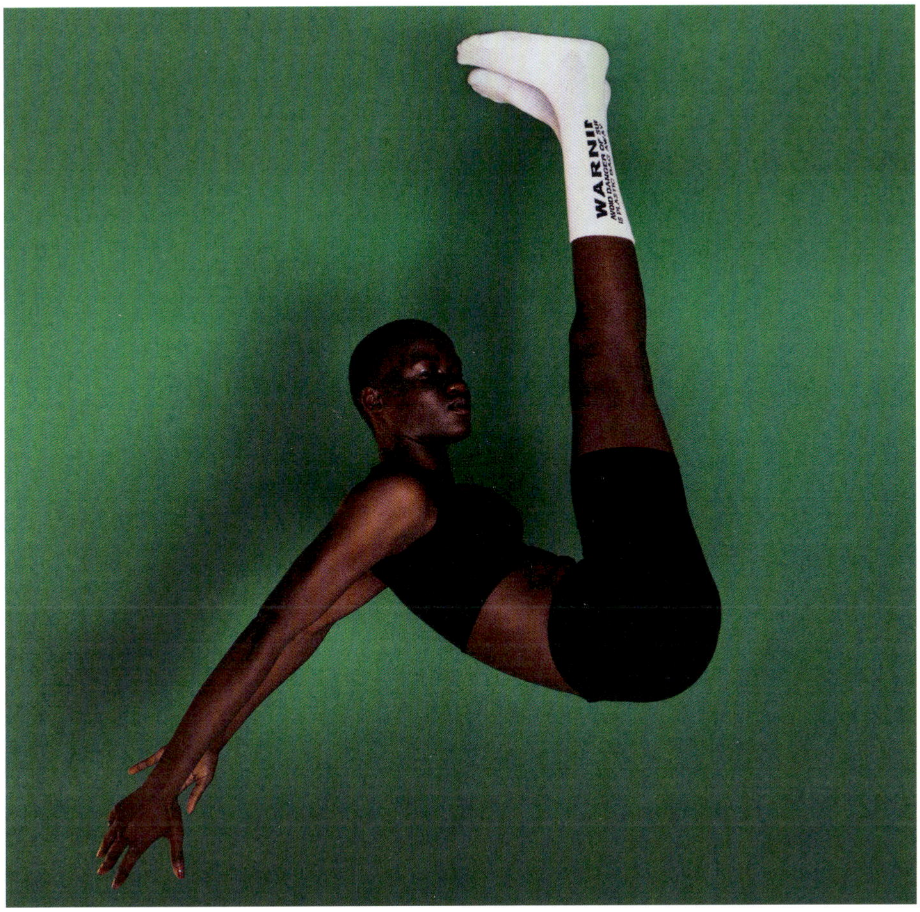

Lena Shkoda's photos are full of irony and beauty. The artist likes to experiment with different films and cameras, and plays with light, shadow, angles, and mood with incredible ease.

Lena Shkoda is a photographer and visual artist with more than 20 years of experience in art and fashion photography. She honed her skills at Studio Marangoni in Florence, Italy, before relocating to New York and establishing her own production studio. Despite living far from home, she makes a point of visiting Ukraine whenever she has the chance. Shkoda enjoys experimenting with themes of fashion and sexuality, approaching them with a lighthearted, often ironic touch. The photographer is currently very fond of bright, contrasting colors, but, as an artist who is constantly trying new approaches and aesthetics, this could very well change. Shkoda works with fashion brands like the Ukrainian company Bevza (see page 314) and has exhibited her work in cities such as New York, Kyiv, Florence, and Berlin. Her photographs have appeared in *Vogue Ukraine, Harper's Bazaar, Schön! Magazine, Wonderland, The Independent,* and the *Editorial Magazine,* among others. Shkoda also co-founded the New York-based non-profit Spilka, which supports volunteers, refugees, and other victims of the war.

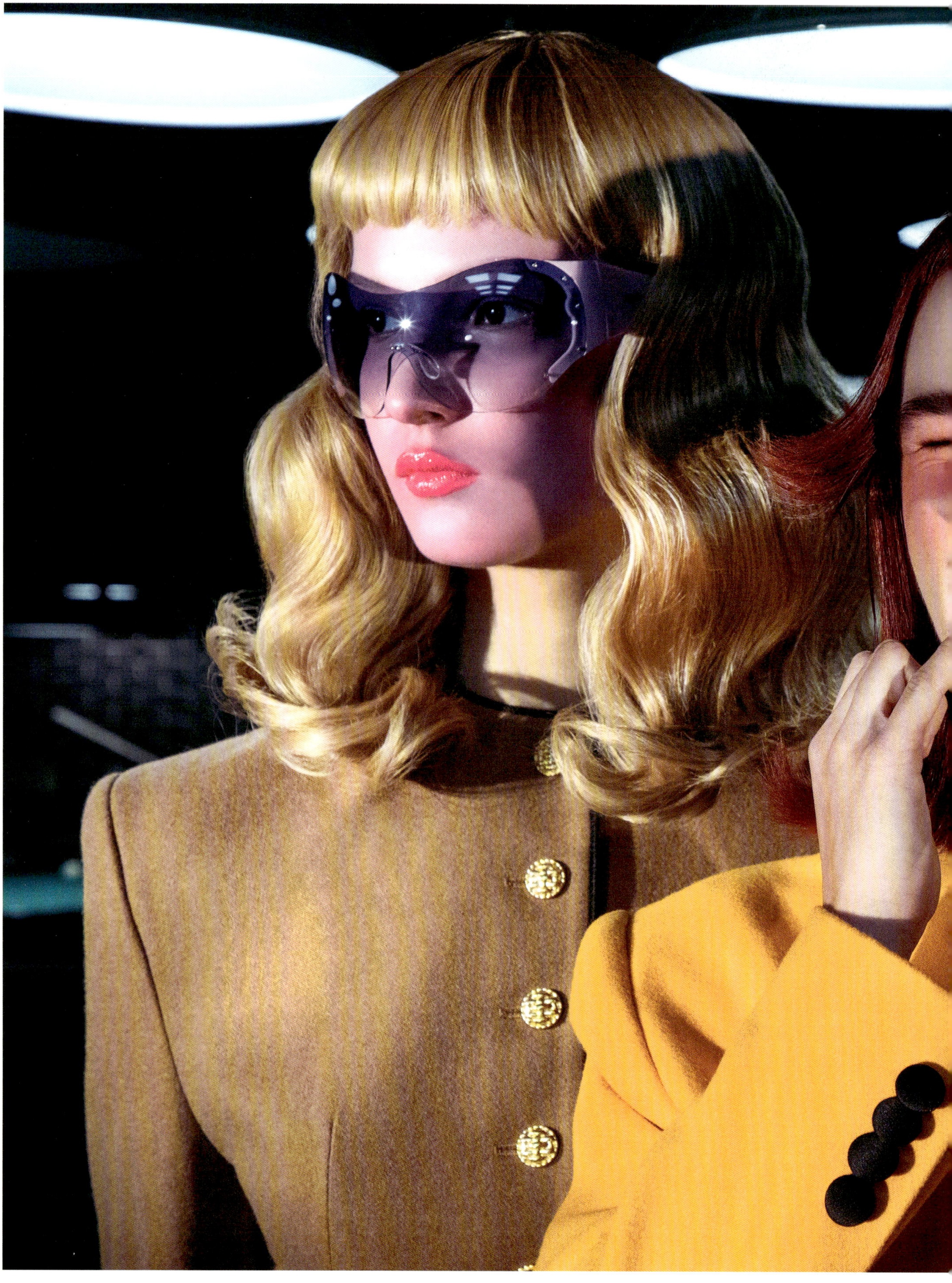

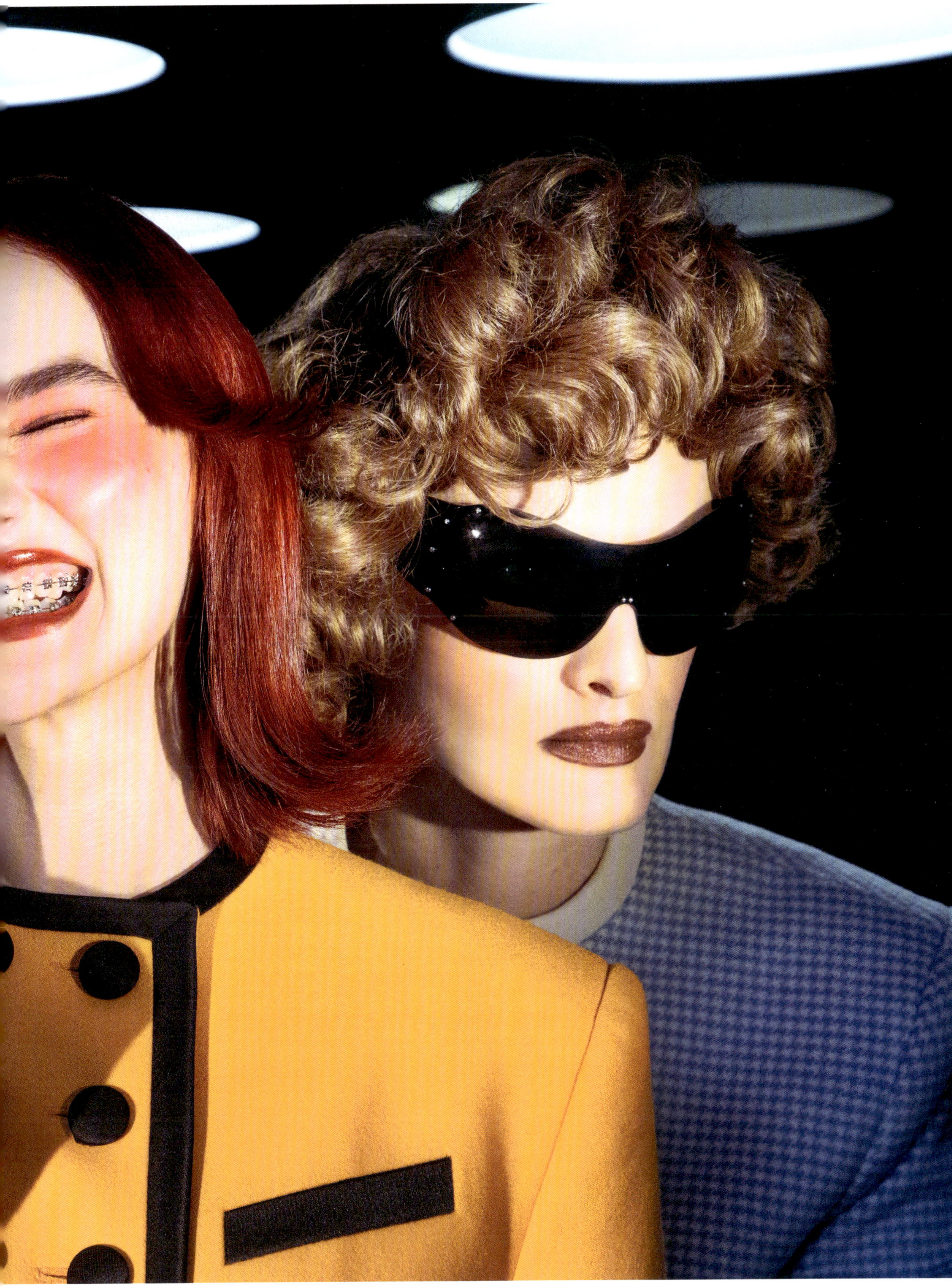

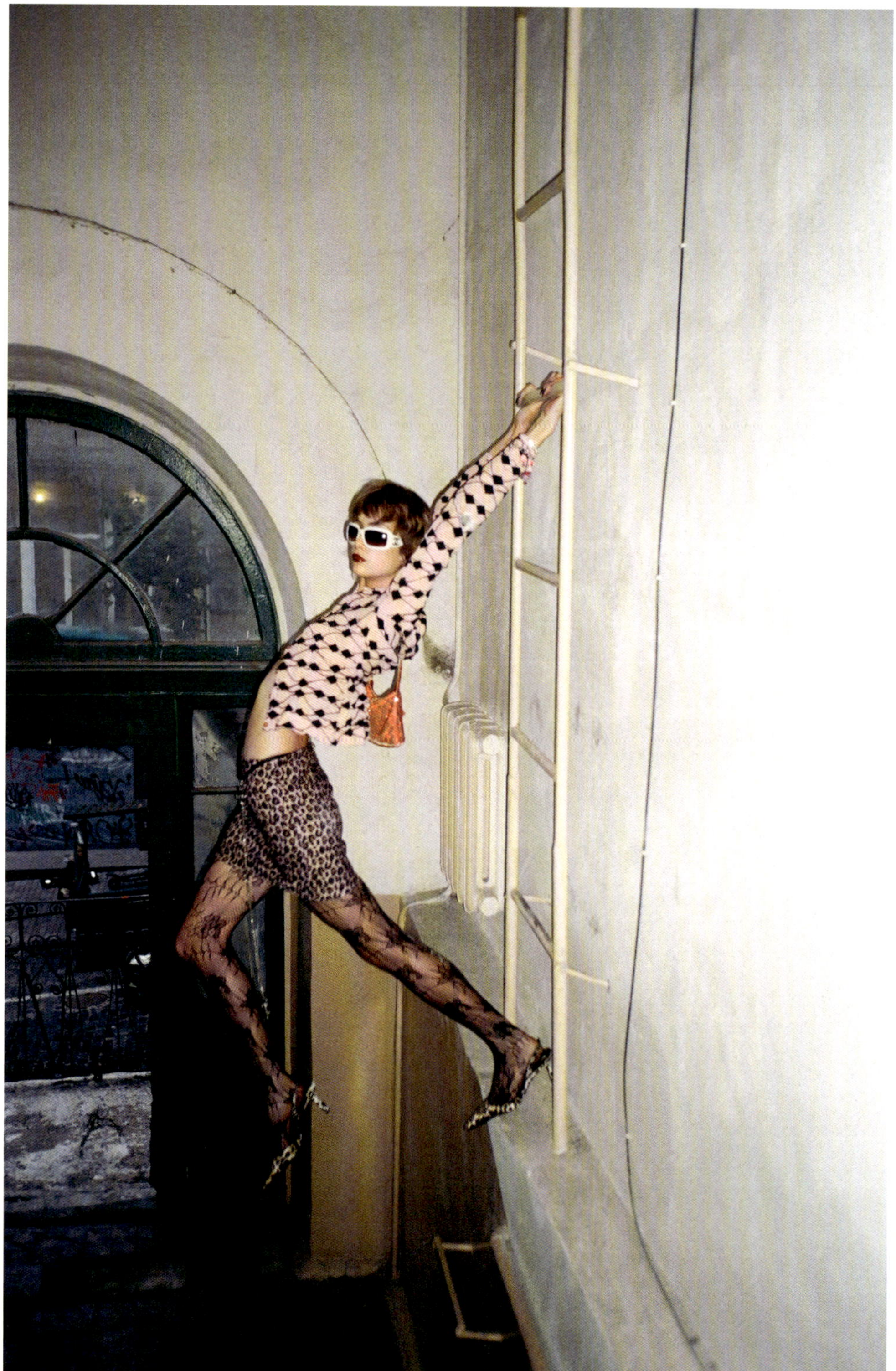

Drawing inspiration from every corner, Lena Shkoda works hard to stay open and perceptive to her environment. Her photography is filled with beauty and irony, and her personal projects often feature her friends, who motivate and inspire her.

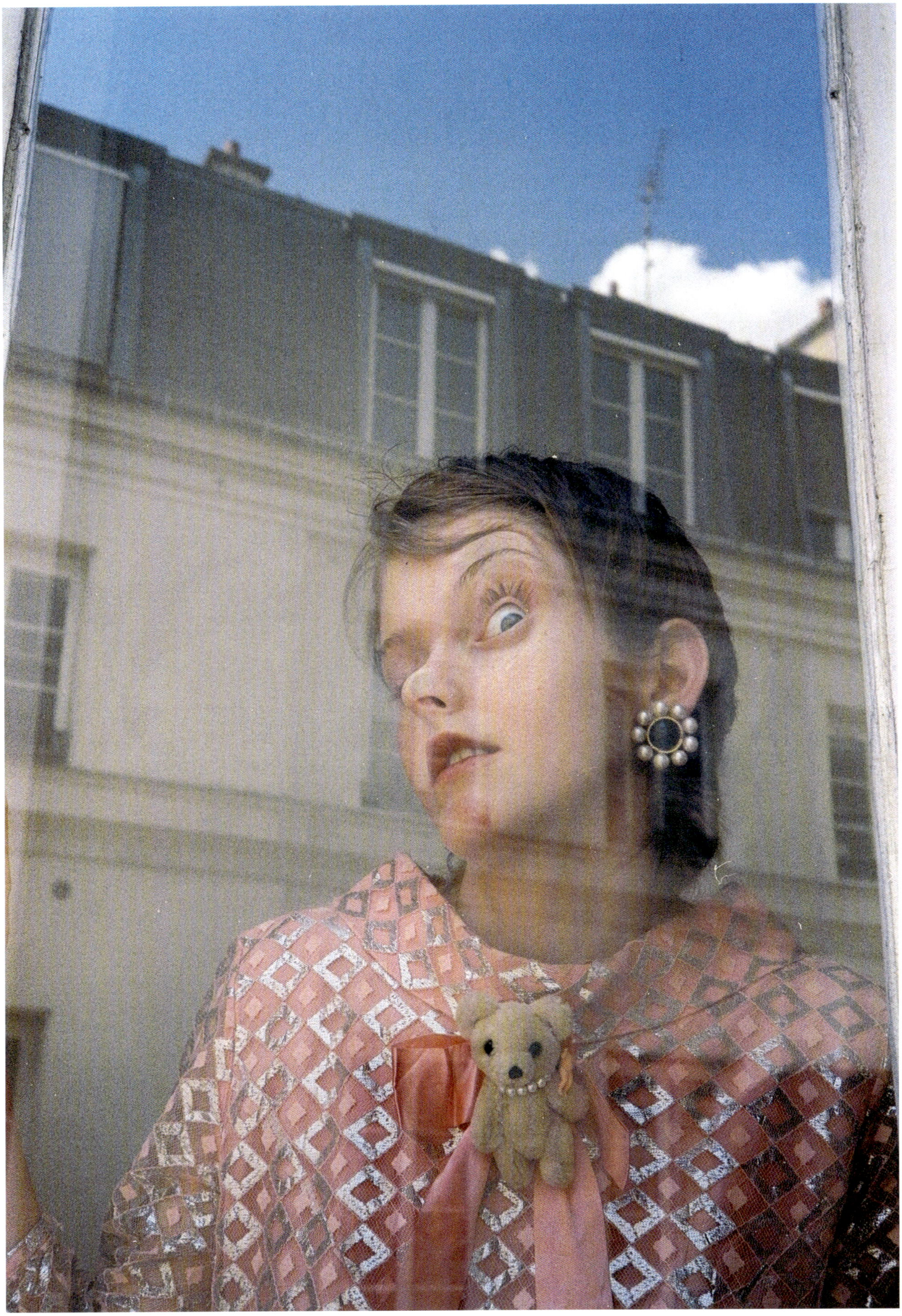

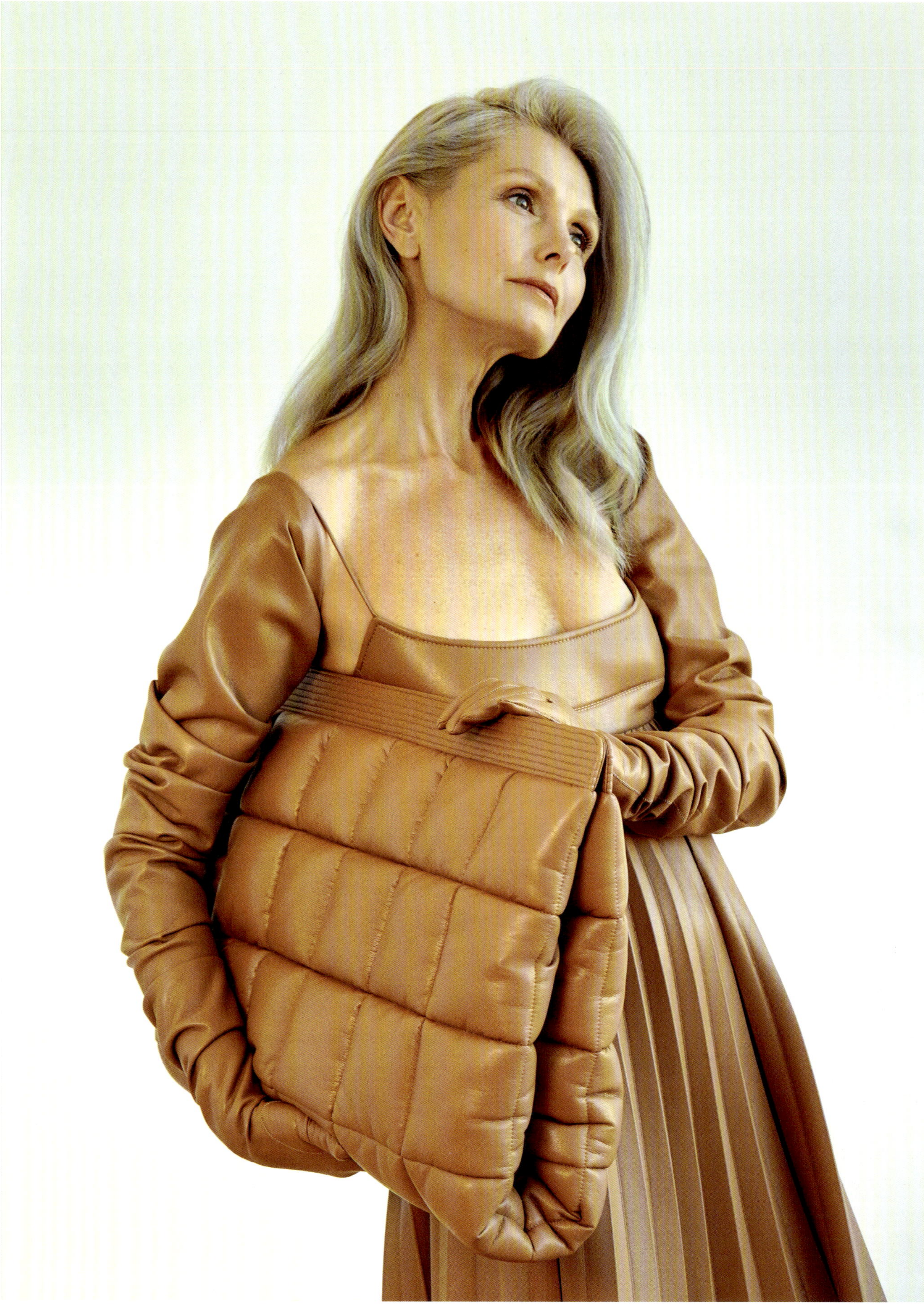

BRAVERY IN EVERY GARMENT

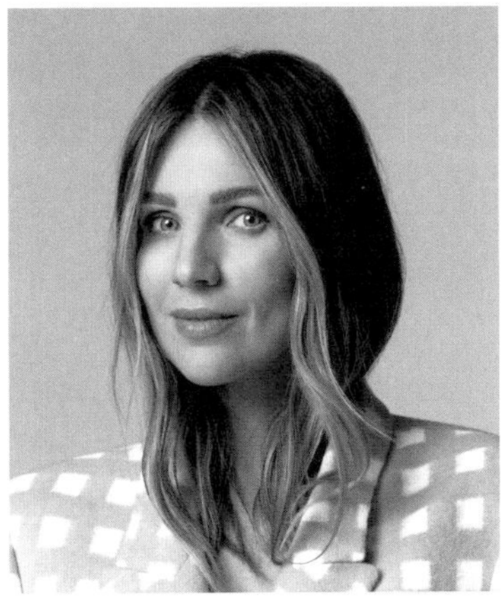

THE COAT BY KATYA SILCHENKO

Each of Katya Silchenko's collections at the COAT is a powerful statement aimed at drawing the attention of world fashion to Ukrainian traditions and modern culture.

The COAT is a Ukrainian brand of ready-to-wear women's clothing, founded by Katya Silchenko in 2014. Silchenko, who is also the creative director of the company, gets her inspiration from women: strong, passionate, and gentle at the same time. With a blend of aesthetics, shapes, and colors unique to the brand, the designer's vision is ever-present, from her very first collection to her most recent collaborations. When Silchenko designed her Spring-Summer 2023 collection, she wanted to depict the originality of Ukrainian culture by using traditional silhouettes, prints, and embroidery, all while utilizing colors inspired by the country's stunning national landscapes. Presented at Copenhagen Fashion Week in 2022 and photographed at the open-air National Museum of Folk Architecture and Life of Ukraine (known as the Pyrohiv Museum), the collection was a bold statement that drew the attention of the global fashion world to Ukrainian culture. Despite facing challenges since the beginning of the full-scale invasion, the COAT has remained steadfast in its mission. The brand has produced two main collections, one pre-collection, two collaborations, and two capsules, all in Ukraine. The COAT has also launched a line of home decor, including jugs made in an eco-village in the Zhytomyr region using ancient techniques. As Silchenko succinctly puts it: "We are brave!" In 2022, the COAT joined forces with Italian partner Noova, producing sneakers in the national colors of Ukraine. The collaboration received a record number of pre-orders, with proceeds going to charity. The COAT has gained the admiration of the First Lady of Ukraine Olena Zelenska, and has been embraced by celebrities such as Maye Musk, Rita Ora, Amanda Steele, Coco Rocha, Kelly Rutherford, Beyoncé, and many others. The brand's commitment to celebrating and promoting Ukrainian culture and craftsmanship continues to resonate with fashion enthusiasts around the world.

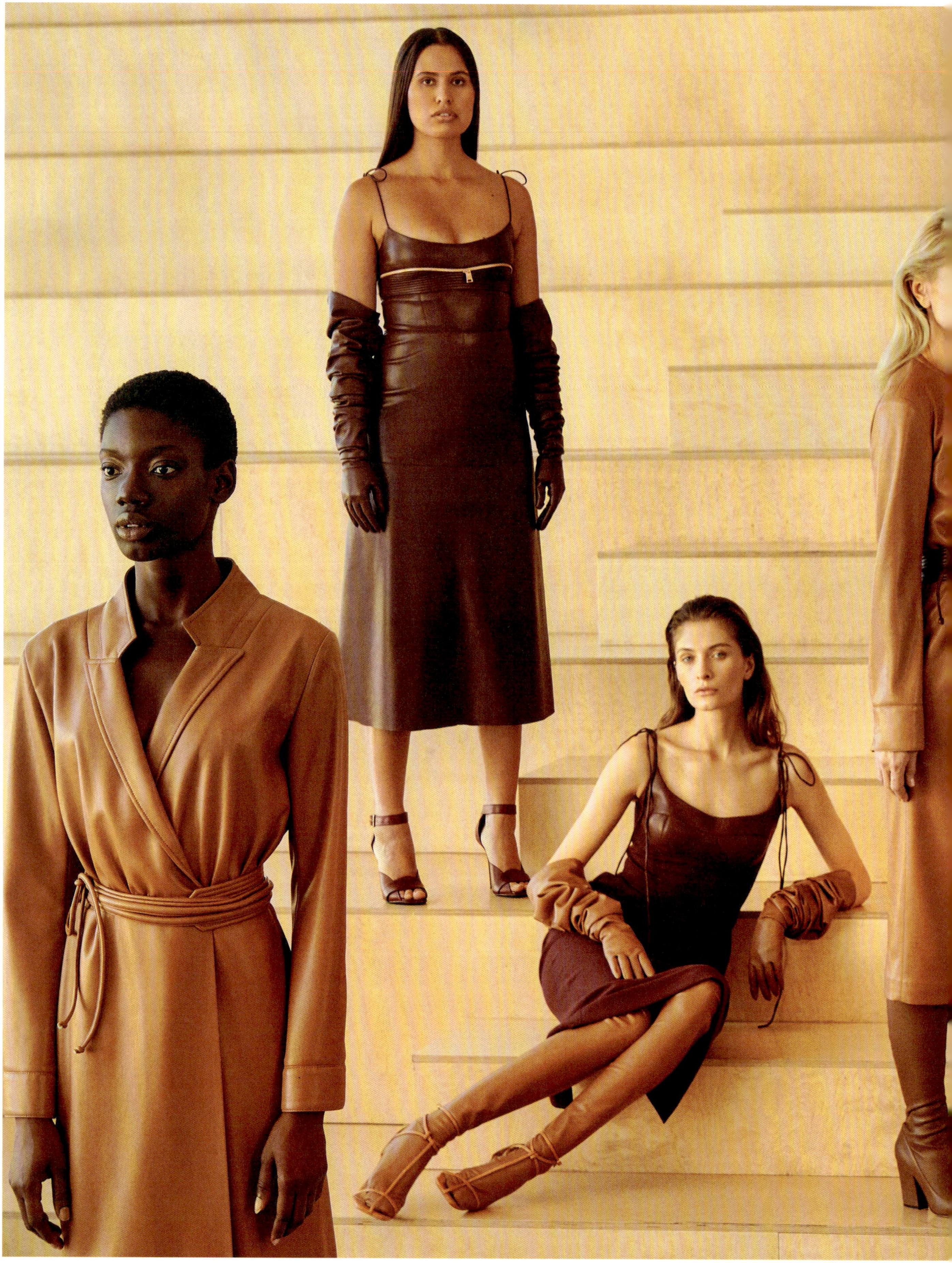

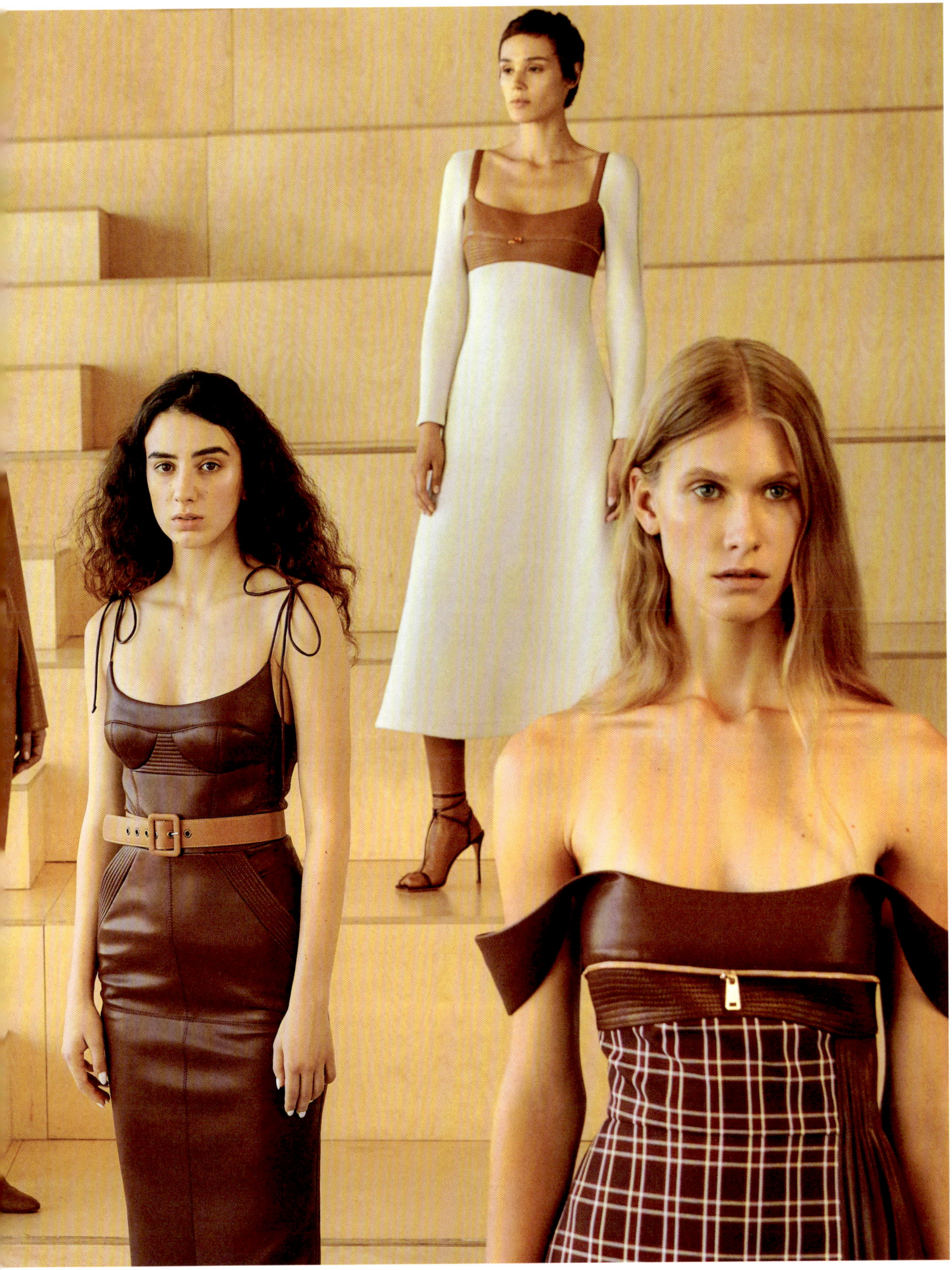

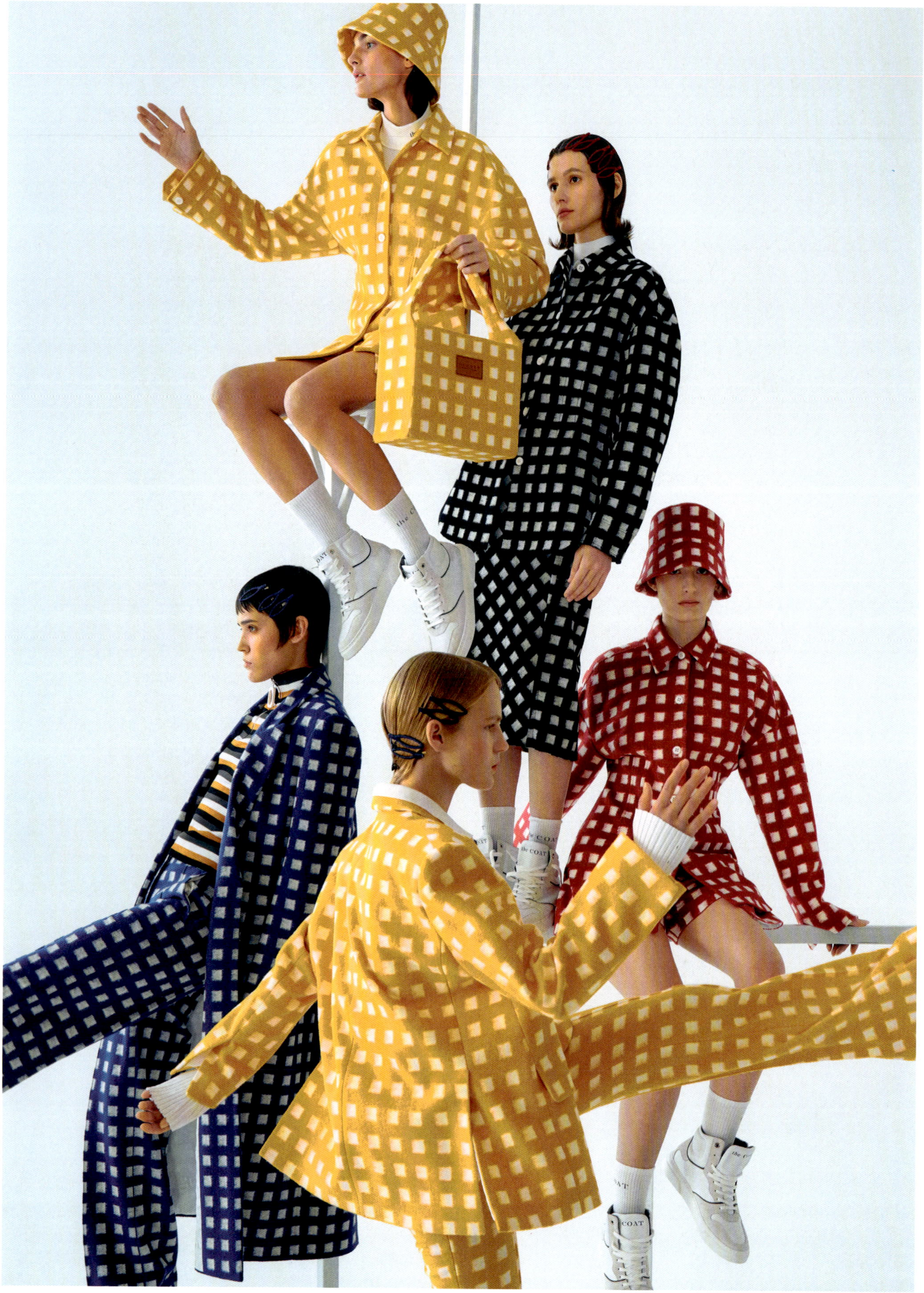
the COAT

“It is quite simple to trace the DNA of the brand in any collection. No need to explore the archive to see my creative vision. It is a common thread from the beginning to the latest collections, collaborations, or drops.”

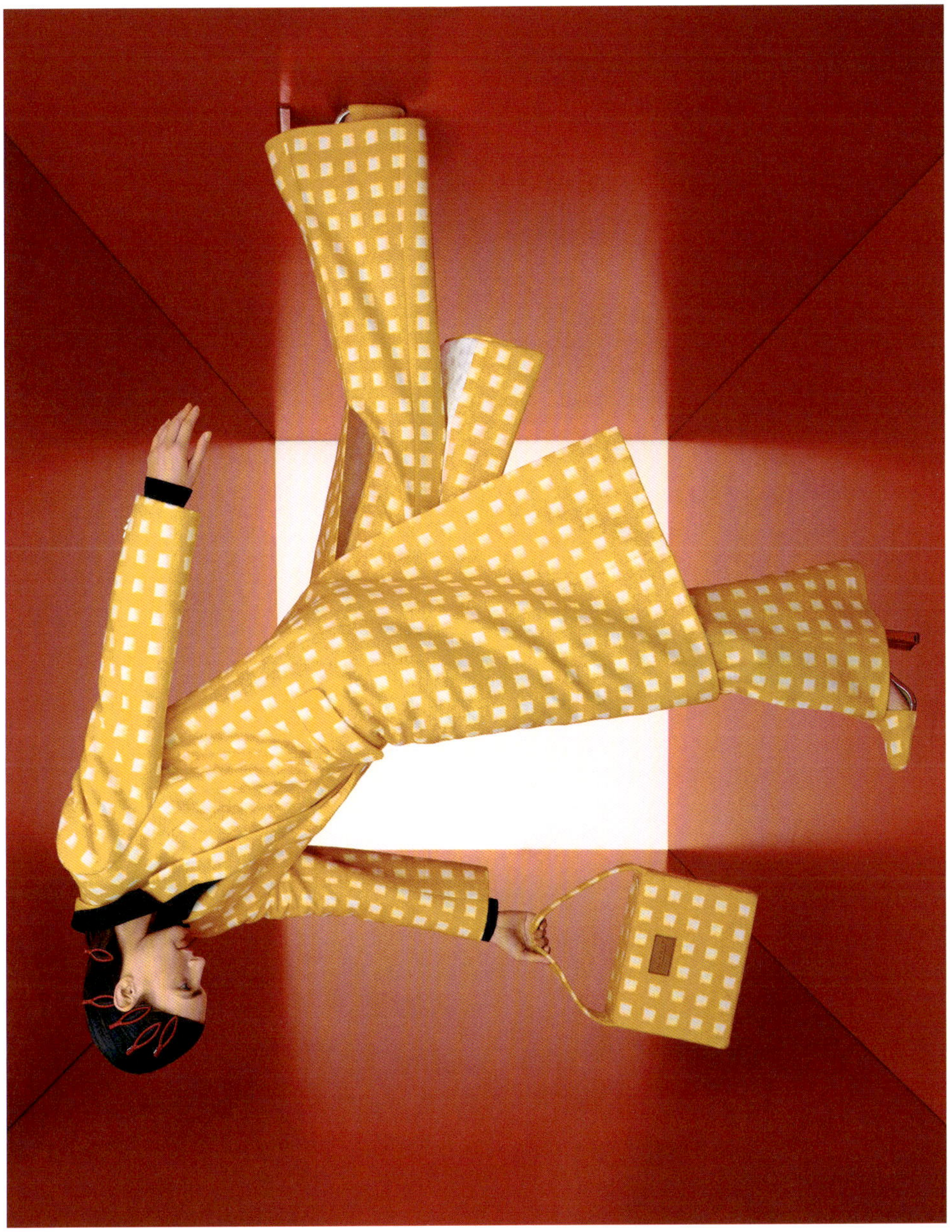

The COAT’s Pre-Spring ’23 collection offers a rush of endorphins with its dynamic geometric silhouettes in eye-catching magenta, sun-soaked yellow, and electrifying blue tones. The brand is known for expertly blending classic tailoring with bold accents.

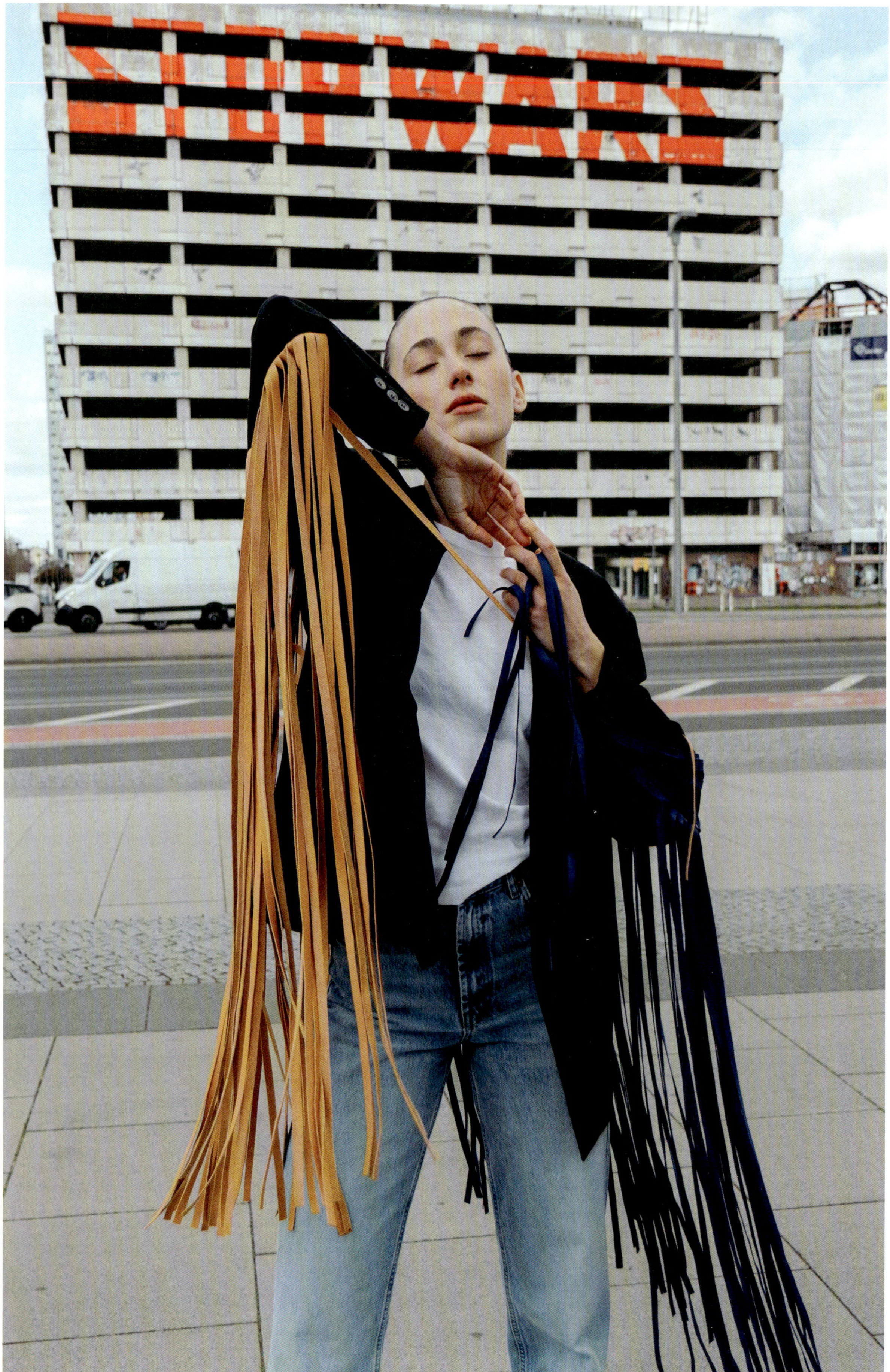

AN HOMAGE TO TRADITION VIA BOLD DESIGN IDEAS

STARCHAK

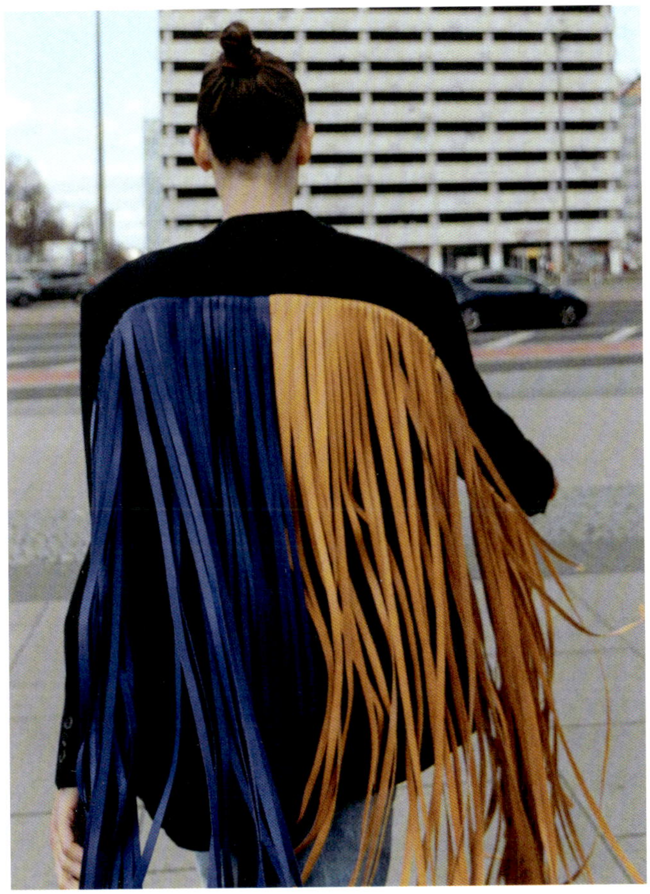

By transforming vintage textiles into modern clothing, Maria Starchak ingeniously blends Ukrainian heritage with contemporary fashion.

In 2019, Maria Starchak founded her upcycling brand in order to advocate for smart consumption. Raised in a village in the Lviv region, Starchak's upbringing was steeped in local tradition. Her fond childhood memories of carpet hangings and vibrant woven designs served as inspiration for the unique Drimota collection, which translates to "nap" in Ukrainian. This collection evokes a dream-like return to one's roots, a chance to revisit old homes and connect with those who have passed away. By blending contemporary design cues with traditional elements, the collection works *kylym* and Hutsul motifs into modern suits, colorful ties, and tailored pants, balancing relaxed androgyny with a pronounced masculinity. According to the designer, her wartime collection for Spring-Summer 2022 was created not from inspiration but from fear, which she then channeled into her work. Each element of the collection tells the story of Ukrainian cities impacted by the Russian invasion.

A CULTURAL RENAISSANCE: THE RISE OF UKRAINIAN DESIGN

Thanks to Ukraine's rich cultural history, the nation has developed a highly distinctive style over the years. This bold, unique aesthetic is on display everywhere, whether in its wood and ceramic dishes, regional embroidery, bright colors, decorative ribbons, or dried flowers—all elements deeply embedded in Ukrainian culture.This colorful cultural legacy, alongside the nation's Soviet past and its numerous political transformations, has given rise to the Ukrainian design scene we see today. Above all else, modern Ukrainian design aims to show the world what was hidden for so many years.

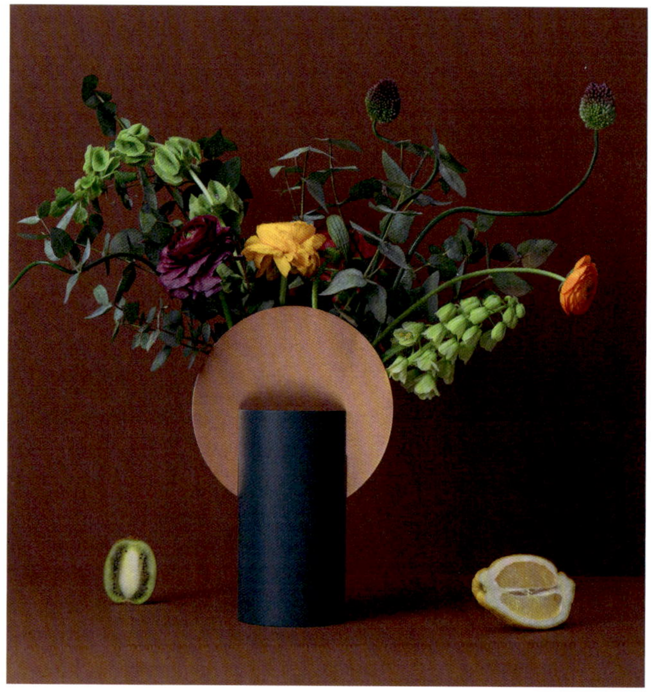

Malevich Vase by Kateryna Sokolova. Below: Levantin Design, an interdisciplinary design studio, implements cosmopolitan design concepts for clients with a creative outlook on the world.

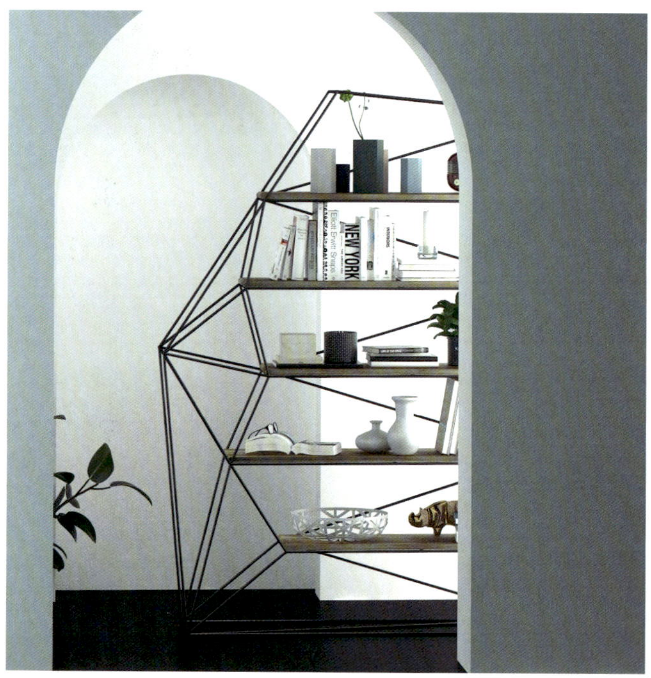

DOES UKRAINIAN DESIGN REALLY EXIST?

One of the most important aspects of the Ukrainian style is its deep connection to Ukrainian culture and history. Many Ukrainian artists and designers draw inspiration from traditional Ukrainian folk art and crafts, like furniture and decor brand Faina, which represents Ukrainian heritage through its organic design and materials.

Ukrainian style is also closely associated with eco-style, as natural materials such as stone, clay, and wood have been used here for centuries. It is very common to see raw, untreated brick and stone in modern designs, following a long tradition of celebrating natural texture. Modern Ukrainian products often integrate traditional motifs and materials into their embroidery patterns, woodcarving, and ceramics. Other essential art forms include pottery, weaving, and *pysanky* (Ukrainian Easter eggs), each boasting distinctive styles unique to each region and made with techniques passed down through generations.

Ukrainian design is also characterized by a deep appreciation for nature and spirituality, reflected in its pattern designs and interior details. Many of these elements come from the Orthodox Christian tradition, which has been an important part of Ukrainian culture

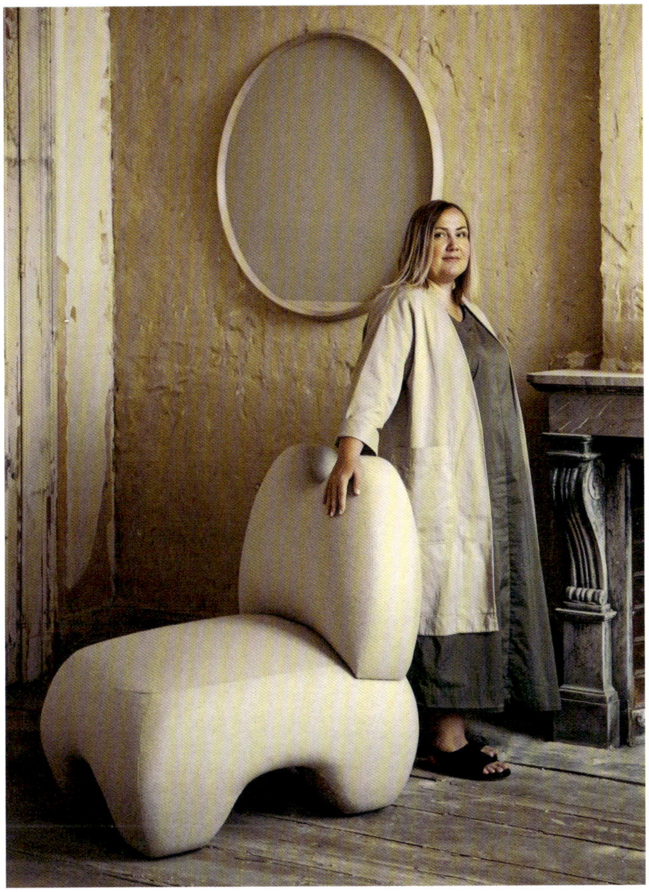

Victoria Yakusha, a designer, artist, and architect, has been inspired by Ukrainian culture and traditions all her life, and has always wanted to give her country a voice. Below: Ceramic plate by Gunia Project.

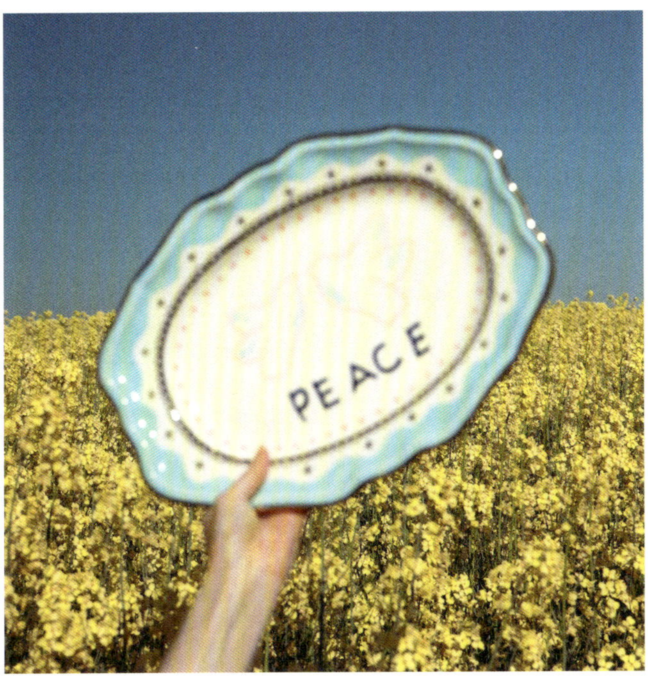

for centuries. The church's influence can be seen in the use of religious iconography and traditional Orthodox Christian motifs in decorative crafts. Simultaneously, Ukrainian folklore and mythology, such as stories of Mavka (a type of female spirit) and the holiday of Kupala also play an important role in design.

The origins of Ukrainian folk art can be traced back to the pre-Christian era, when Slavic tribes first settled in the region that is now Ukraine. Over time, Ukrainian folk art and crafts evolved to reflect various historical and cultural influences, including those of neighboring cultures. Ukrainian folk art adopted elements from Polish, Turkish, and Greek traditions, to name only a few, as well as influence from the Orthodox Church. Overall, Ukraine's cultural roots stretch deep and far into world history. The earliest pottery found in Ukraine dates back to the Neolithic period, around 6,000 BCE.

The 19th century was a historically important period for the development of the Ukrainian national style in handmade design. Ukrainian pottery underwent a revival, as artists began to turn to traditional Ukrainian folk art for inspiration. This movement, known as the "Ukrainian National Revival," helped to popularize traditional Ukrainian pottery styles and motifs. During this era, several collective movements and organizations were created to promote the Ukrainian national style in handmade design. For example, the Kyiv Artistic Society, founded in 1899 to champion Ukrainian art and design, helped organize exhibitions and competitions that showcased the work of Ukrainian artists and artisans.

DESIGN DURING THE 20TH CENTURY

In the early 1900s, Ukrainian artists and designers were influenced by art nouveau and constructivism, two popular design movements in Europe at the time. The Kyiv and Kharkiv Art Schools were established during this period, providing training opportunities for aspiring designers. However, due to the country's turbulent political history, the development of design as a profession was slow and uneven. One of the most important figures in the development of the Ukrainian national style was Ivan Kavaleridze, a sculptor and designer known for his use of traditional Ukrainian motifs in his work. Kavaleridze's designs often featured elements such as folk costumes, embroidery patterns, and folk tales, and were created using traditional Ukrainian techniques and materials. This dedication to tradition extended not only to his sculpture but also to his work as a filmmaker.

With the dawn of the Soviet era, creative freedom suffered under state-imposed regulations that dictated what kind of art could and could not be produced. Many artists whose work didn't align with Soviet ideology saw their artistic visions repressed. This all changed in 1991 with the collapse of the USSR. Ukraine underwent a period of rapid change and transition, and design as a profession began to flourish, with more and more designers setting up studios and agencies. The country's rich cultural heritage and history inspired many designers, who incorporated traditional Ukrainian motifs and symbols into their work. Additionally, as their borders opened to the rest of the world, Ukrainians began to notice differences between Western lifestyles and their own. This sparked considerable shifts in both political perspectives and the pursuit of contemporary design.

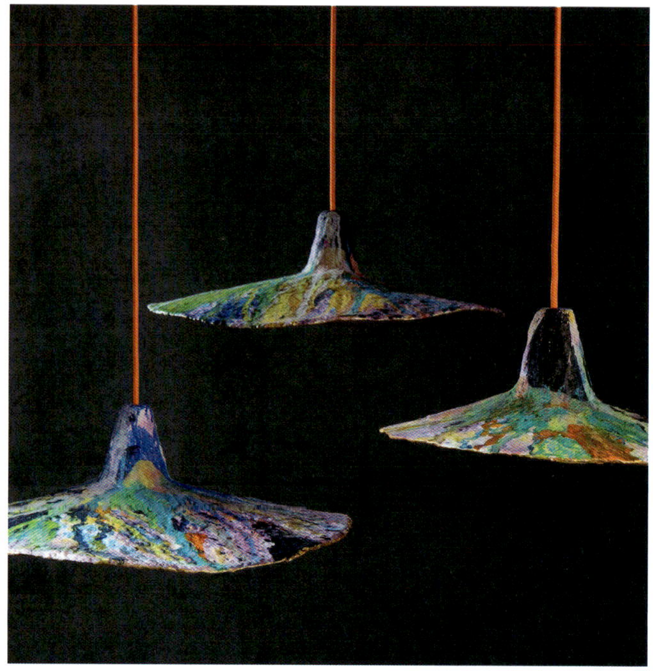

Parasolka lamps created by Makhno Studio. Below: Ukraine's rich heritage serves as a muse for Kononenko ID—they invoke age-old traditions and reinterpret them for the modern world.

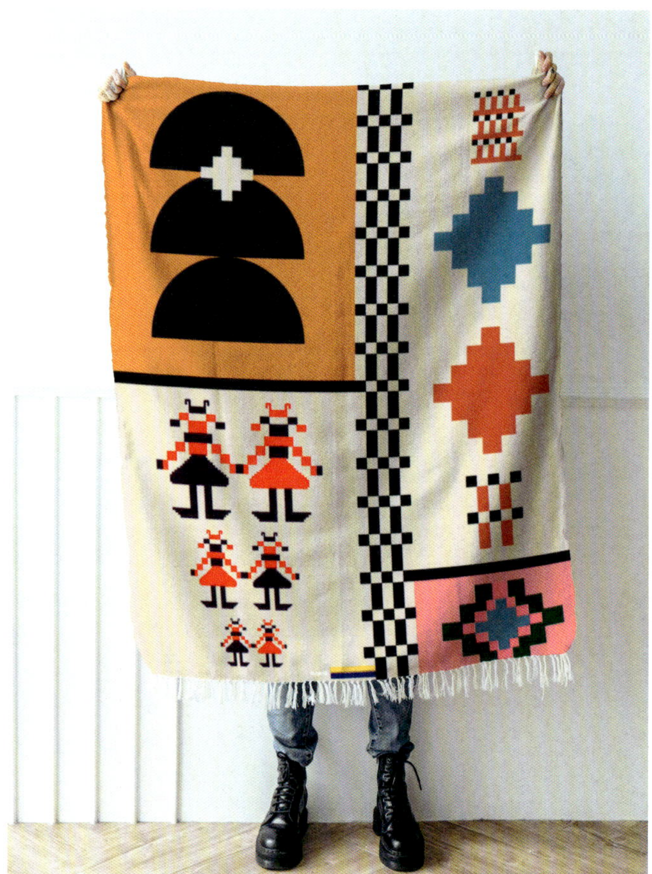

PUTTING UKRAINIAN DESIGN ON THE MAP

Contemporary Ukrainian design is now known for its unique aesthetic, which blends traditional Ukrainian motifs with modern design elements. Ukrainian designers often use natural materials and colors, contrasting them with bright, modern accents. Despite these contemporary touches, floral design and geometrical patterns in shades of red, blue, and yellow remain central to much of the country's contemporary design.

Of course, international design plays a big role as well. Recent years have witnessed a striking fusion of Ukrainian culture and global contemporary trends, merging time-honored techniques with novel materials and modern styles. For example, today we see many concepts that seamlessly combine the similar moods of Ukrainian and Scandinavian design.

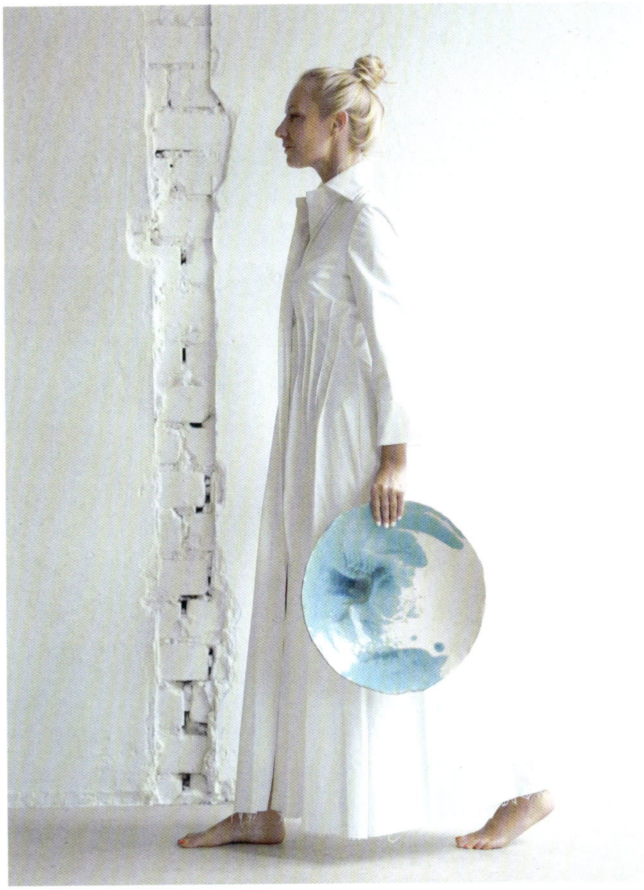

For SaGa Pottery, firing clay is a mystery, a miracle, a burst of emotion. The designers cherish the variety of shapes, colors, and combinations. Below: TUTTU Monteur armchairs, created by Levantin Design.

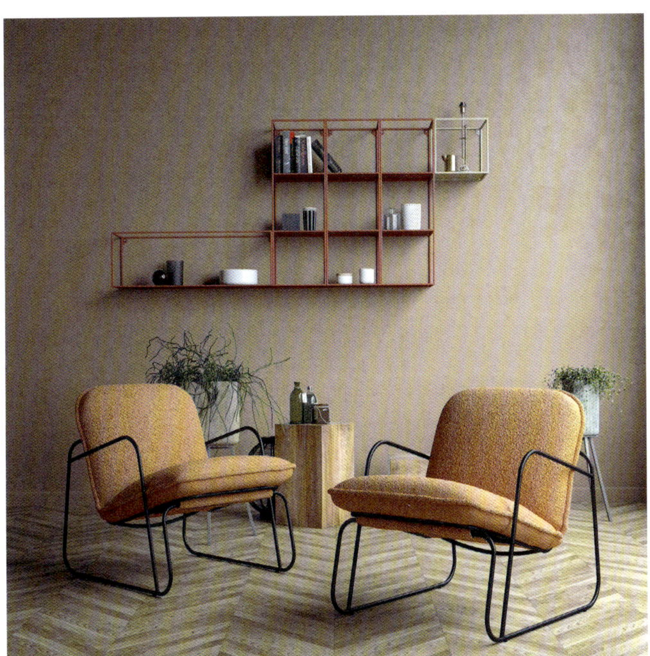

The rise of social media and online platforms, such as Instagram and Behance, has brought about significant changes as well. Ukrainians can now effortlessly share their work with a worldwide audience, attracting international clients, securing features in prominent media outlets, and establishing their brands globally.

Major Ukrainian cities are increasingly hosting international design events and exhibitions, providing a platform for seasoned and emerging designers to showcase their work and network with industry professionals from around the globe. For example, Ukrainian designer Serhii Makhno recently partnered with Japanese brand Raku-Raku to create a collection of ceramic tiles, and Ukrainian design studio FILD (now +kouple) worked with German brand Vitra to create a showroom in Kyiv. Each year, the Ukrainian design awards see more globally renowned names among the jury members. Undoubtedly, Ukraine is emerging as a country with a robust design community.

The Euromaidan Revolution in 2014 also played a crucial role in propelling the design world forward. As the country moved away from dictatorship, the revolution exposed corrupt politicians' lavish homes, which were practically dripping with garish gold decor. People saw this as a clear sign of what they as a country should avoid. From this moment on, the New Design Revolution flourished. And now with European Union borders even more open to Ukrainians, people will further expand their design horizons as they travel. The nation has collectively rejected the old dictatorial ways and embraced the construction of a new contemporary world.

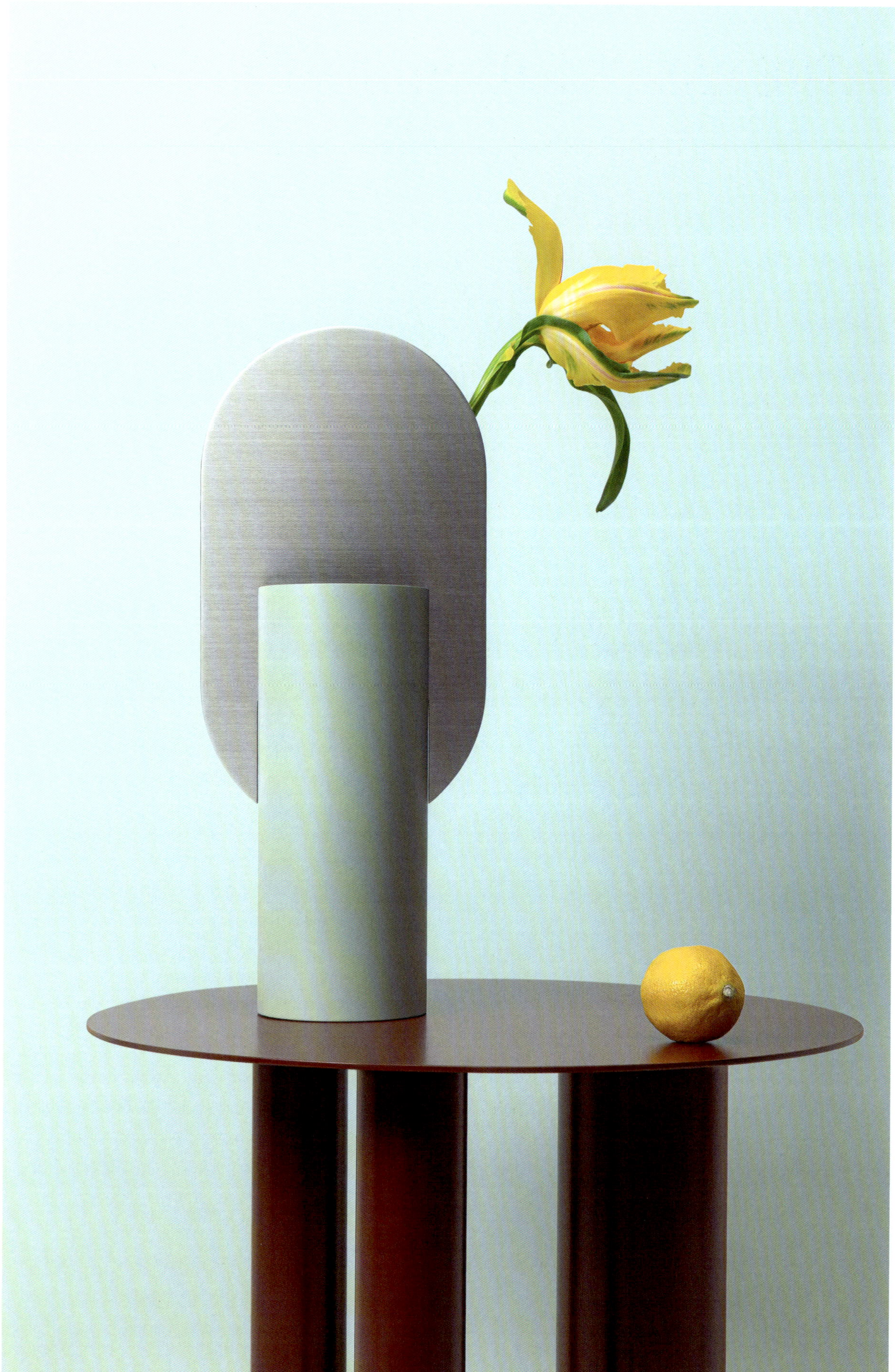

THE ESSENCE OF DISTINCT DESIGN

KATERYNA SOKOLOVA · *КАТЕРИНА СОКОЛОВА*

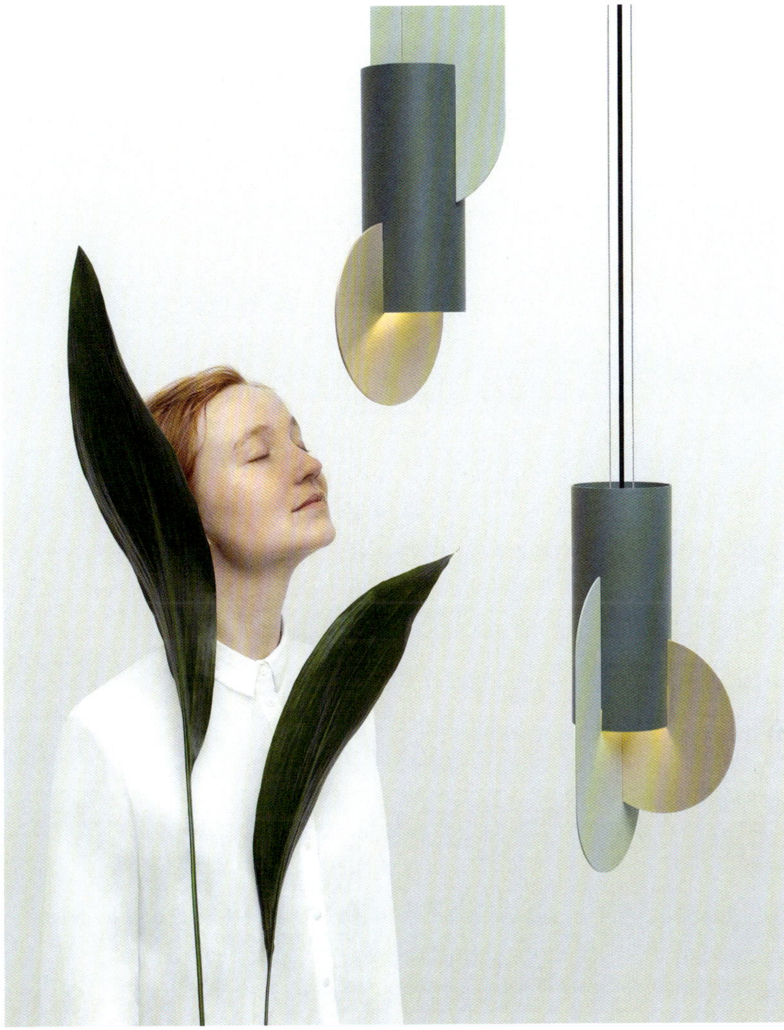

Ukrainian industrial designer Kateryna Sokolova creates objects rich with meaning, combining bold forms, tactile materials, and an intuitive approach. Since the outbreak of the war, her designs have acquired new meaning and function to reflect the turbulent times.

Kateryna Sokolova, co-founder and creative director of the NOOM brand and SOKOLOVA design studio, is an internationally established designer based in Kyiv. She works with manufacturers around the globe, including Ligne Roset, Bolia, Casala, Roche Bobois, and Driade. In 2022, Sokolova designed a new collection for NOOM called Flock, which is based on the idea that home should be a comforting sanctuary and gathering space filled with unique, eye-catching statement pieces. Kateryna and NOOM also presented their wartime product, Gropius Low Chair Military Edition, at London Design Festival 2022. This piece poignantly combines the classic peacetime shape of NOOM's Gropius Low Chair with wartime camouflage netting.

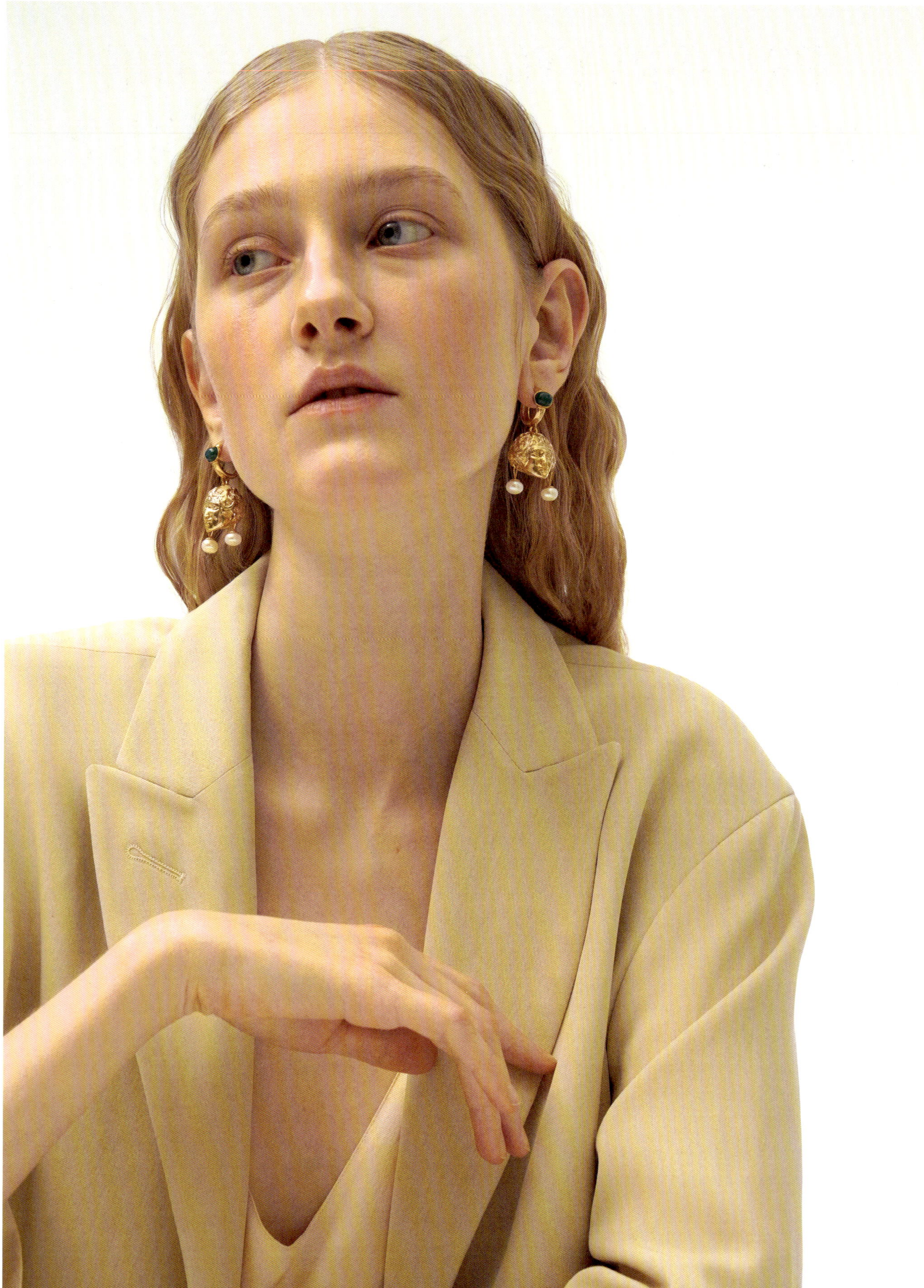

PRESERVING AND REMAKING TRADITIONAL CRAFTSMANSHIP

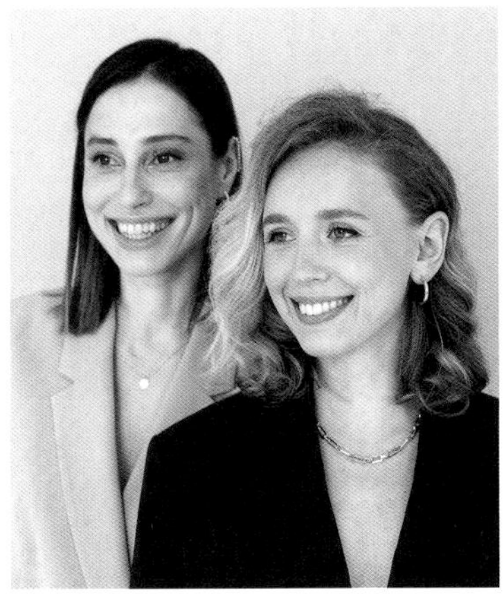

GUNIA PROJECT

The Gunia Project blends modern design, ethnographic research, and artistic craftsmanship in each unique collection.

Following a lengthy period in the fashion industry, Maria Gavryliuk and Natalia Kamenska decided to join forces to create a brand of their own—one that showcased the heritage and cultural traditions of Ukraine. In 2017, Kamenska started a pilot project, designing a modern interpretation of the traditional Hutsul fur coat, or *gunia*. The coat used natural sheep's wool and was handwoven in the Carpathian Mountains on traditional looms. The first joint collection of the duo was focused on scarves. The success of the project led the two to officially launch their brand in 2019, naming it the Gunia Project after their debut product. Today, the brand experiments with a whole range of products, including ceramics, glassware, candles, jewelry, accessories, and clothing. For inspiration, the designers conduct ethnographic research and involve Ukrainian artisans in their work. Gavryliuk and Kamenska have traveled extensively through Ukraine in search of artisans, and have studied the cultural heritage, traditions, and techniques behind ancient artisanal processes. During their travels, they connected with various ethnographers and made ties with employees of the Ivan Honchar Museum, Ukraine's National Center of Folk Culture. Each Gunia product, whether in glassmaking, ceramics, knitting, or weaving, is created using age-old techniques passed down through generations as well as modern technologies. Although clearly inspired by Ukrainian culture, the designers never resort to mimicry and always reinterpret their findings in a modern context. For example, many of their products feature iconographic images rendered as contemporary folk art. As of 2022, the Gunia Project employed a staff of office and production personnel and worked remotely with around 40 craftspeople across Ukraine. According to the founders, finding artists and artisans to collaborate with remains one of their most significant challenges.

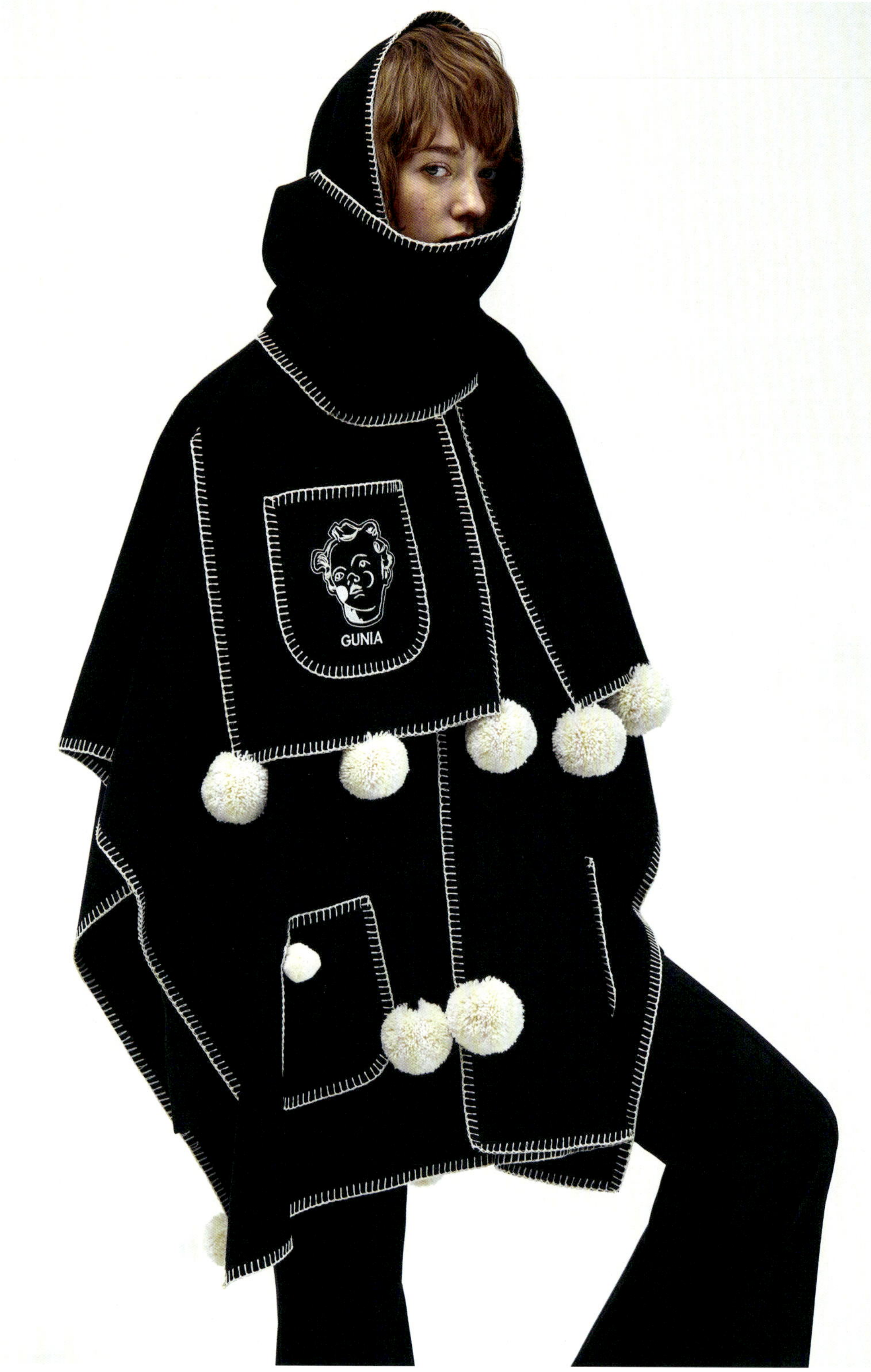

This woolen poncho with pom-poms was inspired by the *guglia*, a traditional outerwear garment worn during festivities in the Hutsul region of Ukraine.

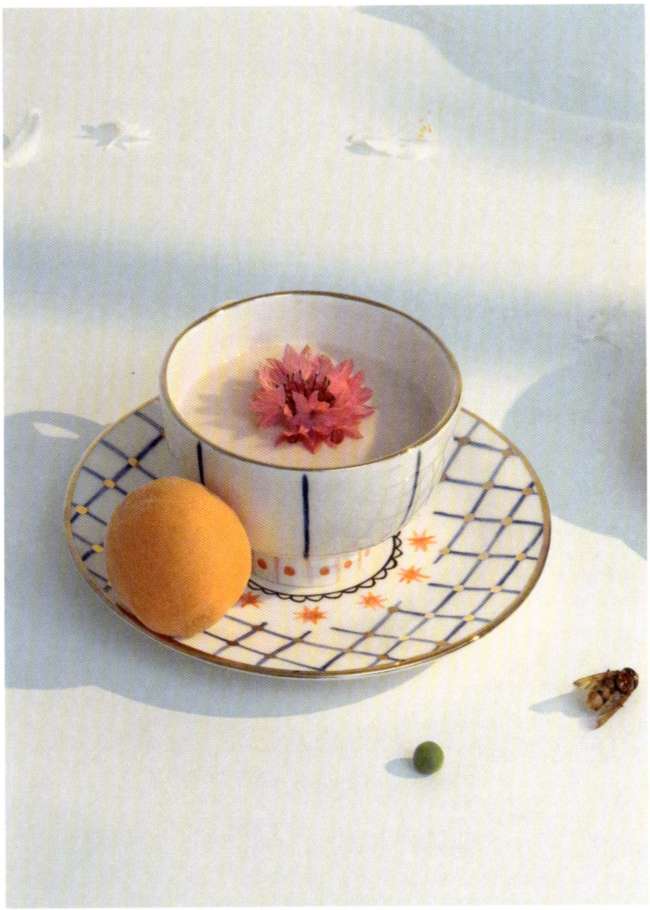

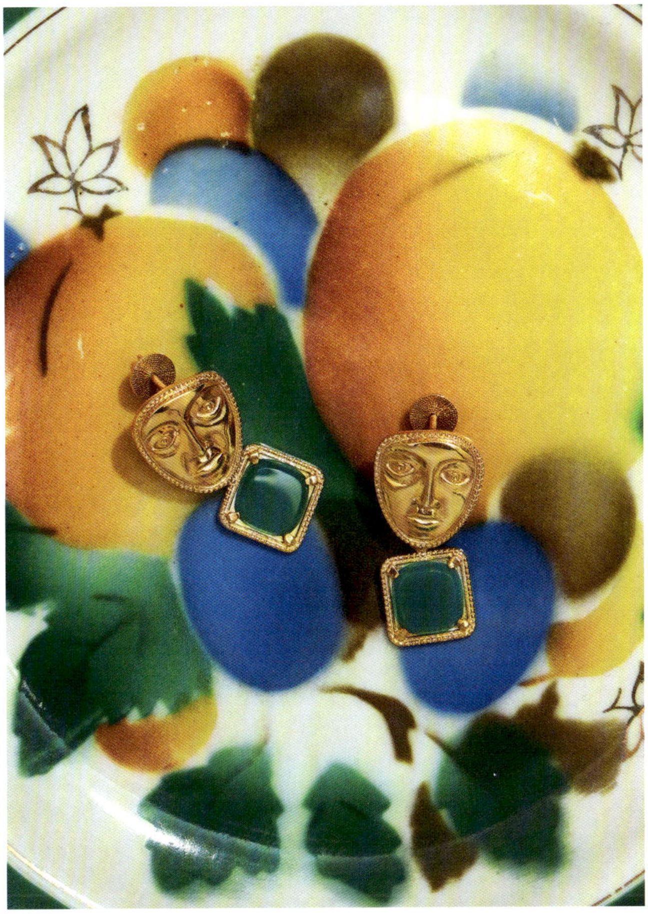

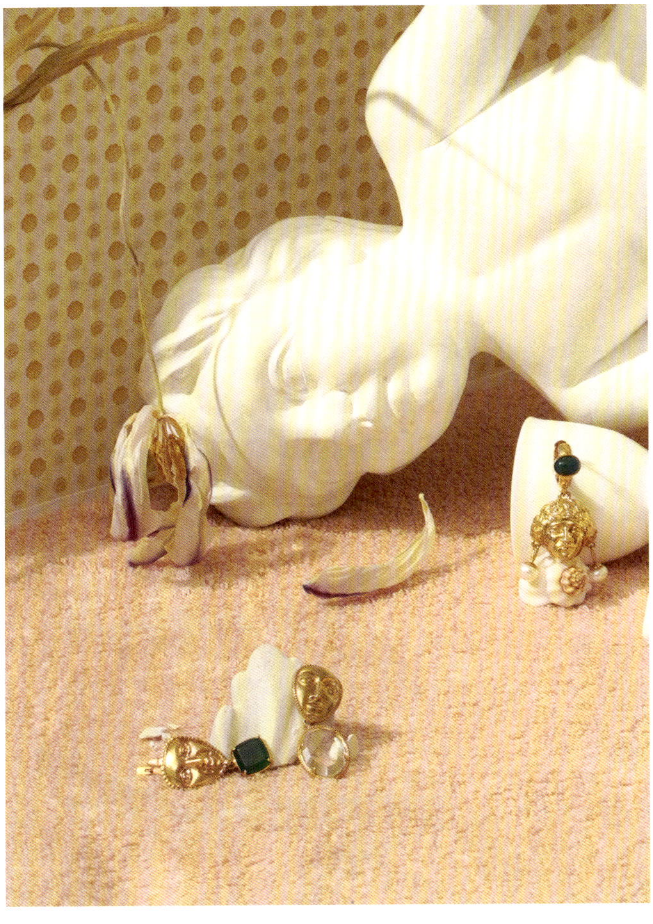

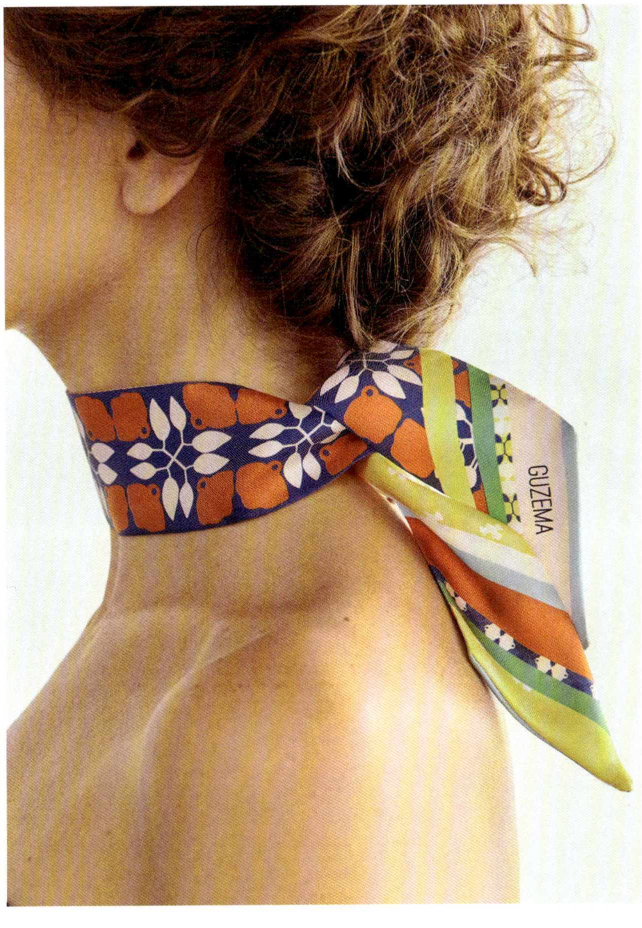
GUZEMA

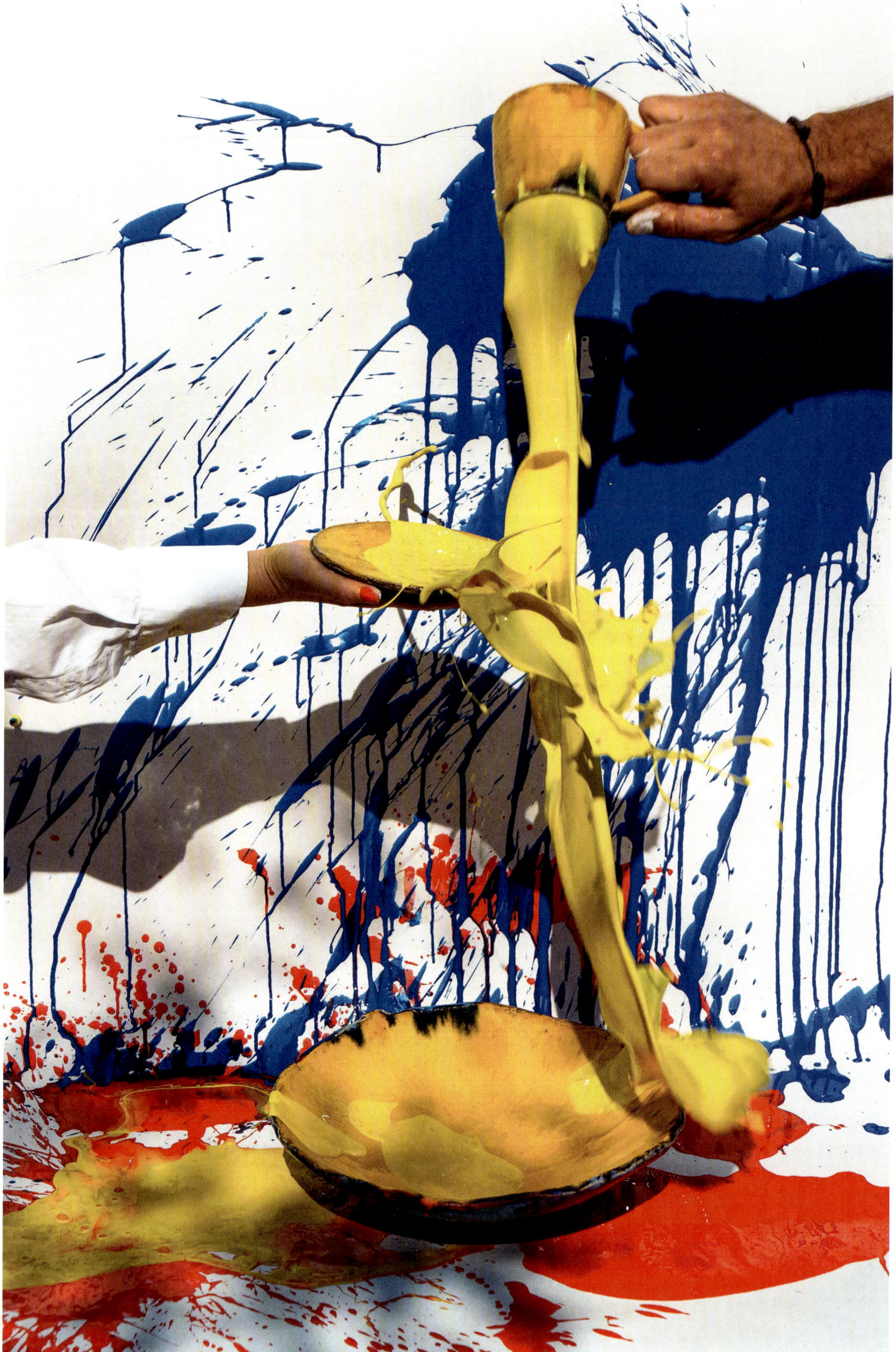

FIRED WITH PASSION

SAGA POTTERY

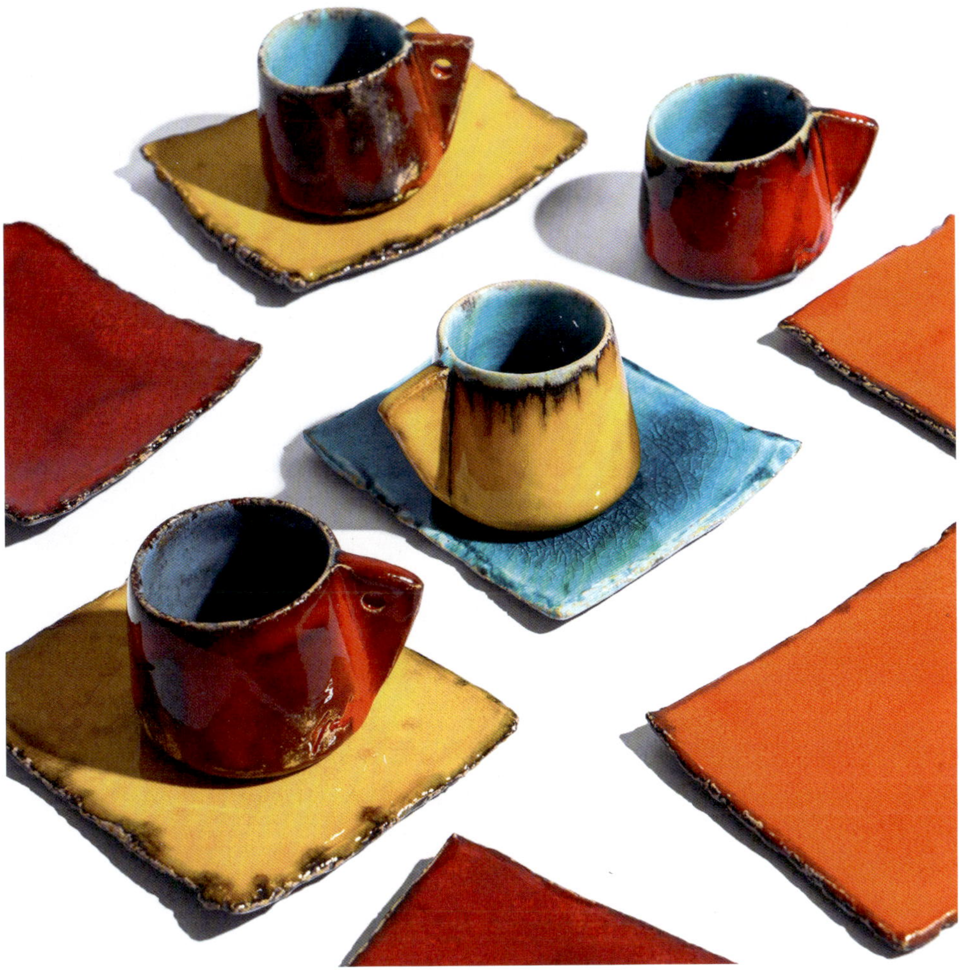

SaGa Pottery's founders harness the unpredictable nature of clay to create stunning, one-of-a-kind pieces.

In 2017, Galina Kaniuka and Oleksandr Barabanov, a married couple with a passion for creativity, founded their handmade ceramics brand, SaGa Pottery. The Kyiv-based couple had been experimenting with painting for several years and were constantly on the lookout for new creative outlets. When they found ceramics, it was love at first sight: they were drawn to the intricacies of the process, the delayed outcomes, and the vast array of techniques to choose from. Their products take 7–10 days to make, during which they delight in trying out new color combinations, playing with new patterns, and mastering the *kurinuki* technique. The war has made it particularly difficult to source materials. Before the war, most ceramicists sourced their clay from Sloviansk in the Donetsk region, home to Ukraine's largest clay deposits. However, as the frontlines drew near to the city, clay production came to a virtual standstill. Despite these and other challenges, SaGa Pottery has continued production in Ukraine.

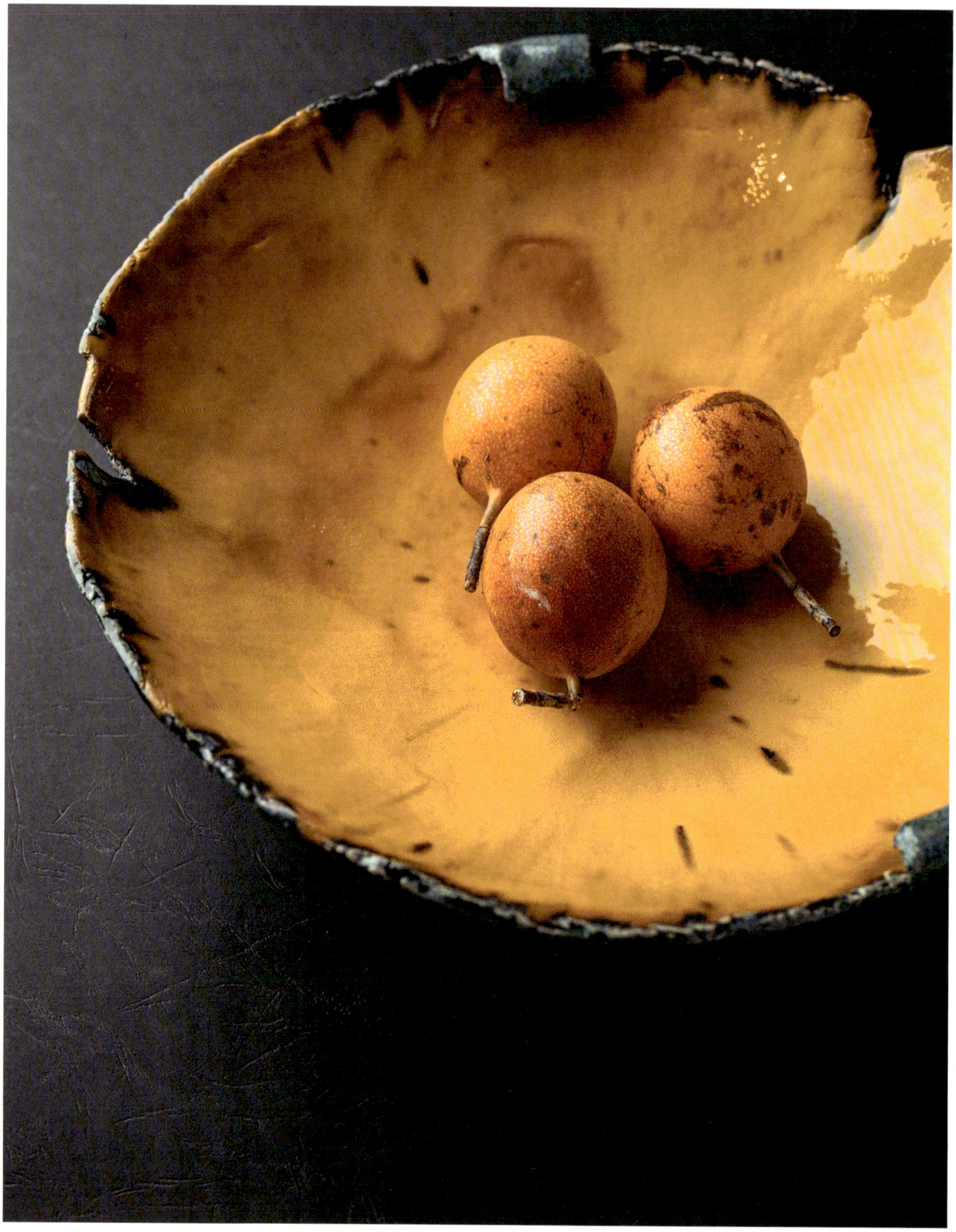

SaGa Pottery has its own recognizable style. The works of the artisan duo can be easily distinguished from others due to their characteristic features: uneven, sometimes jagged edges, original shapes, and an especially bright glaze.

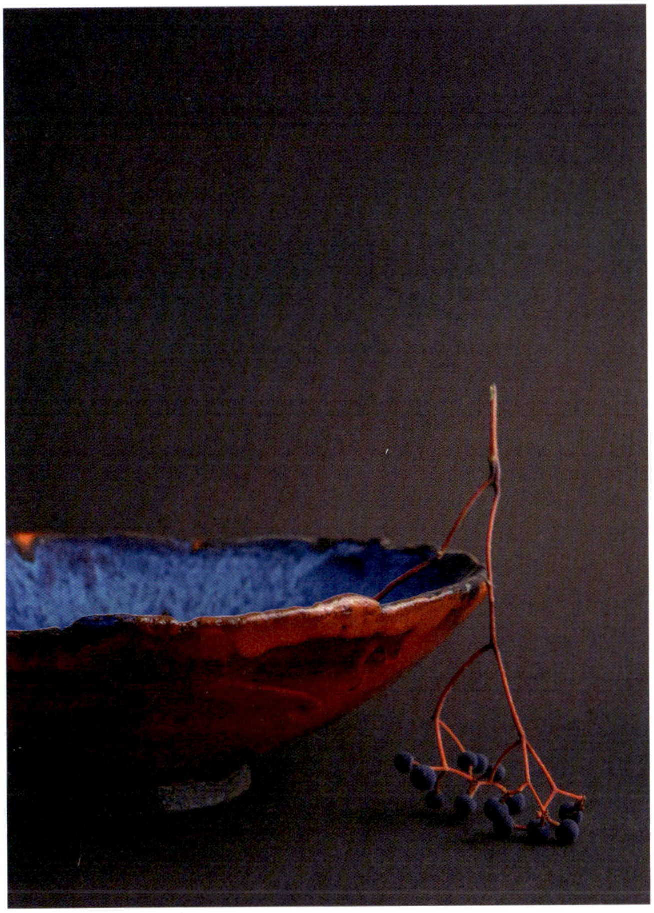
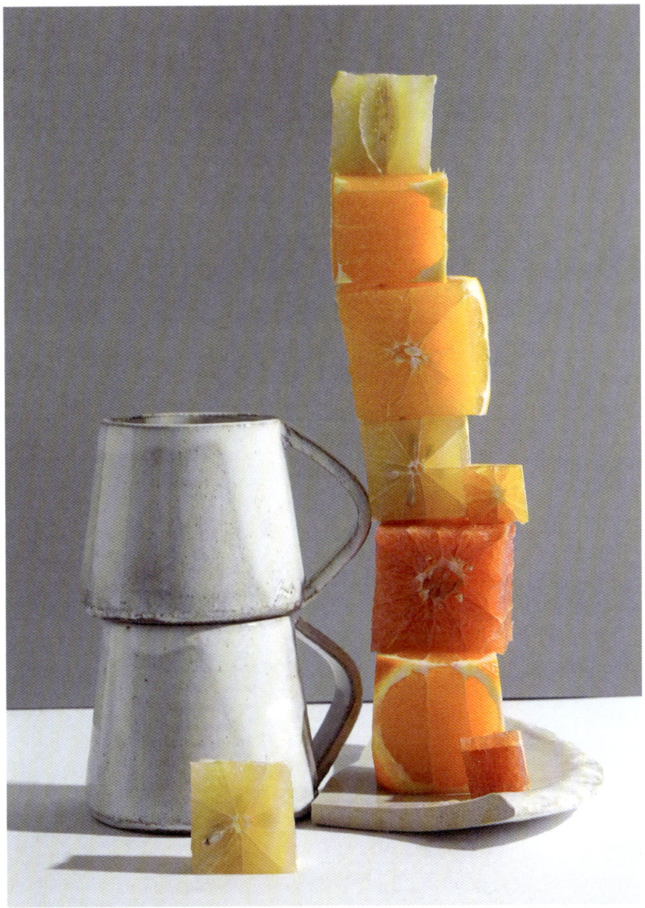
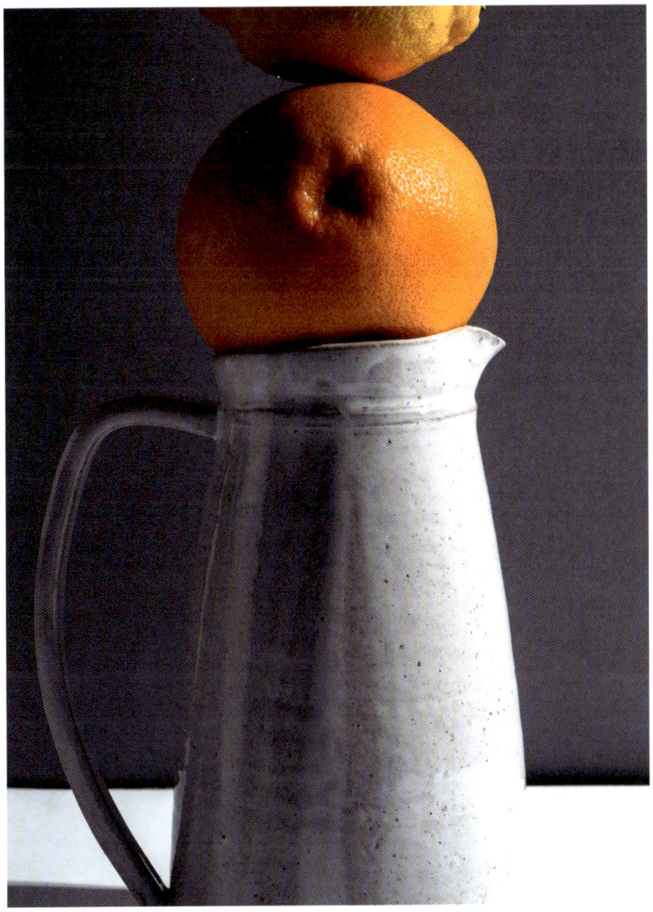
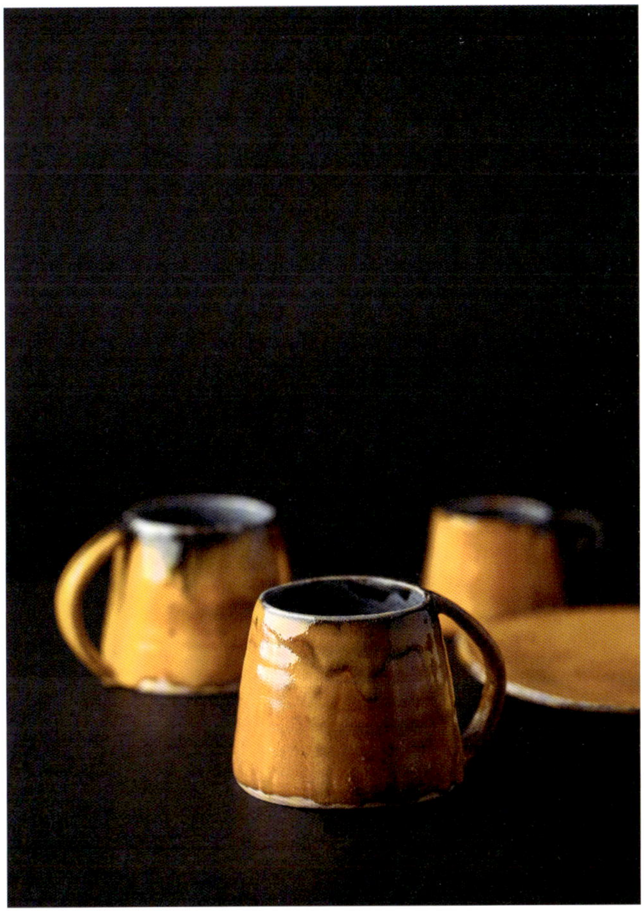

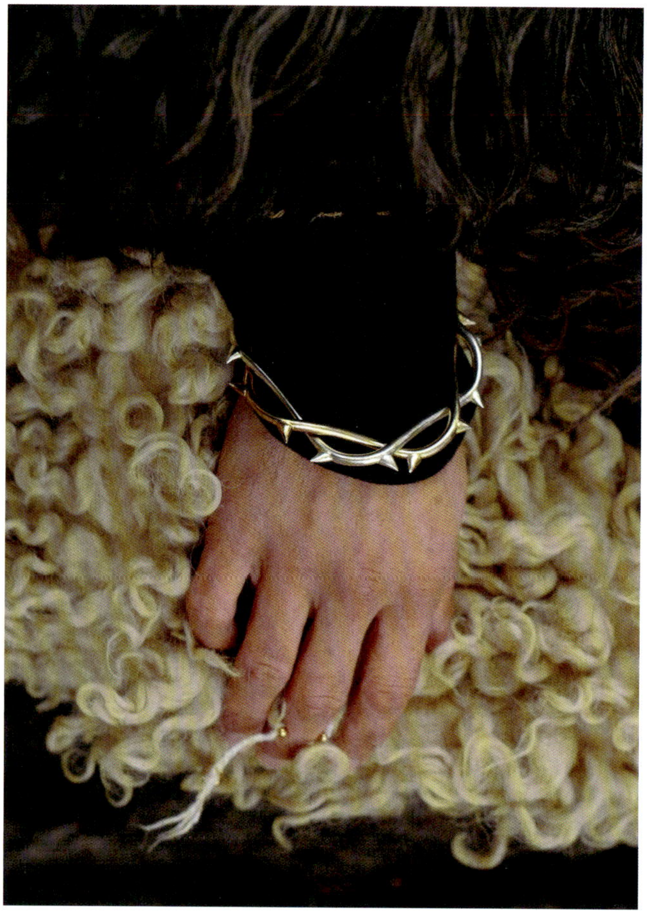
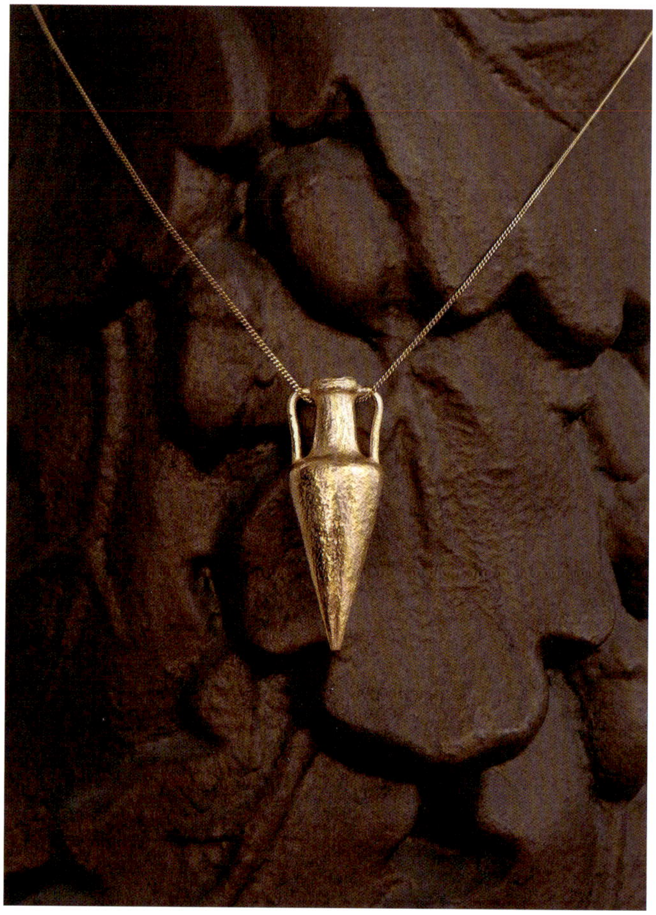
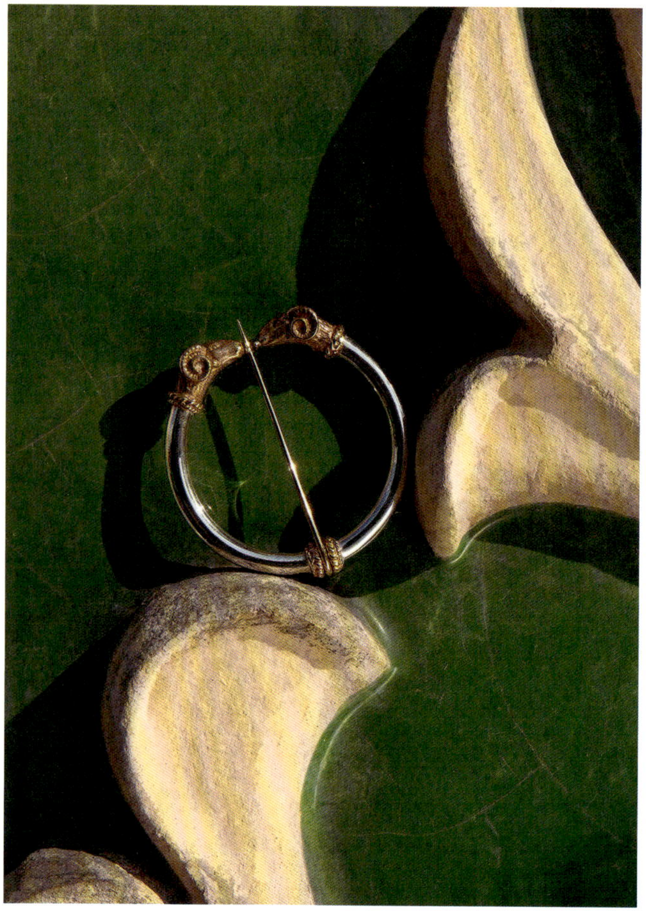
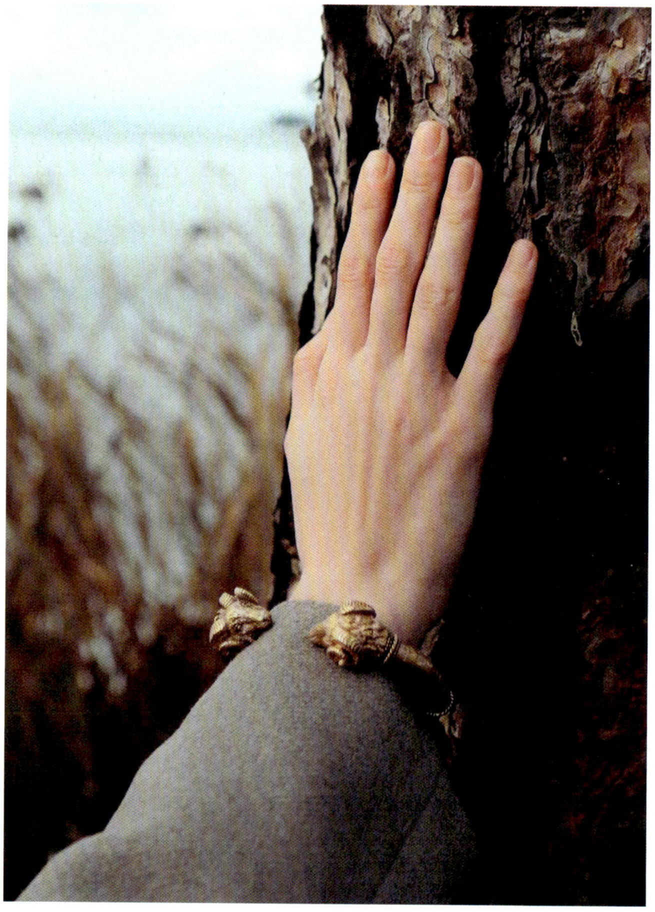

NEW JEWELRY WITH AN ANCIENT TWIST

ROCKAH.BRAND

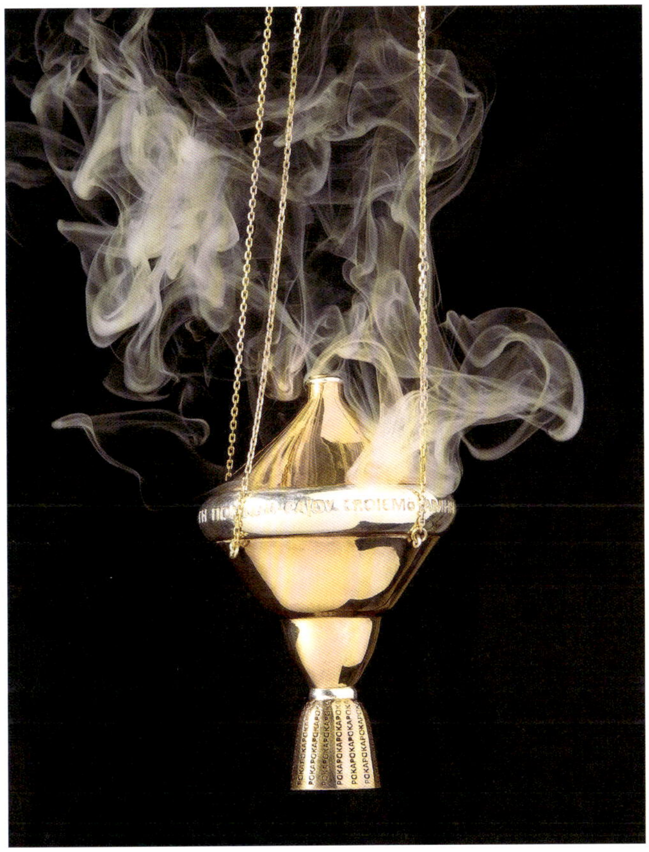

Jewelry design studio rockah.brand recreates the aesthetics of the ancient world, inspired by the artisanal heritage of humanity throughout the ages.

Rockah.brand, established in 2019 by Roxana Romanenko, is dedicated to creating unique jewelry inspired by the cultural heritage of the ancient world. Utilizing natural oxidation and other artisanal techniques practiced by the old masters, rockah.brand creates distinctive, gender-neutral jewelry cast in recycled bronze or silver. The pieces are then gold-plated or hand-patinated, the brand's signature technique. Committed to sustainability, the company uses 100 percent recycled metal and adheres to a zero-waste production model. The brand also supports local craftsmanship by working with artisans across different fields, such as jewelers, potters, painters, and more. The Hemp Amulets collection features hand-woven ritual hemp jewelry with an abstract, convex-cross centerpiece, a reinterpretation of the 17th-century Zaporizhzhia Army flag. Another series, the "BLAGO" collection, focuses on themes of faith and humility, and draws on early Orthodox Christian symbolism, harkening back to an era when the Kyivan Rus adopted Christianity under Volodymyr the Great.

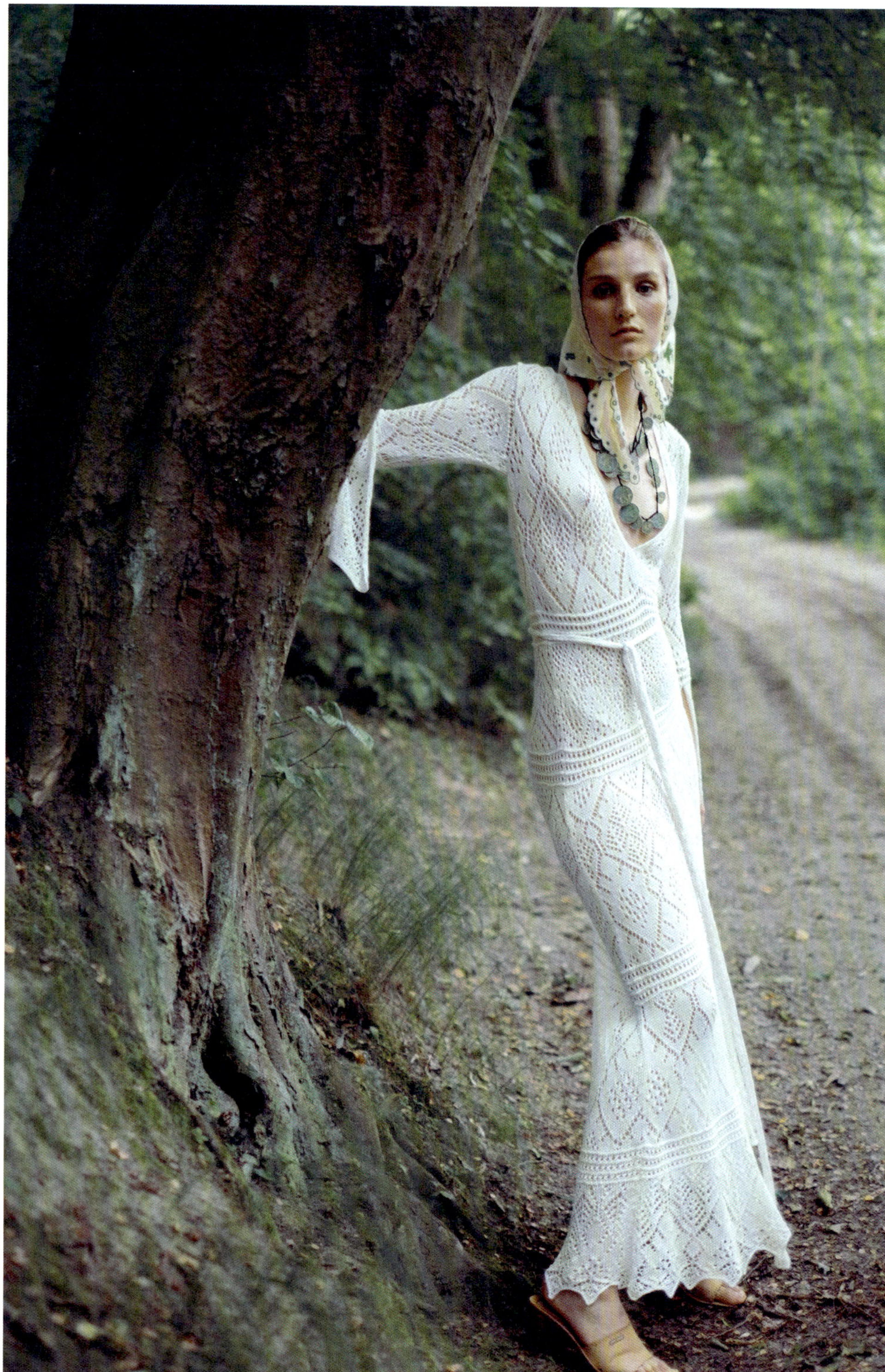

According to Roxana Romanenko, her passion for the ancient world, old masters, and forgotten techniques inspired her to create jewelry. Today, every product of rockah.brand broadcasts Ukrainian traditions and culture.

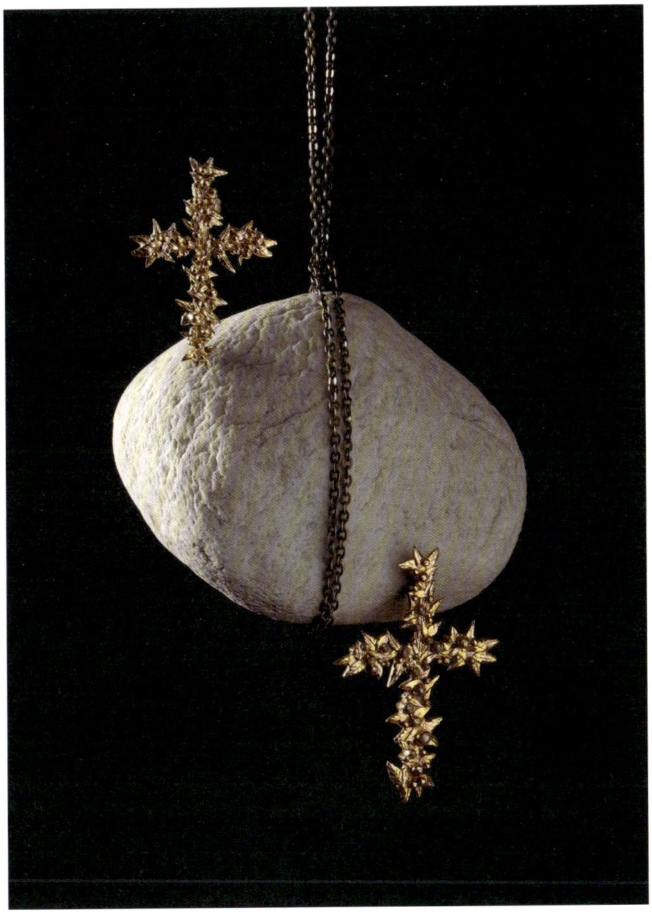
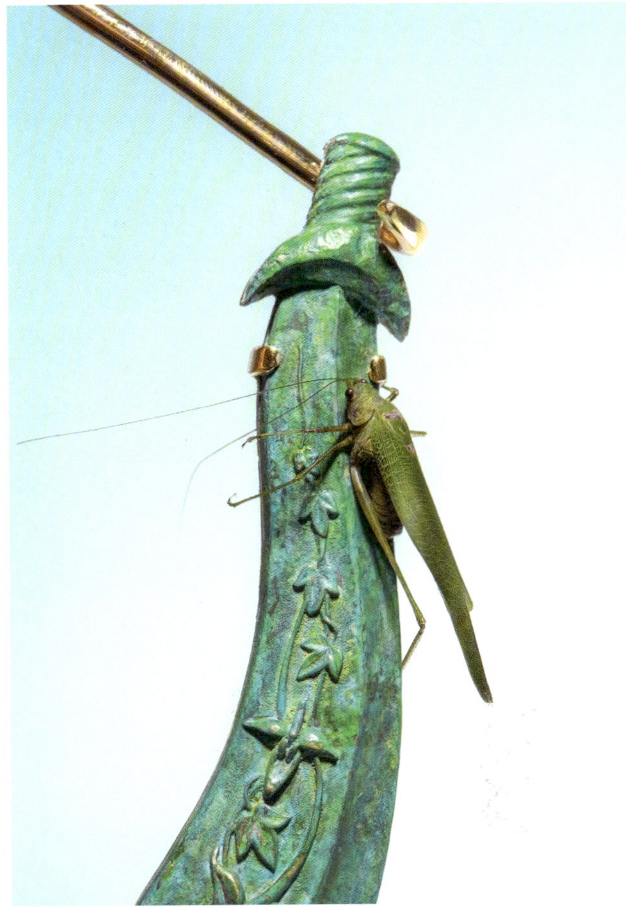
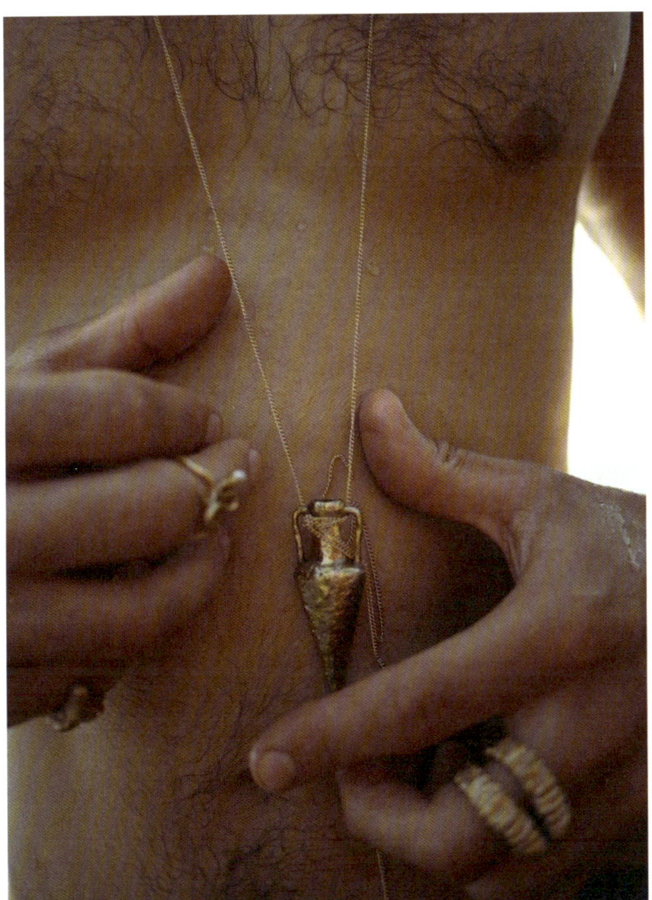
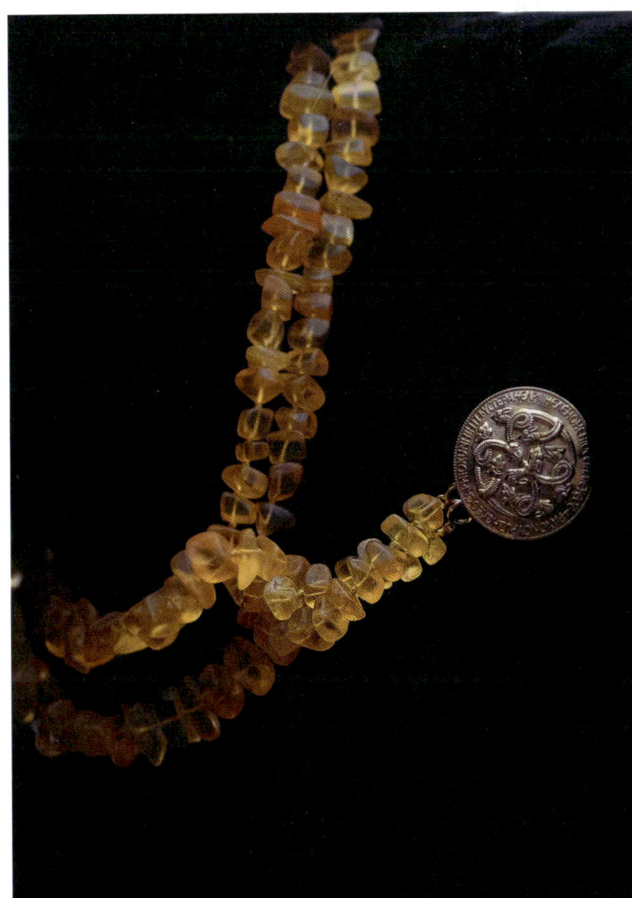

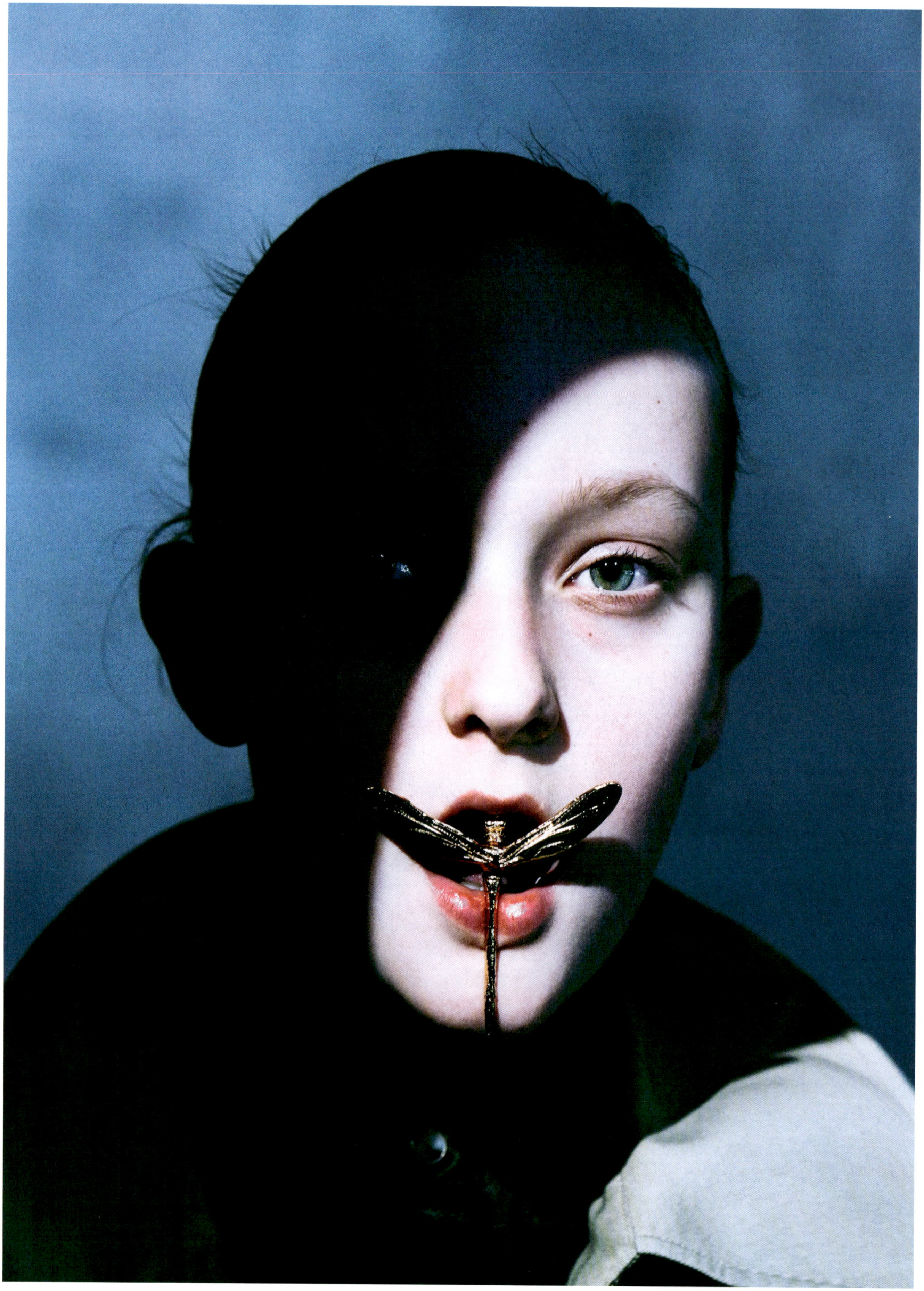

MYSTICAL FAIRIES RISING FROM CHAOS

ZHERNOV ARTIFACTORY

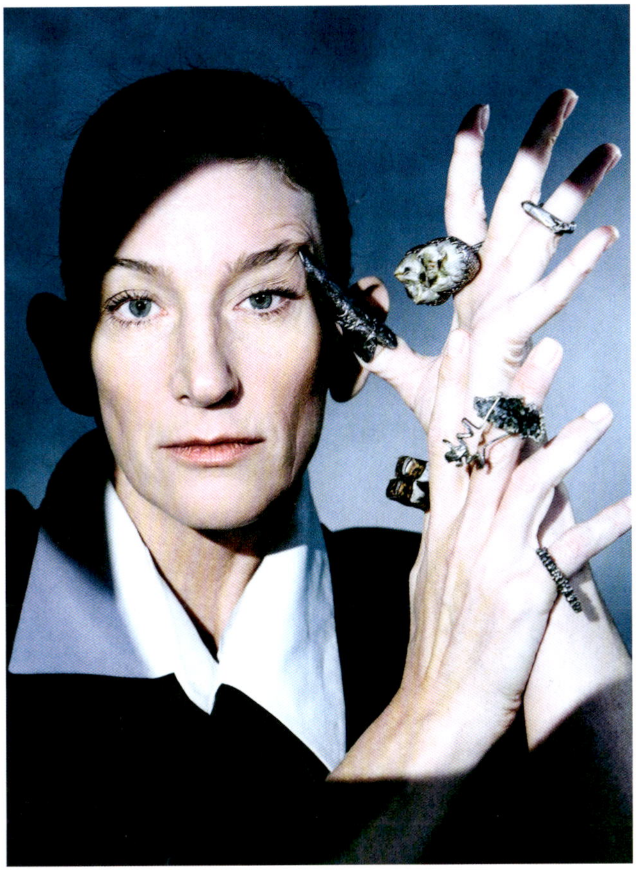

Using unfinished natural minerals that are both rare and collectible, ZHERNOV Artifactory creates jewelry masterpieces that often look like wearable sculptures.

Sergey Zhernov is a Kyiv-born jewelry designer and artist. His father was a metalsmith, and by the time Zhernov was old enough to attend school, he had already begun working in his father's workshop, where he learned the basics of the craft. In 2013, after honing his skills in his family's production factory, Zhernov decided to embark on a solo career. Together with his wife Lilia, he founded the ZHERNOV Artifactory, a niche jewelry brand. Since March 2022, the artist has been working to set up a new studio in Zurich, Switzerland, where he hopes to continue his creative pursuits. Zhernov's work is known for its independent and philosophical style, which blends raw crystals and other natural motifs with more refined elements, such as gold. This striking contrast between the glimmering perfection of gold and the rawness of unfinished (often experimental) materials is a hallmark of the artist's work. For him, this duality symbolizes the primordial moment—long before human existence—when the "higher-powers" created the world: a fleeting, beautiful moment in which chaos and order collided. This vision is also at the heart of Zhernov's series of unique jewelry mini-sculptures entitled "Fairies." Part animal and part insect, these captivating creations are the product of the artist's boundless imagination.

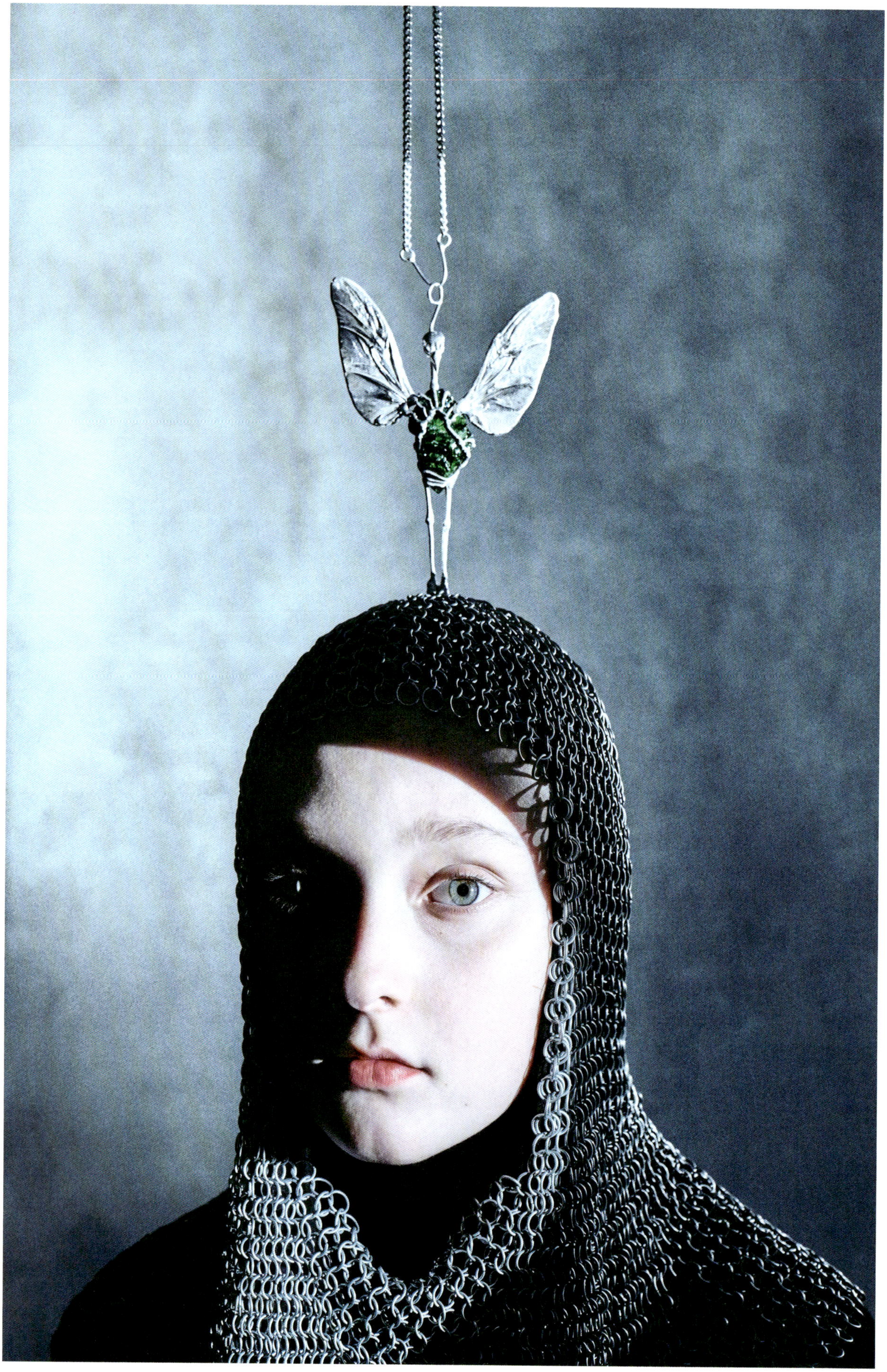

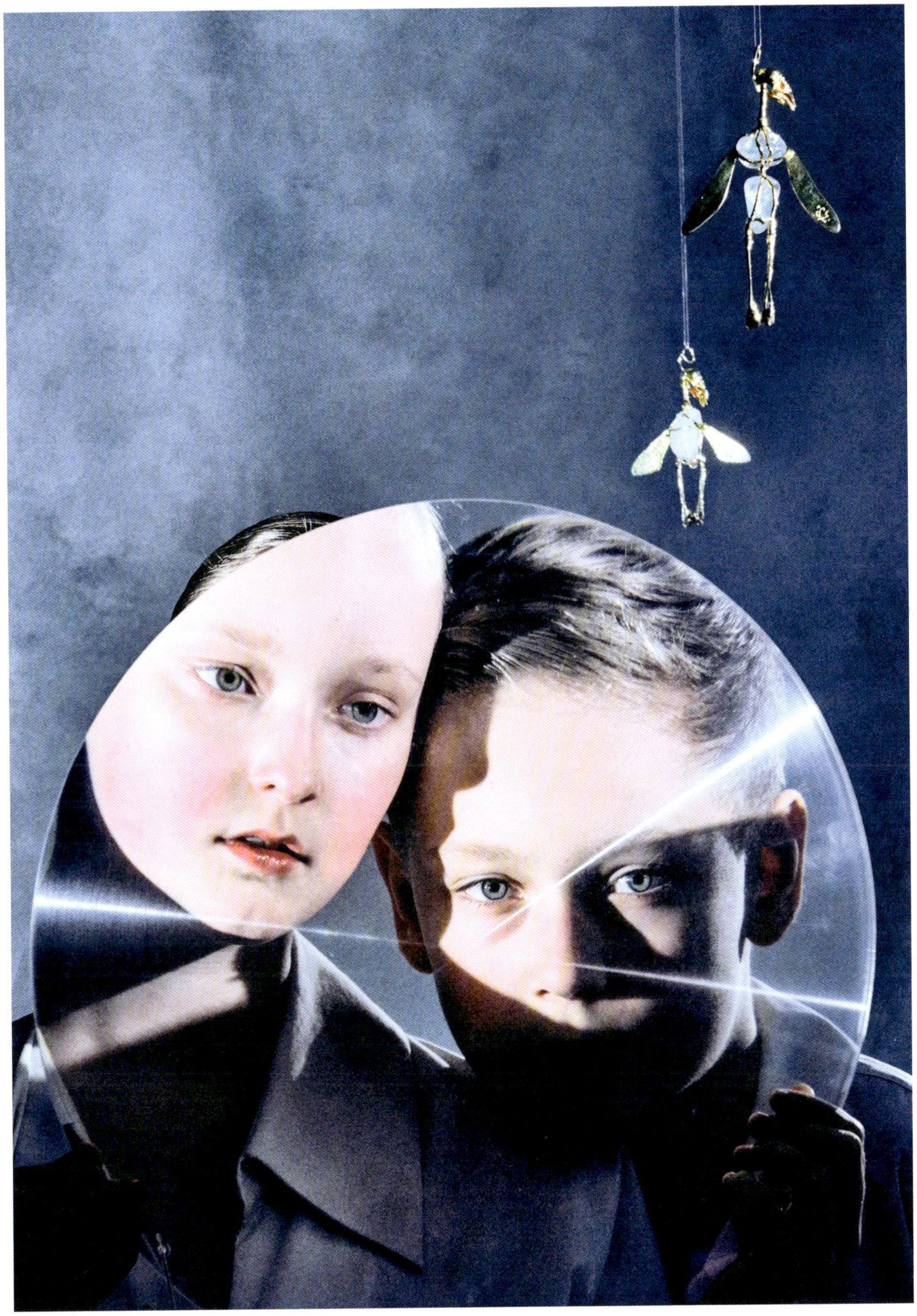

ZHERNOV Artifactory's series of mini-sculptures depicts mystical creatures called "Fairies," part animal and part insect. Each item is made from raw minerals and is completely unique.

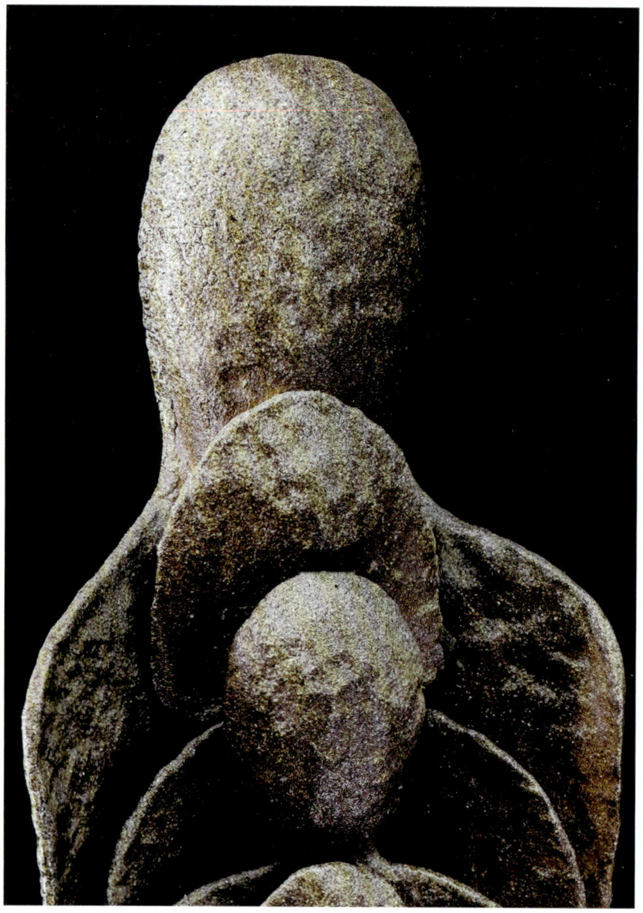
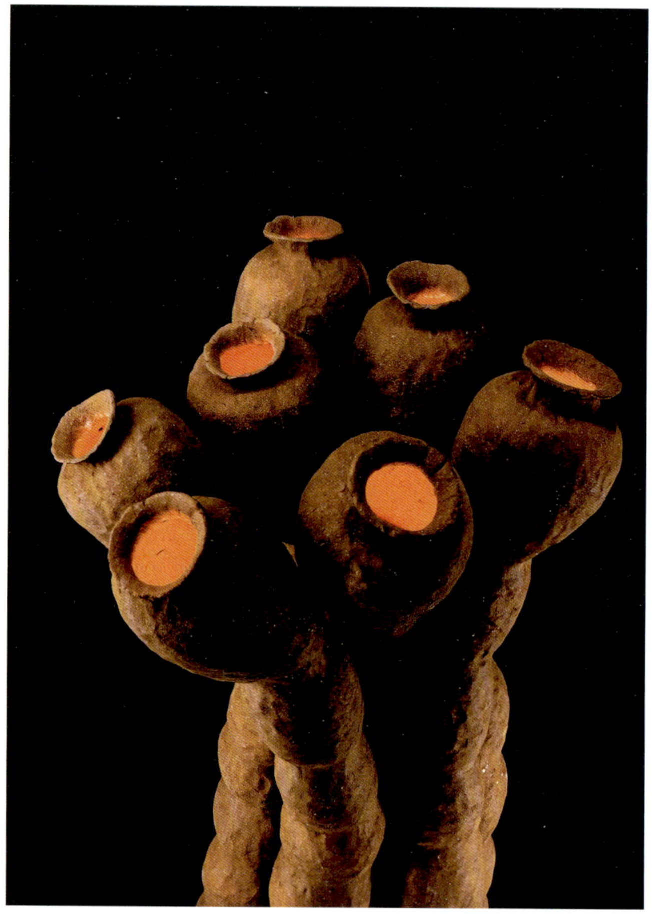
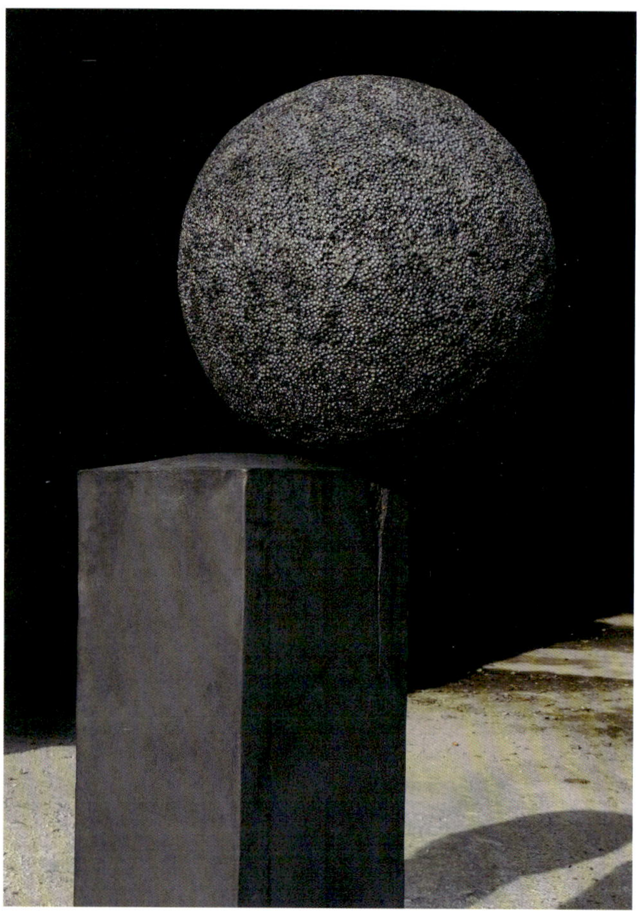
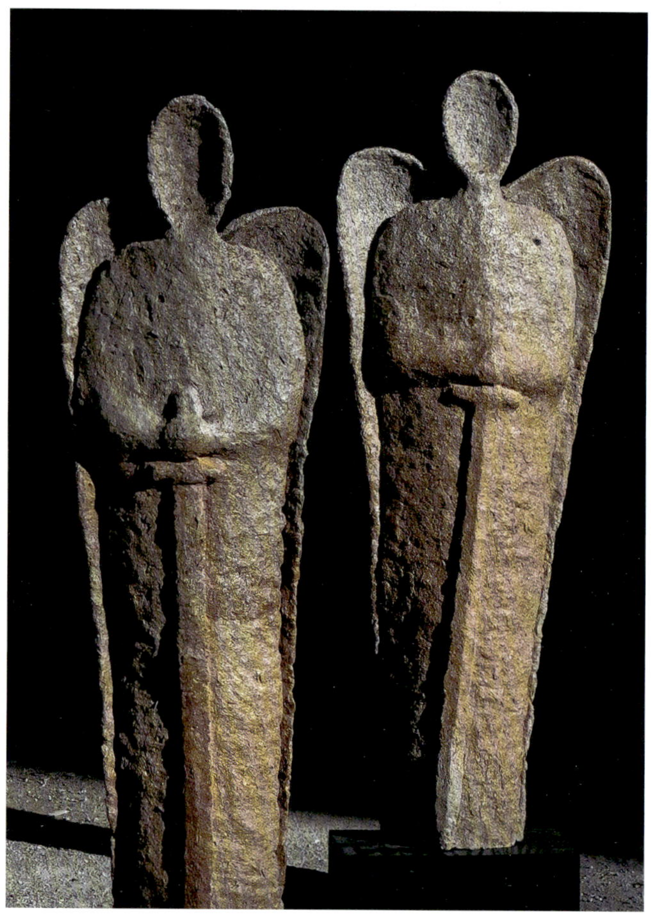

PHILOSOPHICAL CERAMICS

GORN CERAMICS

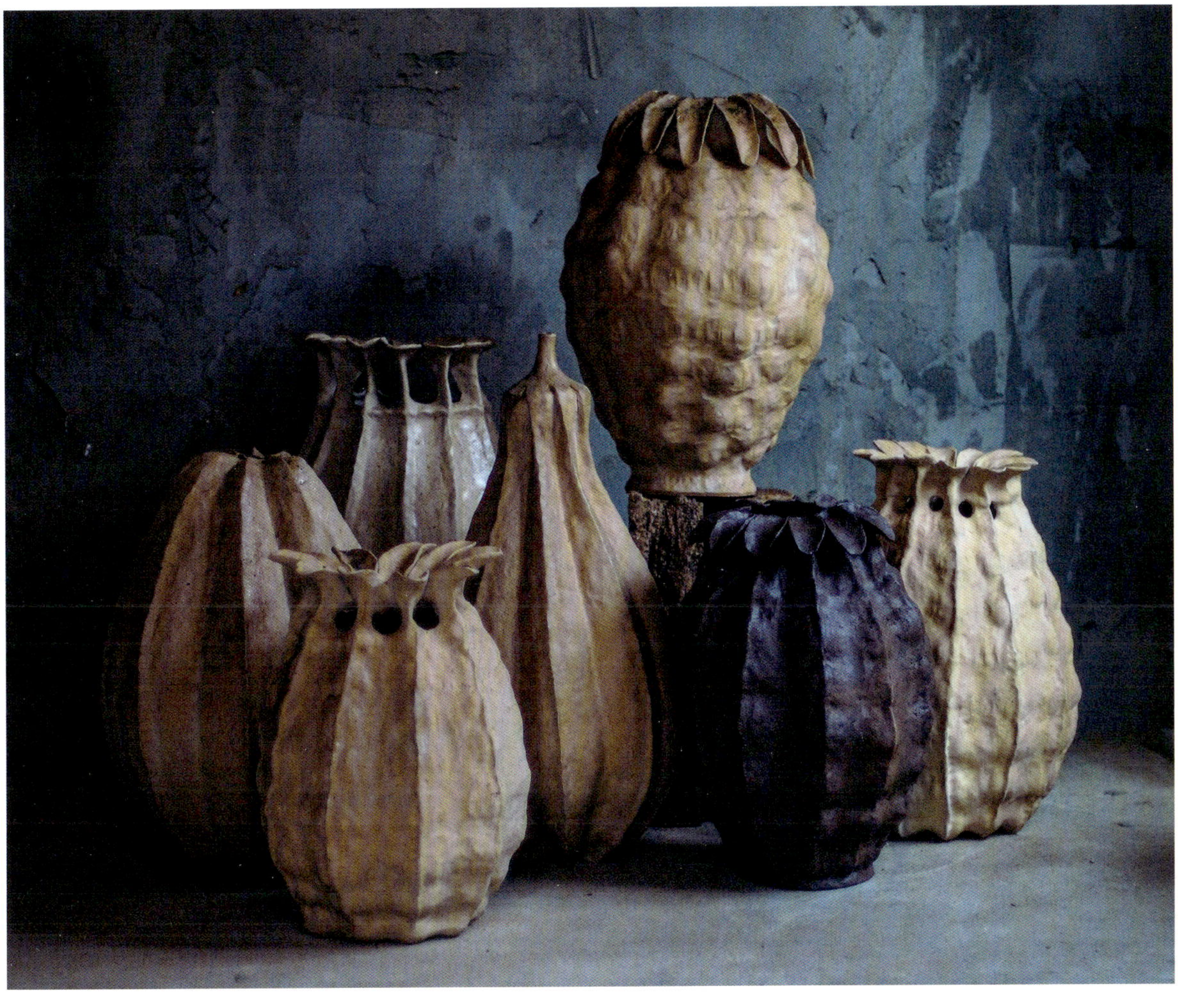

The GORN Ceramics team believes that true art radiates emotions and retains the energy that was embedded in it during the act of creation.

GORN Ceramics is a collective of Ukrainian ceramic artists based in Kyiv. Founded in 2018 by artisan Yuriy Myrko and creative director Bogdan Kryvosheya, the collective produces ceramic decor, design pieces, and art objects. The artists are fascinated by the plasticity of clay, and experiment with countless forms and textures. Throughout every stage of production, they allow the material to express itself through the creative process. In the past year, the ceramicists have had to adapt to the challenges of wartime production, using wood-fired kilns and sculpting anywhere there is light and warmth. With creations they hope will foster cultural growth and awareness, one of their main sources of inspiration is the study of natural forms and eternal values. Some works tackle deep philosophical themes that tap into the more profound aspects of life. The brand's latest collections include the Temples and Makyvky vases, and a collection of sculptures called Guardians.

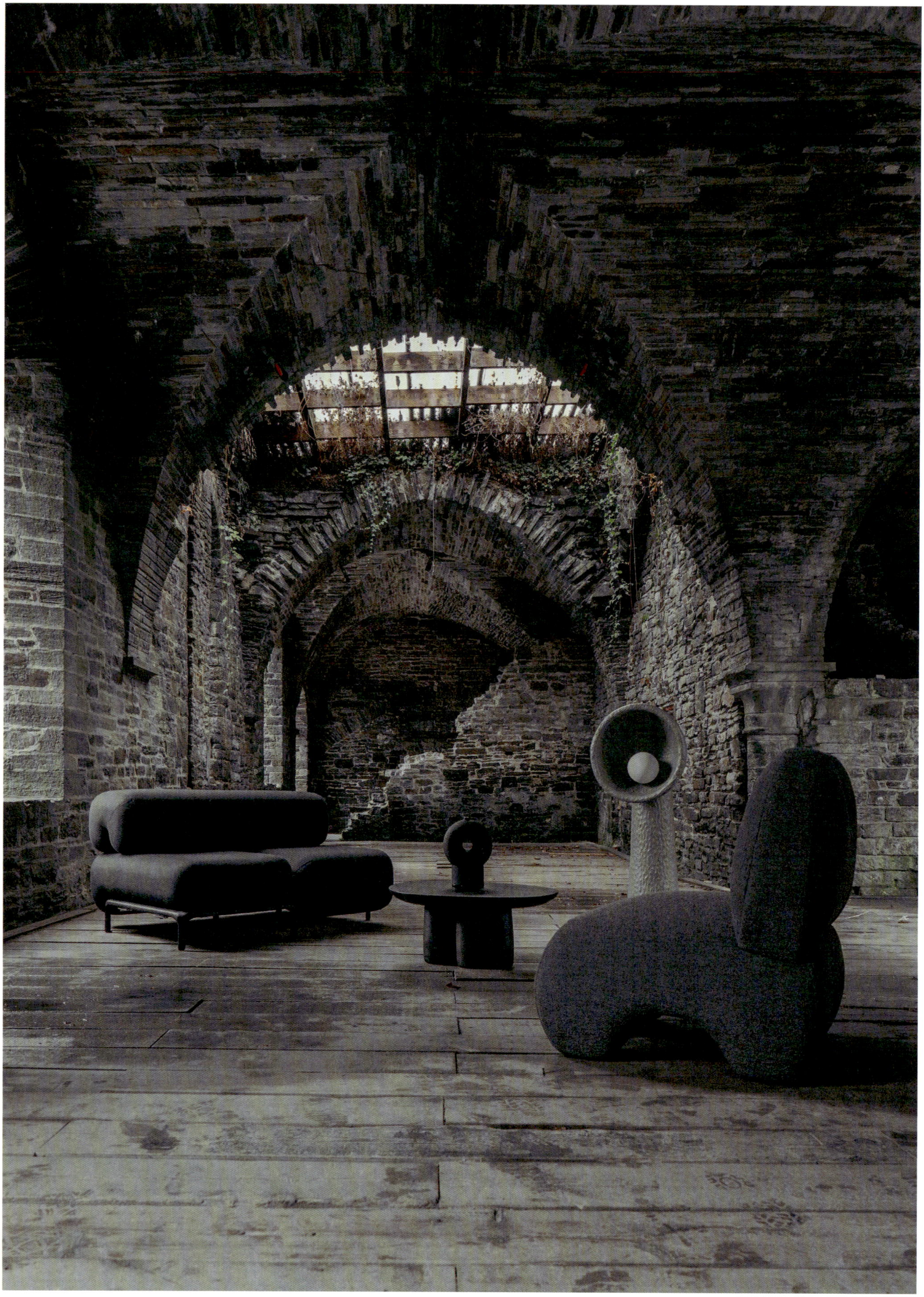

UKRAINIAN LIVE MINIMALISM

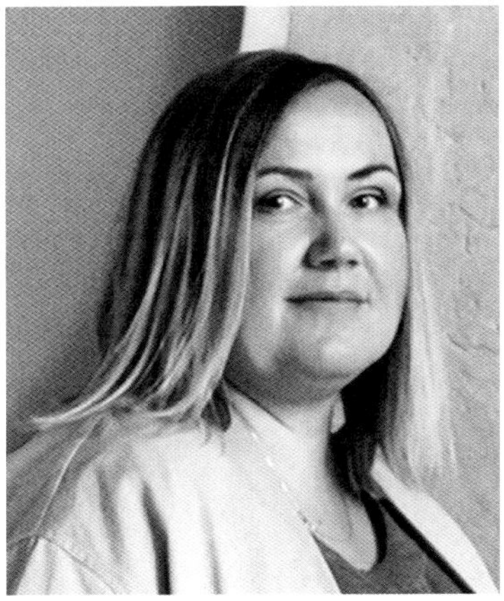

FAINA

The Faina collection is Victoria Yakusha's artistic manifesto, a celebration of modern Ukrainian women's design with a strong connection to its cultural roots.

Victoria Yakusha is a Belgium-based Ukrainian designer, artist, and architect, and the founder of both Yakusha Studio and the Faina live design collection. Yakusha has been inspired by Ukrainian culture and traditions all her life, and has always wanted to give voice to her country and its rich traditions, culture, and beliefs. She works in her own unique style, which she calls "live minimalism" and which has come to embody her fundamental values. Created in 2014 as a natural reaction to the revolution in Kyiv, the Faina brand is an authentic collection of furniture, lighting, and decor. Yakusha believes in connecting with our roots, the power of truth, and authenticity. In interior design and architecture, she reveals these qualities through natural materials, such as straw, wood, and clay. Traditionally, the walls of Ukrainian houses, or *khata*, were covered with clay. Faina manufactures its product using this ancestral technique. The designer invented her own sustainable material based on clay, recycled paper, and other natural components. Yakusha employs artisans to apply this custom material layer-by-layer to a recycled steel frame, creating a unique, living texture. Each Faina product reflects the history of Ukraine, and ancient symbols get a new life in modern times. For example, Yakusha's idea for her Trembita floor vases comes from the Ukrainian musical instrument, the longest wind instrument in the world. The name of the upholstered furniture series "Pampukh" translates as "fluffy bun"—a traditional baked good familiar to every Ukrainian. Speaking about her favorite Faina objects, the designer highlights the Domna armchair, which was inspired by the forms of anthropomorphic Venus sculptures from the Trypillia culture. One of the projects that Yakusha is currently working on is dedicated to Maria Prymachenko, a brilliant Ukrainian artist and a master of folk-art style. In February 2022, the Russian military bombarded the museum containing Prymachenko's works, so Yakusha began a collaboration with the Maria Prymachenko Family Foundation to create an art residency and museum to fill the void left by the destruction.

"At Faina, we use millennia-old techniques to convey history in a new, modern way. Ukrainian crafts and culture are very sincere, authentic, alive. I share this because it comes from within, and I feel it is my mission to preserve and pass on the story."

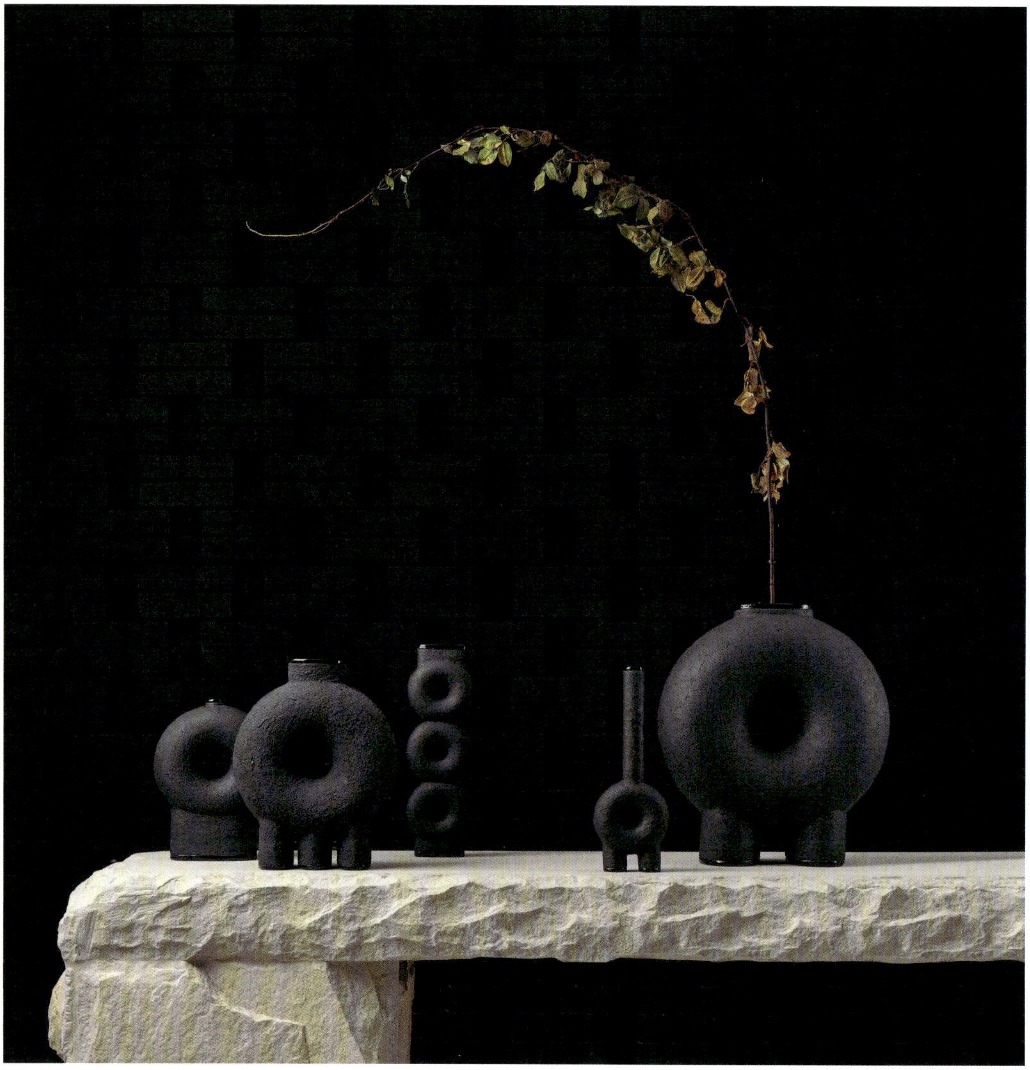

Faina's Kumanec vases revive the form of traditional Ukrainian festive pottery. They are made of clay and have an ancestral shape that pulsates with the animistic presence of live design.

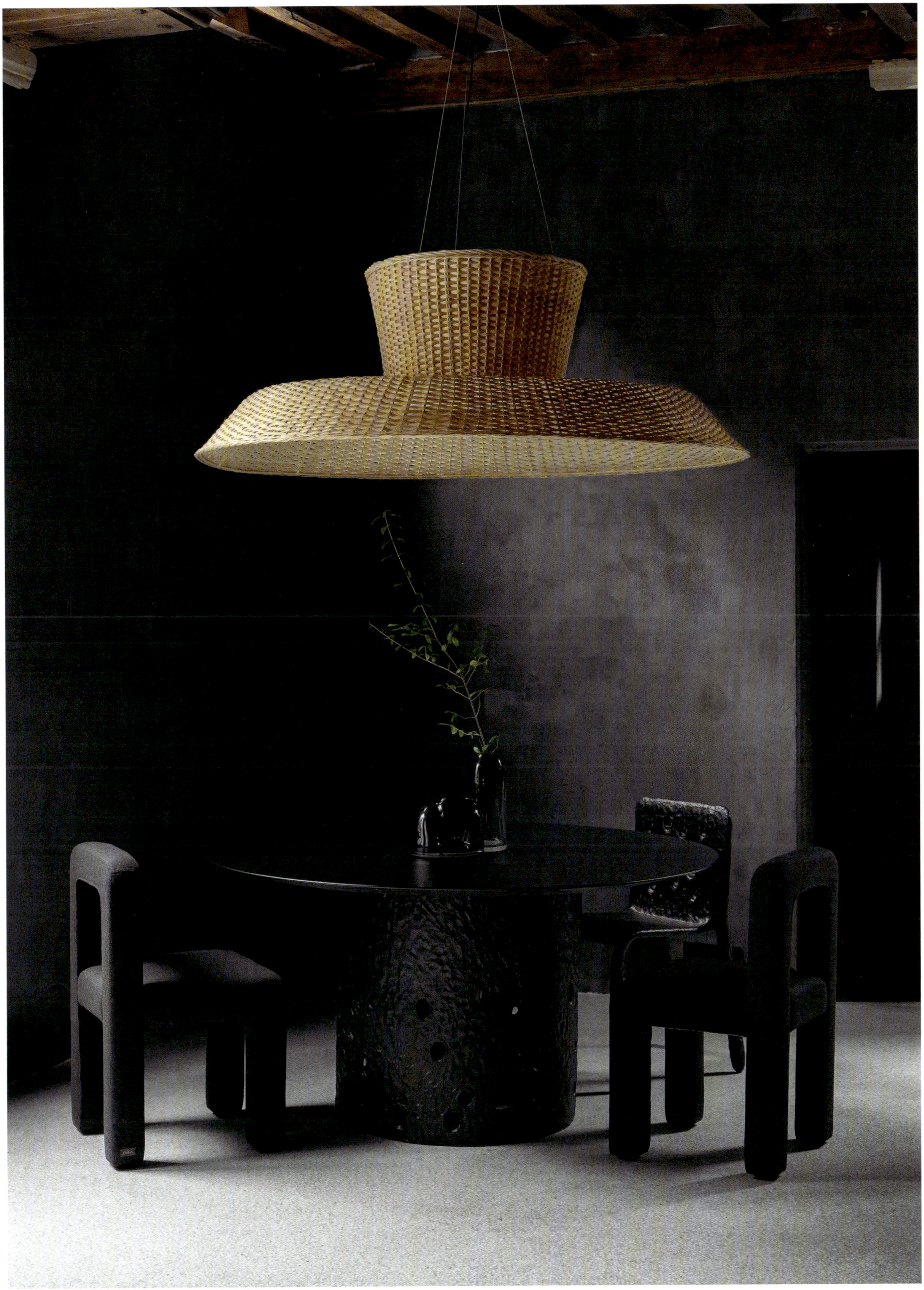

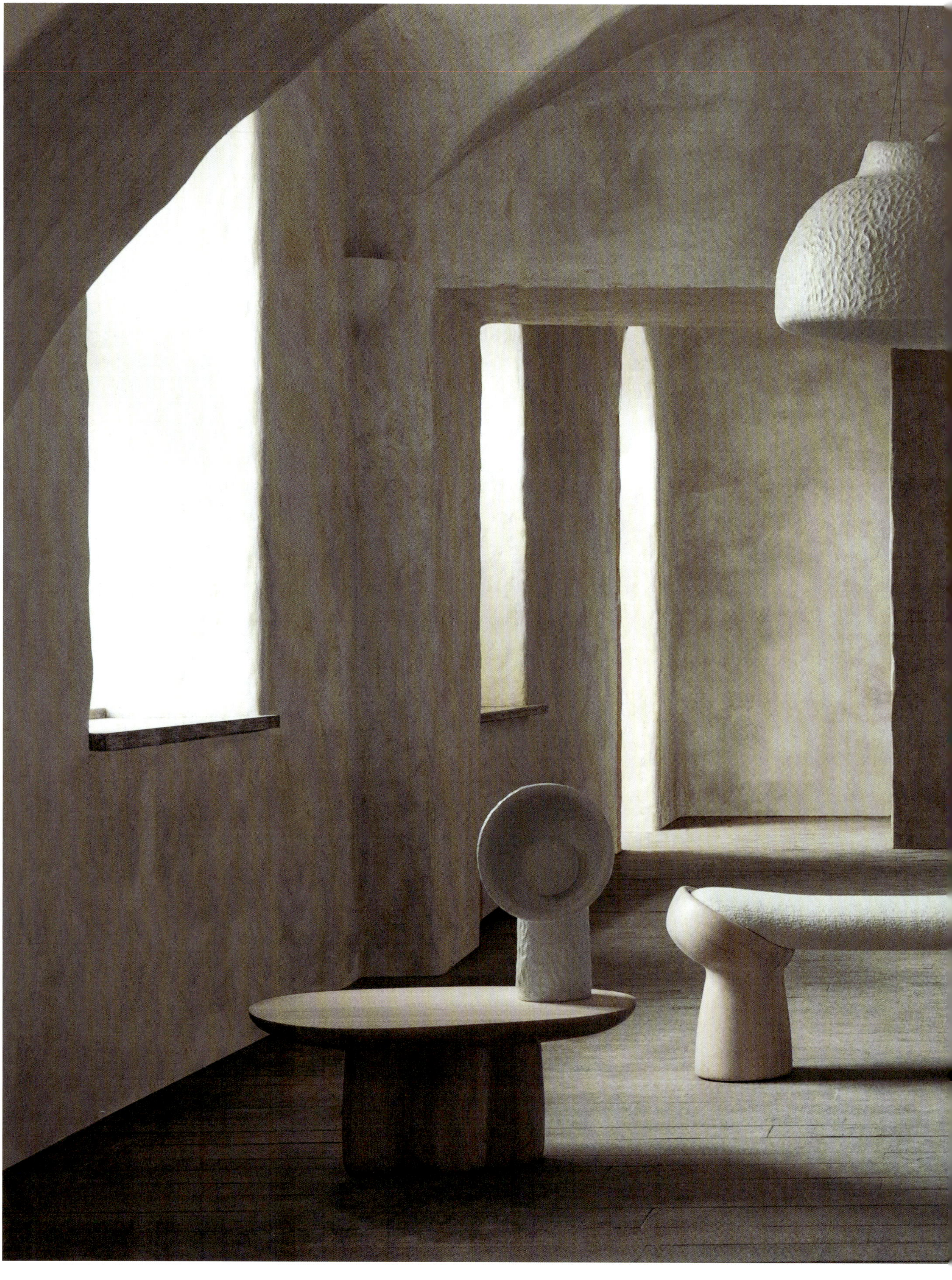

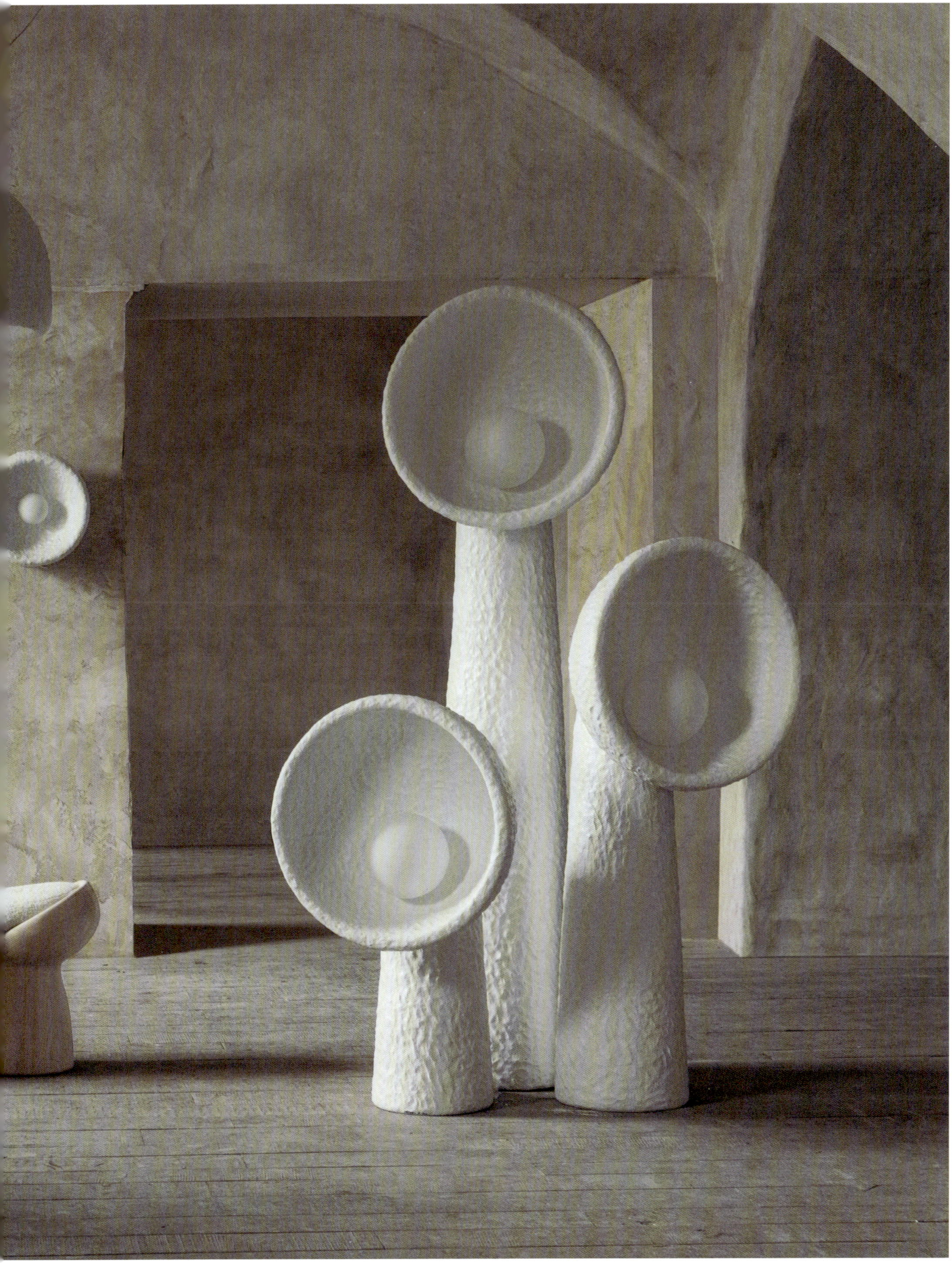

HONORING HISTORY AND EMBRACING CHANGE: A NEW ARCHITECTURAL ERA IS BORN

Three decades of independence have led to a wealth of experimentation and introspection in architecture, as architects work tirelessly to define the essence of Ukrainian design. Throughout the country, many post-Soviet architectural experiments were chaotic and not always fruitful; in response, architects, the design community, and developers are increasingly turning to Ukraine's foundational roots to establish a unique cultural identity. Looking to the past, they are building a future that embraces tradition while taking into account history's many contradictions—all while meeting modern needs and employing cutting-edge construction technologies. This is particularly vital now, as local and international specialists, global organizations, and world-renowned architects come together to plan the reconstruction of Ukrainian cities after the end of the war.

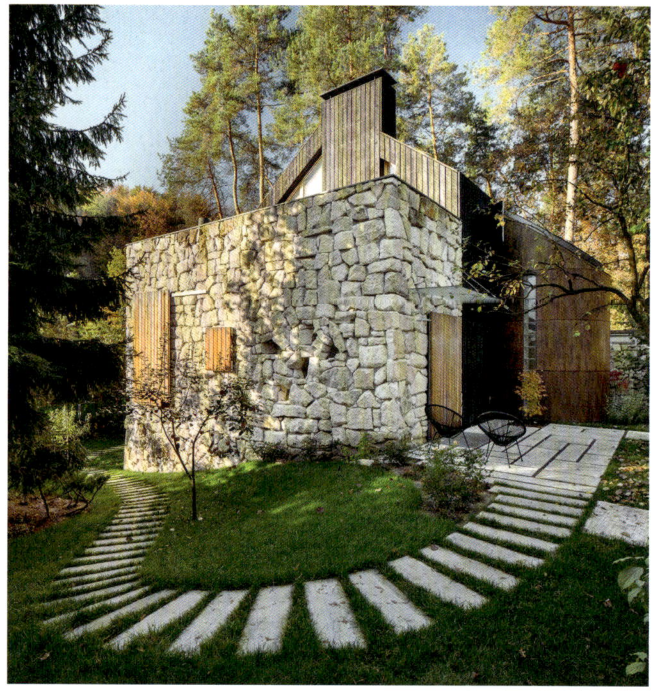

A suburban two-story house in a forest area near Lviv, designed by Replus Bureau. Below: Sivak+Partners' futuristic design for Tanu gelateria, located in a historic building in Odesa.

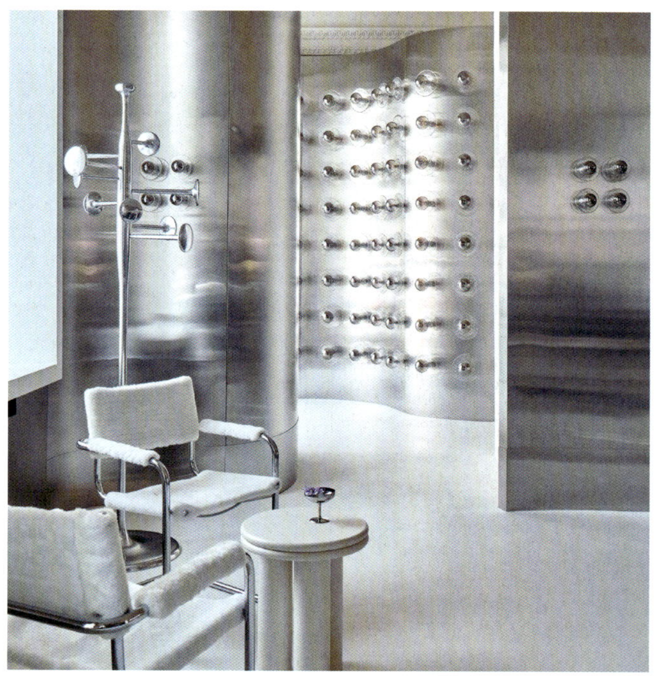

SUSTAINABILITY AND ARTISANAL DESIGN

Today's Ukrainian architects and designers are crafting spaces that are not only carefully designed and functional, but stylish, innovative, and resourceful, too. Ukraine's history, culture, artisanal traditions, and natural environment are increasingly central to the nation's contemporary design landscape. A singular, emblematic style is emerging, rooted in Ukrainians' desire for freedom of spirit and body as well as a longstanding respect for nature, passed down from generation to generation. This new Ukrainian style is exhibited through natural colors and materials, traditional motifs, an extensive use of crafts, and a skillful accentuation of historical buildings' original features. Studios are increasingly promoting sustainability in their projects by using recycled materials and components from older structures, enhancing the authenticity and value of their designs in the process.

The distinct Ukrainian flair of these projects is enriched with elements derived from various cultures and trends. Marked by a passion for innovation and

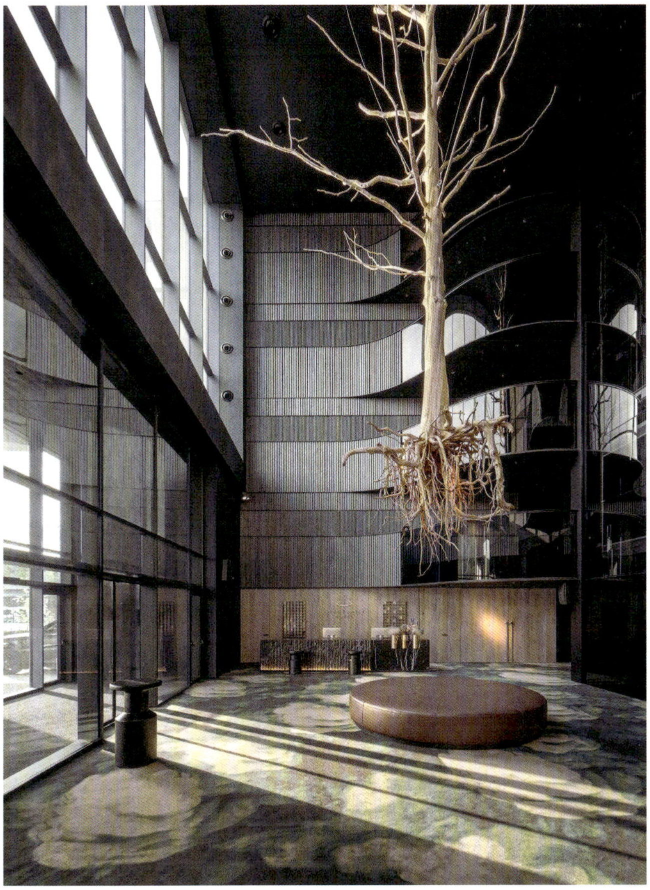

Wood is a recurring motif in all Yod Group projects. Above: a large tree floating in the atrium of Emily Hotel, Vynnyky. Below: an installation in the HAY boutique hotel & spa by Edem Family, Bukovel.

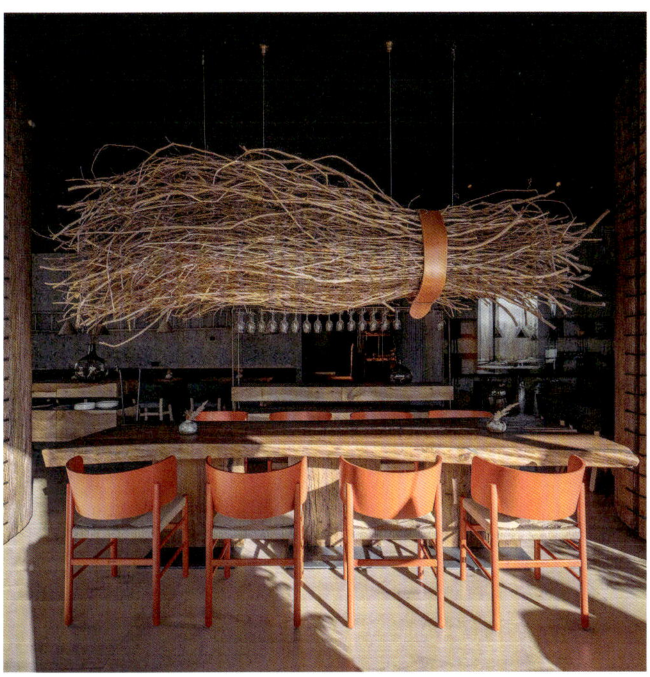

creativity, the generation born in independent Ukraine came of age in the era of information, which allowed creatives to absorb the finest practices from around the world and expertly reapply them in their own, distinctly Ukrainian way.

REVITALIZING THE PAST

Restoring and repurposing old buildings is one of the most sustainable and economically viable ways to shape the future. Ukrainian architects have extensive experience reviving run-down historic properties—in particular, industrial buildings and complexes from the 18th and 19th centuries that were repurposed by Soviet enterprises and then left to decay after the collapse of the Soviet Union. A growing movement focuses on adapting these distinctive buildings to fulfill contemporary needs while showcasing the rich variety of Ukrainian architecture.

An exemplary instance can be seen in A-Station, by the A Development Company in Kyiv, which involves the restoration and redevelopment of the former Arsenal Factory, the Military Commandant's Office, and the historical monument, Mykilska Brama. These restored heritage buildings are taking on new functions and meanings in today's city. For instance, the once-restricted factory grounds have been converted into an accessible, multifunctional space that wide swaths of the public can enjoy. Numerous restaurants, including balbek bureau's Molodist and the Kyiv Food Market projects, coexist with the Creative States coworking hub and various educational institutions in this vibrant space.

EMPHASIZING ARCHITECTURE IN INTERIORS

There is a rich tapestry of architectural styles to be found in Ukraine. Stunning examples of Cossack, or Ukrainian, baroque share the skyline with a variety of late 19th-century and early 20th-century architectural styles. Soviet times brought Soviet modernism, constructivism (particularly in Kharkiv, where many buildings in this style were heavily damaged by recent bombings), and Stalinist architecture, which can be seen in the Office of the President in Kyiv and the monumental buildings on Khreshchatyk Street. These, and many other architectural styles, form the image of large cities in Ukraine.

Throughout Ukraine, architects are revitalizing landmark buildings, filling them with contemporary restaurants, offices, and coworking spaces. Architects take inspiration from these historic spaces to create impressive, original projects, whether that means restoring an early 1900s property in the center of Kyiv, or modernizing an ancient 16th-century landmark in Lviv. By skillfully contrasting design elements, designers preserve and emphasize heritage architectural features, making them the focal point of interiors.

The COOSH Store in Lviv is a great example of this, where the designers at Replus Bureau mixed contemporary furniture accents with an emphasis on old architectural features, such as the arches and exposed brick walls. Another project, This is Pyvbar, designed by balbek bureau, is located in a former furrier manufacturing facility in the very center of Kyiv's Podil neighborhood. This brick architectural landmark was erected at the end of the 18th century, and the 21st-century renovation preserves the geometry of the vaults and the oak wood flooring. The space's textured walls and ceilings also echo the design of a *mazanka,* or traditional Ukrainian home. And lastly, Oleg Volosovskiy from loft buro devised a fresh, contemporary design for Fresh Black Roastery & Bar in the renovated Reytarska Circle building. During construction, the firm unearthed original 1980s accents and incorporated them into their final design, resulting in a highly original space.

In the past few years, an increasingly popular design trend has prominently surfaced in the Ukrainian hospitality industry: free-form spaces with original accents left raw and rough. Architects working in this style leave brickwork exposed and intentionally leave vents, piping, and wires in plain sight. The historic architecture is often complemented by vintage furniture and decor. With relaxed atmospheres and modern touches, these spaces come to epitomize a busy city lifestyle. DOT Coffee Station #1 is a very successful example of this trend. Its eclectic interior—designed by Yod Group—buzzes with a lively urban vibe.

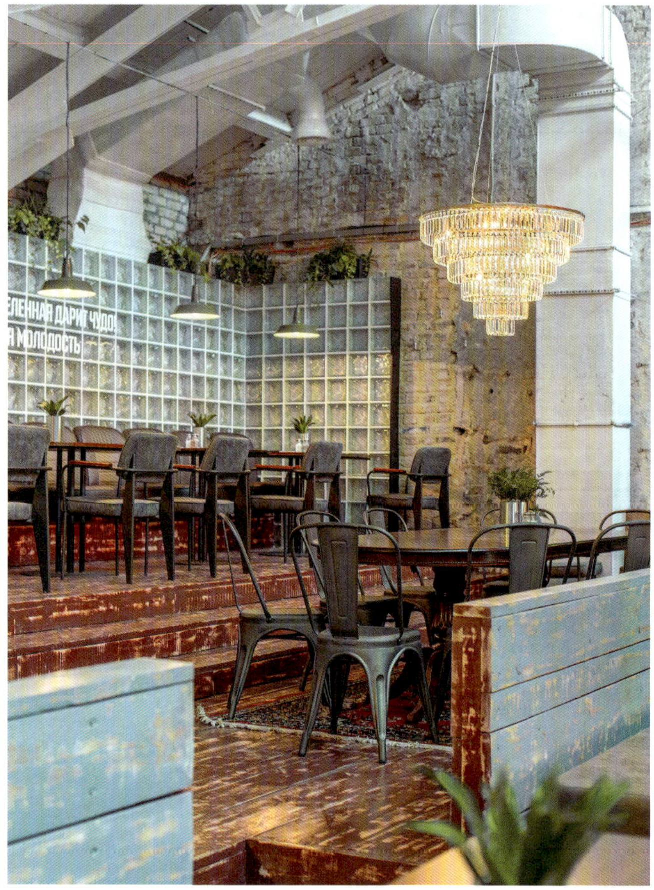

Molodist restaurant, Kyiv, designed by balbek bureau. Below: This is Pyvbar (also by balbek bureau), where lighting solutions perfectly emphasize the architecture of this Kyiv landmark.

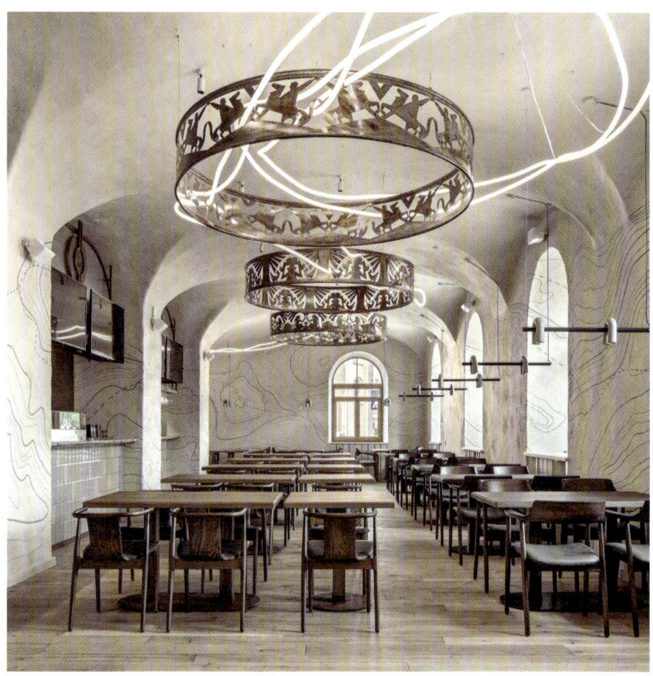

THE DEVIL IS IN THE DETAILS

Many Ukrainian design studios are known for creating complex, sophisticated spaces where even the smallest details have been carefully considered. In some projects, almost every interior element is custom-made by local artisans and manufacturers. Often, designers strive to instill deeper meaning into each detail, with each square inch of the interior filled with symbols. The range of design components is vast and unique, with interiors that combine bespoke accessories made from local materials and crafts, modern product designs, vintage furniture, and authentic antiques imported from around the world. Thoughtful planning goes into custom lighting solutions, and architects carefully select which materials and finishing methods will match their vision for each interior. Perhaps most remarkably, despite the mix of cultures, eras, materials, genres, and styles, these projects maintain an impressive level of cohesion.

In order to effectively meet deadlines and reduce costs, designers frequently have to employ inventive solutions. This resourcefulness enables them to turn ordinary objects into eye-catching interior details, sometimes creating art in the process. For example, in Tin Tin restaurant, designers at loft buro decorated the ceiling with dozens of suspended bicycle wheels, some of which double as lighting fixtures. The end result is attractive and highly dynamic, a veritable art installation. This is a vivid example of how ordinary objects, in the right hands, can create unexpected effects.

Blending authentic vintage elements into new interiors is an important component of this design approach. Balbek bureau packed the restaurant Molodist with a playful mix of eclectic mementos from the '90s. Ukrainians attach a certain stigma to their Soviet past and heritage, so the designers dreamt up almost surreal combinations to add an element of irony to the space.

The theme of nature holds immense significance to Ukrainians, and so designers have learned to organically integrate their projects into the surrounding landscape. The founders of Yod Group even invented their own style, which they call Terroir Design: "We borrowed this term from winemaking. Just as a wine absorbs all the characteristics of the land where the vine grew, our design reflects the local atmosphere of the place where it was created. Such interiors resonate with the environment and expand it," says Volodymyr Nepyivoda, co-founder of Yod Group.

Designers also often use vintage reclaimed wood and other elements from abandoned Ukrainian houses, restoring them and giving them a second life. Replus Bureau even created the Restare Architectural Salvage Warehouse to collect and restore old architectural accents for use in their projects. Kris Badzyan, an architect from Lviv and the founder of Replus Bureau, used to renovate old Austrian houses, and watched in anguish as the new owners threw away valuable features. To remedy this, she and her team began salvaging these items, bringing them to her studio where they cleaned, repaired, and repainted them. This became the impetus for the creation of Restare in 2021. Replus Bureau has since integrated many of Restare's restored items into their designs, including Siaivo Dive Bar's stunning spiral metal staircase, salvaged from an Austrian home. Just as remarkable are the authentic larch beams dating back to the Austro-Hungarian period that Replus installed on the terrace of the Sakae Ramen Bar.

Restare's philosophy is to popularize the love of old things, as this teaches people to feel more connected with their families, communities, land, and culture. And this philosophy is increasingly prevalent in today's development of Ukrainian culture and society—in particular architecture and design. The war, a moment of intense social upheaval, made Ukrainians see that by returning to your roots and by learning to appreciate, protect, and build upon tradition, it is possible to craft a nation's true self-identity. A new generation of talented Ukrainian architects and designers has emerged, each with their own recognizable style intent on combining the past with the future, infusing their heritage with a contemporary perspective.

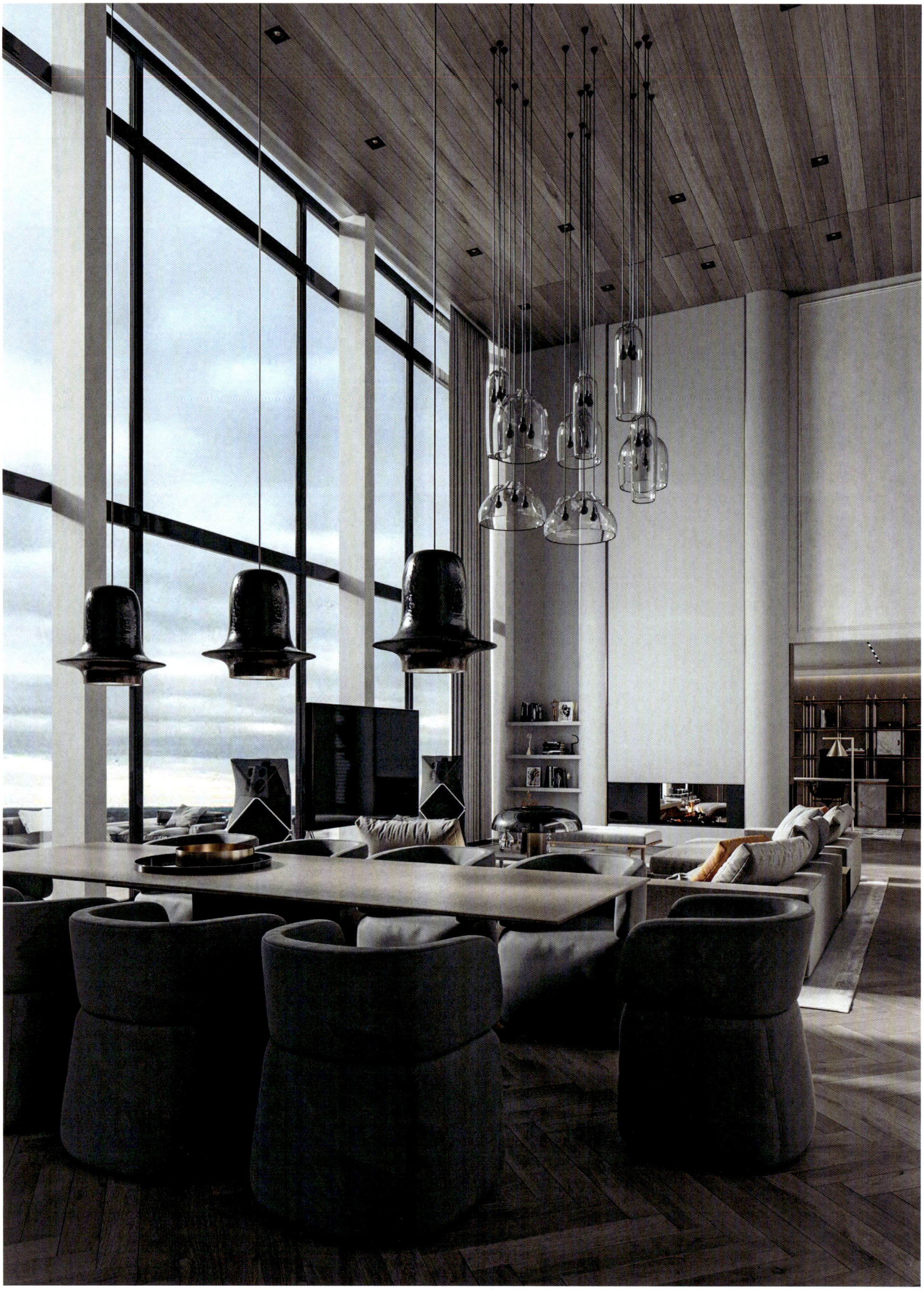

TIME-HONORED TECHNIQUES MEET TRENDSETTING DESIGN

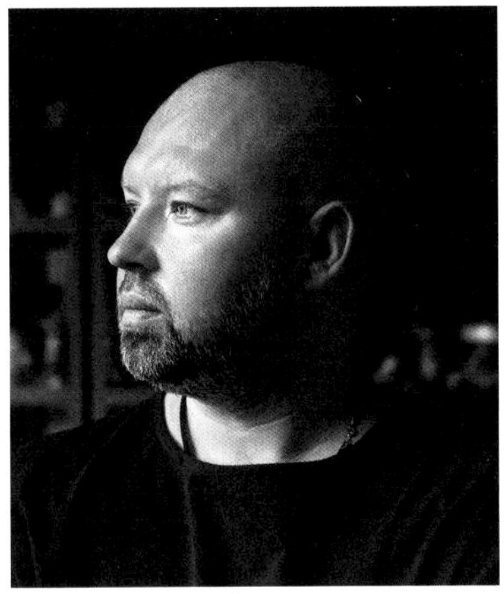

MAKHNO STUDIO

Makhno Studio fuses Ukrainian heritage, global trends, and the principle of wabi-sabi to craft its unique contemporary designs.

Makhno Studio is a design, architecture, and ceramics practice founded by Serhii Makhno in the early 2000s. Its globe-spanning portfolio includes over 600 residential, office, and retail projects, as well as restaurants, galleries, and more. The studio has received more than 70 awards, including International Property Awards, International Design Awards, Restaurant & Bar Design Awards, and a Red Dot Design Award. Makhno Studio aims to highlight Ukrainian design, culture, and artistic heritage while sharing with the world the uniqueness and originality of the country's national aesthetics. Every project incorporates elements of Ukrainian tradition and identity, particularly through the use of traditional materials and ancient craft techniques. For example, the studio mixes local herbs into many of their clay wall finishes, an age-old tradition that imparts a distinct natural ambiance to their interiors. Makhno Studio often uses reclaimed wood and restores old gates and fences, giving these materials a second life. Although Serhii Makhno is a strong proponent of Ukrainian culture, he also blends local customs with global trends and the Japanese philosophy of wabi-sabi, leaving his own unique mark on contemporary Ukrainian design. Another of his passions is product design, with his studio producing a range of lamps, tiles, and home decor items. The products balance traditional craft with modern design, creating "living" objects made from the heart. Some projects, such as the Mureli House, are almost entirely furnished with custom Makhno Studio products, from wall coverings to furniture and lighting. Traditional pottery also plays a vital role in Makhno Studio's creative pursuits, with most items handcrafted in their ceramic workshop. Their famous "Dido" ceramic series consists of art toys and objects made using a modern interpretation of traditional Ukrainian zoomorphic sculpture.

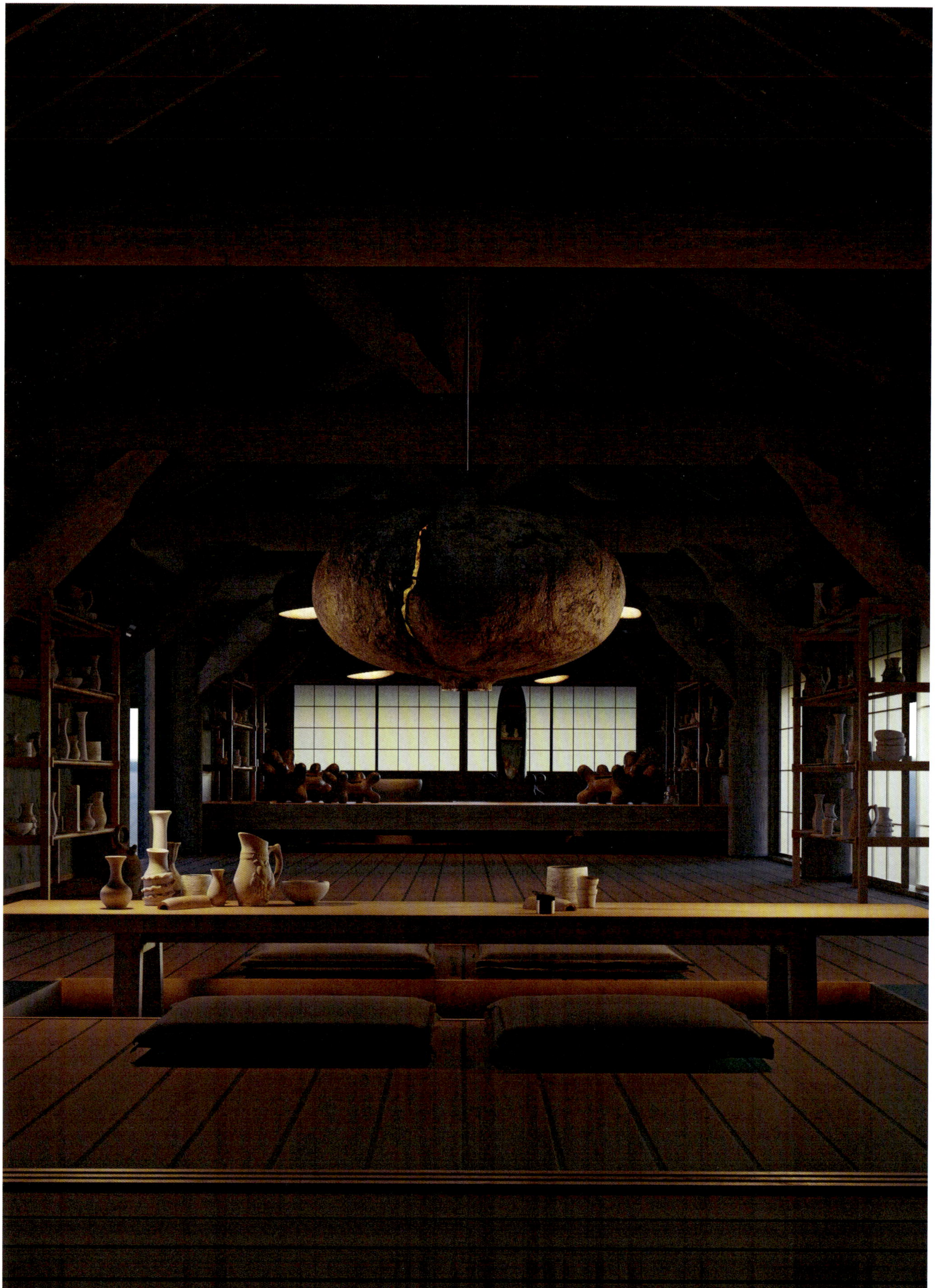

"Makhno Studio has a big goal—to shape and tell the world about Ukrainian design. The most important thing is to convey the uniqueness and originality of our aesthetics and to preserve traditional techniques, adding them to modern interiors."

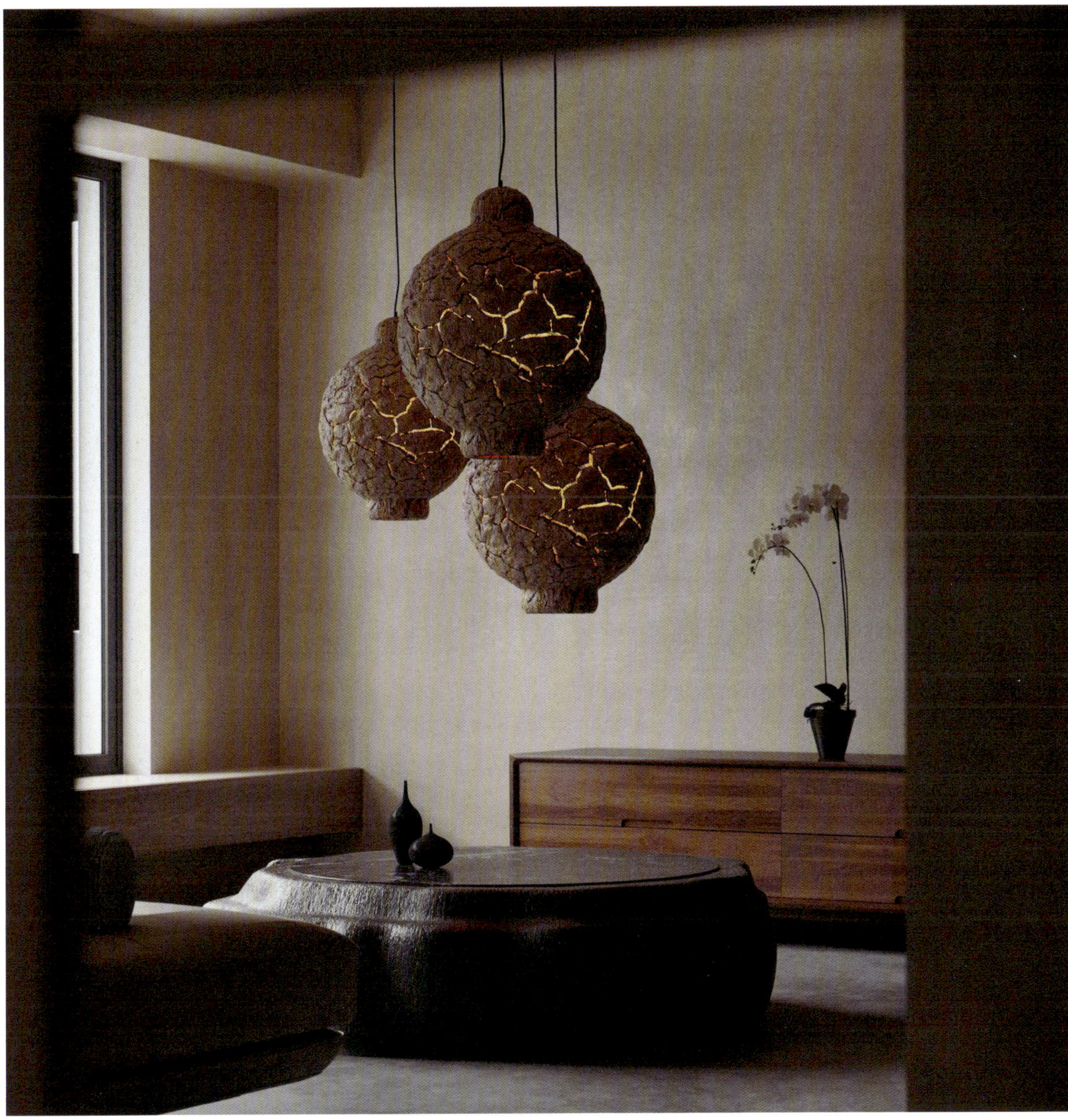

Makhno Studio creates original lighting products using ancient craft techniques. These objects often become centerpieces of the interior. Shown on this page: the Sphera Lamp. Opposite page: Taking its name from the Ukrainian word for "pumpkin," the ceramic Garbuz Lamp perfectly complements the elegant, rugged space.

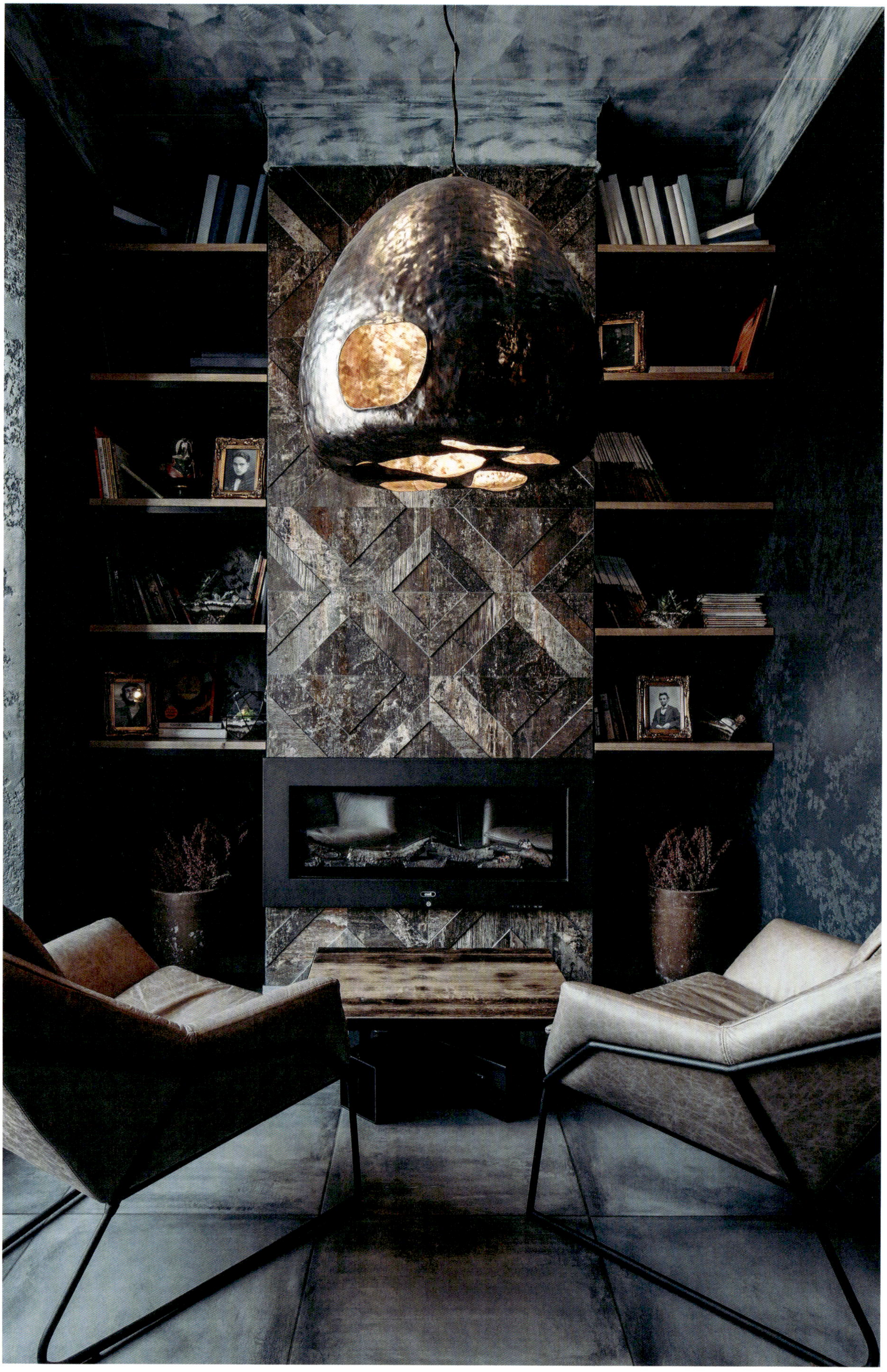

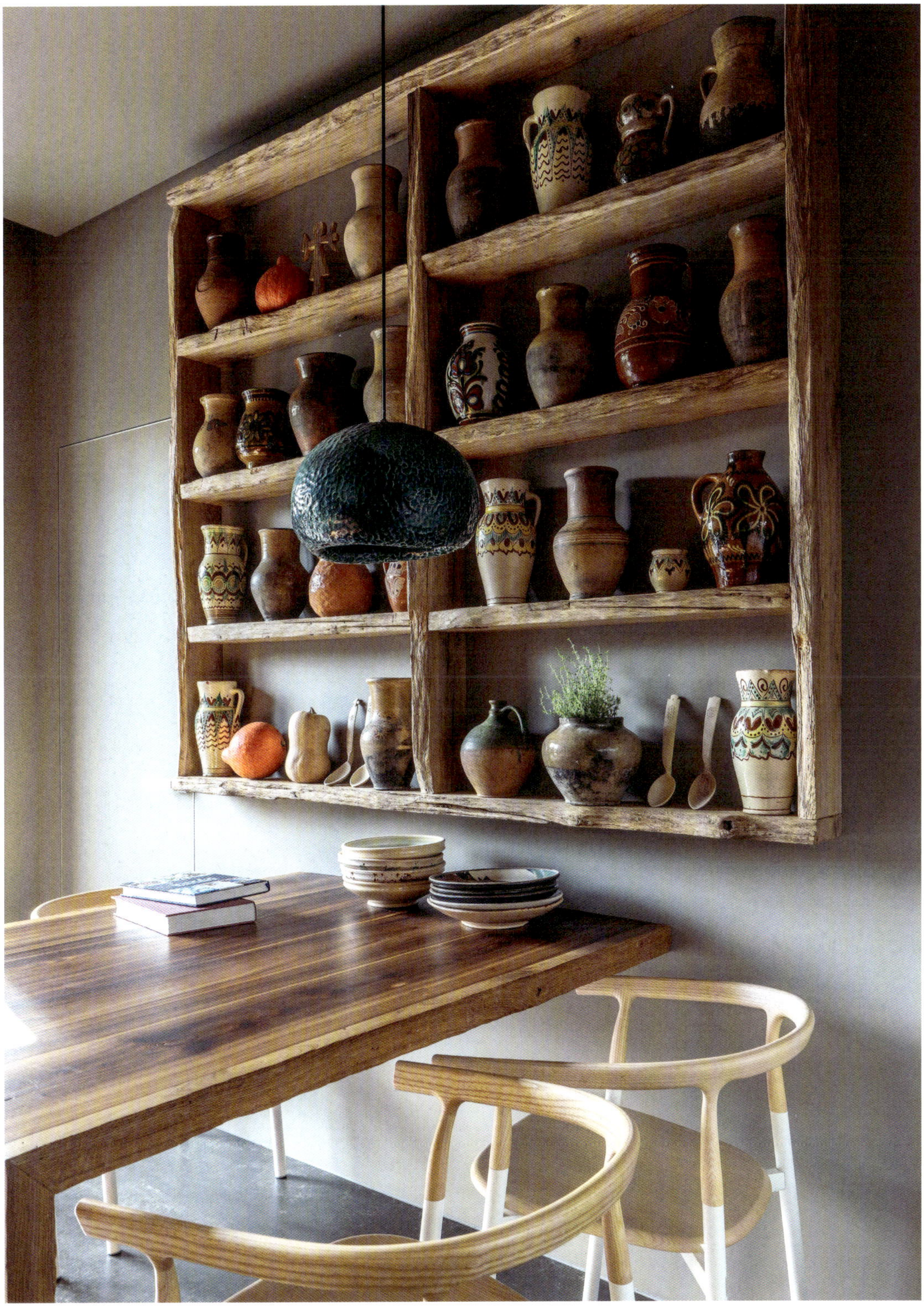

Serhii Makhno has been collecting traditional Ukrainian ceramics for many years. His extensive collection of unique pieces is on display in his office as well as in his private residence, Shkrub House. Opposite page: Makivka Lamp, Makhno Studio.

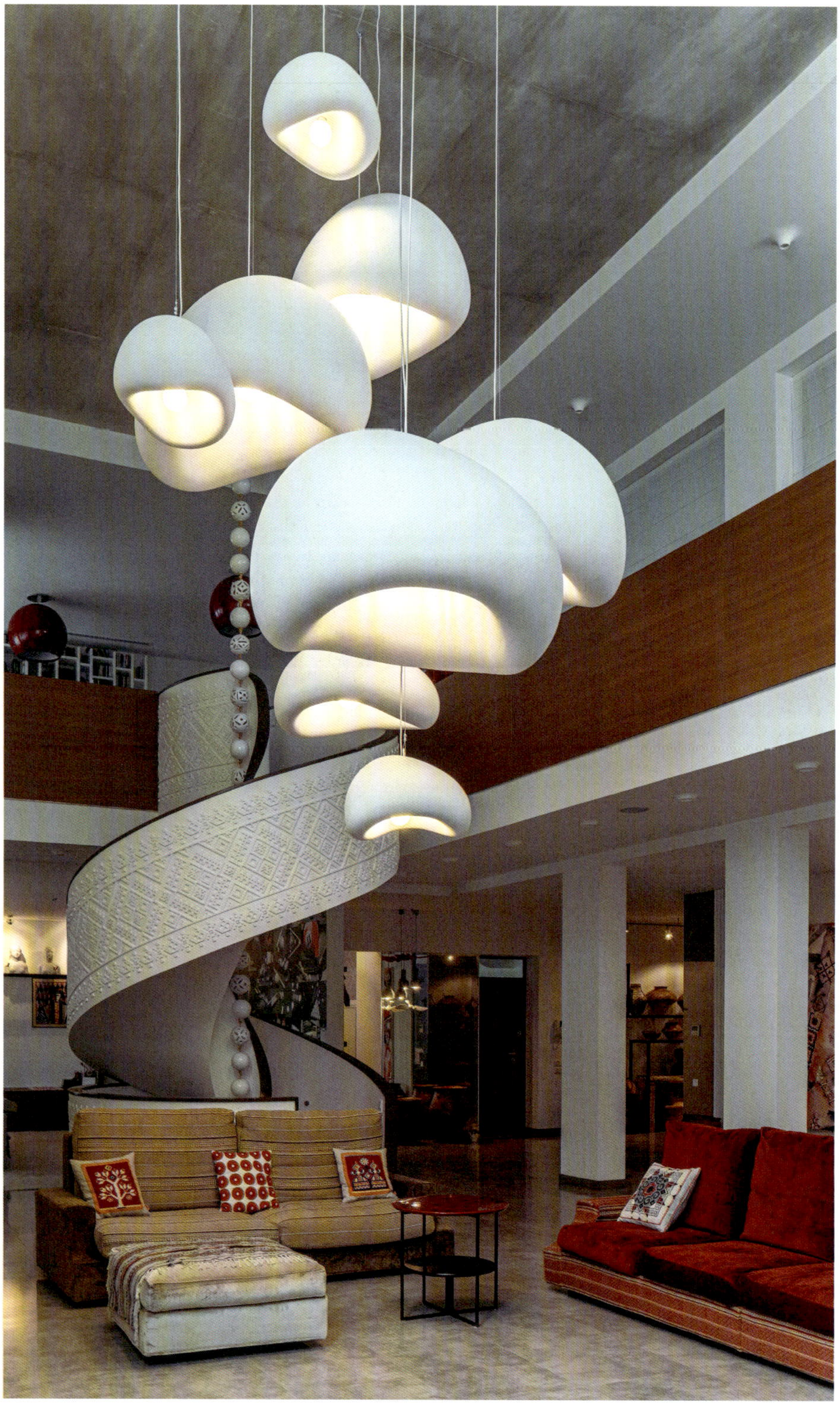

The Khmara Lamp from Makhno Studio has become iconic. Its cloud-like forms, made of a variety of materials, float overhead and fill any interior with a special ambience.

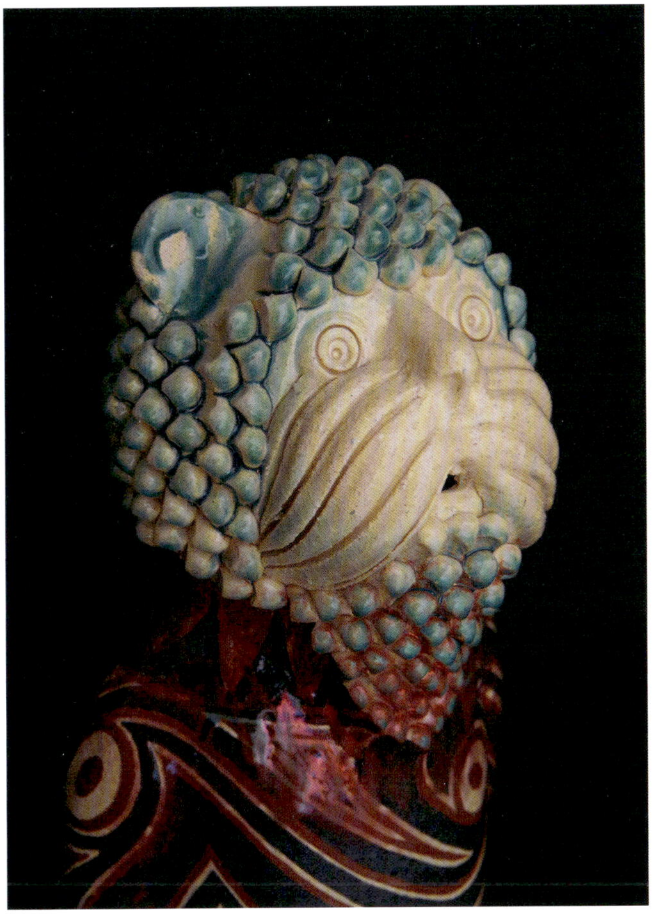
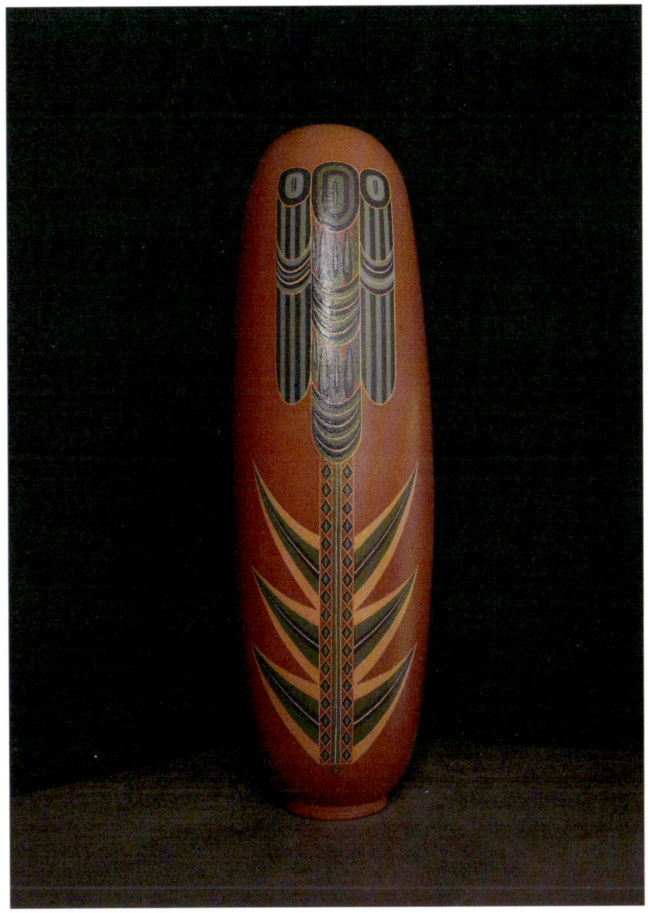
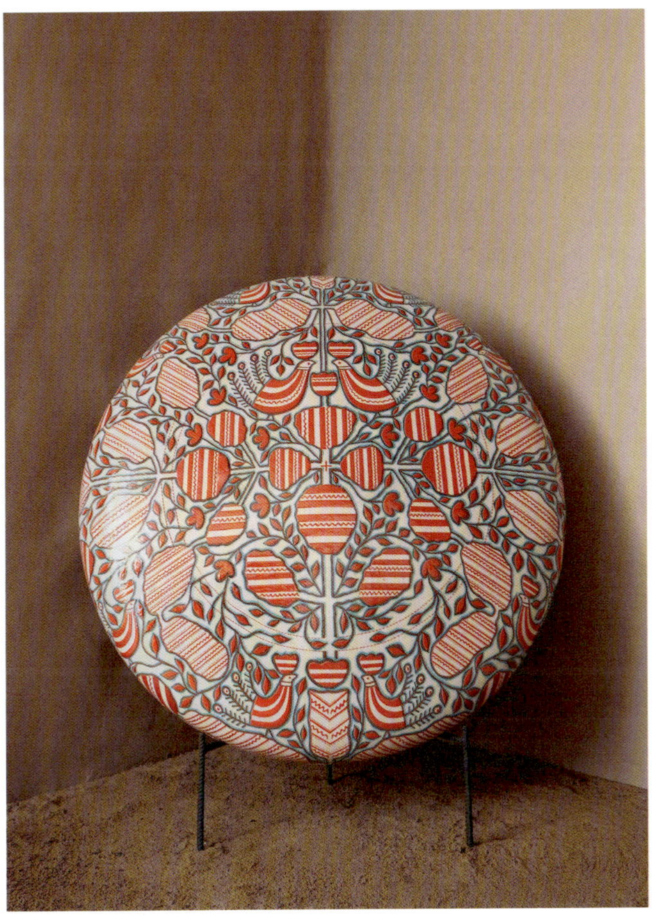
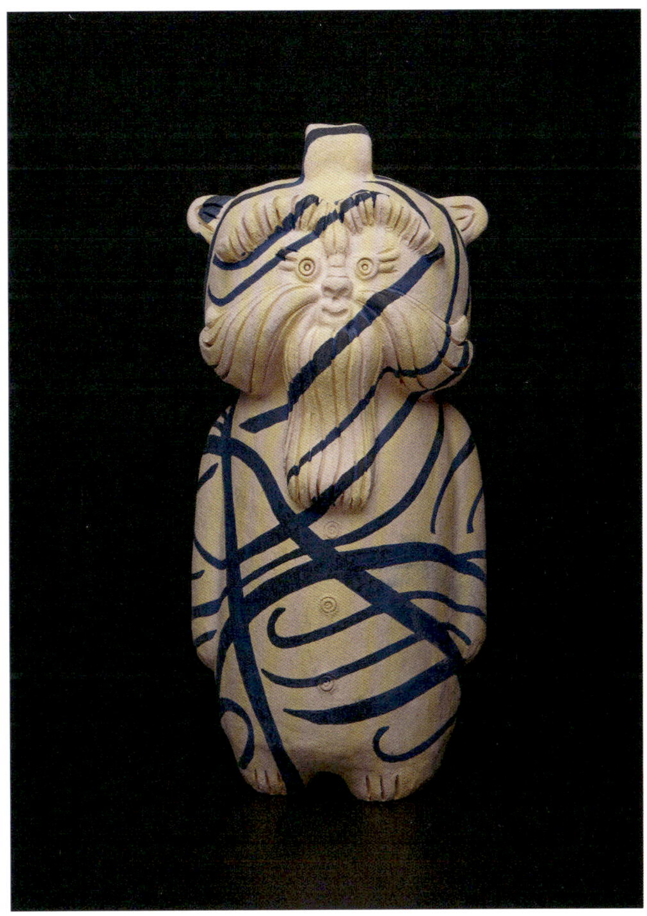

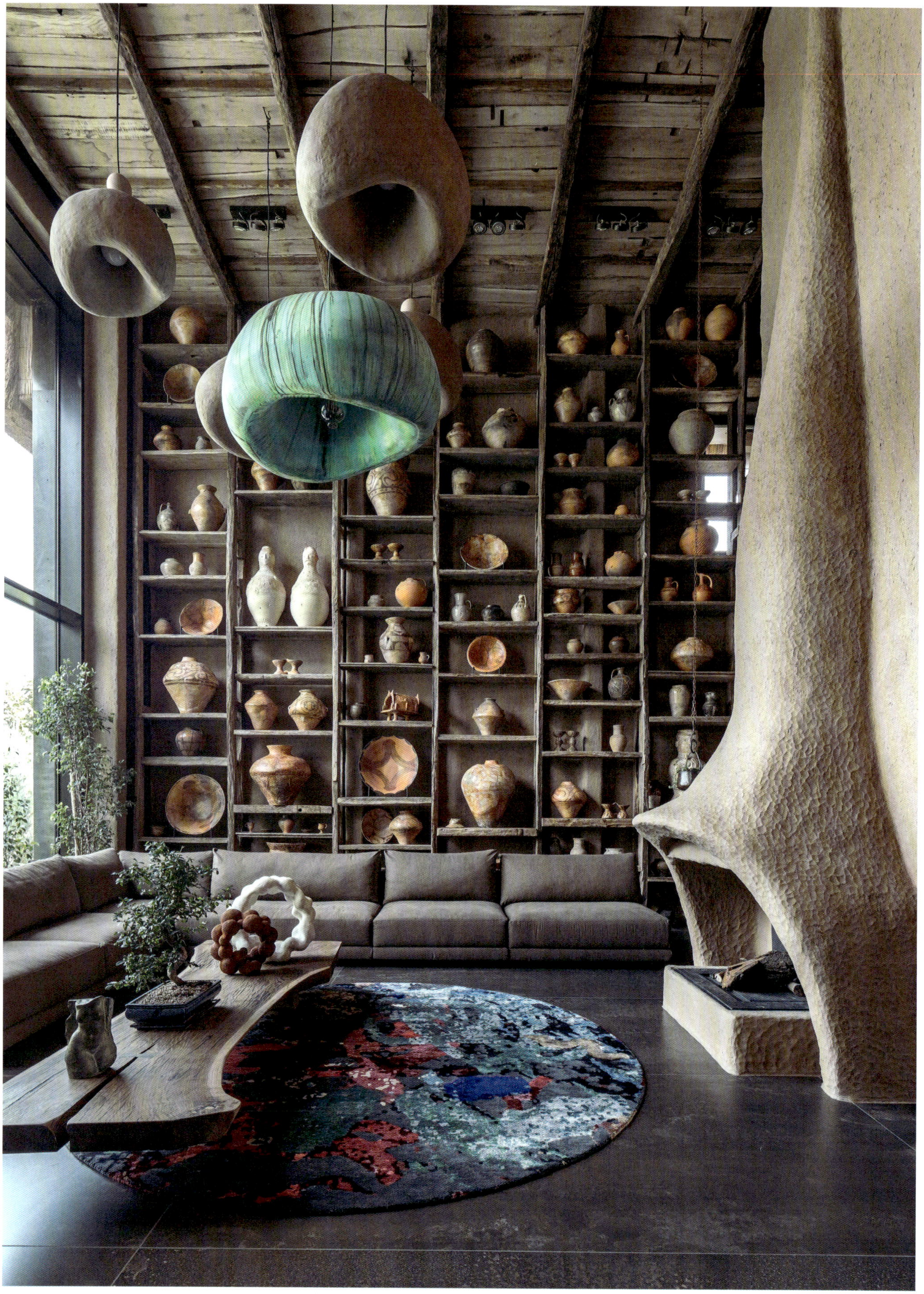

A HOUSE IN MAKHNO'S IMAGE

MAKHNO STUDIO
SHKRUB HOUSE

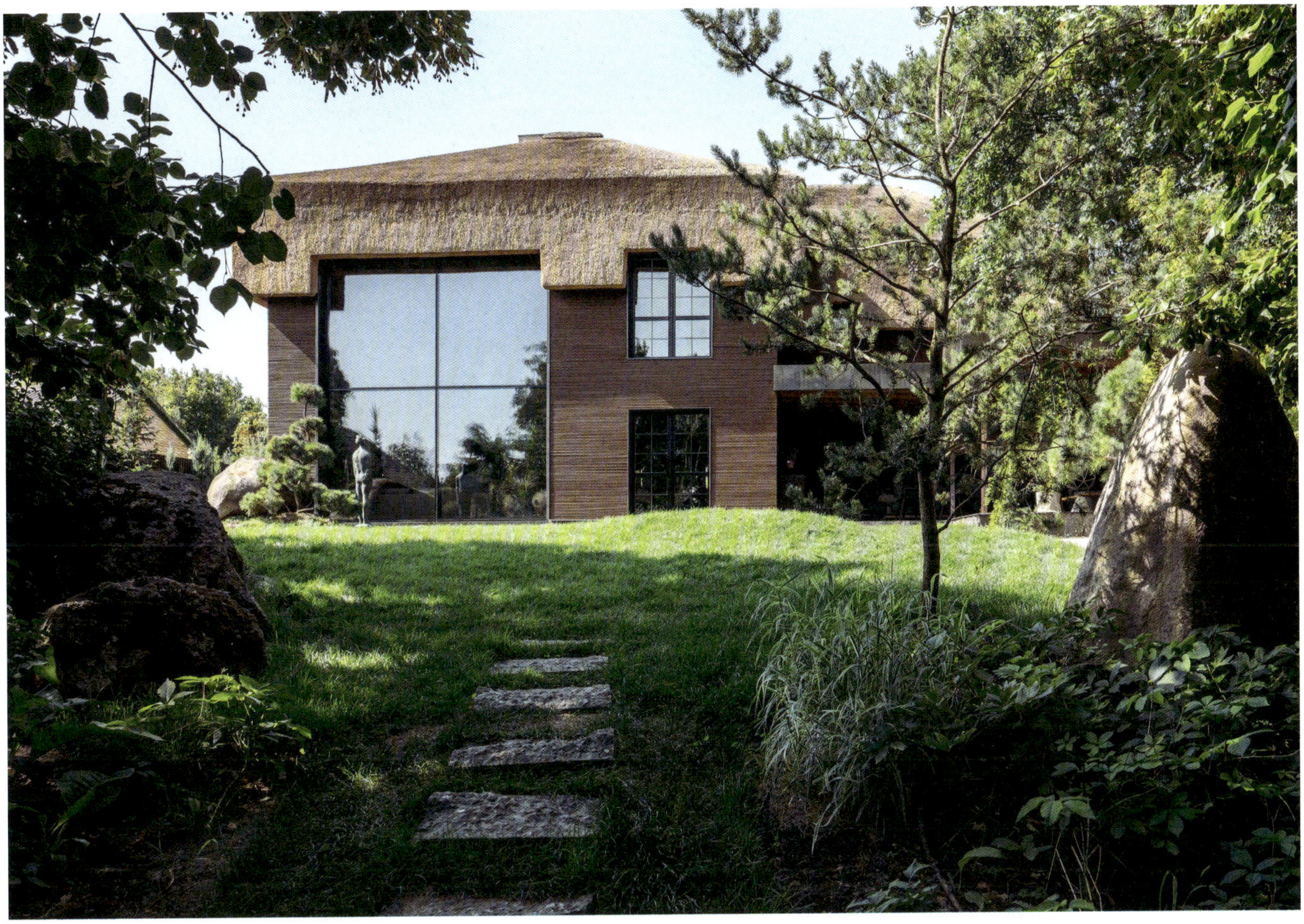

The Shkrub House serves as a testament to the unique design aesthetic of Serhii Makhno, blending Ukrainian tradition and wabi-sabi philosophy.

Serhii Makhno designs his projects with a focus on both Ukrainian traditions and Japanese aesthetics. In the Shkrub House, which he designed for his family, Makhno seamlessly brings these two cultures under one roof: the interior boasts a modern Ukrainian style while mixing in elements of wabi-sabi philosophy. This spacious two-story building features natural materials like wood, metal, and clay throughout. The walls are decorated with several types of clay finish, to which seeds of flax, rye, and wheat have been added—an ancient Ukrainian custom. Meanwhile, an impressive fireplace reminiscent of a traditional old stove adds warmth and comfort to the living room. The interior is further enhanced by Makhno Studio design pieces, such as the Tetrapod, Flapjack, and Grass tiles, or the Khmara lamps. Shkrub House also highlights Makhno's role as a collector, with his extensive collection of traditional ceramics.

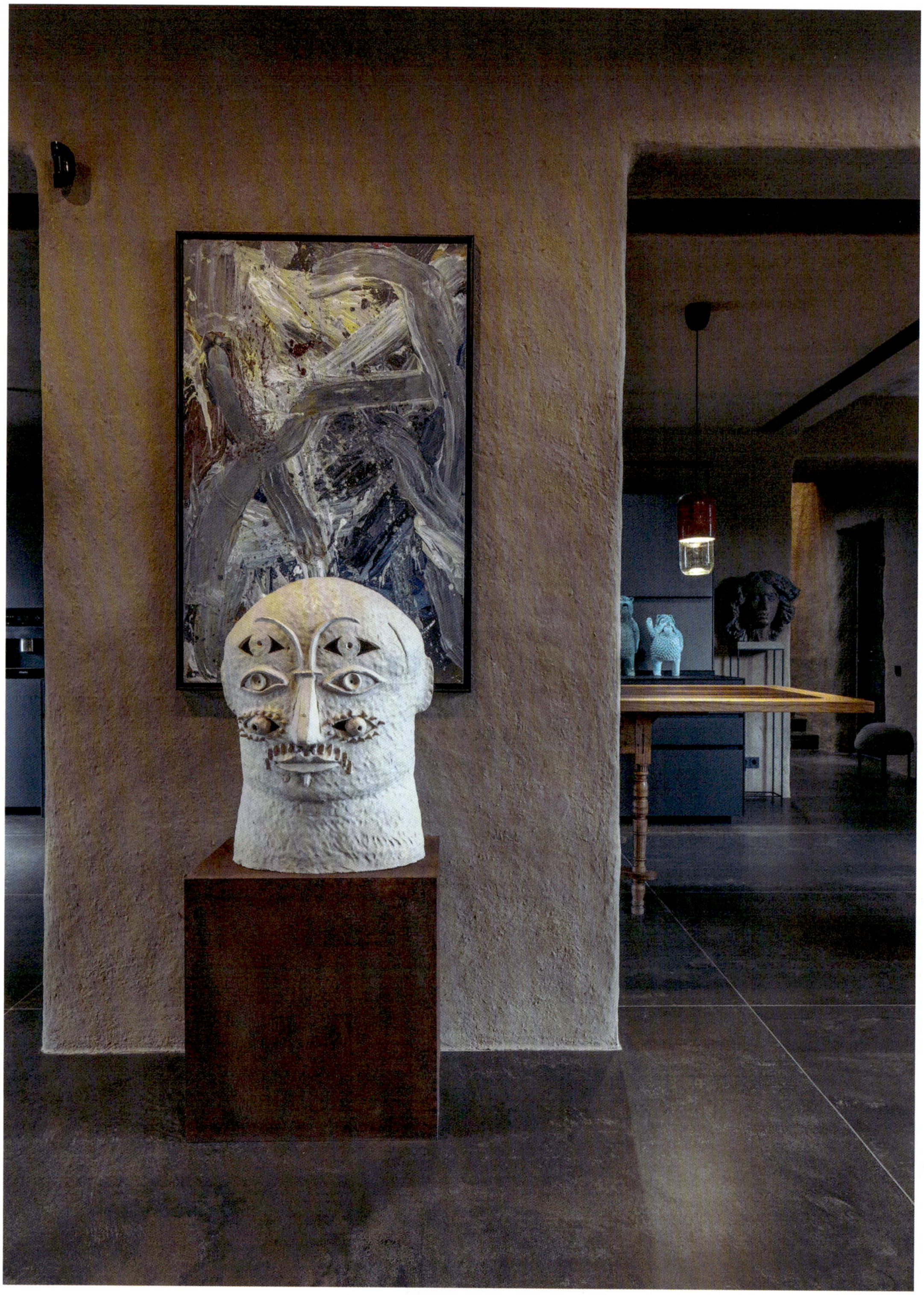

The interior of Shkrub House is filled with Serhii Makhno's collection of contemporary art and ceramics. Made-to-order lighting solutions, a hallmark of the designer's projects, provide an eye-catching accent.

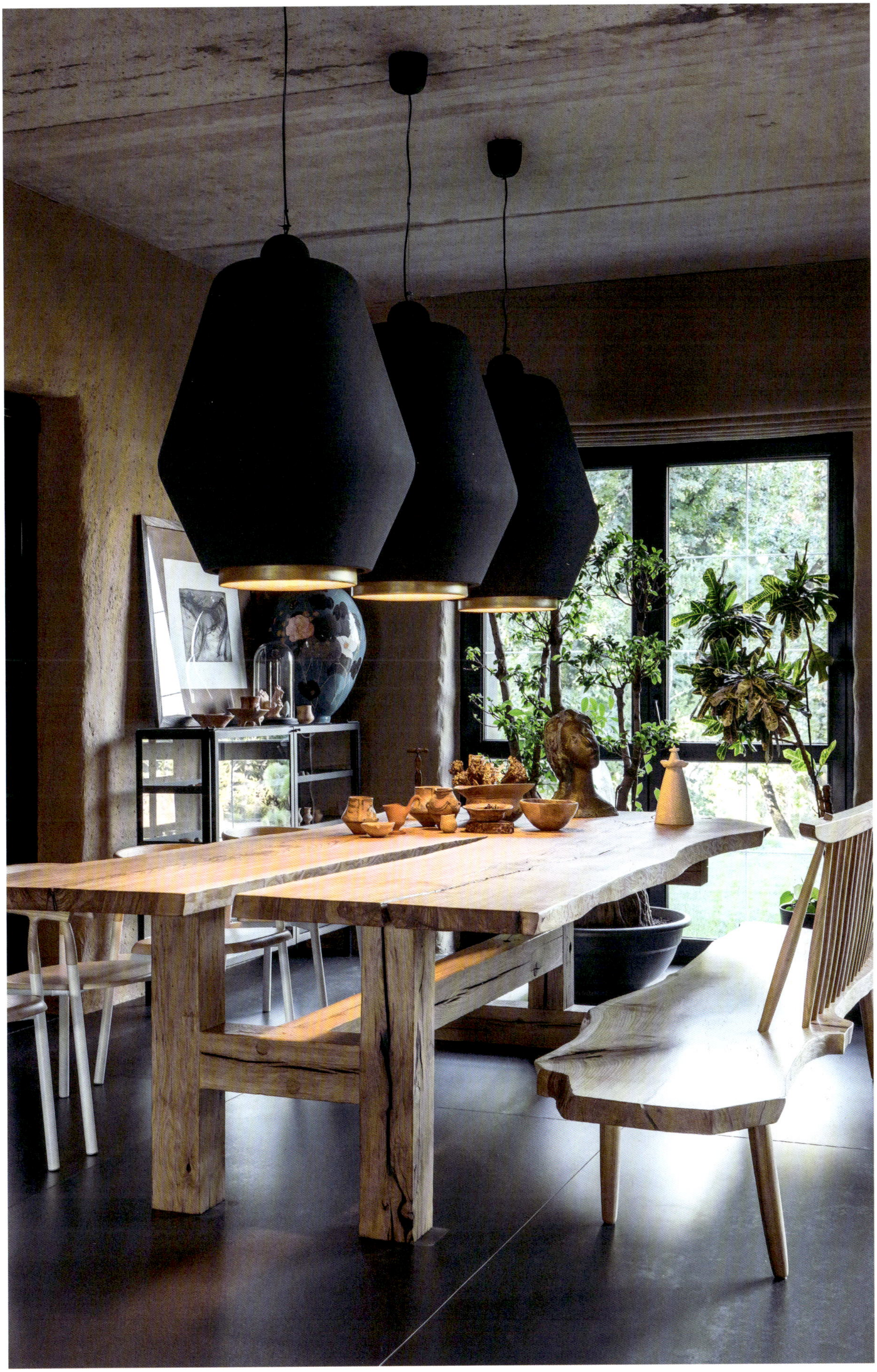

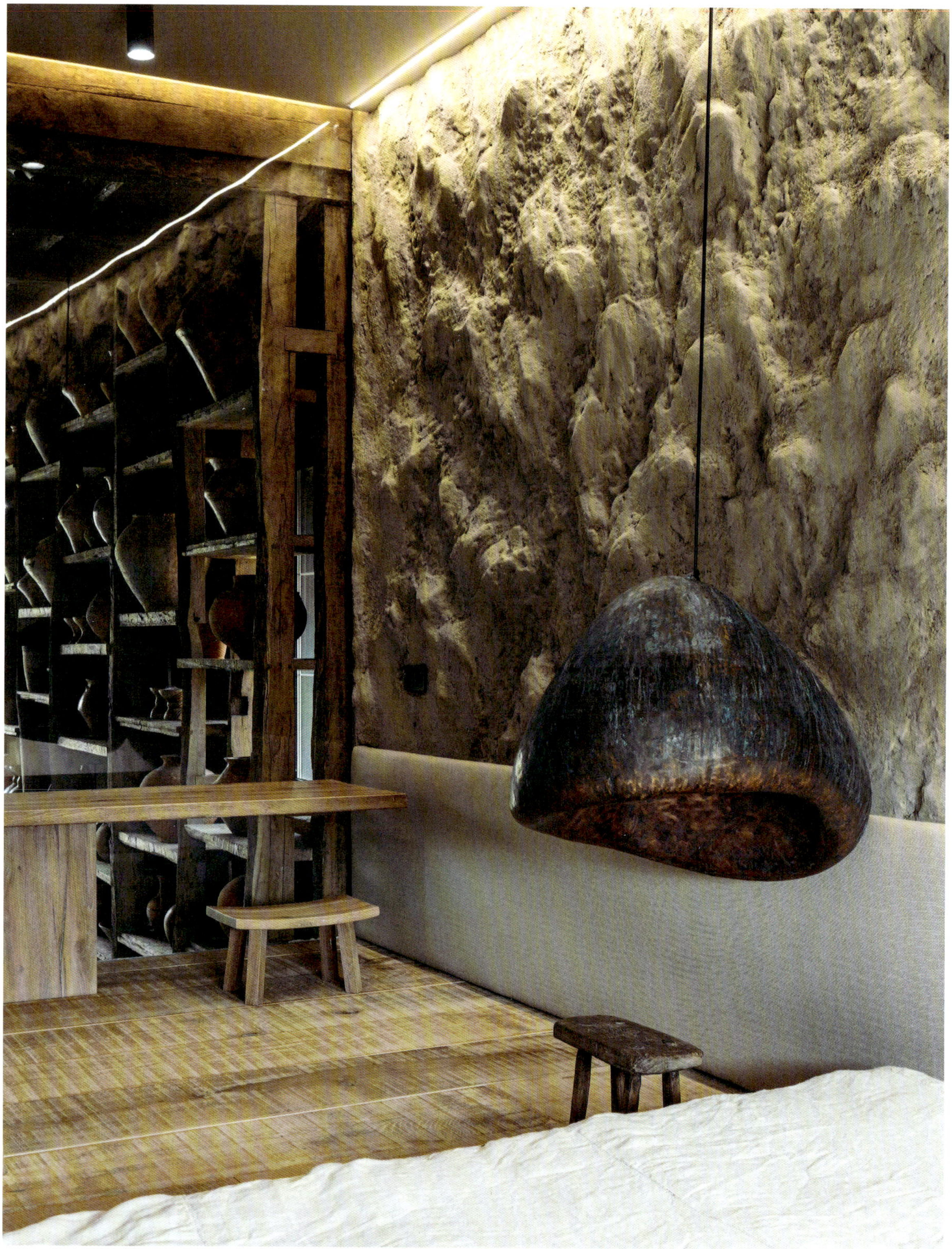

The walls of Shkrub House are decorated with a variety of materials: from clay finishes like those of traditional Ukrainian homes, to elegant, round Flapjack tiles produced by Makhno Studio.

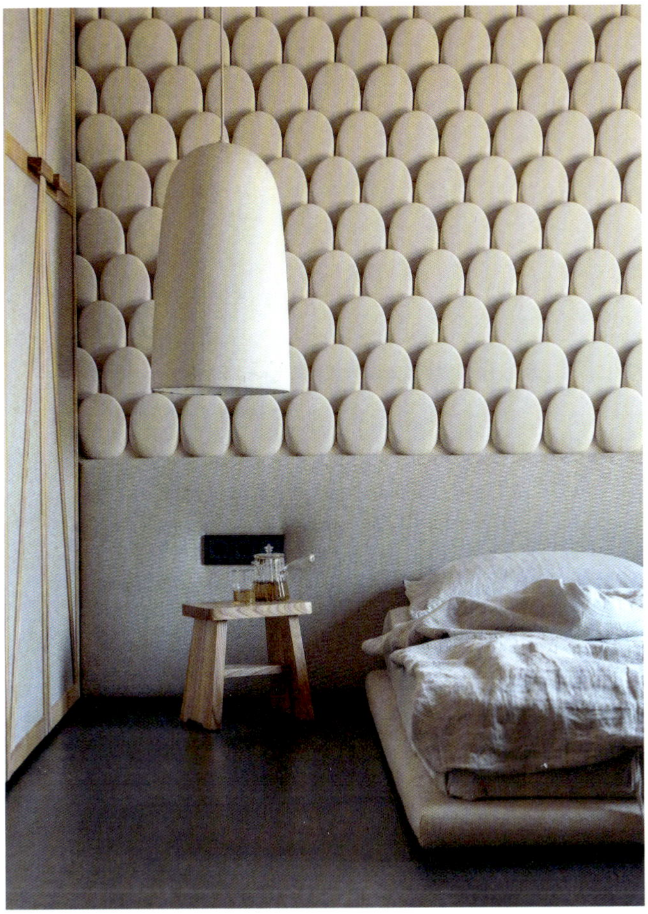
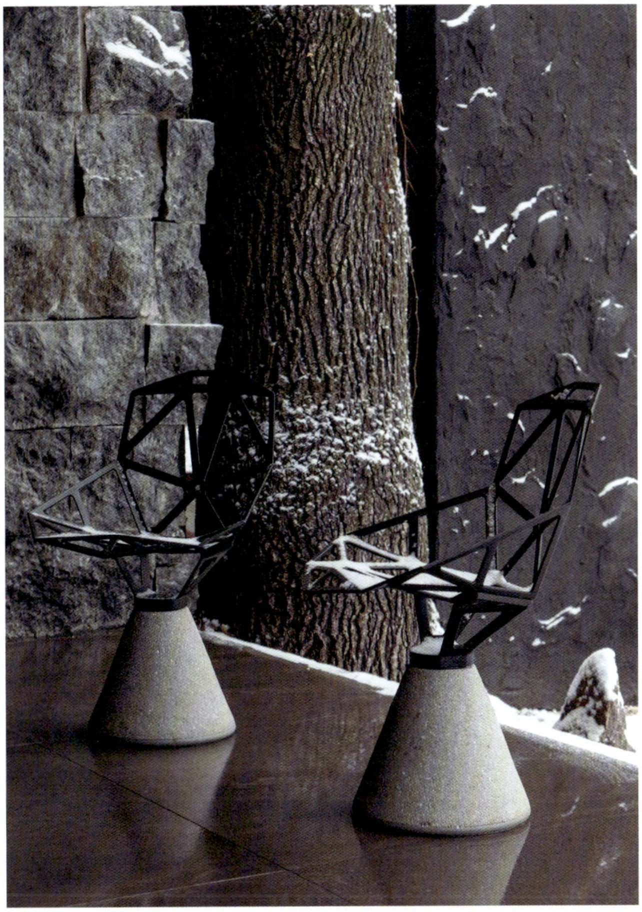
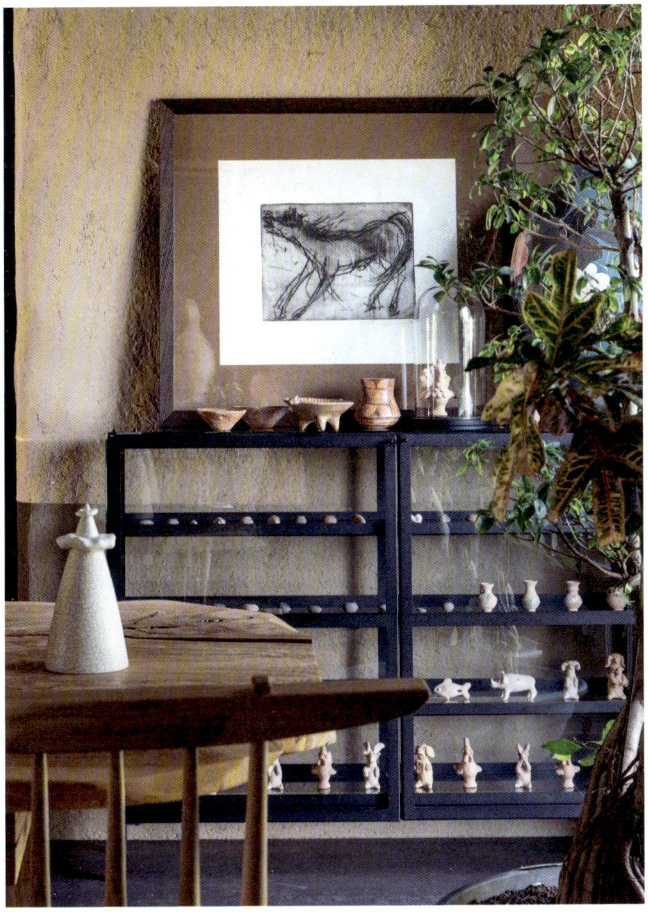
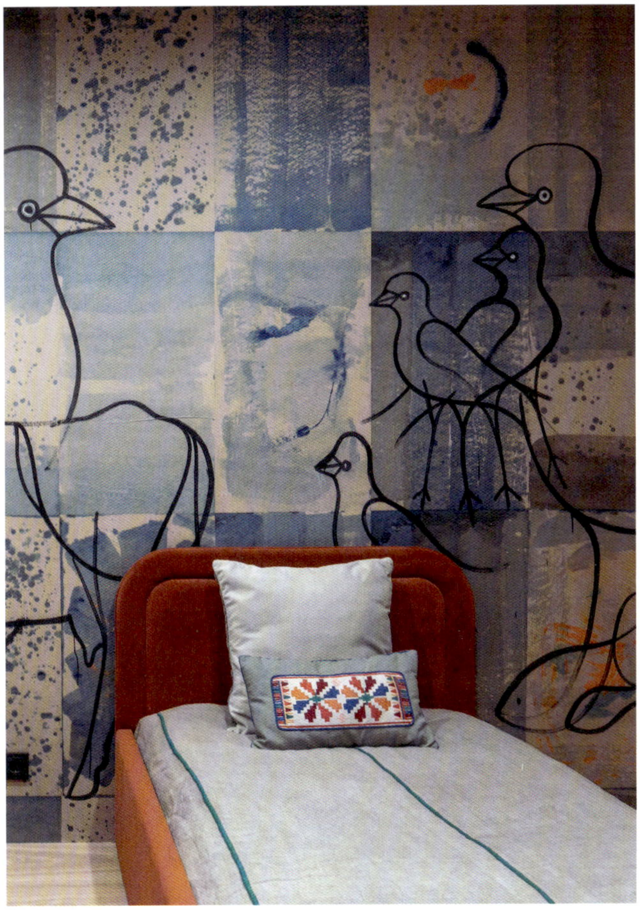

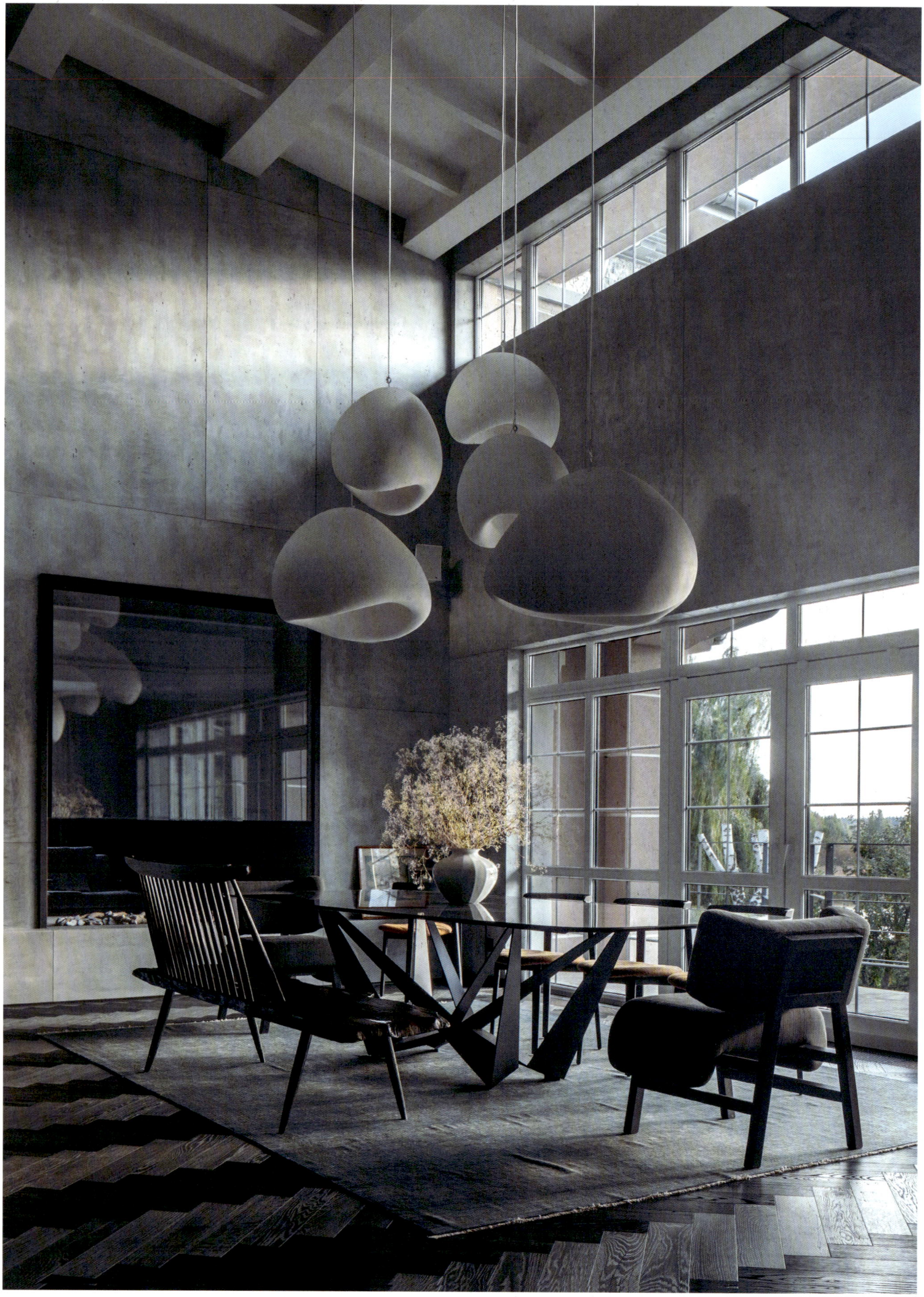

A MIX OF CULTURES AND ERAS IN RIDNYI HOUSE

MAKHNO STUDIO
RIDNYI HOUSE

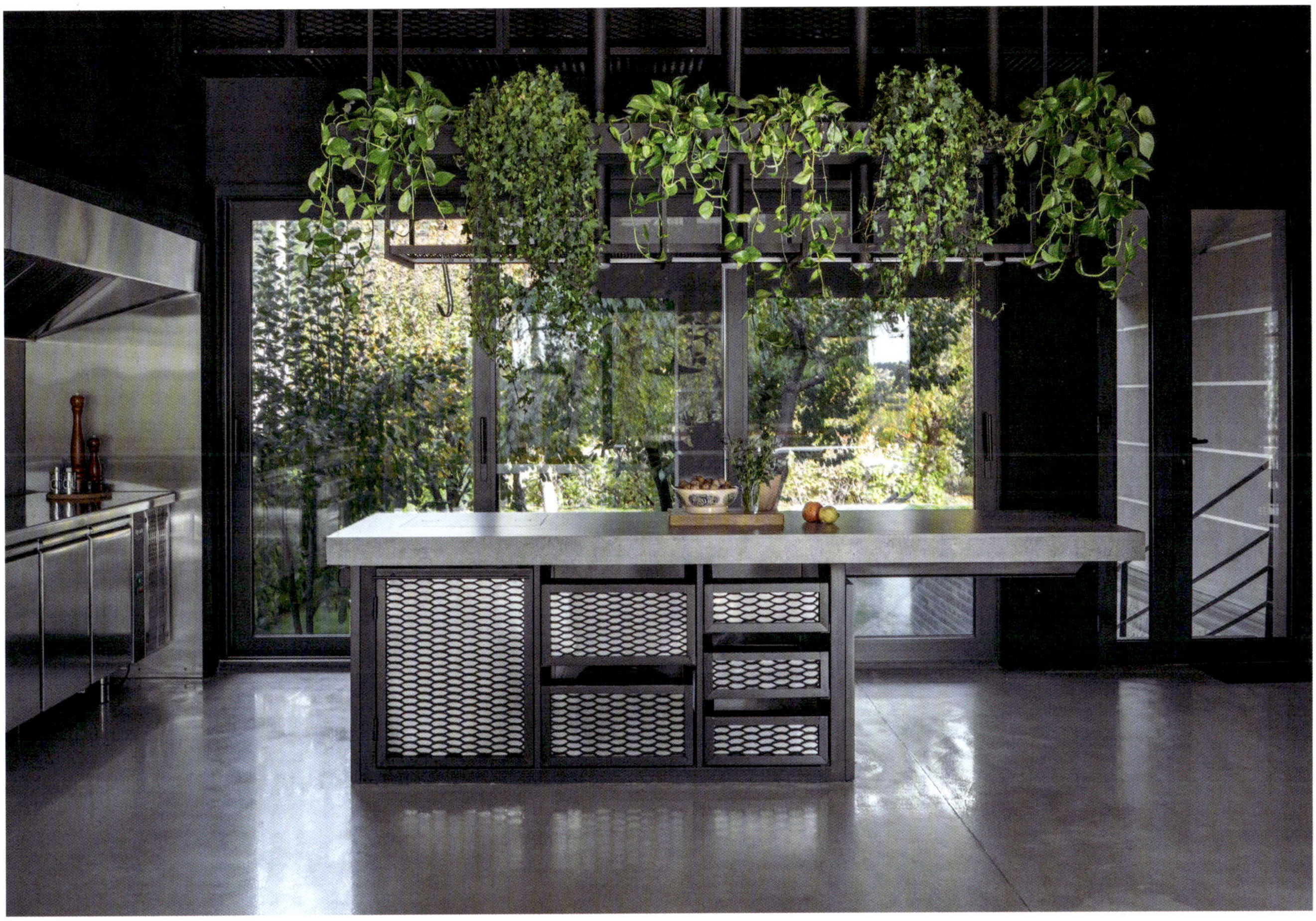

Ridnyi House merges Ukrainian and Japanese influences, blending contemporary art and vintage furnishings to create a striking yet cozy environment.

Developed over a span of six years, the Ridnyi House by Makhno Studio takes full advantage of the studio's signature blend of Ukrainian tradition and Japanese wabi-sabi philosophy. The interior of the three-story building boasts a variety of bold design choices, with stylish elements like concrete and metal surfaces contrasted by the warmth of wood accents, light fixtures, and fireplaces. White Khmara lamps further soften the austerity of the concrete living room. Thanks to large windows and the use of glass partitions, a sense of airiness was achieved, while contemporary artworks enliven the space. The owners' personal items, such as family chests, rugs, travel mementos, and paintings given by friends, were also incorporated into the design.

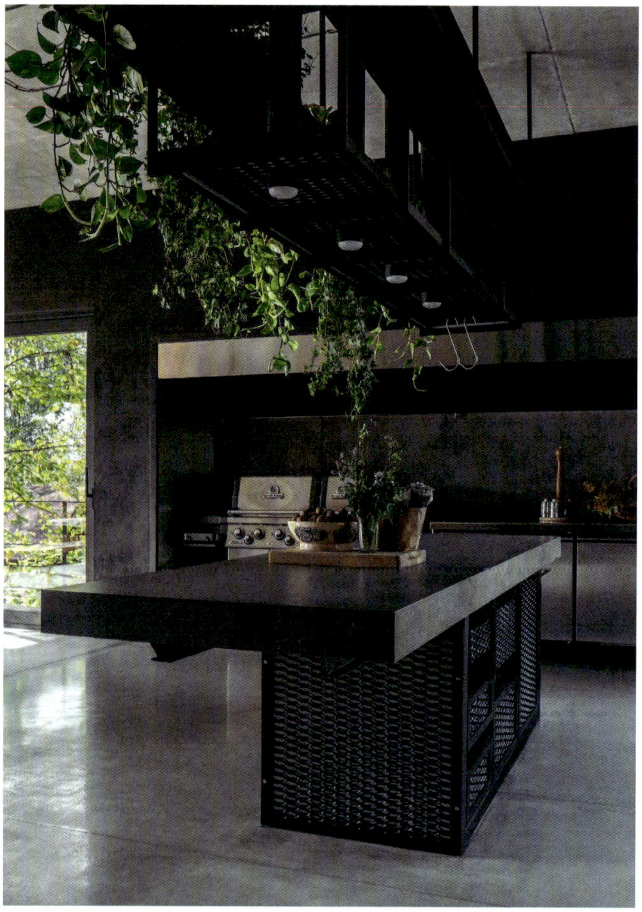
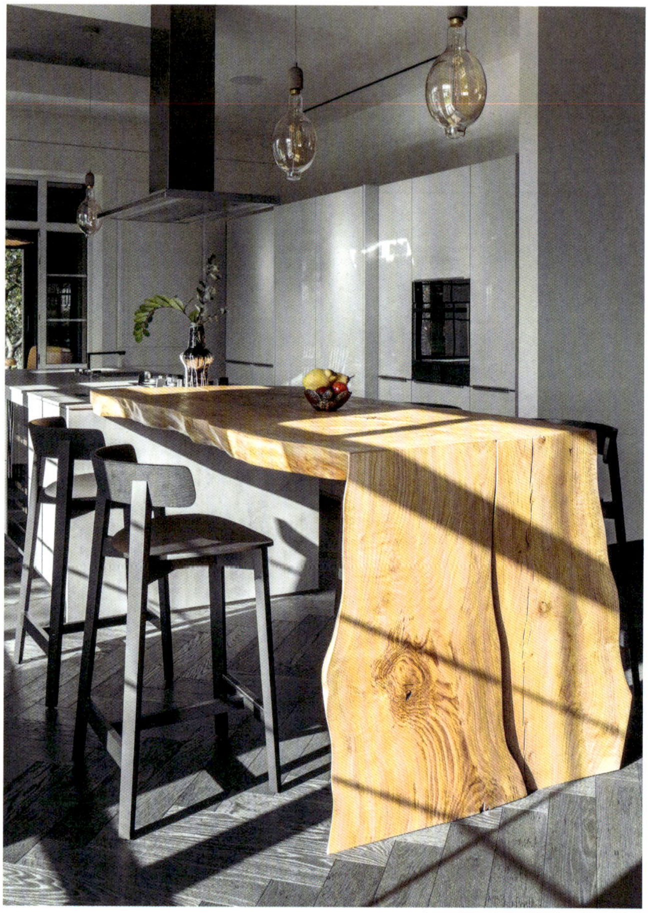
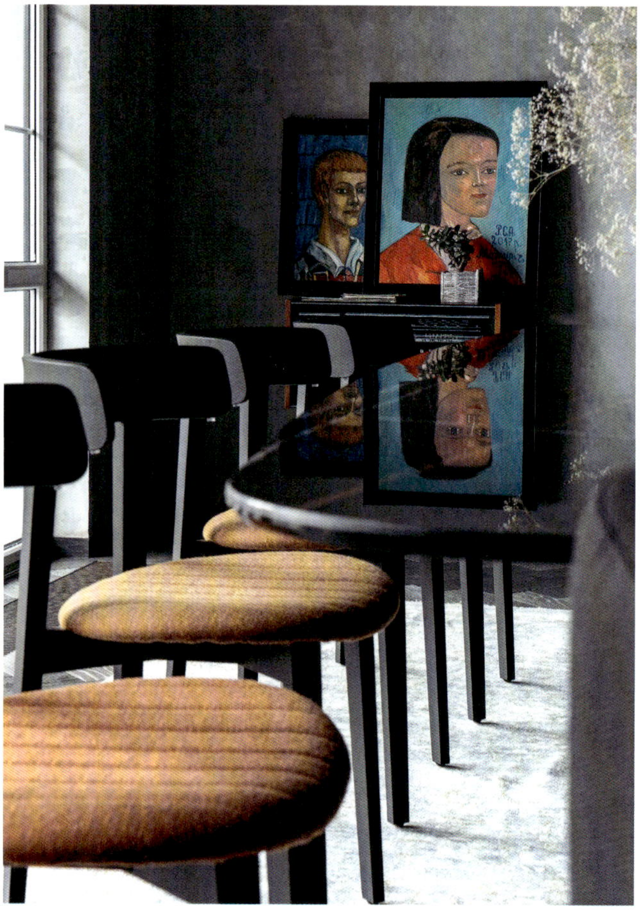
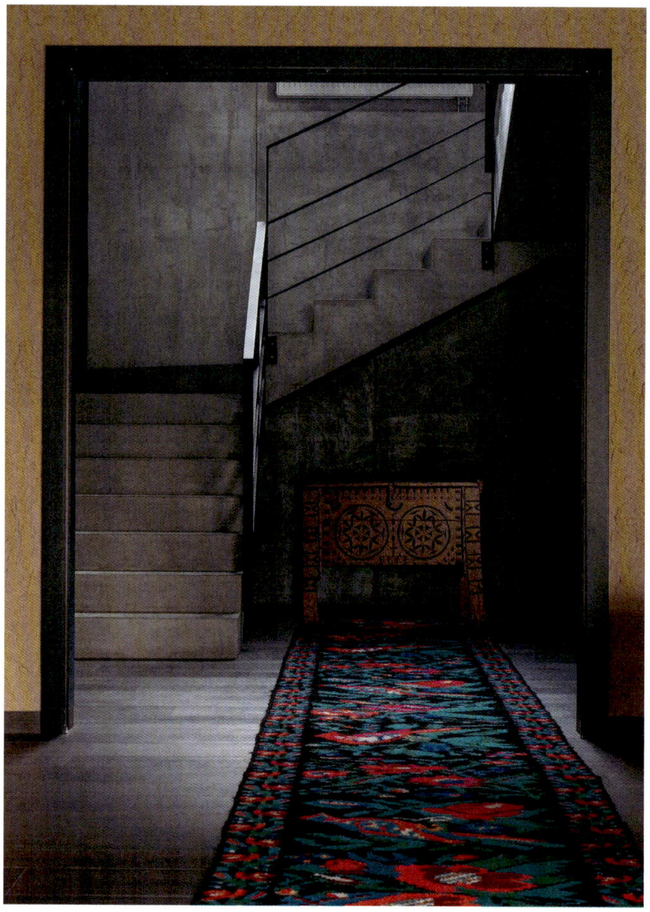

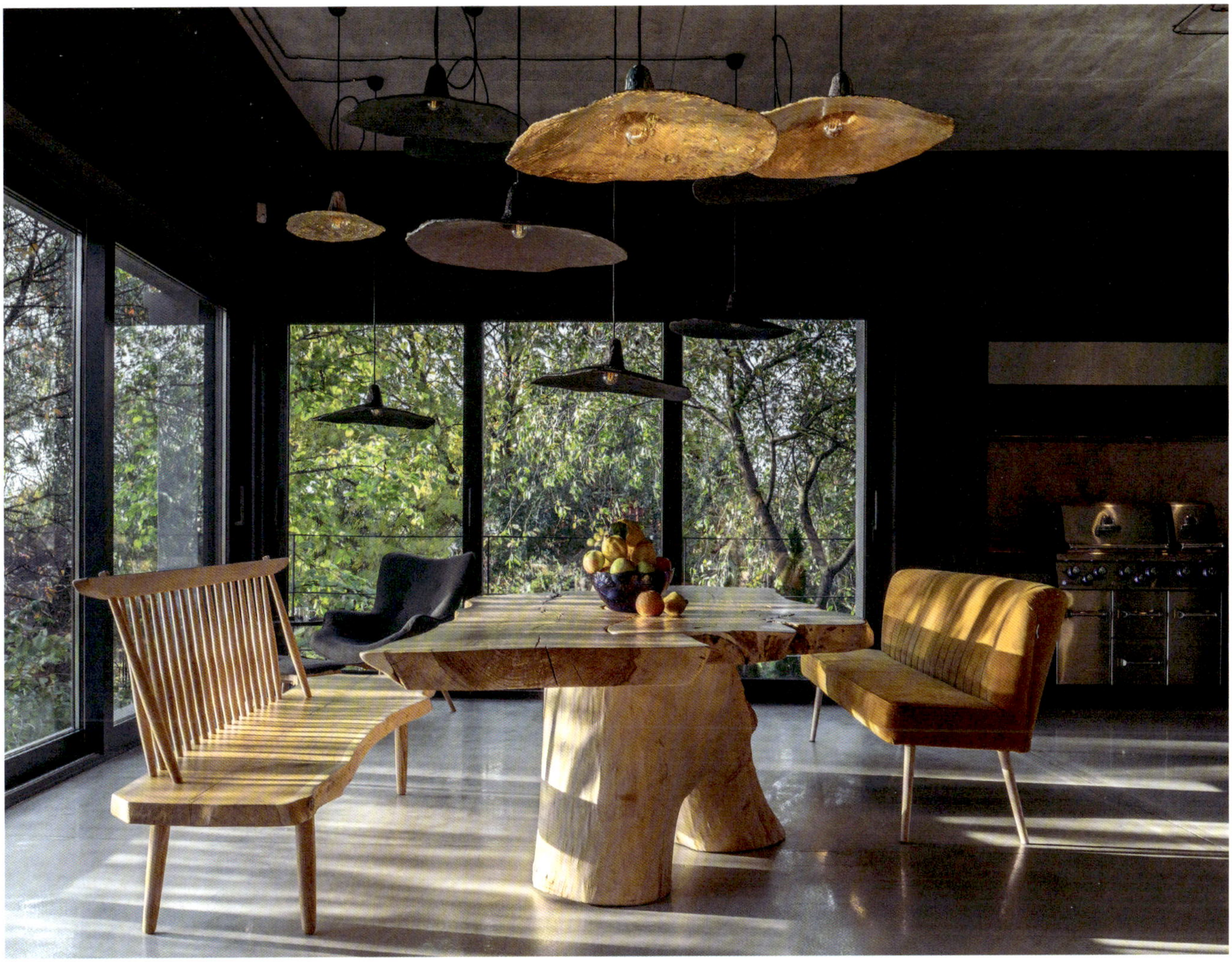

The Ridnyi House showcases numerous pieces of wood furniture, with a deliberate emphasis on preserving the material's natural colors and rough forms. The golden glow of the Parasolka lamps (above) complements the wood, instilling a sense of warmth and coziness.

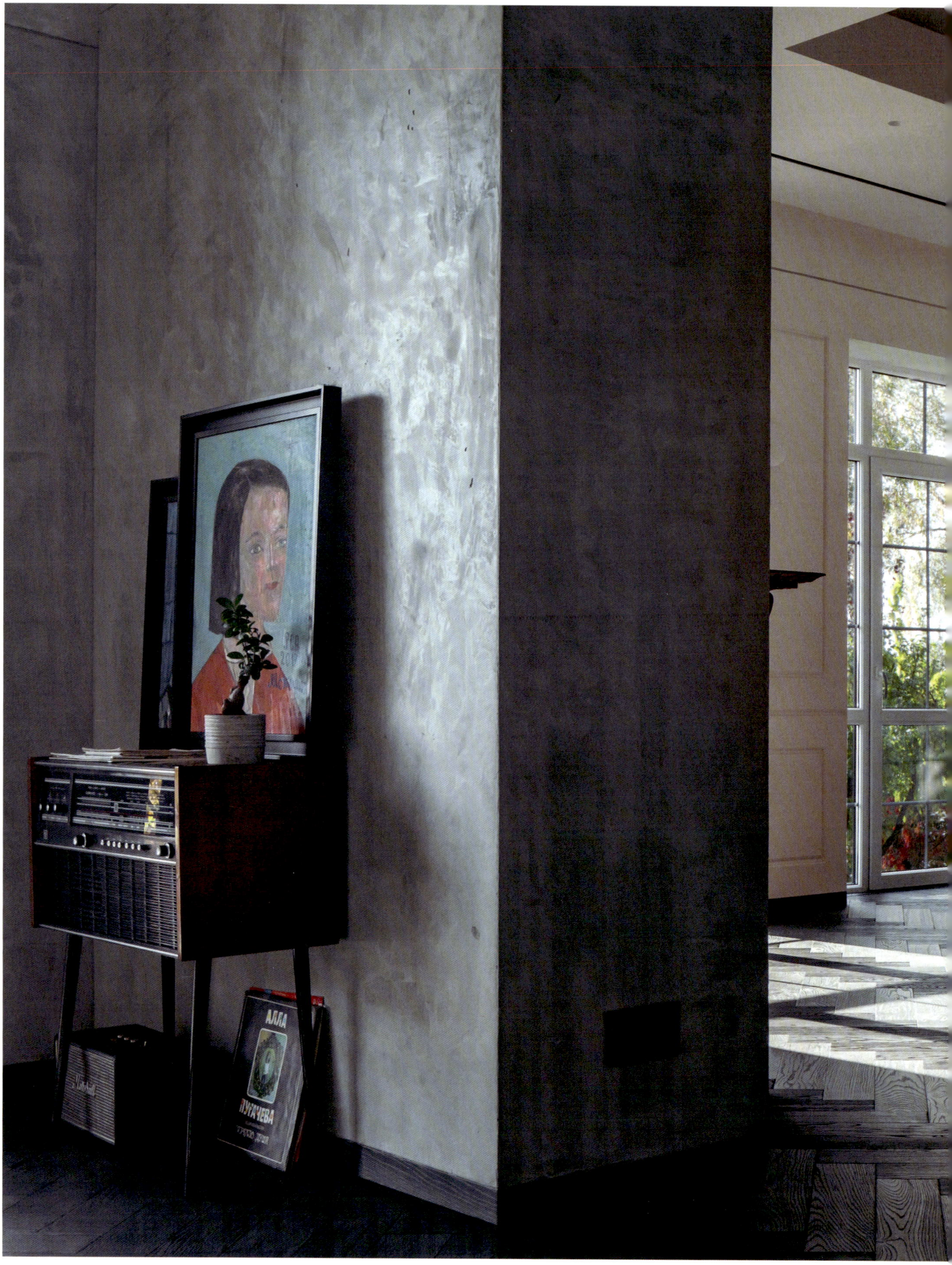
АЛЛА
ПУГАЧЕВА

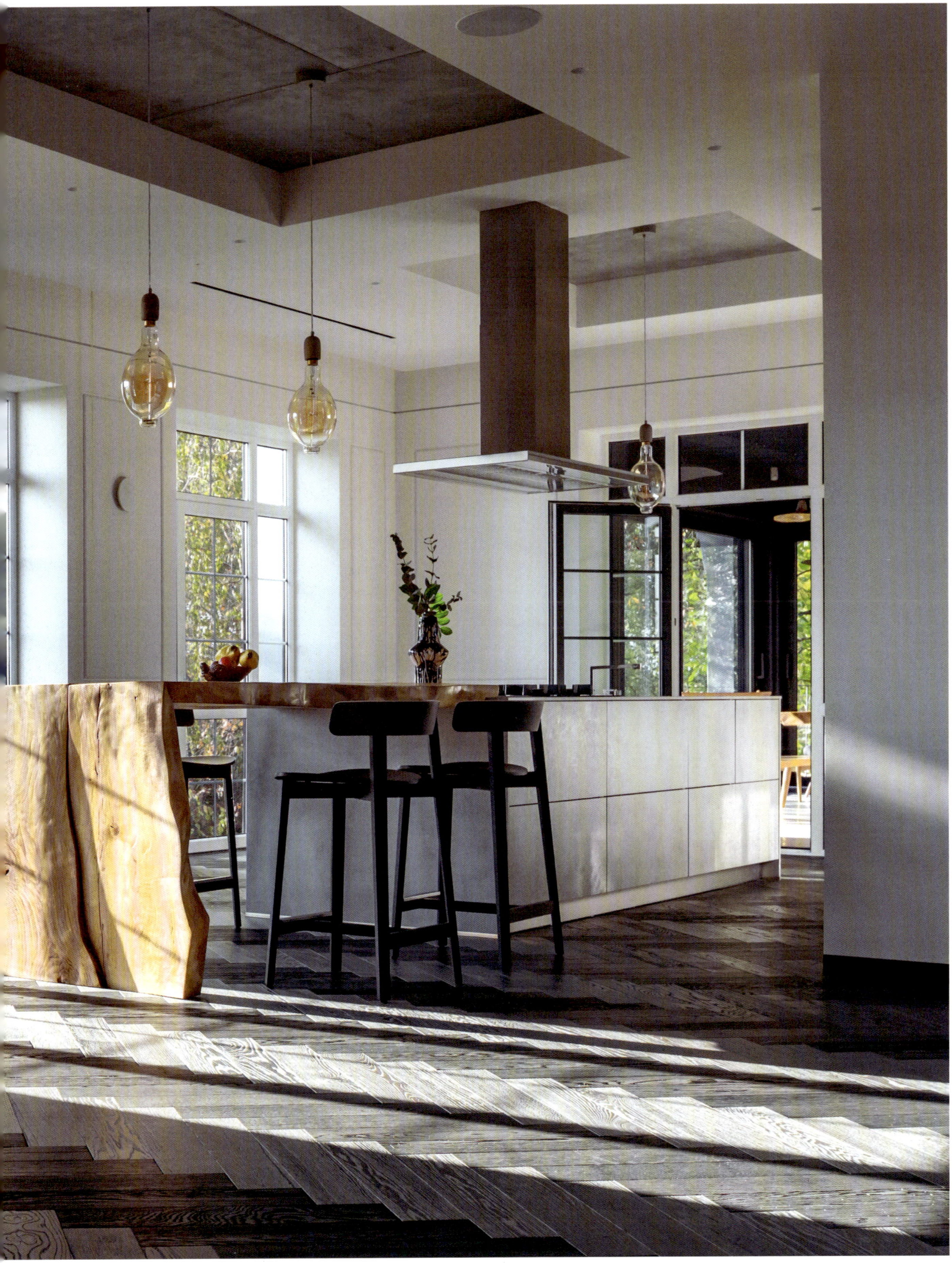

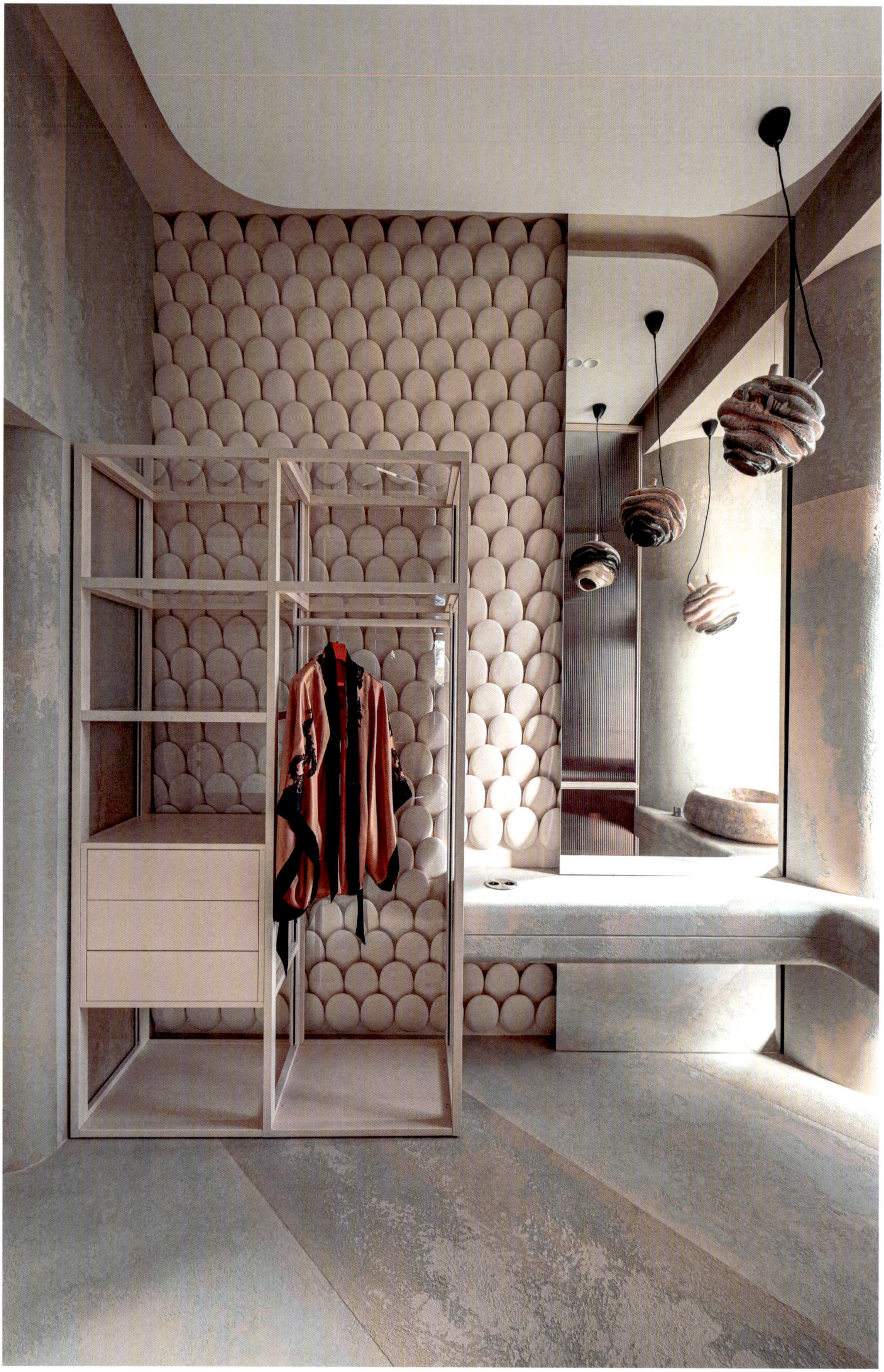

SUMMER DAWN IN THE INTERIOR OF MURELI HOUSE

MAKHNO STUDIO
MURELI HOUSE

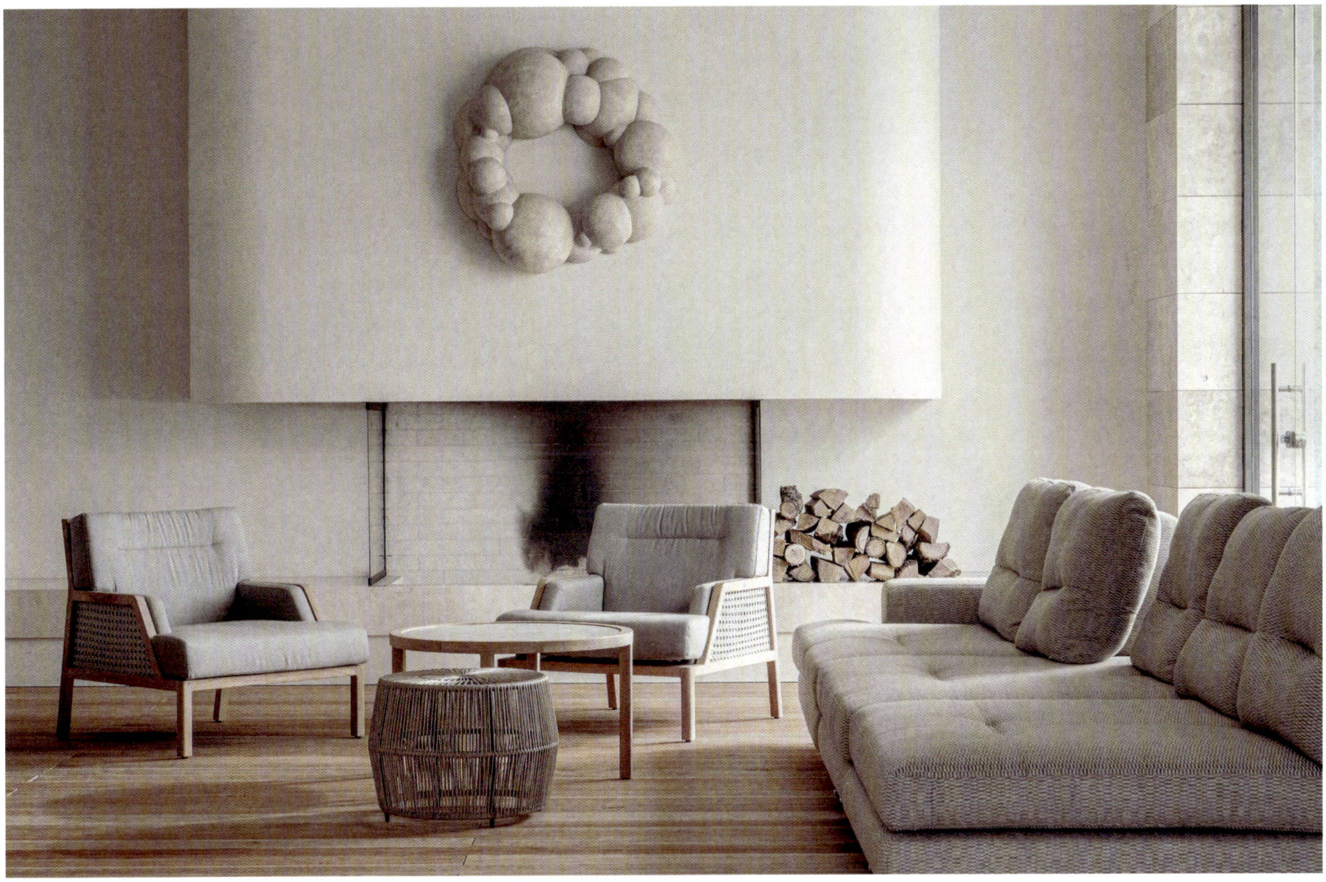

Soft shades of beige in the monochrome interior of Mureli House create a stylistic cohesion and fill the house with an atmosphere of summertime.

Mureli House, designed by Makhno Studio, embodies a modern Ukrainian style, with 90 percent of its furniture and materials sourced locally. The name Mureli comes from an archaic Ukrainian word for apricot, reflecting the design's main feature: a neutral beige color scheme that unifies the house's spaces and imparts a sense of warm, summery joy. A notable exception to the all-beige mood is the pink-hued master bathroom on the upper floor. In the airy, uncluttered interior, design details like Tetrapod tiles and Khmara and Makivka pendant lamps—all designed by Makhno Studio—set accents in the monochromatic color scheme through form. In fact, of all their projects, Mureli House boasts the most extensive collection of Makhno Studio's product designs, including tiles, lamps, bathroom ceramics, furniture, and decor.

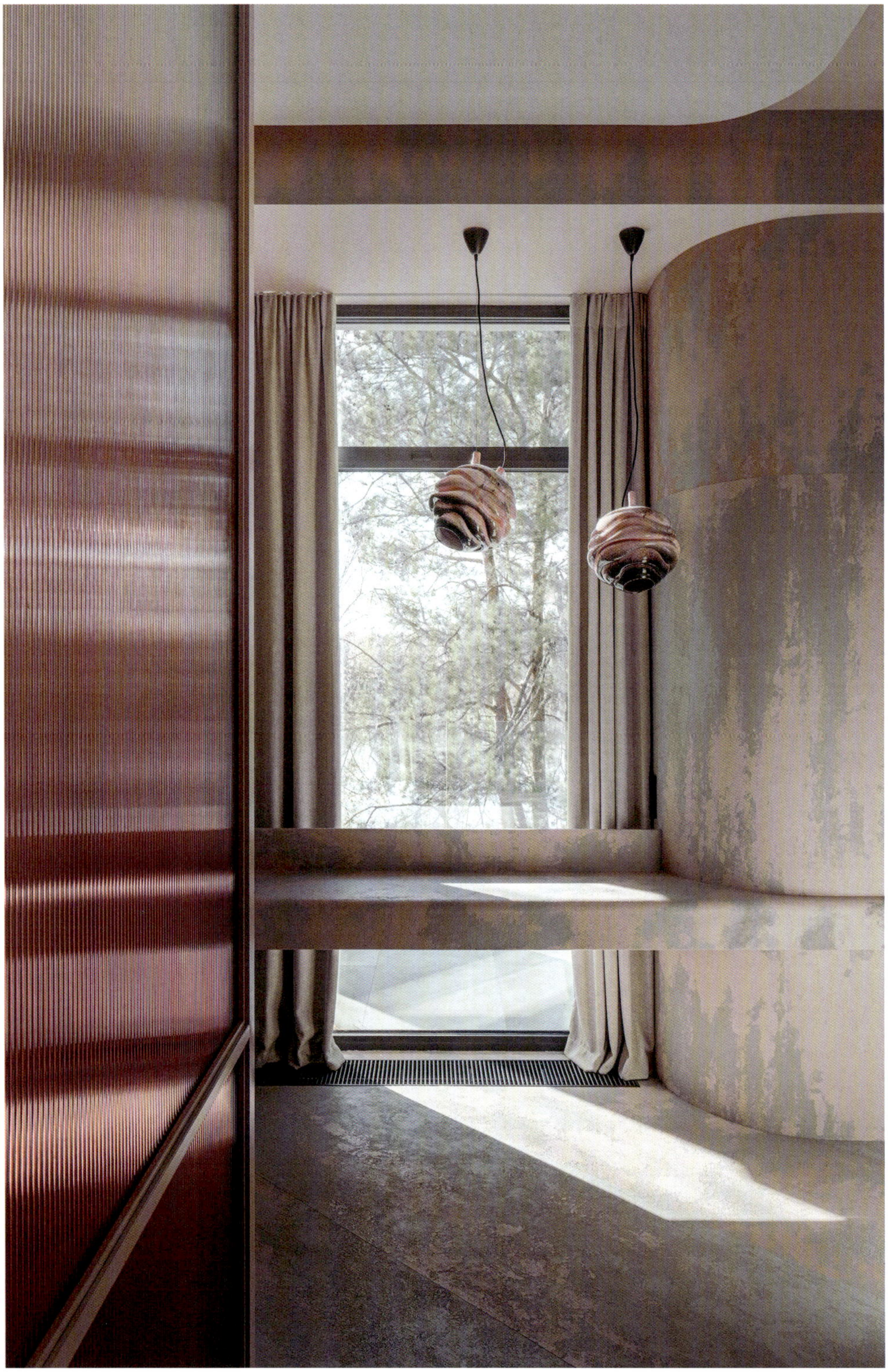

Within the welcoming confines of Mureli House, both the color palette and design exude a gentle touch. Soft, flowing patterns recur all around the home, from the grandiose staircase and rounded edges of the walls to the light fixtures and decor.

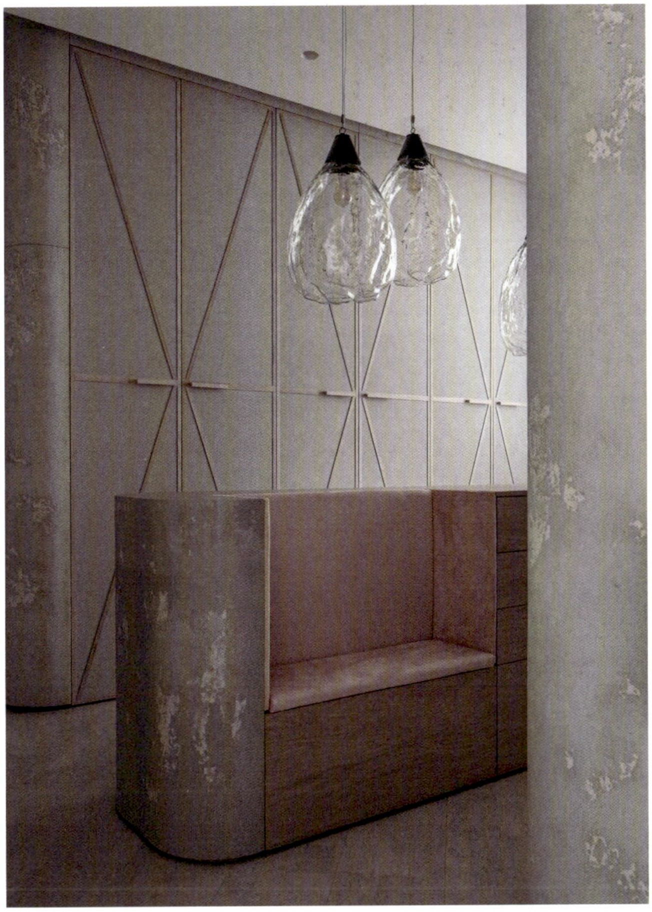
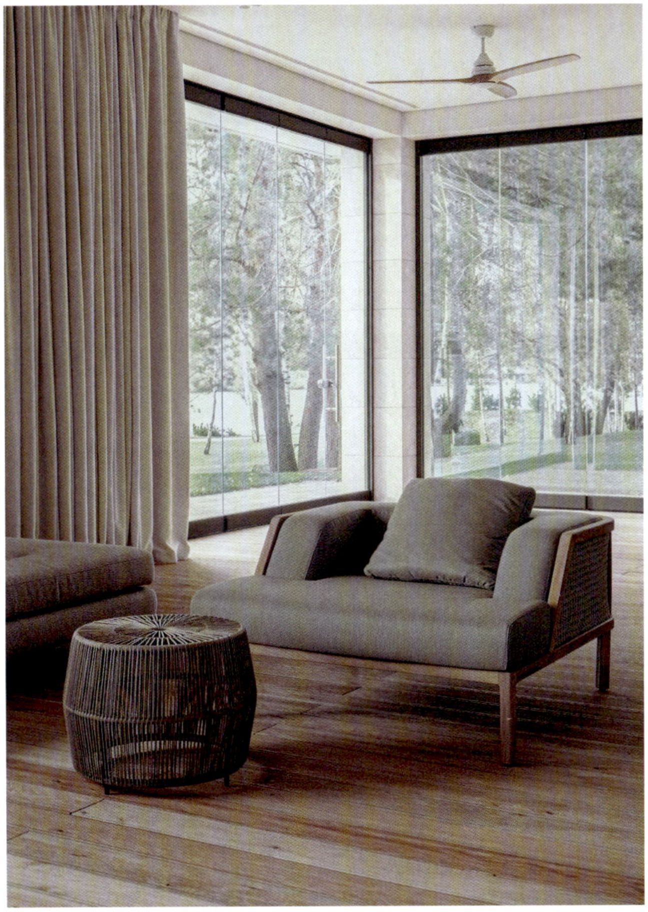
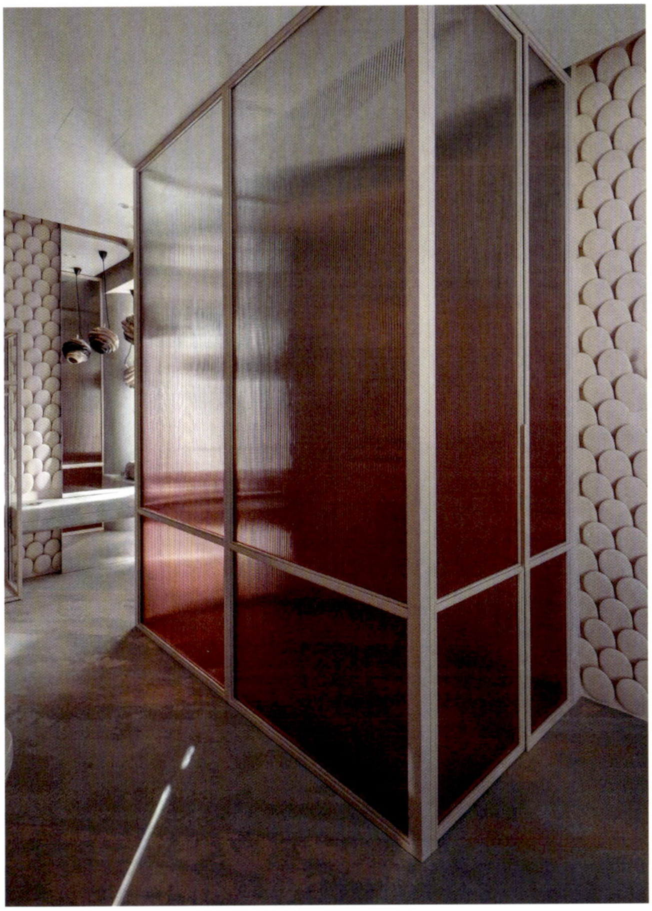
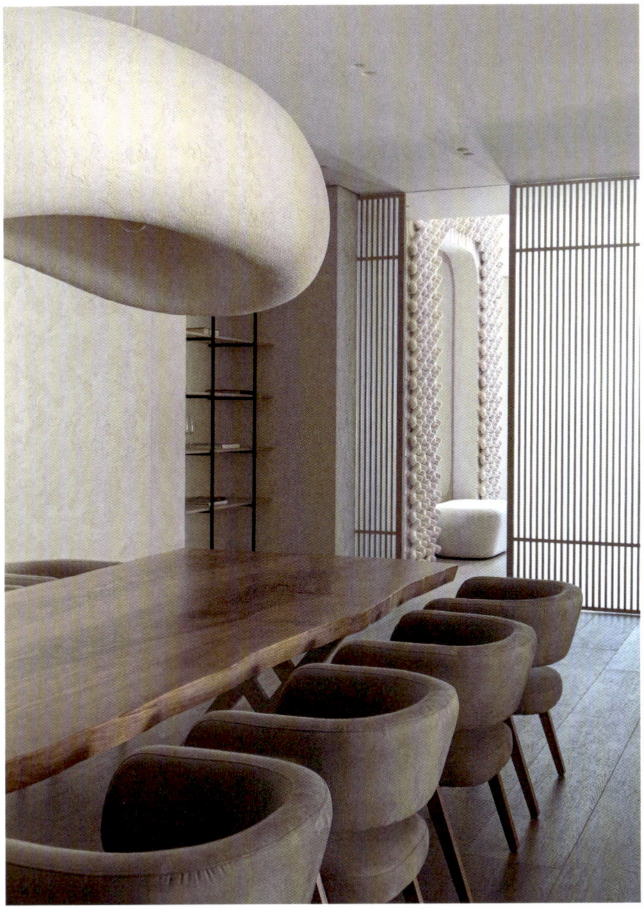

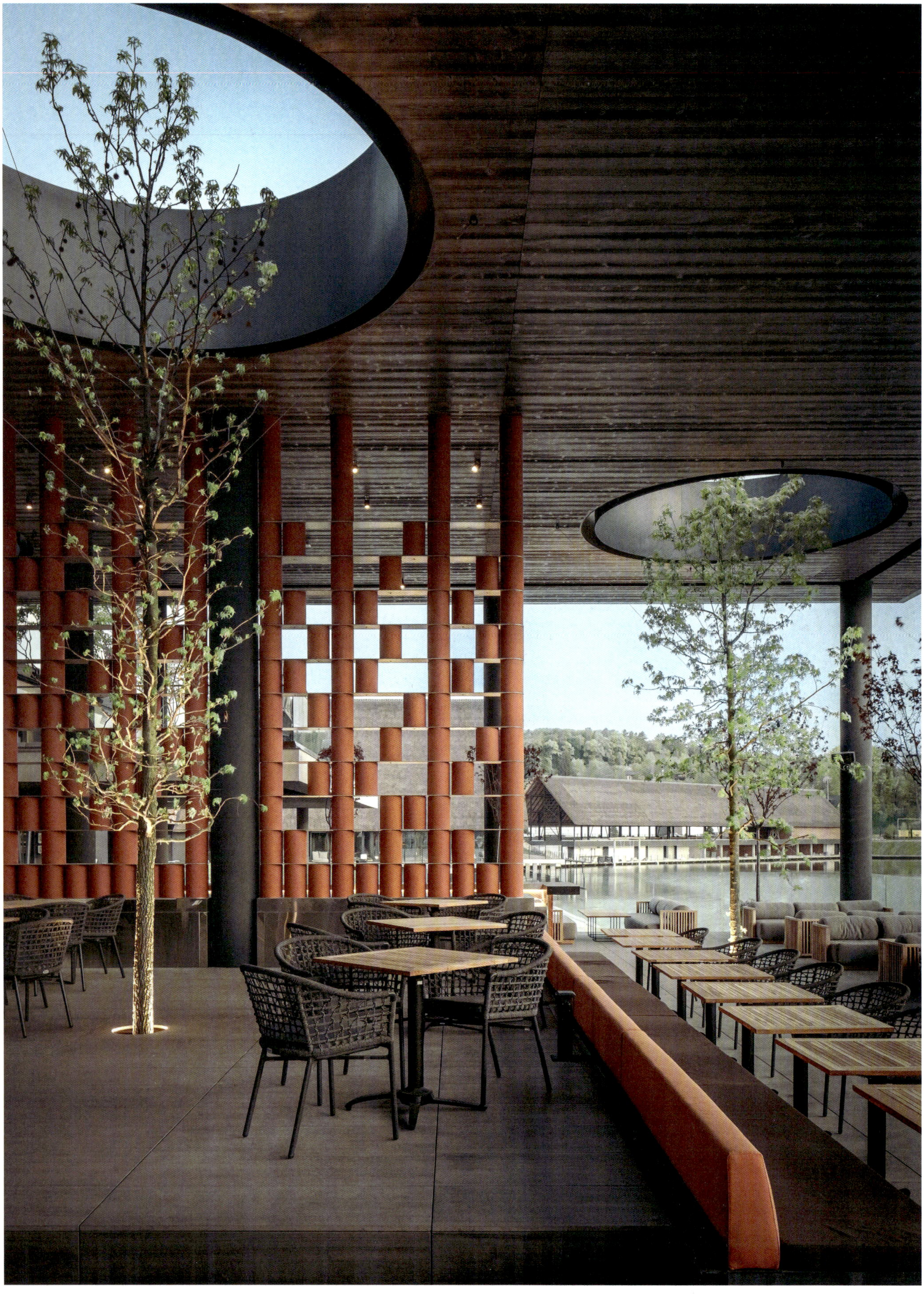

AN ARCHITECTURAL JOURNEY THROUGH WESTERN UKRAINE

YOD GROUP
TERRA

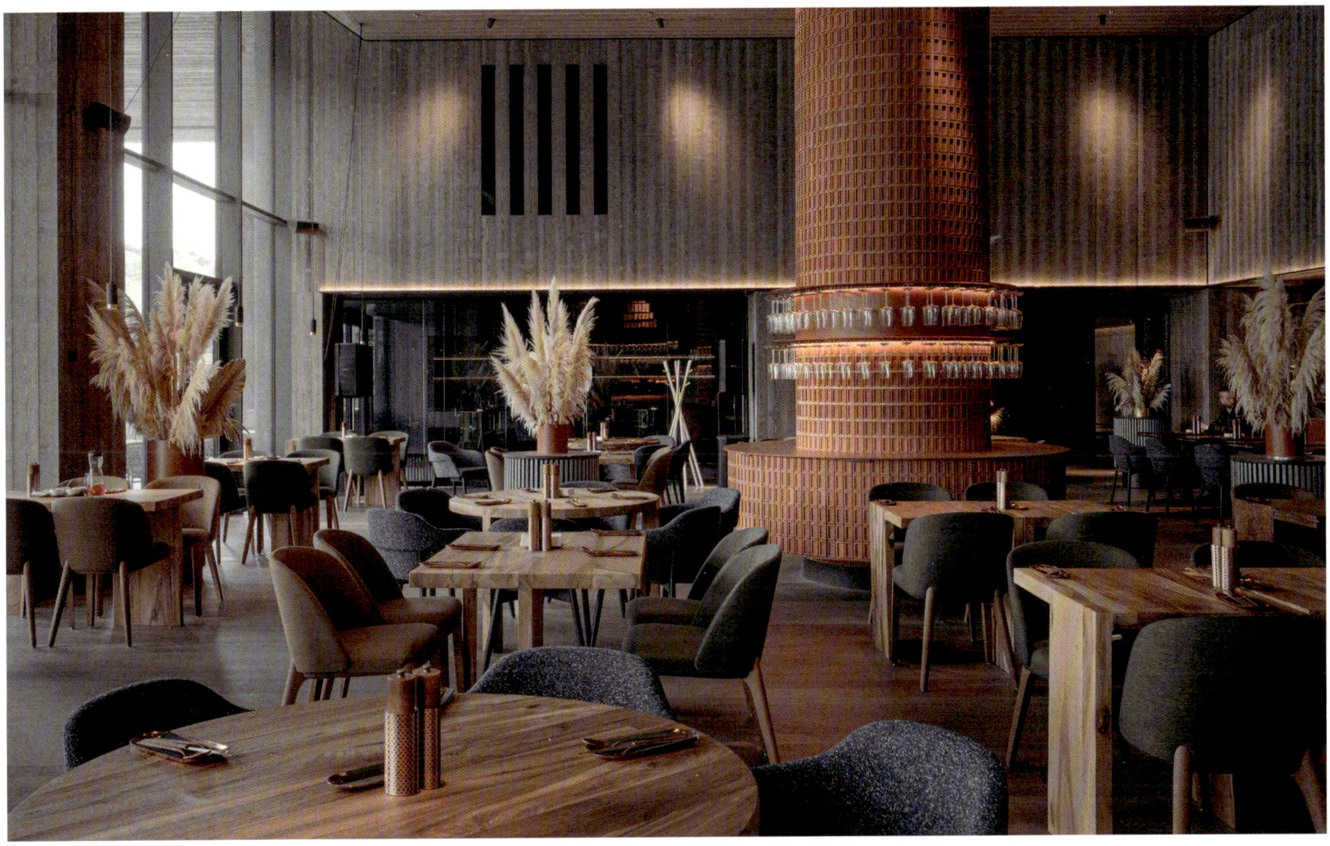

In the interior of Terra restaurant, the design reflects the vibrant nature of Western Ukraine—vast expanses, rich colors, varied textures, and a general lust for life.

When you visit Terra restaurant, it feels like you are embarking on a journey through the picturesque landscapes of Western Ukraine. Located within the Emily Resort in the Lviv region, the restaurant's design was crafted by the Yod Group, who sought to capture the essence of the region's colors, textures, and ambience in their interior design. The space reflects the rolling green hills outside, where shepherds' fires can be seen flickering in the distance, as well as the nearby lake, whose tranquil surface gently ripples in the wind. Setting the visual rhythm of the restaurant are a series of columns made of green glass brick. The columns are lit from within, creating a soft and natural green gradient. Other columns have been lined with small, locally sourced terracotta tiles, a nod to the Ukrainian tradition of adorning fireplaces and stoves with tiles. Another eye-catching design element is a wall of copper-colored glass plates, some of which feature distinctive floral patterns.

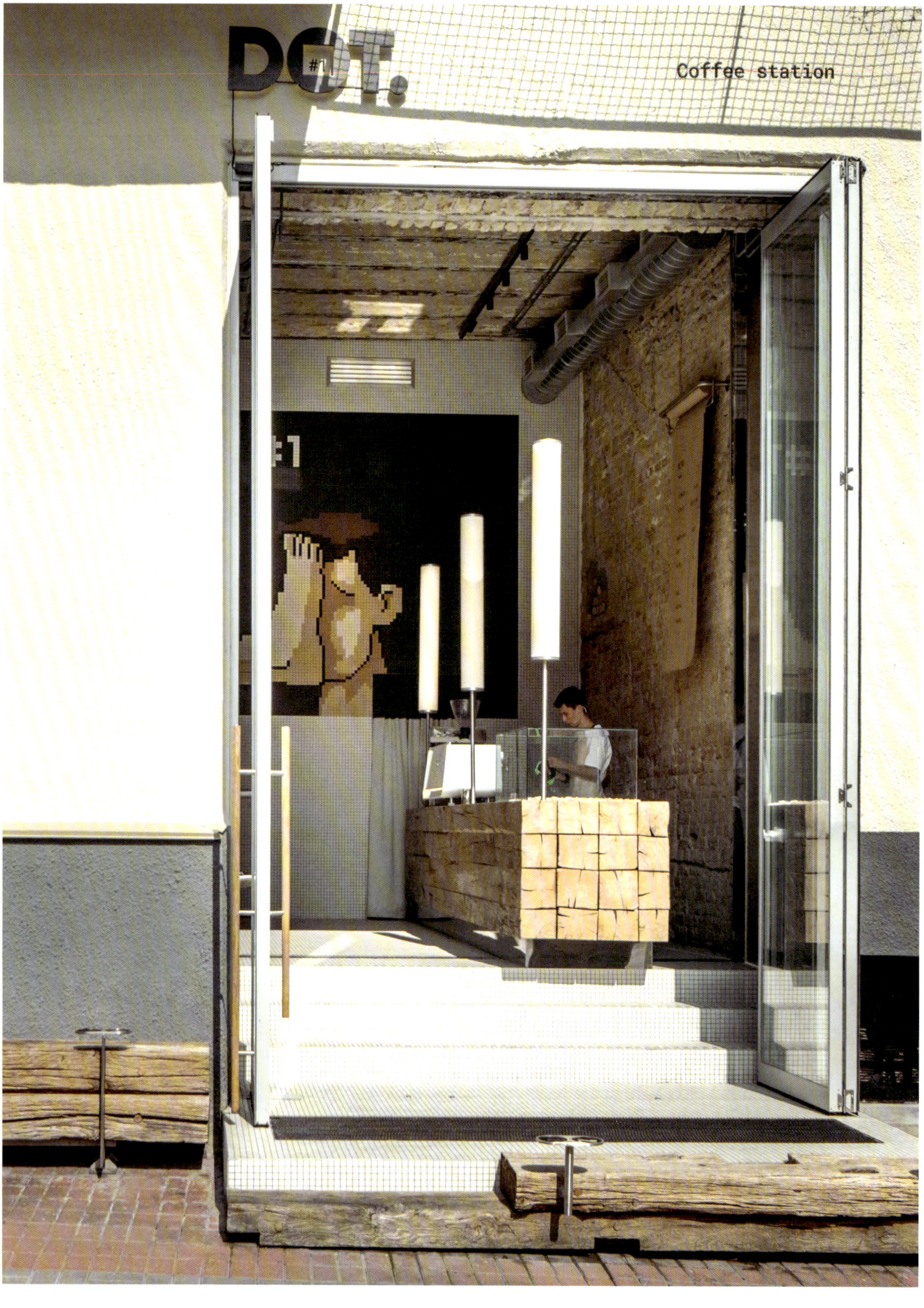
Coffee station

BIG CITY VIBE IN A SMALL COFFEE SHOP

YOD GROUP
DOT COFFEE STATION #1

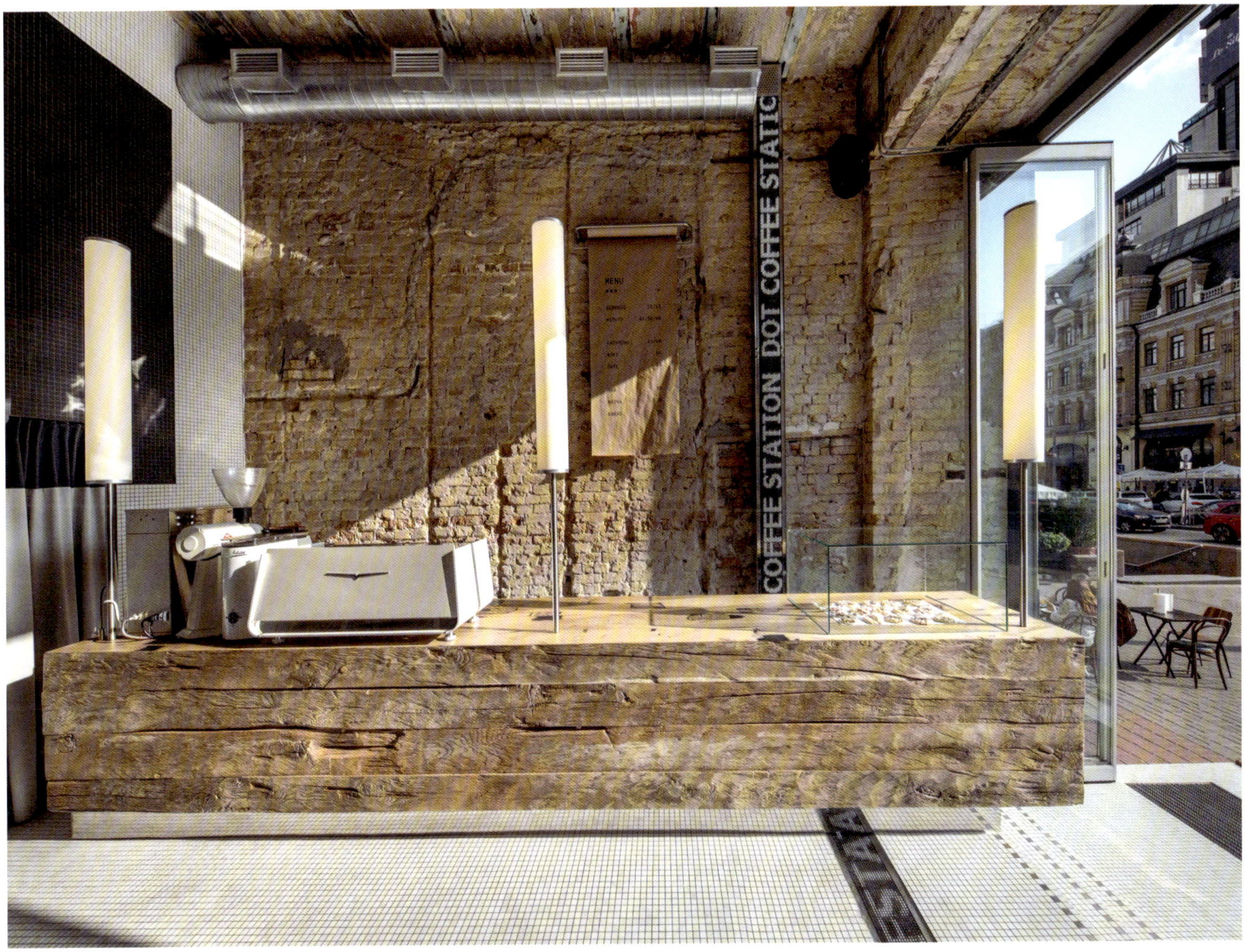

The minimalist design of DOT Coffee Station #1 accentuates the historic building's charm, while its pixel art mosaics capture the essence of a vibrant modern city.

In a bustling area of Kyiv sits DOT Coffee Station #1, designed by the award-winning Yod Group. The cafe's foldable glass wall facade not only invites urban energy into the space, but also enables a complete merging of the interior and exterior when opened, allowing pedestrians to glimpse the exposed brick walls of the structure, which was built in the year 1900. Inside, quirky panels of mosaic pixel art add a modern, yet playful touch, and a narrow screen with scrolling text further enhances the cafe's dynamic vibe. True to the dot theme, the mosaic tiled stairs feature a dotted line on each tread, also rendered in pixel art. Rough timber seating and wooden counters offer a warm contrast to the cold steel accents, striking a balance between ruggedness and comfort.

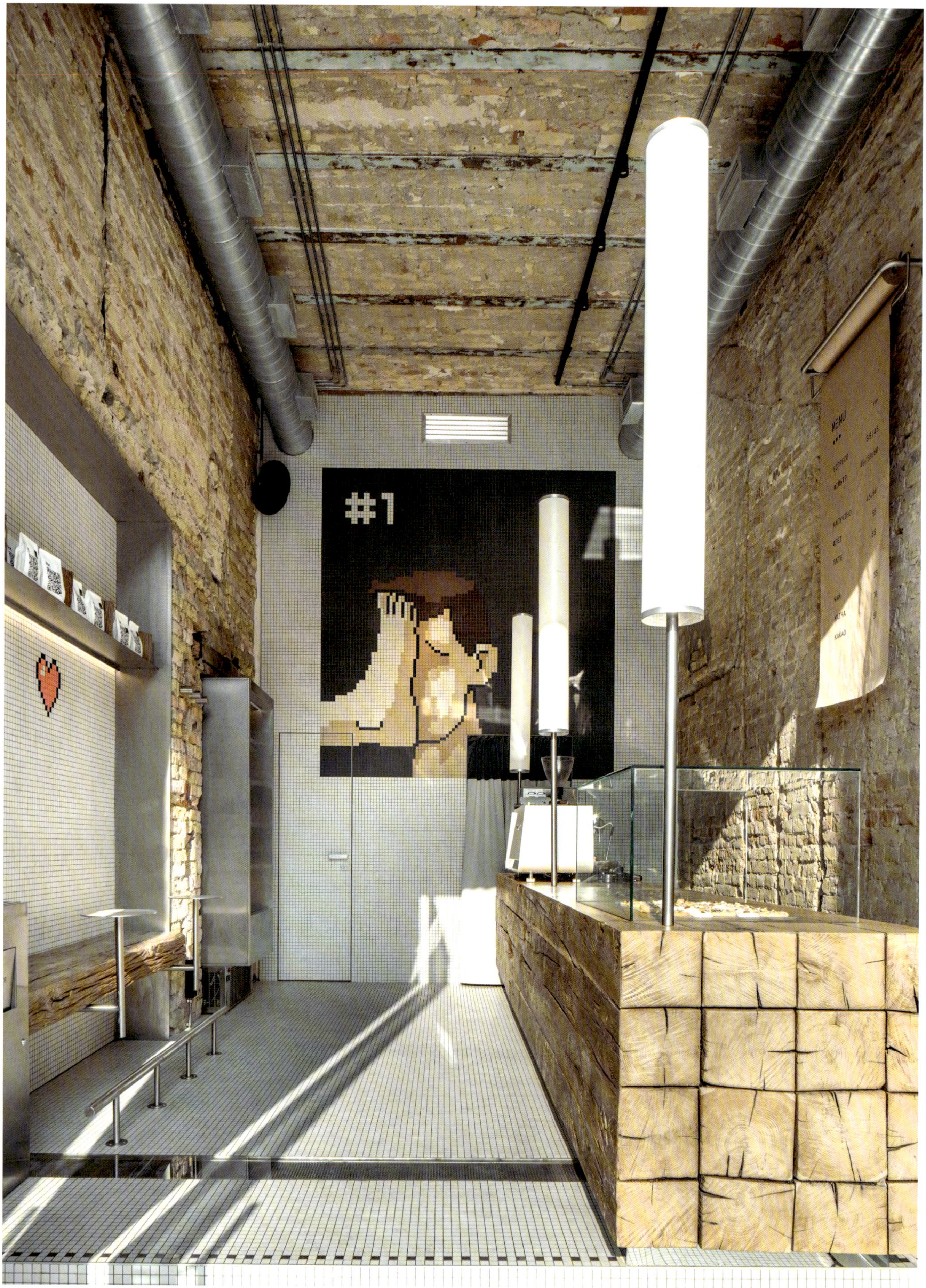
#1
MENU

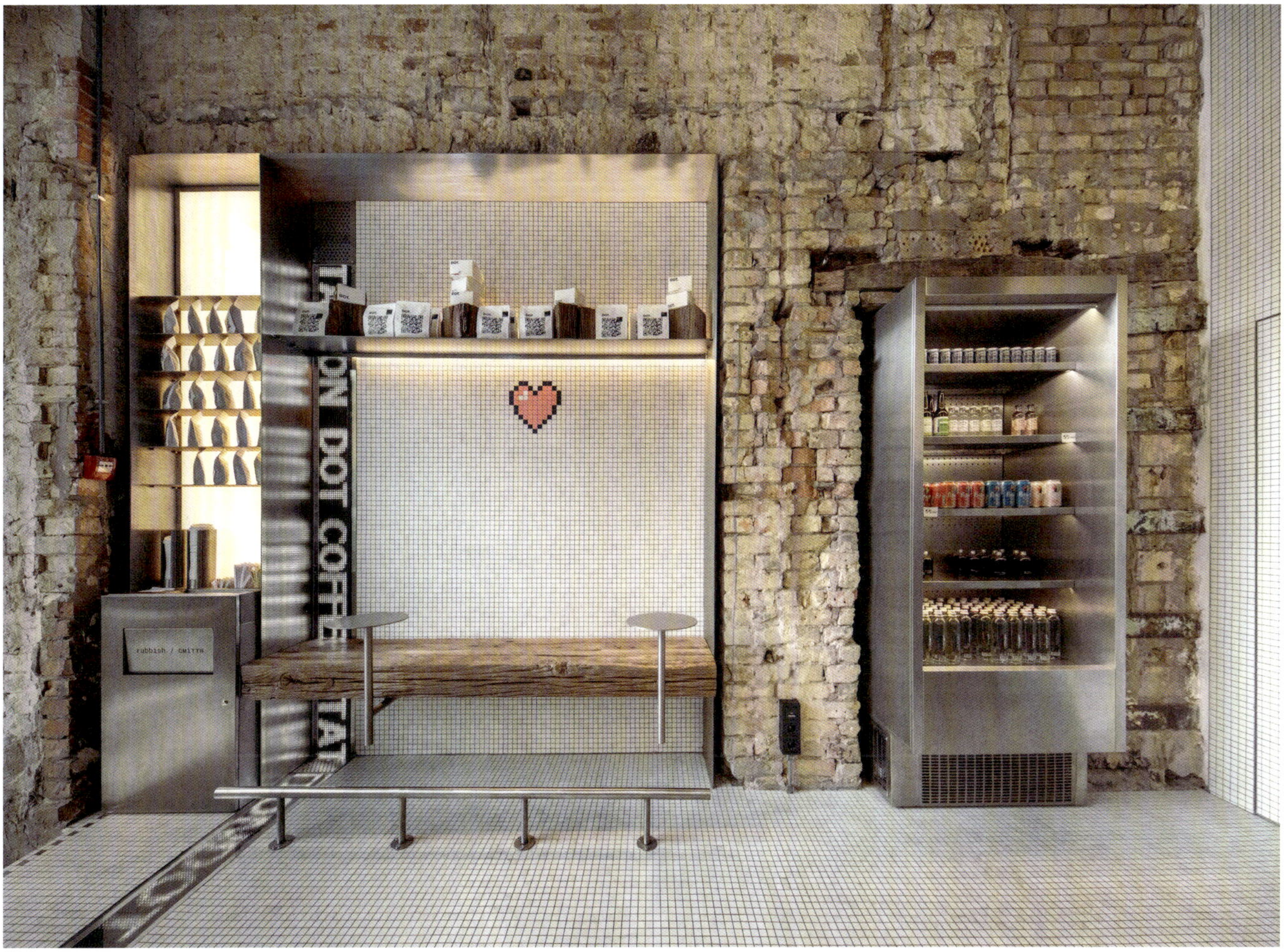

The primary focal point of DOT Coffee Station #1 is the mosaic pixel art on the central wall. A white mosaic partially covers the brick walls, while shiny metal surfaces and rough timber accents produce a vivid contrast.

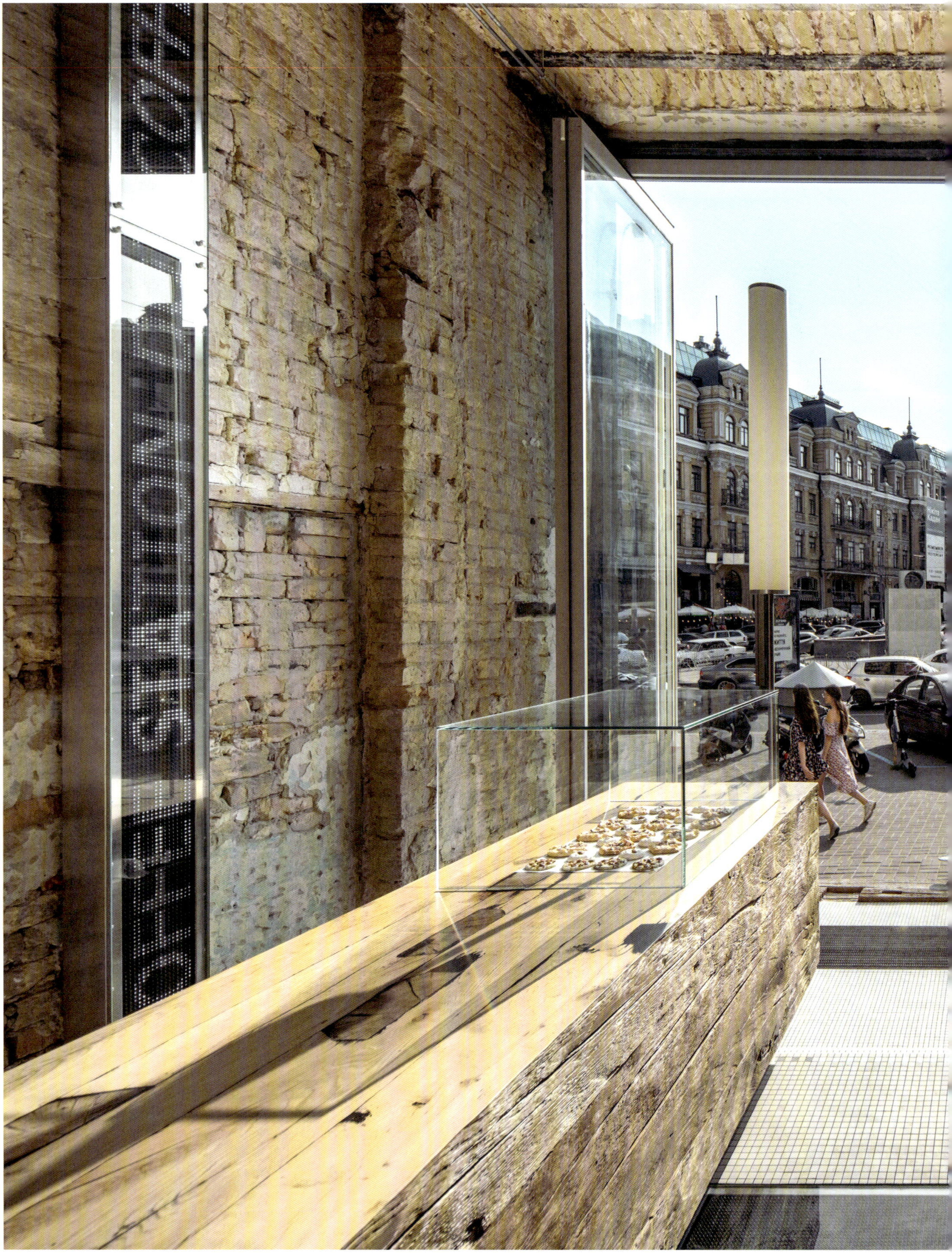

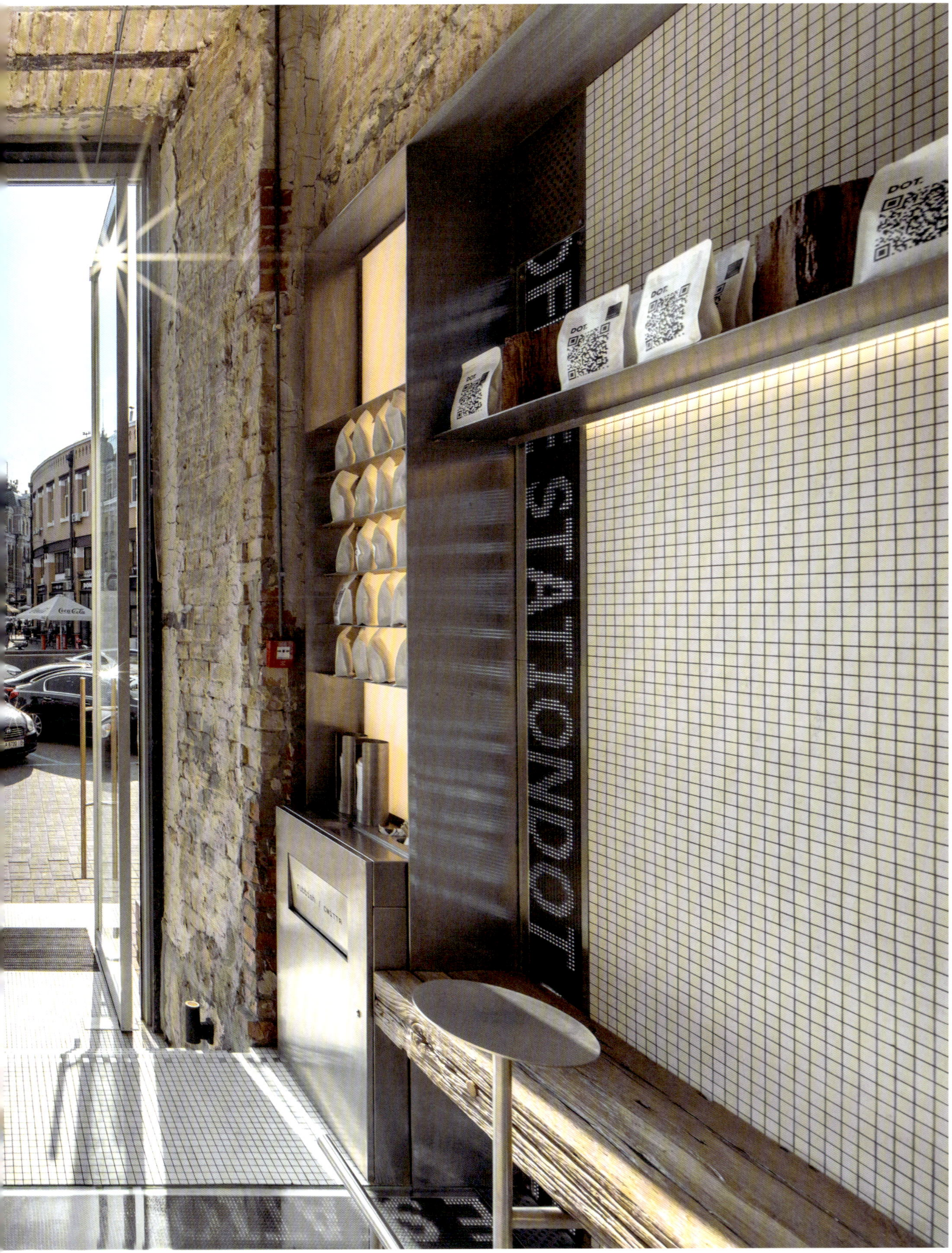
DOT.

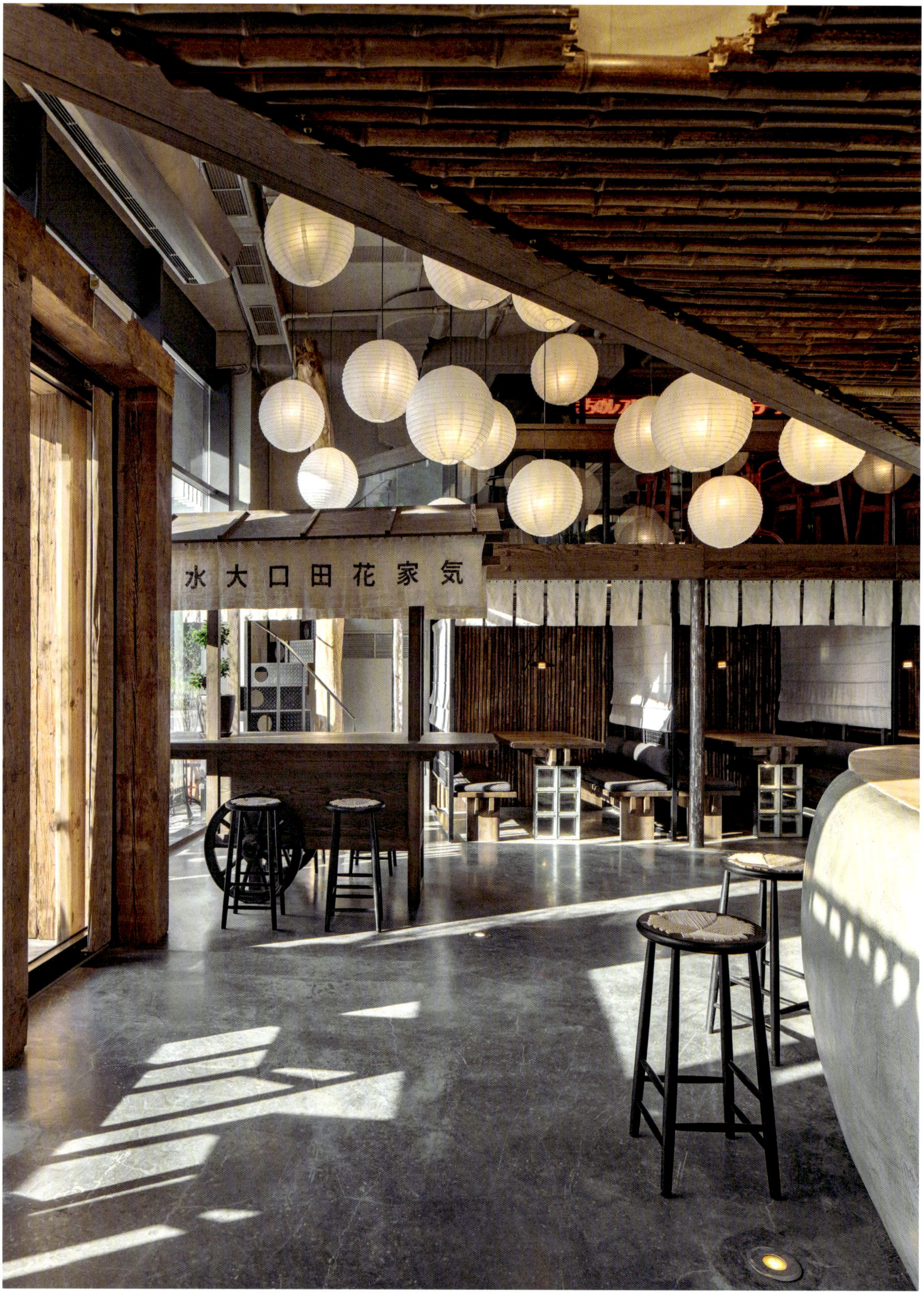
水 大 口 田 花 家 気

MIXING EUROPEAN ACCENTS WITH A JAPANESE VIBE

REPLUS BUREAU
SAKAE RAMEN BAR

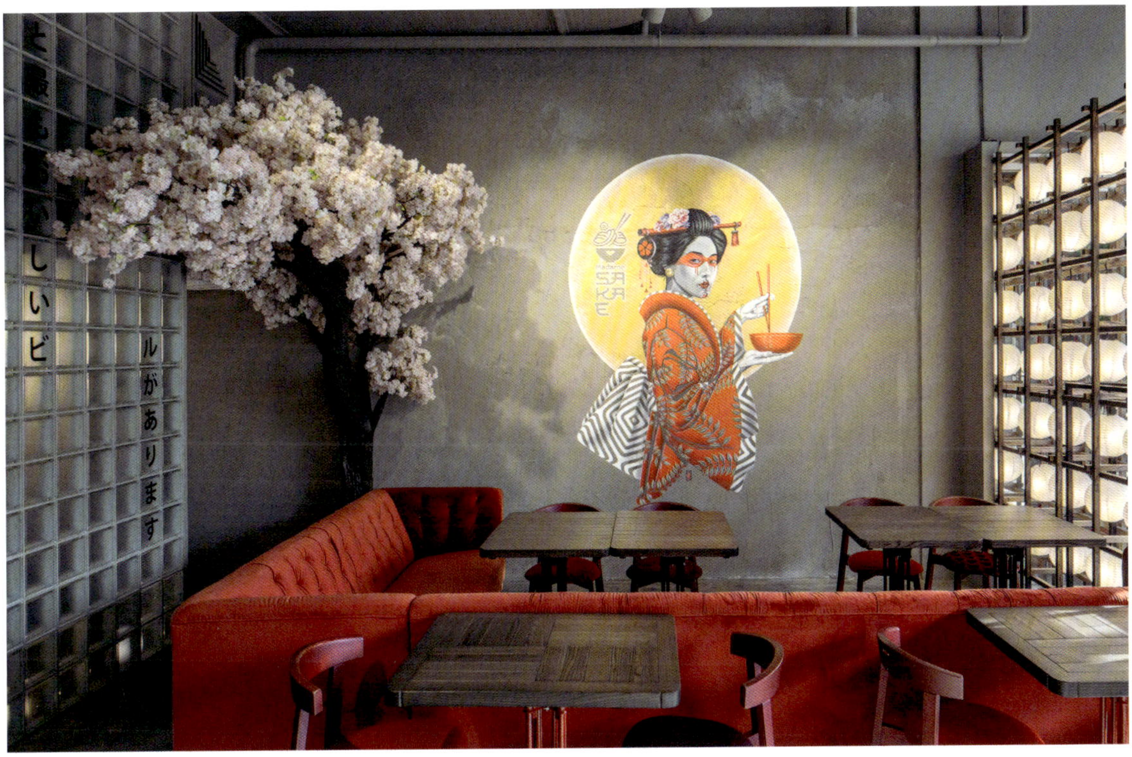

Reinterpreting vintage elements for modern interiors is one of the cornerstones of Replus Bureau's approach—and it is on full display in the design of Sakae Ramen Bar in Lviv.

The restaurant Sakae Ramen Bar, located in the heart of Lviv's IT district, is a sleek, modern take on a classic Japanese ramen bar. The designers were inspired by Japan's customary ceremonies and the country's respect for tradition. They worked hard to highlight these elements in their design, using an attractive mix of natural textures and vibrant color accents. Working alongside Restare Architectural Salvage Warehouse, they brought many of these stylistic concepts to life by sourcing a plethora of vintage furniture and decor, including Japanese silk umbrellas, lamps, and carpets. Local artisans decorated the dining booths and the ceiling above the bar area with natural bamboo, and added a lively touch to the space by adding flags made of vintage home-spun hemp fabric. Custom woodwork features heavily in the design, with Restare installing authentic larch beams from the Austro-Hungarian period on the outdoor terrace. The hallway was also decorated with ancient Hutsul shingles, salvaged from homes in the Ukrainian Carpathians. The design's tasteful blend of cultures makes the charming space truly unique.

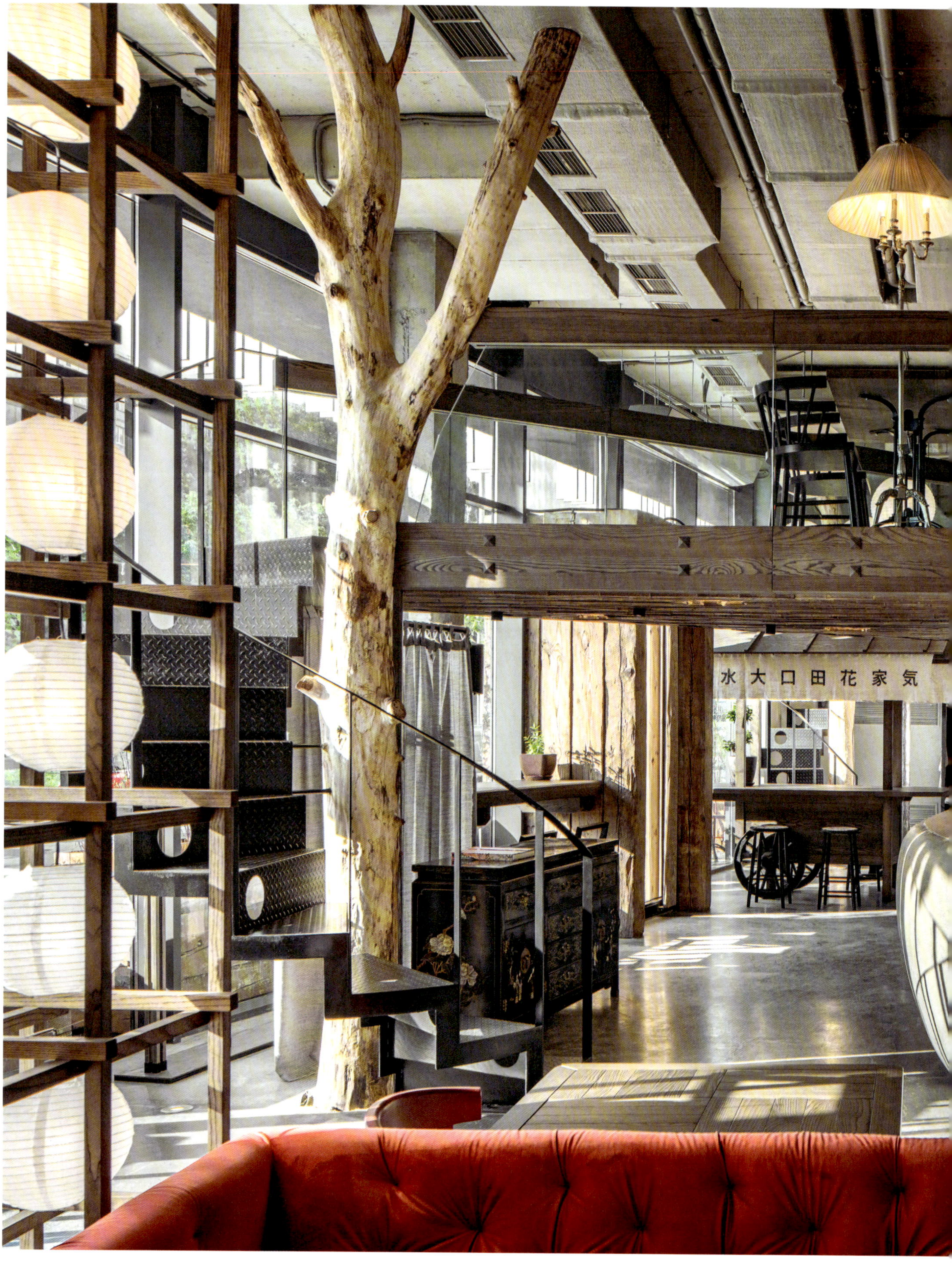
水 大 口 田 花 家 気

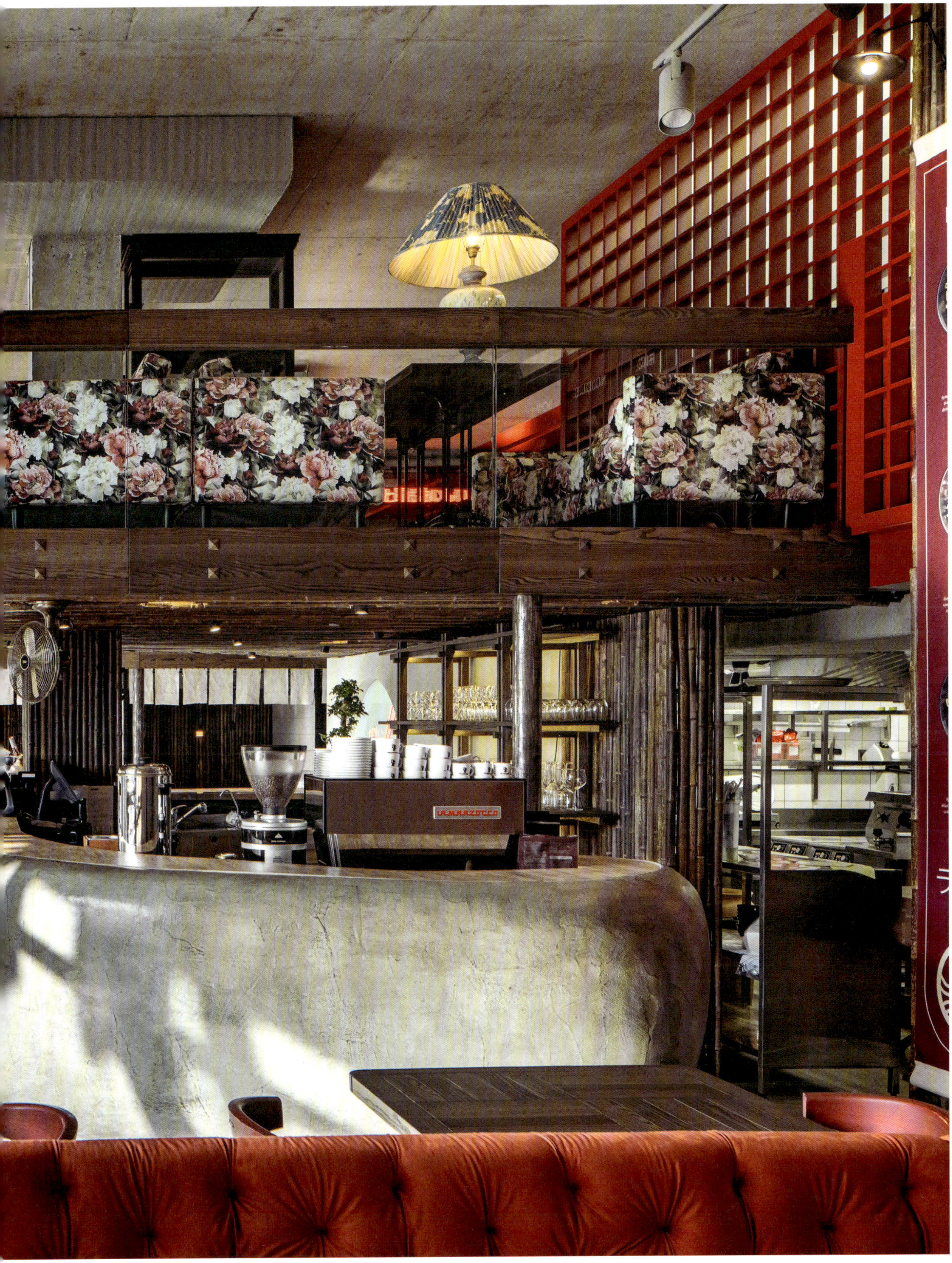

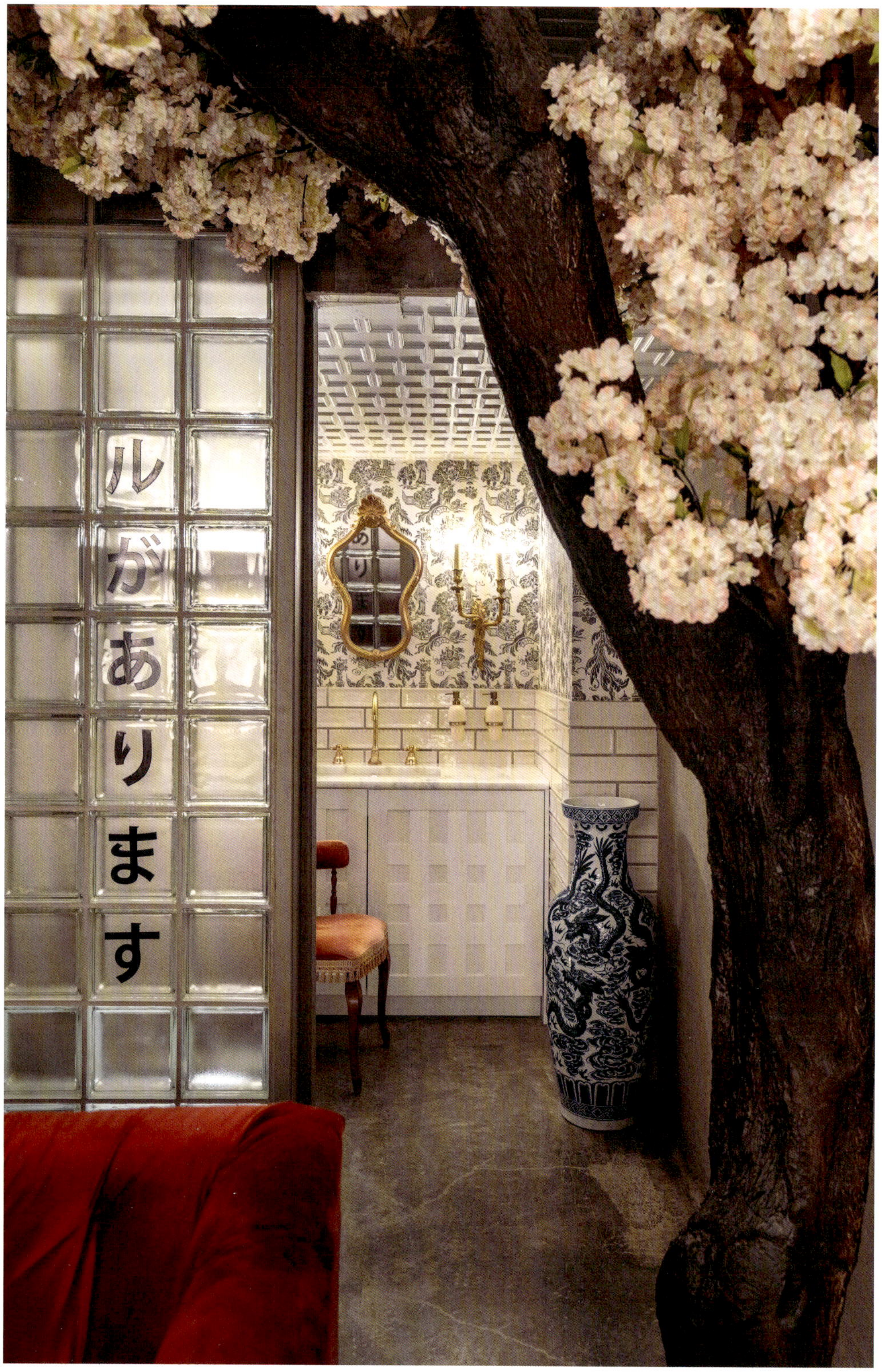

For Sakae Ramen Bar, Replus Bureau carefully chose vintage items from both East and West, combining intricately painted vases and silk umbrellas from Japan with ornate baroque mirrors, sconces, and floor lamps.

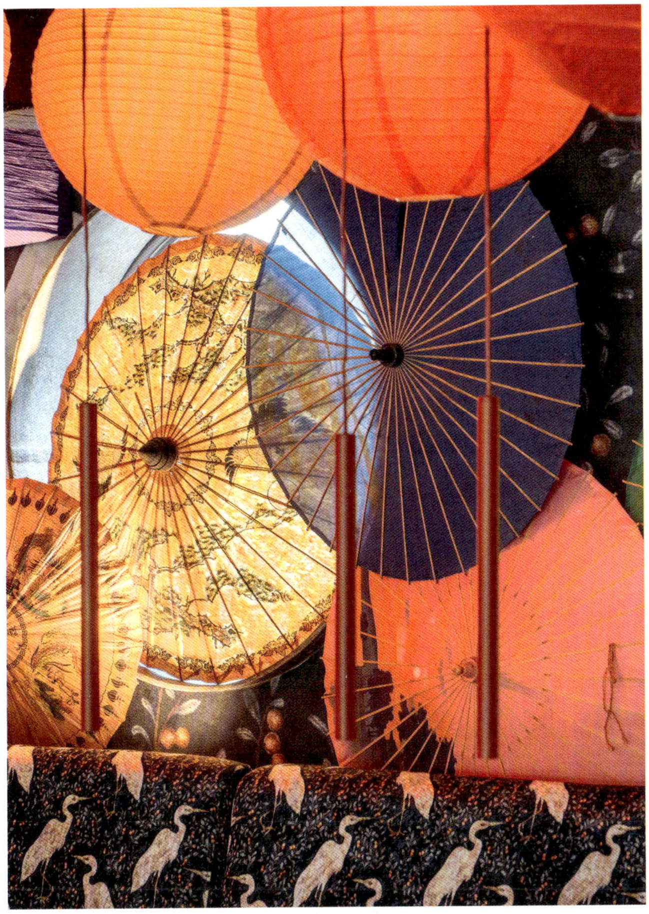
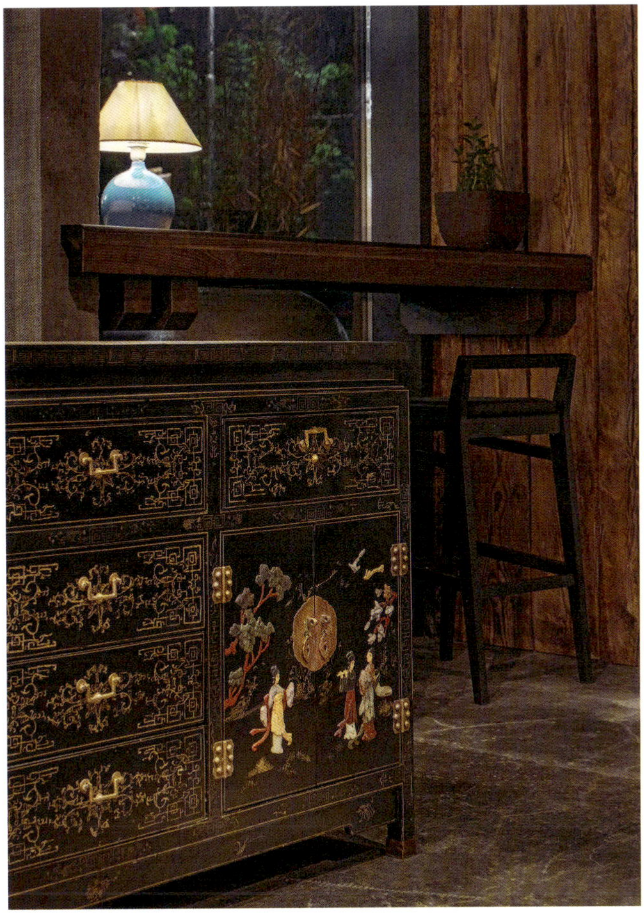
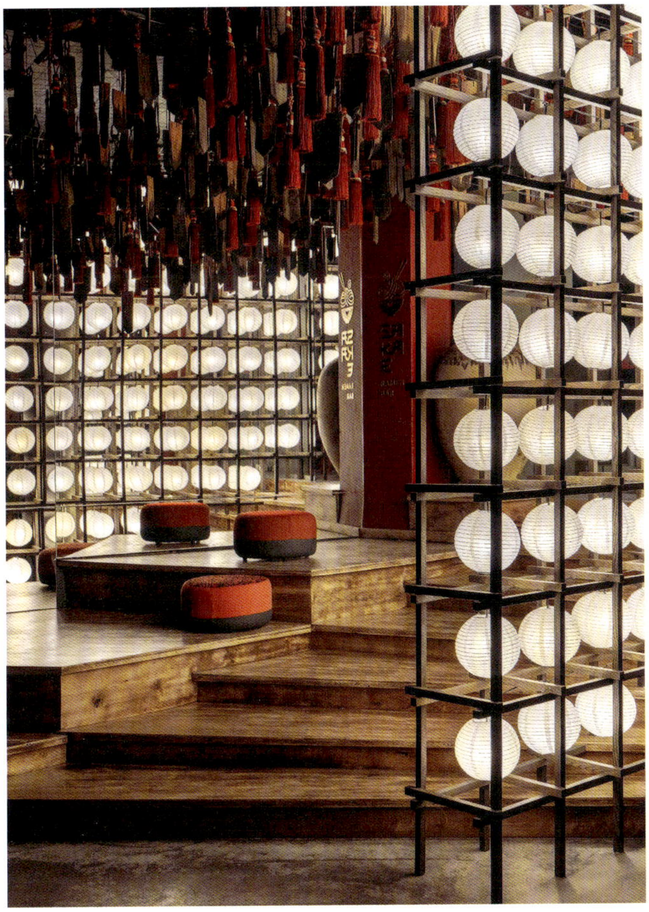
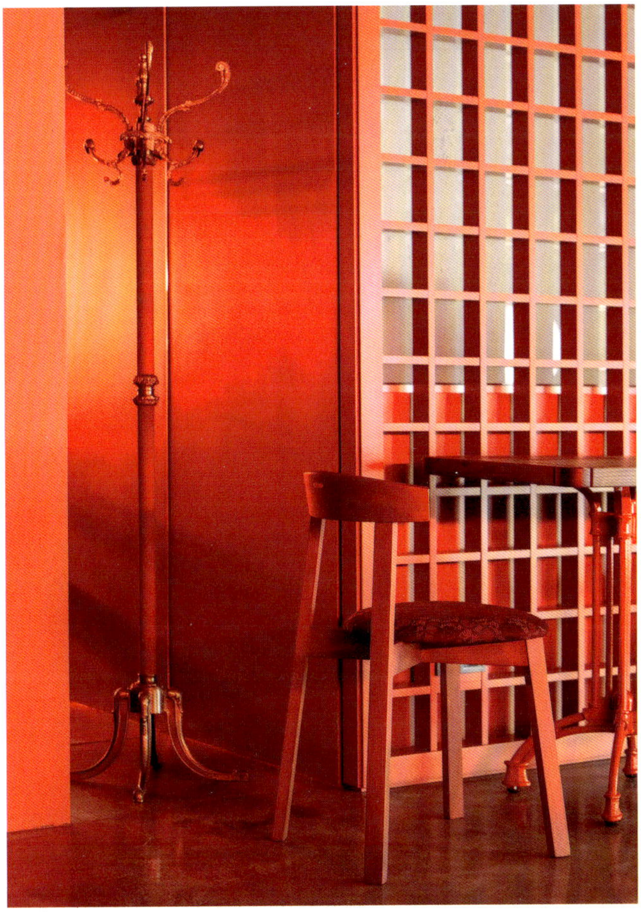

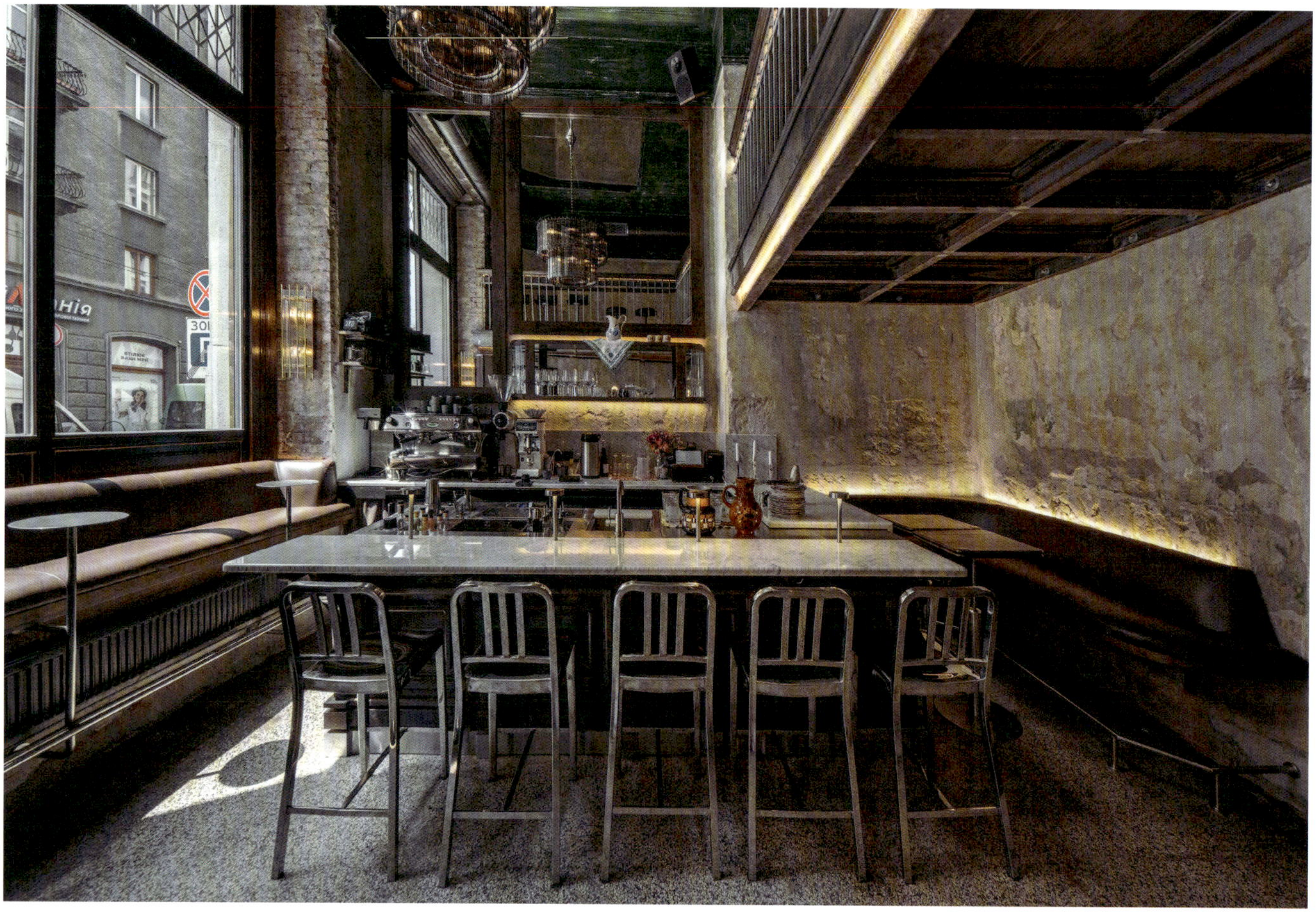

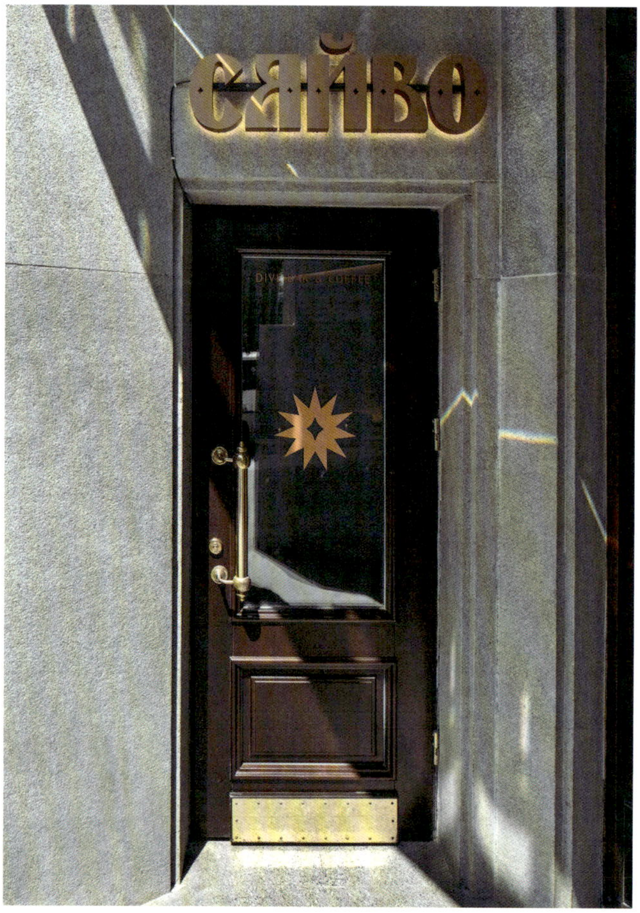
СЯЙВО

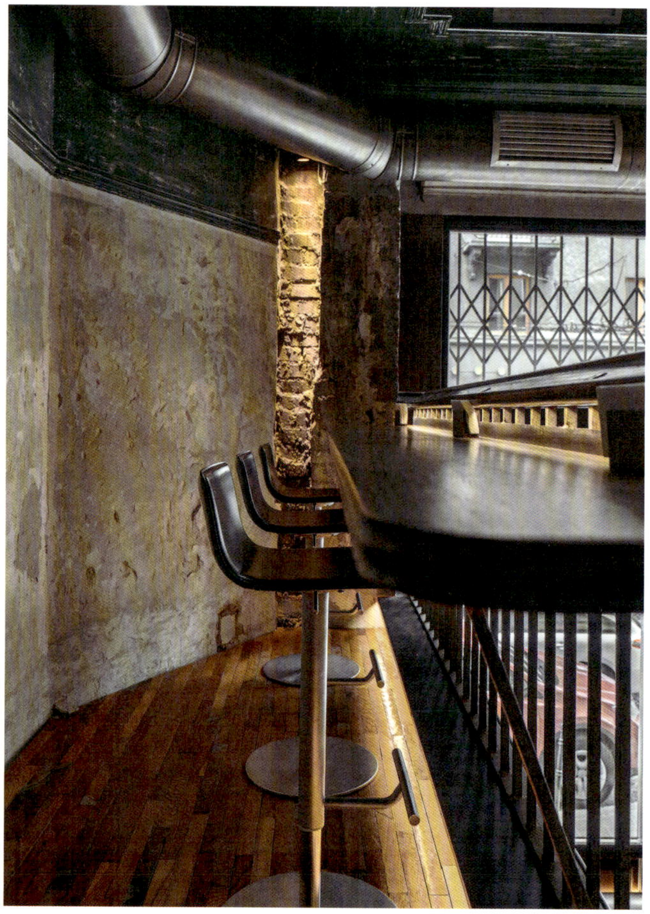

TWO CENTURIES MEET IN A TIMELESS INTERIOR

REPLUS BUREAU
SIAIVO DIVE BAR

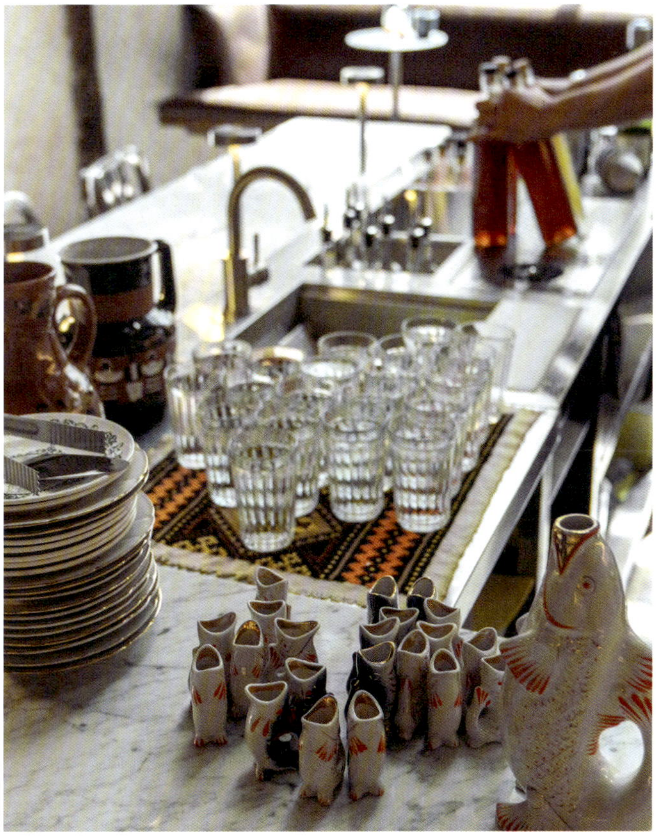

When designing Siaivo Dive Bar, Replus Bureau wanted to create the impression that the bar had been operating, unchanged, since the beginning of the 20th century.

Siaivo, a coffee shop by day and bar by night, is located in the former Prague Bank building that dates back to the early 1900s. For the interior, Replus Bureau used stainless steel and marble for a timeless look, preserving original features and incorporating additional vintage elements. Among these elements is the warm Soviet-era parquet flooring on the second floor and the authentic Austrian terrazzo with mosaic inlays discovered while pulling up tiles during renovation. Restare Architectural Salvage Warehouse, part of Replus Bureau, provided the Austrian spiral metal staircase as well as a balustrade from an old Austrian house of the same period and style, ensuring a cohesive aesthetic. A large chandelier, suspended from a mirrored ceiling for added impact, serves as the interior's central focal point. Replus opted for small lamps on each table, rather than hanging pendants, and installed mirrored walls behind the bar to enhance the space's visual appeal from the street.

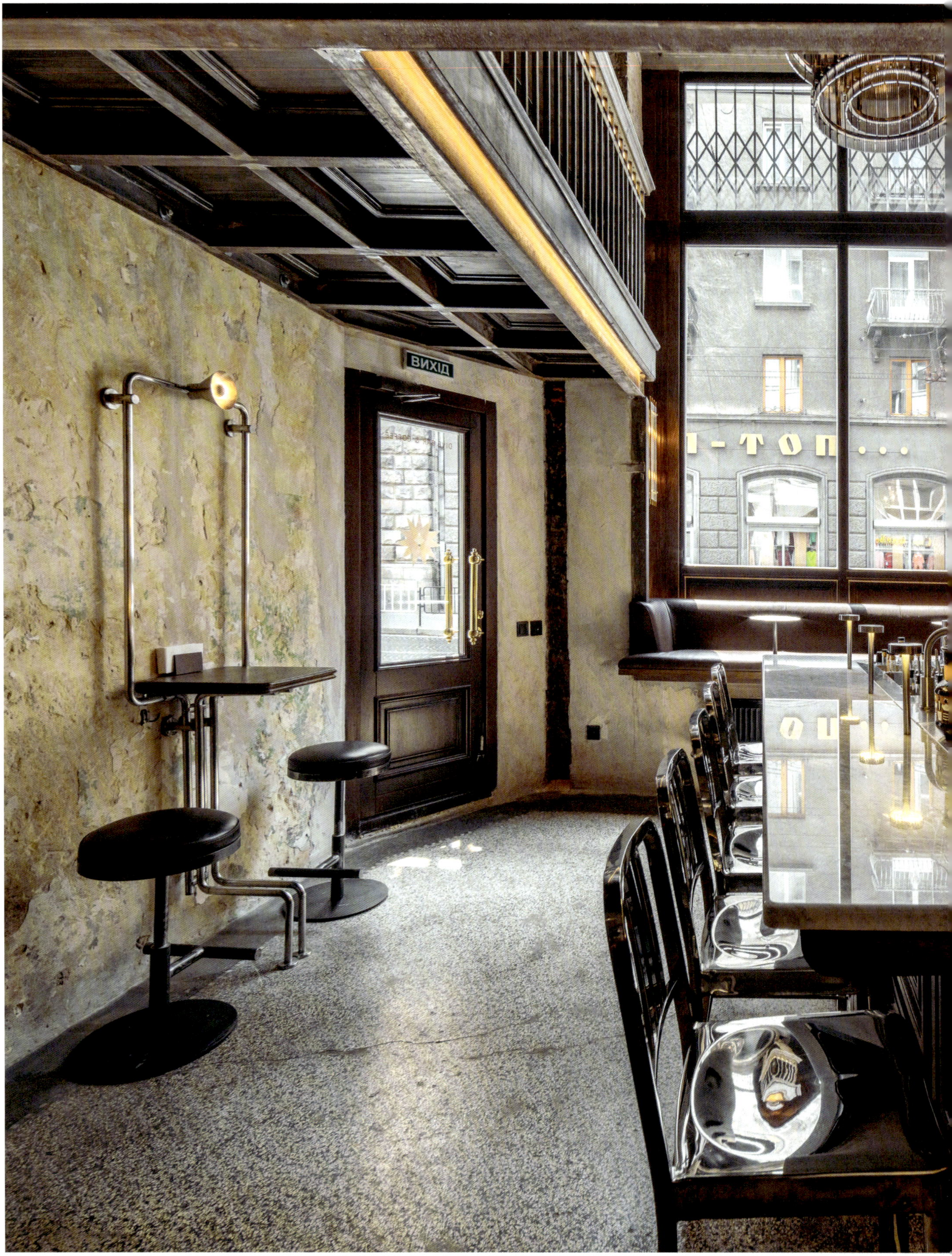
ВИХІД

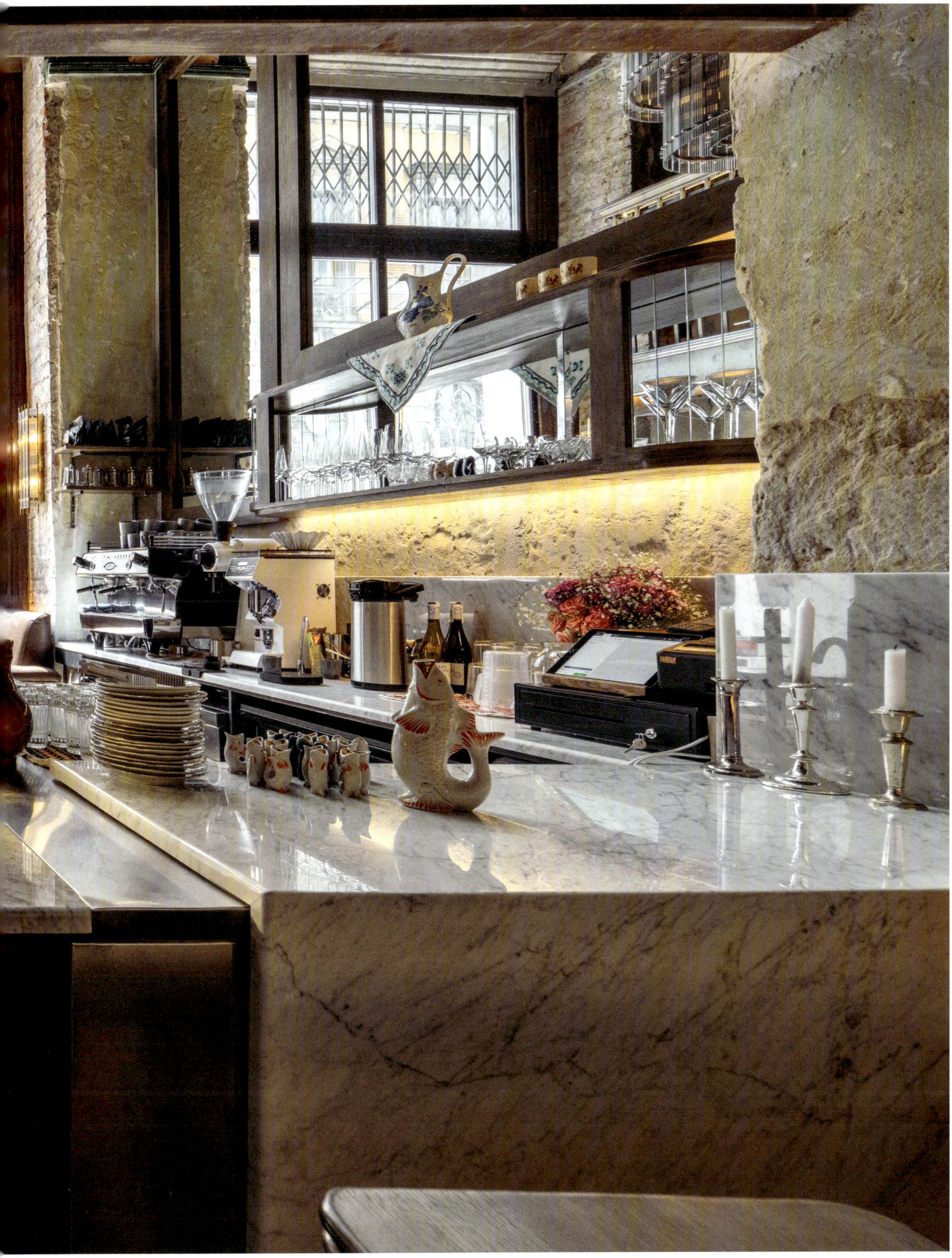

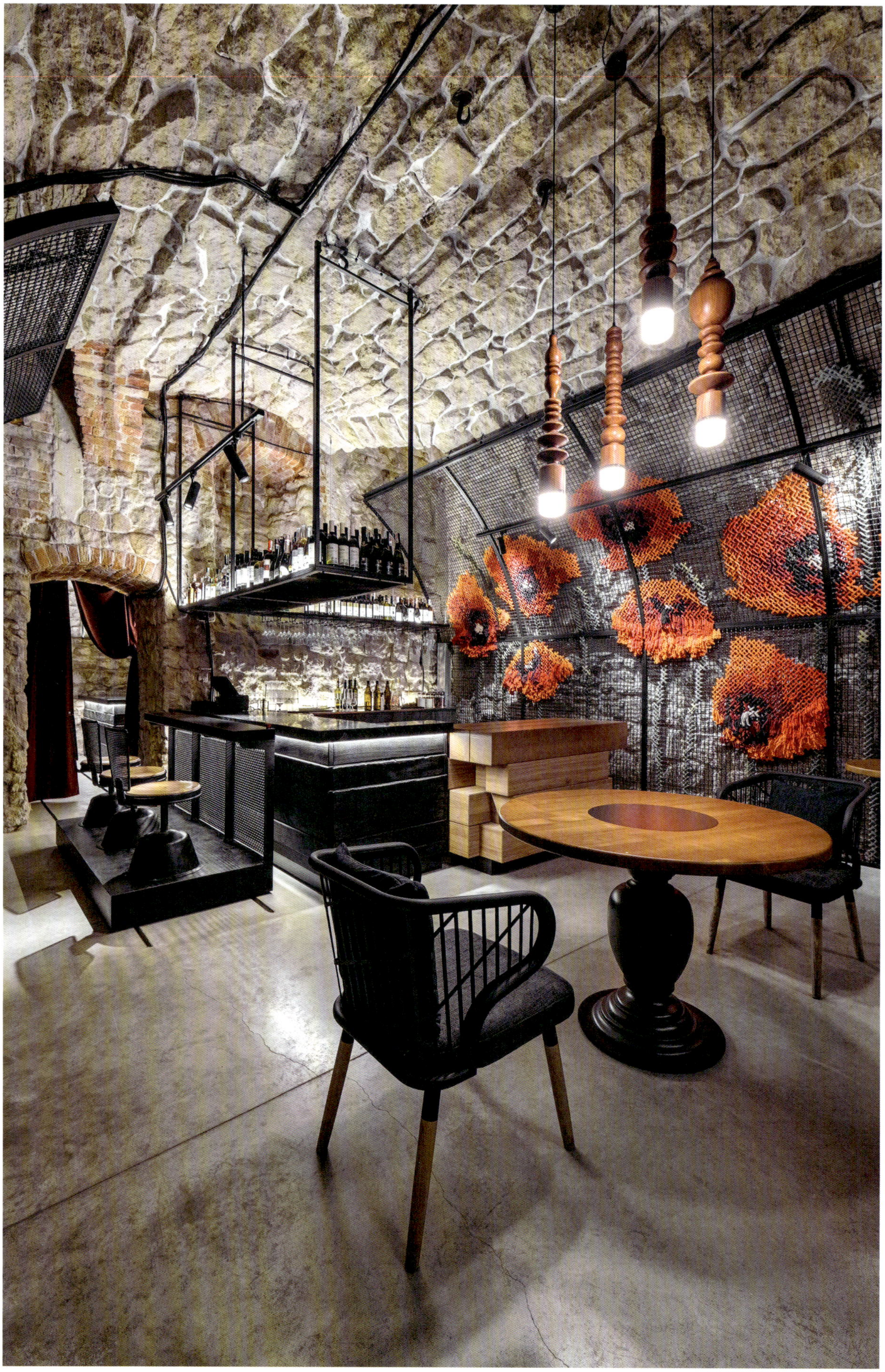

BOLD AND INDIVIDUAL

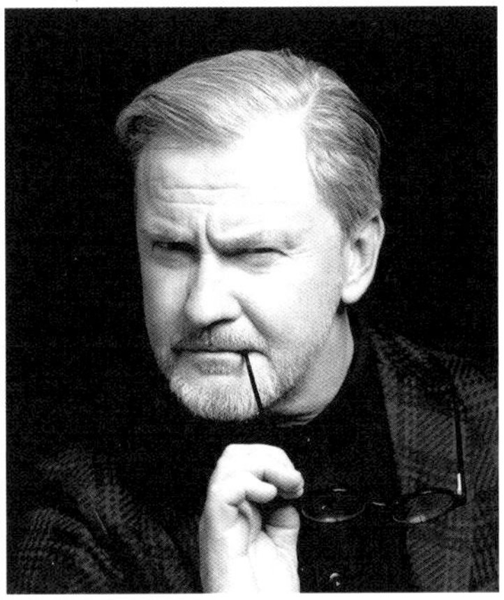

LOFT BURO

According to the founder of loft buro, Oleg Volosovskiy, the main task of the studio is to create a harmonious, cozy space that perfectly sets the mood for every person who steps inside.

Loft buro, led by founder Oleg Volosovskiy, brings together a talented group of architects, designers, artists, and engineers. The studio specializes in spatial, product, and interior design for restaurants, bars, and multifunctional spaces, as well as loft-style residences in the private sector. With over 20 years of experience, loft buro has executed a great number of distinctive projects across Ukraine and abroad, predominantly in the HoReCa sector. For every one of their projects, loft buro creates custom furniture and lighting, bespoke decor, and unique art objects, paying intense attention to detail. Its focus on detail is one of the team's hallmark traits. The studio also prides itself on incorporating historical features of buildings into their designs whenever possible. To bring their creations to fruition, loft buro collaborates with local artisans, manufacturers, and glassblowers. Their interior designs are also known for their "animation"—a reference to their dynamic style, which is created using special mechanisms and unexpected visual techniques. In the difficult year of 2022, the studio continued working, supporting local manufacturers and bringing several standout projects to completion, including the Porto Maltese restaurant in Kyiv and Ostannya Barykada in Lviv. The Fresh Black Roastery and Bar project, created in 2021, was long-listed for a 2022 Dezeen Awards in Sustainable Interior, and in 2022, the studio introduced CAMPUS, a volunteer initiative that provides energy-efficient modular homes to displaced individuals for quick resettlement. In addition, they developed a reconstruction plan for the Mykolaiv Regional State Administration building, which was destroyed by a Russian missile attack.

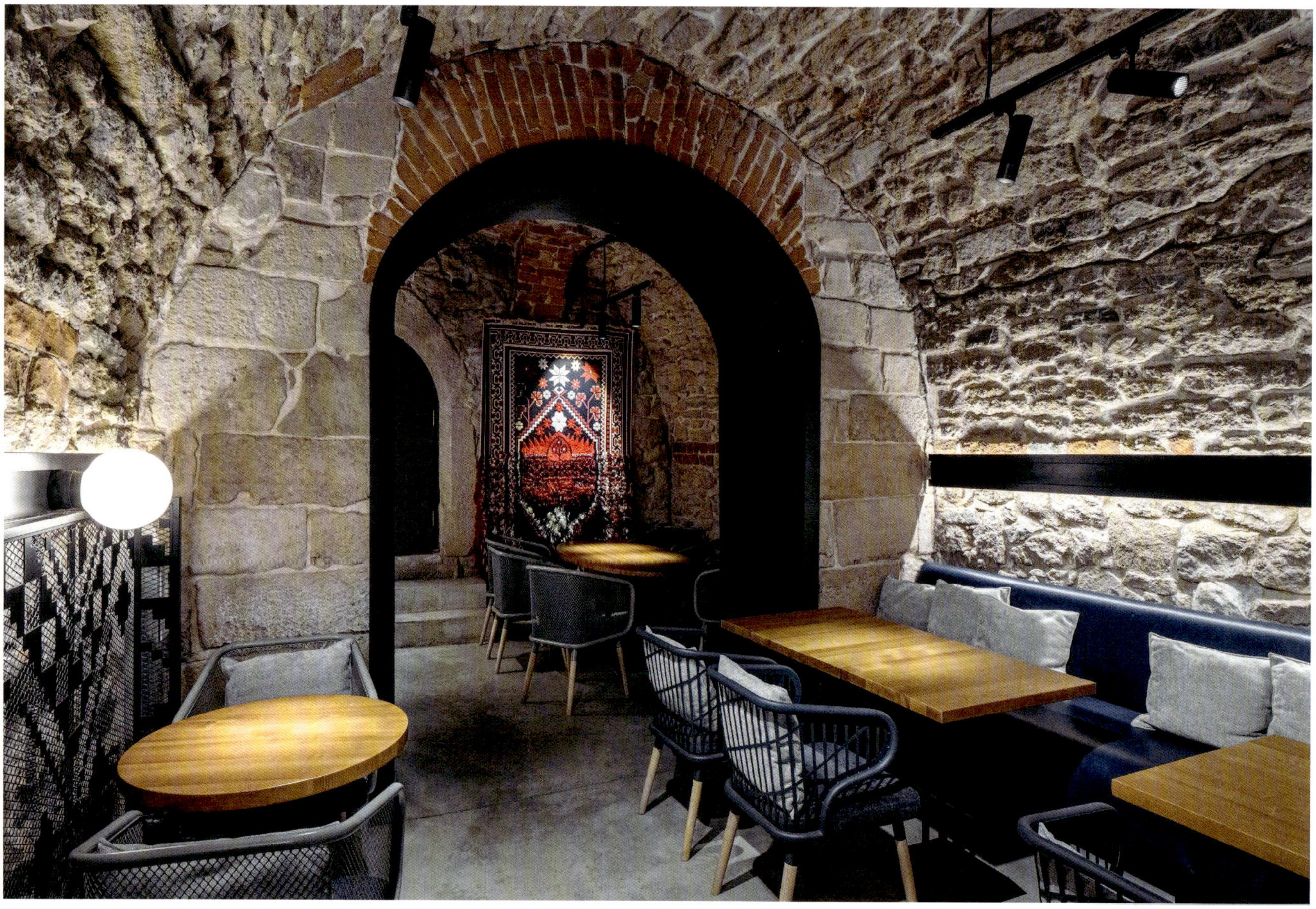

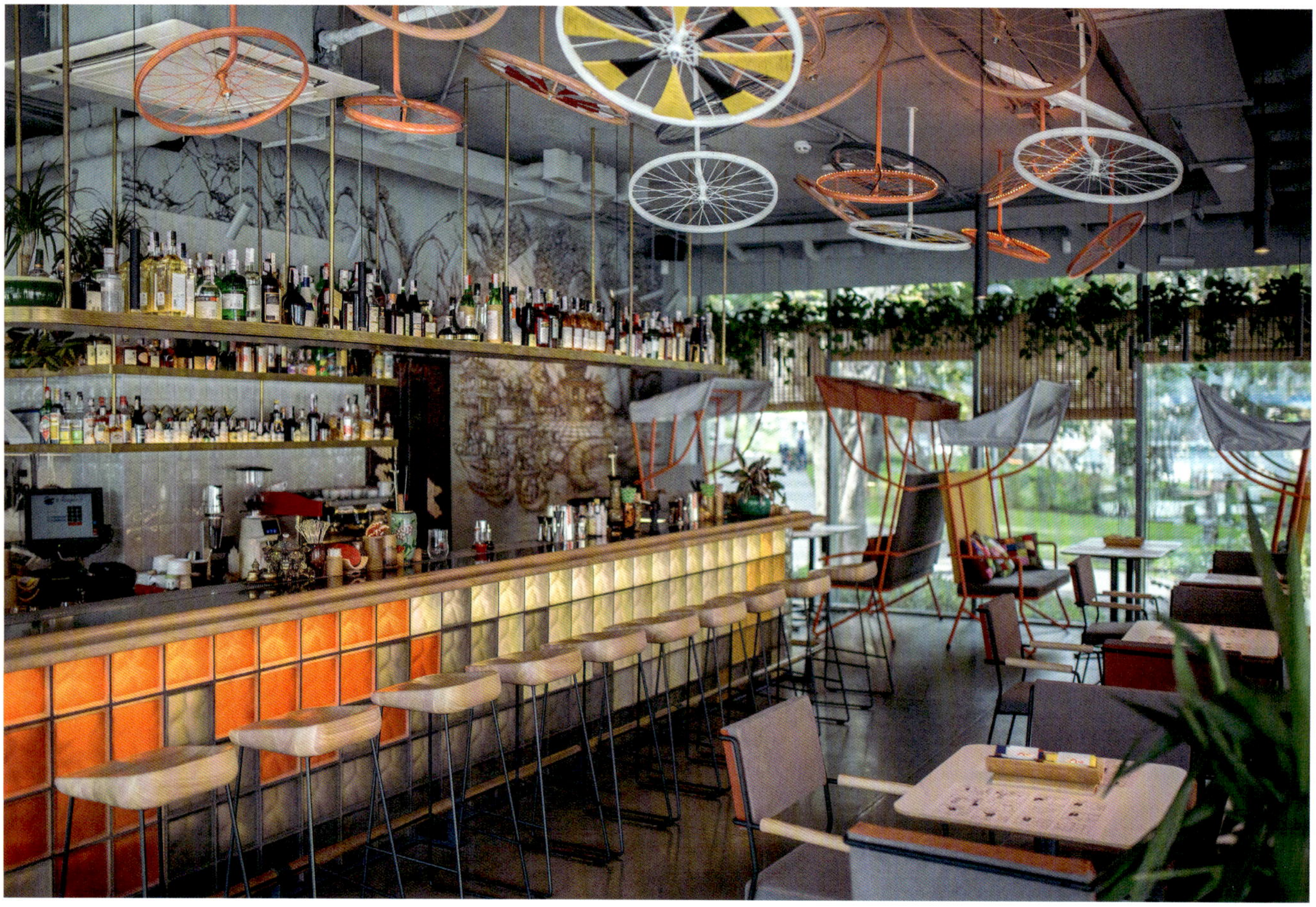

"For loft buro, wartime is hard work. Sometimes beyond human capabilities, but it keeps us going. Traditionally, our projects include many items created by Ukrainian artisans. In this way, we support the work of not only our team, but also local manufacturers."

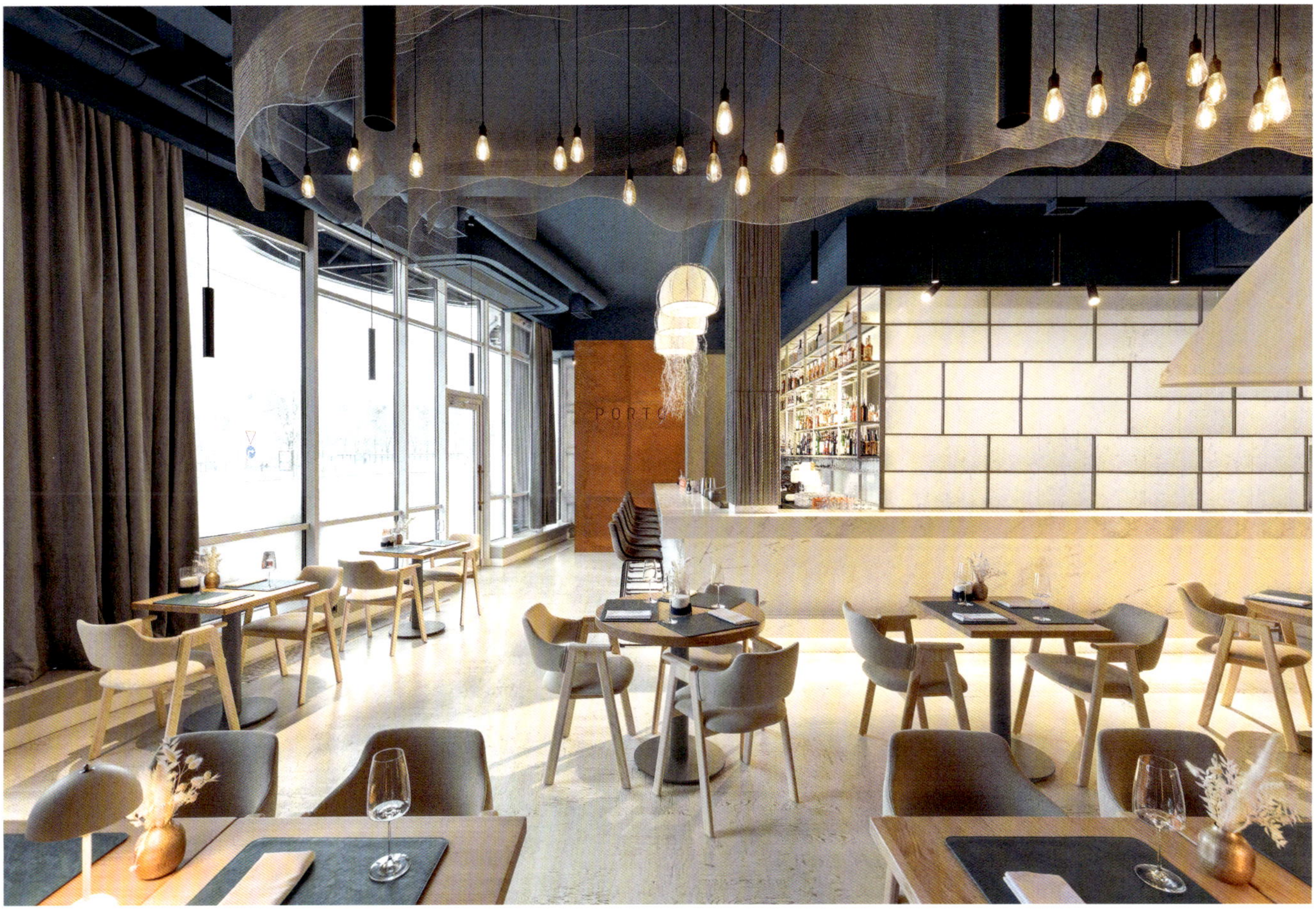

Every design from the loft buro team is thoughtfully considered. The designers develop the general concept and each component separately, resulting in unique, highly detailed spaces that fit harmoniously into the architecture of the premises.

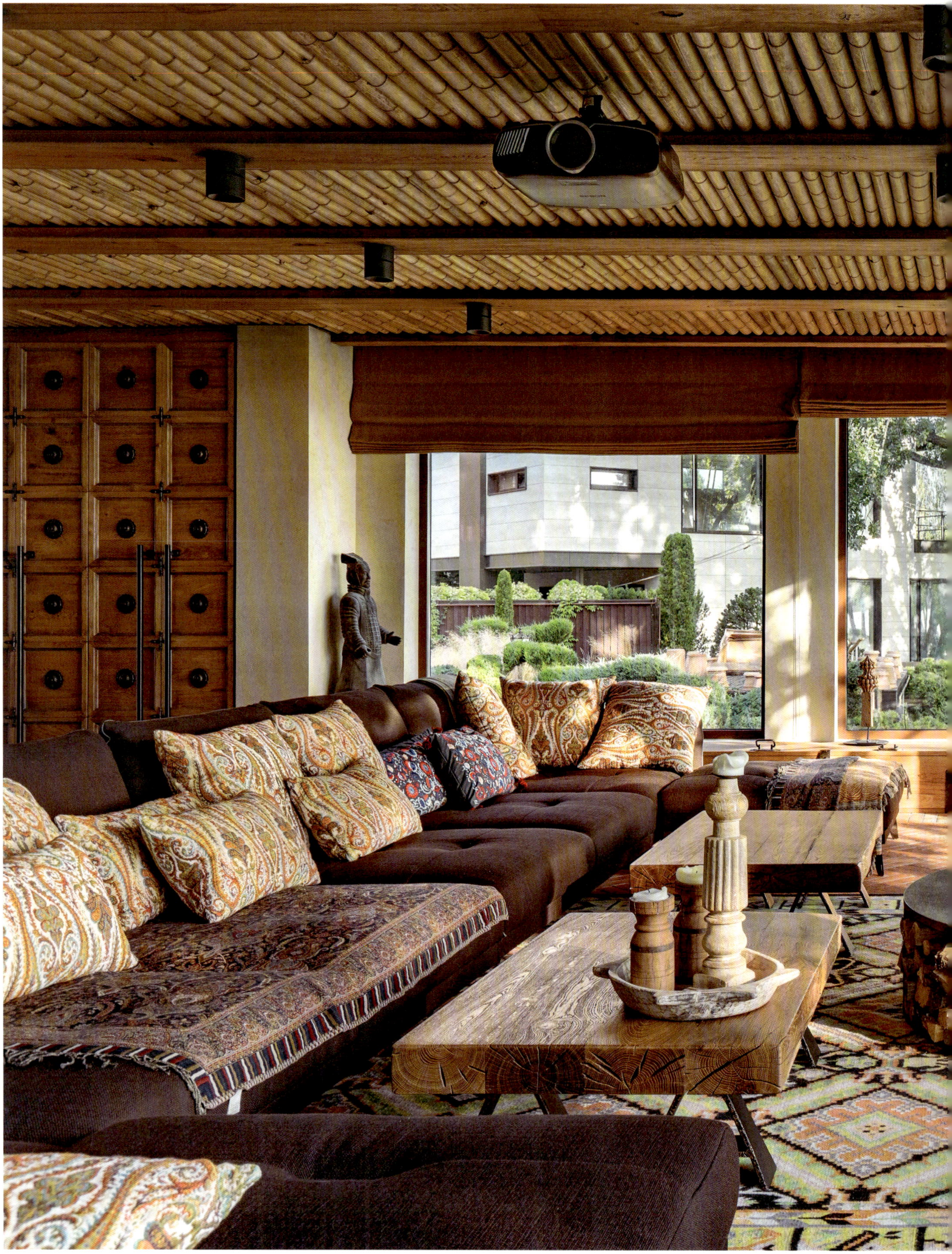

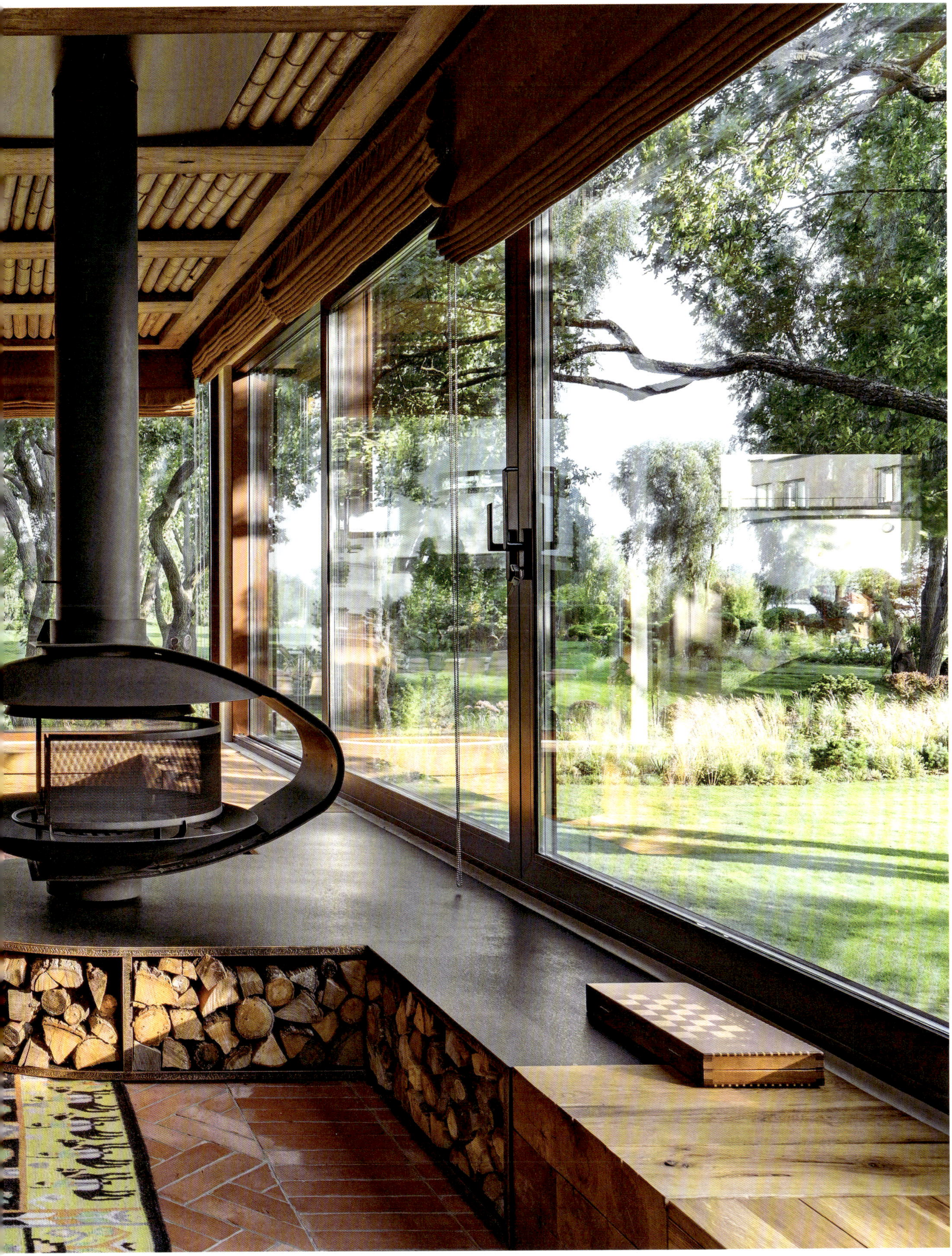

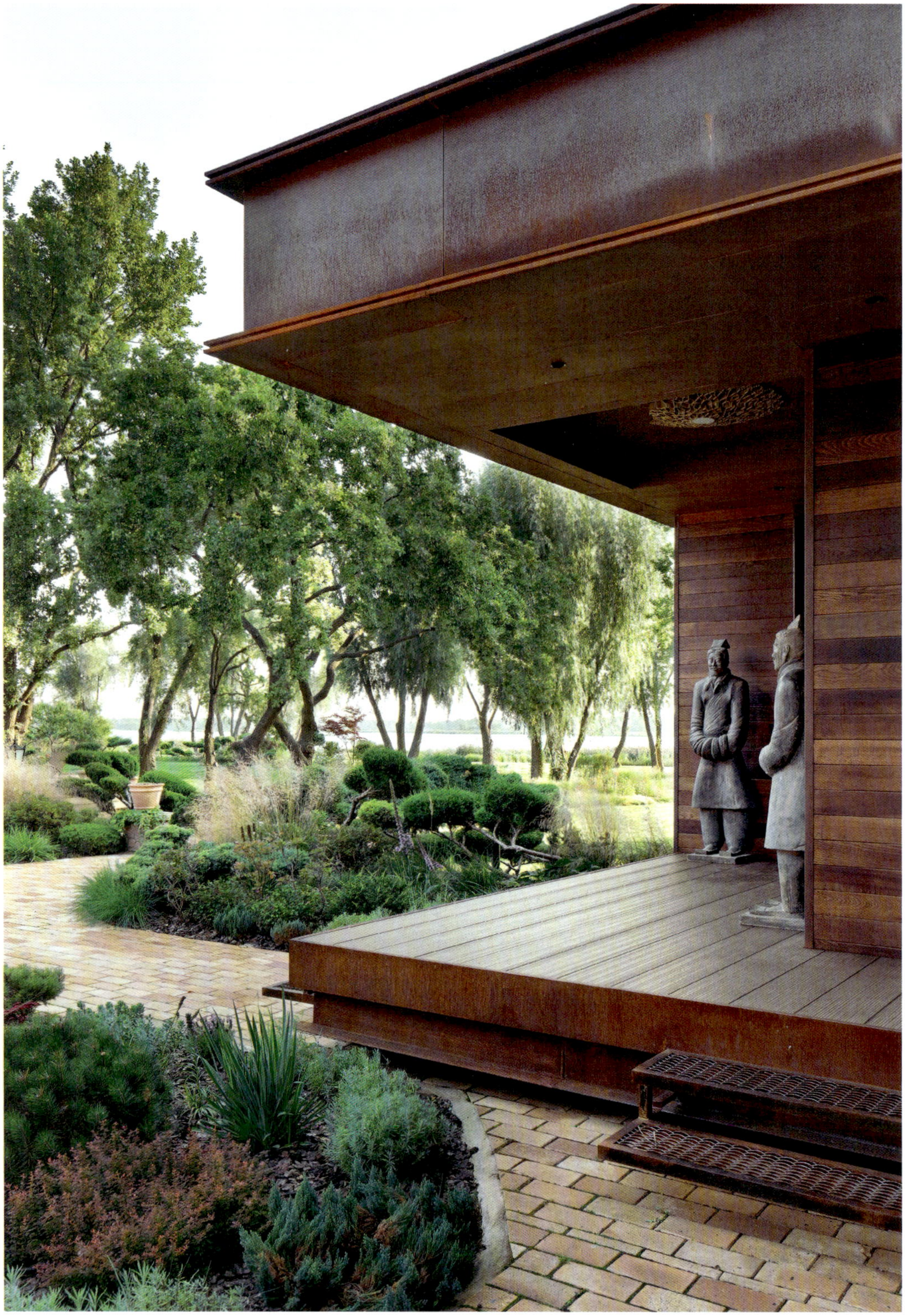

The name Enjoy the Silence speaks for itself—this cozy chalet was created by loft buro as a hideaway for meditation and relaxation. By masterfully combining different cultures, they've allowed the project to blend seamlessly into the local landscape.

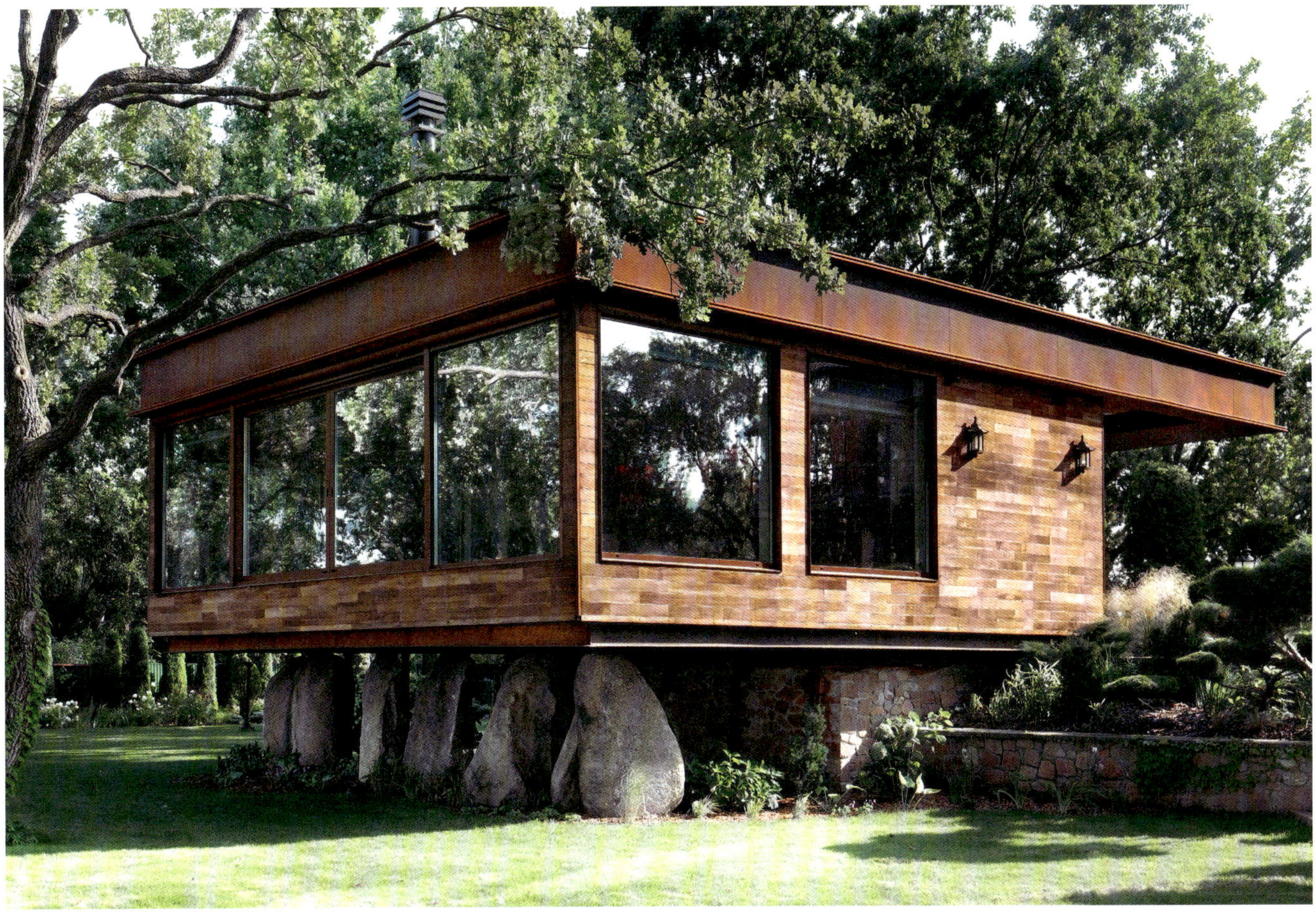

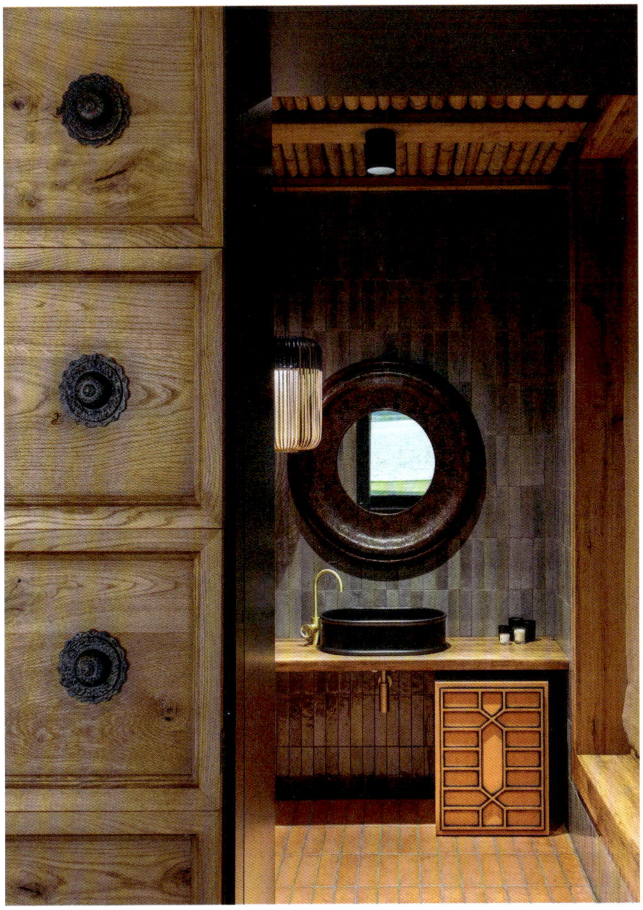

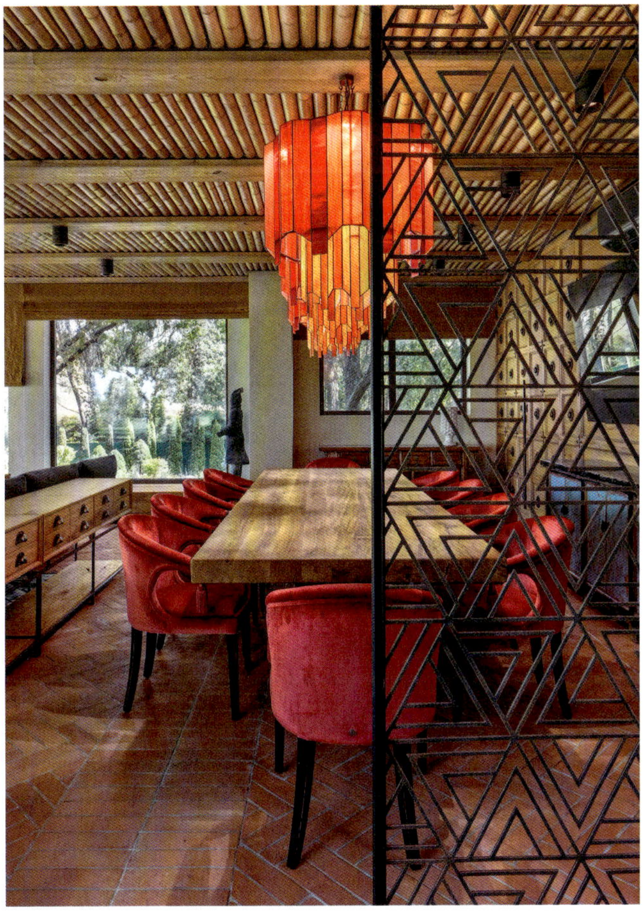

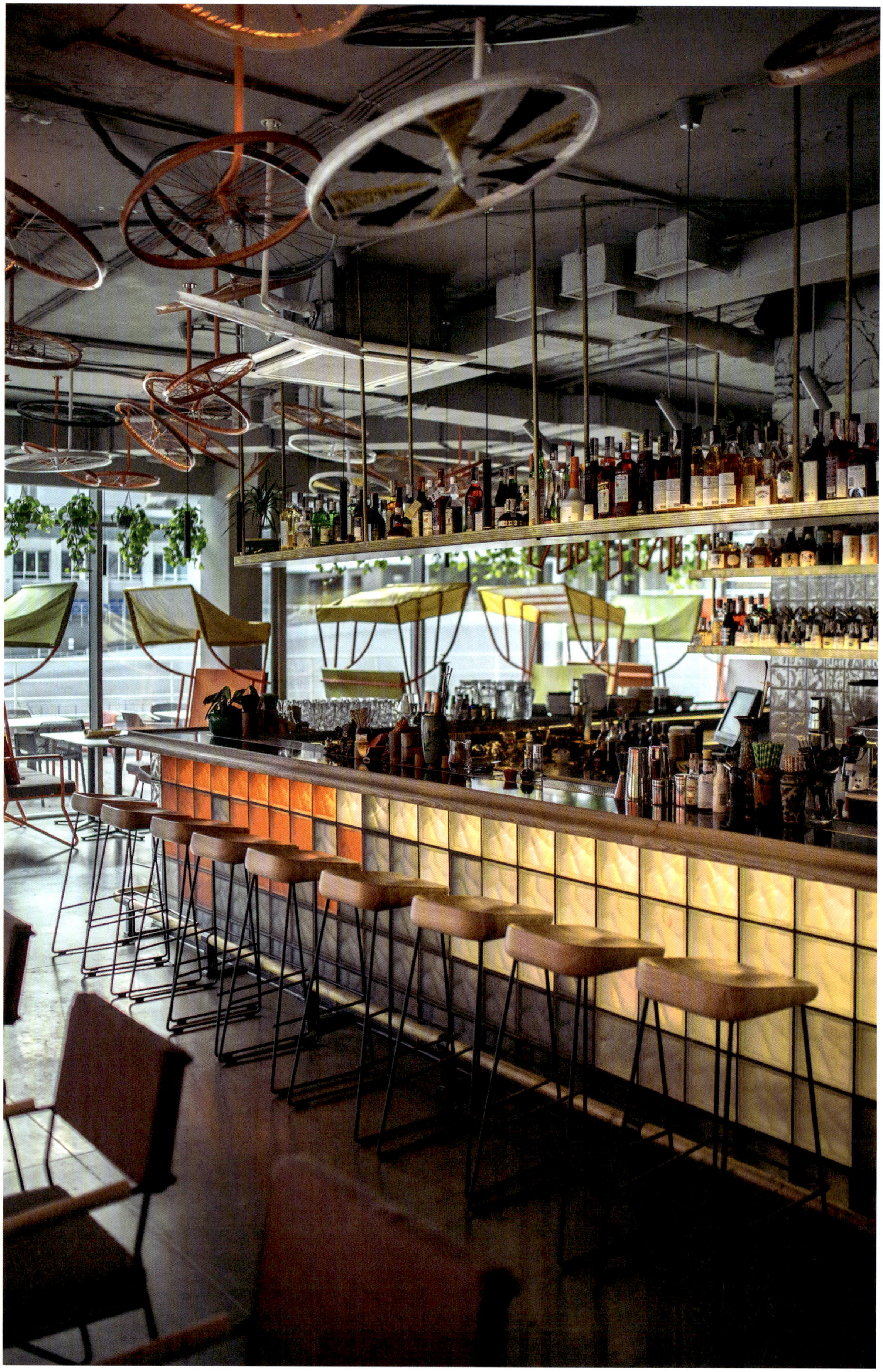

VIETNAMESE VIBES IN THE CENTER OF KYIV

LOFT BURO
TIN TIN

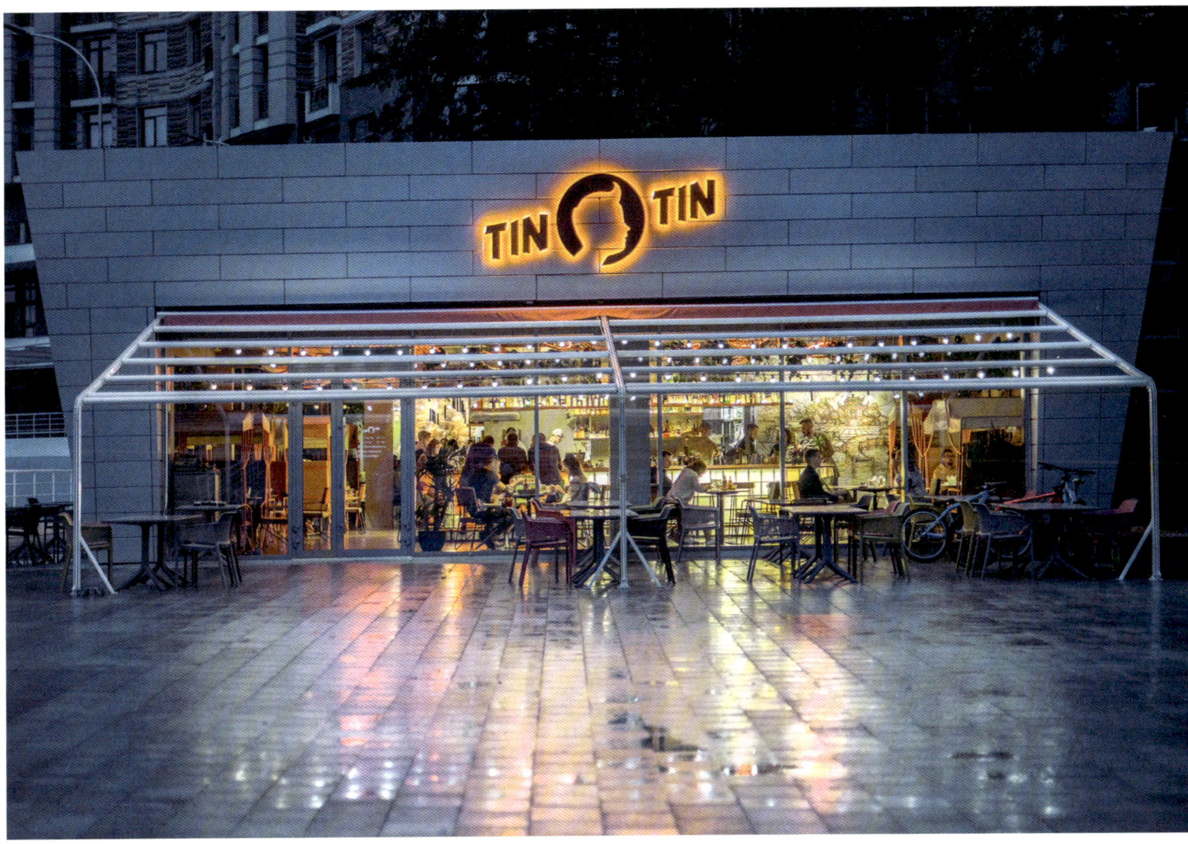

Inside Tin Tin restaurant, loft buro combined Vietnamese street aesthetics with local Kyiv vibes. Transparency effects and light scenography emphasizes the design.

Tin Tin, a Vietnamese bar and restaurant, is situated in the heart of Kyiv, opposite one of the oldest velodromes in Europe, built in 1913. Since its reconstruction in 2017, the Kyiv Velodrome has become a popular destination for cyclists and ordinary residents alike. For Tin Tin's design, loft buro used elements of Vietnamese street culture and blended them with references to the local cycling history. For example, they repurposed vintage bicycle wheels into an art installation and converted rickshaws into comfortable sofas. The sleek, vibrant interior is punctuated with street signs and posters of imaginary cities in Vietnam. The team at loft buro also wanted to connect the street with the interior, so they created a transparent facade. The designers hung plants along the facade to block excessive sunlight while maintaining most of its transparency. The team also worked hard on the inviting lighting concept, which casts a warm glow on the restaurant's surroundings.

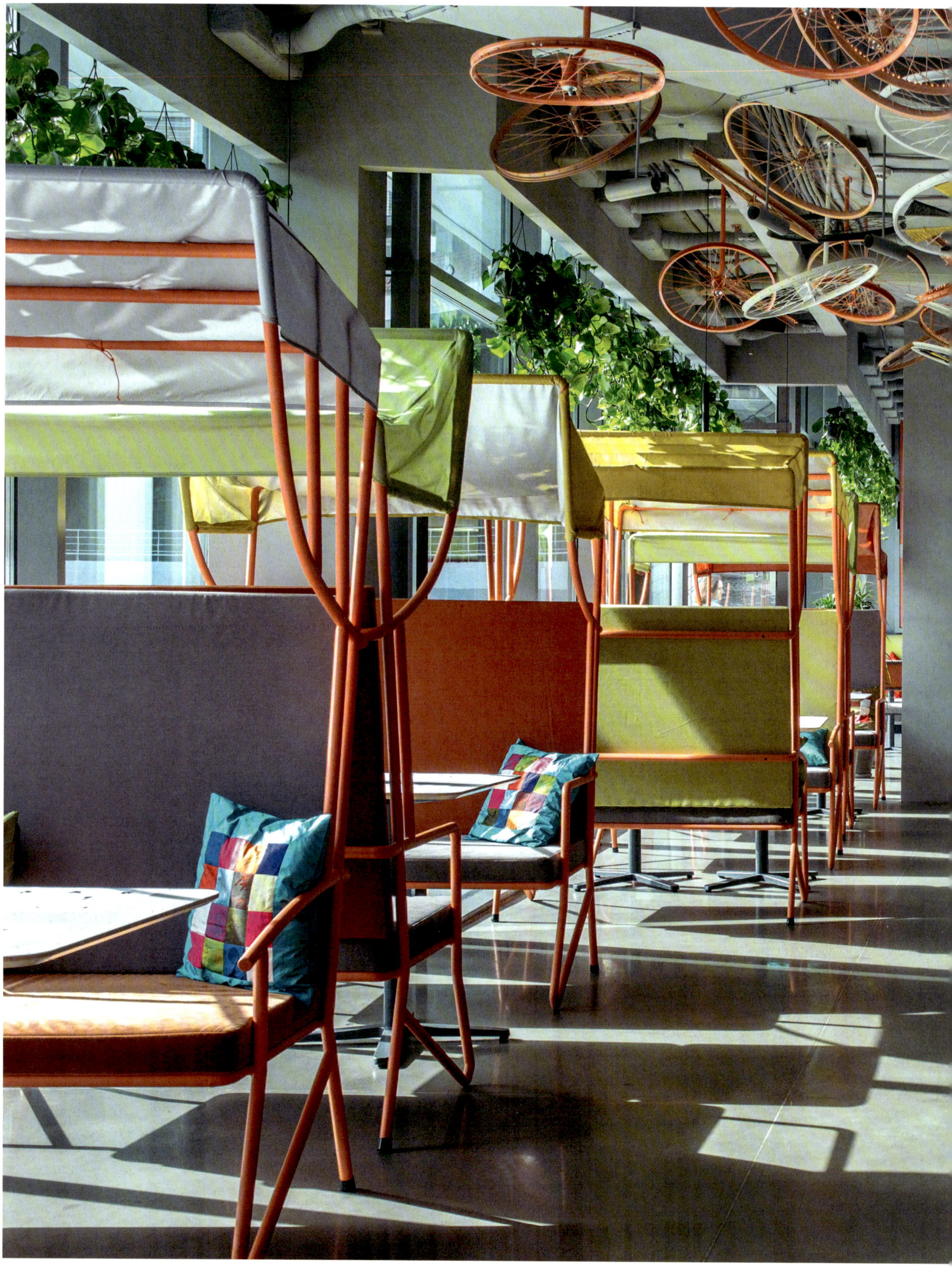

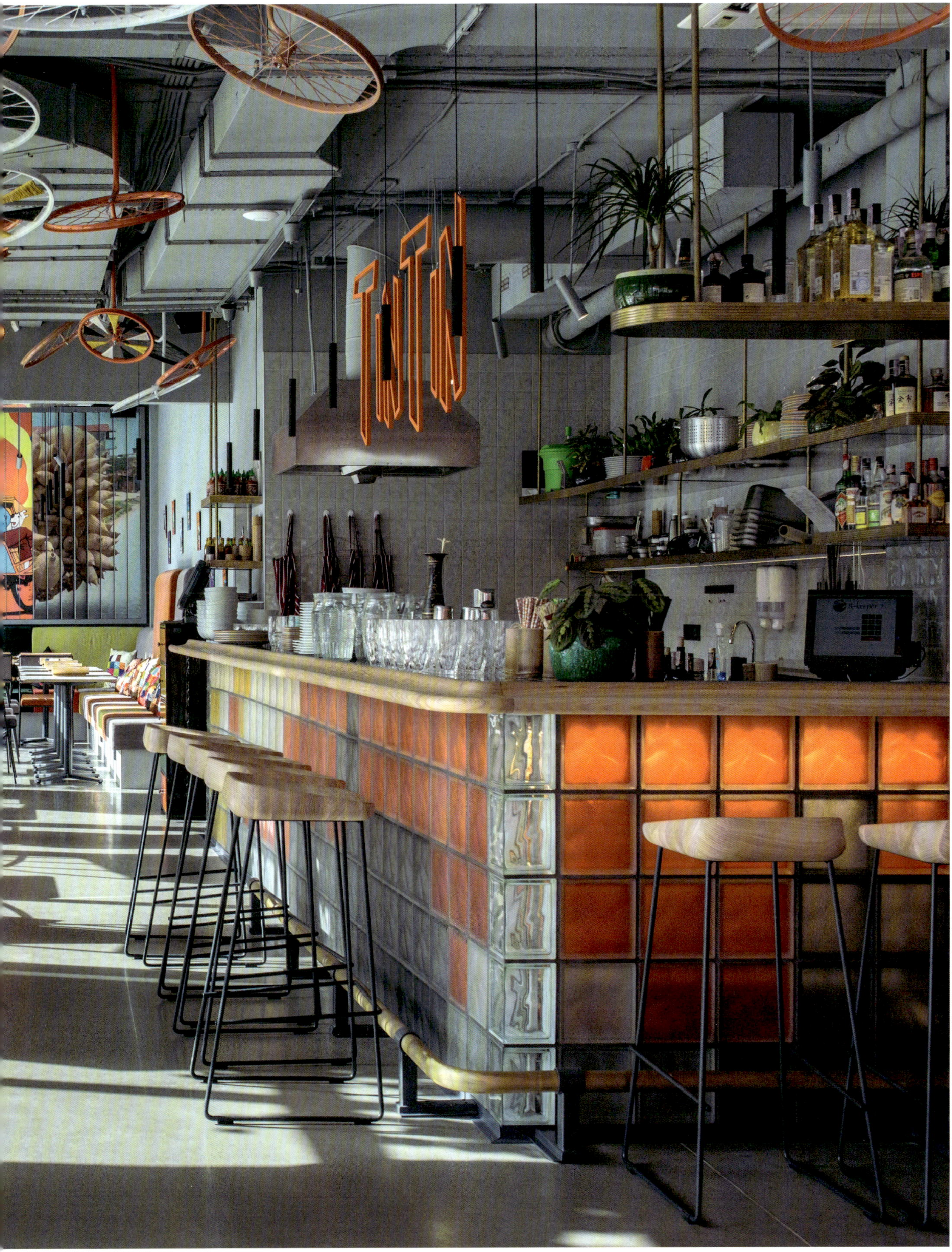

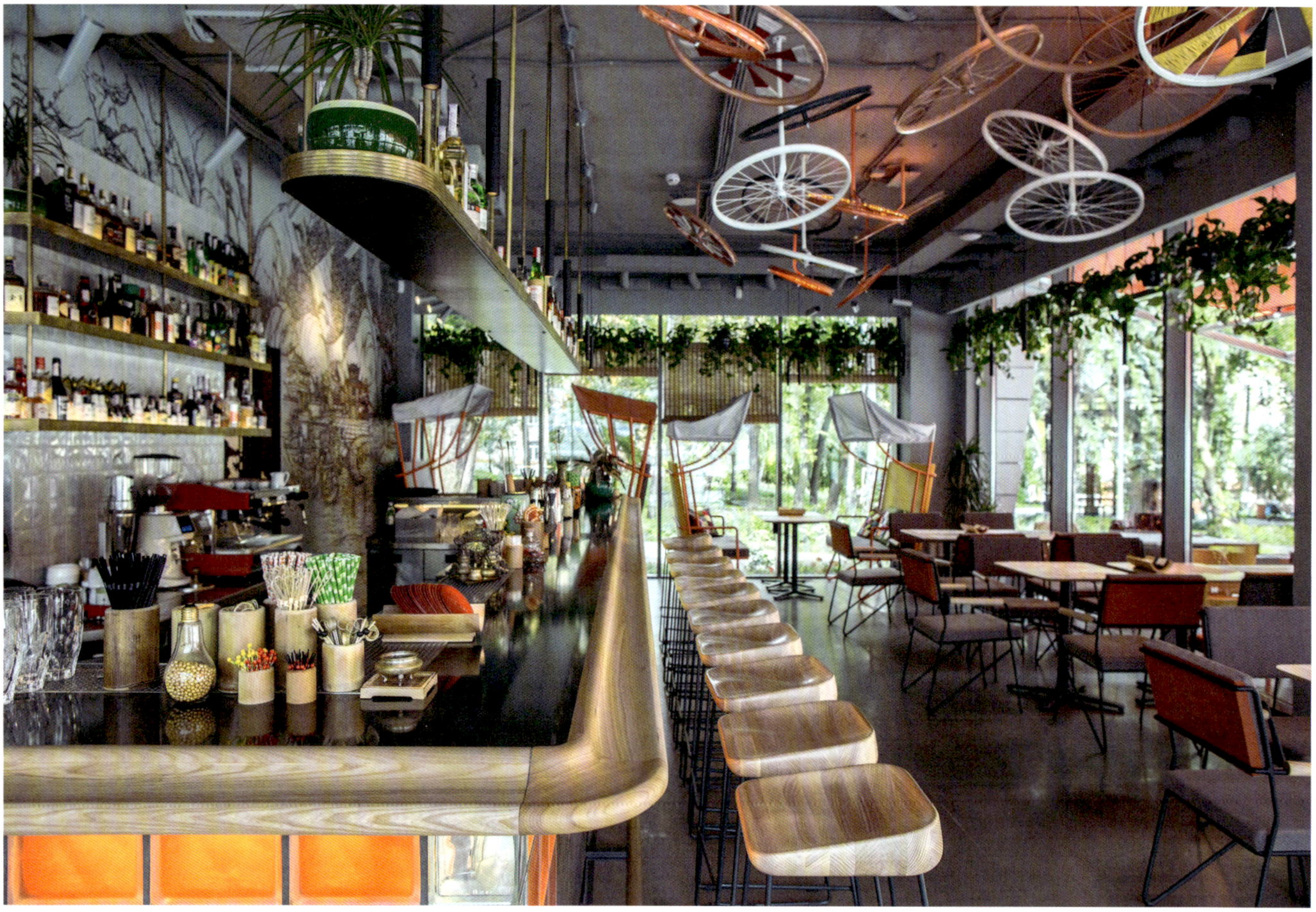

Tin Tin's interior is decorated with rickshaws-turned-cozy-sofas, outdoor signage, and posters with images of imaginary cities in Vietnam.

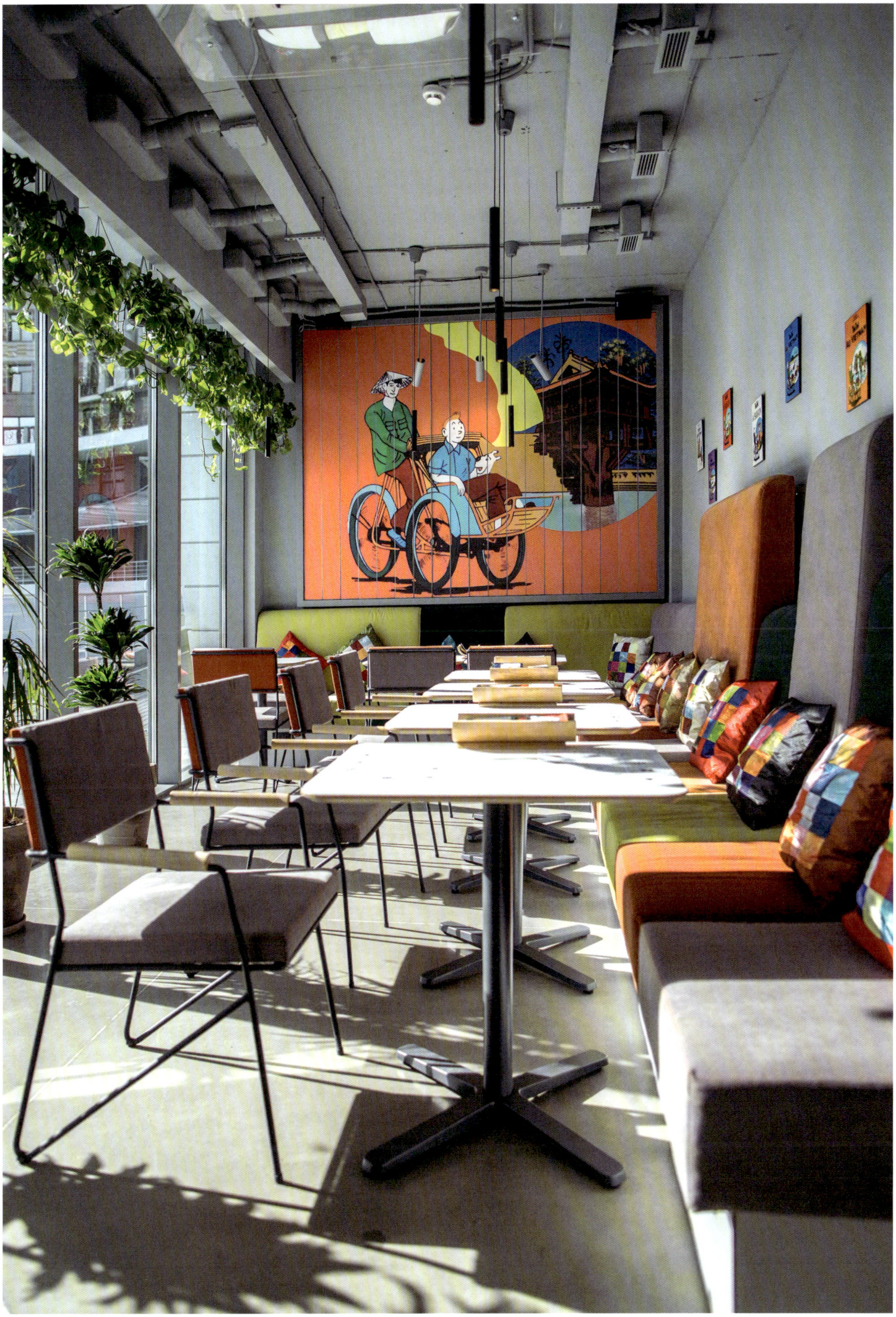

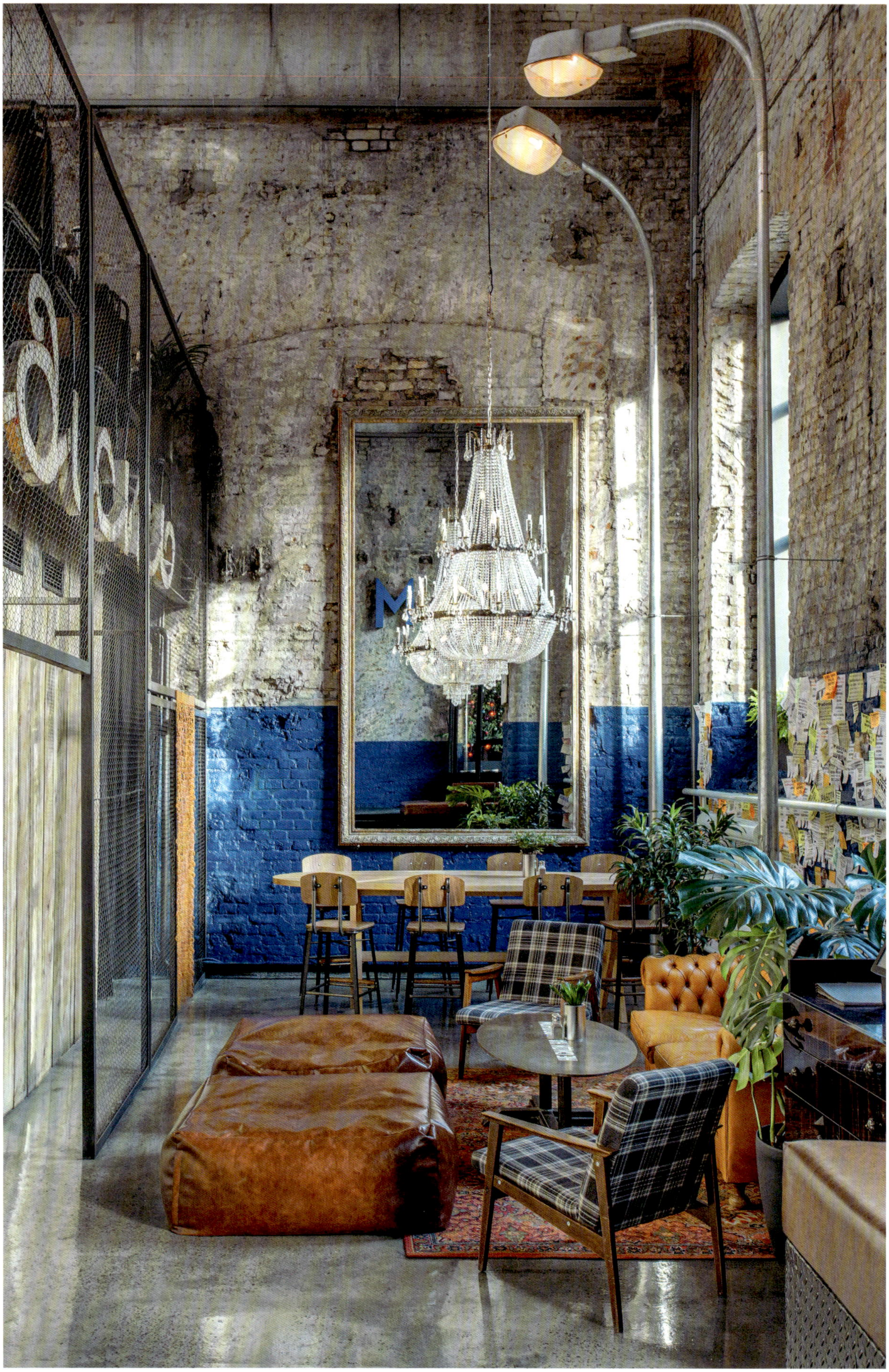

HUMAN-CENTERED DESIGN

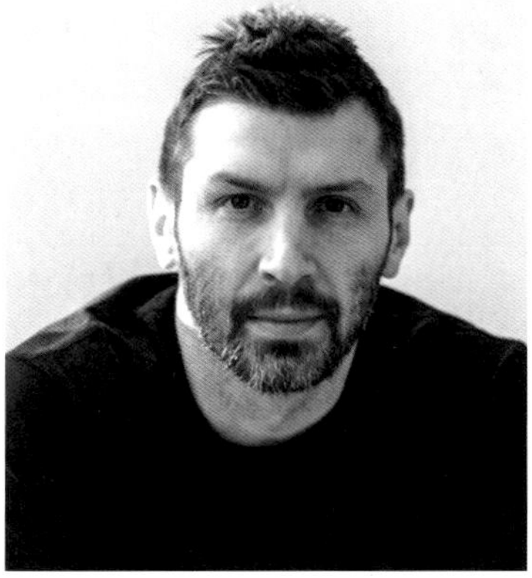 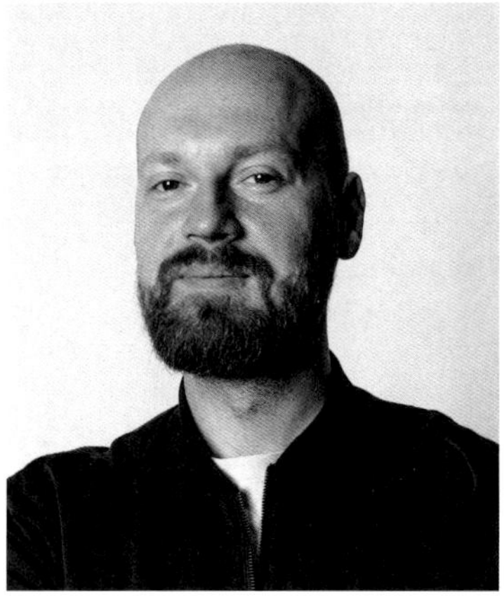

BALBEK BUREAU

While designing bespoke commercial, corporate, and residential properties, balbek bureau is building a community of socially sustainable spaces.

Balbek bureau is an award-winning architecture and interior design studio founded by Slava Balbek and Borys Dorogov. The firm has garnered international acclaim, receiving accolades such as Hospitality Design Awards, Interior Design Best of Year, Architecture MasterPrize, and IIDA Global Excellence Awards. Balbek bureau designs commercial, corporate, and residential spaces throughout Europe, the United States, and Asia. As longtime fans of human-centric design and architecture, the designers of the studio see people as the core value of their projects. Whether it is an office for a global tech company or a temporary settlement for displaced individuals, they always keep those who will interact with the space in mind. As architects, they aim to help people feel welcome no matter where they go. And being a Ukrainian firm, they want to spread the word about their native country. Though architects don't often refer to ethnographic motifs in their interiors, balbek bureau believes that the Ukrainian spirit is already in their design DNA. Since many of their Ukrainian projects are based in historical buildings, they always try to preserve the distinctive elements of a given space. When appropriate, they also like to reinterpret traditional techniques (e. g., *vytynanka* paper cutting craft and *vyshyvanka* embroidery), implement authentic vintage finds (like hand-knitted ornamented rugs), and create custom-made elements with Ukrainian flair. Designers pay homage to the past and, alongside other Ukrainian studios, shape the future of local design. After the outbreak of the war, some of balbek bureau's team joined the armed forces and a few members evacuated to other cities, but overall, most of the team stayed in Kyiv. Balbek bureau now develops social projects in response to the challenges arising from the impact of war, and their RE:Ukraine System covers four areas: temporary housing for IDPs (RE:Ukraine Housing), rural housing restoration (RE:Ukraine Villages), monument protection (RE:Ukraine Monuments), and commemoration (RE:Ukraine Memories).

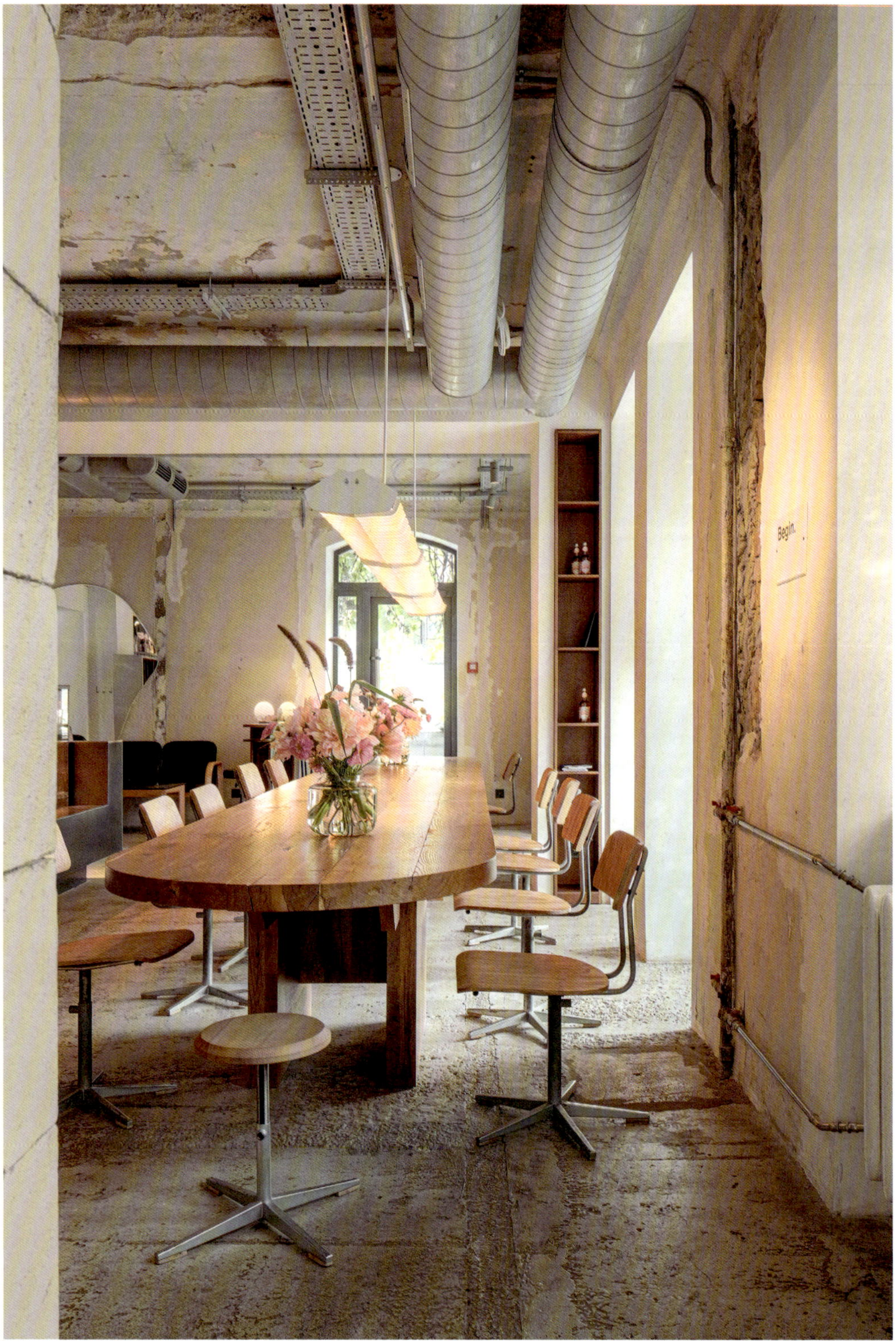

Comfort, innovation, and functionality drive every balbek bureau project. The designers start with essentials and progress to more intricate details, turning their vision into pioneering spaces that honor history while shaping the future of local design.

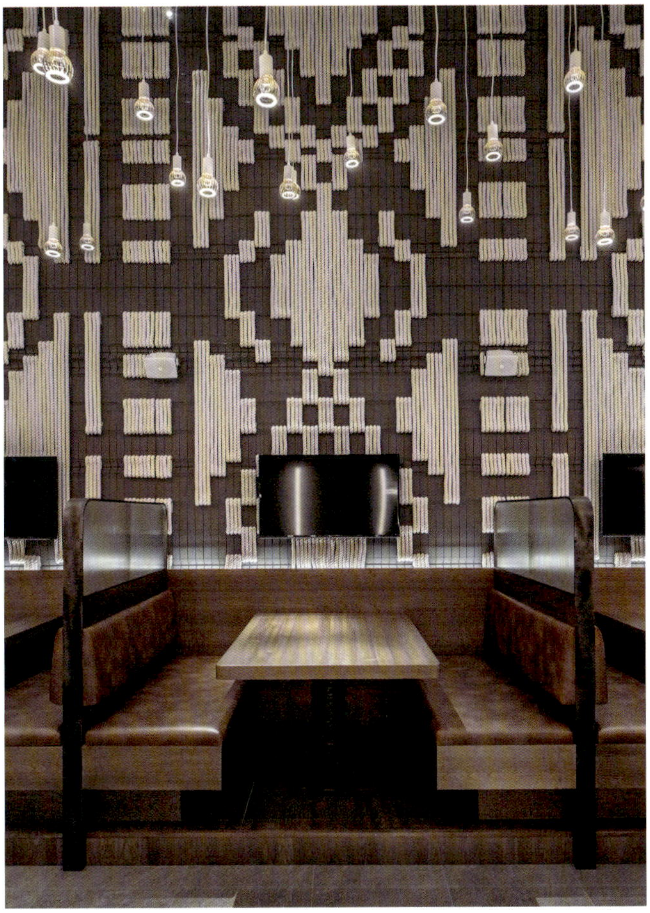

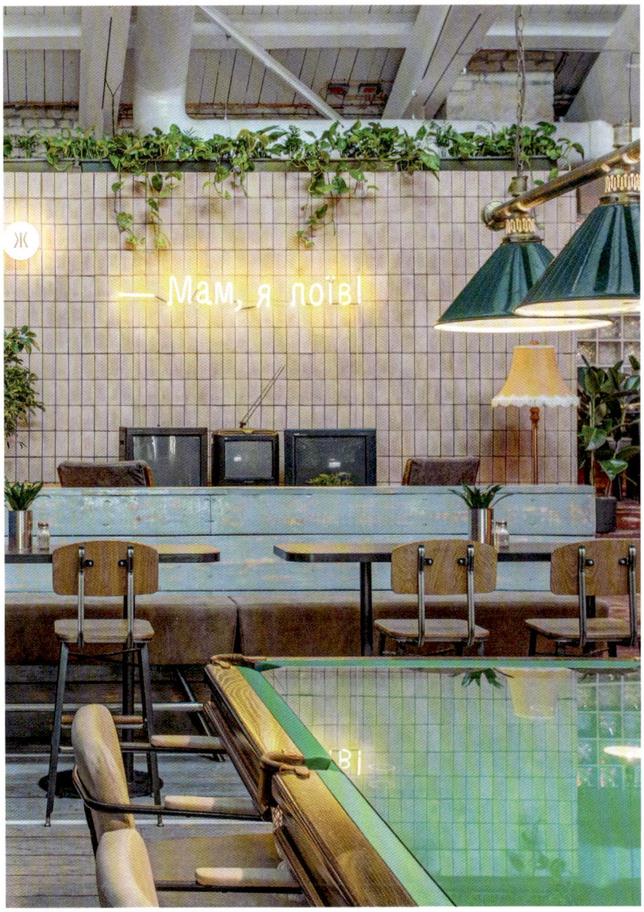
— Мам, я поїв!

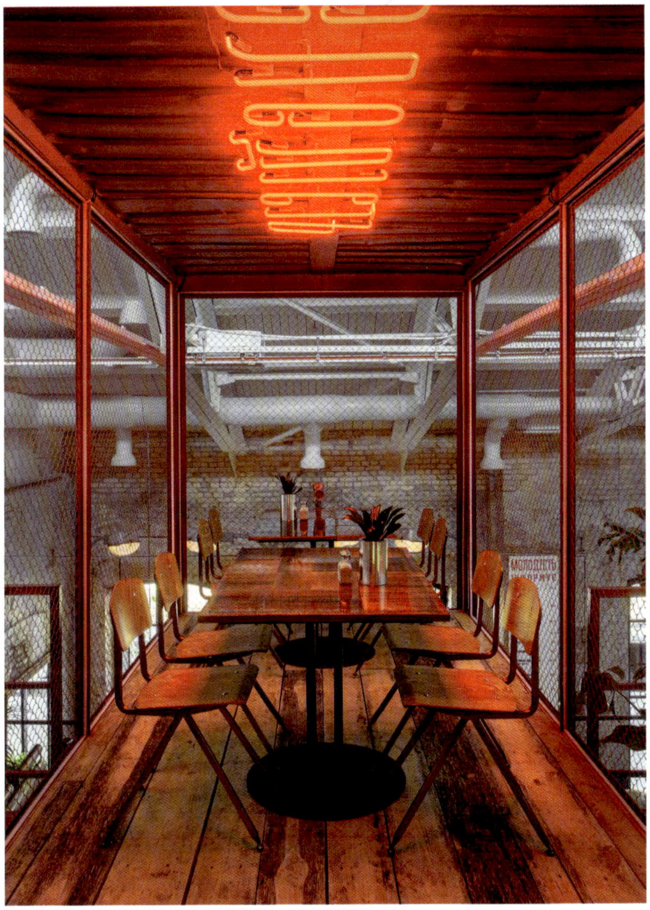

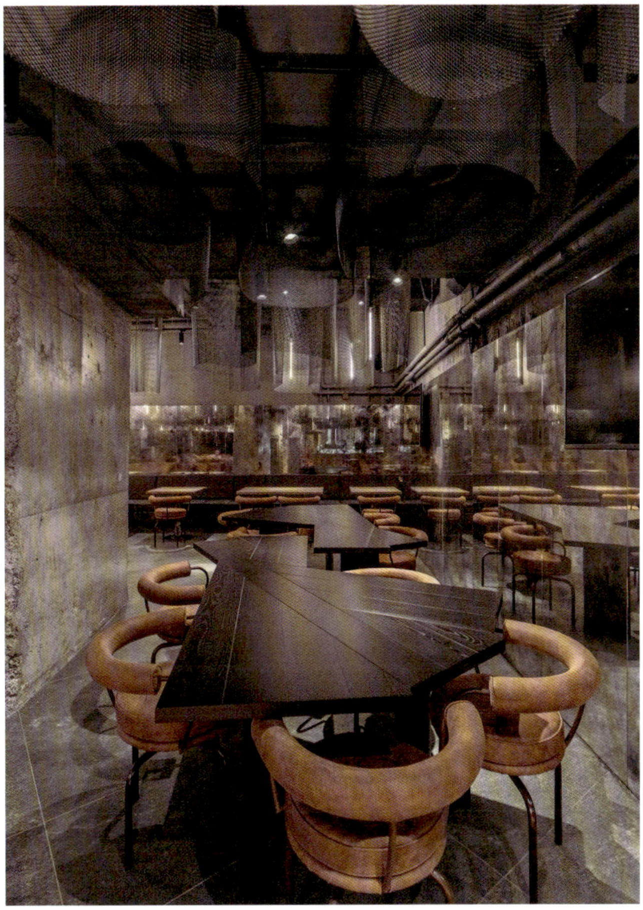

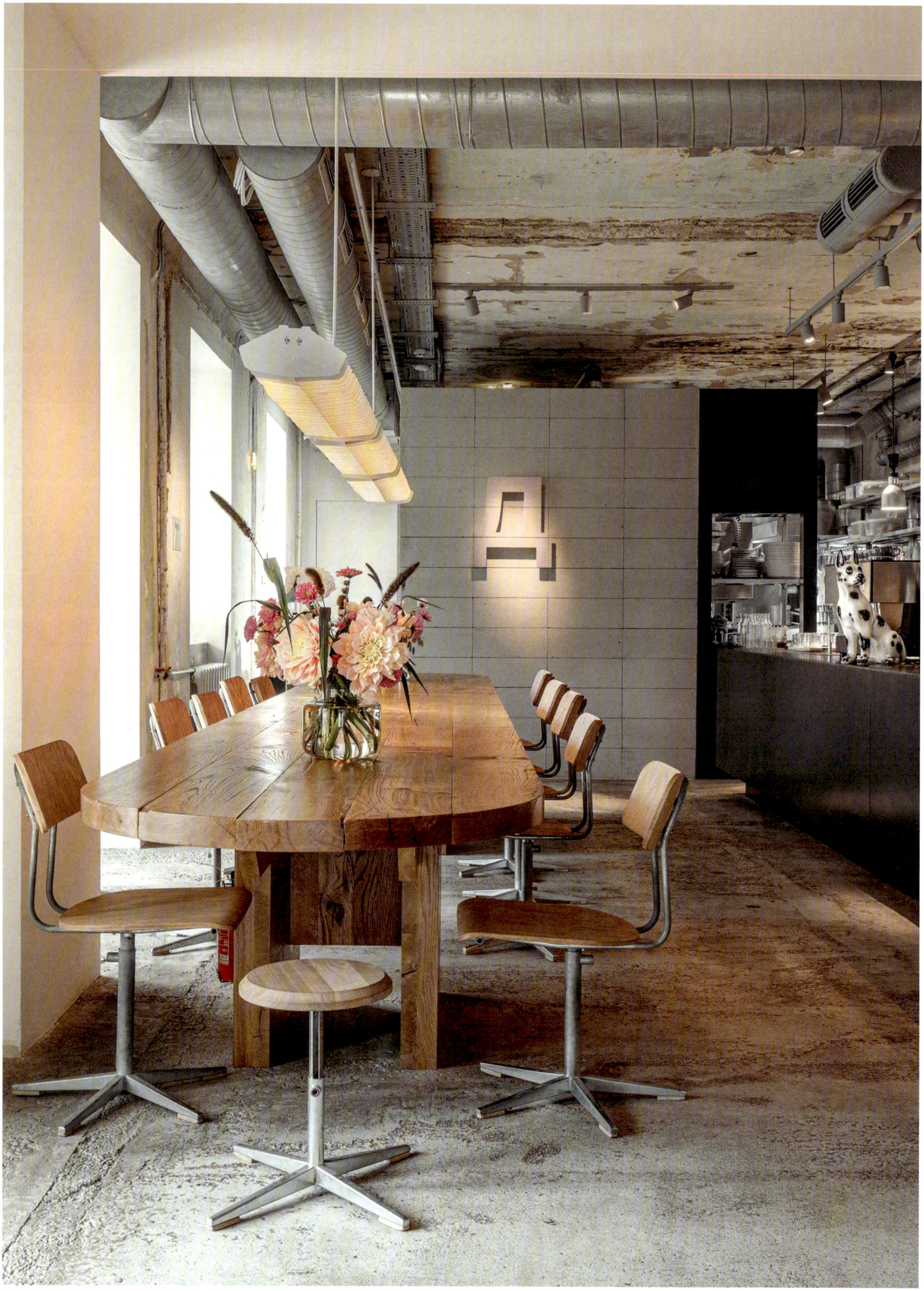

COMMUNITY HEART WITH VINTAGE FLAIR

BALBEK BUREAU
DUBLER

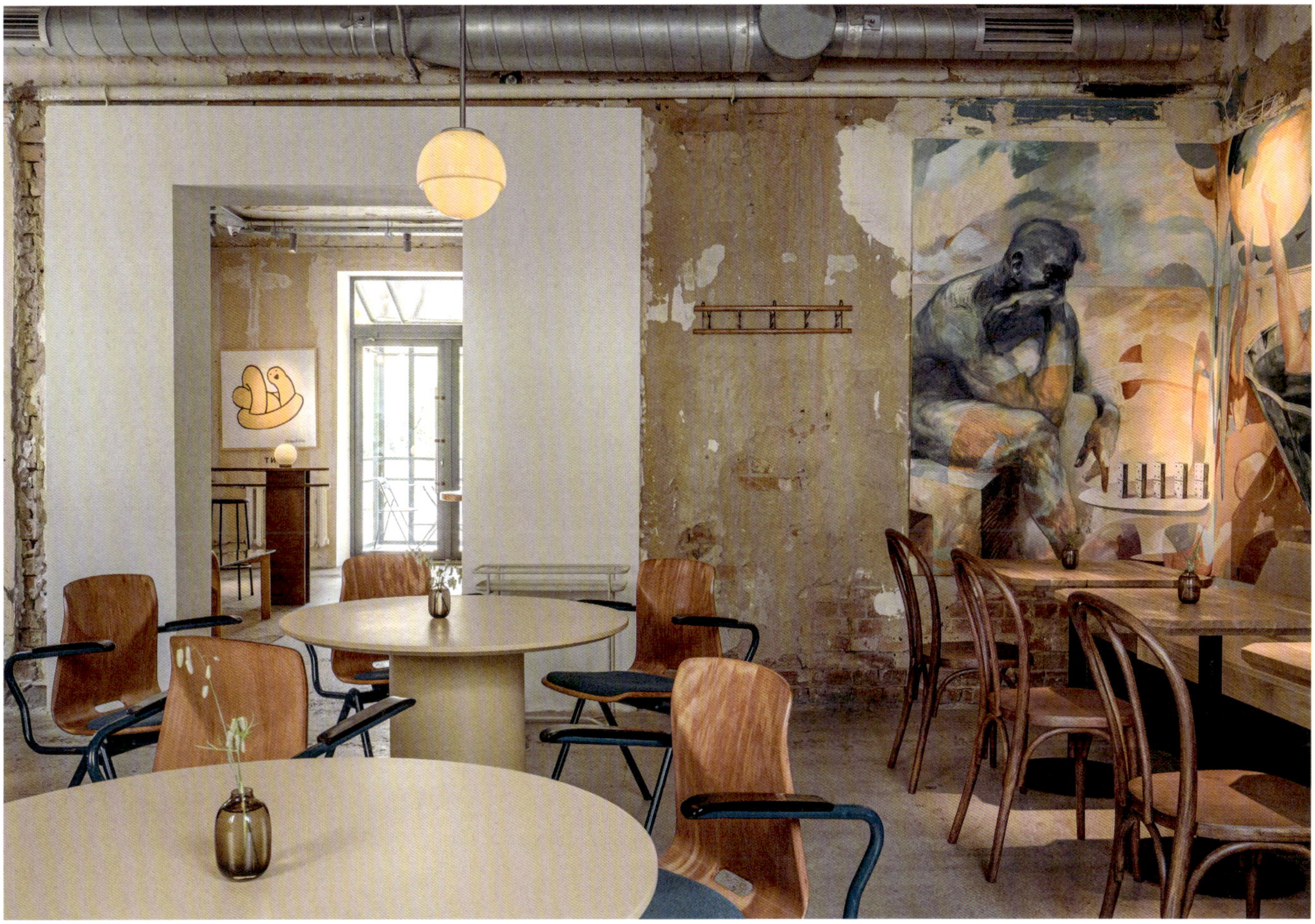

In Dubler, vintage aesthetics highlight the old brick architecture and the atmosphere it conveys.

Dubler is a city café in the Pechersk district of Kyiv, located on the ground floor of a residential building built in the 1970s. The building's arched window facade is partially covered with grapevines, further adding to the space's charm. Dubler's core focus is building a community around its hip cuisine and casual service. With this in mind, the designers decided to create a cozy interior that allows guests to enjoy their food and socialize at the same time. The architecture and atmosphere of the old building was emphasized with the help of vintage furniture and decor. Dubler's vibe is reminiscent of a '70s flea market, but thanks to its simple and clean forms, it never loses touch with the modern world. Upon entering, the first thing that guests see is a bar and a pastry counter. The area is visually enlarged by a mirror that stretches along one of the walls, and by a communal table that runs parallel to the bar (probably the largest the team has designed), drawing the entire space together.

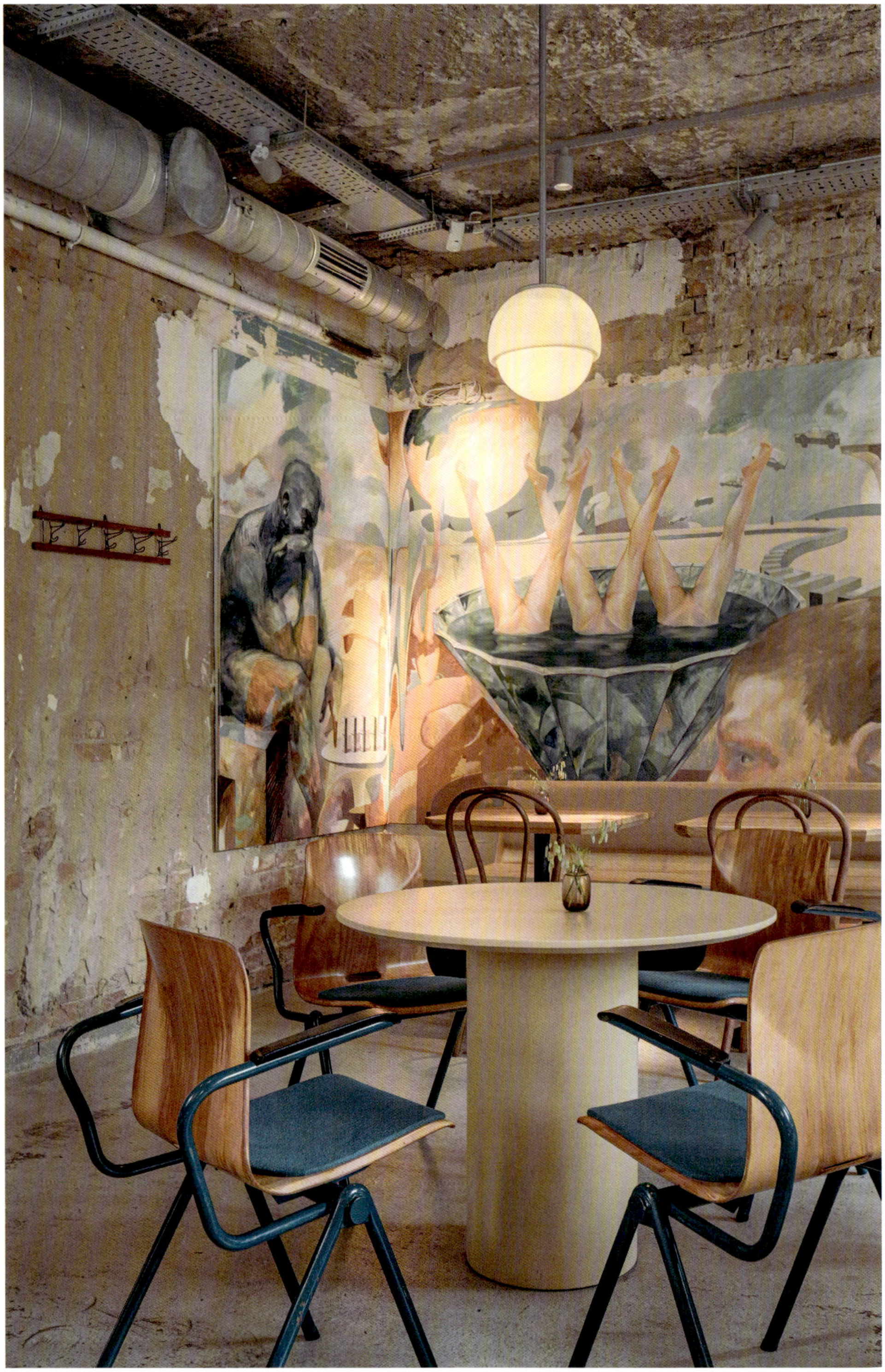

This playful, surrealist mural is the work of Oleksander Grebenyuk. The scene features Rodin's *The Thinker* and an acrobat from a Picasso painting, which, according to the painter, are doubles of each other. The piece also depicts synchronized swimmers diving into a martini glass.

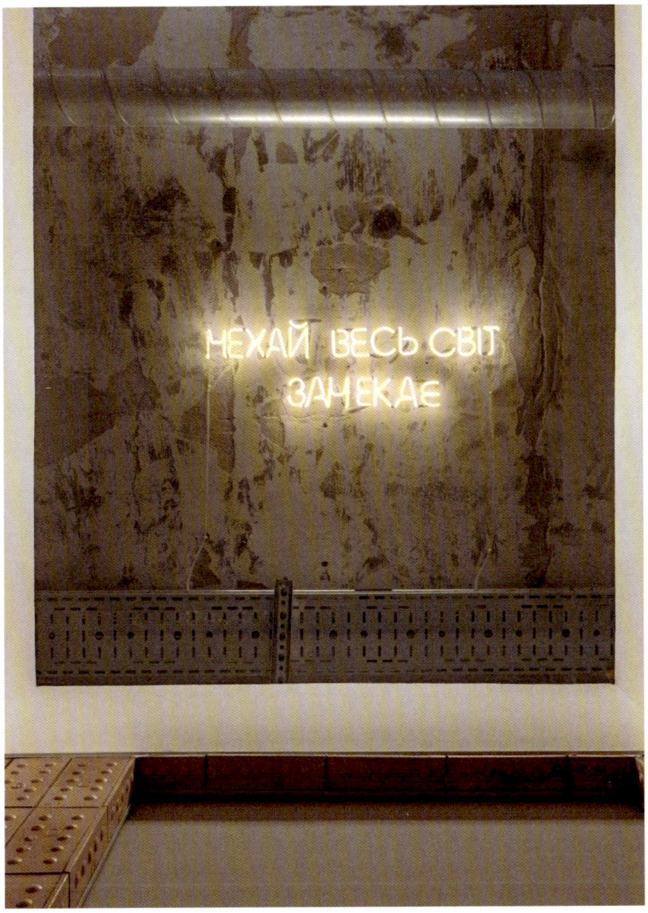
НЕХАЙ ВЕСЬ СВІТ
ЗАЧЕКАЄ

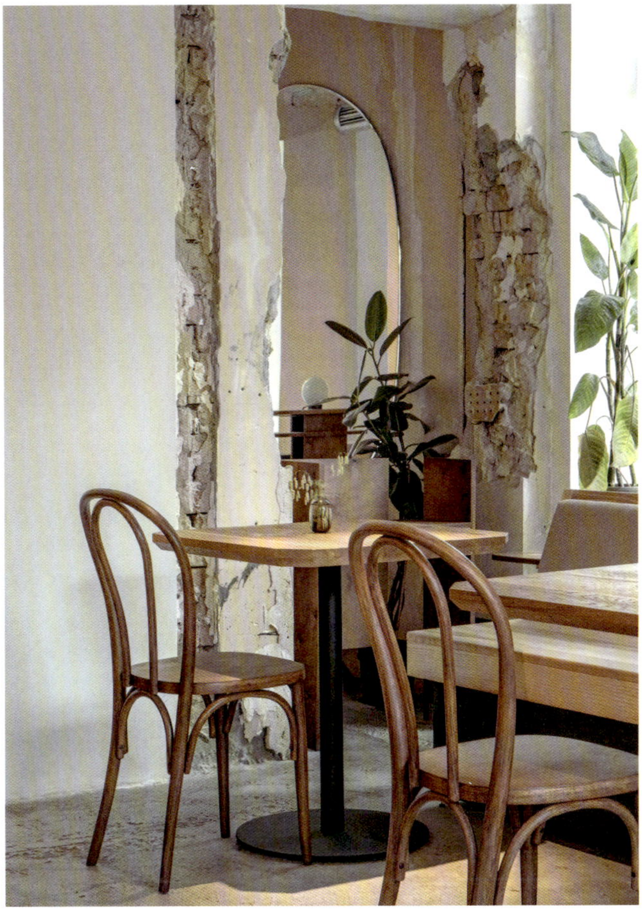

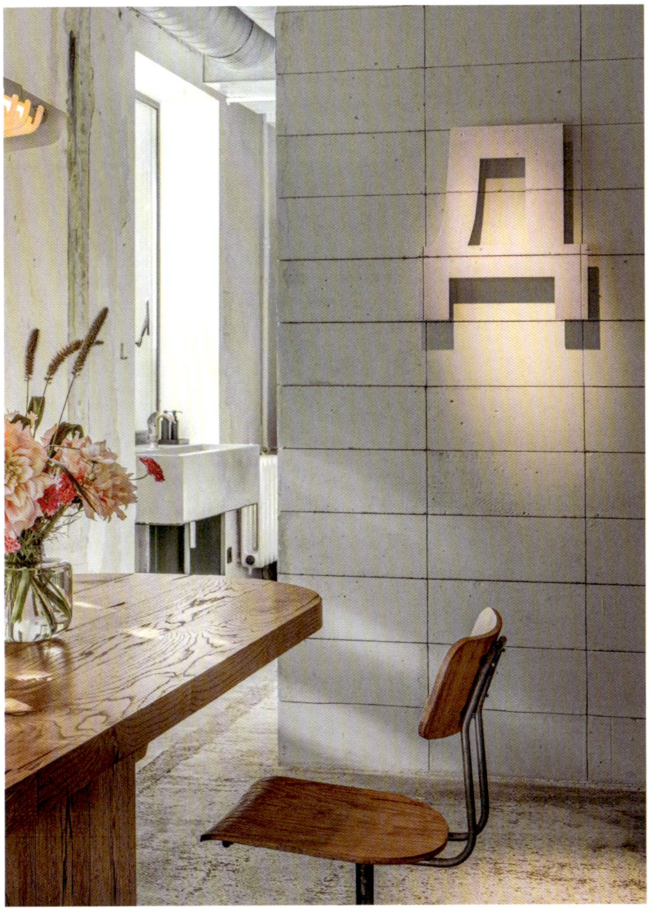
Д

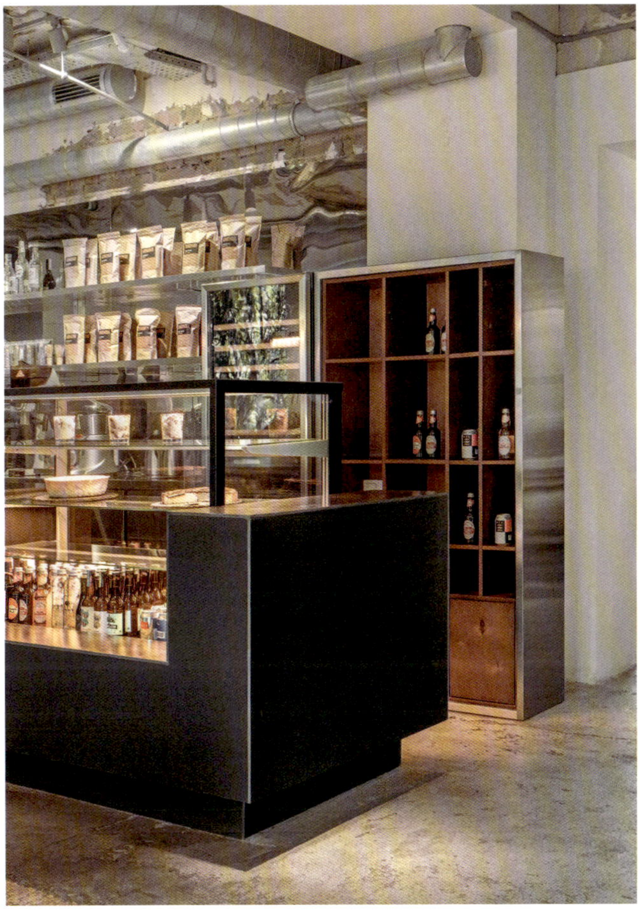

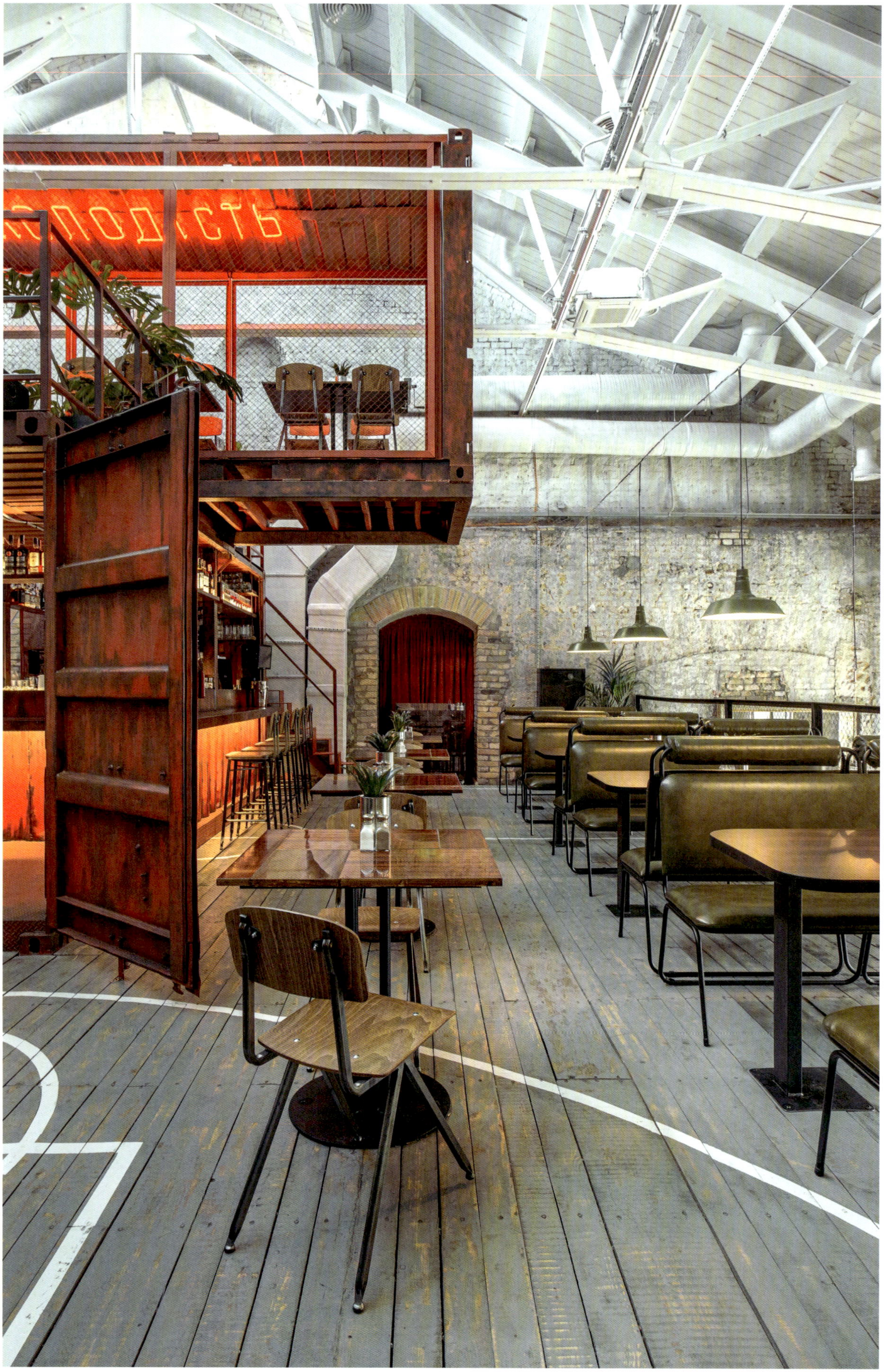

VINTAGE '90S VIBES WITH AN IRONIC TWIST

BALBEK BUREAU
MOLODIST

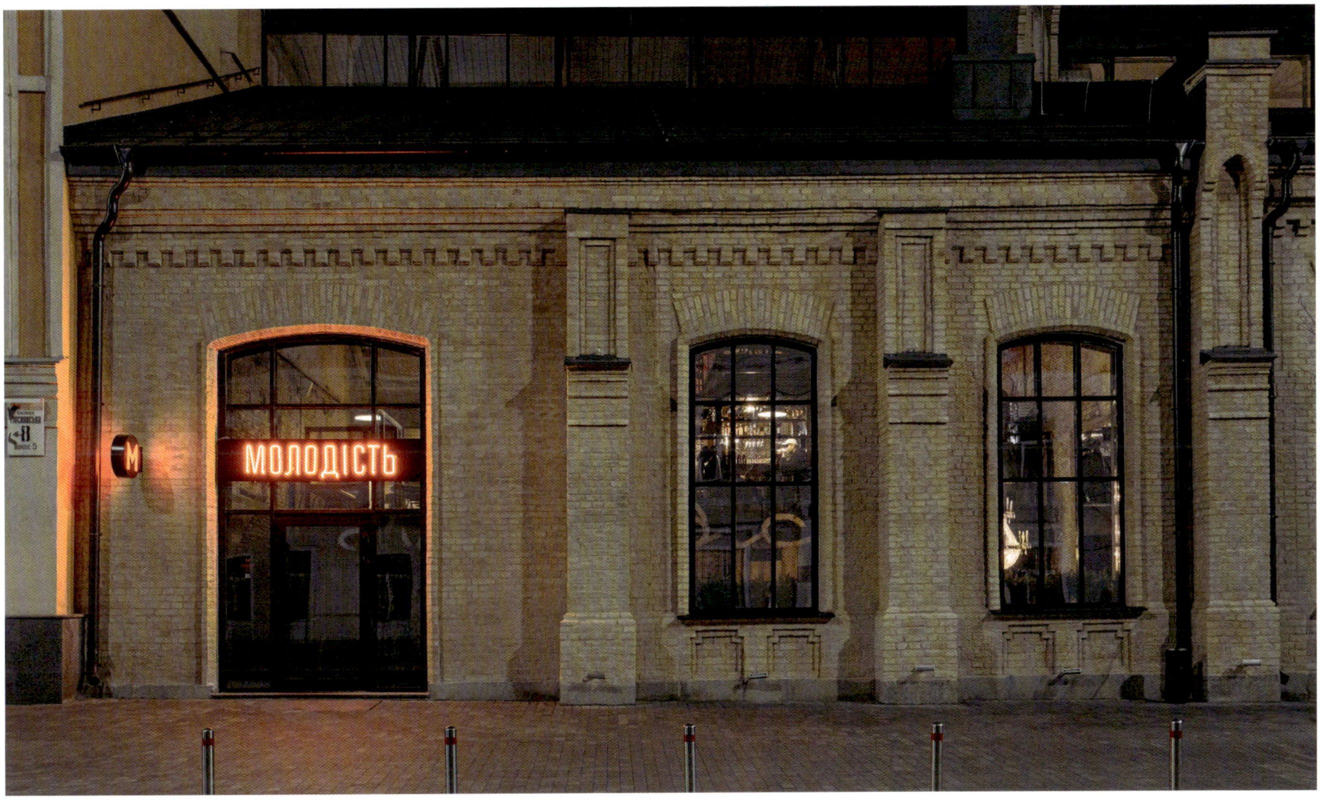

Molodist restaurant is established in an extension of a previous 18th-century military arsenal. Using a mix of vintage items and warm lighting, the designers created a cozy space within the raw industrial premises.

At Molodist restaurant, balbek bureau has thoughtfully curated a diverse collection of '90s post-Soviet memorabilia. Many Ukrainians have negative associations with their country's Soviet past and heritage, so the team wanted to add an ironic touch to the space, placing imaginative, sometimes surreal juxtapositions at the center of their design. The interiors feature real street lanterns, and approximately 90 percent of the furniture is secondhand, including carefully curated pieces purchased from old Soviet apartments. Each detail has its own story: the tabletops were upcycled from old furniture, and much of the seating was reclaimed from decommissioned buses and Soviet-era Lada cars. But then balbek bureau took the design a step further by incorporating freight containers into the layout, creating a central feature from two vertically stacked cargo containers. And finally, a stunning crystal chandelier adds a contrasting touch to the disco ball and the eclectic, vintage-inspired interior.

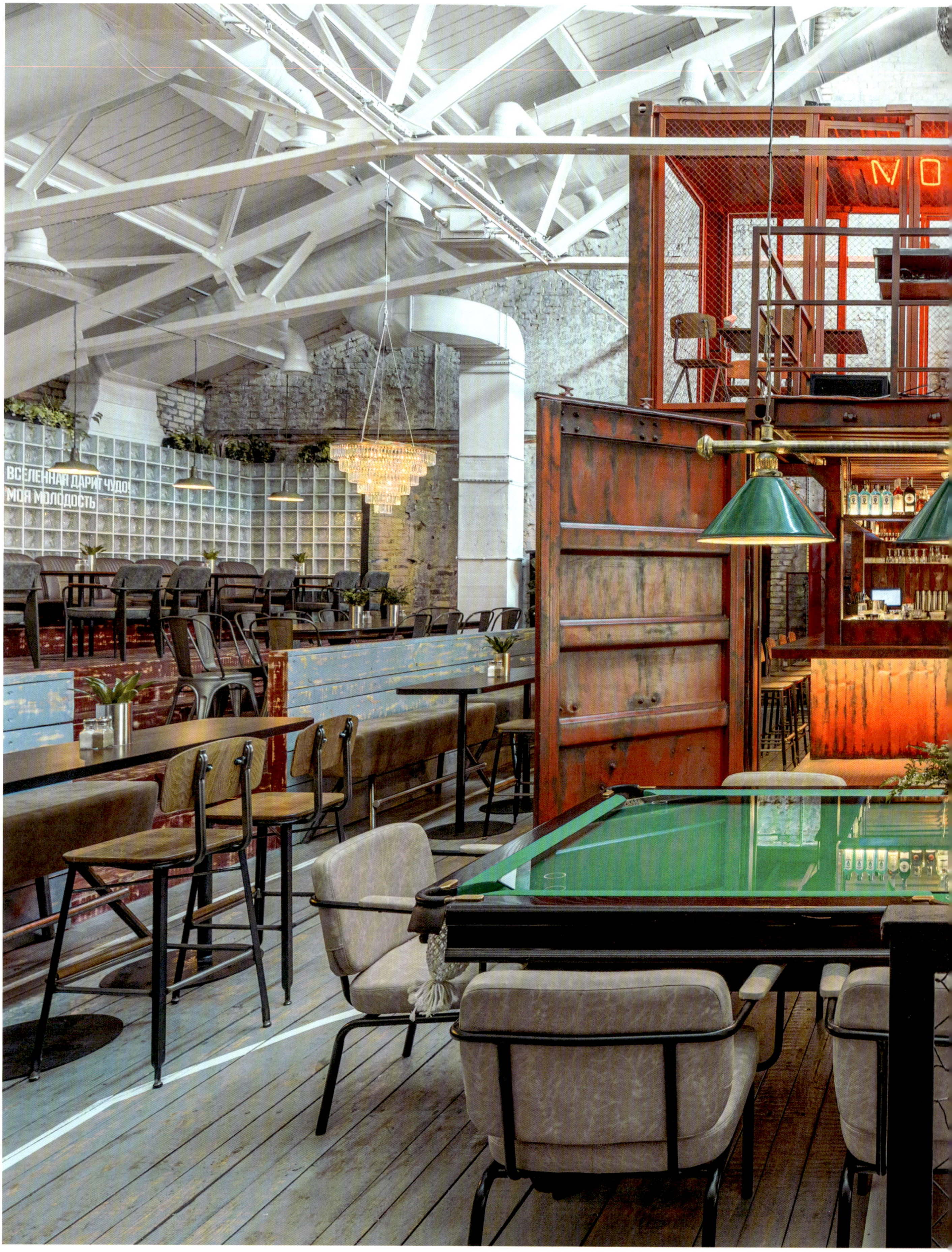
ВСЕЛЕННАЯ ДАРИТ ЧУДО!
МОЯ МОЛОДОСТЬ

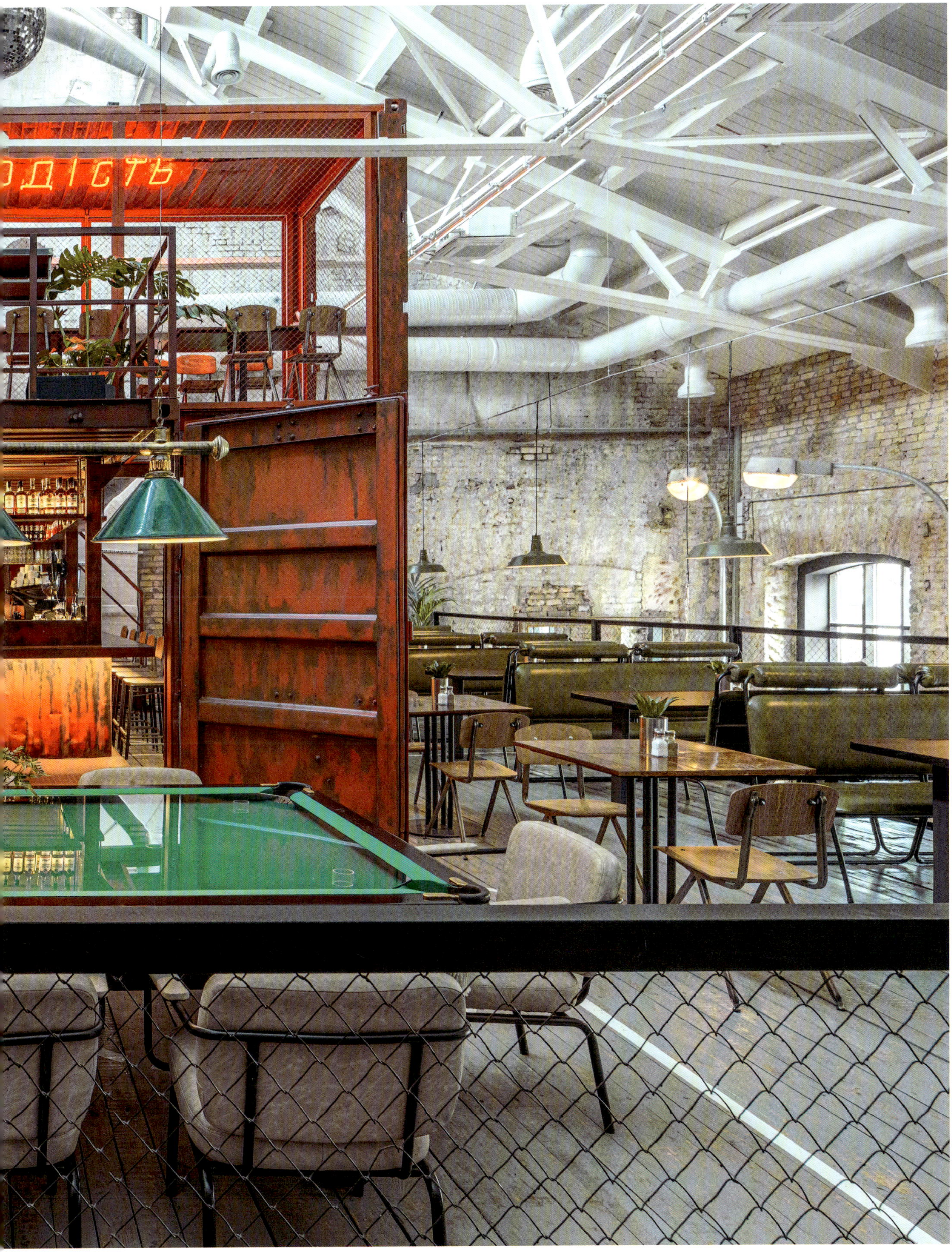

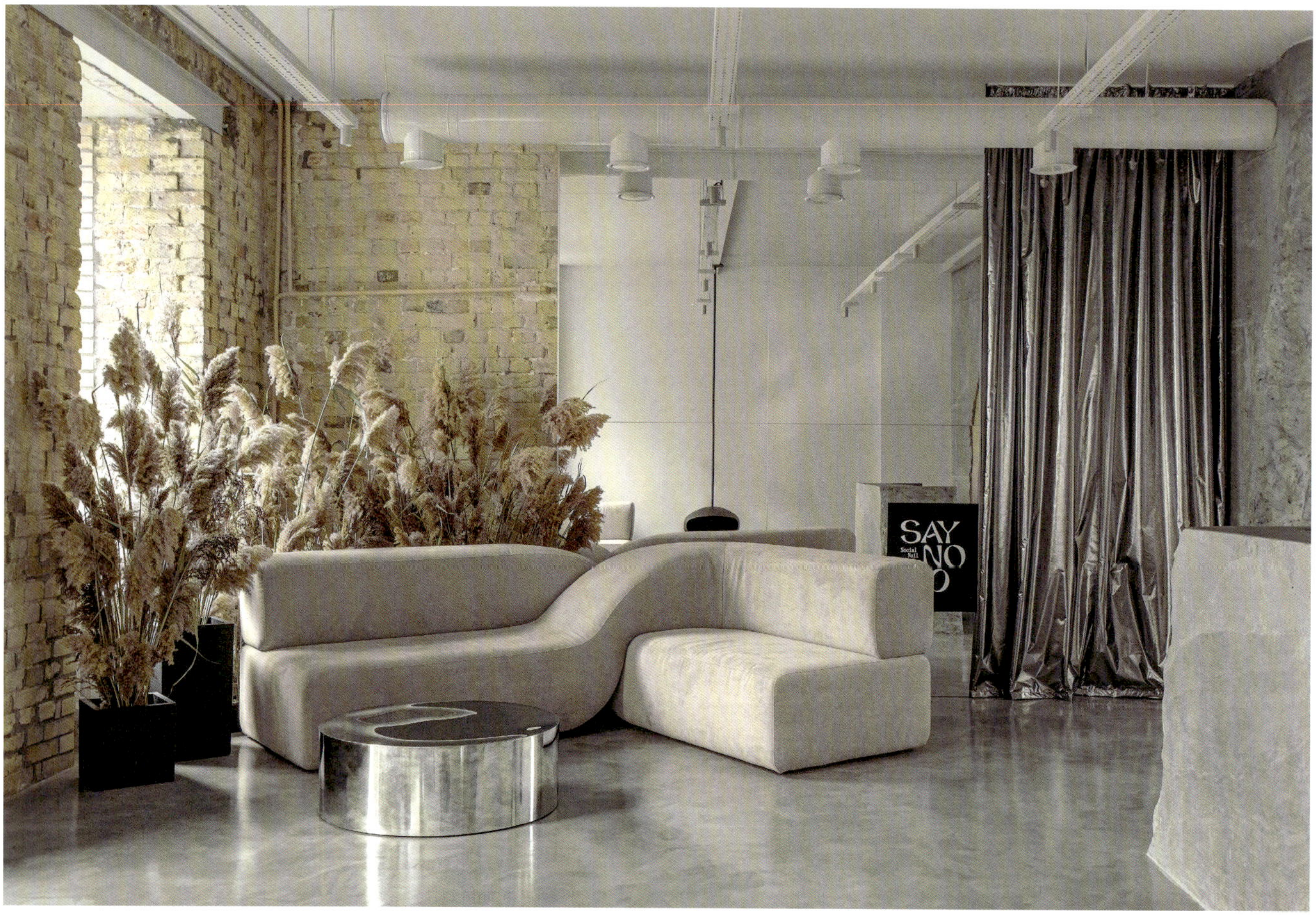
SAY
Social Nail
NO

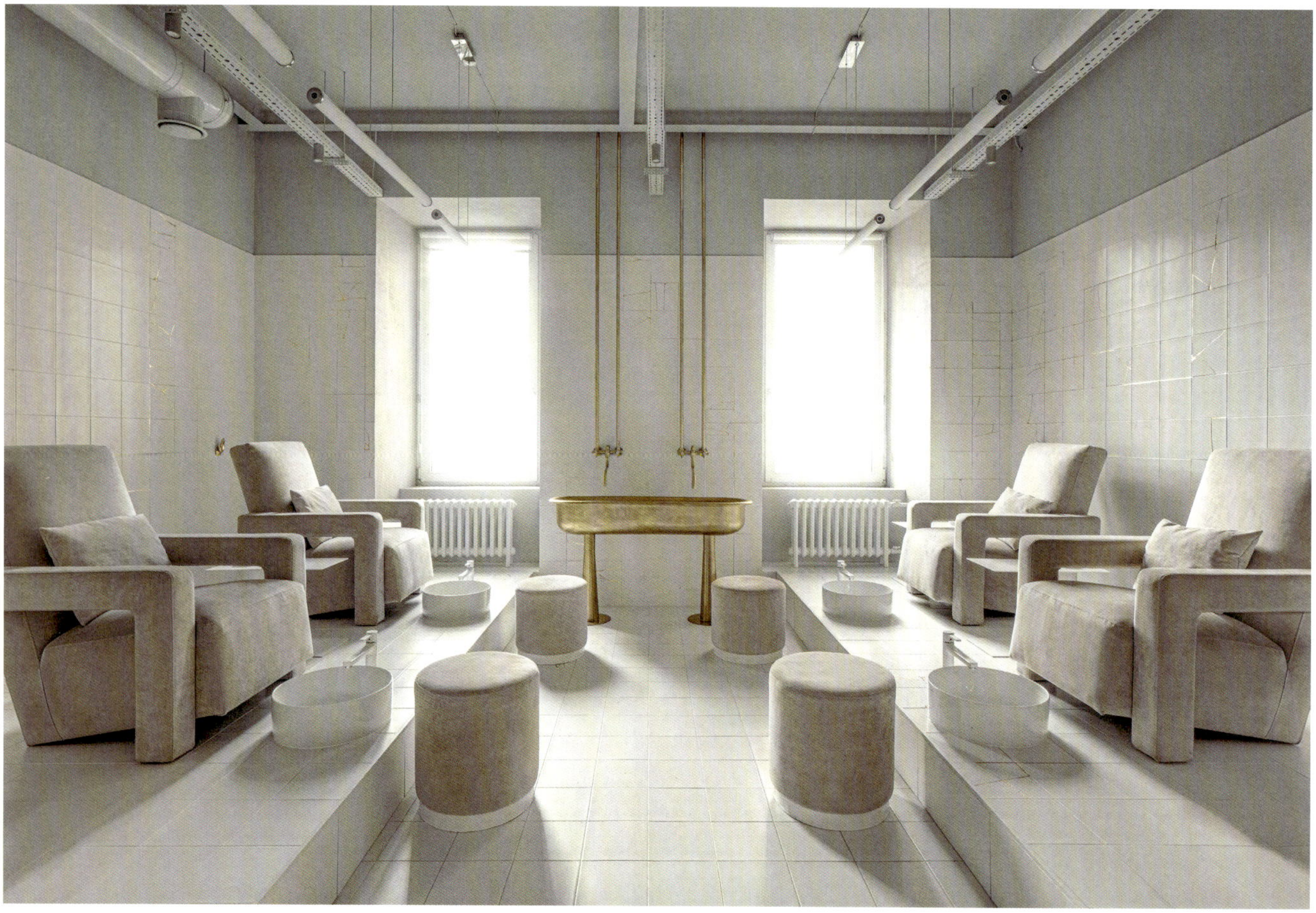

A GENDER-NEUTRAL BEAUTY SANCTUARY

BALBEK BUREAU
SAY NO MO

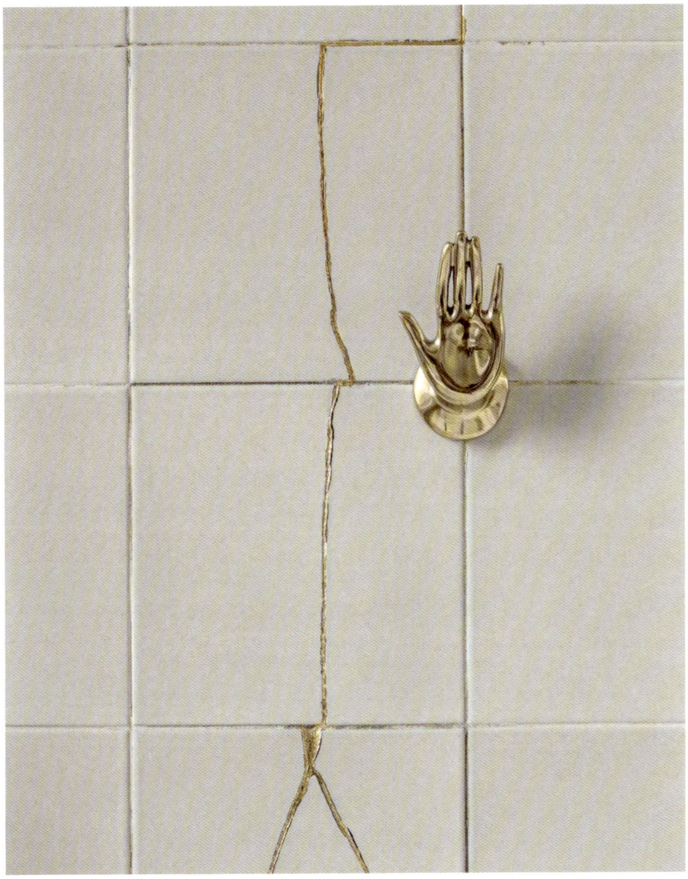

Throughout the entire design process, balbek bureau sought to break away from conventional notions of a beauty salon, including its gender distinction.

Say No Mo was designed by balbek bureau's team as a conceptually new format for a beauty salon. The "heart" of the salon is the bar, which is used for both beauty services and for serving cocktails. Located in a historic building in Kyiv, this stunning 2,153-square-foot (200-square-meter) space spans two levels and boasts a unique geometry of curved walls and a scarcity of parallel surfaces. With lofty 13-foot (4-meter) ceilings and no shortage of quirks (including a free-standing sink assembled from two Soviet-era baby baths), Say No Mo is a salon like no other. One of the main visual accents is a monolithic "broken" arch that looks as if it's been hammered out of an existing concrete wall. The effect is imposing and raw, and the broken appearance serves as a metaphor for shattered stereotypes in the beauty industry. The reception counter, reminiscent of a stone altar, is also made of concrete. To balance the starkness of the concrete, the architects have added large golden panels throughout, lending a warm, luxurious touch to the space.

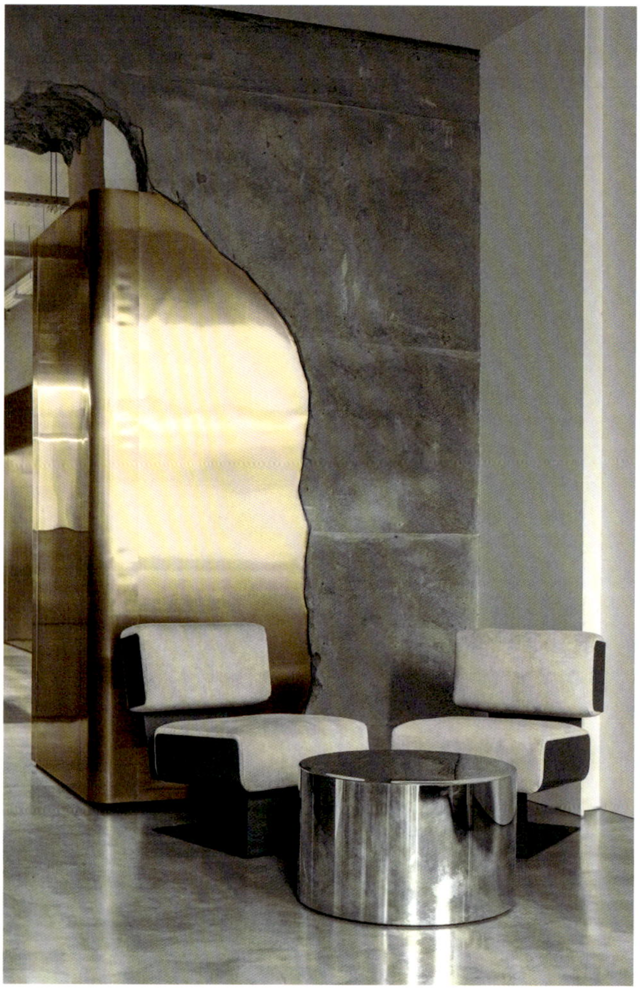

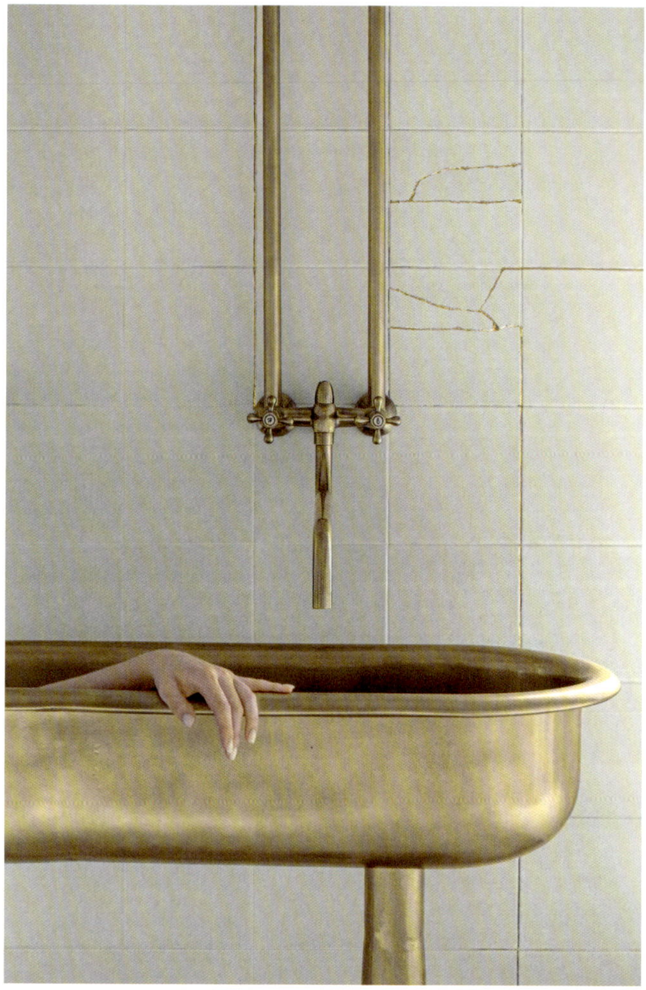

The sleek, imaginative interior of Say No Mo perfectly reflects balbek bureau's approach to design. As its name suggests, the salon has said goodbye to traditional salon design, outdated beauty standards, and strict gender distinctions.

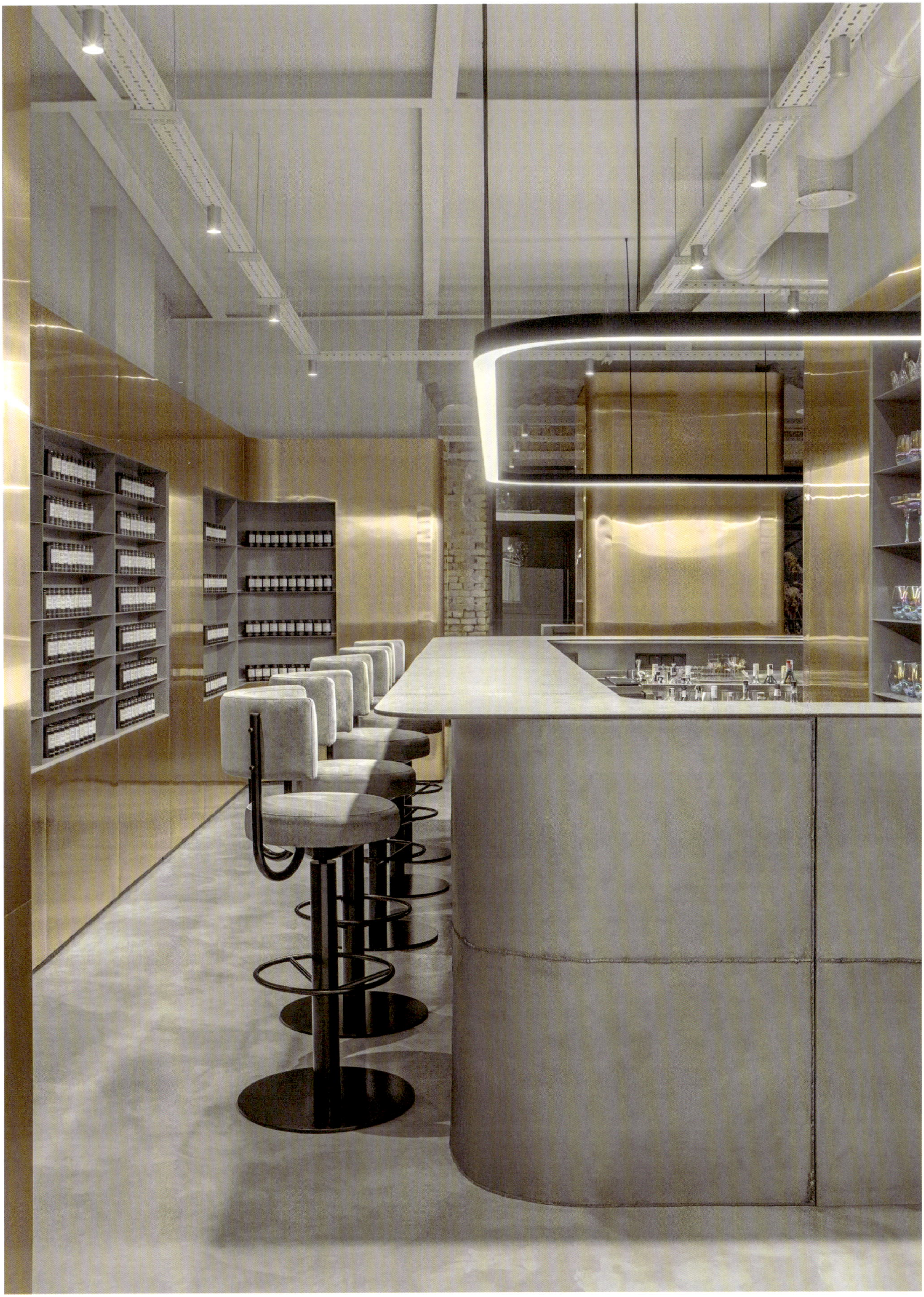

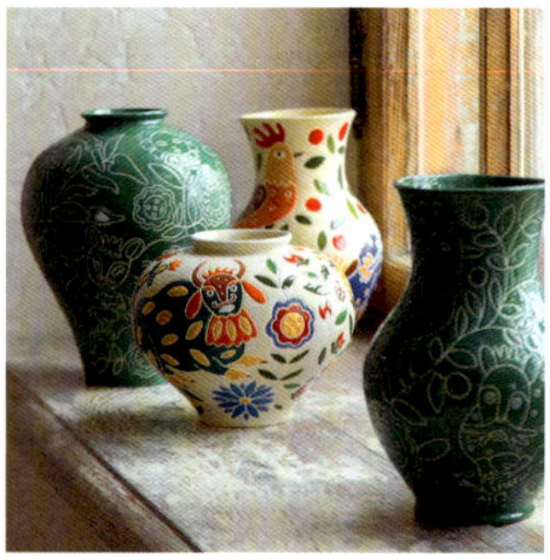

LORASHEN
CERAMICS & FLORISTRY

LoraShen is a Ukrainian company that has been creating original projects in floristry and green design since 2010. The brand's designers, who are inspired by Ukrainian heritage, visit local history museums throughout the country to gain a deeper sense of Ukrainian culture and traditions.

In 2019, the company opened its own ceramic manufactory, employing graduates of the best art schools in Ukraine. In 2020, the company collaborated with the Maria Prymachenko Family Foundation to depict the artist's whimsical animals, birds, and flowers in ceramic form, using ancient etching and glazing techniques.

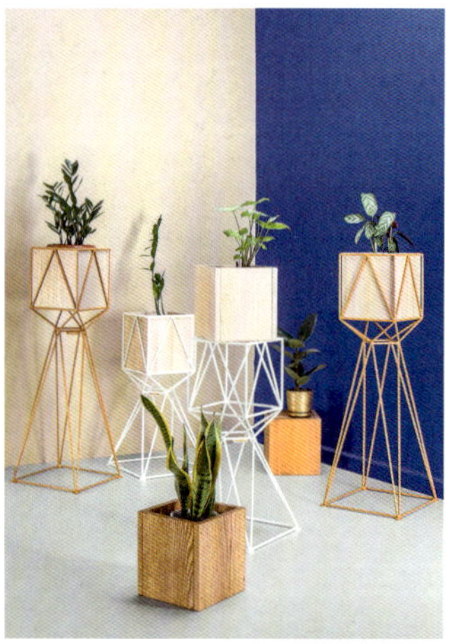

LEVANTIN DESIGN
PRODUCT DESIGN

Levantin Design is an interdisciplinary product design studio founded by brothers Serhii and Oleksandr Lvov. The duo started their venture in 2012 with furniture restoration, but quickly pivoted to manufacturing their own furniture. The studio's approach to design centers around creating a "Wow!" moment in any given space. In the first months of the war, the workshop, located in central Kharkiv, became a shelter for individuals and animals. In July 2022, Levantin Design managed to resume work and continue shipments of finished furniture. In 2022, the studio's products received a multitude of awards at the International Design Awards (IDA) 2022 competition, and were also showcased at Barcelona Design Week 2022, Maison & Objet 2022, High Point Market 2022, and Warsaw Home & Contract 2022 exhibitions.

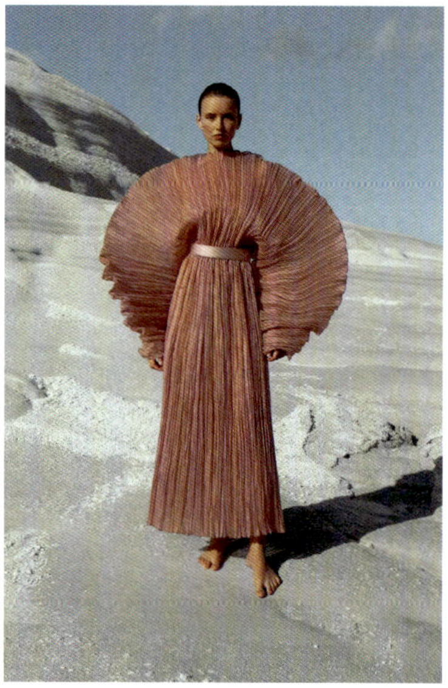

J'AMEMME
FASHION

Julie Yarmoliuk's brand J'amemme is known for its architectural silhouettes and signature pleats. Her dresses have appeared in more than 200 editorials worldwide, graced the cover of *Time* magazine, and have been worn by prominent figures.

With a bold sense of line and a unique range of fabrics and textures, the brand offers a fresh, modern take on femininity. Each pleated couture piece is meticulously crafted by skilled artisans in Ukraine. In addition to pleating, many garments feature stunning hand-embroidery and traditional quilting and knitting techniques. J'amemme pays homage to the hardworking and dedicated people of Ukraine by incorporating spikelets into the ornamentation—a symbol of prosperity and success, underscoring the brand's dedication and solidarity.

The latest collection, FW 22/23, represents a monumental undertaking for the brand, constructed against the backdrop of incredibly challenging circumstances. The collection was a way to offer customers an escape from the harsh realities of war, blackouts, and homesickness.

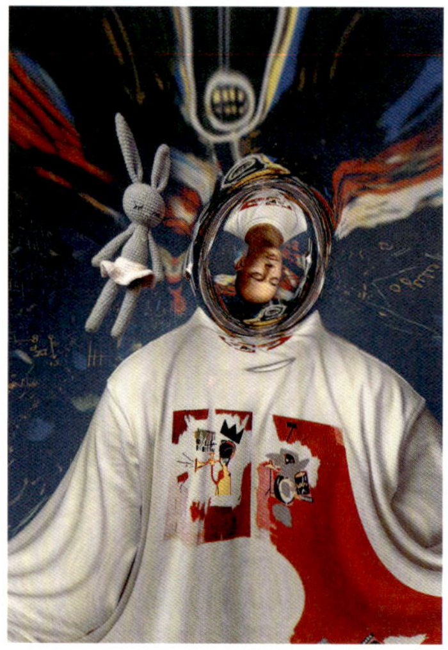

YEVHEN ZAIETS · *ЄВГЕН ЗАЄЦЬ*
VISUAL ARTS

Yevhen Zaiets started working as a photographer in 2011. His work focuses on the human form and color, as well as how visual images can reflect a person's inner world. Zaiets is representative of an emerging movement in art, combining photography and digital images. His works are bright, abstract fantasies that captivate with their shapes, colors, and hidden meanings. Zaiets lives for and through his art, transforming everything that happens, excites, or moves him into images. His passion is driven by the desire to push human boundaries. Living and working in Ukraine, Zaiets says the war has made him feel numb and frozen, and he will only be able to understand its influence on his art with time.

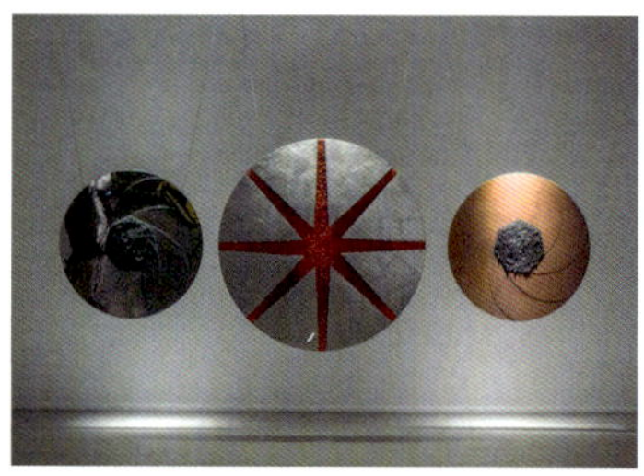

OLEKSII ZOLOTAR · *ОЛЕКСІЙ ЗОЛОТАР*
SCULPTURE

Ukrainians have experienced gaps in their cultural lineage, with traditions being altered or even erased over the centuries. With his art, Oleksii Zolotar is helping to restore historical values and forge a genuine cultural heritage. Working with a range of techniques and materials, he pays homage to former traditions, reimagining and recreating Scythian women and Trypillia motifs in metal and wood.

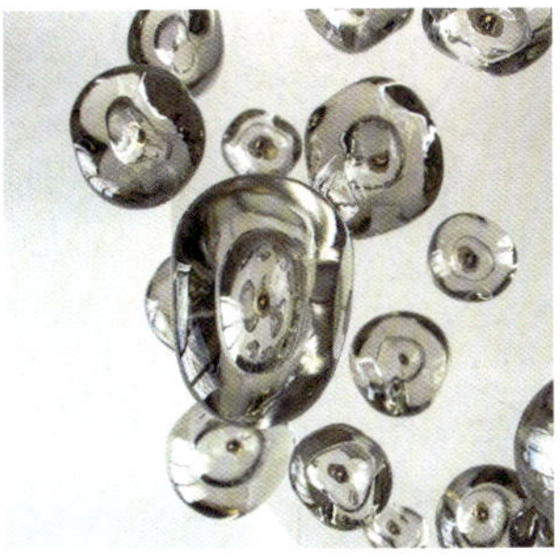

NN ZVIR
PRODUCT DESIGN

The NN ZVIR art glass & lighting brand was founded in 2018 in Kyiv by glass artists Nazarii and Natalia Zvir. Nazarii grew up in a family of talented artists, and now the pair continues the family legacy, hoping to preserve and promote Ukraine's glass industry in the process.

NN ZVIR uses cutting-edge, proprietary technology to craft their exquisite glass decor and custom artistic lighting solutions. Using materials like tempered glass, metal, and stone, each piece is handmade by artisans, lending the products their uniqueness and originality. Numerous traditional motifs are inspired directly by nature.

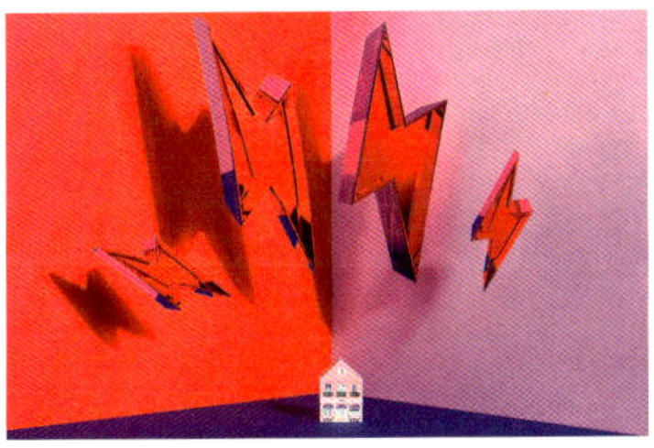

LLIWELL
GRAPHIC DESIGN

LLIWELL established by the husband-and-wife duo Nonna Starushchenko and Glib Kaporikov, specializes in strategic design, branding, book design, and packaging.

The founders started the agency as a form of protest: they rejected the visual and cultural landscape that prevailed in Ukraine in the 2000s, which they saw as a jumbled mixture of decaying post-Soviet aesthetics and pseudo-European influences. The only solution was to take things into their own hands. For the founders, the most valuable aspect of their work is creating projects that leave room for exploration and convey deeper meanings.

When designing the first print issue of *Telegraf.design* magazine, they conducted extensive research and studied the work of great 20th-century Ukrainian artists, including Heorhii Narbut and Vasyl Krychevskyi, luminaries of Ukrainian graphics and design. The magazine included numerous quotes and allusions to these artists, whose creative legacy continues to inspire new generations.

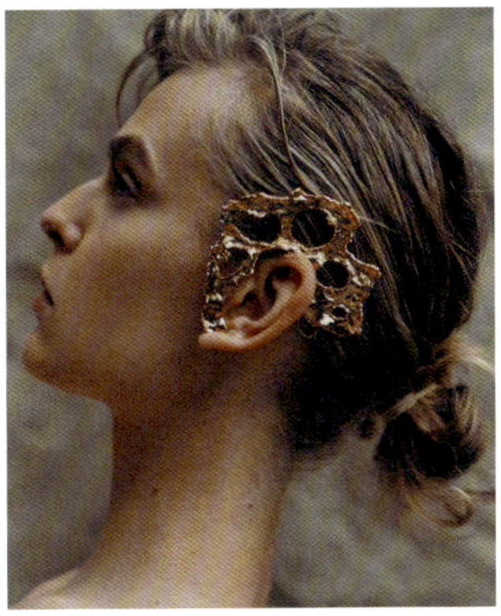

JULIE KLEOM · *ЮЛІЯ КЛЕОМ*
JEWELRY

Jewelry designer Julie Kleom combines artistry with craftsmanship, producing exceptional pieces that are artistic achievements. In the creation process, Kleom studies Ukrainian cultural codes, traditions, and obscure symbols. Kleom blends the ancient with the modern, using a millennia-old method to apply gold to various metals.

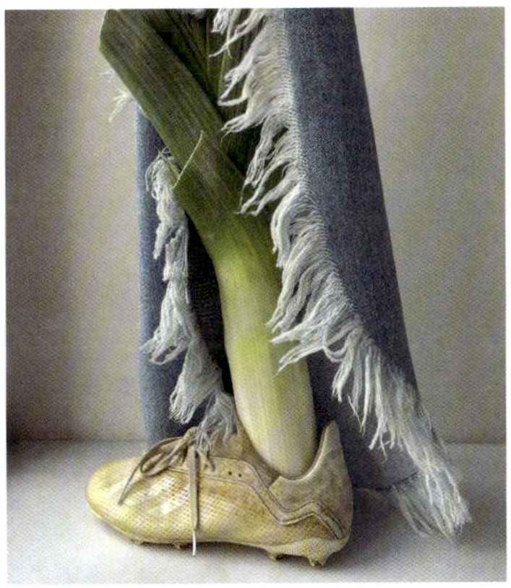

KSENIASCHNAIDER
FASHION

Kseniaschnaider brand hallmarks are sustainable production and "design minus design" philosophy. The design team is an active player in the avant-garde denim niche. The brand's fame skyrocketed when Bella Hadid wore their Demi-Denims, a mix between culottes and skinny jeans.

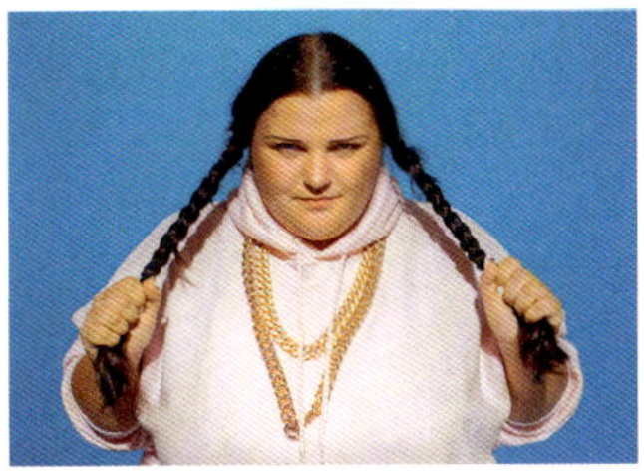

ALYONA ALYONA
MUSIC

Alona Savranenko, better known by her stage name alyona alyona, has made a name for herself with her unique approach to hip-hop and her unconventionally quirky humor. As one of Ukraine's top hip-hop artists, this spirited rapper and songwriter advocates for empowerment and body positivity, and raps about politically charged themes like tolerance and acceptance. In 2019, *Vogue* dubbed her "Ukraine's Most Unlikely Rap Star." Alyona alyona's recent mini-album "Dai Boh," a product of wartime, brings together six artists from five different countries—Ukraine, Poland, Germany, Latvia, and Lithuania—and features lyrics in five languages.

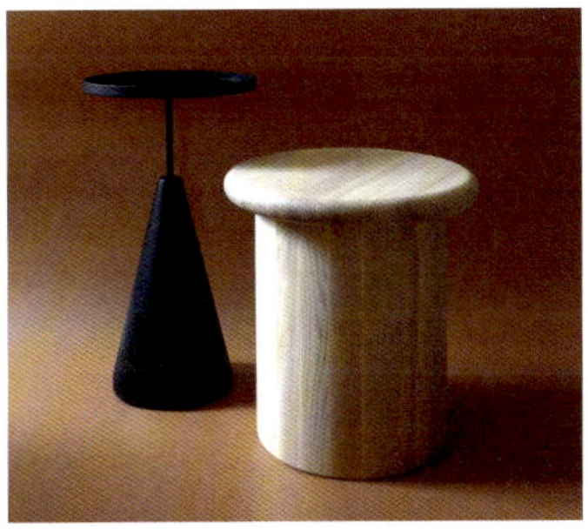

STARITSKA MAYSTERNYA
PRODUCT DESIGN

Staritska Maysternya, a craft furniture and home decor brand, draws its inspiration from nature and traditional Ukrainian crafts. In addition to the core team, the workshop works with independent craftspeople. They primarily work with wood, but also use metal, flax, and woven textiles in their products.

Handcrafted from natural substances, the products are defined by minimal forms, sculptural elements, tactile surfaces, and a fusion of both refined and rustic materials. The studio creates unique items from wild and vintage wood that resemble sculpture more than carpentry. They also use textile elements handwoven from cotton cord, using a traditional weaving technique that has been lovingly and skillfully reinterpreted by textile artist Ira Balbek.

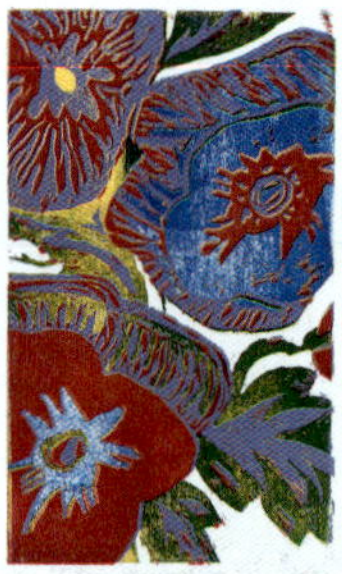

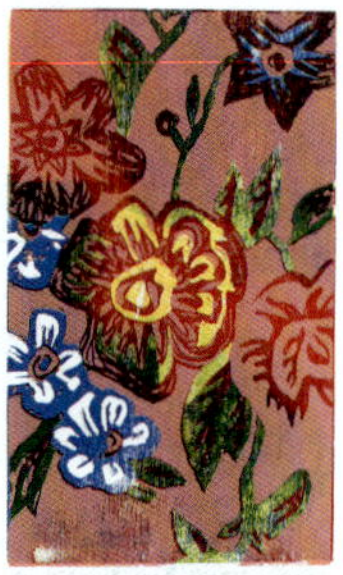

OLEG GRYSHCHENKO · *ОЛЕГ ГРИЩЕНКО*
PAINTING

Oleg Gryshchenko is an artist and illustrator, and co-founder and curator of the Pictoric Illustrators Club. His conceptual project "Florescence. Greenhouse conditions" pays tribute to Ukrainian cultural memory and the work of Ukrainian folk masters. Gryshchenko based his graphic stencil compositions on flowers in folk paintings. Other influences include Petrykivka painting (a traditional Ukrainian decorative painting style), and the art of Hanna Sobachko-Shostak, known for her colorful folk art. The result is a varied, expressive, and visually stunning collection of floral compositions.

Gryshchenko took select fragments of flowers from 20th-century Ukrainian folk art and spun them into new compositions, focusing on previously overlooked details, for his work "Flowers and Fragments."

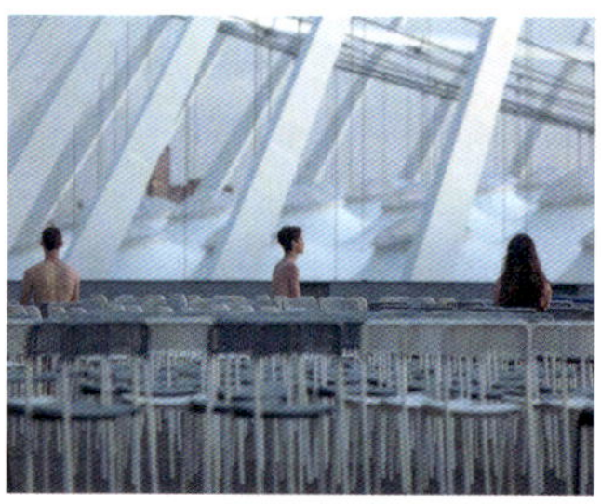

UKHO
MUSIC

The Ukho Agency, a Kyiv-based organization dedicated to contemporary, classical, and experimental music, started with a series called "Architecture of Voice," 19 legendary concerts that took place in various city locations: at the pool, nude beach, botanical garden greenhouse (where viewers were sitting in the tropical bushes), and St. Cyril's Church.

The unique combination between music and place allowed curators to develop a one-of-a-kind rhythmic palette for Kyiv. With the mission to "reappropriate Kyiv back through the music," as co-founder Sasha Andrusyk once said in an interview, Ukho has managed to attract a diverse audience who could hardly imagine being seen together: poets, media artists, musicians, techno club kids, and many more.

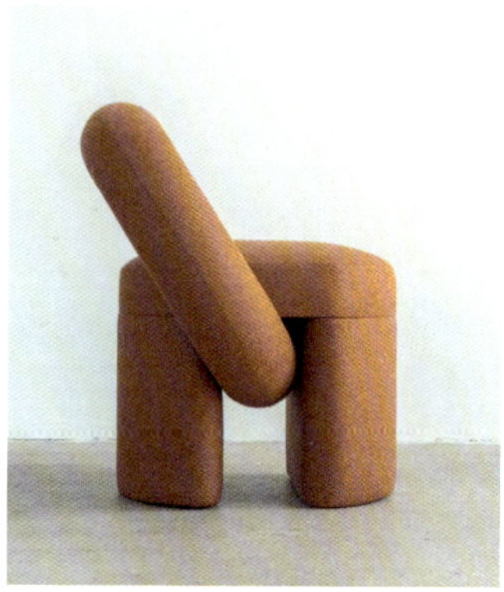

DMYTRO KOZINENKO · *ДМИТРО КОЗІНЕНКО*
PRODUCT DESIGN

Dmytro Kozinenko started his career as a graphic artist before transitioning to product design. He has collaborated with brands such as Roche Bobois, Durame, Breitenthaler, and others. He draws inspiration from Ukrainian rural life; one example is his collection of poufs, DROVA, which resembles a pile of firewood stacked near the stove. Another noteworthy design by Kozinenko is the Play Chair, crafted for the Ukrainian brand WOO. Its playful design won Kozinenko a Best of Year Award from *Interior Design* magazine.

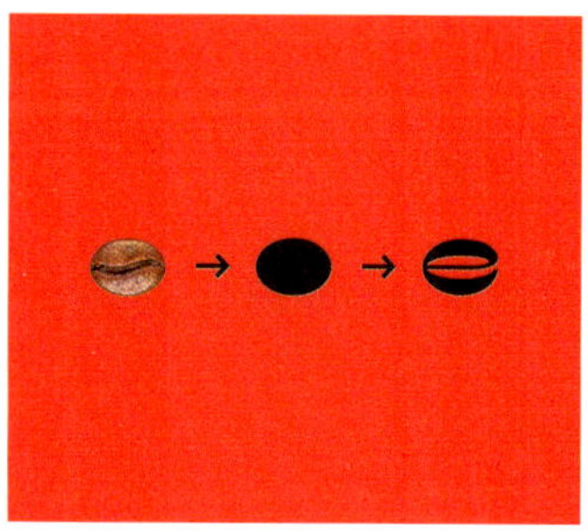

DOZEN AGENCY
BRANDING

Founded by Maksym Lesniak in 2017, Dozen's work can be found in practically any supermarket in Ukraine. The studio specializes in packaging, and its work is diverse, playful, and colorful. Dozen's portfolio includes everything from labels for mass-produced goods to graphic design for a coffee roastery, and even the brand identity for a children's clinic.

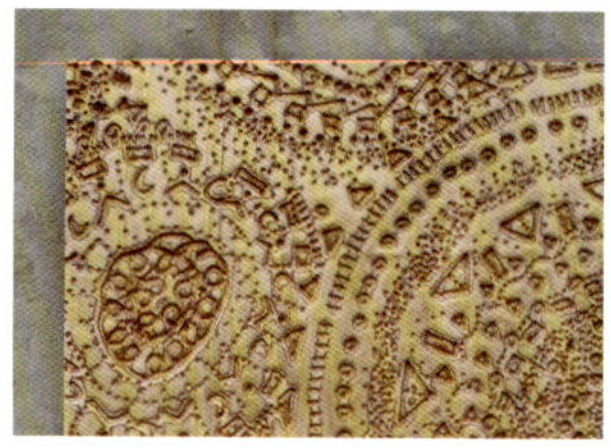

VENKO
PRODUCT DESIGN

Venko started out making custom furniture and assorted plywood structures. In 2018, the founders shifted their creative focus to putting a modern twist on the traditional art of wood carving, creating patterned 3D plywood panels. This method merges machine technology with manual labor, creating a product with distinct handmade charm and the intricate precision of machine processing. Their products can be found in private residences, restaurants, hotels, and offices.

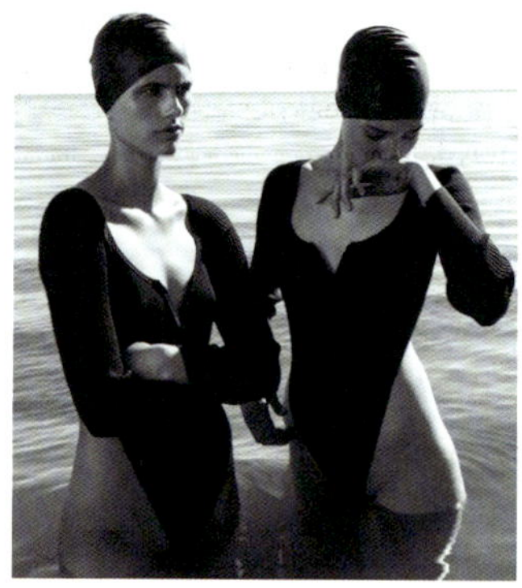

BEVZA
FASHION

Bevza's design aesthetic is defined by sleek, clean silhouettes, sharp tailoring, and a soft color palette. By emphasizing chic and sensual lines, Bevza creates modern minimalist pieces. The key "white dress concept" is built on the idea of a pure, iconic piece of clothing.

The brand also infuses updated folk motifs into its designs, with Svitlana Bevza, the founder and creative director, skillfully incorporating cultural codes and traditional symbols into her modern creations. In 2019, the brand created its signature "spikelets" jewelry, inspired by the age-old Ukrainian wheat motif, a symbol of harvest, prosperity, and fertility. In the Spring/Summer 2023 collection, the symbolic jewelry was reinterpreted with "burned" spikelets, whose more somber details serve as a reminder of what war has done to the fruitful Ukrainian fields.

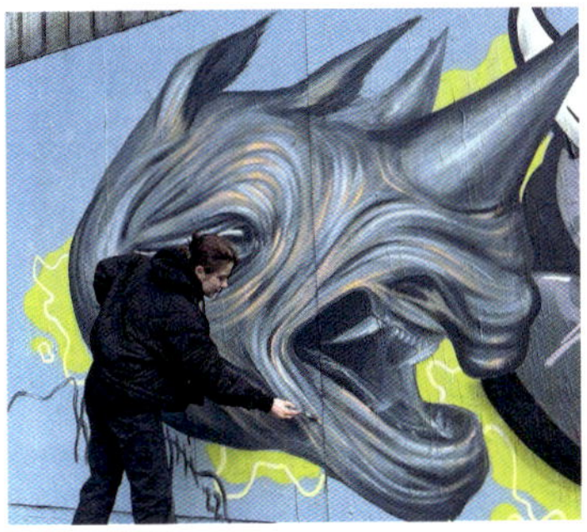

KATERYNA KOMENDANT · *КАТЕРИНА КОМЕНДАНТ*
STREET ART

The artist Kateryna Komendant started her career painting on canvas, but soon gravitated toward street art. After the outbreak of the war, Komendant moved to Sweden and immersed herself in the local creative scene. In the months following the invasion, she was unable to define how she wanted to depict what she felt and saw around her. Komendant believes that the world and society have become so surreal that it is hard to believe that anything is real. As a result, many people, including Komendant herself, resort to escapism to feel more comfortable. This confuses and inspires her; she wants to show people's weaknesses and what they ultimately lead to.

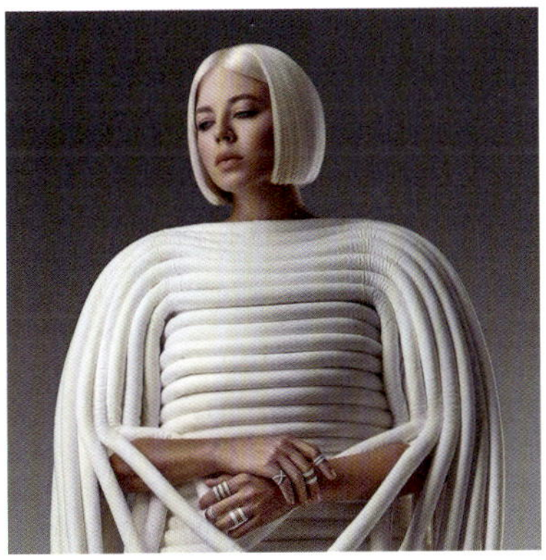

ONUKA
MUSIC

The ONUKA project was created in 2013 by musicians Nataliia Zhyzhchenko and Yevhen Filatov. Using the distinctive sounds of Ukrainian national instruments, which have been echoing from Ukraine for centuries, the band addresses social issues like the war in Ukraine, the Chornobyl disaster, the environmental crisis, and female empowerment.

The band's most recent music video, *Soul of the People*, holds special significance for the group—it was produced in partnership with performers from the Chernihiv region, and released in 2022 to commemorate the Holodomor anniversary. The artists draw parallels between two Russian crimes against the Ukrainian population: the Holodomor of 1932–1933 and the recent full-scale invasion.

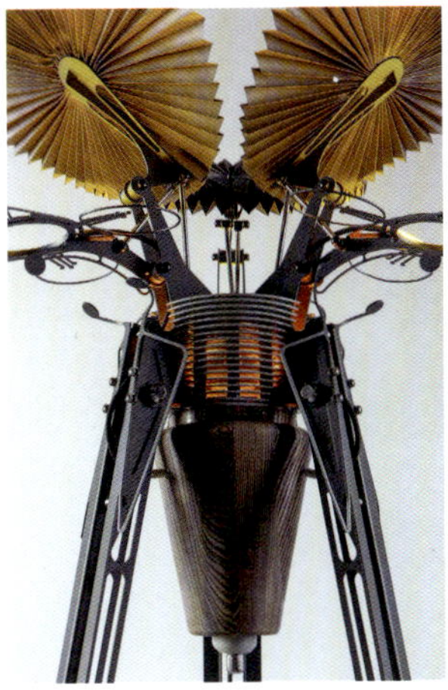

SMITH & WINKEN
SCULPTURE

Established by Valery Kuznetsov and Otto Winken, Smith & Winken is a studio lab that designs kinetic sculptures. The studio's mission is clear: to inspire a mechanical renaissance in this age of electronics and virtuality. Kuznetsov's expertise in utilitarian design and Winken's technical thinking result in pieces that showcase their individual talents and the essence of their shared artistic vision.

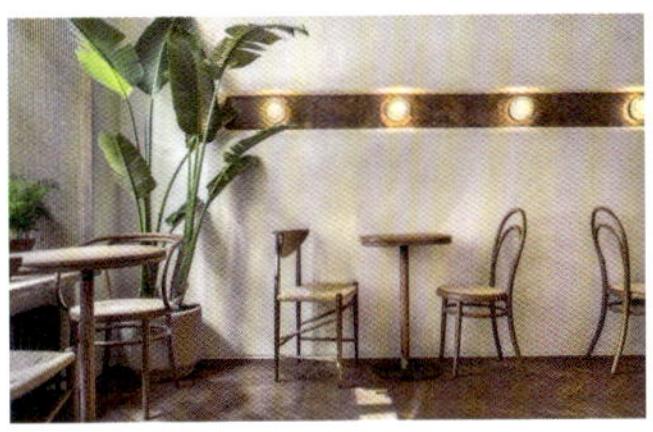

SIVAK+PARTNERS
INTERIOR DESIGN

Dmitry Sivak, Alexey Gulesha, and Maksym Iuriichuk are the co-owners of Sivak+Partners, an architectural and design firm based in Odesa. Their philosophy is grounded in the belief that context is crucial to a concept's evolution. As such the firm strives to integrate design, art, and comfort seamlessly into their assignments. Their projects are notable for their melding of past and present styles from around the world.

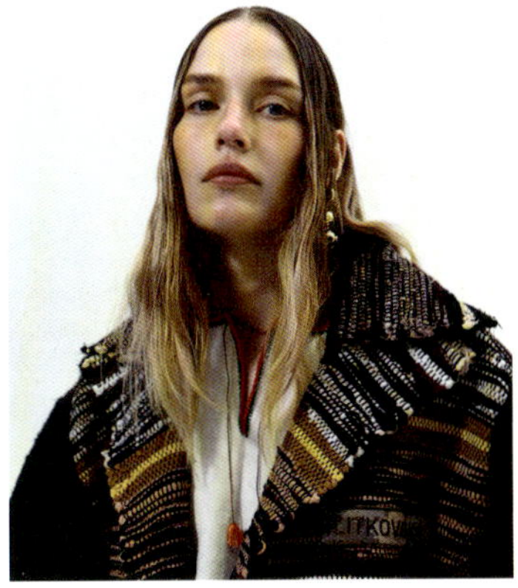

LITKOVSKA
FASHION

Lilia Litkovska, creative director and founder of Litkovska, sees her creativity as an expression of the intangible aspects of life that touch the soul. A key aspect of her work involves traveling through Ukraine, collecting materials and studying traditional craft techniques. The SS23 "Vesnianka" collection pays tribute to Ukrainian spring songs, a traditional way of welcoming new beginnings and expressing hope for a better future.

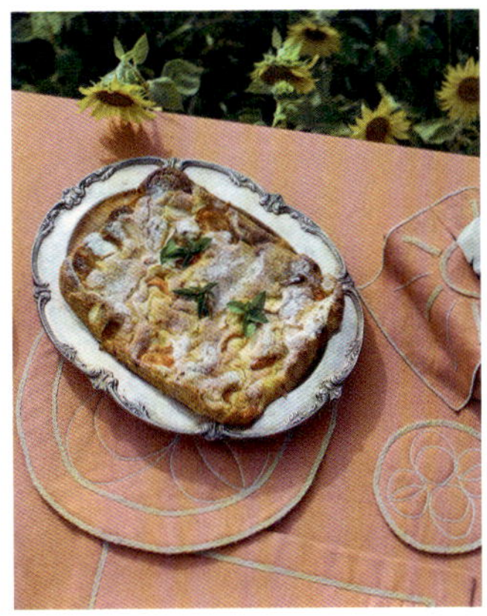

OSELYA HOME AND GARDEN
HOME DECOR

Iryna Kovalchouk, mastermind behind numerous iconic events in Ukraine, is celebrated for her ability to create whole new worlds. Her one-of-a-kind table settings play an important role in this, so naturally, Kovalchouk and her agency partners wanted to create a brand that celebrates the art of home styling while staying grounded in the rich legacy of Ukrainian cultural traditions. And so OSELYA Home and Garden was born. The brand offers a wide range of home furnishings and tableware, including throw pillows, tablecloths, placemats, napkins, and table runners.

LUCIA BONDAR,

a seasoned media manager, journalist, and publisher, presides over CP PUBLISHING, the Ukrainian media company that she founded. She has studied at various institutions around the world, including at Harvard Business School. Lucia's passion for design led her to the Istituto Marangoni in Milan, Italy and the Florence Institute of Design International, where she studied interior design and architecture respectively. She has authored numerous books about contemporary Ukrainian culture, exploring topics from architectural and interior design to art, and photography.

ANNA AVETOVA,

the founder of Tuasho art agency, works as an art manager and curator. After obtaining degrees from the National Academy of Culture and Arts Management and the National Academy of Fine Arts and Architecture, she has worked as a creative director for several galleries. With a curatorial focus on environmental issues, emotional freedom, and interdisciplinary cooperation, Anna has distinguished herself through projects like the national pavilion at EXPO 2020 Dubai and numerous art exhibitions. In addition to her active participation in global art fairs, she is an established researcher, author, and is currently pursuing a PhD at the Modern Art Research Institute in Kyiv.

KATERINA KOVALENKO

is an interior designer, author, and the founder of 725 Design. With over a decade of experience in design, she has completed projects in several countries, including Ukraine, the United States, Italy, and the United Kingdom, where her studio is currently based. In addition to publishing a wide range of articles on design, Katerina's unique interior designs have been featured in numerous publications. She has also served as a jury member for design awards in Milan and has given lectures on interior design trends and design history at various global forums.

TETYANA SOLOVEY

is an experienced editor, journalist, communications professional, and educator working at the nexus of fashion, design, curatorship, and sustainability advocacy. She has held noteworthy positions in magazine publishing, including as Editor-in-Chief at BURO Ukraine and, before that, as Fashion Features & Jewelry and Sustainability Editor at Vogue Ukraine. In 2022, she added being a member of the renowned Chevening Alumni to her credentials. Today, she is pursuing a PhD at the School of Social Sciences at the University of Manchester.

UKRAINE RISING

Contemporary Creative Culture from Ukraine

Support the Ukrainian creative community

This book was conceived, edited, and designed by gestalten.

Co-Creator: Lucia Bondar
Edited by Robert Klanten and Masha Erman
Editorial support by CP PUBLISHING Ukraine

Introduction by Masha Erman and Robert Klanten
Feature texts by Anna Avetova (pp. 50–55), Lucia Bondar (pp. 236–239),
Katerina Kovalenko (pp. 206–209), and Tetyana Solovey (pp. 8–11, 188–191)
Profile and project texts by Lucia Bondar and Tetiana Antonyuk
Copy editing by Kevin St. John

Editorial Management by Lars Pietzschmann

Cover, design, and layout by Stefan Morgner

Photo Editor: Francesca Zoe Paterniani

Typefaces: Alpina by Reto Moser, Panama by Roman Gornitsky

Cover design based on an artwork by Inna Kharchuk
Backcover images by Vladislav Nagornyi (bottom left), Andrey Bezuglov (top right),
Julia Vdovychenko (middle), courtesy of The Coat (middle right), Serhii Polyushko (bottom right)

Printed by Firmengruppe APPL, aprinta druck GmbH, Wemding
Made in Germany

Published by gestalten, Berlin 2023
ISBN 978-3-96704-118-7

Bibliographic information published by the Deutsche Nationalbibliothek.
The Deutsche Nationalbibliothek lists this publication in the Deutsche Nationalbibliografie;
detailed bibliographic data is available online at www.dnb.de

None of the content in this book was published in exchange for payment by commercial parties or designers;
gestalten selected all included work based solely on its artistic merit.

This book was printed on paper certified according to the standards of the FSC®.

FSC www.fsc.org MIX Paper | Supporting responsible forestry FSC® C004592